ADDRESS

TO THE

RT. HON. THE EARL OF AUCKLAND, G. C. B.

&c. &c.

GOVERNOR GENERAL OF INDIA.

MY LORD,

I HAVE at length the satisfaction of presenting the "*Narrative of the March and Operations of the Army of the Indus,*" which you did me the honor to permit me to dedicate to your Lordship.

2. The importance, in a political and military point of view, of the great measure of your Lordship's administration, by which an additionl barrier against foreign invasion, has been secured to the North West Frontier of British India, has induced me to add to this volume, a History of the Dynasty of the "Dooranee Empire;" exhibiting the period of its foundation; the period and splendour of its rule; the dethronement of its sovereign, and loss of its most valuable provinces; the dismemberment of the remaining portion of the country and thirty years of anarchy and misrule: and finally, the restoration, under your Lordship's auspices, of Shah Shoojah-ool-Moolk, to the throne of his ancestors.

3. May I be permitted to add—while the result of the expedition has obtained such present advantages, and has rendered an act of justice to a fallen monarch, who long lived under the protection of a liberal government—that I trust, under Divine Providence, the event may not only cause the regeneration of Affghanistan; but may, in future times, be attended with great commercial advantages to Great Britain.

I have the honor to be,
My Lord,
Your Lordship's faithful servant,
WILLIAM HOUGH.

Calcutta,
25th August, 1840.

⁎ The reader is requested to refer to the *Addenda* at the end of the work for further information regarding the *Invasion of India,* by the Swedish Ambassador.

A NARRATIVE

OF THE

MARCH AND OPERATIONS

OF THE

ARMY OF THE INDUS,

IN THE

EXPEDITION INTO AFFGHANISTAN

IN THE YEARS 1838-1839,

UNDER THE COMMAND OF

H. E. LIEUT.-GENERAL SIR JOHN (NOW LORD) KEANE,

G. C. B. & G. C. H., *Commander-in-Chief:*

ILLUSTRATED BY

VARIOUS TABLES:

ALSO;

THE HISTORY OF THE DOORANEE EMPIRE FROM ITS FOUNDATION (1747) TO THE PRESENT TIME.

DEDICATED BY PERMISSION

TO THE RIGHT HON'BLE

THE EARL OF AUCKLAND, G. C. B., &c.

Governor General of India.

BY

MAJOR W. HOUGH,

48th Regiment, Bengal Native Infantry;

LATE DEPUTY JUDGE ADVOCATE GENERAL OF THE "BENGAL COLUMN, ARMY OF THE INDUS;" AND AUTHOR OF SEVERAL WORKS ON MILITARY LAW.

The Naval & Military Press Ltd

published in association with

FIREPOWER
The Royal Artillery Museum
Woolwich

Published by
The Naval & Military Press Ltd
Unit 10 Ridgewood Industrial Park,
Uckfield, East Sussex,
TN22 5QE England
Tel: +44 (0) 1825 749494
Fax: +44 (0) 1825 765701
www.naval-military-press.com

in association with

FIREPOWER
The Royal Artillery Museum, Woolwich
www.firepower.org.uk

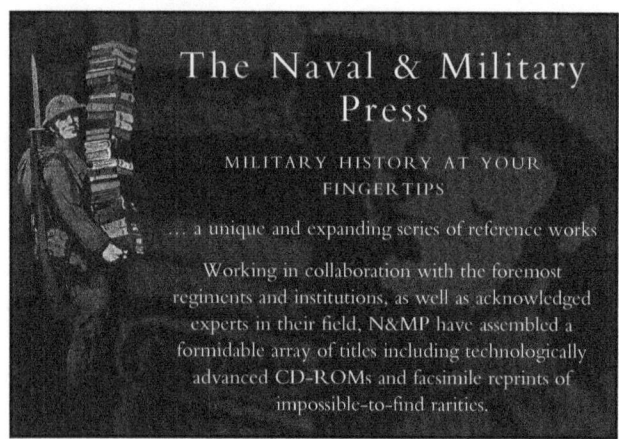

In reprinting in facsimile from the original, any imperfections are inevitably reproduced and the quality may fall short of modern type and cartographic standards.

ADDRESS

TO

THE READER. (1)

I HAVE given to this work the title of the "*March and Operations of the Army of the Indus,*" because it is not merely a "Diary." The details of the march and operations of an Army in the form in which I have given them, appeared to me to be the most simple method, and the notice, as they occurred, of the losses sustained in cattle, &c. by the State or by private individuals, has the advantage of identifying the places where the Army suffered most. The details of the losses sustained by an army marching into a foreign country, may be useful as guides for the future; and I am indebted to friends for many valuable tables to prove the amount in each case.

2. Had I the ability to give a comprehensive political view of so great an undertaking, still as the necessity for the measure is acknowledged by sound politicians, it were useless to argue the point in detail. If the article on the "*Invasion of India,*" and the "*History of the Dooranee Empire,*" will not satisfy the objections of another class of politicians, I plead my inability, on the present occasion, to do more than refer them to the "*Parliamentary*

---

(1) "While you keep the pen of correction running over this work, cover its faults with the mantle of generosity."

Papers." I am of that class called " *Whig ;*" and am of opinion that a mistaken policy towards Persia caused the expedition into Affghanistan.

The expense I believe, will be less than the admirers of another plan would suppose : but the cost should be referred to another period.

3. The nature of the country, in a great measure, prescribed the plan of our marches. Our operations were against fortresses, where the engineers, as a matter of science, had the chief direction of the mode of procedure, and as they declared only one form of attack was available under the existing circumstances, the execution of it only remained to be carried into effect. The daily description of the country we passed through, may serve to show by the relative position of our columns, the means to resist an enemy. If the reports of " advancing foes" often proved fallacious, such will be found to be the case in all warfare ; it is wise to be prepared for their truth : but we must not condemn the "*Politicals,*" because a rumour of such a nature proved untrue. Information obtained in a foreign country must often be uncertain ; the parties giving it may have every inducement to be sincere; but, like Hajee Khan, Kakur, they may prove deceitful.

4. I have commented on several occurrences, from a desire to state, fairly, what took place, and I have endeavoured to do so with a view to elicit a consideration of what I have deemed erroneous, to prevent their recurrence ; but without any intention of hurting the feelings of any one. Where any action of gallantry or conspicuous good conduct occurred, I have mentioned the name of the in-

dividual, which is an act of justice. I have employed the most simple style, which is a type of the old-school: but, if I have rendered the work a useful record of facts, I shall be satisfied; and willingly concede to others, the ability to write in a more fascinating form.

5. From the nature of our operations, Cavalry were less employed than Infantry, the *Affghan* troops are chiefly composed of Cavalry, but do not equal the description given of the " *Candahar Horse*" of former days; though we had no opportunity of testing their military worth. The *Ghiljies* have proved themselves, of late, to be the boldest of the mounted troops of the country.

The *European* troops of our Army had no "*rum*" from the time we left Candahar, till a supply came from India, after the campaign. Owing to eating the fat Doomba mutton which is rich, and drinking the water of the country possessing an aperient quality, they suffered much from bowel complaints. Whatever may be the opinion of the "*Abstinence Societies*," all sound medical men declare the sudden deprivation of spirits to be injurious.

Now that the "*Magnates*" have received the meed of their merits, in the shape of *Honors* and *Rank*, it is to be hoped that the more humble officers, N. C. O. and soldiers may be honored with the "*Medal*" for the capture of Ghuznee, which his Affghan majesty designed to bestow, in high approbation of their services; while the public voice has sanctioned the justness of the expectation.

6. As it appeared to me that some account of a country so little known, and which has been the scene of our operations, should be afforded, and

Address to the Reader.

having possessed the means of effecting such an object; I have in my XVIIth Chapter given the "*History of the Dooranee Dynasty.*" It may, here, not be out of place, to show the ancient dimensions of the *Empire;* now reduced to the *kingdom* of Cabool and its dependencies.

At the death of Ahmed Shah the founder (1747) who died in 1773, the Empire was composed of :—	Under Shah Shoojah-ool-Moolk, 1839.
1. Neeshapoor.	1. Cabool.
2. Meshid.	2. Bameean.
3. Herat.	3. Ghuznee.
4. Cabool.	4. Candahar.
5. Balkh.	5. Jellalabad.
6. Bameean.	
7. Ghorebund.	
8. Ghuznee.	
9. Candahar.	
10. Jellalabad.	
11. Peshawer.	
12. Cashmeer.	
13. The Punjab.	
14. Dera Ghazee Khan.	
15. Dera Ismael Khan.	
16. Mooltan.	
17. Sindh.	
18. Belochistan.	
19. The country as far E. as Sirhind.	

THE INVASION OF INDIA, AND THE MEANS OF DEFENCE.

1. The Invasion of India, has been contemplated at various periods for more than half a century. *Sir John McNeill* (1) states that Prince Nassau Siegen presented to *Catherine* of Russia in 1787, a project, drawn up by a Frenchman, for marching an Army through Bokhara and Cashmeer (2) to Bengal, to drive the English out of India, this was to be preceded by a manifesto declarative of the intention to re-establish the great Moghul on the throne of India; (3) and though *Potemkin* derided it, the plan was favorably received by the Empress: and has never been forgotten in Russia.

2. It is a singular fact that Zeman Shah, (4) brother to Shah Shoojah, whom the British Government has just replaced on the throne of Cabool, should have twice (1797 and 1798) threatened the invasion of India; the last time accompanied with a letter addressed to the minister at Delhi

---

(1) Progress and present position of Russia, (1838,) p. 46.

(2) Then possessed by the Affghans, now belonging to the Sikhs. In our treaty with the Sikh government (25th April, 1809), it was provided (Article 1st) that "the British Government will have no concern with the territories and subjects of the rajahs to the northward of the river Sutlej." But for this article, the Sikhs never would have obtained possession of this valuable province.

(3) Shah Alum was then in the hands of the Mahrattahs. The above measure, it was supposed, would secure the concurrence of the intermediate states, and attract all discontented spirits to the standard of Russia. The Shah was replaced on his throne in 1803, by the British Government.

(4) He was dethroned in 1801, and blinded. Shah Shoojah succeeded him as king, and was dethroned in 1809. Both were pensioners of the British Government, till the result of the expedition placed Shah Shoojah, a second time, on the throne of Cabool.

declaring his intention of returning, on a more favorable occasion, to replace Shah Alum on his throne, and make the Mahomedan the paramount power in India. An ambitious Government would in 1838 have taken possession of Affghanistan, instead of adopting the more generous act of the restoration of a long deposed monarch. Both the above events caused great alarm in India, and occasioned a considerable increase in the Bengal Army. (5)

A Persian of rank was entrusted, by the Government of Bombay, with a letter to the King of Persia to endeavour to secure his aid, which was afforded in the shape of an attack on an Affghan province in Khorasan; which caused Zeman Shah's return from Lahore to his Capital.

3. The Government of India next determined to send an Ambassador to Persia. Sir J. Malcolm was selected. He left Bombay in the end of 1799, arrived in Persia in 1800, and in 1801, commercial and political treaties were signed between the British and Persian Governments. The invasion of Egypt by France about this period, with 40,000 men, though it failed in gaining the object intended, owing to our successes, ought to have opened the eyes of the ministry of that period, to the probability of an attempt to invade India by the way of Persia; but the opportunity was lost. This was the *first* error.

In 1805, (6) the King of Persia being unable to cope with Russia, addressed a letter to Napoleon, desiring to form an alliance with France. *M. Jaubert* was sent to Tehran. *Merza Reza*, in return, went on a mission to Napoleon, accompanied him to Tilsit, and concluded a treaty, which was ratified at Fenkenstein in May, 1807. At the same time *Mahomed Nebbee Khan* was sent as Envoy to the British Government of India, to claim its assistance against Russia; but his mission was unsuccessful; and Persia losing all hope of support from her old ally, had no alternative but to throw herself into the arms of France.

(5) The 4th Lt. Cavy., the present 26th, 27th, 28th, 29th, 30th, 31st, 32nd, 33rd, 34th and 35th Regts. N. I. were raised in consequence.
(6) McNeill, p. 55.

4. This was the *second* error in our policy towards Persia. There was also at this period, a secret treaty signed at Tilsit, between Napoleon and the Emperor Alexander, having for its object the invasion of India, each power to furnish 30,000 men. Napoleon was playing a double game. Probably his plans in Spain and Portugal prevented the execution of his designs on India on a great scale. Probably he was not desirous of sharing his conquest with Russia; and wished, by a successful invasion of Russia, to carry single-handed his views in the East. The next step of Napoleon was to send General *Gardanne* as Ambassador to the Court of the Shah. French officers were sent who first introduced European discipline into the Persian Army. French Engineers built the first regular fortifications.

5. In 1809 *Sir J. Malcolm* was sent on a second mission to Persia. On his arrival at Bushire he was denied permission to proceed to the capital, owing to French influence; (7) in consequence he returned to Calcutta. *Sir Harford Jones,* (8) who had been sent by the Court of London on a mission to Persia, was received at the Persian Court. The Shah apprehensive of the threatened hostilities from India, and more than all, the inability of the French Ambassador to perform the promises his master had made, (9) secured to this mission a favorable reception, and ultimately forced the French Embassy to retire, and procured a Persian Ambassador to be sent to England. Sir H. Jones settled a preliminary treaty on the 12th March, 1809, to the following effect: (10)

(7) He was told to communicate with the Viceroy at Shiraz, which he refused to do. It was expected that an Ambassador should be sent by the crown and not by the E. I. Company.

(8) Since Sir H. Jones Brydges. He was (in January, 1809), entering, as he states, the harbour of Bombay just as Sir J. Malcolm had sailed from it.

(9) Genl. Gardanne had persuaded the Shah to take a French subsidiary force, but *Napoleon* disapproved of the measure, which is most unaccountable.

(10) And returned to England in 1811. A treaty founded on this was settled by Sir Gore Ousley, who was appointed Ambassador extraordinary from the king of England.

Article IV. (11) " In case any *European* Forces shall invade the territories of Persia, His Britannic Majesty will afford a force, or, in lieu of it, a subsidy. That in case the dominions of H. B. M. in India are attacked or invaded by the *Affghans*, or any *other power*, H. M. the King of Persia shall afford a force for the protection of the said dominions." (12.)

But, while the Government of India had, thus, secured the aid of Persia in case of the invasion of British India by the *Affghans*, or any *other power*, it was resolved to be *doubly* armed, on the present occasion, by having a treaty with the *Affghans* themselves. Accordingly, the mission of the *Honorable Mr. M. Elphinstone* was despatched to the Court of Cabool, which resulted in the following treaty. (13).

6. *Article* II. " If the *French* and *Persians*, in pursuance of their confederacy, should advance towards the king of *Cabool's* country in a hostile manner, the *British* state, endeavouring heartily to repel them, shall hold themselves liable to afford the expenses necessary for the above mentioned service, to the extent of their ability. While the confederacy between the French and Persians continues in force, these articles shall be in force, and be acted on by both parties."

So that, while the Government of India entered into a treaty with Persia to defend British India in case of its invasion by the *Affghans*, or any *other power*, it, at the same time, sent a mission to the King of the *Affghans*, and made

(11) Parliamentary papers.

(12) The definitive treaty, concluded at Tehran, by Messrs. Morrier and Ellis, on the 25th Nov. 1814, fixed the subsidy to Persia, if troops were not furnished, at 200,000 Tomauns (£400,000); but the late Abbas Merza, P. R. of Persia, in March, 1828, gave his bond cancelling the subsidy, provided £400,000 were given by the British Government to Persia, towards liquidating the indemnity due by Persia to Russia: this the king of Persia confirmed.

(13) On the 17th June, 1809, at Peshawer. By Article III. the king of Cabool, *Shah Shoojah*, was to receive no individual of the French nation into his territories. He was shortly after dethroned, which annulled the treaty.

a treaty with him to protect India from an invasion by the French and Persians ! While the British Government merely engaged to defend Persia against *European* enemies, and Affghanistan only against *one* European power !

7. Had the British ministry secured the advantages to be expected to result from the commercial and political treaties with Persia, settled by Sir J. Malcolm in 1801, they might have prevented the King of Persia, in 1805, seeking the alliance of France. Our expedition to Egypt had been crowned with success, and there was no war in India. But when in 1809, we obtained the dismissal of General *Gardanne's* Embassy, and induced a Persian Ambassador's being sent to England, then, at all events, was the time to have secured such a political and military alliance with Persia, as to have prevented Russian influence succeeding that of France. It must have been foreseen that, if remote France could gain an ascendancy in Persia, the proximity of Russia rendered it probable that she would exert a more direct and permanent ascendancy in the councils of the Shah.

As observed by *Sir J. McNeill*, (14) "British replaced the French officers in the armies of the Shah, and taught them to combat, on several occasions with success, the battalions of the Czar." At this period too, France was amply engaged in Spain and Portugal.

8. In 1812, Russia was invaded by France. At this time though we were much engaged in the war in Spain and Portugal, still in India there was no war (15) to have prevented our embracing so favorable an opportunity to strengthen our relations in Persia, and prevent Russian influence in that country.

As the greatest commercial nation in the world, it was to have been expected that such permanent relations would have

(14) P. 60.
(15) In 1810, the expedition to the Mauritius had captured that island. In 1811, we became possessed of Java. British officers were sent to accompany divisions of the Russian troops, engaged against the French.

been established in Persia as should have secured to the British nation, a paramount commercial influence; and by such means, some recognised principle of permanent political advantage. (16) But the ministry of the day neglected British interests, and those of her *ancient ally*, and threw her on the mercy of Russia : this was not the Act of a *Whig* ministry.

In 1814, a treaty was concluded between Russia and Persia, by which the latter ceded to Russia, all her acquisitions South of the Caucasus, and engaged to maintain no navy on the Caspian ; which now belongs to Russia : this we might have prevented. By the treaty of 1828 with Persia, Russia established the line of the river Arras (Araxes) as her frontier towards Persia. (17)

9. In 1833, several British officers were sent to Persia (18) to discipline the king's troops. Had Abbas Merza lived, British influence would have prevented the march of a Persian Army to Herat in 1837. The present king of Persia, Mahomed Shah, eldest son of Abbas Merza, having marched to Herat, the British officers in his service were not allowed to accompany the troops; and shortly after returned to Bengal.

Supposing the subsidy of 1814 to have been continued up to the year 1828, £5,600,000 were paid to Persia, and there have been several expensive Embassies; (19) so that eight or nine millions sterling have been paid to our *ancient*

(16) Our war with France, in Spain and Portugal was to support our commerce, and prevent the extension of Napoleon's "*Continental System.*" Napier says (Hist. Peninsular War, Vol. 1, p. 3)—

" He prohibited the reception of English wares in any part of the continent, and he exacted from allies and dependants the most rigid compliance with his orders ; but this ' Continental System,' as it was called, became inoperative when French troops were not present to enforce his commands."

(17) The Persians to have no navy on the Caspian.

(18) Col. Pasmore, (the late,) Majors Todd and Laughton of the Bengal army. They sailed from Calcutta, in July, 1833.

(19) Sir H. Jones Brydges says, Sir J. Malcolm's two missions cost more than £262,000 alone !

ally, for which no adequate political advantage has been gained.

Sir J. McNeill states (20) that the British imports into Persia the last two years amounted to 1½ millions, and the last year (1837) to nearly two millions. But it might be greater if we possessed more influence in that country. (21)

10. When Abbas Merza in 1828, cancelled the subsidy of 1814, with his father's consent, such a fact fully proved the hold which Russia had obtained on Persia, which a more liberal system might have averted. Persia had at one time consented to receive a French subsidiary force, and a British force would no doubt have been received, and at a time when the integrity of the Persian empire could have been assured. The years 1809 or 1812, would have been the best periods for such an arrangement, to have prevented the execution of the Russian and Persian treaty of 1814. But even in the year 1827, important service might have been afforded to Persia; and such a course would doubtless, have rendered our expedition into Affghanistan unnecessary.

11. The failure of the ministry of the above period to act with true policy towards Persia, and the advance of a large Persian army against Herat in 1837 (22) imposed on

(20) P. 119. He writes in 1838. The last two years must mean 1835 and 1836.

(21) We have not very recently learnt what the Committee of Commercial men in Great Britain, &c. have effected towards the extension of trade to the East, &c.

(22) Sir J. McNeill announced to Lord Palmerston that Mahomed Shah's army consisted of 45,000 men and 80 guns. There were besides one Russian Regt. and three European officers exclusive of those in the Russian corps, the staff of the Russian Envoy, and the Envoy himself was there aiding.

The Persian army drove in the garrison outposts at Herat on the 22nd Nov. 1837. There were two very large breaches, four smaller sized, and three difficult breaches; but they were not all practicable at once. On the 9th September, 1838, the siege was raised. The regular, or paid army of Herat was 8,000 men, but the whole city engaged in the defence. There were about 2,000 horse, and these were strong enough to prevent the Persians from foraging. All the guns (seven) were mounted on the walls.

the Government of India the necessity of sending the expedition into Affghanistan; since the fall of the above fortress, would have caused the whole of Affghanistan to become a Persian Province! Treaties had been tried since the year 1801, without success; because treaties, alone, were of no avail. I do not believe the expedition will cost above one-third of the money expended in Persian diplomacy.

If then it were good and sound policy, to prevent the conquest of Affghanistan, by Persia, the next consideration was, whether it were better to restore Shah Shoojah who had been deposed for 30 years, and thus add to the measure an act of justice; or to make Dost Mahomed Khan, an usurper, the head of the Affghan nation?

I think the former measure was the most advisable and legitimate one; as there would be a sense of gratitude to the British Government for its past liberal asylum to a fallen monarch; (23) and *kingly* power was preferable to that of an *usurper*, whose rule was not by the choice of the people. To have made Dost Mahomed the head of the nation, and to have fully effected such a measure, we must have placed him in possession of Candahar, which would have involved a subsidiary force both at Candahar and Cabool, equal to the expense of the Shah's contingent; (24) together with European political officers at both cities; as is now the case. But we could not have placed the same confidence in Dost Mahomed; and it was of importance that the head of the nation should not be on unfriendly terms with Shah Kamran of Herat. (25)

(23) Who had received a pension from our Government for twenty-four years, as well as his brother Zeman Shah, a blind, and also a deposed monarch.

(24) 6,000 men. Though there are more than 60 British officers employed in the Shah's service, many must have been employed in the other case. With respect to the British Regts. now in the country, some must have been employed to have aided Dost Mahomed to establish his rule at Candahar, &c.

(25) Kamran had been accessary to the murder of Futeh Khan, (Vizier of his father, Mahmood Shah,) the brother of Dost Mahomed,

And the Means of Defence.

12. The result of the expedition will prove, that the difficulties of the invasion of India are far greater than have been supposed. The British Army had the resources of the country at its command, or it never could have replaced a great portion of the 33,000 animals which died, &c. during the campaign. (26) This an invading army from Persia could not reckon on. The friends of Shah Shoojah brought cattle to us. Were a Persian Army now to invade Affghanistan, the camels, &c. would be driven away.

We had two convoys of grain sent to our Army from our Provinces; but, had we not, through the Shah's possession of Candahar, obtained grain from the city (having only two or three days' supplies on our arrival) and the coming crops of grain, we must have been starved! The quantity of grain required for our *small* army, (27) and the great number of cattle required for its transport, prove that the feeding an army, in a country where the people only grow enough grain for their own support, is one of great difficulty. We nearly starved the inhabitants of Candahar.

13. The greater the force sent to invade India, the more would the difficulties multiply. The Emperor Baber in 1525 (28) invaded India the 5th, and last time, with only 12,000 men, including followers, and defeated Sultan Ibrahim, at Paneeput, at the head of an army of, it is said, 100,000 men! Baber had guns, the Sultan had not; and the troops of the former were better disciplined: but with Asiatic armies the first success often insured a victory, as in the above case, against very superior numbers. At Herat a Persian army of 45,000 men with 80 guns besieged that fortress for nearly 14 months, against a garrison of 8,000 men. *Napoleon* seems to have thought 60,000 men necessary. He failed in Egypt with 40,000 men.

---

which caused a deadly feud. While Shah Shoojah is Kamran's uncle, and is on friendly terms with his nephew.

(26) See Table, No. 8, Appendix.
(27) See Table, No. 6, Appendix.
(28) Erskine's translation, pp. 293 to 304.

Sir J. McNeill supposes the Persians to attempt the invasion with a larger force still. (29)

The cavalry portion of an invading army would prove the most uncertain of reaching India, as every cavalry soldier requires for himself and horse six or seven times as much grain as the infantry soldier. (30) I say grain, for the sheep would, as well as the cattle of the country, be driven out of reach. The British Government could collect on the Indus a much larger force than the invading one could bring to it, a considerable portion of which would be European Infantry. The native regiments in the Company's army, with European officers, are superior to any

---

(29) He says, p. 120, "50,000 Persian Infantry, composed of what are perhaps the finest materials in the world for service in those countries, and disciplined by Russian officers, with about 50 guns of Persian artillery, in a high state of efficiency, and an almost unlimited number of irregular horse, could be put in motion by Russia, in any direction, within 12 months after the resources of the kingdom were at her disposal."

The late Lieut.-Col. Macdonald in his geographical memoir on Persia, (1813) p. 32, states, that the Persian standing army consisted of the king's Body Guard of about 10,000 men, and the Gholams (or royal slaves) at 3,000. The former were a kind of militia who lived in the capital or its vicinity. The latter in constant attendance on the king. That it was the number and bravery of the wandering tribes which constituted the military force of the empire. That when the sovereign was desirous of assembling any army, the chiefs of the different tribes were commanded to send to the royal camp a number of men, proportionate to the power and strength of his tribe. The army thus assembled was entirely irregular, chiefly consisting of cavalry. They seldom received either clothing or pay, and were only kept together by the hope of plunder. The late king (Futeh Ali Shah) as an extreme measure, might probably have been able to collect a force of 150,000, or 200,000 men.

To the cavalry, which was excellent, the rulers of Persia entrusted the defence of their dominions. Their arms were, a scimetar, a brace of pistols, a carbine, and sometimes a lance or a bow and arrows, all of which they alternately used, at full speed, with the utmost skill and dexterity. He states the revenue of Persia in 1813 at three millions sterling. It is now said to be about one and half million, so that Persia is a poor nation.

(30) See Table, No. 6, Appendix.

troops in Asia, European excepted. The artillery of India is equal to any in the world perhaps, as the guns are chiefly manned by Europeans, and we could produce on the Indus, three times the number of guns any invading force could transport to the banks of that river.

14. Sir J. McNeill (31) says, "the invasion of India by Russia from her present frontier is impracticable; or at least beyond all probability from the facility with which we could multiply impediments on so long and difficult a line, and our power to throw troops into India by *sea*, in a shorter time than Russia could march them by *land*,—possessed of *Herat*, there will no longer be any insuperable impediment to the invasion of India." (32) Herat is alone 370 miles from Candahar. If the reader will peruse with attention, the nature of the route from Shikarpoor to Candahar, he will perceive that owing to the want of forage, we were obliged to move our small army by separate columns, and at times, by small detachments! If he will also read the account of the return of Hd. Qrs. with less than 1,500 men, he will see that we were obliged to march in two separate columns, and that besides the cattle of officers and others, the Government lost 1300 out of 3,100 camels, on the march between Cabool and Peshawer, a distance of only 193 miles. His opinion will, therefore, be confirmed as to the utter impracticability of a *large* invading army reaching India; and I need not insist on the inutility of a *small* force. The other routes are now I believe, pretty well known, and offer many obstacles to an invading army.

15. When *Baber* invaded India in 1525, he was in possession of the intervening countries, so that we will suppose in the view taken by *Sir De Lacy Evans* (33) a

(31) P. 120.

(32) He says, elsewhere, that on his arrival at Herat he was convinced (having before doubted the fact) that between it and Candahar, there would be no difficulty in procuring supplies. But from an account I have seen of the route, there are more difficulties than many suppose, and great want of forage and supplies for an army.

(33) The practicability of the invasion of India, pp. 94 and 95.

start to be made from *Khiva*. (34) He allows of two campaigns from *Khiva, Bokhara,* and *Samarcand* to the *Attok*. He says " Let us suppose, that early in the following year there are 10 or 15,000 Russians, with 20 or 30,000 *newly organised troops,* assembled between Balkh and the ancient *Anderab* at the foot of the mountain; smaller columns being directed towards the Passes leading to Peshawer and Cashmeer. (35)

"From Anderab, through the defiles of the Hindoo Koosh to Cabool, is 100 miles. (36) From Cabool to Attok is about 230 (37) miles. It is strange if they cannot accomplish this within the *second* compaign."

But, as there would be some little to be done in *Affghanistan,* and in the *Punjab,* before they reached our frontier, and a strong one too, we will call the whole, the operation of three campaigns. In the meanwhile that admirable plan of the command of the navigation of the Indus would, by the aid of steamers, throw European troops into India, and, making certain allowances for losses in the invading army, we could present a larger army of fresh troops: while our plan would be, to harass the enemy by light detachments, at certain points; to cut off stores and baggage; and to drive off all the means of supplies; while the *Punjab* would offer many obstacles to the progress of an invading force. (38)

(34) Consult the Map.
(35) I beg him to read the invasion of Cashmeer in 1809.
(36) "It was in commencing this march that *Alexander* caused the private baggage of the army to be burnt, the soldiers being overloaded with booty, according to Plutarch."
(37) 238 miles.
(38) The possession of India by Russia, as observed by a writer at Pondicherry, in 1838, would be of no commercial advantage, while Great Britain kept possession of the sea. Sir J. McNeil has, also, pointed out, that *Circassia* and *Georgia* would be the first sacrifices on the advance of Russia beyond her frontier with a large force. It is clear that the Navy of Great Britain would ruin the commerce of Russia; and that such a result would cause a revolution in that kingdom.

16. Looking at the result of the expedition in all its bearings, I think the operations have been attended with beneficial consequences. I have in my XVIIth Chapter given the History of the "*Dooranee Empire*" from its foundation (1747) to the present period; and while its distracted state, for 30 years, will prove the impracticability of the regeneration of the country under Dost Mahomed Khan, the good effect which has already flowed from the operations of the "Army of the Indus," by the restoration of a kingly Government, with every prospect of the re-establishment of tranquillity and prosperity in Affghanistan; cannot fail to render that kingdom, a real and efficient barrier against the invasion of India; for while it remained in an unsettled state, with a plundering and discontented population, it was desirable to remove the cause: unless, indeed, it be argued that it were a matter of indifference whether Dost Mahomed possessed the country; or that it should become a Persian Province. But, in a commercial point of view, the regeneration of our northwest frontier, is of the very first importance; and the constant intercourse between us and the inhabitants of those countries, cannot fail, ere long, to convince the people, that the change has, in every point of view, been for their benefit.

ACKNOWLEDGMENTS TO CONTRIBUTORS.

Sensible of the great advantages which the present work possesses by the contributions of many friends, I take this opportunity of returning my best thanks for the kind aid afforded me in the progress of the preparation of this volume; which is designed to be a record of our operations.

To Lieut. A. M. Becher, 61st Bengal N. I. and D. A. Qr. Mr. Genl., for a most valuable Map, tracing the routes of the Army.

To Lieut. H. T. Coombe, 1st Bengal European Regt., for the views of Candahar, Ghuznee, and Cabool.

To Lieut.-Col. Sir C. M. Wade, Knt. C. B. Resident at Indore, for materials for the continuation of the Dooranee Dynasty from 1809, &c.

To Jas. Atkinson, Esq. Suptg. Surgeon, Bengal Column, Army of the Indus, for a return of the admissions and deaths in Hospital, for the year 1839.

To Lieut.-Col. T. Monteath, C. B. 35th Bengal N. I. for a return of the sick in his Regt. at Cabool.

To Major P. Craigie, D. A. G., Bengal army, for a return of casualties in the Bengal Column, for 1839; and for access to the Genl. Orders of the Army.

To Major Sage, 48th Bengal N. I. late Post Master, Bengal Column, for the Register of the Thermometer for the year 1839; and also, for access to his Journal of the route, which I have made use of on many occasions.

To Dr. Jas. Thomson, 31st Bengal N. I. for the Register of the Thermometer at Quetta.

To Dr. Geo. Griffiths, Madras Army, for a copy of his Barometrical Heights.

To Capt. A. Watt, A. C. G. Bengal, for the return of a month's supply for the Army, &c. &c.

Acknowledgments to Contributors.

To Capt. E. F. Day, late Commissary of Ordnance, for the return of ordnance, ordnance stores, &c. taken with the Bengal Column.

To Lieut.-Col. N. Campbell, Qr. Mr. Genl. Bombay Army, for the routes of the Bombay Column.

To Lieut.-Col. Sir A. Burnes, Knt., (Bombay Establishment) for information on several subjects.

To the several officers who have afforded the returns of the loss of cattle, &c. &c.

The works of Sir A. Burnes, Dr. Jas. Burnes, K. H., and Major Jas. Outram; Major Leech and Dr. Lord's Reports, have been of great service to me.

Those of Sir John McNeill, Sir De Lacy Evans, and other authors referred to in the course of the work, I duly acknowledge: while the writings of the former, from his personal experience at the Court of Persia, for many years, are of paramount importance in regard to the position of Persia with reference to Russia.

I deem it a duty to acknowledge the above obligations, and I have always made it a rule to show the sources from which I draw my materials; by which I render justice to the authors, and add a value to the work, by the aid of so many authorities, which it, otherwise, would not possess.—W. H.

DETAILS OF THE ARMY OF THE INDUS; AND ITS RESERVES.

H. E. Lieut.-Genl. Sir John (now Lord) Keane, (1) K. C. B., and G. C. H. Comr.-in-Chief, Bombay Army. Comr.-in-Chief of the Army of the Indus.

Lieut.-Col. R. Macdonald, K. H., H. M. 4th Foot, (D. A. G. Q. T. Bombay) Offg. Mily. Secy. and A. D. C.

Lieut. E. A. W. Keane, H. M. 2nd Foot, A. D. C.

Capt. (now Major) Outram, 23rd Bombay N. I. Extra A. D. C.

Capt. T. S. Powell, H. M. 40th Foot, Persian Interpreter and Extra A. D. C.

Asst. Surgeon B. P. Rooke, Surgeon.

General Staff of the Bengal Column.

Major P. Craigie, D. A. G.
Major W. Garden, D. Q. M. G.
Capt. Geo. Thomson, Chief Engineer. (2)
Major J. D. Parsons, Dy. Commy. Genl. (3)
Capt. J. Patton, A. Q. M. G. (4)
Capt. A. Watt, D. A. C. G. (5)

(1) Genl.(the late) Sir H. Fane, G. C. B. Comr.-in-Chief in India, was appointed Comr.-in-Chief to the Army, but on the reduction of the Force, gave up the command to Major-Genl. Sir W. Cotton, who retained it till Sir J. Keane joined on the 6th April, 1839.
(2) And of the Army of the Indus.
(3) And General control of the Bengal and Bombay Depts.
(4) Major W. Sage, 48th N. I. officiated till he joined.
(5) Relieved Capt. H. R. Osborn, A. C. G. who was sick.

Details of the Army of the Indus.

J. Atkinson, Esq. Suptg. Surgeon. (6)
Surgeon R. M. M. Thomson, Field Surgeon.
Asst. Surgeon M. J. M. Ross, H. M. 16th Lancers, Medical Store-keeper.
Capt. B. Bygrave, 5th N. I., Pay Master.
Capt. E. F. Day, Arty., Commissary of Ordnance.
Rev. A. Hammond, A. B., Chaplain.
Bt. Major W. Hough, 48th N. I., D. J. A. G. Dinapore and Benares Divisions, (7) D. J. A. G.
Bt. Major W. Sage, 48th, N. I. Executive Officer Dinapore Division, Post Master. (7)
Capt. C. Troup, 48th N. I. Baggage Master. (8)
Lieut. J. Anderson, Engineers, Surveyor.
Lieut. H. M. Durand, Engrs. ditto.
Lieut. J. Laughton, ditto, Field Engineer. (9)
Lieut. R. D. Kay, Adjt. 2nd N. I., Offg. A. A. G.
Lieut. A. M. Becher, 61st N. I., D. A. Q. M. G.
Cornet W. F. Tytler, 9th Lt. Cavy., Offg. ditto.
Lieut. G. Newbolt, S. A. C. G.
Lieut. G. B. Reddie, ditto.
Lieut. R. S. Simpson, ditto.

(6) Relieved Dr. Playfair who was sick. Surgeon Jas. Thomson, 2nd Lt. Cavy. officiated till relieved.

(7) G. O. G. G. in C. 31st Aug. 1838. "Their full staff salary, provided that other officers are not appointed to officiate for them, and that they hold no staff situation in the Army with which they are serving. In cases where other officers may be employed to officiate, during the absence of staff officers (as above) a moiety of their staff salary will be drawn by the absentees, and the other moiety by the officiating officers." Staff officers whose Regts. were ordered on this service had notice of the fact; and with one or two exceptions they all joined.

(8) Succeeded by Capt. J. Nash, 43rd N. I.

(9) Appointed Garrison Engineer at Bukkur.

Details of the Army of the Indus. xxvii

Cavalry Brigade of the Bengal Column.

Divisional Staff.	Brigade Staff.	Corps.	Commg. Officers.
Major Genl. J. Thackwell, K. H. Comg. the Cavy. of the Army. Major Cureton (10) 16th Lancers, A. A. G. Lt. Roche, 3d L. D., A. D. C. Lt. Crispan, 2d Lt. Cavalry, Do.	Col. Arnold (11) H. M. 16th Lancers, Brigr. Lt. Pattinson, 16th Lancers, A. D. C. Bt. Capt. Havelock, (12) H. M. 16th Lancers, M. B. Bt. Major Hay, 2d Lt. Cavy. A. Q. M. Genl. Lt. Reddie, S. A. C. G.	2nd Regt. Lt Cavy. H. M.'s 16th Lancers. 3rd Regt. Lt. Cavy. 4th Local Hor. and Dett. Skinner's 1st Local Horse. Not attached to the Brigade.	Lt. Col. A. Duffin. (13) Lt. W. Persse. (14) Lt. C. C. Smyth. (15) Capt. J. Alexander.

Artillery of the Bengal Column.

Divisional Staff.	Brigade Staff.	Corps.	Commg. Officers.
Brigr. Stevenson, Bombay Artillery.	Major Pew (16) Bt. Capt. Backhouse, M. B. Capt. E. F. Day Commy. of Ordnance. Lt. Newbolt, S. A. C. G.	2nd Troop, 2nd Brigade H. A. 4th Co. 2nd Bn. Arty. 2nd Co. 6th Bn. (Camel battery.)	Capt. C. Grant. Capt. Garbett. Capt. A. Abbott.

(10) Succeeded by Capt. Bere, 16th Lancers, at Cabool.
(11) Ditto by Lieut.-Col. Persse, on Brigr. A.'s death.
(12) Ditto Capt. F. Wheler, 2nd Lt. Cavy.
(13) On his death, Major Fitzgerald commanded, till Major Salter joined.
(14) Succeeded by Major McDowell, and then by Major Cureton.
(15) Major Angelo commanded till he joined.
(16) Brigr. Graham was appointed Brigr. but Brigr. Stevenson, Bombay Arty., being senior, commanded the whole of the Artillery, and Major Pew the Bengal Arty. Brigr. G. did not go.

xxviii   *Details of the Army of the Indus.*

Infantry Division, Bengal Column.

Divisional Staff.	Brigade Staff.	Corps.	Commg. Officers.
Major Genl. Sir W. Cotton, K. C. B. and K. C. H. (17) Capt. W. Cotton, 44th Foot, A. D. C. Capt. Havelock, H. M. 13th Lt. Infantry, A. D. C. (18) Capt. J. D. Douglas, 53rd N. I. A. A. G. Capt. J. Patton, (4) A. Q. M. G. Lt. Laughton, Fd. Engineer.	*1st Brigade* Col. Sale, C. B. H. M. 13th Lt. Infantry, Brigr. Lt. Wood, H. M. 13th Lt. Infy. A. D. C. Bt. Maj. Squires, H. M. 13th Lt. Infantry M. B. Lt. Simpson, S. A. C. G.	16th Regt. N. I. H. M.'s 13th Lt. Infy. 48th Regt. N. I.	Maj. MacLaren. Lt.-Col. Dennie. (19) Lt.-Col, Wheeler.
Capt. A. Watt, D. A. C. G.	*2nd Brigade.* Maj.-Genl. Nott, (19) Brigadier. Lt. Hammersly, 41st N. I. A. D. C. Capt. Polwhele, 42nd N. I. M. B.	42nd Regt. N. I. 31st Regt. N. I. 43rd Regt. N. I.	Maj. Clarkson. Lt.-Col. J, Thompson. (20) Lt.-Col. Stacy.
	4th Brigade. Lt.-Col. Roberts, Eurn. Regt. Brigr. Lt. Gerrard, Eurn. Regt. A. D. C. Capt. Tayler, Eurn. Regt. M. B.	35th Regt. N. I. 1st Eurn. Regt. 37th Regt. N. I. Two Cos. Sappers and Miners.	Lt.-Col. Monteath. Lt.-Col. Orchard, C. B. Lt.-Col. Herring, C. B. Capt. Sanders. Engrs. and Lieuts. J. L. D. Sturt. N. C. Macleod. R. Pigou. J. S. Broadfoot. Dr. F. C. Henderson.

(17) Commanded the Bengal Column till Sir J. Keane joined; and then Maj.-Genl. Nott commanded the division.
(18) Maj.-Genls. Comg. divisions had a 2nd A. D. C., and Brigrs. one A. D. C.
(19) Commanded the 2nd Brigade, when Genl. Nott commanded the division, when Major Tronson commanded the Regt.
(20) Major Weston (on the Lieut.-Col.'s death) who commanded it at the storming of Khelat.

Details of the Army of the Indus.

The Bombay Column Army of the Indus. Major-Genl. Willshire, C. B. Commanding the 2nd Division of the Army.

General Staff.

Major Keith, D. A. G.
Capt. Hagart, A. A. G.
Major N. Campbell, Actg. Qr. Mr. Genl.
Lieut. J. Ramsay, D. A. Q. M. G.
Capt. A. C. Peat, Chief Engineer.
—— D. Davidson, senior A. C. G.
—— Stockley, S. A. C. G.
Lieut. Threshie, ditto.
—— Wardell, Actg. ditto.
—— Hogg, S. A. C. G. charge of bazars.
Capt. Swanson, Pay Master.
—— Warden, Commy. Ordnance.
—— Bulkley, D. J. A. G.
Lieut. Jephson, Post Master.
—— North, Field Engineer.
—— Marriott, ditto.
R. H. Kennedy, Esq. Suptg. Surgeon.
Surgeon Pinkey, Field Surgeon.
Asst. do. Don, Medical Storekeeper.
Rev. G. Pigott, Chaplain.
Ensn. Malcolm, Baggage Master.

Cavalry Brigade, Bombay Column.

Divisional Staff.	Brigade Staff.	Corps.	Commg. Officers.
Major General Thackwell, K. H.	Lt.-Col. J. Scott, H. M. 4th L. D. Lt. Campbell, 4th L. D., A. D. C. Capt. Gillespie, H. M. 4th L. D., M. B.	Wing H. M. 4th L. D. 1st Lt. Cavalry.	Major Daly. Lieut.-Col. Sandwith, Brigr.
		Poona Local Horse, (unattached.)	Major D. Cunninghame.

Details of the Army of the Indus.

Artillery of the Bombay Column.

Divisional Staff.	Brigade Staff.	Corps.	Commg. Officers.
	Lt.-Col. Stevenson, Brigadier. Lieut. Woosnam, A. D. C. Capt. Coghlan, M.B.	3rd Troop, H. A. 4th Ditto ditto. Horse Field Battery ditto.	Capt. Martin. ,, Cotgrave. ,, Lloyd. ,, Pontardent.

Infantry of the Bombay Column.

Divisional Staff.	Brigade Staff.	Corps.	Commg. Officers.
Major General Willshire, C. B. Comg. 2nd Division, Army of Indus. Capt. Robinson, 2nd Queen's, A. D. C. Lt. Halkett, do. do.	Col. Baumgardt, 2nd Queen's Brigr. (21) Capt. Kershaw, H. M.'s 13th Lt. Infy. A. D. C. Capt. Wyllie, 21st Regt. N. I. M. B.	H. M.'s 2nd Q.'s Royals. (22) H. M.'s 17th foot. (23) 19th Regt., N. I. (24) Sappers & miners.	Major Carruthers. Lt.-Col. Croker. Lt.-Col. Stalker. Lt. Wemyss Engrs.

Shah Shoojah-Ool-Moolk's Force.

Divisional Staff.	Brigade Staff.	Corps.	Commg. Officers.
	Major General F. H. Simpson, Comg. (25) Capt. Griffin, 24th N. I., A. D. C. Capt. McSherry, 30th N. I., M. B. (26)	Horse Arty. 1st Troop. 2nd Ditto. 1st Regt. Cavy. 2nd Ditto. 1st Regt. Infy. 2nd Ditto. 3rd Ditto. 4th Lt. Infy. Regt. 5th Regt. Infy.	Capt. W. Anderson, Bengal H. A. Comg. Lt. Cooper, ditto. Lt. Turner, ditto. Capt. Christie, 3rd Bengal Cavy. Capt. W. Anderson, 59th Bengal N. I. Capt. Bean, (27) 23rd Bengal N. I. Capt. Macan, 16th N. I. Capt. Craigie, 20th N. I. Capt. Hay, 1st Ruropean Regt. Capt. Woodburn, 44th N. I. (28)

(21) Appointed Brigr. at Candahar.
(22) Belonged to the 1st Brigade.
(23) Ditto to the 2nd Brigade.
(24) Ditto ditto.
(25) Succeeded by Brigr. Roberts.
(26) Ditto by Capt. Troup, 48th N. I.
(27) Capt. Griffin, 24th N. I. in command.
(28) The Shah's Contingent has two troops of Horse Artillery;

Details of the Army of the Indus. xxxi

Shahzada Timoor's Force, under Lieut.-Colonel Wade. Lieut. J. D. Cunningham, Bengal Engineers, Mily. Secy. and Political Assistant.

Artillery.—Two 24-Prs. Howitzers and two 6-Prs. (and 2₀ Swivels), under Lieut. *Maule,* Bengal Artillery, 4

Golundaze, ... 40
British.—2 Co.'s 20th (Capt. Ferris) and 2 Co.'s 21st N. I. (Capt. Farmer), ... 320
Cavalry.—Mahomedans armed with swords, shields and matchlocks 400—irregulars 600, ... 1,000
Juzzailchees (rifles), 320. *Infantry* (matchlocks). Regulars 3 Bns. (683)—2,040. Irregulars 820, (29).. 3,180
Affghans, ... 100
Pioneers, ... 200

Total,.. 4,840

British officers with these troops and commanding parties, Lieut. F. Mackeson, 14th ; (30) Lieut. Rattray, 20th ; Lieut. J. G. Caulfield, 68th ; Lieut. Hillersden, 53rd Bengal N. I., and Dr. Lord (31) Bombay establishment, Dr. Alexander Reid, Bengal establishment, in medical charge.

and since the arrival at Cabool, Garrison Artillery has been formed at Ghuznee with a mountain Train of 12 3-Prs. There are also, Affghan and Kohistan levies amounting to about 4,000 men, principally horse. 2 Local corps of Infantry besides the king's guards; all commanded by British officers. So that the Shah's own force amounts to about 13,000 men; while, including the British force, (H. M. 13th Lt. Infy. and 1st Bengal Eurn. Regt., 2nd Regt. Lt. Cavy., the 2nd, 16th, 35th, 37th, 42nd, 43rd and 48th N. I., the 4th Co. 3rd Bn. Arty. (European), 4th troop, 3rd Brigade H. A., and the camel battery (natives); there is an organized force in Affghanistan, of 20,000 men, with between 70 and 80 guns including the mountain train, forming a much larger, regular, and superior force both at Candahar and Cabool, than in the time of Dost Mahomed.

(29) Under native Commandants.
(30) Political Assistant.
(31) Ditto to Lieut -Col. Wade.

xxxii   *Details of the Army of the Indus.*

The Sikh Contingent with the Shahzada's Force, under Colonel Shaikh Bussawun.

                                                                                 Numbers.

Artillery. 1 Howitzer and 1 Mortar (French Legion).
Horse Artillery guns (8—6-Prs. and 2—9-Prs.) 10,   12

Artillerymen, ...   100

Regulars.

Cavalry.—1 Squadron of Cavalry (French Legion) half
    Lancers and half Dragoons, ...   174
Infantry.—1 Battn. of 5 Cos., ...   602
        2 Battns. (529 and 522), ...   1,051
        2 Cos. Poorubees, (Hindustanees,)   215
                                           ——— 1,868

Irregulars.

Cavalry.—Missildars (feudatories) Moosulmans, ...   893
Infantry.—2 Bns. Nujeebs (820 and 455), ...   1,275
        1 Corps of Hill Rangers, Rajpoot, and Moo-
           salmans, from hills N. of Sutluj,   1,000
        1 Battn. of Ramgoles (32), ...   686
        Pioneers, or Beldars, ...   50
                                        ——— 3,001

                                          Total,..   6,046

Total.

Guns, ...   12

Cavalry, (Regular 174—Irregular 893,)   1,067
Infantry, (Ditto 1868—Ditto 2,961,)   4,829
Artillerymen, ...   100
Pioneers, ...   50

                                        Total,..   6,046

(32) Aligoles are Moosulman soldiers. The Sikhs (or Hindoos) call them Ramgoles.

Details of the Army of the Indus.

Lieut.-Col. Wade's Force.

	Guns.	Artillery men.	Cavalry.	Infantry.	Pioneers.
Shahzada Timoor's Force, (4,740)	4	40	1000	3500	200
Sikh Contingent, (6,146)	12	100	1067	4929	50
Total,...	16	140	2067	8429	250
Total,...	16	10,886			

Average strength of Corps, &c. of the Bengal and Bombay Columns which marched into Affghanistan.

Bengal Column.	No.	Bombay Column.	
Park—Mortars, 8 inch, ...	2	The Park not brought on to	
5½	2	Candahar.	
Howitzers, 24-Prs.	1		
12 do.			
Guns, 18-Prs. (33)	4		
9 do.	2		
Field Pieces, 6 do.	2		
Camel Battery, (native) 9 do.	6		
1 Troop Horse Artillery, 6 do. (34)	6	—2 Troops H. A. 6-Prs.	12
1 Co. Foot Artillery, 6 do. (34)	6	—2 Field Batteries, (38)	12
	32	Total,	24
Artillery—Horse, and } Foot, (35)	200	Artillery—Horse, ... Foot, ...	200 200
Cavalry—1 Eurn. Regt.	480	Cavalry—Wing Eurn. Regt.,	300
2 Native ditto, (36)..	950	1 Native Regt.	500
1 Regt. L. H. & Dett.	1,000	Local Horse,	400
Infantry—2 Eurn. Regts.	1,080	Infantry—2 Eurn. Regts.	1,080
7 Native ditto, (37)	5,000	1 Native,	750
Sappers and Miners (native), ..	250	Sappers and Miners (native),	100
Pioneers, ...	240	Pioneers,	100
Total,	9,400	Total,	3,630

(33) Left at Candahar.
(34) Howitzers included.
(35) Left at Candahar.
(36) Did not take their recruits.
(37) Ditto, nor additional men per Company.
(38) One Battery, drawn by mules, left at Quetta.

Details of the Army of the Indus.

Recapitulation of the Force.

	Guns.
Bengal and Bombay Columns, ... (39)	50
Shah's Force, (39)	4
Shahzada Timoor's and Sikh Contingent, ...	16
Total,.. (39)	70

	Men.
Bengal and Bombay Artillery, Horse 400—Foot 400,	800
Cavalry, ...	3,630
Infantry, ...	7,910
Sappers and Miners, ...	350
Pioneers, ...	340
	13,030
Shah Shoojah's Force, ...	6,070
Force to act viâ Candahar and Cabool, total, ...	19,100
Shahzada Timoor's, and Sikh Contingent, to act viâ Khyber Pass and Cabool, ...	10,886
Total,..	29,986
Left at Bukkur, &c. under Brigr. Gordon, 1st Grenrs., 5th and 23rd Bombay N. I., ...	2,200

Sindh Reserve force under Brigr. Valiant, K. H. 40th Foot. At Kurachee—(with the park.)

	Men.
Artillery.—3rd Co. 1st Bn. Arty. and 5th Co. Golundaze Bn., ...	200
Detail of Pioneers, ...	100
H. M.'s 40th Foot, ...	550
2nd Grenrs., 22nd and 26th Bombay N. I., ...	2,200
	3,050

(39) Or 56 for the Bengal and Bombay Columns, including mortars and howitzers. The Shah's two troops (12 guns, &c.) of Horse Artillery had not joined. Therefore add 18 guns, &c. to the 70, making a total of 78 guns, &c. for all the forces.

Details of the Army of the Indus.

Major General Duncan's Reserve Force at Ferozpoor. (40)

Artillery.—3rd Troop, 2nd Brigade, H. A. and 3rd Co., 2nd Bn. Arty., ...	200	
Cavalry.— Skinner's Hd. Qrs. Local Horse, ..	600	
Infantry.—3rd Brigade, 27th N. I.; H. M.'s 3rd Buffs; 2nd N. I.,	2,000	
5th Brigade 5th N. I.; 20th N. I.; and 53rd N. I. (Bengal,)	2,200	
	4,200	
		5,000

Total forces, for the operations in Sindh and Affghanistan, (See also page 5 of the work.) 40,186

N. B. The total force now in Affghanistan, (including British troops) 20,000 men, and 70 to 80 guns. See note 28.

(40) These corps had their recruits with them.

TABLE OF CONTENTS.

	Page
1.—Address to the Earl of Auckland, Governor General of India,	iii
2.—Address to the Reader,	v
3.—The Invasion of India, and its Defence,	ix
4.—Acknowledgments to Contributors,	xxiii
5.—Details of the " Army of the Indus ;" and its Reserves,	xxv

CHAP. I.—March of the "Army of the Indus" from Kurnal to Rohree on the Indus—Movements of the Bombay Troops,   1

CHAP. II.—March from Rohree to Lower Sindh, and back to Sukkur, crossing the Bridge of boats—March to Shikarpoor—Movements of the Bombay Troops,   15

CHAP. III.—March from Shikarpoor to Dadur near the Bolan Pass—Movements of the Bombay Troops,   35

CHAP. IV.—March from Dadur—Through the Bolan Pass to Quetta,   47

CHAP. V.—Quetta, and march from it through the Kojuk Pass, to Candahar,   63

CHAP. VI.—Arrival at Candahar—Detachment sent to Girishk —Arrival of two grain convoys—Occurrences, &c.—Preparations to leave it,   99

CHAP. VII.—Description of Candahar,   131

CHAP. VIII.—March from Candahar towards Ghuznee,   143

CHAP. IX.—March on Ghuznee—Operations before ; Assault and capture of the Fortress—Reports of operations—Despatches, &c. &c.—Description of Ghuznee,   163

CHAP. X.—March from Ghuznee towards Cabool—Dost Mahomed Khan's flight—Pursuit after him—Arrival at Cabool,   239

Table of Contents.

Page

CHAP. XI.—Arrival at Cabool—Shah Shoojah-ool-Moolk's entry into the Capital—Return of party from the pursuit of Dost Mahomed Khan, unsuccessful—Medals proposed for the capture of Ghuznee—Arrival of Shahzada Timoor and Lieut.-Col. Wade with his Troops. Review of H. M.'s 16th Lancers—Review of the Bengal and Bombay Horse Artillery—Grand Review—Races at Cabool—Durbar—The Dooranee Order—Attack on Ghiljies—Troops to remain in Affghanistan—Arrival of 2 treasure convoys—Disposition of Troops in Affghanistan—Troops to return to India—Mahomed Hyder Khan, and Hajee Khan, Kakur, return to India, ... 251

CHAP. XII.—Description of the country of Cabool—Trade—Fruits—Climate—Grain—The city of Cabool—Revenue—Population—Army—Provisions—Police, ... 275

CHAP. XIII.—March of the Hd. Qrs. and Troops returning to India, from Cabool, through the Khoord Cabool Pass—to near the Khyber Pass, ... 293

CHAP. XIV.—March through the Khyber Pass to Peshawer—The Khyber Pass and its defence—Payments to the Khyberees. Tax, or Toll, levied—Commercial and Military use of the Pass—Arrival at Peshawer, ... 309

CHAP. XV.—Peshawer described—Revenue—Troops—Attacks in Khyber Pass—Battle of Noushera (1823). Cross the Indus over a bridge of boats—Arrival at Attok, ... 321

CHAP. XVI.—March from Attok to Ferozpoor viâ the *Punjab* to—Rawul Pindee—The Tope of Muneekyala—Rhotas—Jheelum—Loss in crossing the river—Cross the Chenab—The true site of Nicæa; Bucephalia; and Taxila. Sir John marches to Lahore. Cross the Ravee—Rumour of attempt to rescue the state Prisoners—The visit at Lahore—Display of the Sikh Army and extensive Artillery—Their state of discipline and knowledge of tactics—Cross the Sutluj—Camp near Ferozpoor—Orders breaking up the "Army of the Indus"—The longest Indian march ever known—Sir J. Keane embarks on the river for Bombay, with Mahomed Hyder Khan—The Troops proceed to their destinations, ... 337

CHAP. XVII.—The History of the Dooranee dynasty, from its foundation (1747) to the present period, ... 365

Table of Contents.

xxxix

	Page
Chap. XVIII.—Tables of routes of the Bengal column, from Kurnal to Cabool, and of Hd. Qrs., back to Ferozpoor—Of the Bombay Column from the landing in Sindh, to Dadur—Of the Bombay Column from Cabool, by a new route, on its return to Sindh,	423

APPENDIX.

No. I.—Proclamation declaring the object of the expedition into Affghanistan,	3
No. II.—Report of the Envoy and Minister of arrival at Candahar,	8
No. III.—Sir John Keane's order on arrival at Candahar,	11
No. IV.—Report of arrival at Cabool,	15
No. V.—G. O. by the Govr. Genl. of India regarding the termination of the expedition,	26
No. VI.—Despatch regarding the operations and capture of Khelat,	23
No. VII.—Honors conferred on Lord Auckland, Sir John Keane, and on officers of the Army of the Indus,	32
No. VIII.—Lord Auckland's letter on the fall of Khelat to the Secret Committee of the E. I. Company,	36
No. IX.—Letter of Lord Hill, Comg.-in-Chief H. M.'s Forces, to Lieut.-Genl. Sir J. Keane, regarding the capture of Ghuznee,	37
No. X.—G. O. by the Comr.-in-Chief in India, expressive of the Queen's satisfaction (through Lord Hill) at the capture of Khelat,	ib.
No. XI.—Directions regarding the Family Remittances of officers,	38
No. XII.—The Queen's permission to wear the order of the "Dooranee Empire,"	39
No. XIII.—List of officers killed, and who have died in the course of the expedition,	41

TABLES.

No. 1.—Return of Death Casualties of Men, Horses, and Bullocks, in the Army of the Indus,	43

Table of Contents.

	Page
No. 2.—Monthly numerical return of the Admissions into Hospital, and Deaths of the Bengal Column, Army of the Indus, for the year 1839,	46
No. 3.—The range of the Thermometer during the year 1839,	58
No. 4.—Barometrical heights in feet—Observations with an Englefield's Barometer, without an attached Thermometer,	74
No. 5.—Return of Ordnance stores, and grain, captured at Ghuznee, &c. &c.,	75
No. 6.—Return of a month's supply for the Army of the Indus,	77
No. 7.—Return of Ordnance, Ordnance stores, Musket, Carbine, and Pistol Ammunition, and Powder, which accompanied the Bengal Park, Army of the Indus,	78
No. 8.—Loss of public and hired cattle in the Bengal Column, " Army of the Indus." Also, the loss of cattle by officers and men in the Bengal and Bombay Columns, " Army of the Indus"—during the Affghanistan expedition,..	79

The Index after the Tables.
The Errata last.

MARCH AND OPERATIONS

OF THE

ARMY OF THE INDUS.

CHAPTER I.

1. *Kurnal* (31st Oct. 1838).—The restoration of His Majesty Shah Shoojah-Ool-Moolk to the throne of Cabool having been determined on by the Government of India, a proclamation was published, dated the 1st October 1838, explaining the motives of the British Government in undertaking the expedition into Afghanistan. (1) The Governor General (Lord Auckland) had on the 10th Sept. directed the formation of an Army to be employed on the expedition into Afghanistan; and the Commander-in-Chief in India, (General Sir H. Fane) issued orders dated 13th Sept. 1838, appointing the several regiments to compose the army, to rendezvous at Kurnal:—while His Excellency was himself solicited to assume the command.

2. *March to Ferozpoor.*—The troops were directed to march from *Kurnal* to *Ferozpoor*, in the following order. The 1st, 2nd and 3rd Brigades of Infantry to march on the 8th and 9th Nov. by Kythul, 16 marches. The 4th and 5th Brigades on the 8th and 9th, viâ Kotla Mullair, 17 marches. H. M. 16th Lancers and 2nd Lt. Cavy. from Delhi, on the 4th Nov. via Termana, Nughara, Moonuk, &c. The 3rd Lt. Cavy. the Arty. and 21st N. I. (the latter not attached

(1) See Appendix, No. I, Copies were sent to Dost Mohammed Khan, to the Ameers of Sindh, to Maharajah Runjeet Singh the ruler of the Sikhs, to Shah Kamran of Herat, and to the Native powers of India generally; while Shah Shoojah addressed the Chiefs of Kandahar and of the Ghilzye country; and issued a Proclamation on entering Afghanistan.

B

to the force) marched on the 8th Nov. viâ Umballah and Loodianah to Ferozpoor 18 marches: and by the 29th Nov. the whole were assembled in one camp. (2)

3. *Ferozpoor* (29th Nov. 1838).—The whole of the troops were encamped to the W. and N. W. of the town, (3) and the camp of the Governor General, who had come to be present on the occasion and to have an interview with Maharajah Runjeet Singh, was pitched some distance to the N. W. of the army, and about four miles from the Ghat on the left bank of the Sutluj, over which His Highness had thrown a bridge of boats, and on the right bank of which were the camp of the Maharajah and of the Sikh troops.

Before the march of the Army from Ferozpoor, Lord Auckland received a visit, in state, from the Maharajah, which his Lordship returned in due form; and the "*Army of the Iudus,*" then amounting to between 14 and 15,000 men, commanded by H. E. Sir H. Fane, in person, passed in review before the Sikh Chieftain and the Governor General, and performed a series of movements. The Sikh army, consisting of 25 or 30,000 men, commanded by one of their Generals, was, on a subsequent day, paraded in review order before Lord Auckland and Sir H. Fane, and performed many manœuvres in very good style.

4. *Reduction of Force* (30th Nov. 1838).—The following notification, dated Ferozpoor, 30th Nov. 1838, in the Secret Dept., by the Governor General of India, was published on the 4th Dec. by H. E. the Commander-in-Chief in India. " The retreat of the Persian Army from before *Herat* having been officially announced to the Government as notified to the public on the 8th instant, (4) the circumstances no

---

(2) A detail of the Regiment and Brigades, &c. is given in the introduction.

(3) The 2nd, 3rd, 4th and 5th Infantry Brigades were in one line. 1st Infantry Brigade, the Cavalry Brigade and Skinner's horse were in another line, on the right, thrown back.

(4) The king of Persia raised the siege on the 9th Sept. 1838, and marched from Herat towards his Capital. It was known to Government about the 22nd Oct.; but Runjeet Singh transmitted the intelligence in a letter from Peshawer, dated the 10th October 1838.

Shah Shoojah's and Sikh Forces.

longer exist which induced the Right Honorable the Governor General to solicit a continuance of the services of H. E. the Commander-in-Chief, with a view to his conducting military operations to the west of the Indus." H. E therefore published the following order, that "under these altered circumstances the command of the detachment of the Bengal army is to be assumed by Major General Sir W. Cotton, K. C. B. and K. C. H. ;" and in an order dated the 11th Dec. 1838, directed that, " under the orders of the Right Honorable the Governor General, the 2nd Division of Infantry of the Army of the Indus is to remain till further orders near the Sutluj, the Head Quarters at *Ferozpoor;* and to facilitate supplies, the 5th Brigade and the troop of H. A. may be placed at *Loodianah,* the other Brigade, and field battery, to remain at Ferozpoor." This reduced the army to about 9,500 men. (5)

5. *Shah Shoojah's Force.*—A Force had been raised for Shah Shoojah only about five months before, the contingent consisting of 6,000 men, (6) officered by British officers; the whole commanded by Major General Simpson. This force, as intended, preceded the march of the Army. The Shah quitted *Loodianah* on the 15th Nov. and proceeded to *Ferozpoor,* from which he marched on the 2nd Dec. with the contingent, while the British army did not leave Ferozpoor till the 10th Dec. 1838.

6. *The Sikh and Shazada's Forces.*—Maharajah Runjeet Singh having signed the treaty by which he agreed to furnish his quota of troops, (7) it was decided that after the

---

(5) To decide upon the Brigades, &c. to be left behind, lots were drawn; and the 3rd and 5th Brigades of Infantry (including H. M.'s 3rd Buffs) the 3 T. 2 B. H. A., 3rd Company, 2nd Battn. A., and Skinner's 1st Local horse, were destined to remain at Ferozpoor.

(6) 2 Regts. of Cavy. of 1,000 each, and 5 of Infy. of 800 men each with a troop of horse Artillery. In one Regt. there were 200 Ghoorkhas afterwards increased to 400; and more of that excellent class of soldiers are being entertained. There are two British officers to each corps, the rest being native officers.

(7) Though Runjeet Singh was willing to aid Shah Shoojah in his restoration, as evinced by the treaty of 1834 between them, still he did

army had marched, the Governor General should pay a visit to His Highness at the court of Lahore, and the 21st N. I. and other troops accompanied his Lordship as an escort. On the 6th Dec. Lieut.-Col. Wade, Political Agent at Loodianah, left that place to proceed to Lahore to introduce Shahzada Timoor (Shah Shoojah's eldest son) to Runjeet Singh: and after the Governor General quitted Lahore, the Lieut.-Col. moved to Peshawer with the Shahzada for the purpose of forming and organizing a force of about 4,800 men, (8) with British officers; the whole to be under the Colonel's command. Two companies of British N. I. formed part of the force, and of the personal guard of the young prince.

The Sikh contingent, amounting to about 6,000 men, (8) was assembled under General Ventura, at Peshawer. Both bodies were composed chiefly of *Mahomedans,* as the *Sikhs* were known to be disliked by the *Afghans,* as well as by the *Khyberees* through whose country and the famous pass, lies the road between Peshawer and Cabool. The general political and military control was vested in Lieut.-Colonel Wade: while a Sikh army of observation, under Koonwar Nao Nihal Singh, (9) was assembled on the frontier at Peshawer. The Shahzada's force was organized by the 7th, and by the middle of May 1839, both forces were prepared to commence operations.

7. *The Bombay Force.*—The Government of India had directed the formation of an army at Bombay consisting of about 5,600 men, (10) which, under the command of H. E. Lieut.-Genl. Sir J. Keane, Commander-in-Chief,

not like to have a British force march through his country, and he remarked that " he had been for many years adding to his dominions; but that this expedition would prove a bar to future conquests." But he did more than fulfil his engagement by the amount of force which he furnished. The treaty was *tri-partite,* the parties being the British Government, Shah Shoojah-ool-Moolk and Runjeet Singh.

(8) See the introduction for the details.

(9) Grandson of Runjeet Singh, and son of the present Maharajah Khurruk Singh.

(10) See the introduction, for details.

Bombay Army, was to land in *Sindh*, with a view to compel the Ameers of Hyderabad to sign a treaty agreeing to pay Shah Shoojah a certain sum in consideration of tribute due to him, and for the purpose of obtaining the *free navigation* of the river *Indus;* and to aid if required in the operations of the Army of the Indus in Afghanistan.

The Head Quarters embarked at Bombay on the 21st and reached the *Hujamree* mouth of the *Indus* on the 27th of Nov. 1838, where they found Major General Wiltshire, and a portion of the 1st Brigade; and the rest of the troops landed at *Vikkur* near the mouth of the *Indus,* on the 30th Nov. 1838, with the loss of some horses. "No preparations whatever had been made by the Ameers of Sindh, either for carriage for the troops, or for provisioning them."(11)

8. *Total Bengal and Bombay, &c. Forces.*—It being found necessary to send more troops to Sindh, a reserve force of about 3,000 men was despatched from Bombay, and landed at Kurachee on the 3rd Feb. 1839, after a slight resistance. (12)

I will here give a summary of the whole of the troops which were available for employment in the Afghanistan expedition.

	Men.
1st.—The Army of the Indus (*Bengal*) under Major General Sir W. Cotton,	9,500
2nd.—Major General Duncan's reserve division, at Ferozpoor, &c.,	4,250
3rd.—Shah Shoojah's Contingent,	6,000
4th.—The *Bombay* force under H. E. Lieut. Genl. Sir J. Keane,	5,600
5th.—The *Bombay* reserve *Sindh* force,	3,000
To act in *Sindh* and in *Afghanistan,*	28,350

(11) See Capt. Outram's narrative. He was an extra A. D. C. to Sir J. Keane.

(12) H. M.'s Ship Wellesley, 74 guns by her fire, nearly destroyed the fort; upon which the troops landed without further opposition.

6th.—The Shahzada's force,	4,800	
7th.—The Sikh Contingent,	6,000	
To move from Peshawer on Cabool,		10,800
	Total,	39,150
8th.—The Sikh army of observation at Peshawer (13)		15,000
	Grand Total,	54,150

9. *Herat, if threatened.*—Though the Bombay force under Lieut.-Genl. Sir J. Keane had to settle affairs with the Ameers of Sindh, still the main object of the expedition was to replace Shah Shoojah on the throne of Cabool, and to settle the country of Afghanistan. Now, though the Persian army had marched from *Herat,* still there was a contingency to be provided for in case of its falling into the hands of enemies; for owing to the gallant defence of the place, under the skill and science of Lieut. (now Major) Pottinger of the Bombay Artillery, and the long protracted siege of nearly a year, some danger was to be apprehended for its safety. (14) In the event, therefore, of it being deemed advisable to detach a force to its aid, instructions were given by the Governor General to do so; provided that the sending such force did not compromise the ulterior design of the expedition in Afghanistan—the securely re-seating Shah Shoojah on the throne at Cabool.

10. *Disposable Force.*—Of the 28,350 men above detailed, about 19,000 actually marched through the Bolan Pass into Afghanistan, (15) so that there were 9,350 men to form the force to be left in Sindh, and for Depôts between it and the pass, and including General Duncan's division; for the troops under Lieut.-Col. Wade, were to operate in a different direc-

(13) This was beyond his promise, see note 7.

(14) It was afterwards ascertained that there were seven breaches in its walls, the fort almost in a defenceless state; and the inhabitants were almost starving, the country having been laid waste all round the place.

(15) 9,500 under Sir W. Cotton, Shah Shoojah's of 6,000 and Sir J. Keane's of 3,500; total 19,000 men, from which we could not safely have spared any sufficient body of troops.

tion (16) and were not available. So that it might have been practicable to send about 4 or 5,000 to *Herat*, and as the army did not leave Candahar till the 27th June, 1839, such an object might have been attained as far as *time* and *troops* were concerned; but the difficulty would have been to furnish *carriage* for the stores, baggage, and *provisions* of such a force. The Bombay troops on landing in Sindh, found no carriage or provisions had been furnished by the Ameers. (17) Had it been necessary to detach any force to *Herat*, the circumstances under which such necessity existed, would have, most probably, caused delay in the operations in *Sindh*, by giving confidence to the Ameers; and might have induced them to resist our demands, and thus have rendered it necessary to attack *Hyderabad*; after which the Bengal column might have marched on *Candahar*, and have there awaited the arrival of the troops destined to march to Herat, distant 370 miles. I state this to prove the importance due to the defence of *Herat*, and to show that it is easier to furnish troops, than to *feed* them, and carry the munitions of war!

11. *March of the Army of the Indus from Ferozpoor* (18)

(16) The Bengal troops were to move S. W. from Ferozpoor to Sindh and thence N. W. The Bombay troops to move N. on landing, and through Sindh, while Lieut.-Col. Wade was to move from Peshawer more than six degrees N. and a little E. of Shikarpoor, which is nearly on the N. frontier of Sindh.

(17) See para. 7.—There had been a famine in the N. W. Provinces of India in 1838, and the collection of grain to any great extent was a difficult operation. The districts from which camels are procured, had been drained by the great demands of Government and private individuals for carriage, so that, as the *Bengal* Commissariat must have supplied carriage for the additional 4 or 5,000 men, and had been called on to furnish camels, &c. for Sir J. Keane's force, it would not have been easy to have answered the demand.

(18) The Journal of the route from Ferozpoor to Cabool with the Army, and that from Cabool back to Ferozpoor with the troops which returned with Sir J. Keane and the Bengal column Head Quarters, as well as that of the Bombay column through Sindh to Dadur (whence they followed the route of the Bengal column to Candahar, &c.) will be found at Chapter 18. The route of Lieut.-Col. Wade from Peshawer to Cabool, and that by which we returned, were the same.

(10th Dec. 1838.)—Preparations having been made (19) for the advance of the troops, (Shah Shoojah having preceded) they marched in five columns, preceded by the engineers, sappers and miners in advance. The Hd. Qrs. (Major Genl. Sir W. Cotton, commanding) H. A. and Cavalry Brigade moved on the 10th. The 1st, 2nd and 4th Infy. Brigades; and the park of Artillery and 4th Local horse and the Commissariat supplies and stores, in separate columns, in succession, keeping a march between each column; and this was the order of march till the Army reached Rohree *(Bukkur)* in Sindh. The Commissariat supplies which accompanied the Army (amounting to about 9,500 and about 38,000, including camp-followers) were as follow : 30 days' supplies of all kinds, slaughter cattle for 2½ months ; additional quantities of grain were sent down by water to Rohree, and Depôts were formed at Bhawulpoor, Shikarpoor, &c. A Reserve Depôt was established at Ferozpoor containing 50,000 maunds,(20) and two months' supplies of other grain. 14,235 camels were employed *(for supplies only)* with the army on leaving Ferozpoor. Each column carried a certain quantity of supplies with it.

The sick and principal hospital stores were sent down by water. It was intended, had it been practicable, to have sent the ordnance stores, &c. by water, but boats could not be procured in sufficient numbers. Indeed, boats were required to be sent down to *Bukkur,* on the Indus, to form the bridge of boats; for which purpose timbers were floated down. (21) It would have been desirable to transport all

(19) The road from Ferozpoor to Bhawulpore, and through that country, was made by Lieut. Mackeson, Pol. Assist., who, as well as Dr. Gordon (Pol. Assist.) were, for a long time, employed in collecting grain, and experienced great difficulty, owing to the neglect of Bhawul Khan's people. Dr. G. was afterwards engaged in a similar manner at Mooltan, where Capt. W. Thomson, S. A. C. G. was subsequently sent, on the march of the troops, for the same purpose.

(20) 4,000,000 lbs.

(21) Many boats were sent to Ferozpoor from Bhawulpoor for the grain, &c.; but the boats for the bridge were chiefly obtained on the Indus.

the heavy stores by water and thus have saved the cattle. The march of the army down from Ferozpoor to Rohree, on the Indus, never being above 20, and often within a few miles of the river (which assumes the names of the *Sutluj*, *Gharra*, and *Punjnud* till it falls into the *Indus*) enabled the troops to have communications with the fleet of Boats.

H. E. Genl. Sir H. Fane, Commander in Chief in India, on the march of the army, embarked on board his boats, and proceeded down the river.

The Bombay army at this time, having landed in Sindh, were engaged in procuring carriage to enable it to move on Hyderabad, the capital. On the 24th Dec. the Bombay troops marched from Bominacote towards *Hyderabad*.

12. *Camels and Carriage of the Army.*—There must have been from 25, to 30,000 camels with the army (public and private) and so early as the 26th of Dec. (22) it was found necessary to allow the camels, &c. to quit camp some hours before the troops, as they fell off in condition, owing to their arriving late in camp and being unable early enough to get forage or to graze. This will account, in some degree, for the loss of camels with the Army, as we often could not allow them to proceed in advance of the troops, owing to the danger of being attacked by plunderers or by the enemy; and so numerous were the camels, that though we marched in several columns, forage could not be obtained in sufficient quantity in many places, after we marched from Shikarpoor. The fact is, that most of the officers had too many camels, too large tents, and too much baggage: though Sir H. Fane had issued an order to caution all against taking large tents, or establishments.

13. *Money Rations to the Native Troops* (27th Dec. 1838).—When within two marches of Bhawulpoor we were all gratified by the receipt and publication in orders of the following extract of a despatch from the Secretary to the Government of India in the Mily. Dept. (No. 138), dated the 18th Dec. 1838. "The same advantages are extended to

---

(22) Some of the Camels had marched nearly 500 miles, at this period; but many camels were overloaded by the men.

the Native troops serving with the Army of the *Indus,* as were granted to those who served 'beyond the *Eastern-*frontier of the British Dominions, during the war with *Ava,*' from the date of crossing the *Indus.*" (23)

We were now within 22 marches of the Indus, and while all were pleased at the liberality of Government, we still regretted that the measure had not been promulgated previous to the march from Ferozpoor. Before the army marched from Ferozpoor, several Native officers were invested with the order of *British India,* which was a well timed measure. It is a *Boon* attended with some extra expense to Government, but one which is amply repaid by the zeal of the Native troops; which has never been greater than on the service on which they were now employed in a foreign

---

(23) "The Native troops and establishments, who served beyond the *Burrampooter,* by G. O. G. G. in C. No. 358, of 1824, 25th Nov. 1824" (vide Pay and Audit Regulations, pages 420-21). However, the field pay-master (who had served in the Pioneers in Ava) suspecting a mistake might occur, the following *memorandum* was published in G. O. on the 16th Feb. 1839 to explain *who* were entitled to the gratuity, viz. "To extra and permanent authorized establishments attached to the Local Horse" (an irregular corps); "and not to the establishments of other corps, and of other branches of the service; which last, if entitled to batta in Cantonments, received" (in Ava) "extra batta, and money rations; but no increase of ⅓rd pay."

The Pay and Audit Regulations, p. 420, para. 2, state that "such money rations will be drawn in regular abstracts of troops and companies, under the head of *extra charges,* at the rates regulated in public orders by Commanding Officers of divisions and detachments at the end of each month, on a certificate from the Commissariat officer of the correct prices of the articles in the bazar; or the rates at which they have been issued from the public stores; with a calculation of the value of each man's ration for the month, on the publication of which the officer commanding the troop or company will draw for the amount due to it."

Under para. 4.—The money rations are to be drawn for "all Native officers, N. C. O., Drummers and Privates, Gun or Tent Lascars, or other permanent establishments, drawing half or full batta, and regularly enrolled."

The expense to the Government and the advantage to the soldier, depends on the price of grain; according to the dearness of which is the soldier's gain.

country; and with the prospect of a long absence from their Native land.

14. *Arrived at Bhawulpoor,* (29th Dec. 1838.)—The Head Qrs. of the Army of the Indus arrived at Bhawulpoor to-day under a salute from the town, and found that Sir H. Fane had arrived in his boats. The army encamped to the W. of the town. The rest of the columns moved up on the following days. On the 30*th,* Sir H. Fane held a Durbar and received the Khan in state ; presents were given to the Khan who did not seem quite at his ease, the fact is, that neither he nor his people *(kardars)* had been at all active in procuring the supplies required for the Army (24) though ample notice was given.

On the 31*st Dec.* 1839.—Sir H. Fane returned the Khan's visit in company with Sir W. Cotton and the staff; when a a salute was fired from the town. In the evening the order of *British India* was conferred on three native officers, and we buried Lieut.-Col. Duffin, Comg. 2nd Lt. Cavy., the first officer who had died with the army. Lieut. Mackeson joined us here as the Asst. Political agent.

(24) Indeed the Government was obliged to remonstrate with the Khan himself : perhaps he was afraid of displeasing the Ameers of Sindh, his neighbours. There was said to be a deficiency in the N. portion of his territory, when he was told that there was plenty of grain in the S. districts, from which he could transport it, having a great number of boats at his command ; we did not find the quantity of supplies we expected on our arrival, though it is a fine grain country. The excuse made was, that he had understood the troops of Shah Shoojah were to precede our march two months. Bhawul-khan even said he was afraid the advance of the army would cause his people to desert ; though it was well known that, when *Shah Shoojah* went on his expedition in 1834 through his country, the people did not then desert their villages. The discipline of British troops and the precautions used against plundering, could not be unknown to him ; while it was known that the *Kardars* and people of his country, dared not to disobey his orders. Arrangements had been made by Dr. Gordon to procure grain from *Pak Puttun* on the other side of the Sutluj, in the Punjab ; and Lieut.-Col. Wade also induced the grain merchants of *Loodianah* to enter into contracts, to furnish supplies : supplies were required both for the troops of Shah Shoojah, and for the British Army.

15. *Bhawulpoor.*—The town of Bhawulpoor, is on the left bank of the Gharra river, distant 229 miles from Ferozpoor, and about halfway between it and Rohree *(Bukkur)* on the Indus. The town has a mud-wall all round it, without ditches, or bastions. It is said to contain about 4,000 houses, and 20,000 inhabitants. (25) It is about 4 miles from the river. It is a wretched place, the houses and huts being of mud; and in a military point of view of no consideration. Bhawul-khan has about 4,000 infantry and some horsemen, and though dressed in uniform they do not make a very formidable appearance, but answer the purpose of preserving the tranquillity of the country; which the Khan keeps in good order. The place is rich in woollens, carpets, and fruit: pears, apples, oranges and grapes; all except the grapes, are brought from Cabool. There is a manufacture of carpets and durrees. Indigo is exported from it to Mooltan. It is cultivated between this place and Khanpoor, which is 90 miles distant—to the annual value of 3 or 4 lakhs of rupees; and at Mooltan to the value of 6 or 7 lakhs of Rs. Indigo is sent from Mooltan to Sindh. The road between Ferozpoor and Bhawulpoor is jungly, the roads sandy; and we found several deserted villages, though the strictest discipline was maintained, and safeguards furnished to every village.

The Head Quarters marched from Bhawulpoor on the 1*st January,* 1839; and Sir H. Fane proceeded in his boats down the river towards Bukkur.

16. *Ahmedpoor,* (3rd Jan. 1839.)—The Head Quarters arrived here to-day. Halted on the 4th and marched on the 5th Jan. The town is large and contains about 6,000 houses and 30,000 inhabitants. (25) It has no kind of fortification, but there is a pukha enclosure where the Khan (of Bhawulpoor) lives when in the vicinity; and the great bazar is pukha, and contains a handsome mosque with four beautiful minarets, seen for several miles before you reach

---

(25) There may be a doubt as to the number of inhabitants, as it is easier to ascertain the number of houses, than that of the people who dwell in them.

the town. This place exports coarse cotton cloths and indigo, and imports silks, woollens, fruit and grain. The country all round is a rich plain, covered with turnips, carrots, wheat, indigo;—and fruit trees of the apple, orange, pomegranate, grow in the fields; the oranges were covered in with matting, to protect them from the frost. There is a house built by Lieut. Mackeson, in which he resided here, as the British agent for the navigation of the Indus.

17. *Khanpoor*, (8th Jan. 1839.) The Head Quarters arrived here to-day. Camp one and a half miles beyond the town. The place is said to contain 10,000 inhabitants, and has many pukha houses in it. A salute of 21 guns was fired from two guns on our arrival. There is a canal running through the town. It comes from a branch of the river, which is about 18 miles off, and expends itself in a jheel. There are two Battalions of Bhawul-khan's in the town. There is a mart for rice, and brass utensils. The canal fertilizes the soil which produces rich crops of wheat and barley. We marched from Khanpoor on the 10th Jan.

18. *Enter the Sindh Country*, (14th Jan. 1839.)—Sir A. Burnes (26) joined us yesterday, and to-day the Head Quarters arrived at Subzul ka kote, which is just on the frontier between the Bhawulpoor and the Sindh territories. The distance from the river is about 18 miles; two-thirds of this place belong to the Ameers of Hyderabad, and one-third to Roostum Khan of Khyrpoor (cousin to the Ameers). It formerly belonged to the Khan of Bhawulpoor.

19*th Jan.* 1839.—We, at this period, found that the Commissariat camels were dying faster than the grain was consumed; for though we had supplies at each stage, still not to the extent required for all the columns: and many of the carriage camels were carried off by the owners, which obliged the Commissariat to employ some of the hired or rewaree camels carrying grain, to carry the baggage of the men of one of the Regts. The owners of camels did not like the notion of crossing the Indus!

(26) He had been engaged, for several months at Shikarpore, (Sindh) in arranging for supplies for the Army, re-coining some old rupees, and for other purposes.

23rd Jan. 1839.—We heard this day that Sir H. Fane had been requested, from England, to remain as Comr.-in-Chief in India.

24th Jan. 1839.—The Head Quarters, to-day, reached Rohree (*Bukkur*) on the Indus, where we found Sir H. Fane. The Engineers had been sent on in advance with the sappers and miners, to prepare materials for the bridge of boats across the Indus. The *Shah* who had preceded us seven or eight days had arrived here, and crossed the whole of his force in boats in seven days, by the 17th January.

The Bombay army under Lieut.-Genl. Sir J. Keane, was within three marches of Hyderabad (Sindh); and Lieut.-Col. Wade with the Shahzada, was proceeding on his march towards Peshawer.

CHAPTER II.

THE ARMY ARRIVES ON THE INDUS—MOVEMENTS OF THE BOMBAY TROOPS.

1. *Arrival at Rohree,* (24th Jan., 1839.)—Major-General Sir W. Cotton, with the Head Qrs., the H. A. and Cavalry brigade under Major-General Thackwell, (1) arrived this day at Rohree, where we found H. E. the Commander-in-Chief Sir H. Fane, on board his boats. The other brigades, &c. moved up on the following days. The Engineers had made considerable progress in making the bridge of boats for the passage of the troops. (2) In the afternoon Sir H. Fane held a Durbar to receive the son of the Ameer of Khyrpoor, at which the Major-Generals, &c. and staff were present, together with Sir A. Burnes. The young man and his attendants seemed much alarmed; no doubt, owing to the presence, of our troops, and the unsettled state of affairs at Hyderabad, being connected with the Ameers of that place.

25th Jan. 1839.—By subsequent intelligence (3) it appeared, that Sir J. Keane with the Bombay troops, was at *Jirrikh,* only two marches from *Hyderabad,* which are both on the other side of the river, and I mention it here, to

(1) He joined the army on the 13th December, 1838, having been appointed to command the whole of the Cavalry of the Army of Indus, (Bengal and Bombay.)

(2) Shah Shoojah, who reached the Indus before us, crossed at the *Hossein Bahleh* ghat, which is four from Uzeezpoor, and about seven miles from Rohree, as the bridge was not ready. They commenced on the 11th and finished crossing the whole force (6000 men,) camels, cattle, and baggage, in seven days.

(3) We only learnt this on the 5th February, 1839, on our march from Rohree down towards Hyderabad, as those who brought letters were obliged to take a circuitous route; but our movements must have reached the Ameers very quickly; as they had the command of the whole country, on both sides of the river.

show how far a knowledge of the proximity of the two forces operated on the minds of the Ameers of Sindh, regarding the treaty proposed for their signature; while the *Shah's* force having crossed on the 17th January, had reached Shikarpoor, which is only two marches from Rohree; so that there were three forces to act against Hyderabad; two of which were about twenty marches from their Capital. (4) This night arrived the treaty from the Governor General ready signed, and addressed to Colonel Pottinger, the resident in Sindh, but it was sent, immediately, to Sir A. Burnes, the Political Agent with the force; by it the Ameer of Khyrpoor was to deliver up the fort of *Bukkur* situated on the island in the centre of the Indus, and near the town of Rohree; by which we obtained command of the river.

2. *Visit of the Ameer of Khyrpoor*, (26th Jan. 1839.) —To-day was appointed by H. E. Sir H. Fane to receive the visit of the Ameer of Khyrpoor himself, at half-past 7 A. M.; but he did not make his appearance till about 11 A. M. preceded by his minister, who was anxious for H. E. to go and meet his master, which was not complied with. He came in state, and was received by a guard of honor, consisting of four Cos. H. M.'s 13th Light Infantry, one troop H. M. 16th Lancers, and a party of the Bengal 3rd Light Cavalry. As soon as the old man reached the carpet, Sir H. Fane rose and welcomed him; then arose a confusion of tongues; then commenced struggling, pushing, and screaming for the seats of honor. At last silence ensued,— speeches were made—then the duly ratified *treaty* was produced, upon which the Ameer said *he* would insist on *Noor Mahomed Ali*, of Hyderabad, agreeing to our terms. Sir H. Fane replied, (5) " I have wasted time enough in treating; I will *now* march down, and attack him; and if you like, I will show you the troops I shall send to do it." The review of the Cavalry brigade, and 2nd T. 2nd B. Bengal H.

(4) Sir J. Keane's force was about 5,600, Sir W. Cotton's 9,500, and Shah Shoojah's 6,000, total 21,100 men, of which 15 or 16,000 might have been employed against Hyderabad.

(5) Sir A. Burnes was the interpreter on the occasion.

A. took place in the evening. The Ameer was astonished at the Military array, but expressed his fears on seeing the *Europeans !* As affairs were in an unsettled state at Hyderabad, Sir H. Fane suggested the propriety of detaching a considerable portion of the *Bengal* Column to Lower Sindh.

3. *The Bridge—Order for march*, (27th Jan. 1839.)—The river rose to-day 18 inches, and the bridge opened to some extent, and caused a good deal of anxiety, for it was not yet finished; the portion over the strongest part of the stream, i. e. on the left bank, was to be constructed, and it was highly important to have it ready as soon as possible. To-day the 1st and 2nd Infy. brigades marched into camp.

The troops in orders yesterday, to march to lower Sindh were as follows;—1st, The H. A. and Cavalry brigade to march on the 28th—2nd, The 1st Brigade of Infantry on the 29th, with the camel-battery—3rd, 2nd Brigade on the 30th Jan. 1839, a total of about 5,600 men, equal to Sir J. Keane's force; who would thus have had more than 11,000 men with which to act in Sindh. The 4th Brigade of Infantry, the 4th Local Horse, the Park of Artillery, and the Engineers, Sappers, and Miners, (the latter required to complete the bridge) were to remain at Rohree, the whole under the command of Brigadier Roberts. (6) The order for the march was postponed, as we had not yet got possession of the Fort of Bukkur. Sir W. Cotton invested certain native officers with the order of " *British India*," in the afternoon.

(6) Major General Nott went in command of the 2nd Brigade. The sick horses and those out of condition, and sick men were left at Rohree ; and officers and men were recommended to move as light as possible; and with such servants and baggage only, as were essentially necessary. The infantry took 150 rounds with them; of this 25 rounds in pouch, and the rest packed in boxes. A spot was fixed on for a Field Hospital at Rohree.

No baggage was allowed to precede the troops, the first day, but we afterwards found it was not necessary to prevent its going on in advance. Servants were cautioned as to the danger of quitting the line of march ; and of the risk of stragglers being ill-treated.

4. *Orders for march repeated—False alarm in Camp.*—
(28th Jan. 1839). The orders for the march were repeated to-day. Both yesterday and to-day many armed persons were observed to leave the town of Rohree, and from certain indications, it was supposed by some that an attack would be made on us. Enemies were talked of—picquets were strengthened after sunset—sentries were doubled, and their muskets were loaded. At 12 o'clock at night, a musket went off by chance, when the whole line turned out under arms, in the course of a few minutes, (7) as the alarm spread through the whole Camp in a moment. It was a fine moon-light night, and the movements of an enemy could easily have been seen. On an examination at the picquets, and in the vicinity of the town, no enemy could be seen—it proved a *false alarm*. The real cause I believe to have been this. The people in the town most probably were in a state of alarm at the presence of an army near them, though guards to protect them were placed in the town, and were leaving the place, as we afterwards heard, with their families and property, through fear, but neither with an intention of attacking us, nor of proceeding to Lower Sindh, to join the Ameers at Hyderabad. (8) In fact all

(7) Orders had been given to the sentries to fall back on their picquets on hearing any firing, and to give the alarm. The sentry whose musket went off belonged to a Regt. N. I. of the 4th Brigade.

(8) Sir W. Cotton praised the vigilance of the troops, and the alacrity with which they turned out, and published the following order next day: "on a sentry, or vidette, finding it necessary to fire upon any object advancing, it is the duty of the officer Comg. the picquet from which the sentry is posted, to ascertain, by personal examination, the cause of the alert; and should he discover that any ground exists for apprehending an attack on his post; he will sound the '*alarm ;*' and take the usual steps to repel it." He should likewise, send to report to the field officer of the day of the Brigade to which he belongs.

The beating of *tom-toms*, &c. after 7 o'clock at night was prohibited; and the Provost Marshal and his Deputy, were ordered to patrol at uncertain intervals during the night, and to cause people disobeying, to be arrested.

Possession of Bukkur. 19

the people of the country are armed, and their going away in considerable bodies gave rise to the reports.

5. *Possession of the Fort of Bukkur; and order for march*, (29th Jan. 1839).—The Fort was to be given up to us by the Ameer of Khyrpoor to-day at half past three in the afternoon, four Cos. of the 35th Bengal N. I. under Lieut.-Col. Monteath, and the flank Companies of the 16th N. I. under Capt. Graves, were paraded for the purpose of taking possession of it. At about 5 p. m. the troops entered the boats, accompanied by Major Genl. Sir W. Cotton and staff, and the boats reached the fort in about half an hour. When two-thirds of the way across the river, we saw the garrison in their boats, half across the river. The troops landed, and the setting sun shone on the British Flag. A bag of gunpowder was taken by the party in the boats to blow open the gate had it been required, under the superintendance of Capt. A. Abbot, Arty. The treaty for the possession of the fort had arrived on the night of the 25th; so that four days had elapsed, and the delay was imputed by some to a desire on the Ameer's part, not to fulfil his agreement; but, I believe, he had no such intention. The people in the fort did not like, as I was informed by Sir A. Burnes, to give up the keys of the fort to any but to those from whom they had received them: this caused delay on the 29th: but resistance was quite out of the question; because there were only about 20 or 30 men in the place, with one old gun; and besides, we could have crossed over in boats and have breached it from *Sukkur*, where the river is narrow. (9) The troops were in orders to march for lower Sindh on the 30th Jan. Brigadier Roberts was ordered to

---

(9) Or have attacked it from *Rohree* (see para. 7). Lieut. Wood of the Indian Navy, Supt. of boats, went in his boat, and it was agreed that he should make a signal when they left. The fort was evacuated, the signal was not seen. It was agreed that the flag of the Ameer should, also, be hoisted as well as the British; for we were only to have possession of the fort during the war. The real cause for the delay was, I believe, owing to some dilatory forms, or etiquette, on the part of the people, for there was not the least show of resistance.

assume command of the Posts of *Rohree* and *Bukkur* (in which a force was placed) and adjacent country, on the left bank of the *Indus;* and to move his brigade nearer to *Rohree* and the river, and take up a military position. The stores, &c. left by the different brigades were directed to be placed in the fort. The treasure not required, was left here, likewise. (10) It was at one time suggested to send down some troops by water, to Hyderabad; but a sufficient number of boats were not procurable: and it would have been unwise to have broken up the bridge for such a purpose.

6. *The town of Rohree.*—The streets of the town are full of filth and so narrow, that meeting a camel, &c. you are obliged to turn into a cross-street. The houses are all built of sun-burnt bricks, some have 3 or 4 stories, particularly those looking towards Bukkur. Descending a steep slope through the gateway, you come to a sandy-road, with the rock on which Rohree is built, on your left, and several isolated rocks on your right; and in front is a grove of date-trees on a rising slope. The river when filled by the freshes has washed the rock on which Rohree stands, so completely away, that men could walk under the over-hanging town. The rocks to the right were accessible, though evidently islands in the time of the freshes: and on one of them were the bones of all the chiefs and warriors of Rohree and Bukkur; passing these, you come to the river. The boats used are flat-bottomed, high in the stern, and the hull out of all proportion to the upper works, built in three pieces; the bottom and the two sides nailed together; so that if heavily laden, the bottom is apt to fall out, unless there be a pressure on the upper part of the sides, to keep them bearing on the bottom.

---

(10) 3 Guns of No. 6, Field (or Camel) battery were to-day ordered to be attached to the 4th Brigade, and a Regt. of N. I. from it was directed to march back to Uzeezpoor (one march) to escort the train to camp. The Brigadier was authorised to appoint a Post Master to keep up the communication with the army; and to report to Hd. Qrs. direct.

Fort of Bukkur.   21

The town of Rohree has been of much consequence, and wide-spread ruins prove its former extent and magnificence. At present, it is said to contain 2,000 houses and about 8,000 inhabitants; six miles from it is the still more ancient capital of *Arore,* where a Hindu Raja once reigned in great splendour; the ruins occupy a space of four miles in depth, and the same in length. " The *Meerwah* canal runs from the Indus S. for 90 miles, and is lost in the sands." (11) Rohree is seen 3 or 4 miles before you reach the river, and all at once strikes the mind in an imposing manner. (12)

7. *The Fort of Bukkur.*—When within 3 or 4 miles of the Indus, all at once Rohree, Bukkur, and the deep, broad winding Indus, burst on the view. From the right flows the mighty stream, sweeping from a magnificent reach, round the island of *Bukkur,* and dividing it from the town of *Rohree.* Pile above pile rear their heads on the island. This is the fort built by *Alexander the Great,* to bridle surrounding nations. *Lieut. Leach,* of the Bombay Engineers, gives the following description of the fort in his report to Govt. in 1838.

" It is situated on an island in the *Indus,* between *Rohree* on the E. bank, and the village of *Sukkur* on the W. near to the latter; it is conveniently situated, and if remodelled, would be an excellent situation for troops; it is built in the usual manner, partly of burnt and partly of unburnt bricks, and its walls are 30 to 35 feet high; the elevation of the island on which it stands above the river is 25 feet; it is loopholed, and has a weak parapet; on the E. there is an unfinished *fausse-braye* without a *terreplein,* acting merely

---

(11) Burnes, vol. III. p. 260.
(12) " Here is the castle built by *Craterus* to awe *Musicanus* and his city. From this he marched out with his elephants and state, to do homage to *Alexander,* and from this, after his revolt, he was led forth in chains by *Python,* and crucified in his own dominions, with the Brachmanes," *(Brahmins)* " who had induced him to rebel." (*Arrian,* Book 6th, chapters 14 to 19.)

as a screen to part of the fort walls; it looks, however, imposing from without, with its turrets and loop-holes; there is a low parapet wall to the west. It is commanded by the city of *Rohree,* where an enfilading battery would be advantageously erected, to cover the occupation of the island to the N. of the fort, well screened by large trees, from which island the escalading party could cross with no difficulty; as there is no current. There is at present a garrison of about 10 men and *one* gun on the ramparts, (13) which have been partly destroyed by its discharge! The inside is in ruins, there being only a few huts, and a bungalow of the Ameer of Khyrpoor; the magazine in time of siege." (14)

8. *March towards Hyderabad,* (30th Jan. 1830).—Major Genl. Sir W. Cotton with the Hd. Qrs. marched this morning from the camp at Rohree; while Sir H. Fane, with a suitable escort, accompanied by the staff, went to Khypoor to return the Ameer's visit. This place was a few miles to the left of our route. After the visit Sir Henry returned to his boats at Rohree; and Sir W. Cotton and Staff joined the camp.

(13) This gun was on a bastion (where the flag was hoisted) facing towards our camp.

(14) He adds, "the Sindhians have a knowledge of sand-bag-batteries; and of driving galleries, which they support with framework in loose ground."

The walls are said to be ten feet thick, and ages of accumulated filth had raised the platform inside so much, that the ascent by the gate-way, was one of great difficulty to some who went to take possession of the Fort on the 29th January, 1839. The fort is about 800 by 300 yards long.

Sukkur is about half a mile from the right bank of the river. The place is one of extensive ruins; but towers, bastions mosques, and minarets, are still standing, the latter in perfect order, and giving an extensive view of the surrounding country. The present village has about 100 houses and 500 inhabitants. Shah Khair Deen ke Durga, is a mosque built to commemorate the memory of Khair Deen, who made himself Shah; and that of his son Peerun Peer Ka, who lies beside his father.

The order of march was as follows:—

1. 1 Squadron of Cavalry.   5. 1 Regt. N. I.
2. H. M.'s 13th Lt. Infy.   6. 2 Regts. of Cavy.
3. The Artillery.   7. The Baggage.
4. 3 Squadrons of Cavalry.   8. 1 Regt. N. I. (15)

The road for the first six miles was so strong with enclosed walls, ditches, and forest, that 3 or 400 resolute men might have annoyed us much on our march, by firing from behind the walls; as we could not, as it was, move on quickly. The road was narrow, and very bad; the camels of the 9-pr. field battery fell into a ditch; and before the water-courses could be crossed, the pioneers were obliged to be employed. We saw a small camp of horsemen at a short distance on the right of the road, after we had passed the most enclosed part of the road, but met with no enemy, or opposition, on our march towards Hyderabad. We encamped on rather open ground; and found the rest of our march in Lower Sindh, to require the aid of the pioneers.

9. *The Bombay Reserve Force in Sindh.*—On the 3rd Feb. 1839, the Bombay reserve force of about 3,000 men landed at *Kurachee* on the Sea Coast, about 50 miles to the N. and a little to the W. of the *Hujamree* mouth of the Indus, where Sir J. Keane had landed on the 27th November, 1838. *Kurachee* town, according to Col. Pottinger and Capt. Maxwell, of the Indian Navy, lies a considerable distance from the anchorage, and the channel to it is narrow, and very shoaly even for boats at low water; the fortifications of the town are very mean and irregular, being in some places not above five or six feet high, and even there so broken down, that a horseman might ride to the top of them; while in others they are lofty and kept in excellent repair; the whole are built of mud and straw; and the side towards the creek, which flows up from the head of the harbour, the works are faced, to a certain height, with masonry. A fort built in 1797 on the promontory that forms the western side of the

---

(15) On subsequent days, the H. A. and Cavy. went in advance, and the rest of the troops in separate columns.

Bay, is judiciously placed to defend the entrance. (16) The Sindh reserve force landed under the fire of H. M.'s ship *Wellesley* of 74 guns (17) with slight opposition. The fort fired into her, when she brought her broadside to bear, and *it is said* nearly reduced the parapets and bastions to one level. (18)

10. *Operatioms on right bank of the Indus*, (4th Feb. 1839.)—At about the time that the Bengal column was ordered to march down the *left* bank, Major General Simpson, with a part of the *Shah's* force, marched from *Shikarpoor* down the *right* bank of the Indus, and took *Larkhana*, belonging to the Ameers of Hyderabad. This place is 52 measured miles from Shikarpoor, and our column was pretty nearly parallel to Larkhana. We took the direct

---

(16) There were various opinions as to the practicability of the approach of a large ship so as to cover the landing of troops. *Col. Pottinger* supposed that no ship could approach it with impunity, and certainly not with effect; for her guns would require to be so elevated, to avoid striking the hill, that nine shots out of ten would pass over and fall into the sea on the opposite side.

Lieut. Leach (Bombay Engineers) remarked, " The same cause would undoubtedly screen her from the fire of the *fort*, but as she would be close under the hill, her *decks* might be cleared by matchlockmen, who would be completely protected by the masses of rock ; and, therefore, in the event of its ever becoming necessary to take this place, the only plan would be, to land troops at some distance from it, and carry it by *escalade*."

Dr. Lord who visited Kurachee in 1838, says that, " there were 11 guns in the fort, which could have no effect on a vessel going into the harbour, owing to the partial degree of their depression ; there was then, no garrison, but a few days after 13 men arrived to defend it; after passing the fort, however, there is a three gun-battery level with the water. There is no road from the fort to the town, the ground being a *marsh*. There is no hard road when the tide is out, from the landing-place to the town, which is there three miles distant; the only hard road by which troops, when landed, could approach the town, is from the E.; but the possibility of landing there, has not been ascertained by sounding."

(17) Rear Adml. Sir F. Maitland commanded the Naval Force ; and Brigr. Valiant, the troops.

(18) This news only reached Sir W. Cotton's column on the 9th February, 1839.

route for Noushera, instead of marching by the river route. The place was found evacuated on the General's approach; it is a great mart for rice; and the place where the Ameers kept their artillery.

Sir J. Keane had been detained at Jerrikh (19) two marches from Hyderabad ever since the 25th January; but this day he reached Kotre near Hyderabad.

The horses had commenced to fall off in condition, and this day an order was issued for the commissariat to serve out rations of eight seers (15 lbs.) of kurbee (20) per horse of the H. A. and Cavalry, whenever there was a scarcity of grass, or forage of inferior description. (21) The Bengal European Regt. attached to the 4th Brigade, and the Engineers had been ordered to join our column, as *Sir J. Keane* had now directed our advance, it being considered that operations against Hyderabad, and a siege were inevitable. The Engineers and supplies were ordered down by the river; and supplies were, also, to be sent by land, to join us.

11. *Countermand of our March—Treaty signed—ordered back*, (6th Feb. 1839.)—We had to-day arrived at Khundearee seven marches from Rohree, and four from Noushera, at which latter place the country of the Ameers of Hyderabad commences; and which is about half-way between Rohree and Hyderabad. At half-past 10 o'clock at night, our march for the next day was countermanded; and the baggage, which had gone on in advance, was ordered back. (22) The Ameers of Hyderabad had signed the treaty which Col. Pottinger was anxious to effect, without having recourse to hostilities. The columns in our rear were

(19) This we heard on the 5th February, 1839.

(20) It is the stalk of a grain, and given to bullocks in Bengal, and often to horses in the south of India.

(21) The officer at the head of the Qr. Mr. Genl.'s Dept. to ascertain and certify the necesssity; and the Dy. Cy. Genl. to make arrangements for its collection, and issue, on indents duly vouched.

(22) The country between Rohree and Noushera, belongs to the Ameers of Khyrpoor, with whom we had made a treaty.

ordered to stand fast; and the troops, &c. ordered to join us, were directed to stand fast at Rohree. On the 9th February, we were ordered to retrace our steps, and the *rear* columns now became the *leading* ones, on the march back to Rohree.

12. *Orders for crossing the Bridge of Boats over the Indus*, (9th Feb. 1839).—Brigadier Roberts, Comg. at Rohree, was directed to move the ordnance and commissariat stores across the river. On the 10th February, the Baggage Master was ordered to proceed to Rohree to arrange with the Chief Engineer in communication with the Dy. Qr. Mr. Genl. for the passage of the troops and baggage across the river.

The *Artillery and Ordnance Stores* were ordered to be passed across the Bridge by manual labour, or to be ferried over the river in rafts, as the Chief Engineer might think fit. The troops crossed by Brigades. The baggage of Brigades was to be collected by regiments, and to move in rear of the troops, in the order of corps, the baggage of each regiment under an European officer, with a small detail of local horse.

The whole of the troops, baggage, bazars, and cattle, had all crossed by the 18th February, over the Bridge, without a single accident; for which the Baggage Master, *(Capt. Troup)* was thanked in orders. (23)

13. *The Bridge of Boats.*—The Bengal Engineers, under Capt. G. Thomson, and the two companies of sappers and miners, under Capt. E. Sanders of the same corps, had preceded the head-quarter column, under Major General Sir W. Cotton, about a week, for the purpose of cutting and collecting wood, and preparing materials (24) with which

---

(23) The troops from Lower Sindh moved across the Bridge and encamped at *Sukkur*, to which the road lay to the left. We left the town of *Rohree* to our right. The troops were directed to march from Sukkur. The 2nd Brigade was ordered to move on the 16th. The 1st Brigade on the 17th. The 4th brigade on the 18th instant; and the H. A. Cavalry and Head-Quarters on the 19th February, 1839.

(24) There were plenty of *khujoor* (palm) trees in the vicinity of Sukkur on the right bank of the river; to which side they crossed over.

to form a road across the boats to form the Bridge. Boats had been previously collected there. The Bridge was commenced first over the narrowest part of the river, or from the right bank at *Sukkur* to the island on which the fort of *Bukkur* stands. The advantages of this selection were as follow:—1*st*, Materials were most easily procured close to *Sukkur*. 2*nd*, Shikarpoor being only two marches from the right bank, it enabled them to hold communication with that place and the Shah's force; and as we were encamped at *Rohree*, on the left bank, operations could be aided from both sides of the river. 3*rd*. The water being slack on the right bank, the operation was more easily effected. 4*th*, It established a direct communication from the right bank to the island on which the fort of Bukkur stands. Now as this portion of the Bridge was finished before we got possession of Bukkur; it is clear that, the plan adopted would have enabled us to attack it from *Sukkur*, as well as from *Rohree*. (25)

The extent of river bridged was 500 yards; 74 large boats were used in its formation, being 19 from Sukkur on the *right* bank to the Island, and 55 boats from the Island to Rohree on the *left* bank.

There were two pier-heads and 19 boats of an average of 220 maunds (about 80 lbs. each) on the smaller or western-stream, 400 feet broad; and two pier-heads and 55 boats, average 500 maunds, on the largest or eastern-branch of the river, which was 1,100 feet broad.

The two branches being 1,500 feet, or 500 yards of river bridged.

The western-branch was bridged in four days. On the eastern, it took 16 days; but had all the boats been ready, it might, and would have been completed in ten days. So that the operation was the actual work of 14 days; and the two bridges were ready on the 3rd February, 1839.

14. *Thanks to the Engineers.*—On the 15*th Feb.* 1839, on the arrival of Major General Sir W. Cotton, with the

(25) See *Lieut. Leech's* opinion at note 16.

staff at *Sukkur* on our return from Lower Sindh, he issued an order praising Capt. Thomson, the Chief Engineer, and Capt. E. Sanders, Comg. the sappers and miners, for the admirable manner, in which they had performed the arduous undertaking in forming the bridge of boats over the Indus, and for the military skill and abilities evinced on the occasion; and returned his thanks to the officers and men engaged on the work. On the 16*th February* H. E. General Sir H. Fane, Commander-in-Chief in India, issued the following order: (*Para.* 4.) " He feels it just, more particularly to notice the Corps of Bengal Engineers, and the sappers. The manner in which they have completed the important work of throwing a Bridge over the *Indus* (490 yards), (26) reflects great credit on their skill and their industry; and H. E. requests that Capt. Thomson, the Chief

(26) The ground between the two bridges was about 300 yards. The best boats and materials, were used in the large bridge which extended from the left Bank to the island, where the stream was rapid, with many eddies. The smaller bridge from the island to the right bank, had the planks covered with earth. Great precaution was used by the Baggage Master to prevent crowding on the bridge. H. M.'s 16th Lancers rode over. The great object, in crossing a bridge, is to avoid *crowding* on it, so as to have the *whole* of the road-way covered at *once*.

Infantry, if in a very close compact order, weigh more than the same space occupied by *Cavalry*, as the spaces between the horses, being greater than between men, the weight of Cavalry is proportionably less. It is even said, that if a given extent of bridge be occupied by a *gun, horses, &c.* they bear with less weight on it, than a *close* column of *Infantry*. In many cases, Cavalry dismount, if the bridge has a weak road-way, or the boats are not strong. *Cavalry*, therefore, should pass over by single files, as if the stream be strong and rushes with violence against the boats, the horses are apt to be frightened. *Infy.* should generally pass over by *threes*, or by small sections, with proper intervals between. *Camels*, &c. should pass over singly, and if unsteady, their loads must be taken off. If horses are unsteady and likely to fight by going two abreast, confusion will be created. See Capt. Macauley (Rl. Engineers) on Mily. Bridges. The river rose on the 27th Jan. before it was finished; and afterwards on the 3rd Feb. 1839, when danger for its safety was apprehended.

Engineer, and the commissioned, N. C. O. and soldiers under his command, concerned in the work, will accept his thanks."

15. *Sir H. Fane's order on taking leave.*—G. O. by H. E. Genl. Sir H. Fane, G. C. B. and G. C. H. Comr.-in-Chief in India. Hd. Qrs. Bengal Column of the Army of the Indus, Camp, Bukkur, 16th Feb. 1839.

1.—" H. E. the Comr.-in-Chief being about to leave the Bengal Column of the Army of the Indus, in his progress where his duty calls him; feels it due to the troops, previous to his departure, to record what he has witnessed of their conduct, during their march from *Ferozpoor* into *Sindh*, (27) to hold it up, as an example for their brother soldiers, on all occasions.

2.—" The excellent discipline and good behaviour of the troops have conciliated the inhabitants of the country wherever they have passed, and he is glad to be able to point out the consequences. These have been, not only the exaltation of their fame and character as soldiers, but these circumstances have greatly conduced to their personal advantage, because the confidence of the inhabitants, which such good conduct has produced, has led to their freely resorting to our camps with the produce of their villages, by which means we have been free from all wants and privations.

3.—" H. E. desires, that the officers of all ranks and departments will accept the expression of his approbation of their zeal, and of the good example they have set." (28)

16. *Bukkur—Force left in the Fort.*—The 35th Bengal N. I. was directed to stand fast in the fort of Bukkur, until arrangements were made for its relief; and Lieut.-Col. Monteath ordered to correspond direct with the Head Quarters of the column.

(27) The Army had marched 600 miles, including 145 miles down to lower Sindh and back to Sukkur.

(28) Sir H. Fane left us on the 18th Feb. 1839, and proceeded by water down the Indus to Bombay; where he established his Head Quarters. His leaving the army was much regretted by us all. He had an interview with Sir J. Keane, on his way down.

A sick Depôt was directed to be established at *Sukkur*, and a proper supply of medicines and surgical instruments to be left. The recovered men in hospital were sent to join their corps.

A Fort Adjutant was appointed, and Lieut. Laughton, Bengal Engineers, to be Garrison Engineer, to receive instructions from the Chief Engineer; and to be under the commandant of the fort.

The heavy baggage of the Cavalry Brigade, which could not conveniently be carried on, was directed to be deposited in the fort; and to be sent in empty boats proceeding to Ferozpoor, where it was to be lodged.

The Commandant of the fort of Bukkur was authorized to disburse treasure from the military chest (29) for the public service, without reference, on any emergency; payments to be made in presence of the Ft. Adjt. (30)

The *Bridge of Boats* was directed to be made over to Lieut. Wood, of the Indian Navy, and to be kept up till Shah Shoojah's Artillery should have crossed to the right bank; the larger bridge, or that in the main branch, was then to be broken up, 10 most suitable boats to be used for a *Ferry*, either at *Rohree*, or *Uzeezpoor*. (31) The remainder of the boats to be made over to the Commissariat Department for transport of grain, &c. The other materials to be deposited in the fort, under charge of the Garrison Engineer, for the public service. The smaller bridge to be kept up as long as practicable, to facilitate the communication with Bukkur;

(29) Treasure was left in the fort, and was to be afterwards forwarded to the army in charge of the 35th N. I. when relieved by a Bombay corps.

(30) Triplicate receipts, the original and duplicate to be sent to the Field Pay Mr. the triplicate, retained by the Comdt.

(31) Distant about 11 miles higher up the river. On the 8th March it was published in orders that Lieut. Wood I. N. had made arrangements for a boat to leave Sukkur on the 15th, and another on the 1st of April; after which, a boat was to leave on the 1st of each month; and that as soon as a boat leaving Sukkur could reach *Ferozpoor*, the same arrangement would take place *there*.

and when necessary to break it up, the boats to be transferred to the Commissariat, and the materials to the Garrison Engineer.

17. *The Bengal and Bombay Columns—Army of Indus.*—Lieut.-Genl. Sir John Keane, K. C. B. and G. C. H. Comr.-in-Chief of the Bombay army, and in command of the forces in Sindh, was now, to assume the command of the "*Army of the Indus,*" which occasioned the following arrangements to be made. The whole of the Cavalry (Bengal and Bombay) as originally intended, were to form a division under the command of Major Genl. Thackwell. The whole of the Artillery (Bengal and Bombay) to be under Brigr. Stevenson, Bombay Army. The Infantry of the Bengal column, to be denominated the 1st Infy. Division, under the personal command of Major Genl. Sir W. Cotton; (32) the infantry of the Bombay column, to be the 2nd division under Major Genl. Willshire.

Major Parsons (Bengal) Dy. Commy. Genl. was directed to assume a general control over the Commissariat of the Bengal and Bombay columns; and Capt. G. Thomson, Chief Engineer of the Bengal column, became the chief Engineer of the "*Army of the Indus.*" There were no other staff arrangements made. (33)

It was subsequently notified (34) that the 15th Feb. 1839 was the period from which the Native Troops, and permanent establishments of *both presidencies,* were to be placed on a footing of perfect equality in regard to pay and allowances: being the date on which the Head Quarters of the

(32) Sir W. Cotton commanded the Bengal column till Sir J. Keane joined us at Quetta on the 6th April, 1839, when Sir W. C. assumed the command of the 1st Division; and Major Genl. Nott, reverted to the command of the 2nd Brigade.

(33) The late Major Keith, D. A. G. Bombay Army, and Major N. Campbell, Depy. Qr. Mr. Genl. Bombay Army, were *seniors in their Depts.* to Major Craigie and Garden, of the Bengal army, which is the rule by which departmental seniority is governed, while Lieut. Col. R. Macdonald, was D. A. G. Queen's troops, Bombay, and Mily. Secy. to Sir J. Keane.

(34) On Sir J. Keane's joining us (6th April 1839).

Bengal column were established on the right bank of the *Indus*. (35)

18. *Bengal Column arrived at Shikarpoor.*—The train of artillery marched into Shikarpoor on the 16th of Feb. 1839. The 2nd Brigade of Infantry reached it on the 17th Feb. The 1st Brigade of Infantry on the 18th Feb. The 4th Brigade on the 19th : and the Head Quarters, the H. A. and Cavalry Brigade on the 20th Feb. 1839, where we found the Shah, Mr. MacNaghten, the Envoy and Minister at his court; and the Shah's contingent, commanded by Major General Simpson.

The Chief Engineer was direced to entertain 300 bildars for the purpose of making roads ; as the sappers and miners were required for other duties. Preparations were now to be made for the advance of the troops. The Bombay column was about 15 marches in our rear at Lukkee, one march on the other side of Sewun. The Dy. Commy. Genereral, Major Parsons, wished to have remained about 20 days at Shikarpoor, to enable us to start with the greatest possible quantity of supplies ; but it was urged, that it was highly expedient to push on to the *Bolan Pass* to secure it as soon as possible. We were just 10 marches from Dadur at the entrance to the pass, 18 marches from Quetta, and 32 marches from Candahar. No doubt it was expedient to move on to the pass, and to move through it, but as the Shah had reached Shikarpoor a month before us, the Chiefs of Candahar had ample time to have made 22 marches to occupy the pass, to which they must have known the invading force to be so near. It was proposed by one party that a brigade of Infantry only should be sent on in advance to occupy the pass ;. but as it could not be known whether Dost Mahomed Khan would join the Candahar Chiefs, (36) and whe-

(35) The Bombay troops were on the *right* back of the Indus the whole time.

(36) In 1834 when Shah Shoojah went to Candahar, in his last attempt to recover his throne, Dost Mahomed did march from Cabool to Candahar, where he defeated, and put the Shah to flight. The dis-

ther they might not *both* have contested for the possession of the Pass;—great caution was required in risking an advance without the means of an immediate support. (37) The Bombay column halted at *Larkhana* nine days (from 3rd to 11th March), and 10 days at *Gundava* (21st to 30th March) after the treaty had been signed at Hyderabad : and if Sir J. Keane could have pushed on with his escort from *Larkhana*, (38) he would have reached *Quetta* by the time we did—whereas we had to halt there, from the 27th March to the 6th April 1839—11 days, by which we consumed our supplies, and were obliged to be put on half rations. (39)

19. *Shikarpoor.*—The town of Shikarpoor contains about 6,000 houses and 30,000 inhabitants, the houses are all built of mud, and it is a dirty place. It is a place of much resort, and the first of importance between Rohree and Dadur, near the entrance to the Bolan Pass. It has some pretensions to trade, but none to consideration from its

---

tance from Cabool to Candahar is 29 marches. Had he done so he might have effected more for his cause than making a stand at Ghuznee!

(37) From the nature of the pass, the cattle would have been starved had any force been kept many days in it. The pass was known from the written report of *Mr. Masson*. In a Mily. point of view, a Brigade of Infy. and a few guns could have defended the Head of the pass!

(38) Leaving Larkhana on the 4th of March he might have reached Shikarpoor by the 8th, then Dadur (10 marches) on the 18th March, while we only marched from Dadur on the 16th March, 1839.

(39) His Excy. was anxious to ascertain the practicability of the *Gundava Pass*, which it was desirable to do. It is to be regretted that he did not join us sooner, as we did not obtain one day's supplies either at Bhag or at Dadur, nor even at Quetta, where we awaited his arrival.

The Bombay column made 12 marches from Larkhana to *Dadur*, and the Bengal column 10 marches from Shikarpoor to Dadur, so that the march was a little shortened by moving by the *Gundava Pass*, but much time was lost. Capt. Outram (*Rough notes, &c.* p. 39) makes the distance from Larkhana to Shikarpoor, 52 miles, equal to four marches, so that about two marches were saved: but from 15 to 17 days more time were consumed by the route viâ *Gundava*, while the Bengal troops were already in advance from Shikarpoor.

buildings. There are a number of Jews here, from whom Bills can be obtained or negociated, on any place in India, or even on Constantinople, China or any place almost in the world :—in fact money transactions are the chief employment of the wealthy people of the place, and the merchants will contract to furnish large quantities of grain. Being so near the Indus, whenever the free navigation of the river increases the commerce of Sindh and Afghanistan, Shikarpoor will become a place of great commercial importance.

When Shah Shoojah visited Sindh in his last expedition to try to recover his throne in 1834, (40) he obtained possession of this place, with the consent of the Ameers of Hyderabad. He tried to obtain money from Ameers, which they would not at first comply with. The Shah threatened to plunder Shikarpoor and Larkhana, if not supplied with money. A very severe action took place on the 9th Jan. 1834, seven koss (14 miles) beyond *Rohree*. The Sindhians lost 1,370 horse and foot soldiers, and a considerable number were killed and wounded on the Shah's side. The army of *Talpoorians* fairly fled from the field of battle; and the Shah obtained firm possession of Shikarpoor. They consented to the pecuniary aid in preference to hazarding another battle: and agreed to farm the place from the Shah at from 5 or 7 lakhs of Rupees. (41) There were, now 15,500 troops at Shikarpoor; so that with camp-followers, there must have been nearly 100,000 people to feed.

(40) His departure from Loodianah was reported to Government as having taken place on the 17th Feb. 1833.

(41) The only European officer with the Shah, was a Mr. Campbell, who was made prisoner by Dost Mahomed Khan on the defeat of the Shah at Candahar on 2nd July, 1834, and afterwards entered his service.

CHAPTER III.

MARCH FROM SHIKARPOOR TO DADUR NEAR THE BOLAN PASS.

1. *Preparations to leave Shikarpoor,* (20th Feb. 1839.)—On the arrival of the Head Quarters with Maj. Genl. Sir W. Cotton at Shikarpoor, the whole of the *Bengal* column, and the Shah's contingent, were present,—a force amounting to about 15,500 men. Consultation was held between Sir W. Cotton and Mr. MacNaghten, the Envoy and Minister, the principal staff being present, as to the time of marching onwards to the Pass. Mr. MacNaghten had received a report that the *Bolan Pass* (10 marches distant) was occupied by the enemy; (1) he, therefore, on the 18th Feb. had addressed a dispatch (2) to Lieut.-Genl. Sir J. Keane, Commander-in-Chief of the army of the Indus, then in Sindh, pressing him to push on. It was resolved to march towards the Pass, *at once,* to secure its possession. The Dy. Commy. Genl. had represented that it was necessary to remain at Shikarpoor for about 20 days, to enable the commissariat to obtain the greatest possible quantity of supplies for all the troops; while halting at this place, the troops would not consume their stock of supplies, but procure their grain, &c. from the city, where a large quantity had been collected; and more was procurable for the rear columns, Bombay troops, &c. on the arrival of an expected convoy, with wheat, gram, &c. coming from Mooltan, &c. The *Bengal* Commissariat were to supply the *Bombay* troops, not only with *grain*

---

(1) It turned out to be a mere report.
(2) It reached Sir J. Keane on the 23rd Feb. 1839, when he was about 12 marches distant from Shikarpoor.

but with *Camels*. (3) Before the resolution to move on immediately, was known, the Dy. Commy. Genl. had detached 4,000 camels to bring up from the rear grain, &c. He was also led to expect 10 days' supplies would be ready at *Dadur* (4) (10 marches in advance), and 20 days' supplies at *Quetta* (5) (18 marches in advance); while *Candahar* was 32 marches distant from Shikarpoor: so that, including halts, &c. 45 or 50 days' supplies were required for the troops up to Candahar: (6) and as we marched with carriage for and with only a month's supplies from Ferozpoor, (7) more carriage was required than could be procured at the time, both for the Bengal and Bombay columns, (8) as well as for the Shah's force.

(3) It was well known that the Bombay troops had great difficulty in procuring 3000 camels in Sindh. As on their march from *Shikarpoor* they would be deprived of their *Water-carriage*, it was estimated that 10,000 would at least be required for the Bombay Army alone. Of *grain* there was plenty to be had, but the difficulty was, thus unexpectedly, to supply the *camels* for the Bombay column. Undoubtedly, the supplies and cattle were properly to be used by *both* columns. The *Bengal* Commissariat did not know, till now, that it would have to supply both columns—or previous arrangements would have been made, of course, in due time, to procure a greater number of camels. It was not to be expected that the Ameers of Sindh would be very zealous in their exertions to supply camels; but if the Govt. of Bombay could not well rely on the army procuring carriage in Sindh, it would have been better to have intimated to the Bengal (supreme) Govt. their fears on this head. *Sir J. Keane* could do nothing less than share the supplies and cattle, between the two columns. I say thus much to exonorate, as is but just, the Bengal Commissariat from any supposed want of exertions. Neither do I attribute any blame to that of Bombay; they could not bring with them any cattle but horses—by *sea*. The error committed was, timely notice not having been given. Between Shikarpoor, and up to the time of the Bombay column leaving Cabool, on its return, the Bengal Commissariat supplied it with 6,830 camels.

(4) And even at *Bhag*, eight marches only in advance.

(5) We were deceived in our expectations. We only obtained about 300 maunds there.

(6) Not *one* day's supplies were obtained between Shikarpoor and Candahar, at any *one place*!!!

(7) See p. 8.

(8) We left Shikarpoor, leading column and Hd. Qrs. on 23rd Feb.

Supplies with Bengal Column.

Supplies taken with the Bengal Column.—The Bengal Column marched from Shikarpoor with *one and a half* month's supplies, and a similar quantity remained in depôt there, to follow if required. Rum for three months, accompanied the Bengal column.

2. *Order for march from Shikarpoor*, (21st Feb. 1839.) —The troops of the Bengal column were directed to march in the following order, in columns, and on the following dates:

1st. *On the 22nd Feb.*—The Engineer Dept., Ressalah of Local Horse, and a Company of Infy.

2nd. *On the 23rd.*—The Head Quarters. Cavy. Brigade and Horse Arty. and a wing of Native Infy.

3rd. *On the 24th.*—1st Brigade Infy. and Camel battery,

4th. *On the 25th.*—4th Brigade of Infy. and a Regt. from 2nd Brigade (temporarily attached.)

5th. *On the 26th.*—The Park, 4th Local Horse, and a Coy. N. I.

6th. *On the 27th.*—Field Commissariat stores, escorted by one Ressalah of Local Horse, and one Coy. of Infy.

7th.—The 2nd Brigade, with H. M. Shah Shoojah-ool-Moolk. (9)

8th.—The field hospital with the 4th Brigade. A portion of treasure, and a party of Local Horse, attached to each Brigade.

Maj. Genl. Sir W. Cotton, inspected the Park of Arty. and the H. A. Cavy. and Infy. Brigades and Camel battery, on the 21st and 22nd Feb. previous to the march of the troops.

Review of Troops.—The troops were paraded in *Review order* before H. M. Shah Shoojah-ool-Moolk, who was

and reached Candahar on 26th April, 1839, a period of 63 days thus elapsed; and our staying 11 days at Quetta, partly, and not obtaining supplies on our march, were the causes of our being so early placed on half rations.

(9) Though His Majesty took the lead up to Shikarpoor; it was decided that the British troops should move in advance, being better able to cope with an enemy. Had any check been given to the contingent raised but recently, it might have been serious; and besides, we should have been deprived of the best of the little forage to be expected, and we had more cattle to provide for.

pleased to present a donation of 8,000 Rs. (£800) to be divided, in equal proportions among the corps, European and Native.

3. *March from Shikarpoor*, (23rd Feb. 1839.)—Marched this day 17½ miles, the road through a jungly country to Jagan. 24*th Feb.* marched 11¾ miles to Janeedera, through a jungly country, but, except in a few places, open on both flanks. To prevent the Rewaree camels falling off in condition by coming late to the ground, they were allowed to go on at any hour during the night, under parties of Local Horse. Scarcity of water reported at next stage (Rajhan): Hd. Qrs. directed to halt to-morrow. The 1st Brigade to halt till further orders. The 4th Brigade to close up to it at Jagan. The Park and Field Commisst. to stand fast at Shikarpoor; till columns in advance have moved on in the order already directed.

Of the Shah's force, the 2nd Regt. of Cavy. and a Provisional Battn. of Infantry (900 strong) were left at Shikarpoor, on the march of H. M. from that place.

Major Leech joined the Hd. Qrs. to-day. He had been engaged in collecting supplies between Shikarpoor and Dadur.

Post office.—The Post Master, under the directions of the Envoy and Minister, agreed to lay dâks and establish a post along the line of march, using horsemen, camels, and men, as the obstacles to be overcome, and the nature of the country and circumstances might dictate.

New order of March, (10) (25th Feb.)—On the 27th Feb. H. A. and a Regt. of Cavy. to march; on 28th, remainder of Cavy., a wing of Infy., and the Hd. Qrs. of the column; on 28th Feb. 1st Infy. Brigade; on 1st March, 4th Infy. Brigade and Field Commisst; on 2nd March the Park and 4th Local Horse.

26*th Feb.*—Report of only three wells at the next ground. The Engineers in advance; H. M.'s 16th Lancers marched by wings.

(10) This was rendered necessary, owing to the reports of the scarcity of water in advance, and to there being a "*marshy desert*," to cross. (See Journal, chapter 18.)

27*th Feb.*—Hd. Qrs. marched to Rajhan, 11¼ miles. The road passed over the edge of the *Desert*. Scarcity of forage.

28*th Feb.*—The Hd. Qrs. halted.

1*st March.*—The 3rd Cavy. to march to Barshore to-morrow. The 2nd Cavy. and Dett. 48th N. I. to march to-morrow, from Janeedera to Rajhan.

The supply of *Kurbee* (11) unequal to the demand, limited to rations for officers' chargers. Infantry officer for one horse only.

The mails going to and coming from Hindustan, plundered; one runner killed and two wounded. Heard of a Convoy coming on with grain, having been attacked.

2*nd March.*—The 3rd Cavy. marched over the desert. The Hd. Qrs., one Squadron 2nd Cavy., and one Coy. of N. I. to move to-night to *Barshore*, across the desert; and to wells near *Cundah* on the following day. Remaining two Squadrons of 2nd Cavy. and remainder detachment of Infy. to Barshore, on the 4th, and to wells on the 5th,—where the whole were to remain till further orders.

1st Infy. Brigade, with camel battery to Jagan on the 4th; remainder of troops, to stand fast till further orders.

4. *Supplies and Forage*, (3rd March.)—Supplies ordered to be pushed on to the Army, as a scarcity was found on the march hitherto. Capt. Lawrence 2nd Cavy. sent with a party to *Cundah* (eight miles W. of Meerpoor) to collect forage for the Cavy. (The *Bombay* Column to-day at Larkhana.)

The Desert (called the *Putt*). The distance over the *Desert* was 26½ miles. The troops moved at night to prevent the men suffering from the heat, or the reflection and glare caused by the rays of the sun, striking from the hard sandy soil. It was a clear moon-light night, and after leaving camp the desert appeared interminable. The troops, by the above arrangements, did not suffer in the least. (12) There is not

---

(11) Supplied when a deficiency of grass or bad forage.

(12) Detachments which crossed this *desert* late in *April*, and in the month of *May* suffered dreadfully.

a drop of water to be had, and when in the centre of the desert, if the traveller loses the proper direction, he may wander about, and die of thirst, as many others have done. We found strings of camels moving across in several lines with guides, so that we could not lose our way.

We found bad water at Barshore. There were a number of small wells, but the water so salt and muddy, that the horses refused to drink it, though they had marched so many miles without drinking. A large pukha well was ordered to be made here. (13)

4th March.—The Head Qrs. moved to-day to Meerpoor, distant, 14½ miles. The road much the same as that of the desert: wells in any number dug in the bed of the river, but water salt and bad.

Two Squadrons of 2nd Cavy. and three Cos. 48th N. I. march to Meerpoor to-morrow.

Intimation received of a party of *Jahranee Belochees* having descended from the mountains to carry off camels, and plunder stragglers. The Maj. Genl. warns officers Comg. columns, to take precautions to protect the baggage, &c. on the march. They usually move in parties of five or six men. (14)

Commsst. Cattle.—The Camels were obliged to be allowed to travel over night, as otherwise, owing to the long marches, want of forage, and heat of the weather. (98° to-day at 3 P. M.) they could not carry their loads of grain; to be protected by small parties of horsemen in front, on the flanks, and in the rear, and not to go far from Camp to graze, without a suitable escort.

5th March.—Head Quarters to-day at Ustad, distance 13¾ miles. There is a lake of fresh water here. The country on this march as barren as last march; a desert within a few miles of the hills. A chief of the Belochees has a

---

(13) Each soldier should carry a canteen to hold a quart of water. Every Bombay soldier had one. A certain quantity of water should be carried for each troop of Cavy. &c.

(14) It was owing to these Belochees, that we found so many deserted villages, since our leaving Shikarpoor

fort in the hills, and about 20 miles distant. A number of camels carried off in the night. (15)

5. *Cavalry Horses*, (6th March).—The Head Qrs. to-day at *Bhag*, distant 9½ miles from last ground. The Hd. Qrs. and Cavy. to halt to-morrow. Obtained 300 or 400 maunds of grain here.

Comsst. unable to furnish full rations of Kurbee; to issue an extra ration of one seer (two ℔s.) of Jooar (barley) to each horse.

A number of more camels driven off by the Belochees to-day. The Governor paid the General a visit in the afternoon.

The camp-followers who went beyond the picquets, were plundered, and their cattle stolen.

The Crops, (7th March).—Warning against depredations committed on fields of growing wheat, and severe punishment denounced. Whenever necessary to assign growing wheat, or barley, as forage for Cavalry, (16) a portion of a field to be marked off for each corps, by an officer of the Qr. Mr. Genl.'s Dept., and the owner paid by the Executive Commissariat officer of the Brigade, on statements of the number of rations, by Qr. Mrs. of the Regts., countersigned by Comg. officers.

The *Shah* marched from Shikarpoor on the 7th March, with 1 Regt. of irregular Cavy. and 5 Regts. of Infantry, (each 820.)

8th March.—Hd. Quarters marched to-day to Myhesur (or Myhsur) distance 16 miles, across a wretched country. The village stands on the bank of the *Bolan* river, which issues from the *Pass*.

Half-rations to Non-Combatants.—There being a difficulty in bringing on supplies from the rear, the Comsst. Dept. for the present, to issue *Half-rations* to men of the mustered establishments; paying compensation in money in lieu of

---

(15) A horse-artilleryman shot himself to-day, and died in the night.

(16) This was often found necessary; so I here give the mode of carrying the plan into operation, to save repetition.

the other half: this order not to affect the *troops*. We were now, within 23 miles of the Pass.

9th March.—The Hd. Quarters moved to-day to Noushera 15¾ miles; road over a bleak, barren desert for 15 miles. Crossed a Pass about five miles from the last ground. If great care be not taken, the road may be blocked up at this Pass for hours. After quitting the narrow gorge of the pass, the road, though bounded on each side by low hills, is good. The country throughout is a *desert*. Plenty of good water from the *Bolan* river. The baggage to-day crowding at the pass, delayed the march of the troops for a long time.

9th March.—Camels with the treasure, &c. over-driven; orders not to force them on.

6. *Arrive at Dadur*, (10th March).—The Hd. Quarters, to-day, arrived at Dadur, a distance of 7½ miles. At 4½ miles from the last ground, crossed the *Bolan* river. Hence over a good road (the mountains closing in on all sides) three miles is Dadur near the entrance to the *Bolan Pass*.

Reconnoitring—Detachment in Advance.—A detachment of one troop of Cavy. (17) and three Cos. 48th N. I., (18) under Major *Cureton*, (19) was directed to move into the pass to-morrow, to escort the Dy. Qr. Mr. Genl. (Major *Garden*) to make his observations on the forage, and grass procurable; and on the obstacles to the passage of the troops. (20)

The Engineer Dept. also to move to *Drubbee* (21) to-mor-

(17) Under Capt. Wheler, 2nd Cavy.
(18) Under Major Thomas.
(19) 16th Lancers, and A. A. G. of Cavy. Sir A. Burnes accompanied this party.
(20) Major G. was recalled when he had proceeded half-way. We got, afterwards, reports from Major C. the Chief Engineer, and from Sir A. Burnes.
(21) This place is only seven miles from Dadur; has a fine green sward and a clear stream of water running past it. The Engineers did not move on with Major Cureton, but encamped short of his stages, with the two Cos. of sappers and miners. They were to remove any obstacles on the road.

Preparations to advance. 43

row; and proceed with their operations, in facilitating the passage of the Army through the Defile.

11th March.—To supply six or seven days forage for the Cavy., &c. horses, a quantity of green barley was directed to be supplied to each corps, to be cut, dried, and mixed with grass. (22) Reports from the rear, of Camp-followers being robbed and cut down by the Belochees.

12th March.—Forage reported to be in the Pass. In the rear columns, the Qr. Mrs. of H. M.'s 13th Lt. Infy. (23) and 16th Bengal N. I., attacked by a party of Belochees, while riding on to take up new ground.

13th March.—The Maj. Genl. intimated to Comg. officers that the country, through which the army was now passing, abounds in a good description of carriage-bullocks, and afforded a good opportunity to complete the transport for their several bazars, to carry three days supplies; as required by the Regns. of the service. (24) From the reports from the advance, it was stated that there were occasional patches of dry, coarse grass, to be found in the Pass. Caution published against lighting fires in or near the grass; all transgressors to be severely punished.

The *Dâwk* robbed, and the letters destroyed. Reports of more thefts in the 4th Brigade, in the rear. Good reports from the advance.

7.—*Order for March into Pass, &c.*—(14th March)—The Hd. Qrs.—2 T. 2 B. H. A.—a Regt of Cavy. and 2 Regts. of Infy. from 1st Brigade, and half a Ressalah of Local Horse—to march on the 15th;—remainder of Cavy. and remaining Regt. of the 1st Brigade, No. 6 Lt. Fd.

(22) The A. Qr. Mr. Genl. of Cavy. arranged this with Major Leech. Asst. Pol. Agent, by a field near camp, being assigned.

(23) His Sergt. not being so well mounted was cut up and stripped. The Qr. Mr. of the 13th (Lt. Fenwick) charged seven of them.

(24) It was found impracticable to keep up this Regtl. arrangement. By the orders of the 14th March 1839, the supplies were to be served out through the buneahs attached to the different Brigades; and it was directed that "if *they* cannot carry the whole, indented for, the *Commissariat*. Dept. must lend the aid of Rewaree camels."

Order of March into the Pass.

Battery, and half a Ressalah of Local Horse, on the 16th;—2 Regts. of 4th Brigade, and a Ressalah of Local Horse, and the Field Hospital, on the 17th;—The remaining Regt. of the 4th Brigade, in charge of Commissariat Field Depôt, on the 20th inst.

The Columns actually marched a day later than the above dates, viz.—on 16th March, and following days.—Each Column to carry with it its proportion of Commissariat supplies.

Order of March.—The order in which the leading Columns will enter the Defile.

The *Infantry* by Sections, right in front; the *Artillery* and *Cavalry,* conforming.

1. H. M.'s 13th Infy.
2. Horse Arty.
3. 2nd Lt. Cavy.
4. Wing 48th N. I.
5. Treasure.
6. Led horses of Cavy. &c.
7. Hd. Qr. baggage.
8. Regtl. baggage, according to Regtl. seniority.
9. Local Horse. (25)

Two Cos. of Infy., when practicable, to move parallel with the guns; ready to afford aid to them, in getting over difficult parts of the road.

The *Baggage Master* to reconnoitre the gorge of the Pass, to make the necessary arrangements, for regulating the march of the baggage. A detail of Local Horse at his disposal. (March countermanded, at 10 p. m.)

The 1st Infy. Brigade, and the Camel battery marched into Dadur. Orders received from Sir J. Keane.

Yesterday the Dhoolee bearers of the 3rd. Lt. Cavy. ran away. (26)

---

(25) The baggage of Hd. Qrs., Divisional, and Brigade staff, to be collected under the Provost Marshal—of Regts., under an officer from each Regt.; with a party to preserve order, and protect the camels, &c. from plunderers. The baggage packed and loaded in one hour.

The baggage of each Regt. to be conducted to centre of its lines; awaiting its time for moving off.

(26) G. O. 15th March 1839.—" Symptoms of discontent, and insubordination having occurred among the Dhoolee bearers, and other camp-followers (notwithstanding the very great consideration shown them

15th March.—The 1st Column to march to-morrow, the rest on subsequent days, in the order above indicated.

Memo.—Compensation, in money, will be disbursed in lieu of the moiety of their rations, while on *half-rations*, to those belonging to mustered Establishments,—the difference between the price of Attah (flour) in the *Suddur bazar*, and the rate issued from the Commissariat stores.

Full rations to be restored as soon as supplies, in transitu, reach the army. (27)

8. *Position of the Forces*, (15th March 1839).—At this period the *Bombay* Troops were nine marches from Dadur. The *Shah* had marched from Shikarpoor towards Dadur, and Lt.-Col. *Wade* was within five marches of Peshawer.

We did not find *here* the 10 days' supplies of grain which we expected, and had been promised. Before leaving Shikarpoor, *Mehrab Khan* of *Khelat* wrote to say that the grain was collected for the Army, and " to send people to receive it, as he could not take care of it." (28) The people at Dadur were under his authority, and from the way in which we were supplied here, we might somewhat judge of the conduct to be expected from *this chief.*—The Dy. Comy. Genl. left Camels and people with money to purchase grain in the Valley of *Seistan*, which is close to Dadur, but

during the March from the Provinces); officers Comg. Brigades, or detached Columns, have the power to inflict the *summary punishment* of *flogging*, on all followers, who hesitate to do their duty."

" Officers in command to take precautions against followers, &c. deserting; and it is to be explained, that the A. P. A. (Major Leech) has been requested to give a reward of five Rs. for every mustered follower who may desert, and whom his *Belochees* may secure, and bring to camp.

(27) A Dâk in the *Balan* Pass cut up, and others in the *Rear*; two Artillerymen and two camp-followers, *(unarmed)* attacked by the mountaineers; one European was dragged into the mountains, and stripped, his jaw broken, and his arm cut with a sabre.

(28) Major *Leech* was at *Kelat*, as late as August 1838, urging the Chief to supply us; and I must say *he* never was very sanguine as to his keeping his promise to furnish supplies.

only obtained about 500 maunds—not a *tenth* of what had been promised us.

A *Depôt* was, subsequently formed here, on the advance of the Troops, and a force was left here.

CHAPTER IV.

MARCH FROM DADUR—THROUGH THE BOLAN PASS—TO QUETTA.

1. *Country between Shikarpoor and Dadur.*—The distance between Shikarpoor and Dadur, is 146 miles, and 10 marches; but owing to the want of water on the road, the Hd. Quarters did not reach Dadur in less than 16 days, as it was found necessary to send the troops by detachments, and sometimes by wings of Regts. of the Cavy., as they require three or four times more water than Infantry Regts. From *Rajhan*, or after our 3rd march, we found the whole country between it and *Noushera*, a distance of 96 miles, and only six marches, a desert almost the whole way, except a little cultivation round the villages. The marches were long, and no water to be had at intermediate places; so that we found the troops much fatigued and the cattle much knocked up, owing to the length of the distance they daily travelled, and the difficulty of procuring water, and forage. A party of Cavalry was sent out to collect forage for the horses, and strict orders were given to prevent the columns closing up on each other. After crossing over the "*Marshy desert,*" we left *Sindh*, and entered, at Barshore, *Belochistan*, the country which produces such numerous bands of plunderers, (1) by which the troops were so much annoyed, so many of our followers killed and wounded, so many of our cattle carried off, and property lost and destroyed. It

(1) The Belochees inhabit the country to the W. of Sindh, and the *Hala* mountains which run N. and S., divide Sindh from Belochistan. We found Janeedera (the 2nd march though in Sindh) was deserted, and had been for a long time, owing to the depredations committed by these robbers.

is to be hoped that one of the benefits to be derived from our operations in *Sindh* and *Affghanistan*, will be the restoration of the country, between Shikarpoor and Dadur, so necessary to keep up our communications in that quarter, to some order, and to free it from these pests, and enemies to civilization. (2)

2. *Entrance of the Bolan Pass to Kohan Delan*, (16th March, 1839.)—Thermometer at 3 A. M. 62°. The Hd. Qrs. left Dadur this morning at day break, with the 1st Column. Dadur is 743 feet above the level of the sea. The road lay over the Bolan river after leaving camp. The entrance to the Pass might be disputed for a short time, by parties being stationed on the broken hills on each side ; but an irregular enemy could not long oppose regular troops— who would dislodge those occupying the heights before the advance of the column was made ! They might much annoy the rear, baggage, and cattle. It would be necessary to crown the heights to protect the advance of the troops, and the passage of stores, baggage, &c., and to post parties at such points, as those from which the enemy could descend from the hills to make an attack. Our column was not attacked, but the rear columns were.

After entering the Pass the road lay N. W., and after marching about four miles, the mountains began to close

---

(2) The treaty was signed at Hyderabad on the 3rd Feb. 1839. Capt. Outram says (p. 34) in his notes, that 16 or 17,000 Belochees had occupied the opposite (Hyderabad) bank, for two miles. The Ameers "(who had called them in to their assistance)" had great difficulty in inducing them to withdraw. *Sheer Mahomed*, having expressed his determination to oppose us, was joined by the followers of all the other Ameers. " *Meer Sobdar Khan* (since favorably distinguished in the new treaty) prevailed on *him* to retire, and by distributing upwards of five Lakhs of Rs. (£50,000) induced them to depart."

But the Belochees were much under the influence of the late Mehrab Khan, the Belochee chief of *Khelat*, to whose instigation we owed the attacks of this people. There being a British force in Sindh, and our influence now extending to Khelat, will be the means of imposing a check on these people, and will render the country safe to merchants and travellers.

on us from N. E. to S. W. The hills which immediately enclose the pass, are not very high—are irregular in height and barren; their strata most confused, and their formation of coarse pudding-stone, changing near the surface, to loose clay and pebbles. The distance from hill to hill, on each side, varied; but in few places within the command of *musketry*, though shots from *Juzzails* (rifes) would have reached us more frequently. (3) The road lay over rough loose stones and shingle. We to-day crossed the Bolan river eight times, never deeper than three feet in any place. At about eight miles we came to a spot called *" Drubbee,"* where there is a small valley, and green sward, as the name imports, where the Engineers had encamped. A clear stream runs by it, and 1,500 men might have their camp here. From this, the distance between the hills contracts again.

On the left hand side and close to camp, we saw six trees, not having seen one before. We found our camp at the distance of 11 miles from Dadur at Kohan Delan, (4) where the valley of stones widens. But little forage here.

The H. A. and Cavy. were in one Camp just beyond the six trees. The five Cos. 48th N. I. in another across the river, which was fordable. The Hd. Qrs. near some grave stones, near a height situated between the two camps. (5) We found nothing to prevent our tents being sent on in advance, with a party to protect them. The elevation of this place above the level of the sea was 904 feet, or 161 above Dadur—which, in a distance of 11 miles gives a rise of 1 foot in 360—Thermometer at 3 P. M. 86°. On entering the Pass you are in *Khorassan*.

(3) The native Rife with a fixed rest, it is said will kill at 800 yards. The common rifle is only 4 feet 10 inches in the barrel, the larger Juzzails are six or seven feet in the barrel.

(4) Kundyee of Conally. From this place there is said to be a road out of the Pass, which goes to Dadur, Khelat, &c.; the Dâk went by this road, or path, over the hills.

(5) A Sergt. of the 16th Lancers was drowned by his horse getting into deep water. Subsequently, we were obliged to wait for day-light.

3.—*March to Kirta*, (17th March, 1839.)—Marched before day-light; thermometer 3 A. M. 60° crossed the river on leaving camp, (6); the darkness of the morning was increased by heavy clouds, and rain, with a cold cutting wind. Crossed the Bolan river 13 times, at no place deeper than three feet. The distance between the hills greater than on the last march, and on reaching Kirta, we found our camp. The village of Kirta was about a mile in advance, to the right, and did not contain many houses or inhabitants. (7)

The valley, here, is from 3 to 4 miles broad, and 6 or 7 miles long, in the direction of the next stage. The whole length of the valley about 10 miles. A Kalifa of merchants from Candahar came into camp at noon, on its way to India.

The same kind of road as last march, over loose stones, and shingle. Crossed the last time about three miles from camp just where we entered the valley. The country has the same sterile appearance; there is some long dry grass, and a few stunted bushes: little forage.

The distance marched 10 miles, 5 furlongs; the elevation above the level of the sea 1081 (8) or 177 feet above Kohan Delan, which gives in to-day's march, a rise of one foot in 304; thermometer at 3 P. M. 80°: very close and cloudy weather.

4.—*March to Beebee Nanee*, (18th March, 1839.)—Thermometer at 5 A. M. 60°. Marched at 8 A. M. owing to the rain, early in the morning. The clouds hid the barrenness of the mountains, rolling down towards their base. The valley barren except a few bushes of coarse grass, *Lanna*, (9) and dwarf Tamarisk. The march from Kirta for the first 6 or 7 miles, lies through the valley which is

---

(6) We were obliged to fasten the tent-ropes to stones; could not use tent-pins. *Iron*-pins are used in a rocky soil.

(7) It was made a Dâk station.

(8) This is the elevation of Gurm-ab a little beyond Kirta. A little grain was procured at Kirta.

(9) A bush which the camels eat, but not the camel-thorn.

here from 3 to 4 miles broad. The route lay close to the left towards the hills, and at the termination of this valley, which runs to the right to a considerable extent; entered another and smaller valley about a mile or 1½ mile wide, by crossing a small range of hills of clay and sand-stone, by a short gorge, about 18 or 20 feet wide. (10) Up this second valley the road is better, at the distance of 3 miles from the gorge, saw our tents at *Beebee Nanee*, about a mile from which, we came to numerous tombs of stones, and one of brick, on both sides of the road. It is considered a *Holy place*, and the dead are brought to it for interment from a great distance, said to be the bodies of travellers, murdered by the *Murhees*; a tribe of lawless, cowardly robbers, who live in these wastes, who will not attack armed men, but will kill travellers when asleep, or entrap them and stone them, without running any risk themselves. (11) Our camp at the further end of this valley, where we crossed the *Bolan*, at Beebee Nanee, much swollen and discolored by the rain of this morning. There are two caverns in the mountain, on the left, after crossing the river, which go by the name of *Beebee Nanee*; (12) but no human habitation to be seen.

The *Camp*.—The Hd. Qr. and Infy. camp were across the river; that of the H. A. and Cavy. on the Kirta side of it. There were graves near Hd. Qrs.

Distance marched 9 miles, 1 furlong. The elevation to-day above the level of the sea 1695 feet, or 614 feet above Kirta, (13) this gives the increased rise of 1 in 77 feet: thermometer at 3 p. m. 72°. Thunder and lightning

---

(10) You can enter the second valley without going through this gorge, by passing to the right and round it.

(11) A description of *Thug*. About 30 attacked a hackery this morning, and were beaten off by three horsemen who accidentally came up.

(12) Which we may translate to be the "Old Lady of the mountain." In Hindustani, Beebee (lady) and Nanee (grandmother).

(13) Gurm-ab beyond it, the place at which the rise was calculated.

and rain at sun-set; a gale of wind, and some heavy showers during the night, and very cold: many tents blown down. (14)

5.—*March to Abi-goom*, (19th March, 1839).—Marched at 5 A. M., thermometer 50°. The road this morning had much more of ascent than heretofore, and the gusts of wind were so violent, that it was difficult to keep our seats on horseback. The same dreary waste was around us, and we saw *snow*-capped mountains, which we shall approach to-morrow. The road passed through two valleys, between which the distance of the hills which bound the road, may be 2 to 300 yards in some places; crossed the river several times; at one place it was 3½ feet deep, passing through thick grass, and marshy ground, about 3 miles from our new camp.—The site of our *camp* is the same from which the engineers, sappers and miners were driven a few nights ago (15), and every table, chair, and tent, was washed down by the sudden rising of the river, or mountain torrent. We encamped in higher ground. Running streams of good water, close to camp: strong wind at night. There are some houses on the left-hand side of the road. The distance marched to-day, 8 miles, 5 furlongs. The elevation above the level of the sea was 2,540 feet, or 845 feet above Beebee Nanee; being a rise on this march of 1 foot in 51—much greater than in the last march. The gale in full force, and thermometer at noon 60°. Strong wind during the night. There were low hills to our right, and close to camp, from which we could see the open road in advance for a considerable distance.

(14) Obliged to fasten the tent-ropes to large stones, and pile stones on the ropes, to prevent the tent-pins being forced out of the ground. It was impossible to sleep, expecting every minute the pole of the tent to break, or the pins to be pulled out of the ground, by the sudden and strong gusts of wind.

(15) The 15th of March; the day before we marched, and on which it blew a gale of wind all day. They had encamped in the bed of the river, which we found quite dry. About one or two miles further on, is the real Abi-goom, (turn of the stream,) where the ground is more open.

6.—*March to Sir-i-Bolan*, (16) (20th March, 1839.)—
Thermometer at 4 A. M. 52°. Marched to-day at 5 A. M. with
a N. W. wind which pierced to the bone. The ascent this
morning was greater than we had yet found it, while the
road was still stony and pebbly, and lay through the bed of
a mountain torrent. A slight descent, at first, in the road.
The valley narrowed a good deal, and precipices of sand-
stone, pudding-stone, and loose earth and pebbles, over-
hung our route ; while in our front glistened in the morning sun, the snow-capped mountains ; the streams had
lost their depth, and every thing indicated an increased
elevation.

At about 6 miles came to *Sir-i-Khujoor*, where are some
Khujoor (Date) trees on the right of the road, on a rising
ground and some green fields, and a spring of water.
Except " *Drubbee*" on the first march, this was the only
green spot we met with in the Pass. There was some snow
on the mountains a few miles off.

After marching 3½ miles more, we came to the camp at
Sir-i-Bolan, distance from the last ground 9 miles and 5
furlongs. The elevation above the level of sea this march
far exceeded that of the last, being 4,494, or 1,954 feet
above Abi-Goom, giving a rise of about 1 in 25 feet, the
greatest we found in the Pass. Thermometer at 3 P. M. 66°.

The destruction of animals, and camels, this day, has
been very great, and the horses of the Artillery were greatly
distressed—8 horses (2 additional) to each gun and the
assistance of the Infantry, hardly sufficed to bring them
into camp. The Horse Artillery were five hours in marching
from the last ground (9½ miles). (17)

(16) Or, *Head*, or *source*, of the river Bolan. When Major Cureton's advance party was here on the 15th March, 1839, there was a
snow-storm which killed a great number of camels and other animals, and occasioned great loss of property. It is not safe to enter
the Pass very early in March; as there is great danger of having snow-
storms, and very cold weather.

(17) The *Camel battery* got on very well ; the camels in this Pass
performed their work with more ease than the horses. Some of the

Here there is not a blade of grass to be seen. The road from Sir-i-Khujoor to Sir-i-Bolan was constantly intersected by the stream of the river. There is a spring in the rock at Sir-i-Bolan, on the left of the road, close to where our Camp was; and it is from this spring that the Bolan river has its source. (18)

Lt.-Colonel Wade this day arrived at Peshawer.

7.—*March to Head of and beyond the Pass*, (21st March, 1839.)—Thermometer at 5 A. M. 44°. The troops having a long march before them, they were ordered to cook and eat their dinners and be ready to march. The order yesterday was, " Camp to be struck at day-break, tents loaded, and sent to the mouth of the Pass, and the camp to be pitched in the valley; an escort to be sent with the baggage, which is to be allowed to move off till 11 A. M.—after which, not till the troops shall have marched. (19) The troops to cook, and be prepared to move at 2 P. M."

camels of officers were preserved by being fed with flour, goor, and ghee; the mode of feeding suwaree *(riding)* camels. There was very little camel forage at this place.

(18) The Hills near camp were of no great height; picquets were placed on each during the evening, and remained there all night. Parties of the enemy might have annoyed us from these heights, but we saw no enemy. From the height to our right, fields of cultivation were seen. The distance between the hills on the right and left was about 300 to 400 yards. The camp was obliged to be a very straggling one.

(19) The grain-camels to be sent off before 11 A. M. or after 2 P. M. as least harassing to the cattle, the object being to enable the troops and baggage to clear the Bolan Defile before night; and be prepared to pass the sterile plain to *Sir-i-Ab* with as little inconvenience to troops and followers as possible. It was supposed that there was no water at Dusht-i-Bedowlut, 12¾ miles hence and 2¾ beyond the Pass. The March to Sir-i-Ab, would have been 28½ miles. The mushuqs, &c. were ordered to be filled with water, and sent with the troops. In to-day's orders extra drams were ordered to be given to the 3 Cos. H. M.'s 13th Lt. Infy. employed this afternoon as a working party with the Artillery; and also to the men of the 2 T. 2 B. H. A. The Chief Engineer went with the S. and M. in advance into the Valley. Major Leech gave the déjeuné staff a *déjeûne a la fourchette* consisting of a lamb, roasted whole and stuffed with raisins, &c. in the true *Affghan* style.

March out of the Bolan Pass.

The morning was clear and still. The camp laid before us, with the snow-clad mountains on the right, and the stream gushing from the mountain on the left, (20) which gives the name to the Pass—the picture was fine and even grand; while the stream was tainted with the dead bodies of camels, &c. The road lay through the same bed of pebbles, until we passed the river *Bolan*, when the hills closed; and reduced the valley to about a quarter of a mile in width.

At about five miles there were some stunted trees on each side of the road, the precipices became more abrupt, and the confusion of the different strata was beyond description. The ascent was considerable, and the Pass gradually narrowed, until it wound through some high hills, the shadows of which left us cool for a little while; the sun and radiation of heat were far from pleasant.

There were groups of starved camels, and here and there a horse, and a bullock; men, women, and children crowded the road, and lay among the stones basking in the sun; every thing indicated our gradual approach to the head of the Pass.

The last three miles to the head of the Pass, the road is good in many places; but this is the most commanding part of the Pass. The road is in some places not more than 40 to 60 feet wide, with perpendicular rocks 100 feet high; from which an enemy could give a most destructive fire. (21)

(20) A valley is also to be seen from the height on the left, just above the spring.

(21) It was from this part of the Pass that the Belochees, or rather *Kakurs*, (having crowned the heights) annoyed the column marching with the 37th N. I. The Comg. officer was obliged to send up parties to dislodge them. This part of the Pass consists of a road varying from 40 to 60 feet, and flanked, on each side, by high perpendicular hills, which you can only ascend at either end; so that, if the precaution of crowning the heights be not used, and you be caught in the centre of the pass, or distant from either end of it, an enemy is within pistol-shot of you; he can fire from behind rocks, and retire, and you cannot return one shot, with any effect. Capt. *Barstow*, 37th N. I. was badly wounded in this Pass.

At 10 miles, we reach the *Ghaut*, or head of the Pass. The ascent of the ghaut was gradual and only about 100 yards in length. The camels loaded, walked up and down it without stopping or resting. (22)

Descent from Pass.—After the descent, which is not great, a *Plain* covered with wild thyme lay before us, hills covered with snow, sparkled in the sun (near setting), and a cold, piercing wind from the N. E. swept over it, and took from the scene, its fierceness. (23) The distance to camp was 2¾ miles; the road took a turn to the right; and we did not see the camp on first entering the valley, or *Dusht-i-Bedowlut*. (24)

The distance from *Sir-i-Bolan* to *Dusht-i-Bedowlut* was 12¾ miles. The elevation above the level of the sea is 5,793 or 1,299 feet above Sir-i-Bolan, which gives a rise of one foot in 41 in this march.

Marches in the Pass.	M.	F.	Level above the sea.	Rise at each stage.
Dadur, ...			743 ft.	,,
1. Dadur to Kohan Delan	11	0	904	1 in 360 ft.
2. Kohan Delan to Kirta (or Gurm-ab,)	10	5	1081	,, 304
3. Kirta to Beebee Nanee,.........	9	1	1695	,, 77
4. Beebee Nanee to Abi-i-Goom,	8	5	2540	,, 51
5. Ab-i-Goom to Sir-i-Bolan, ...	9	5	4494	,, 25
6. Sir-i-Bolan to head of Pass, ...	10	0	5793	,, 41
	59	0	(25)	(25)

(22) Parties were sent here to prevent the crowding of the camels, &c. You do not see the Ghaut till you come upon it; it lies to the right, and the road winds round to it. It is said that there is another road to the right, into the valley; and just before you turn to the right to the ghaut, there is a road to the left, and in continuation of the road you are leaving.

(23) The skin was peeled off our faces, the effects of a hot-sun, succeeded by a cold wind.

(24) The *barren-plain*. This place is also called, Munzilgar, or halting-place.

(25) The whole rise is 5050 ft. from Dadur to Dusht-i-Bedowlut, making the latter the same height as the head of the Pass; this divid-

The *Bombay* army was this day at Gundava, five from Dadur, and 11 marches from this place. Water was found at Dusht-i-Bedowlut, a collection of rain-water, after a fall of rain, two days before; otherwise, we must have made a march of 28½ miles. Thermometer here at 5 P. M. 60°; at day-break it was as low as 26°.

8. *March to Sir-i-Ab,* (26) (23rd March, 1839.)—Thermometer 38° at 4 A. M. Marched at 5 A. M. (27) The road, consisting of numerous foot-paths of sand and pebbles, lay, N. W. over the Dusht-i-Bedowlut, on which nothing but wild thyme was seen. The valley is extensive to the right and left, after leaving Dusht-i-Bedowlut. To the N. and S. were hills covered with snow; bleak mountains, crags, and steeps, bounded the plain on every side. The traveller may picture to his mind, the horrors of a winter in such a place. At 1½ miles from last camp, crossed two ghauts over dry ravines. Within two miles of the new ground near the

---

ed by 59 miles will give a general rise of about one in 63 feet, fractions omitted. I have given the daily rise in each march, to enable the reader to judge of the increased labor of horses, camels and bullocks drawing guns, wagons, hackeries, &c.

From Shikarpoor to this place we had marched 206 miles, of which 96 miles of a Desert country between Shikarpoor and Dadur, (See para. 1) and thence to this place 59 miles of Pass, or total of 155 miles of road, furnishing but scanty forage for our cattle.

We were obliged to carry our supplies, not getting a day's supply any where on the road. If we had entered the Pass with fresh cattle, or animals not jaded after a march of 833 miles from Ferozpoor, (1038 from Kurnal; indeed some of the cattle had marched nearly 1,200 miles,) the animals would not have been so knocked up; but they were worn out by a long march, bad water, and want of food, and therefore our loss was very severe, and those remaining had strength only equal to the carriage of half loads. As the Rewaree camels (of which class they chiefly were) are not fed on grain, it will be readily imagined what numbers would die on a march, where their food was to be derived from a *barren*-country.

(26) The *Head* or source (of *water*), of the *Shahdezee Lora* river; the spring gushes from the mountain to the right, in a crystal volume.

(27) Baggage not sent in advance.

I

road, and by the sides of the hills we found some wheat-fields. At Sir-i-Ab, there were no human habitations to be seen. On the mountains were a few black sheep-skin tents, and a flock of sheep and goats. The plain is a wilderness covered with southern-wood (or old man). The crocus and tulip, bloomed in the waste.

There was a slight descent in the country at about 12 miles from the last ground.

Here for the first time, we saw a long line of *Karezees* (28) running across the valley from N. to S.

To the left of Sir-i-Ab and S. from our camp is a valley which leads to the road to *Khelat* about 112 miles distant. (29)

The troops did not reach this ground till 11 A. M., and the whole of the baggage not till 2. P. M. About a mile before we arrived at Sir-i-Ab, (or near the *Karezees*) there was a dry nullah, over which the Pioneers had to make a road. (30) Comg. officers of corps and Heads of Depts. reminded of the order against the destruction of growing crops of wheat, &c.

Distance marched to-day was 15 miles, 5 furlongs. The thermometer at 3 P. M. 75°.

To-night, unexpectedly, H. M.'s 16th Lancers marched into camp from Sir-i-Bolan, 28½ miles. (31)

9. *Halt 23rd, 24th, and 25th March, 1839.*—On the 23rd

(28) Subterranean water-courses, by which water is conveyed from a spring, &c. in any direction to irrigate lands, &c. A well is first dug of sufficient depth, and then a channel to the spring excavated; then other wells are made, and the channel continued in the whole line of direction intended. Water is thus procured from a great number of wells, which are, usually 30 or 40 feet distant from each other.

(29) Captain Outram says in his journal, p. 138, " The road from Quetta (i. e. one march in advance from this) *to Khelat* is excellent, both water and forage so abundant that the whole Division (Maj. Genl. Willshire's) might have marched without the smallest difficulty."

(30) One of the Bengal H. A. horses came down, and very nearly injured the rider.

(31) They lost many camels. The baggage was coming in all night, the men left their quilts behind, owing to the camels falling down.

March, 1839, Sir J. Keane marched from Gundava, 12 marches behind, to join us. This morning the 16th N. I., the 3rd Cavy. and camel battery, marched into camp.

At the request of Major Leech (P. A. at Hd. Qrs.) attention of officers Comg. Brigades, Corps, and at the head of Depts. called, requiring the troops and followers to be " careful not to interfere with, or insult the prejudices of the people of the country, through which the army is about to advance."

" The mosques not to be entered by any one, not of the faith of those by whom they have been erected."

" The poles and flags, by the way-sides, are considered sacred by the people, being emblematical of the grave of a pilgrim; these are, on no account to be removed."

" The surwans and others, are to be directed to abstain from cutting fruit trees for forage, for their cattle, or for other purposes; and signal example will be made, on the spot, of any one who may be detected, in the act of committing this offence."

" Caution to European and Native soldiers from interfering, when in the bazars, or villages, with the women of the country ; quarrels, and loss of life will attend a disregard of this warning."

" The substance of the above order to be particularly explained to the troops ; and proclaimed by *Tom-tom* throughout the different bazars, and lines of the camp."

24*th March.*—The 4th Brigade marched into camp. Few of the corps have their baggage up, and in several the men have lost their quilts.

The wind rushing down the crannies in the mountains, sweeps clouds of dust into camp, and nearly blows down our tents. Hence, no doubt, the natives live in the caves in the side of the mountains, or in small, low tents. The 37th N. I. still at the head of the Pass.

To-day the Cavalry horses were put on half rations. Officers allowed none. Brigadiers to-day, directed to protect their own camps.

Order for March.—The whole of the troops (except the 4th Brigade, under Major-Genl. Nott.) will move to-morrow morning towards *Quetta*, in the following order; right in front.

1. The Cavy. Brigade.
2. Troop of H. A.
3. 2 Regts. of Infy.
4. No. 6 Lt. Field battery.
5. A Regt. of Infy.

The March countermanded; the Engineer Dept. and a Compy. of N. Infy. alone to march to Quetta, to-morrow.

10. *March-order repeated*, (25th March.)—Thermometer at 5 A. M. 44°. The order of yesterday repeated, except that no baggage animals to precede the column, or proceed over night; the baggage to follow the troops. The crops on the line of march to be preserved, and parties posted to prevent animals going over the corn-fields. On the arrival at *Quetta*, guards to be posted at each of the gates of the town, and orders given to prevent any soldiers, or followers, except the buneeahs of the different bazars, entering it. (32)

The Post, or Dâk, having been cut off for 10 days, 4 mails came in at once. One of the runners had been shot dead, and the blood-stained packet left on the road, and picked up by the next. Attah at 1½ seers per Rs. Gram, none. (33) Thermometer at 3 P. M. 66°.

This afternoon Sir A. Burnes, accompanied by Lieut. Pattison, (16th Lancers and A. D. C. to late Brigr. Arnold) Lt. Simpson, S. A. C. G., and Moonshee Mohunlal, started for *Khelat*, the object being to induce Mehrab Khan to come to tender his submission to H. M. Shah Shoojah-ool-Moolk;

---

(32) On the arrival of the troops at Quetta, Major Cureton's details to rejoin their respective Brigades.

Memo.—1 H. and 8 Troopers, 3rd Lt. Cavy. with rations for man and horse for seven days, to be sent at 2 P. M. for escort duty, with Major Craigie (D. A. G.). This officer went back through the *Bolan Pass*, to meet Sir J. Keane. He did not meet him till he arrived at *Dadur*, having been only three nights on the road travelling a distance of 74 miles. He was obliged to leave one trooper's horse in the Pass. He returned to Quetta on 3rd April, having marched 158 miles in 8¼ days, over wretched stoney-roads.

(33) Indian corn sold for 15 Rs. for 20 seers; ½ maund (40 lbs.) of Bhoosa for 2 Rs.

Arrival at Quetta. 61

and to obtain a supply of grain. Sir A. B. intended to reach his destination, a distance of 112 miles, in 3 days: an escort of 1 Duffadar and 15 troopers, 1st Local Horse, went with him.

March to Quetta, (26th March, 1839.) Thermometer at 4 A. M. 34°. Marched at day-break; the road was by an old foot-path, or bullock track; it wound up the valley, which, after a march of 3 or 4 miles, exhibited signs of cultivation. The mountain peaks, on our right and left, were covered with snow. These mountains divide the valley of Pesheen from Candahar. The route, had a straight line been drawn, would have been N. N. W. to N. W. by N. After a short but cold march, we reached *Quetta*—a most miserable mud town, with a small castle on a mound, on which there was a small gun, on a ricketty carriage. The peach and almond trees were in blossom. There is a garden, enclosed by a mud-wall, surrounded by poplars; numerous streamlets watered the valley, only a few inches broad, and as many deep; except a broad one near camp, which was deep. Camp N. E. of Quetta. Thermometer at 3 P. M. 60°. (34)

The elevation of this place above the sea is 5,637 feet, or 156 feet *lower* than *Dusht-i-Bedowlut*.

Sir J. Keane, to-day, met Shah Shoojah at Noushera, one march from Dadur, near the entrance to the *Bolan Pass*. Halt until further orders.

Brigr. Arnold (Comg. Cavy.) and Brigr. Sale (Comg. Infy.) were directed to protect their Camps, while at Quetta. (35)

---

(34) The thermometer at 4 A. M. to-day was 34°, the lowest we have yet had it. At 3 P. M. 60° the same as in the valley just beyond the Pass, while the intermediate days, it has ranged several degrees higher.

(35) Patrols to be sent every two hours to prevent camp-followers, or others, entering the town, by scaling the walls, &c.

CHAPTER V.

QUETTA, AND MARCH FROM IT TO CANDAHAR.

1. *Quetta*, (27th March, 1839.)—To-day H. M. *Shah Shoojah-ool-Moolk*, the Envoy and Minister, and Sir *J. Keane*, arrived at Dadur, 8 marches in our rear. H. M.'s force had been attacked by the Belochees, between Shikarpoor and Dadur, and at one place lost 250 camels. They likewise suffered much from want of water and forage.

28th March.—The want of grain now began to be severely felt. After our arrival, we found the shops which contained grain, shut. Recourse was had to a strict search in the town, and at last, Major Leech, the Pol. Asst., ordered the grain-shops to be forced open; but the Commissariat only obtained a supply of about 3 or 400 maunds of flour, not equal to a day's supply for the troops. Some condemned this measure as likely to prevent people coming to the camp; but we were in want of grain. (1) The following order was, therefore, to-day published: " In consequence of the limited quantity of supplies at present in camp, and the country so destitute as to afford nothing to replenish the Commissariat stores, Sir W. Cotton is sorry to be under the necessity of placing the European and Native troops and followers

---

(1) We had here the H. A. Cavy. brigade, Camel battery and 1st. Lt. Infy. brigade. The 4th Brigade was left at Sir-i-Ab, a march behind; but required to be supplied from Quetta, and the Shah, Sir J. Keane and his escort, and the Bombay column, were on their way to join the camp here.

on the following rations, until supplies come in: *European* soldiers, ½ seer (1 lb.) of Attah (flour) in place of bread; except to men in hospital. *Native* soldiers and followers *half* of their *present* ration." (2)

"The Native troops and followers will receive *compensation* in money, in lieu of their *half*-ration of Attah, at the Nerikh (price) of the day. Major Genls. Thackwell and Nott will cause it to be explained by Brigadiers, and by Officers Comg. Regts. to the Native Commissioned and European and Native N. C. O., rank and file, the urgency of the case; he fully relies on the military spirit which has always animated the Bengal soldier, and that they will meet him, willingly, in overcoming this difficulty; which he trusts will be of short duration." (3) This gave the soldier a pound

---

(2) Which was *one* seer to the troops, and *half* a seer to the followers. It will be seen that both the European and native soldier were limited to *half* a seer. While the Europeans had meat served out to them besides (one lb. a day). I mention this to show the mode of feeding troops in India; while there were plenty of *Doomba* (or fat-tailed) sheep to be had. The Mahomedans eat meat; the Hindus do not generally. . Officers were directed to inquire, through their Native officers, if any and what number of sepoys, &c. would take rations of meat. Some did take them, but the sheep were too dear (3 Rs. or 6s.) for the camp-followers to purchase often.

The soldiers and natives of all classes were on the look out daily, to see for a casual seller of grain, which might be brought to the camp from the villages.

I should observe that the native soldier received *one* seer daily from the Comsst. stores, paying for the same; but that the followers (servants, &c. not mustered persons) only received *half* a seer, so that the reduction gave the followers only a *quarter* of a seer (¼ lb.) of flour—too little for men who live chiefly on this food, and in a country where (except meat) they could procure nothing else; and often making long marches!

(3) "The followers whose pay is not drawn in Abstract, and who are entitled to rations from the godown, will receive their compensation from the Executive Comsst. officer; those attached to Regts. to be drawn for by Comg. officers, and those belonging to Depts. or public establishments, by officers in charge of them." "Brigadiers, and officers in charge of Depts. or public establishments, to muster their respective followers, and forward, without delay to D. C. G., certified *Returns* of the numbers entitled to rations from the godown." It was

of flour and 2 ounces of *Dhall,* (4) and the servants half a pound of flour, and half an ounce of *Dhall.*

29th March.—Grain selling at 3 seers, and flour 2½ seers per Rs.; a small bundle of Lucerne for 5 Rs.; a maund of Bhoosa, 4 Rs.; a grass sheep, 3 Rs.

30th March.—(Genl. orders) " The store of grain for H. A. and Cavy. horses being consumed, and the Commissariat Dept. being unable to collect a sufficient quantity of Bhoosa, (5) or other forage for a general issue of rations to troop horses; to preserve their condition, till a further supply of grain reaches the army, Officers Comg. Corps to make arrangements, under instructions from Maj. Genl. Thackwell, for the purchase of such forage as may be procurable, to serve out to the horses, at a rate not exceeding the Govt. ration." " Statements certifying the quantity of forage, and rate of purchase, countersigned by Comg. Officers, to be sent to D. C. G., who will cause a refund to be made."

"To be clearly explained that no interference with the inhabitants of the country is to take place; armed-men not to enter their villages under any pretext. If conciliatory means be used, the Major Genl. is confident they will readily bring supplies to camp. Major Genl. T. to hold Comg. officers responsible." (6)

intended to give compensation to the servants of officers, on furnishing statements duly vouched : but it was countermanded in orders, next day, and suspended, pending the sanction of Government, for which urgent application was made. No compensation was granted; but afterwards Government liberally, gave six months extra full batta to officers; and many officers who could procure grain, bought it and gave an extra *quarter* seer of Attah, or the same quantity of meat, to such of their servants as would eat mutton, or the flesh of goats.

The mustered establishments had been put on *half*-rations on the 8th March, 1839.

(4) Split-peas.
(5) The Chopped straw of wheat, &c.

The Shah, in consequence of the misconduct of the *Cazy* of *Quetta,* gave up the fields of green barley belonging to *him,* for the use of the Cavy. &c. horses. The horses went in marching order daily from 3 to 5 P. M. to forage in the fields.

(6) The people who went unarmed were murdered, or wounded.

" The Arty. Park, on reaching Sir-i-Ab to remain halted there till further orders; the 37th N. I. with it, to rejoin its brigade."

" Comisst. Dept. to entertain an establishment of 10 *Domes*, (7) to remove and bury all dead animals found near camp."

A dâk runner murdered in the Pass, but the mail found.

2. *Camels driven off, &c.* (31st March, 1839.)—About mid-day the enemy came down from the hills and drove off 200 camels. The history of the case is this: the Cazy or Governor of Quetta, (8) in the valley of Shawl, had, for a certain consideration received from Major Leech, agreed to protect the gorge of a pass to the N. E. of our camp, distance five or six miles; he *did* post his people, and while there we had no attacks from that quarter; but they deserted last night, and the Governor also disappeared! (9) Parties went out from camp in pursuit, (10) but the camels were carried off, and the troops returned to camp in the evening. This was by the facetious called the battle of *Cockatoo*, the valley being near a hill called *Tukatoo*.

1st April.—The Major Genl., though he complimented the zeal of officers, directed that, " when a party is detach-

---

Armed foraging parties are the best to send, they preserve order, and can defend themselves, and the people soon learn not to be alarmed, if well treated.

(7) They are the lowest class of Hindus. We found it difficult to procure them, and officers were often obliged to pay people to remove dead animals found near their tent. In a standing camp, the stench from dead camels, was dreadful.

(8) An appanage of Khelat.

(9) Mehrab Khan of Khelat had this man under his influence, and the Kakurs, always ready for plunder, readily obeyed the order to annoy us in every way, and hence the people did not come in with provisions and grain, so frequently at first.

(10) Lt. Coy., 48th N. I., a troop of Cavy., re-inforced by the whole of the 2nd Cavy., a Wing of H. M.'s 13th Lt. Infy., the Camel-battery, and a number of officers of rank, among others. The Cavy. advanced, found the enemy to be 12 Kakurs (robbers), halted for the Infy. The Lt. Coy., 48th N. I. dislodged them from the hill. Lt. Hasell, Adjt. 48th N. I. had a shot through his hat!

ed, or ordered out, no officer, except those belonging to it, to proceed with it, as he may be wanted with his own corps."

A picquet was sent early this morning, consisting of two Cos. of Infy., (one of H. M.'s 13th Lt. Infy.) and a troop of 3rd Cavy. to the gorge of the Pass, to prevent camels entering the valley beyond it, to graze; or the ingress of the Kakurs.

The people appear alarmed, and are deserting their villages. Many camp-followers killed and wounded in the villages, to which they go to purchase grain, (11) and the cultivation near them often destroyed in retaliation.

2nd April.—The picquet at the pass allowed their own camels to go into the proscribed valley, when the Kakurs came down, and drove them off. The Cavy. pursued, and returned in the evening without a camel; but they overtook the fellows, killed three, wounded four, and made one prisoner. (12)

The Arty. Park ordered to close up to the 4th Brigade to-morrow.

Provisions, (G. O.) "As the price of provisions daily increases, owing to *private* competition, (13) the Maj. Genl., at the recommendation of Major *Leech,* A. P. A., publishes the following nerikh (price-current), and requests no higher prices may be given. Wheat or uncleaned rice, $2\frac{3}{4}$ seers—wheat flour, or cleaned rice, $2\frac{1}{2}$ seers—barley 3 seers, and Indian corn 3 seers per rupee."

3rd April. A party with treasure and camels ordered to be sent from Sir-i-Ab, on the 5th instant, with Lieut. *Marsh,* 3rd Cavy. to the valley of *Mooshtung* and *Nooshky,* to purchase and transport grain for the army.

(11) Those who had *Affghan* servants easily procured grain by sending their *Yaboos* (ponies) The Natives of Hindustan, were of no use on these occasions, as they could seldom speak Persian.

(12) These *dours* (pursuits) greatly knocked up our Cavy.

(13) It is difficult to prevent men half-starved from buying at any price to satisfy the wants of nature; if *all* would, or could, refuse to buy except at a certain price, they might make more favorable terms; but they will *not* do so.

Repeated the order against armed people going into villages, under penalty of severe punishment. Officers Comg. Corps, and at the head of Depts. to explain the personal risk run, by people wandering about, or into the deserted villages. (14)

"The picquet at the gorge of the Pass to be withdrawn this evening; to be replaced by a troop of Native Cavy. to come on duty at sun-rise, and to fall back on camp at dusk."

Major Craigie, D. A. G. returned from his trip through the *Bolan* Pass, to meet Sir J. Keane.

Bearers and other camp-followers brought in during the day, killed or wounded while plundering. The people retaliated, and camels were stolen. They brought in beams and rafters for firewood from deserted vilages. These people were severely punished when caught. Camels carried off and recovered by a party under Lieut. *Meik*, H. M.'s 16th Lancers.

Two Serjts. of Arty. trepanned while out shooting, and mutilated, while in the act of giving a Kakur, a pinch of snuff. (15)

3. *To meet the Commander-in-Chief, &c.* (4th April, 1839.)—Sir *W. Cotton*, and principal staff, rode with an escort to meet Sir *J. Keane* at Sir-i-Ab, where the Shah and Envoy and minister also had arrived. "The Arty. Park, its escort and the 4th Brigade of Infy. to move from Sir-i-Ab to Quetta, on the 6th instant."

5th April.—Regtl. Qr. Mrs. to employ their Bildars (16) to remove and bury all dead animals found in or near the encampments.

Some camels were stolen and driven off towards a village. Cornet *Toone*, with a party of the 2nd Cavy. picquet pursued, when the thief was overtaken. The Cornet with one cut,

(14) They often decoyed our servants into the villages saying they had grain to sell, and then murdered them.

(15) The *Kakur* snatched the gun from the Serjeant's hand, which was the signal; and they were surrounded by armed men. The Serjts. killed several before they were cut down.

(16) Men who use shovels, &c. attached to Regts.

took off his head, and brought three prisoners, and the camels back. The *Bombay* column to-day reached *Dadur*, eight marches in our rear.

6th April.—A salute of 19 guns announced the arrival of H. E. Lieut.-Genl. Sir *J. Keane*, Comr.-in-Chief of the *Army of the Indus*, who marched in with his Escort of a Wing of the 1st Bombay Lt. Cavy., and of the 19th Regt. N. I.

A guard of Honor of Infy., with the *Royal* colors of H. M.'s 13th Lt. Infy. and the Band, with No. 6, Light Fd. battery, marched to Sir-i-Ab, this morning, to salute H. M. Shah Shoojah-ool-Moolk, on his arrival there. A salute of 21 guns on his reaching his camp. The Shah and the Envoy and Minister, encamped to-day near the town.

Order of Thanks.—" H. E. the Comr.-in-Chief having arrived in camp, and assumed command, in person, of the Army, and having directed Maj. Genl. Sir W. *Cotton* to resume command of the Bengal Infantry, of the 1st Division, he (Sir W. C.) cannot give up charge of the Bengal column, without expressing in the strongest and warmest terms, his thanks to Maj. Genls. Thackwell and Nott, Brigrs. Sale, Arnold and Roberts, to officers Comg. Corps, and to the Officers and men generally, and to Maj. Craigie, D. A. G., Maj. Garden, D. Q. M. G., and Major Parsons, D. C. G., and to the officers of the several Depts., for the admirable manner in which their duties have been conducted, and for the good conduct and soldier-like behaviour of the troops during a march of more than 1,100 *miles.*"

Order for March.—The Cavy., H. A., and 1st Brigade of Infy. No. 6, Lt. Fd. battery, with the sappers and miners, to move to-morrow, in the following order.

The sappers and miners, under an escort of 2 Cos., will quit camp at 4 A. M. (17)

---

(17) The cattle carrying their tools only, to accompany them: remainder of their baggage must remain till the Column quits the ground.

Order of March from Quetta.

1. H. M. 13th Lt. Infy.
2. 2 T. 2. B. H. A.
3. 2 Regts. of Cavy.
4. No. 6, Lt. Fd. battery.
5. A Regt. of Cavy.
6. The Treasure.
7. Remg. Regt. of Infy.

(Column right in front.)

Baggage to move in the following order.

1st. Of H. E. the Comr.-in-Chief, and Staff of Divisions, and Brigades—under Provost Marshal.

2nd. Baggage of Regts., collected, under an officer from each corps; and marched to new ground, in the order in which Regts. move in the column.

3rd. Commissariat Field Depôt, and grain cattle.

Rear Guard.—Of 2 Cos. of N. I. and one troop of Cavy., will bring up the whole, and the officer Comg. it will not quit camp till the baggage is off the ground. (18)

4. *Order by Sir J. Keane, &c.*—1. " H. E. the Comr.-in-Chief, having established his Hd. Qrs. with the advance column, cannot but express his gratification at the proud position in which he is placed by the command of such fine troops; also at having received charge from his friend, and former companion in the Field, Maj. Genl. Sir W. *Cotton,* to whom his thanks are due, for the able and judicious manner in which he has conducted the march of the Bengal column, over a great distance of country, from Ferozpoor to this, crossing the *Indus;* and overcome the difficulties between Shikarpoor to Dadur, and passage of the *Bolan Pass,* with Arty., Cavy. and Infy., and arrived in

(18) " Capt. Watt will direct his treasure-camels to move with those of the Fd. Pay-office, in front of the rear Regt. of Infy. in the column. The ressalah of Horse at his disposal, will afford ample protection to the stores of the Depôt."

" The Local Horse will be posted, at convenient distances, along the line of baggage animals."

" The Baggage Master held responsible that no baggage precedes the troops. A party of L. H. will be at Capt. Nash's disposal, to give effect to these orders."

Afghanistan in a highly creditable order, and the Comr.-in-Chief will not fail to report his sentiments, in these terms, to his lordship the Govr. Genl."

3. "Maj. Genl. Sir W. *Cotton*, will resume command of the 1st Division; and Maj. Genl. *Nott* of the 2nd Brigade, from which these officers were, temporarily, transferred in G. O. of 4th December 1838."

4. "Lt.-Col. Dennie, will deliver over the command of the troops at Shikarpoor, and proceed to join his Regt. the first favorable opportunity."

5. "Brigr. *Gordon*, Comg. in Upper Sinde, will receive orders, to send on to the advance, as occasions may offer, the 3 Regts. of *Bengal* Infy. now at Shikarpoor; they will be sent by strong detachments, guarding provisions and treasure: the 35th Regt. to be the first sent on."

6. "*Depôts* for ordnance and Comsst. stores, will be formed at *Dadur*, and at *Quetta*, and at each of those posts, a Regt. of N. I. will be quartered, with a ressalah of Local Horse, and such details of H. M. Shah Shoojah's troops, as may hereafter be specified."

7. "Maj. Genl. Nott, with the Hd. Qrs. of the 2nd Brigade, to remain at Quetta; and will exercise a general superintendence and military control within the province of *Shawl*. (19) The 43rd N. I. to stand fast at Quetta, and 1 Regt. of Infy., with a ressalah of Horse from H. M. Shah Shoojah's force, also, will be left at that place."

8. "On the arrival of the 35th N. I. at Dadur, the 3 Cos. of the 37th N. I., now there, will be replaced by a similar detail from that corps; which, in its turn, will be relieved, and pushed forward on the arrival of the Regt. of the 2nd Brigade, destined to occupy that place."

10. "In a service of this kind, having in view the interest of the public, as well as that of the Army, and followers, it seems inexpedient that two distinct Comsst.

(19) Capt. Bean, 23rd N. I. was appointed Pol. Agent at Quetta, and in the province of Shawl. This province was the gift of a king of Affghanistan to one of his nobles, for service performed, as a *Shala* (Shawl) or dowry with his wife.

Establishments, drawing in connexion one with the other, should exist; it is therefore ordered that *Major Parsons*, the D. C. G., *Bengal Army*, shall take on himself the *general* direction of the Comsst. Depts. both of Bengal and Bombay." (20)

11. "*Returns* by the Heads of Depts. with troops of each Presidency, to continue ; and all periodical *papers* and *reports* required by the Regns. of the service to the Hd. Qrs. of the Army of Bengal and Bombay to be transmitted."

12. "Maj. Genl. *Thackwell* and Brigr. *Stevenson*, Comg. troops both from *Bengal* and *Bombay*, will report for the information of H. E. the Comr.-in-Chief through the Staff officers of the Presidency to which the corps, or detachments happen to belong."

13. "The officers Comg. at Shikarpoor, Dadur, and Quetta, will report direct to the D. A. G. of the Presidency to which the troops belong, all casualties, and occurrences ; and use their utmost influence to aid the officers of the Comsst. Dept., or their Agents employed in the collection of *grain* for the troops; and afford adequate escorts, when provisions are forwarded to the army."

14. "Officers, of whatever rank, must not fail, in passing through those stations, to report their arrival and departure, to the officers Comg. the posts in question, for the information of the Comr.-in-Chief."

5. *Occurrences and state of affairs*, (6th April, 1839.)— The *Lancer* patrol this morning was fired on from a loop-holed mud building ; the picquet came up; a few of the men dismounted, and ran up to the building, and as the garrison presented their matchlocks, the Lancers seized

---

(20) "Capt. *Watt* is, at present, at the Head of the Field Comsst. and office of Accts. of the *Bengal* troops ; and Capt. *Davidson*, at the Head of the *Bombay* Comsst. will act in the same situation for the Bombay troops; under the orders of Major P."

"Capts. W. and D. will have superintendence over the Comsst. officers in charge of Brigades ; and exercise control over their Accts. : all matters relating to provisioning the troops, will be referred by the latter to the former. The above not to interfere with the Regns. of the respective Governments."

them; wrenched them out of their hands; unroofed the building, and pistoled the six men inside, killed 5 and wounded 1; the rest, outside, ran up the mountains.

Sir A. Burnes returned about this time from *Khelat*, but without any supplies. Mehrab Khan made many excuses for not furnishing grain, saying that he could not force the grain merchants to sell, while it was known that *they* were willing to sell, but dared not to do so without *his* orders. Another object of Sir A. B.'s mission was, to try and bring the *Khan* to tender his submission, in person, to the *Shah*. Here too, he interposed obstacles; he said he was a *poor Beloch*, and what harm could *he* do, that he was attached to the King's service, (21) and that if the Envoy and Minister would give him the "*Istiqbal*" (or meeting) he would come. (22) There were several interviews, during which the Khan would not allow even his *minister* to be present. The Khan, moreover, before he entered into any treaty, wanted to obtain *Kurachee* and its port in Sindh, but he waived this claim on the British Govt. agreeing to stand between him and the king, and giving him 1½ Lakh of Rs. (£15,000); for which he said he would protect our supplies, convoys, &c. (23)

Not much grain was obtained by the Convoy which was sent to the valley of *Moostung*. To judge of the conduct of Mehrab Khan, who said to Sir A. B.—"*You have brought an Army into the country; but how do you propose to take it out again?*"—it is necessary to state, that it was, afterwards, ascertained, that the night before the departure

(21) *Khelat* always belonged to the *Dooranee* empire, and it is quite true as the Khan said, " When the Shah was defeated in 1834, at Candahar, and sought shelter *here*, I gave it to him; and when urged by the chiefs of Candahar to give him up, *I* refused."

(22) This would not have been according to etiquette, and was tantamount to a refusal.

It is said he was afraid the king would seize and imprison him; however, he was told no such thing should occur, and that he should be escorted back to Khelat in safety.

(23) He could have brought about eight or 10,000 Belochees into the field if they were united, and if he had money.

L

of Sir A. Burnes, a plan had been formed to *murder* the whole party, which was defeated by their unexpected departure. (24)

Distress of the followers.—So scarce and dear had grain become, that some of the camp-followers were known to have fried the skins of the sheep, and to have eaten them, and also to have devoured the congealed blood of animals, roots, &c. The thermometer, here, at 5 A. M. averaged from 30° to 55°; and at 3 P. M. from 58° to 76°, while we had, at times, heavy rain and cold cutting wind. The *Bombay* Column was now at *Dadur,* near the entrance to the Pass, 8 marches in our rear. There were detachments of *Bengal* troops also there. The Belochees were daily attacking and carrying off the cattle belonging to the troops of both.

" All open communication with their *front* and *rear*, was entirely cut off, except by large detachments; and these were invariably menaced by strong bodies of Beloch horse." (25)

(24) I was told so by Lt. Simpson, S. A. C. G., one of the party. The Khan said, " Your army will be starved, and the water of the country will kill your people."

(25) Capt. Outram says, p. 59, that the *Bombay* column " was obliged to wait at *Dadur* for supplies from *Shikarpoor*." Shikarpoor to Dadur is 10 marches. The Bombay column made 12 marches from *Larkhana* to *Dadur*. Had it marched from Larkhana viâ Shikarpoor (52 miles, or four marches) it would have made two marches more; but would have saved time, and have procured supplies *at* Shikarpoor. The object of the march viâ the *Gundava Pass* was, to try and move by *Khelat*, and thus, avoid the *Bolan Pass* and the route between Shikarpoor and Dadur. The march of troops viâ Khelat, would have been useful, but we could not afford the time it took; which caused delay, and a consumption of our provisions.

There was *one* person who thought our advance fraught with great danger, from the certain prospect of starvation ! The contents of a letter written by this person were, by mere accident, made known to another person. It contained a proposal to counter-march the *Bengal* column by double forced marches, from Quetta to Shikarpoor, and one Regt. with two guns, was destined to be intrenched at the Head of the Pass, till the column had got through it to Dadur. The *Bombay* column was to leave guns, &c. behind; and push through the *Gundava* Pass to

I must not omit to mention that while Sir J. Keane, was at Sir-i-Ab, one march in our rear, his camp was attacked by plunderers, when 11 were seized in the act, and the fact being proved, were summarily dealt with and shot. This example was necessary to deter others, and was warranted by the *custom of war* and by *necessity*. (26)

6. *March from Quetta to Koochlâk*, (7th April, 1839).— Leaving the force, above detailed (27) at Quetta, the troops marched this morning. Shortly after leaving camp, we heard repeated firing, which turned out to be the shooting of 60 horses belonging to the Cavalry, which had been reported, by a Committee, as too weak to proceed on the march!

There are three roads or passes from Quetta towards Candahar; one to the right N. E. (28), another to the N., and a third to the N. W. We marched by that to the N. W. The road lay down the valley over water-courses, ditches, and fields of corn. We saw a number of the dead bodies of camp-followers on the road, and the barbarous savages of such deeds, scowled on us, from their mountain-peaks.

Larkhana!!! This because we had only about nine days *full* rations in camp. We should have been in a pretty position, with hordes of Belochees, &c. attacking our rear and flanks!!!

(26) Sir A. Wellesley (Duke of Wellington) wrote to Col. Murray, letter dated Bombay, 1st April, 1804, as follows: " However, I think that *Bheels*, and people of that description, whose profession is plunder, and who come armed into the camp for that purpose, ought not to be considered and treated as *common robbers*. They are *public enemies* and rebels against all authority, and I recommend that when one of them is caught in the camp, whether it be situated in the Company's territories, or in those of the Rajah, he may be *shot* by the nearest rear guard if he should be taken in the *act* of robbery. If something of this kind be not done, the robberies and outrages of the *Bheels*, will reduce the troops to the greatest distress." (The Wellington Manual, p. 61.)

(27) See para. 4, No. 7 of the G. O. 6th April, 1839. Capt. *Bean* was ordered to raise a local (Kakur) corps, which has proved to be a useful body.

(28) Whence the camels were driven off, see para. 2.

At about 7 miles a slight ascent towards the gorge of the Pass. There are two ghauts, descended by both, (the guns went down by that to the right,) down to the dry bed of the river.

The road lay N. and N. W. to the Pass of Koochlâk. Moved through the bed of the river for about a mile; high hills on each side; then, turning to the right, entered the valley. The Ghauts were not very steep, and about 100 yards long. The bed of the river was stony. The heights near the Pass, command the road: we found no enemy. (29)

Two miles from camp crossed a deep water-course. The village of Koochlâk, W. of camp, deserted. Our rear (E.) was covered by the hills, and a deep water-course ran along our front (W.): distance marched 10¾ miles.

8th April.—Marched at 5 A. M. to Hyderzye. The road bad; crossed the Shahdeezy-Lora twice; the banks precipitous, and difficult for the guns and cattle. After a tedious march, came to a fine plain and the considerable village of Hyderzye. Most of the people had fled. The guns and baggage not up till 1 P. M. There are two roads hence, by one of which it is said you save a march.

Some baggage camels got in advance to-day, before the troops moved, which caused delay; the order of the 6th inst., repeated.

The *Kakurs* attacked the Shah's baggage, and were severely handled; six were killed, and the rest fled.

Distance marched 10¼ miles. This place is 5259 feet above the level of the sea; 378 feet below Quetta.

9th April.—Marched at 5 A. M.

The order of march this morning was as follows:

1. 2. Regts. Cavy.
2. H. A.
3. 2 Regts. Infy.
4. Camel-battery.
5. A Regt. Infy.
6. A Regt. Cavy.
7. Treasure between the 2 rear Regts.
8. Rear Guard, 2 Cos. of Infy., and a troop of Cavy.

(29) The subsequent column, H. C. 1st. Bengal Eurn. Regt. and 37th N. I. were fired on; they were obliged to send up parties, and a sharp firing took place. A Sergt. of the European Regt. was wounded, and disabled: and a Sepoy was wounded.

At 8 miles crossed a narrow river with high banks, and shallow water, and the spur of a hill, into the valley of *Pisheen*.

Grain is coming into camp; and the people have remained in the villages, and asked for guards. A Company of Infy. was posted in the town.

The Park of Arty., under the Escort of the 4th Brigade of Infy. and 4th Local Horse, marched this day from Quetta.

The *Bombay* Arty. (H. and F.) and H. M.'s 17th foot marched to-day from Dadur into the Pass.

The distance to Hykulzye 10 miles, 7 furlongs. The elevation 5063 feet, or 196 feet less than yesterday.

7. *To left bank of the Shahdeezy-Lora*, (10th April, 1839).—Marched at 5 A. M. The sappers and miners in advance. No baggage allowed to move in advance. At six miles crossed a dry nullah. At 7½ miles crossed the Shahdeezy-Lora river. The ravines near the river precipitous, and the banks so high and perpendicular, that the troops were obliged to pile their arms, and lower the guns, and drag them down and up the steep Ghauts, made for their passage. (30) The river not broad, and not above two feet deep. The horses were taken out of the guns, and the camels from the camel-battery. There was a descent of about 150 yards, and after crossing the stream, a steep bank to ascend; then, at the distance of 150 yards, a second ascent, not very steep. The baggage, thus kept in the rear, did not all come up till 5 P. M. Distance marched 7¾ miles.

After crossing, the Cavy. and H. A. were ordered to move on immediately, as there was here, no forage, to Arumbee, distant 7 miles and 5 furlongs.

The Shah and his force, &c. remained encamped on the other (right) bank of the river.

The Envoy and Minister wrote to Sir J. Keane, to inform him that an attack on the camp at night, was threatened by 3000 men. The troops slept on their arms all night: no

(30) Working parties H. A. and H. M.'s 13th Lt. Infy.

attack was made. Grain brought into camp more freely to-day. (31)

11*th April.*—To Arumbee; distance 7 miles, 5 furlongs. The road over a level track of jungle of Tamarisk, interspersed with cultivation. The road good.

The Engineers went on in advance to the head of the *Kojuk* Pass, to prepare the Ghaut for the passage of the guns, &c. The 1st Brigade Infy. and Camel-battery marched this morning to Quilla Abdoollah Khan.

Lt. Simpson, S. A. C. G., left camp with a company, and went to the rear to purchase grain.

We to-day heard of a very gallant affair which occurred in the Bolan Pass, some days ago, while the 35th Bengal N. I. were marching through it;—a large body of *Belochees* and *Murhees* attacked the Rear Guard of the corps (one company) commanded by Lt. *Towgood*. The Belochees fired a volley with their matchlocks, and then rushed on the guard, sword in hand. The guard waited till they came within about 40 paces, when Lt. T. fired a volley; and, under cover of the smoke, came to the charge. They fled leaving 40 killed and wounded on the spot, and never again ventured within the range of the musketry!

12*th April.*—The Hd. Qr. marched to Quillah Abdoolah Khan, distant 7½ miles. The road lay over a flat, broken by small hills and the dry beds of mountain-streams, covered with loose stones, till we saw Quillah Abdoolah on our left, (N.) about 4 or 5 miles distant. The camp in a little open valley of stones, bounded by low hills. The fort was deserted. A Battn. of the *Shah's* Infy. was left here, and withdrawn on the formation of the "*Bolan Rangers.*" (32) A grove of trees, and a fine stream of water close to it. There is a tank in the fort, and a garden, and

(31) There is said to be a straight road by which you can march from Hyderzye to the river in one march. Major Leech said so; he marched, alone, however.

(32) Lt. *Bosanquet*, 16th N. I. was left at Quillah Abdoolah Khan, in political charge, and directed to raise a corps of *Achukzyes*, which took some time to effect. It is a useful body, but it is a lonely position, he being the only European there.

room for a Battn. The Cavy. and Arty. order to encamp between this and the entrance to the Pass.

The remainder of the 16th N. I. pushed on to join the Sappers and Miners. The troops at Head Quarters halted to-day.

H. E. Sir J. Keane went this morning to look at the entrance to the Pass, where he breakfasted, and staid sometime. (33) This day the remainder of the *Bombay* troops entered the *Bolan* Pass. Major *Daly*, Comg. the wing H. M.'s 4th L. D. saw a party coming in force towards him, and trying to surround him; *he* retreated from them till he enticed them on, and then, he charged *them*, and killed many of them.

13th April.—The troops at Hd. Qrs. halt to-morrow.

The sappers and miners, and the 16th N. I., in advance, were established to-day on the northern extremity of the Pass, in the valley.

The whole of the Cavy. and the two batteries marched into our camp.

8. *Passage of the Kojuk-Pass*, (14th April, 1839.)—The order of march published yesterday for to-day was as follows:

1. *Baggage* of H. E. the Comr.-in-Chief—Genls. of Division, and Officers at Hd. Qrs.	At 3 A. M. the 1st Brigade of Infy. and Camel-battery will quit camp, followed by the baggage, in the order detailed in the *margin;* which is to be protected by the Dett. of Local Horse on duty with 1st Brigade; and a Coy. of Infy., as a rear-guard.
2. Baggage of corps, according to position in the Brigade.	
3. Fd. Comsst. and grain cattle. (34)	

(33) The late Brig. *Arnold* went to the Pass and was fired at by a well-dressed mounted man, supposed to be a chief. A sentry of H. M. 13th Lt. Infy. to-night, shot an Achukzye (mountaineer of these hills) who came up to his post and did not answer the challenge; he ran off up the hill, but his body was found next day in the hills.

(34) All the baggage was to be off the ground this morning by six A. M. after which hour nothing was to quit camp till 1 A. M.

"The brigade of Cavy. with its Arty., to move on to the Pass."

"Working parties from the Cavy., and Infy., on the arrival at the ascent near the Sapper's camp, to be told off, to drag the *Arty.* of their respective brigades, across the Pass."

"The *Baggage Master* to be on the alert, at the commencement of the ascent, to prevent crowding, and to take care to stop the baggage, at intervals, before it enters the narrow gorge, to admit of the animals filing over with regularity; only *one* camel can pass up at a time, and H. E. impresses upon Officers, the necessity of having their own animals, as well as those of the men, as lightly laden as circumstances will admit; this will be the only mode of preserving their baggage; as every camel that falls, must be removed with his load, out of the path, and the eventual loss of property must be the result."

Thermometer at 2 A. M. 60°. At 3 A. M. the 1st Brigade of Infantry, and Camel-battery marched, and 5 A. M. the wing of 1st Bombay Cavy. (escort) and Hd. Qrs.

After leaving our last ground, the mountains soon closed on us, and the troops filed up a water-course, dry and stony, with a few stunted trees here and there.

At about 6 miles, the ascent of about 1½ miles in extent to the entrance to the Pass, commenced; the distance between the hills, here, was not more than 80 or 100 feet, the road confined by banks. The centre road had been made for the guns; it was very steep and difficult: there is a steep ascent first up to the left, then there was a turn to the right (35) after the ascent; thence there was a descent, with a precipice on one side of the road, which rendered the operation of dragging the guns, &c. a service of great labour and

---

(35) Guns with horses, or with men and drag-ropes, cannot make a sharp turn; there must be a considerable sweep in the road. It was necessary to *make*, as well as *cut* the road at the turn, to prevent guns falling over the precipice; one H. A. gun fell over, horses and all; a wheel only slightly injured. The ascent was very steep for 800 feet.

fatigue. There were two other roads, one to the left, and another to the right.

The *left* road, though the longest and circuitous, was the best for camels, being easier of ascent.

The *right* road was not fit for the passage of camels with loads; some men, bullocks and ponies went by it; it lay over a rocky path.

All the three roads met at the bottom of the Pass. The descent was about a mile by the centre road, and more by the right and left roads.

From the top of the Pass, you behold the road which leads to the valley of *Candahar* below; and distant hills, beyond which that city lies.

The elevation above the sea, at the halt in the Kojuk Pass was 6,848 feet; the summit of the Pass, 7,457 feet, the summit is 1,780 feet above the valley below, which gave us a commanding view.

9. *Confusion in the Pass.*—The Cavalry brigade and H. A. were ordered to march to-day at 1 p. m. Thus there were two batteries and six Regts. with their baggage, to move through the Pass, and make a march of 11 miles included in one day's operation! The Camel-battery was overtaken by camels and baggage. The Pass only admitted of *one* camel passing at a time. (36) The ascent was so steep, that some did not like to ride up it; nor, for the like reason, to ride down the descent, for this was more difficult still; some camels fell, and stopt the rest behind. This state of things caused the march of the Cavalry and H. A. to be countermanded; but it was too late, their baggage was in the Pass; and it was clear, as it turned out, that it would take the whole day to cross and pass down the H. A. guns and troops, already in the Pass; for each gun, each tumbril, wagon, &c. was to be separately *handed* down by manual labor. Orders were given to turn back the camels, and make them go by a different route—that by the left.

---

(36) Sir W. *Cotton's* buggy got upset, but it made the *grand tour* to Caubool and back to Ferozpoor. The ascent and descent of the right road were fearfully dangerous.

M

This augmented the confusion, and the whole became one accumulated mass of troops, guns, and baggage. The ammunition wagons came into camp. Troops were ordered back to protect the baggage for the night. The whole of the Comsst. stores were in the Pass.

The Hd. Qrs. were established at the foot of the Pass at *Chumun Chokee* in the valley, which is about 2½ miles from the top of the Pass. The road down to the valley, runs between commanding hills, which may be distant 5 to 800 yards from each other. The camp at the *Chumun Chokee* was 5,677 feet above the level of the *sea* (40 feet above Quetta), 1,780 feet below the summit of the Pass. This would give, in 3 miles a fall of about 1 in 9 feet, but, as the *descent* only occupied about 1-3rd of the distance from the top of the Pass to the Chumun, the fall in it must have been about 1 in 3 feet. Thermometer at 3 p. m. 94°.

The troops at Hd. Qrs. directed to halt to-morrow.

15th April.—(G. O.) "The Brigade of Cavy., and its Artillery, to encamp to-day at the foot of the Pass. The 1st Brigade (excepting the 16th N. I.) to be employed in bringing the heavy ordnance across the heights."(37)

16th April.—The Cavy. Brigade and H. A., the Engineer Dept. and the 16th Bengal N. I. marched this morning to the *Kudany* river (Dundee Goolaee), the first march towards Candahar, to obtain forage and water. (38)

(37) *G. O.* 16*th April.* " Every soldier who can be spared from camp belonging to the 1st Brigade Infy. to be detached as a working-party, to the top of the Pass to-morrow morning, to aid in bringing over the heavy Artillery. A party of sappers with the pioneers to move at the same time to the top of the Pass.

" The men of *one* Coy. of N. I. proceeding to the Pass are to have their arms with them." In such cases I think *all* should take their arms, and pile them near the working party.

(38) There are some springs at the Chumun, but not enough for a large body of troops, they were to the right of our Camp, distant about 800 yards. There were springs in the Pass, between the summit and the Chumun, but it was not a safe position for troops, or baggage cattle; there was not forage in it, but coarse grass; and the hills, on each side, perfectly commanded the road! At *Chumun Chokee* the for-

Some of the *Bombay* troops arrived at Quetta to-day. Mehrab Khan of *Khelat* was, *then,* said to be in close communication with Dost Mahomed Khan. (39)

17*th April.*—" A working party from H. M.'s 13th Lt. Infy. to be sent to the Head of the Pass to-morrow morning. Every soldier in the 14th Brigade (40) who can be spared from the duty of camp, to be detached to-morrow morning as a working-party, to assist in bringing over the heavy *Artillery.*" *A report of* 3,000 *of the enemy in the Plains.*

The 4th Brigade and battering train were at the Pass. The *Shah* passed down the Pass this morning, and took up ground between the Hd. Qrs. and the Cavy., or a little in advance of us. (41)

The mules of the Bombay 9-pr. battery (at Quetta) were found to be completely exhausted, and arrangements were made for leaving it behind.

10. *Head Qrs. march to Dundee Goolaee,* (18th April, 1839.)—The Hd. Qrs. with H. E. and escort (wings of 1st Lt. Cavy. and 19th N. I. Bombay), and Staff, marched this morning. Before day-light we heard the sentries firing at the *Achukzyes* (mountaineers) ; 5 camels carried off from the

age for camels was not very good, and scarce; our camels were constantly carried off. Captain *Outram* says, p. 72 " there are some fine springs, but scarcely a blade of *grass.*"

It may be here mentioned, that these only admitted of obtaining water at a great expense of time. They dry up for a time if used all day ; so that troops from the rear coming in during an evening, would not find much, and that muddy ; and we had great experience of these facts! There was some water in advance about four or five miles to the left of our next march.

(39) Major Todd was there, and must have known it. Some kind of treaty had been made by Sir A. Burnes, but the Khan was acting a part!

(40) Arrived to-day at the top of the Pass.

(41) Two bullocks were carried off close to camp, and three water-carriers dreadfully cut up. The springs ought at first to have been enclosed within the picquets. While at dinner, a saees of Capt. *Lowe's* (16th Lancers) came to the door of our (staff) Mess-tent dreadfully cut on the head, and robbed of every thing, and this not 100 yards from the tent!

Hd. Qrs. camp. There was a considerable descent over a sterile plain. At about half-way, crossed the dry bed of the *Kudany* river. The road was over a succession of undulating, stony ground. At this point, about 3 or 4 miles to the right of our track, we perceived what we thought to be a cloud of dust. It had the appearance of *Cavy.*, at a distance, charging down on us! Some officers rode out to see what it was, while we halted, to be prepared. All our glasses were in requisition to ascertain the cause. There was no enemy. (42) Had there been, we were between the camp of the *Cavy.*, and that at the *Chumun Chokee*. There was a long string of camels, with baggage, on our left.

The distance to Dundee Goolaee, where we found the Cavy. &c., was 14¼ miles. The elevation above the sea, at this place, was 4,036 feet, or 1,641 feet lower than the Chumun Chokee; so we descended considerably this march.

Found on the road the mutilated bodies of many camp-followers.

The 4th Brigade hard at work at the Pass to-day. Maj. Genl. *Willshire*, with part of the Bombay Column at Siri-Ab, to-day. His baggage attacked with considerable spirit at the head of the *Bolan* Pass; 49 camels' load of grain carried off, 5 horses killed, and 3 troopers wounded, many of the enemy said to be killed.

The Hd. Qrs. to halt to-morrow. A good tank of water to the right of camp, fed by the Kudany river; the stream got dry by the evening. The stream had been turned up to the next ground. Thermometer at 3 A. M. 62°, at 3 P. M. 97°.

(42) Some grass had caught fire, and the smoke moved rapidly towards us with the wind which was light, in a waving, undulating form; (we know that grass once catching *fire*, that *it* will force a passage even against the wind, if a patch of grass to windward be near it, as if lighted to lee-ward the heat bends down the dry grass towards it, and thus communicates with that unburnt.) A little further on, we found some camels from the Cavy. camp out at graze, moving quickly and kicking up a dust, which had a different appearance.

19*th April.*—Thermometer at 5 A. M. 54°., at 3 P. M. 102°. The first Brigade Infy. with its Artillery marched from Chumun Chokee into our camp to-day. Halt for the 4th Brigade and Arty.; they are at the Pass still; hard work for the 1st Bengal European Regt. Twelve men and two women killed by the villagers, and two elephants belonging to the Envoy and Minister, carried off. A party sent to bring back the stream of water, but returned unsuccessful. A party should have been kept there. The D. A. Q. M. Genl. (Lt. *Becher*) and a troop of the 1st Bombay Cavy. went out to feel for the enemy; but none seen within the distance of 11 miles. The Bombay Column at Koochlâk to-day seven marches in our rear; the enemy fired long shots at them.

The *Shah* this evening made a tour round the whole camp.

11. *G. O. Camp duties, Crops, &c.* (19th April, 1839.)— Heard to-day, that the Candahar chiefs, with 1,500 horse, were near our camp, and meant to attack us. " H. E. the Comr.-in-Chief directs that the duties of camp, shall for the future he conducted in the following manner."

1st. " A Brigadier of the day, who will be in charge of the whole of the picquets of the camp."

2nd. "A Field Officer from each Brigade, who will be in charge of the picquets of the Brigade, and who will report to and receive instructions from the Brigr. on duty."

3rd. " A main-picquet of a troop of Cavy. and two Cos. of Infy., will, when the camp is halted, mount every morning at day-light; from which will be detached to a distance of 2 or $2\frac{1}{2}$ miles, in advance, according to the nature of the ground, at sun-set every evening, a subaltern's party of Cavy."

"This party must be particularly on the alert, and no followers of any description to accompany it." (43)

---

(43) " *Patroles* from the main picquet will move up to it, at intervals, throughout the night, and on halting-days, it will rejoin the main picquet at sun-rise."

"On marching days, the main picquet, coming on duty, will form the

4th. "*In*-lying-picquets equal in strength to the *out*-lying-picquets of Brigades, are to be told off for duty." (44)

5th. "The Brigr. of the day when coming off duty, will report, in person, to H. E. the Comr.-in-Chief." (45)

6th. "Brigades will, alternately, furnish an Adjt. of the day, to be, in attendance on the Brigr."

7th. "The main-picquet will mount this evening at 5 o'clock."

8th. "The officer Comg. the troops, forming H. E.'s escort, will communicate to the Brigr. of the day, the strength of the picquets they may have mounted, and will comply with such requisitions as he may make for additional men, to ensure a communication with the sentries in front and rear of the encampment."

"The Brigr. of the day will be furnished, by the D. Q. M. G., with a *Plan* of the encampment, which, on halting days, he will transfer to the Brigr. who may relieve him." (46)

9th. *(Preservation of Crops.)* "As the country through which the army is now moving, affords *forage* for the camels and good *grass* for the horses, H. E. the Comr.-in-Chief deems it necessary to require the strictest observance of the G. O., which have been issued prohibiting the cutting of

---

Advance-guard; and the picquet coming off duty, the *Rear-guard*." (The main picquet consisted of 1 Coy. of Eurn. and 1 of N. Infy.; and 1 troop of H. M. 16th Lancers.)

"In addition to the main-picquet, the Maj. Genls. Comg. the Cavy. and Infy. will direct such picquets and guards to be furnished from the brigades at their Hd. Qrs. as they may deem expedient ; and require the F. O. on duty, to communicate to the Brigr. of the day, the strength of the different details. They are likewise authorized, on his requisition, to increase the number of men on duty, should circumstances render the measure necessary."

(44) They were to join the *out*-lying-picquets, when ordered by the Brigr. or F. O. of the day, being intended as supports to those in front.

(45) The Brigr. coming on duty commanded the *Advance* guard; the F. O. coming off duty, the rear-guard.

(46) He was also, to explain the orders he had received, and what had occurred during his tour of duty; and to communicate any intelligence he was acquainted with, reports, &c.

growing crops; and he desires officers Comg. mounted corps, distinctly to understand, that when circumstances may render it necessary to assign *green crops* for the Cavy. horses, the same will be duly notified to the troops in a G. O. but, without this authority, they are, on no account, to allow the grass-cutters to encroach on the fields." (47)

To-day died poor Lt.-Col. *Jas. Thomson,* Comg. the 31st (Bengal) N. I. The Regt. had just made its first march from Shikarpoor; the heat was intense. The thermometer at 135° in the *sun.* This Officer died of apoplexy. He was an excellent officer, universally respected and esteemed, and regretted as a great loss to the service, as well as to his family. I mention this fact, here, to prove the state of the weather between Shikarpoor and Dadur, in the month of April!

12. (*20th April,* 1839), *Hajee Khan, Kakur.*—To-day no water in camp. A party went and opened the bund: the enemy came down, when our party left, and closed it again. The 4th Brigade still employed at the *Kojuk Pass.* This afternoon came into camp, with a party of about 200 horsemen, the celebrated *Hajee Khan, Kakur,* (48) chief of that

---

(47) " The *Provost Marshal* and his Assts. are required to be on the alert, to apprehend followers transgressing this order; and it is to be proclaimed by beat of *Tom-Tom* in the different Bazars that, if they persist in disregarding it, the Comr.-in-Chief will order a signal example to be made of the offending party."

(48) " Properly *Taj Mahomed Khan,* a Kakur by caste, a man of considerable note in the country, both as being one of the chiefs of a large, independent clan, and as having distinguished himself in the *field* and *counsel;* has lately sought service with *Rahm Dil Khan,* 2nd of the three Chiefs of Candahar) who has allowed him, nominally 60,000 Rs. (£6,000) a year, and the command of 300 horsemen; merely to prevent him joining the Sikhs, or Persians. On account of a supposed intrigue with the former during the late war, *Dost Mahomed* discharged him; he is a man of a ready address, and from the time of Vizier *Futteh Khan,* has been constantly handed backward and forward, between the *Barakzye* brothers; his arguments are heard in council, though his *sincerity* is often doubted." (Lt. Leech's report (1838) to Govt. while at Candahar in 1837; para. 37.) Dost Mahomed is known to have said that the only mistake he committed in regard to this man was, not having taken his life!

tribe, who tendered his submission; and was graciously received by the Shah; he pitched his tents in the king's camp.

The *Hajee* informed the King how he had arranged to get quit of the chiefs of Candahar! (49) He said the chiefs intended to make an attack, at night, *(Chuppao)* on our camp; that he told them that *they* might expect to be attacked themselves; " You have" said he, " carried off two of their *elephants;* (50) the *English* are not the people to allow this to be done with impunity. They will march with a large force, and guns, against you, and you are unequal to a contest with such troops. Stay where you are, and I will go and see if I can find out from what direction they are coming." " I got them to retire; I then moved off with my party, and so got rid of them; and I have now come to join your majesty !"

H. M. Shah Soojah wrote to Lt.-Col. Wade, before he left Loodianah, that the Cossids despatched to Candahar and to the Ghiljie country, had returned with letters from the Ghiljie chiefs, and added, " The Ghiljie, Dooranee, and other tribes are ready with *heart* and *soul* to serve me." " The Cossid delivered a *verbal* message from *Hajee Khan, Kakur,* who, out of fear, addressed no letter, but sent a message alluding to a *silver dagger* which he got before the Persian war, and that, " *he* will either seize the disloyal and present them before me; or induce all the servants to come along with him to the *presence.*" He did not like to commit himself by writing, 10,000 Rs. (£1,000) were sent to the Hajee, before the king left Loodianah, as a *retaining fee !*

(49) Capt. Outram says in his notes, p. 74, Deh Hajee (28th April, 1839)—" a considerable village lately plundered by the Sirdars of Candahar, who had come thus far to oppose our army; and dissensions among themselves, and the defection of an eminent chief, (*Hajee Khan, Kakur*) on whom they principally relied, had broken up their army, and they returned to Candahar, flying from the city with scarce 200 followers, on the 24th April, 1839." From Dundee Goolaee to Deh Hajee is 46½ miles, so that it would appear, that their principal force was not near us on the 20th April. Deh Hajee is 19½ miles from Candahar, so it is probable that the chiefs left Deh Hajee on the 22nd April. Said to have been between 2, and 3,000; see No. 2, Appx. para. 11.

(50) They belonged to the Envoy and Minister; and were taken off while out to get forage.

Two other influential men came in, also, to-day. G. O. "H. M. Shah Shoojah, having intimated his desire that the *Cavalry* be permitted to forage on the *crops* of *growing corn*, in the tract of country through which the army is now moving, and having deputed an Officer (Capt. *Hutton*) to apportion them to the several encampments (an equal distribution to each); H. E. the Comr-in-Chief appoints Maj. *Hay*, A. Q. M. G. of Cavy., to receive from that Officer, the portion assigned to the *Bengal* and *Bombay* troops; Maj. H. will then deliver over to Qr. Mrs. of corps a proportion according to the number of troops of which each is composed; and any infringement on that assigned to the *Shah's* force, on the part of the followers of the regular Army, is strictly prohibited. (Maj. H. to set apart a proportion for the Cavy. and gun-bullocks, still in the rear.) The prohibition to the destruction of the crops by the followers, and to camels, tattoos, &c. going into the fields; to be in full force."

"The three Cos. 37th N. I., not having been relieved by the 35th N. I. as contemplated in G. O. of the 6th inst., are to be sent on from *Dadur* with the first considerable despatch of stores, after the arrival at that place, of the corps of the 2nd (Bengal) Brigade, destined to occupy it."

The *Bombay* column to-day at Hyderzye, six marches in our rear. Their rear-guard was fired on by fifty men, crowning some little heights to the left of the column; no harm done. They found the village deserted. Thermometer at 5 A. M. 54°, at 3 P. M. 102°.

21*st April*, (Quilla Futtoolah.)—Marched to-day at daybreak. (At 3 A. M. Thermometer 54°.) The main-picquet, coming on duty, with the sappers and miners leading. (51)

The *Cavy*. Brigade, with its Arty., followed, and then came the *Infy*., with No. 6, Lt. Fd. battery.

The old main-picquet, reinforced by a squadron of Cavy.,

(51) "To occupy such a position, on arrival at the new ground, as the Brigr. of the day may think fit, in communication with D. Q. M. G."

formed the *rear*-guard; and the Local Horse was distributed along the line of baggage animals. (52)

Marched over an immense plain to Quilla Futtoolah, distant 10½ miles; there is a small square mud fort, with bastions at the angles, about ¾ of a mile from camp. It was empty, and the village deserted; we heard that the head chief, Kohun-dil-Khan, had returned to Candahar, (53) taking Mr. MacNaghten's elephants with him. At 11 A. M. no sweet water in camp; great distress. There was a salt spring, of clear water, to the rear of camp, and about two miles off. The *Bombay* column when here, on the 26th April, discovered a small well; and opened other wells which had been filled up. The Fort was about ¾ mile from the front of camp. At 3 P. M. no water in camp. The thermometer in the tent at 3 P. M. 102°; in the Sun 130°; great suffering among the soldiers, &c. European and native, and the cattle.

The elevation above the sea, here, 3,918 feet; only 118 feet lower than yesterday's camp (Dundee Goolaee).

The Park of Arty. over the Kojuk Pass to-day. There were 27,400 rounds of musket ammunition and fourteen barrels of gun-powder lost in the Pass, and destroyed to prevent their falling into the enemy's hands; and an immense quantity of baggage, and a great number of camels, tents, &c. The men of the 1st Bengal European Regt. were great sufferers; much of the sickness in the corps, is attributed to the very great exertions the men underwent in this Pass.

The *Bombay* column to-day at Hykulzye, still 6 marches behind us. Their Artillery horses beginning to knock up; no grain, and very scanty forage. (54) They had a despatch from Sir J. *Keane* dated 19th inst. " No opposition

---

(52) " No baggage to quit camp till the rear of the column of Troops, fairly in motion. No animals to crowd upon either flank."

(53) See note 49.

(54) " Of a kind to which they are unaccustomed, and it disagrees with them. Seven horses shot to-day, and the last few days several of the Poonah Auxy. horse have been shot."

then, expected; two Sirdars had left Candahar; route unknown."

Our D. Q. M. G. (Maj. *Garden*), accompanied by 60 troopers, did not return from his trip to the next ground till near ten to-night.

13. *March to Mehel Mandah,* (22nd April, 1839.)—Thermometer at 2 A. M. 52°. Marched at day-break. (55) After quitting camp, our road lay a little to the left of the fort, and passed up the Pass (56) which the fort protects. The road lay in the front of our centre. A deep ravine ran between the fort and the camp. The Pass between the mountains was from ¾ to 1 mile wide, over broken, stony, undulating ground. The length of the Pass was about five miles (a complete desert). At about half-way crossed the dry bed of the Kudany river. The country after quitting the Pass had such great ascents and deep descents, that it represented a *sea of rocks and stones.* As you ascended you lost sight of the troops descending, and when at the top of the ascent, you could not see those in the descent, to the front or rear, unless close on the brow towards it; thus we could only see the troops near us; the rest were lost to our view.

At about two miles from camp, crossed over several deep ravines; to our right the river Kudany in a small valley below.

Our camp was about two or three miles to the right, off the road to Candahar. We reached our ground at Mehel Mandah after a march of 12 miles.

When the Cavalry (Bengal) came up, not finding water immediately, the Brigadier asked for and obtained leave to go in advance to seek for some. (57) We had marched 12,

(55) It was at first intended to halt the Brigade of Cavy. with its Artillery, at Quilla Futtoolah, but countermanded.

(56) There was another Pass to the *left,* distant about three or four miles, by which it was proposed to march the 1st Infy. Brigade and Camel battery, and the Shah's force; (it leads to *Lower* Mehel Mandah;) while the Cavy. halted and followed: on account of the scarcity of water. We all marched by the same route.

(57) The Brigadier acted with the best intention on the occasion;

and he marched ten miles further, before he found water at the *Doree*-river, which lay to the left of our road. They procured plenty of water and forage ; but not till both men and horses had suffered dreadfully ; 50 or 60 horses fell down on the road and died. (58) The Lancers were obliged to dismount, and to goad on their horses with their Lances.

Much of the baggage belonging to our camp went on with the Cavalry; and did not come into camp till late in the evening.

The Park of Artillery and the 4th Brigade at the Chumun Chokee. Thermometer, at 3 P. M. 102°.

23rd April.—To the Doree river, (*Tukht-i-Pool.*)—Marched at day-break ; thermometer at 3 A. M. 60°. H. M.'s 13th Lt. Infy. led, followed by the H. A., the other two Regts. of 1st Brigade, Camel-battery, &c. After leaving camp, and marching about three miles we got into the high road to Candahar; a fine road, and through a cultivated country. The river Doree lay to our left about five miles, and when we had marched about eight miles, we saw the Cavy. camp to the left, so that they must have marched across the country to the river. We had some trifling ascents and descents ; we found several Karezees (wells) of good water at about two miles before we reached camp. We encamped on the bank of the Doree river, the water of which is brackish ; there was a sandy-desert on the other side of the river. The river was deep in some places. The hill called " *Lylee Mujnoon*" about three miles N. E. of camp. The distance marched to-day was 15½ miles. This place is 3,630 feet above the level of the sea, or 288

---

but it was found afterwards that there was water sufficient for all, in our camp ; there being several water-courses, with good water.

(58) Those who were present, describe the scene as most appalling. The moment the horses saw the water, they made a sudden rush into the river as if mad ; both men and horses drank till they nearly burst themselves. Officers declare that their tongues cleaved to the roofs of their mouths; the water was. very brackish which induced them to drink the more. The river was 3 feet deep and more in some places; and was 5 or 6 miles off the proper road. Many dogs and other animals died. No officer present ever witnessed such a scene of distress.

feet below Quilla Futtoolah; the thermometer at 3 P. M. 102°. (59) The Park of Arty. and 4th Brigade at Dundee Goolaee to-day, at 6 P. M. The king went on in the afternoon to Deh Hajee.

14. 24*th April.* To *Deh Hajee.*—Thermometer 3 A. M. 62°. The Shah and the Envoy and Minister went on to-day to Khoosh-ab, within seven and a half miles of Candahar. (60) We marched at day-break. The Cavy. and H. A. led, followed by the Infantry, and No. 6, Lt. Fd. battery. A good road, though rather stony. The rear of our camp, close to the walled village of Deh Hajee, by which runs a good stream of water. Candahar reported to be deserted. The 4th Brigade and Park of Arty. at Quillah Futtoolah. It was to this place the Candahar chiefs came; and not beyond it.

25*th April.*—To Khoosh-ab. Thermometer at 3 A. M. 68° Marched at day-break, over a desert-like plain. At 7 A. M. heard a "*Royal salute*" and firing at Candahar, in honor of Shah Shoojah-ool-Moolk's entry into the ancient Dooranee capital of Affghanistan. There were several villages on the right and left of the road on this march, and small distant hills. The last two or three miles, the country covered with fields of grain; the village of *Khoosh-ab* (61) close to the rear of camp. There were a number of Karezees close to the front (N.) of camp of clear pure water. We had a distinct view of Candahar from the front of camp. The village of Khoosh-ab is a large place, with mud-walls and houses. The people had not all left it; a good number appeared on the roofs of the houses to gratify their curio-

---

(59) The Cavy. were ordered to join us in the morning before we moved! They halted to-day. They had 8 miles to march to join us, so that they travelled 18 miles from Mehel-Mandah, or about $2\frac{1}{2}$ miles more than we did to the Doree river. Two men and a woman killed near the Karezees, and many others plundered; and in a narrow glen, not far from them, 100 camp-followers were said to have been butchered!

(60) It was reported that the chiefs had fled from the city. See note 49.

(61) *Pleasant,* or *sweet,* water.

sity. All round the village the crops of wheat, and barley, were plentiful, and extensive. Part of our camp was pitched in fields of barley. The crops were all in ear. (62)

The orders of to-day directed for to-morrow's march; protection to the growing crops, to orchards, and villages. " The officer Comg. the advance-guard, to post videttes over any villages or gardens, he may pass on the road; with orders to remain till the arrival of the rear-guard."

" No soldier, or follower, to enter the city of Candahar, till permission be granted, which will be announced in G. O.; and *passes* afterwards given."

" On the arrival of the troops at Candahar, the Brigr. of the day will post '*safety guards*' from the advance, in the different villages in the vicinity."

People bringing Provisions to camp—Marts. (63)—G. O. " A. Qr. Mr. Genls. of Divisions to assign convenient spots, in the vicinity of the different Brigades, where *marts* may be held for the sale of provisions, and of articles of country produce."

" The Provost Serjts. of brigades, and any steady soldiers who may be available for the duty, must be required to be on the look out for men bringing in supplies for sale, in order to conduct them to the different marts; at which places guards must be posted, that the Sutlers may not be molested, and that no injustice be done."

" If there be any plundering, H. E. will require the loss to be made good by the Brigade in the Mart of which the robbery may be committed." (64)

" Prohibition to enter the city of Candahar, for the present, to be published by beat of *Tom-Tom* in the different buzars."

(62) This I think should have been avoided, as there was ground for our camp without encroaching on the fields; there was a desire to get near the Karezees. This was no fault of the D. Qr. Mr. Gl., as he had pitched the flags on other ground.

(63) Having been plundered.

(64) The Duke of *Wellington* did so in the Peninsula. He made officers and men both pay. It is an admirable plan; as it operates on the purses of all—the most effectual check.

Effects of the length of the March. 95

"The order for the march of the troops to-morrow, countermanded; the Hd. Qrs. alone to move to Candahar."

The 4th Brigade and Park were halting to-day at Quillah Futtoolah.

The *Bombay* column at the entrance to the *Kojuk*-Pass, to-day. (65) Thermometer 3 P. M. 99°; elevation, above the level of the sea 3,484 feet.

15. *March to Candahar*, (26th April, 1839.) *State of affairs.*—The Head Qrs. arrived at Candahar this day. The 4th Brigade and the Park, were four marches in our rear. The *Bombay* column was not quite out of the Kojuk Pass; and Lt.-Col. Wade was with the Shahzada Timoor, and his force, waiting at Peshawer.

The Bengal column, on reaching this city, had made a march of 1,005 miles from *Ferozpoor*, and 1,210 miles from Kurnal; while some of the troops had marched a greater distance. (66) The people of the "*Mustered Establishments*" had been on *half*-rations since the 8th of March last, or for the preceding 48 days. (67) The Cavy. and H. A. horses had been put on *half*-rations since the 24th March, so that they had been on reduced rations, with scanty forage, for 32 days. The troops and camp-followers had been on *half*-rations since the 29th March, and had now been 28 days on these rations, without having much opportunity to purchase grain, or obtain any vegetables as a substitute.

The Cavy. and H. A. horses had *no grain* since the 30th of March, so that for the last 26 days they were subsisted

---

(65) They found a good road had been made by the Bengal column; but the ascents and declivities for $3\frac{1}{2}$ miles were so steep, as to present a most formidable undertaking to their artillery and jaded cattle. A portion of the baggage and of the 4 T. H. A. passed over during the day, assisted by H. M.'s 17th foot and camp-followers, who worked at intervals, also, during the night—flanking parties of the 17th foot, killed several of the hill people. (Capt. Outram, p. 71.)

(66) The 31st N. I. which remained at Quetta had, on its arrival there, marched 1,377 miles, having started from Allahabad in Sept. 1838.

(67) See p. 41.

on such *green* forage as might be procurable, and often on very bad grass. (68)

In this state of affairs, our *Cavy.* much reduced in amount by the loss of a great many horses, and owing to the weak condition of the rest,—were not fit for *Service* on our arrival at Candahar; and had the Sirdars come to attack us, we must have opposed them with *Artillery* and *Infantry;* (69) as we could not have effected any thing with the Cavalry. But *Hajee Khan, Kakur* turned the scale in our favor; his defection occasioned the flight of the chiefs from Candahar on the 23rd April towards *Girishk,* a fort 75 miles distant, situated across the *Helmund* river, and belonging to one of the chiefs.

(68) Horses accustomed to five seers (about 9½ lbs.) of gram, naturally got out of condition on such food. The *Affghan* horses eat green forage (lucerne, &c. chopped up with Bhoosa) in great quantities, and seldom get any grain. " The *Toorkmuns* prefer *dry* food for their horses, and give from eight to nine lbs. of barley a day. If *green* barley be given, the horse has no grain. Clover and artificial grasses are used for feeding horses, and are given in a *dry* state. Juwaree *(Holcus Sorghum)* is preferred, contains much saccharine juice." *Burnes's Bokhara,* vol. 2, p. 272.

The Cavy. &c. gave clover *dried,* (when procurable) mixed with grass, when they could not obtain *Bhoosa.* Large quantities of clover given alone, is considered bad for horses. Even *barley* is a grain which, in its whole state, gives but little nourishment, and is particularly bad if the barley be new, and of *gram* we had not had *one* grain for more than two months. Recourse was had to frying the barley, and, sometimes, making it into flour, or to boiling it; but this could not be done for 2,500 horses!

The *Toorkmuns* usually give the barley flour made up into balls, with the fat of the *doomba* sheep. Even the camel-men gave balls of this kind, mixed with water, declaring that 4 lbs. in this form, were of more nourishment than 8 lbs. of the barley whole. In fact it was observed, that the barley passed *through* the horses and cattle, in a *whole* state.

(69) It seems that the chiefs had not on the 13th April, abandoned the hope of raising a religious war against us, as discovered by intercepted letters. Our approach to the *Kojuk* Pass on the 14th April, had stirred up the Sirdars to move forward; a small advanced party came there; on the 18th and 19th April, two of the chiefs were said to have

The rest of the troops were moving up from our rear. The pursuit of the chiefs was not deemed, at present, advisable by the Envoy and Minister. (70)

The thermometer at 3 A. M. 62°; at 3 P. M. 94°. The elevation above the level of the sea, 3,484 feet, or 146 feet below Tukht-i-Pool, three marches in our rear.

Herat understood to be secure at this period.

---

been within 12 miles of the British camp at *Dundee Goolaee* with from 2 to 3,000 good horse. It is believed that they never came nearer than *Deh Hajee*. On the 20th April *Hajee Khan, Kakur,* and two others of consideration joined us in our camp, and this broke up the Candahar army.

(70) See Appx. No. 2, para. 5.

CHAPTER VI.

THE ARMY AT CANDAHAR—OCCURRENCES THERE—PREPARA-
TIONS TO LEAVE IT.

Candahar, (1) 26th April, 1839.—*Thermometer* at 3 A. M.
62°. On the arrival of the Hd. Qrs. at Candahar, we
had only *half*-rations for the troops for about two days,
and the Cavalry horses had no grain; but there was plenty
of lucerne, and good grass to be procured. We were now,
to lay in a stock of grain, to recruit our horses, and to
purchase others to complete our complement, to be prepared to move towards Cabool. Rest was required both for
man and beast. *Thermometer* 3 P. M. 94°.

27th April. The Camp.—Thermometer 5 A. M. 62°. The
troops left at Koosh-ab, marched in to-day, and a camp was
formed. The Bengal Infantry and Artillery, had a camp to
the S. E. of the city, distant about 2 miles. (2) Maj. Gen. Sir
W. *Cotton,* and the *Bengal* Staff camp, was close to the S.
of the city; and half-way between these camps was that
of Maj. Genl. *Thackwell,* Comg. the Cavy. H. E. the
Comr.-in-Chief, *Sir J. Keane,* pitched his camp to the S.
W. of, and in a garden near, the city. The 3rd and 2nd
Regts. Bengal Cavy. were encamped about half a mile
to the W. of the city; and H. M. Shah Shoojah's contingent was encamped in their rear. The *Cavy.* Brigade was
at first encamped on the right of the *Infy.* The *Bombay*

(1) For an account of *Candahar,* see Chapter 7th.
(2) The corps in one line from right to left; 4th Local-Horse, (and
on its arrival) the 4th Infy. Brigade (35th N. I. 1st Eurn. Regt. 37th
N. I.); H. A. The Park, the Sappers and Miners. 1st Infy. Brigade
(16th N. I.; H. M.'s 13th Lt. Infy.; Camel battery; 48th N. I.)

o 2

column, on its arrival, had its camp, in front of the Comr.-in-Chief's. (3)

The whole of the camels of the army were ordered to be sent out to grazing ground at a distance, protected by a Wing of Native Infy. and a Ressallah of Local Horse, completed to 100 men. (4)

A special committee (5) was formed for the purpose of admitting horses into the service. The committee were directed to record their opinion as to the fitness of the remounts, for H. A. Dragoons, or Bengal, or Bombay, Light Cavalry; but this committee was found not to work well, and Regimental committees (6) were ordered to be formed; limited to the purchase of the number of horses

(3) By corps from right to left in one line. The Park; H. A.; Cavalry Brigade; Infy. Brigade; Poonah Auxy. Horse; H. M.'s 16th Lancers.

(4) They were relieved weekly, and took seven days' supplies with them. When out grazing during the day, parties were sent with them; and at *sun-set* they were ordered to be brought within the picquets. "The officer Comg. the escort directed to inflict summary punishment on any Surwan who disobeys his orders; or who permits his camels to stray into any cultivation. To report all casualties and occurrences every three days."

(5) Consisting of Brigr. *Arnold,* President; and a Field Officer from H. M.'s 16th Lancers; from the Bengal Cavy.; from the Bombay Cavy., and officer Comg. 2 T. 2 B. (Bengal) H. A. To meet at the D. C. G.'s tent, on his notification to the President.

(6) G. O. 3rd May, 1839. "Under the authority of Comg. officers. But no horse to be branded with the Regtl. mark till inspected and approved of by the Brigr. Comg. the Brigade." The President of the committee gave the seller an order for the price, on the D. C. G.: to whom he sent a descriptive Roll of the horse; the officer Comg. the H. A. held a similar committee. Weekly reports were made of the number of horses purchased, and the prices paid.

This committee answered best; as the attention of each was directed to the description of horse, best suited for the particular branch of the service; and time was saved; not having to assemble officers from the different camps. The Regns. of the Bengal and Bombay Govt. differ as to the price given for horses; in Bengal, 450 Rs. are given for horses for the H. A. and Dragoons; and for the Native Cavy., 400 Rs. At Bombay, 500 and 450 Rs. are given for horses. This difference should not, I think, exist on service in a foreign country, or

actually required to complete. But it was found difficult to procure horses in sufficient numbers of the standard height, (7) and the Comr.-in-Chief, at the recommendation of the Maj. Genl. Comg. the Cavy., authorized (8) committees to pass, into the service, horses somewhat under the standard ; provided they were satisfied that the horses possessed sufficient bone, strength, and activity, and were unexceptionable in other essentials. But no horse admitted as undersized, to be hereafter rejected, or cast, on the score of being undersized.

There must have been a loss of more than 500 horses in the *Bengal* and *Bombay* columns. Capt. *Outram* states that there were 350 lost in the Bengal army, (9) and about 150 horses (10) of the Artillery and Auxiliary Cavalry of

out of the Company's dominions, as the Cavy. of one establishment does not come into the market on the same terms. Indeed, it may often be necessary to give more than the regulation price for one horse, while by purchasing a great number, the average price may not exceed the Regn.

The Bombay Cavy. are usually mounted on small Arab horses which are more expensive than country horses; they, also, use the Cutch, and Kattywar horses.

(7) 14½ hands ; the Affghan-horses are rather short and thick-set, and have heavy shoulders.

(8) G. O. 11th May, 1839.

(9) " While the remainder are so reduced in condition, as to be barely able to move from their picquets." p. 75.

(10) " Dropped on the road from exhaustion. The survivors have suffered much, but are in better state than the horses of the Bengal army." But it must be recollected that the horses of the Bengal Column had marched 293 miles more than those of the Bombay Column ; and that the latter had been on *grain* -rations till within 2 *or* 3 *marches* of Candahar ; while *ours* had had no grain for 27 *days !* I merely state the fact to account for the result.

Capt. O. adds : " It is now fully proved, and admitted by all parties, that the *Arab* and *Persian* horses stand their work better than *stud* and *country*–breeds ; the latter though younger, stronger, and in far better condition, at starting, have invariably been the first to give in ; while they seldom rallied afterwards. A few *Cape* horses lately introduced into the Bombay army, have also proved themselves superior to our stud-breeds."

the Bombay: this does not include the Wing of H. M.'s 4th L. D., nor the 1st Bombay Light Cavy.

The *Bengal* column had about 2,560 horses ; so that the loss of 350 was about three in twenty-two horses. (11) The *Bombay* column had about 1930 horses, and the loss of 150 would be about five in sixty-four horses. We lost more than two-fifths; and the Bombay column are said to have lost one-fifth ; nearly 1,500 horses (Bengal and Bombay) were lost in the whole campaign ! (12) Thermometer 5 A. M. 50°. At 3 P. M. 88°.

2. 28*th April* 1839.—Passes were granted by officers to private servants, in limited numbers, to enter the city to purchase supplies. " All passes to be returned on the same evening to the person signing them, that they may be destroyed." *Thermometer* 3 P. M. 90°.

30*th April.*—Thermometer 5 A. M. 64°. The 4th Brigade and the Park of Artillery arrived to-day. Provisions were sent to meet the Bombay column. Cossids reported to-day, that the *Persians* were advancing on *Herat.* Thermometer 3 P. M. 96°.

1*st May.*—*Thermometer* 4 A. M. 54°. The Cavalry this morning, moved to new ground at *Mergaum*, about 4 miles on the road to *Herat,* for the greater facility of procuring forage. H. E. Lt.-Genl. Sir J. *Keane* held a *Levee* to receive, and be introduced to the *Bengal* officers, at half past 5 P. M.; and afterwards had an interview with the Shah, to concert measures for procuring supplies ; and as to the pursuit of the Sirdars of Candahar, then at Girishk, 75 miles off ; who were said to be raising troops. *Thermometer* at 3 P. M. 98°.

Some say the *New South Wales'* horses are equal to those of the Cape.

(11) The total loss from 10th Dec. 1838 to 31st Dec. 1839, was 1072, of *Bengal* horses; being a loss of 5 out of 12 horses !

(12) The Bengal Column *rendezvous'd* at Kurnal, on the 31st Oct. 1838. The Hd. Qrs. and the returning troops reached Ferozpoor on the 1st Jan. 1840, after a march of 2070 *miles*. The troops marched some distance to join at Kurnal ; from 70 to 120 or more miles.

2nd May.—Thermometer 5 A. M. 54°. It had been proposed to send a detachment of two Cos. of Europeans, 1,000 N. I., 300 Cavy., and two guns, to *Girishk*, to pursue the Sirdars; but owing to overtures received from the fugitives, its march was delayed for the present. (13) *Thermometer* 3 P. M. 94°.

3rd May.—Thermometer at 4 A. M. 55°. Preparations were being made for the *King's* first *public* appearance. *Thermometer* at 3 P. M. 96°.

4th May.—Thermometer 5 A. M. 54°. The *Bombay* column, under Maj. Genl. *Willshire* arrived in camp to-day; consisting of two troops of H. A; the Wing of H. M.'s 4th L. D.; Wing 1st Light Cavy.; (14) H. M.'s 2nd and 17th foot; Wing 19th N. I.; (14) the Sappers and Miners and Dett. Poonah horse. It was estimated that 500 Belochees, Kakurs, and Affghans, had been slain by the Bengal and Bombay columns, since leaving Shikarpoor and Larkhana; the loss on our side being thirty or forty killed in open combat; besides some hundreds of followers murdered. (15) *Thermometer* at 3 P. M. 99°.

5th May.—Thermometer at 5 A. M. 56°. The Shah's Artillery was at this time in the Bolan Pass, escorted by the 42nd N. I. and had hard work from the 3rd to 5th May, in protecting the guns, tumbrils and carts, as the cattle were unable to proceed. Five Cos. of the 37th N. I. were, also, engaged on this harassing duty. (16) We heard that Mehrab

(13) Outram, p. 76.

(14) The other Wing, as part of H. E.'s escort, had arrived with us.

(15) On our march from Quilla Futtoollah on the 22nd of April, 150 or more followers were killed, and the Bombay troops on the march from Mehel Mandah lost 100.

(16) Brigr. *Dennie* was proceeding to join his Regt. and was with the party. Orders had several times been given to the men to leave the carts which could not proceed, the cattle being incapable of moving, and to bring on those that could.

The men of the 42nd N. I. were from 10 o'clock on the night of the 3rd until the afternoon of the 5th May, without food, and had only about a pint of water. They suffered dreadfully from thirst and

Khan, of Khelat, was desirous of coming to Candahar to tender his submission to the king; but it was too late. *Thermometer* at 2 P. M. 102°.

6th May.—Thermometer at 4 A. M. 60°. Permission given to the men entering the city, with *Passes*, to a limited number of well-conducted soldiers, daily; to make purchases; the indulgence if abused, to be withdrawn, on the first occasion of any misconduct. Comg. officers to make their own arrangements for N. C. O. being present in the city whilst the men are there on leave; to check irregularities.

The advance of our troops, or a part of them, to *Herat* was to have taken place, had the *Shah* of *Persia* returned to besiege it. Major *Todd*, P. A. and certain Engineer and Artillery officers, are to be sent to Herat, on a mission to Shah *Kamran* ; and to repair and strengthen the fortifications. Thermometer at 3 P. M. 100°.

7th May.—Thermometer at 4 A. M. 62°. The Cavy. Brigade moved nearer to the city.

A convoy of camels with grain came in to-day from Shikarpoor; the convoy when it left Shikarpoor, consisted of 2,000 camels, and 8,000 maunds (17) of grain ; of which grain a little more than ½th reached Candahar.

This was a great loss and disappointment to the army. The convoy was occasionally attacked on its route ; but the misfortune was, that too much trust was placed in the *Native* agents. (18) The news of the occupation of Candahar

fatigue, and there was great difficulty in inducing them to abandon the carts under their charge, even under the severest privations and hard labour. Both these are excellent Regts., and they well maintained their character on this occasion.

(17) 640,000 lbs.

(18) The officer in charge was acting in the Comsst. Dept. from which he was removed ; an inquiry was held to investigate into the circumstances attending this loss. He was wounded during an attack made by the Belochees on the rear of the convoy ; but, the camels ought to have been inspected and counted, as well as the loads, before taking charge ; and in all such convoys, the camels and grain bags should be collected, each day, after the march, in one spot, and ranged in lines ; by which plan they could be counted in a short time.

Installation of the King. 105

by H. M. *Shah Shoojah-ool-Moolk,* and the British army, was brought to Lt.-Col. *Wade* at *Peshawer* to-day; when a Royal salute was fired, by the *British* and *Sikh* Artillery in camp; and the Shahzada *(Tymoor)* held a Levée at 6 o'clock in the evening, to receive the congratulations of the officers of the British Mission and of his own party. *Thermometer* 3 p. m. 100°. At this time the force at *Peshawer* was ready to advance.

3.—*Ceremony of the King's Installation,* (8th May, 1839).—*Thermometer* at 4 a. m. 62°. The whole of the British army (Bengal and Bombay) was drawn up in line, at the dawn of day, in front of the city of Candahar to the N. amounting to about 7,500 men (19). A platform, or throne, was erected in the midst of an extensive plain. At sunrise, the guns of the palace announced H. M.'s departure. H. E. Lt.-Genl. Sir J. *Keane*, with the Staff were awaiting the egress of the procession, at the *Herat* gate, whence the King proceeded on horse-back, through a street formed by his own contingent. On his coming near the line, a Royal salute (twenty-one guns) was fired, and on his passing down the line, there was a *general salute*, and the colors were lowered, as in the case of crowned heads. On his ascending the throne, a *salvo* was discharged from 101 (20) pieces of Artillery. Sir J. Keane, and the Envoy and Minister at his Court, offered presents on behalf of the *British* Govt. of 101 Gold-mohurs each (21), and then the officers, British, and native, in the King's Service, offered nuzzars (presents). The "*Army of the Indus*" then marched round, in front of the throne, in review order; this grand ceremony presented an imposing spectacle. There were about 3 or 4,000 Affghans assem-

---

(19) The British Force then present at Candahar was about 9,000 men, and there were about 3,000 of the Shah's contingent, besides some *Affghan* Cavy.

(20) The royal salute with Indian kings, &c.

(21) £80 16s. An odd number usually given by the natives of India.

p

bled to view the scene, but they did not come on the parade. (22)

Hospitals.—Buildings having been found in the vicinity of camp, to afford accommodation to the sick of 2 T. 2 B. H. A.; of the Park; and of H. M.'s 13th Lt. Infy. H. E. authorized their immediate hire, at a suitable rent. (23) *Thermometer* at 3 P. M. 102°.

9th May.—Thermometer 5 A. M. 60°. The Sirdars having rejected the terms offered them, a detachment ordered to march against them; *thermometer* 3 P. M. 98°.

10th May.—Thermometer 4 A. M. 56°. The Bombay camp-followers in the greatest distress; flour at only 1½ seer (3 lb) per rupee. *Thermometer* 3 P. M. 98°.

11th May.—Thermometer 4 A. M. 56°. A riot at the city gates, and several merchants plundered. The unfortunate people shut up their shops, and fled, and many of the villagers fled to the mountains. Grain had become very dear, and though scarce, its excessive dearness was owing to the cupidity and rascality of the *old Kothwal* of the city. He insisted on high prices and large profits on the grain; this increased the dearness, and the camp-followers were almost driven to desperation (24). A party was sent into the city, to afford protection to the grain and public stores collected by the Commissariat. *Thermometer* 3 P. M. 100°.

4. *12th May*, 1839, (Dett. to Girishk.)—*Thermometer* 4 A. M. 56°. This morning a Detachment of the following

(22) It was expected that there would be an immense crowd, and the Local Horse were stationed "to prevent a pressure towards the throne." This expectation was raised from having observed the cordial manner with which his first arrival was greeted (see Appx. No. 2, para. 3); he, then, came with a few attendants, and on this occasion a large Mily. force was drawn up, a sight to which the people were unaccustomed.

(23) This was a great comfort for the sick, they were living in a temperature of 82° instead of 102°. There being a difference of 18 or 20 degrees, between the tents and these buildings.

(24) Forty men were flogged on the 12th instant for having been caught among the plunderers. There is no doubt that we caused much distress to the people, as the presence of our army, doubled the number of persons to be fed; and we were there two months!

details marched for *Girishk*, under the command of Brigr. *Sale*: 2-18-prs., 2-5½-inch mortars, manned by Europeans, and the Camel battery (4-9-prs. and 1-24-pr. Howit.), with a portion of the Engineer Dept. (Capt. *Sanders*), and detail of sappers and miners. A Squadron of Cavy., made up by selections (25) from the 2nd and 3rd Regts. of *Bengal* Lt. Cavy.; 100 men of H. M. 13th Lt. Infy.; and the 16th Bengal N. I., with a detail of H. M. Shah Shoojah's Infy. to complete it to 1,000 men; and 300 of the Shah's Cavy., Capt. *Christie's*—a total force of about 1,700 men. (26) *Girishk* belonged to *Kohun-dil Khan* (the head chief and is distant 75 miles from Candahar. (27) If the chief refused to surrender the place, it was to be stormed, and the garrison put to the sword, giving no quarter. The Post Master ordered to lay a dawk to convey letters to and from the above detachment.

Intercepted letter.—An intercepted letter was found in the city, said to be written to *Dost Mahomed Khan*, by *Hajee Khan, Kakur*, stating that our force consisted of 2,500

(25) So knocked up were our Cavy. that there was not any one troop fit for detached duty.

(26) Twenty days' provisions (*half*-rations) and 200 rounds per musket, and proper proportion of rounds for the Arty., were sent.

(27) The Fort of *Girishk* is an insignificant place; the defences might be taken by 9-prs., were battering found necessary, and the place carried by escalade; or a favorable spot, where there is no ditch, might be selected for mining, and the wall breached without difficulty. The gateways were weak and the gates badly constructed. The river *Helmund* is crossed from the left to the right bank, on which stands the fort, about a mile distant.

The river was obliged to be crossed by rafts made of rum casks, which were towed across by the sappers. Capt. *Sanders* thinks a suspension bridge of ropes, supported on trestles, should be used when the river is in flood. Girishk is on the road to Herat, and when the mission crossed it on the 27th June, 1839, the river had fallen four feet.

This fort, in our possession, might be rendered serviceable against the *Affghans*.

It is a very unhealthy place in August and September; one of the Shah's Regt. there lost 40 men, and had 4 or 500 sick; and was obliged to be withdrawn!

Cavy. and 7,000 Infy, (28) and advising him to advance to oppose us. Subsequent events induce a belief that he was the writer of the letter.

Flour *one* seer per rupee ! Thermtr. 3 P. M. 102°.

13*th May*.—Thermtr. 4 A. M. 56°. The people returned to-day and opened their shops outside the gate of the city, to sell provisions, &c. Thermtr. 3 P. M. 102°.

14*th May*.—Thermtr. 4 A. M. 56°. The grazing ground changed. Thermtr. 3 P. M. 102°.

16*th May*.—Thermtr. 4 A. M. 60°. " Intelligence received that the chiefs at *Girishk* have fled, with only 100 horsemen and the same number of Infy. ; but in what direction not known." (29) Thermt. 3 P. M. 104°.

17*th May*.—Thermtr. 4 A. M. 62°. The Europeans are going fast into hospital. (30) Three or four deaths occur daily.

Shah Shoojah-ool-Moolk's Levée.—All the British officers and those attached to H. M.'s contingent, were introduced to the king at his palace in the city. H. E. Sir *J. Keane,* Mr. *Macnaghten,* the Envoy and Minister, gave a present each, of 101 gold mohurs, Maj. Genls. 21, Brigadiers 11, Field officers 5, Captains 2, and Subalterns 1 gold mohur, each.

Khujawahs for the sick. (20th May.)—Khujawahs (31) for the carriage of the sick on the march ordered to be made

(28) This was about the amount of the *British* force *then* at Candahar, exclusive of the Shah's contingent and the *Affghan* horse in his service. *Dost Mahomed* did advance, in 1834, to Candahar, when the Shah came there on his last expedition.

(29) We afterwards learnt that they fled, with precipitation, to the frontier of Persia.

(30) The 1st European Regt. had 86 ; H. M.'s 13th Lt. Infy. 80; H. M.'s 16th Lancers nearly 100. See Table, No. 2.

(31) The Khujawahs were made of a wooden frame-work, about 4½ feet long, by 3½ broad, with a seat at the back for two men. The sides of the frame-work were filled up with gunny cloth. Each camel carried two khujawahs, one on each side ; so that each camel carried four sick men. This mode of travelling is very uncomfortable for *very* sick men, as the motion throws the body forward and then backward, at every step the animal takes.

up: for each *European* Regt. ten pairs ; for each *Native* Regt. five pairs, and two pairs for a troop of H. A., and one pair for the Camel battery. (32)

A gun was ordered to be fired, daily, at noon.

Grain for horses.—The Commissariat Dept. having obtained a sufficient supply of grain for the horses, of mounted corps, directed to issue 3 seers (6 lbs.) of barley to each horse daily from to-morrow; and the purchase of it by Regimental committees, to be discontinued. (33)

5. *Camels carried off*, (23rd May, 1839.)—*Thermometer* 4 A. M. 56°. A great number of camels carried off from the grazing-ground; and from the report of the officer Comg. the detachment on duty, there being reason to suspect that the *Rewaree* (hired) owners had exaggerated the numbers carried off, or had been grazing in a forbidden direction; the Comr.-in-Chief desired that *Compensation* (34) should not, on the present occasion, be passed to the claimants; and to secure Govt. from imposition, on the part of the camel-owners, H. E. directed (35) all claims for

(32) On the 20th June, an order was issued to make up *pads*, to prevent the khujawahs from galling, or injuring the camels' backs. The price of each pair of khujawahs, including the pads, was 25 Rs. 12 as.

(33) They had commenced reaping barley (the earliest crop) about the 10th to 12th May, so that the horses had not had grain for many days, since the 30th of March, 1839.

The Horse Arty. horses were kept on *half*-rations, longer than the Cavy. horses were.

(34) Twenty-five Rs. were paid by Govt. for each camel. There is no doubt that many of the Surwans went into the gardens, or cultivation, and that the camels were thus carried off by the villagers. We lost a great many camels, owing to the Surwans going beyond the *Cordon* placed for their protection.

(35) G. O. 26th May, 1839. The Committee to be held on the requisition of the Comsst. officer, and to record their opinion on the claim. Proceedings sent to Hd. Qrs. D. C. G. not to pay on his own authority. Where a camel died, the surwan, or the owner, was obliged to cut out the *mark* and bring it to the Comsst. officer. There is no doubt that many of our camels were carried off, and sold again to us by the *Affghans!*

camels, alleged to have been carried off by robbers, to be sent before a committee of officers, to be assembled in the brigade in which the loss may have occurred.

Commissariat. (24th May, 1839.)—Officers Comg. European corps and Detts. of the Bengal division, were directed to send the names of one steady N. C. O., and three privates, for selection for employment under the orders of the D. C. G. (36)

A Dram of Rum was about this time, issued out to each of the *officers,* who chose to indent for it; as we had long been without any wine, or spirits of any kind. (37) *Thermometer* 3 P. M. 92°.

24th May.—Thermometer 4 A. M. 58°. Being the anniversary of Her Majesty's birth-day; a royal salute was fired at noon; and an extra allowance of liquor issued to each European soldier. *Thermometer* 3 P. M. 95°.

28th May.—Thermometer 4 A. M. 62°. This evening Lts. *Inverarity* and *Wilmer,* H. M.'s 16th Lancers, were returning from a fishing party near the Urghundab river, unarmed, (38) they were attacked by a party of armed-men, but separately; for Lt. W. had gone on in advance, and had despatched his servant with his gun;—Lt. I. staying a little behind for some purpose; at this time no persons were observed. Lt. W., having a stick, beat off the people and escaped to the nearest (the Shah's) camp, and gave the alarm, when a party was sent back with Lt. W. who, on his return, found his companion so dreadfully

---

(36) These Europeans were found very useful. They acted as a check on the Native Agents; but on such an expedition they are absolutely necessary, to see the camels are kept in a compact order on the march, and that the bags are daily counted.

(37) Issued to Staff Serjts. of N. I. Regts. by G. O. 1st June, and to medical *Warrant* officers by G. O. 20th June, 1839. These Drams were paid for by the parties indenting for them.

(38) All officers had been directed not to appear out of camp, without their swords. The king was much annoyed at the murder, and took much trouble to find out and seize the murderers. They lived near a *Sanctuary,* which was razed to the ground.

hacked and cut through the back, that he only spoke a few words; asked for water, drank a little and expired. *Thermometer* 3 p. m. 98°. (39)

6. *Order for march towards Cabool*, (1st June, 1839.)— *Thermometer* 4 a. m. 52°.—*G. O.*—" The whole of the troops except 1 Regt. N. I., to be held in readiness to march."

2. " Brigr. *Gordon*, Comg. in Upper Sindh, to require four Cos. 42nd N. I., now at Shikarpoor, and a Regt. of Bombay N. I., to march as an escort to treasure consigned to the army; together with any Detts. of H. M. Shah Shoojah's horse which may still be in the District; and such details of *Sindh* Cavy., recently raised, as may be available."

3. " On the arrival of the treasure at *Dadur*, the two Cos. 31st Bengal N. I. now there, will be relieved by a similar detail of Bombay N. I., and the former will join the escort, and proceed to *Quetta*; where the whole of the 2nd brigade of Bengal N. I., will be assembled."

4. "The Bombay Battn. will not move beyond *Quetta*, till F. O.; but Maj. Gen. *Nott* will despatch the treasure to Hd. Qrs. under charge of a Regt. of Bengal Infy., the *Sindh* Cavy., and such details of Shah Shoojah's horse, as are available."

5. " Maj. Gen. *Nott* will also send forward one troop of the Shah's Arty., now in *Shawl*; and two Cos. of the Shah's Infy.; these are to be attached to the guns, and to assist in passing them over difficulties."

6. " *Candahar* to be garrisoned by 1 Regt. Bengal Infy., 1 troop of the Shah's Arty., 1 Regt. of the Shah's Infy. and Capt. *Anderson's* Ressalah of horse."

7. " A Regt. from the Bengal Infy. brigade, now at Hd.

(39) Capt. *Outram*, (p. 134) after having captured and razed the different Ghiljie forts between Candahar and Cabool, sent back the Shah's Affghans, viâ *Mukoor* (16 marches from Candahar and six from Ghuznee) in order to apprehend certain persons residing *there*, who stood accused of this murder. I have not heard if they were apprehended.

Qrs., will be detailed for this duty, and Capt. *Timings's* (Native) troop H. A., for the present, to remain at Candahar; to which will be attached a Regt. of the Shah's Infy."

8. "On the arrival of the treasure from *Shikarpoor*, the Regt. of the second Bengal brigade, which affords it escort from *Quetta*, will be relieved from the charge, by the Regt. now here, and will remain at *Candahar;* the latter, till F. O. with Capt. T.'s troop H. A., and such details of horse (not less than 300) as may be available, will proceed with it to Hd. Qrs. of the army."

"The 4 18-*pr. guns* and such ordnance stores as the Brigadier may see fit, to be left at *Candahar*." (40)

2nd June.—Thermometer 4 A. M. 54°. A number of camels carried off. *Thermometer* 3 P. M. 104°.

3rd June.—Thermometer 4 A. M. 54°. The camels sent out to graze at *Goondoo Memsoor Khan;* the escort taking ten days' provisions. Thermometer 3 P. M. 105°.

4th June.—Thermometer 4 A. M. 66°. The public cattle called in from the grazing-ground; from the 5th to 10th June, was the time fixed for the march. The Govr. Genl., it is said, directed that we should not march with less than six weeks' full rations. (41) As respects the health of the troops, there was more sickness at Candahar than we had before experienced, (42) and we should be marching into a country with a lower temperature; so that, in fact, it was *advisable,* if we had secured the required quantity of supplies, to move as early as possible; since, having been here

---

(40) See further orders, 10th June, 1839.

(41) The crops at Candahar were ripe and ripening, while at *Ghuznee* and *Cabool* the crops were green. The object was to collect the crops here (which the Shah permitted us to take); and not to be too soon for the crops at *Ghuznee* and *Cabool*, unless we could carry a very large supply with us, which was impossible; and in carrying away what we did, we half-starved the inhabitants; (all the old grain appeared to have been consumed,) besides we expected daily, a convoy of *Lohanee* merchants with 20,000 maunds (1,600,000 lbs.) of grain.

(42) See Table, No. 2.

thirty-nine days, we had recruited our men, horses, and cattle; (43) and by a delay, the well-affected might cool in their zeal; and we were affording *Dost Mahomed Khan*, so much more time to strengthen himself at *Ghuznee*, and at Cabool: while we knew that *Herat* was not threatened.

7. *Occurrences in our Rear.*—On the 23rd May, 1839, a party consisting of detachments, and a wing of the 23rd Bombay N. I. marched from Shikarpoor, with treasure and stores. Dr. *Hallaran (Bombay* army), Lt. *Chalmers*, 43rd (44) and Ensign Ste. *Beaufort*, 42nd Bengal N. I., who accompanied the party, fell victims to the *tremendous heat;* as, also, Conductor *Havilland* (Bengal), and Mr. *Jervis*, (Agent of Mr. Frith's, *Bombay.*) An expedition had been planned from *Bukkur*, (45) of which some Europeans who had been left behind from the army, sick in hospital, formed a part. A subadar and nine sepoys, *(Bengal)* died in one day, near *Meerpoor.* (46) The above events took place between the 2nd and 4th June, 1839. Thermometer 3 P. M. 106°.

Govr. sent to Tirhun, (5th June).—*Thermometer* 4 A. M. 58°. H. M. Shah Shoojah, sent a new Governor to *Tirhun*, about two or three marches from *Candahar*, to displace the old Governor; the latter resisted and killed twenty of the new Governor's followers; the king then sent a detachment against the place, when the new Governor was allowed to assume his office.

(43) We had to purchase 3 or 4,000 camels!
(44) Just come out from England.
(45) 26 miles to the rear.
(46) Lt. Corny, H. M. 17th Foot, (proceeding to join) started with 49 Europeans from *Bukkur* for *Shikarpoor.* He, with 12 of the men, lost their way and remained under a tree all day. Natives were sent out to look for them, and in the course of the day, seven Europeans were brought in dead. Lt. C. died of cholera the following day; two of the party, not found, were of course dead; the remaining three were brought in such a state, as to require their being sent to *Bukkur* immediately—the *sun* killed them all. The heat was 115° in tents, and 100 in a house with tatties.

Lt. *D. Ramsay*, 17th Bengal N. I. died in the *Bolan Pass* on the 26th March, 1839; but not from the effects of the heat.

Peshawer.—About this time there was a good deal of sickness among the officers (47) and men at *Peshawer.* Thermometer 3 P. M. 106°.

Affghans tried for Camel stealing, (6th June).—Thermtr. 4 A. M. 60°. The four *Affghans* tried by a Native General Court-Martial, for having stolen and carried away on the 2nd instant twenty-three camels belonging to the *Bombay* army (48) and sentenced to be *hanged*, were to have been executed to-morrow morning, on the spot where the late Lt. *Inverarity* was murdered; but the *king* claimed them as his *subjects!* H. M. was not satisfied with the sentence, and appointed a *Meerza* to rehear the evidence, when the *king* pronounced them *not* guilty, (49) upon the evidence taken

(47) Lt.-Col. *Wade*, was sick with a fever, and Dr. *Lord*, (Bombay,) Lt. *Corfield*, 2nd Eurn. Regt. had been obliged to leave the camp.

(48) Said to be Sir *J. Keane's.*

(49) The facts of the case were these. The four men had driven off these camels from the grazing ground, putting the drivers in bodily fear; one Surwan ran back to give information, when a party of the 4th Local Horse went out after the robbers, and seized them, and recovered the camels, just as the robbers were on the point of reaching some hills close by; where had they gone, the camels would never have been recovered. An example was necessary, and they were sentenced accordingly. The *Meerza* examined the *prisoners* themselves; *they* said that when they saw the Local Horse, that *they* beckoned to them to come and take the camels, which *they* had recovered from robbers, and that the *heads of the camels were turned towards our camp*, as if returning!!! The *Mirza* made one of the witnesses for the *prosecution* state in his evidence, that the heads of the camels were turned towards them (the Local Horse).

As I was the D. J. A. G. who tried these *Affghans*, Sir *J. Keane*, ordered me to draw up a report as to the discrepancy between the evidence before the *Court-Martial*, and that taken before the *Meerza*. I sent for the witness above alluded to, who denied that *he* ever stated that "when the Local Horse came up, the camels' heads were turned towards them." The Envoy and Minister (now Sir *W. H. Macnaghten*), declared that the evidence recorded on the proceedings of the Ct.-Martial, warranted the conviction.

These robbers, called themselves the "cultivators of the soil," but the people all round Candahar, were incited by the *Ghiljie* chiefs to plunder and rob us in camp, and out of camp. The latter lurked about

by the *Meerza*. Had the king wished to save the lives of these men, he might have asked Sir *J. Keane* to pardon them. For though *Shah Shoojah* was the sovereign of the country, still there were no Courts of Justice; the country was in an unsettled state. His authority was not firmly established. He was placed on his throne by a *British* army, and we had a perfect right to punish offenders, by whom the safety of that army might be endangered, if such offences were unpunished. The Duke of *Wellington* would not under such circumstances, have made over robbers to the *Spanish* or to the *Portuguese* Government.

Capt. *Prole*, 37th Bengal N. I. arrived to-day with treasure, and an escort consisting of 102 Europeans belonging to H. M.'s Regts., 3 Cos. 37th N. I., and 2nd Regt. *Shah Shoojah's* Cavy. *Thermtr.* 3 P. M. 106°.

8th June. Thermtr. 4 A. M. 54°.—To enable the D. C. G. to collect a supply of grain for the horses when on the march, obliged to limit the daily issue to mounted corps, from to-morrow, to three seers of barley per horse. *Thermtr.* 3 P. M. 106°.

9th June. Thermtr. 4 A. M. 62°.—Order for the pay of the troops before the march. (50)

Eighty camels carried off by the villagers. The escape of the four *Affghans* from their sentence, has induced these people, *"not having the fear of Death before their eyes,"* to take to their old trade of thieving, &c.

The camels ordered to be in from the grazing ground, by the 12th instant, to enable the D. C. G. to distribute them to brigades. *Thermtr.* 3 P. M. 106°.

---

in strong parties at some distance from our camps to protect the robbers, and to be ready to carry off the camels into the hills; and then both would share the booty. Now, under these circumstances, a severe example was required to be made; and it was a pity the example was lost.

(50) Statements sent in to know how much *specie* would be required, for some part of the pay was absorbed by *Drafts* on *India*, and money was, now, a scarce article.

8. *Order of march from Candahar,* (10th June 1839).—
Thermtr. 4 A. M. 74°. " The 4th Co. 2nd Bn. *Bengal* Arty.
added to the garrison of *Candahar,* till F. O.; remaining
troops to march in the following order :—"
 1st *column,* " on the 15th (51) under the personal command of H. E. the Comr.-in-Chief."
 " 2nd T. 2 B. Bengal H. A.; 1 T. Bombay H. A.; the
Cavy. Division (Bengal and Bombay); the Camel battery;
the Engineer Dept.; 1st Brigade Bengal Infy.; 4th (Bengal) Local Horse; Comsst. Field Depôt."
 " H. M. *Shah Shoojah* signified his intention to march
on the 16th instant. (52) 1 T. Bombay H. A. to march
with H. M."
 " The 2nd *column* (53) under Brigr. *Roberts* to quit
Candahar on the day subsequent to that on which H. M.
the *Shah* may move; consisting of—The *Bengal* Park of
Artillery; the 4th Brigade *Bengal* Infy; a Ressalah and a
half of Local Horse, and the field hospital."
 " The 3rd *column,* on the succeeding day, consisting of
the remainder of the troops (54) and establishments of
the " *Army of the Indus,*" under Maj. Genl. *Willshire.*"
 " The Genl. Staff of the *Bengal* army, to march with the
1st column. That of the *Bombay* army, with the 3rd
column. (55) Column right in front, (order of march.)"
1.—Cavy. leading   4.—No. 6, Lt. Fd. battery *(camel.)*
2.—Horse Arty.   5.—1st Brigade Infy. (to which
3.—Engineer Dept.   1 Regt. 4th Brigade added.)
                      6.—4th Local Horse.
 " Camp colormen of the mounted corps, and Qr. Mrs. of

---

 (51) Did not move till the 27th June, 1839; waiting for the
arrival of the *Lohanee* grain-merchants.
 (52) Moved on the 28th June.
 (53) G. O. 24th June, 1839.
 (54) 1st Brigade Bombay Infy., a battery, and the Poonah Local
Horse.
 (55) Maj. Genl. Willshire's column, changed from the 2nd to
the 3rd column.

corps formed on the *reverse* flank of leading squadron, ready to move with the D. Q. M. G." (56)

Rear Guard.—"A rear-guard of one troop Light Cavy. and one Coy. N. I. to remain on the ground till the baggage be loaded and in motion; and to afford protection to the camp."

Baggage.—" To protect the baggage on the march, the Maj. Genl. Comg. the Cavy. to leave N. C. O.'s parties of Cavy. alternately on the *right* and *left* of the road, at intervals of *one* mile from each other, (57) and to prevent straggling."

" A Ressalah of Local Horse at the disposal of the baggage Master, to prevent baggage or followers preceding the column, or moving on its flanks."

" Baggage of H. E. and Staff at Hd. Qrs., to follow the column, under the Provost Marshal, of corps, (under an officer from each) as corps stand in column."

" *Comsst.* camels, under the *Sergts.* at the disposal of the officers of that department, to follow the baggage of Regts."

Treasure.—" The Treasure between two Regts. of the Infy. brigade, covered by flanking parties of Infy."

Main Picquet. (58)—" On the arrival at the new ground, a main-picquet of two guns, (59) a squadron of Cavy., and two Cos. of Infy., under a field officer, to be posted as the Brigr. of the day directs; from this picquet, a subaltern's party of Cavy. to be detached, at sun-set, four *miles in advance,* on the main-road; to fall back on the main-picquet if *felt* by the enemy. With this party, no syces or grass-cutters must be sent, the horses to remain bridled up." (60)

(56) Tindals and classies to remain in the rear.

(57) They were posted on hillocks, or rising ground, to command a view of the country and baggage, &c. These to join the rear-guard; on its passing by them.

(58) Formed the advance guard; see G. O. 19th April, 1839. The Brigr. of the day accompanied it.

(59) H. A. guns.

(60) "On halting-days the picquets to come on duty at sun-rise, when the advance party will be withdrawn. *Tents* of the main picquet to be struck at 6 o'clock every evening. The Brigr. of the

"Parties from the main-picquet will patrol up to the advance, at intervals, throughout the night."

In-lying picquets.—" An in-lying picquet of one troop or company, from each Regt. to be told off for duty, ready to move out in support, when called for."

Cordon at grazing ground.—"The Maj. Genl. Comg. the Cavy., will form as soon as possible after the arrival of the troops, a *Cordon* around the spot selected as grazing ground for the cattle, the troopers to drive back, with blows, (61) any surwan attempting to push camels beyond the line." (62)

" Officers Comg. Regts. and Detts. to send parties of their own men with their cattle, promptly to oppose the attempts of robbers (63) to approach the grazing ground. Camels to be brought in before *sun-set*; those of brigades to be carefully *parked* near the bazars and within the rear-guards. Of the field Depôt, in rear of the Local Horse."

Dismounted cavalry.—" The dismounted men of the Cavy. (64) must take the duties of the Cavy. brigade, on what, under other circumstances, *Infy.* would have been employed. (65) *Thermtr.* 3 p. m. 100°."

9. *Party and Mission to Herat,* (11th June, 1839.)— Thermtr. 4 a. m. 56°. The details (66) of officers and men to day to be furnished with a *sketch* of the ground, by D. Q. M. G., and to make arrangements to protect the camp through the night, by ordering a connecting chain of sentries from Qr. and Rear, guards of corps. Officers Comg. Regts. to comply with requisitions from the Brigr. of the day, for flank picquets, or additional men for duty."

(61) This is the only plan to adopt. Had it been adopted sooner, we should not have lost so many camels at Candahar, and elsewhere; we had not before a proper *Cordon* formed.

(62) The D. Qr. Mr. Genl. selected the grazing ground.

" The Comr.-in-Chief warns officers of the necessity of sending camels to graze, at the same time and place, to which the *public* camels move out, to take advantage of the guard specially assigned for their protection; and in the event of their neglecting to do so, they need expect no aid from H. E. in replacing cattle carried off."

(63) We were about to enter the *Ghiljie* country.

(64) Not having been able to complete the complement of horses.

(65) " During the separation of the columns, a Ressalah of Local Horse to be attached to the 4th Brigade."

(66) Published in G. O. 26th May, 1839.

Girishk Dett. returns—Mission to Herat. 119

be in readiness to march towards *Herat*, under Capt. *Sanders*, Bengal Engineers; except Capt. *J. Abbott* (Bengal Arty.) appointed in the Pol. Dept., Assist. to Major *Todd* (the Envoy) the officers were—

Capt. E. Sanders, Bengal Engr.   Lt. C. F. North, Bombay
Br. Capt. J. Abbott, do. Arty.   Engineers.
Lt. R. C. Shakespear, do. do.   Dr. Ritchie (Asst. Surg.)
Dr. J. S. Login (Asst. Surg.)   Bombay;
do. Estt.

One European Sergt. and 25 Sappers (Natives); one Naick and three Golundaz, (Bengal Arty.) (67)

Girishk Detachment.—The Girishk detachment under the command of Brigr. *Sale,* returned to Candahar about the end of May, 1839. The Sirdars had quitted the place a day or two after our troops marched. The Brigadier had some difficulty in crossing the troops on rafts made of *Rum kegs.* (68) It was, at one time, contemplated to swim over the Cavy. horses, but it is said that there would have been great risk, as the water was deep, and the stream rushed with such violence, that some few who tried it riding bare-backed, were carried more than a mile down the river. The *Shah's* governor being placed in possession, H. M.'s troops went into the fort, (69) and one Battalion of H. M.'s Infy. and 200 irregular horse were left at Girishk when we marched from Candahar. *Thermtr.* 3. P. M. 102°.

12th June.—Thermtr. 4 A. M. 52°. The *Ghiljies* being in our neighbourhood in some force our picquets were increased. The mail again cut off in the *Pisheen* valley. *Thermtr.* 3 P. M. 100°.

---

(67) Two pairs of khajawahs for the sick, a suitable proportion of camp-equipage, small selecton of sapping, mining, and blasting tools, and one camel load of spare fuzil ammn. accompanied the Dett.

(68) Rafts of this kind are so far out of the water and so light, that great care must be taken in troops getting on them; they are liable to npset.

(69) The people did not like our troops going into the place, which was garrisoned by the king's people; the troops were encamped outside the fort.

13*th* June.—Thermtr. 4 A. M. 62°. Pay to be issued to the troops for May. (70)

Capt. *McGregor*, the Mily. Secy. to the Envoy and Minister, gave notice of 30 recovered camels having been brought into the city, and all were allowed an opportunity of seeing them, to try and recognise their own. (71) Thermtr. 3 P. M. 104°.

14*th* June.—Thermtr. 4 A. M. 62°. The march of the troops postponed. The *Lohanee* grain convoy not yet arrived.

The king about this time sent 10,000 Rs. (£1,000) to the *Ghiljie* chiefs, in the hope of inducing them to join him. He, also, sent a *Koran* with a messenger to them, which is a custom among the *Affghans*; and had they sworn allegiance to the Shah, and *retained* the book, it would have been held to be a perfect assent to join the royal cause; but, they kept the cash, and *returned* the Mahomedan sacred volume, which was a certain sign that they would not support him. The kings of *Affghanistan* requiring the services of any clan, have usually sent money, as it is termed, for "*shoeing the horses;*" in other words, to enable them to prepare for a march; such people often not having the means. So that we were to consider them as our enemies. *Thermtr.* 3 P. M. 100°.

10. *Preparations for the march—Reports, &c.* (15th June, 1839.)—*Thermtr.* 4 A. M. 60°. The Infantry ordered to complete their ammunition in pouch to 30 rounds per man, and a proportion to be taken out of the Regtl. reserve ammunition boxes, and placed in the empty treasure boxes; these being light loads for camels, they could easily keep up with the troops.

---

(70) Beginning with the troops to be left at Candahar, then with those of the 2nd column, while, as the Pay Mr. was with the 1st column, he could pay those belonging to it, on the march, if we marched before all were paid.

(71) All the prudent people marked their camels; but the *Affghans* often contrived to deface the mark, (perhaps aided by some of our camel-drivers.)

Thirty-nine horses of H. M.'s 16th Lancers reported, by a committee, unfit for the service.

The accounts from *Cabool* stated that, owing to our delay at Candahar, *Dost Mahomed* did not believe that we should attack him this year, and that conceiving we should direct our views to *Herat*, he had posted a portion of his army at Jellalabad, (72) (between Peshawer and Cabool.) Hearing however, since, of our intention to advance, he was in the greatest alarm; pressing people to labour on the defences of *Ghuznee*. (73)

The reports from *Herat*, describe the Persians to have abandoned all intention of coming against that place again. (74) Thermtr. 3 p. m. 100°.

16*th* June.—Thermtr. 4 p. m. 52°. A Post-office notice published of the dawk from Candahar having been robbed on its way from Quilla Abdoolah Khan; but of what date, unknown. (75) Our post was so uncertain, that duplicates and even triplicates were obliged to be sent of letters of consequence, and we often got letters of two or three months date with our regular mails; as they were picked up on the road the runners having been killed, or robbed, the packages

(72) Mahomed Akbar was there. His force was stated by his brother *Hyder Khan* (Govr. of Ghuznee) to have been 2,500 men, 1,000 horse, 1,000 Eljarees *(militia)*, and 500 foot, and 14 guns.

(73) This we afterwards found to be the case; and that he had commenced fresh works at the *Bala Hissar* at Cabool. He had disgusted the inhabitants by destroying the orchards and vineyards, to clear the approaches to *Ghuznee;* he distrusted all about him, and not long since had assembled all his chiefs, and followers, endeavouring to exact an oath of allegiance. He had deputed one of his sons *(Mahomed Ufzul Khan)* to urge the *Ghiljie* tribes to oppose our passage. (See Outram, p. 81.) Had Dost Mahomed marched to Ghuznee, there is no doubt that the Ghiljies would have joined him there.

(74) There was a rumour that *Kamran*, (or his minister) had demanded Candahar and Cabool, in right of his father having been the elder brother of Shah Shoojah; this must have been a Russian movement to endeavour to prevent Kamran entering into our views.

(75) The Post to *India* was sent from Candahar viâ Quetta, between which and the Kojuk Pass (Quilla Abdoolah Khan lies,) and the Bolan Pass to Shikarpoor.

being opened and the letters scattered about, and recovered by accident, the envelopes often destroyed; no doubt expecting to find money or valuables concealed inside.

A report was said to have been brought to-day from *Cabool*, that Dost Mahomed had signified his intention of accepting a pension, and a residence in Hindostan.

A great number of camels belonging to the 3rd Bengal Cavy. were stolen last night, a surwan killed, and a trooper cut down. Various reports have superseded those of the morning. *Runjeet Sing's* death (76) reported, and a war in the *Punjab* talked of, no doubt under the belief that the Sikh territories would become a scene of contention on the *Maharajah's* death. The newspapers also declared war with *Nipal*, and with *Burmah*, to be inevitable. These rumours were calculated to give some degree of confidence to the expiring hopes of Dost Mahomed.

Want of cash felt at this period. The Comsst. were obliged to make purchases on *credit*, and at one time to *suspend* them. Upwards of 30 *lakhs of Rs.* (£300,000) had been disbursed in the city of Candahar; but every attempt to negociate a loan failed. (77) *Thermtr.* 3 p. m. 100°.

(76) He died on the 27th June, 1839, and was, at this time, dangerously ill. His army was employed at *Peshawer*, at this moment; partly to aid in the expedition; and partly as an army of observation. His illness, at this critical moment, and his subsequent death, were events to be much regretted; for had his successor withdrawn his troops from Peshawer; our force in that quarter would have been much reduced, and would have made *Dost Mahomed* less fearful of an advance from that frontier.

(77) *Outram*, p 82. Money to a certain extent was obtained at a discount of six per cent.; but as 10 Lakhs Rs. which left Shikarpoor on 23rd May, were daily expected, recourse was not had to the above measure to any great extent, and that in the *Shah's* force only. But till we completed our purchases we could not move. The people of Candahar did not like bills on India. Much money was made and saved by natives and others, and paid to *native shroffs (brokers)* who gave orders on *India;* and thus remittances were effected through native agency. In such cases, the Govt. must hold out equal or superior inducements: and at starting should state, that for all monies paid into the Mily. chest, bills would be granted at certain rates, and thus prevent the money getting into the hands of native agents.

11. *Executions—the Ghiljies collecting,* (17th June,1839.)
—*Thermtr.* 4 A. M. 54°. To-day, at 12 o'clock, the king caused one criminal to be blown away from a gun, and three others were deprived of life in another way, and their bodies were exposed in the market place. The *Affghan* mode of execution is usually by blowing away from a gun. More camels carried of. *Thermtr.* 3 P. M. 106°.

18*th June.*—Thermtr. 4 A. M. 60°. Capt. J. P. Ripley, 1st Eurn. Regt., appointed Ft. Adjt. and Post Master, at Candahar.

The Envoy and Minister informed the Comr.-in-Chief that the *Ghiljies* were bent on hostilities, and had assembled with a design to attack our advanced Cavy. picquet; (78) or of cutting off the *Lohanee* convoy advancing from the rear.

In consequence, a detachment consisting of the 3rd Bengal Cavy. and 48th Bengal N. I. with two guns, the whole under Lt.-Col. *Wheeler,* marched this morning to meet the *Lohanee* merchants, as it was reported that a body of 1,500 *Ghiljies* had thrown themselves between them and the city of Candahar; (79) it was highly important to prevent the convoy being captured by the *Ghiljies.* Thermtr. 3 P. M. 106°.

19*th June.*—Thermtr. 4 A. M. 70°. At 2 P. M. an attack was made on the camels at graze. The guard, two N. C. O. and eight sepoys (16th Bengal N. I.) were attacked by 20 horsemen in front, and some foot soldiers in the rear. The sepoys fired on the horsemen and killed three men and two horses. One musket missed fire, and the poor sepoy was sabred across the forehead; he, however, primed again (80) and shot his man; a second volley brought down several,

---

(78) A troop of the 1st *Bombay* Cavy. under Capt. *S. Poole,* was posted 14 or 15 miles off on the *Cabool* road. The picquet was ordered to fall back, if menaced.

(79) It was rumoured that Dost Mahomed's son (Mahomed Ufzul Khan) had advanced with 1,000 Infy., 500 Cavy., and four guns towards our advance post on the Cabool road.

(80) A Surwan gave him a cartridge from behind.

and the *Ghiljies* fled, leaving five men and two horses dead on the ground; and not *one* camel was carried off.

G. O. A piquet of Infy. was directed to be posted in front of the right of the line. The Brigr. of the day was directed to post a second picquet, of a Coy. of Infy. and a Ressalah of Local Horse, on the *extreme right* of the *Bengal* line, (81) with instructions to patrol down to the *main-picquet* on its *left*. (82)

"A *standing order* that an *in-lying picquet* of a troop, or company, each Regt. shall mount daily; and remain on duty through the 24 hours, ready to turn out when called for. A field officer furnished, daily, from each brigade, is to command its picquets, and to assemble them, under arms, at sunset, every evening, and again in the course of the night."

"A *main and flank picquet* of the usual strength (83) will mount at sun-set, and be withdrawn, at sun-rise." *Thermtr.* 3 P. M. 108°.

12. *Camels carried off.* (20th June, 1839)—*Thermtr.* 4 A. M. 66°. To-day about 150 camels belonging to one of H. M.'s Regts. were carried off, while grazing close to camp; one of five unarmed Europeans in charge killed, and the rest severely wounded. (84) A guard of a Sergt. and eight men was sent out as a protection to the camels, but they went into a village to escape from the heat of the sun; (85) and knew nothing of the camels being carried off till too late. The five unarmed men went down to the rivulet to

---

(81) This was the direction in which the *Ghiljies* would come, in moving down from the *Cabool* road, to attack the convoy.

(82) Both to be withdrawn at sun-rise.

(83) *Main picquet* one squadron of Cavy., two Cos. Infy. *Flank picquet* one Coy. Infy. and one Ressalah of Local Horse. (G. O. 21st June, 1839.)

"The duty of *Brigade Major* for the day discontinued, and each M. B. must parade the details for duty in his own lines, and make them over to the senior officer of his Brigade, going on picquet." The M. B. had many other duties to perform, and could well be spared from remaining on the ground.

(84) One died that night, and another the next day.

(85) Thermtr. 100° to-day at 10 A. M. and 108° at 3 P. M.

water the camels; a gang of mounted *Affghan* robbers, rushed from concealment, and drove off the camels. The Europeans behaved as well as men could do, without arms, in defending the camels. The Brigr. of the day went out immediately, with the picquets, but the camels were off to the hills, and could not be traced. (86)

21*st June.*—Thermtr. 4 A. M. 68°. Another attempt at camel stealing, three of the thieves taken. Heard to-day that the detachment had not been able to fall in with the *Lohanee* grain convoy, and the *Ghiljies* being reported to have moved to intercept the convoy, this evening the 35th Bengal N. I. (Lt.-Col. *Monteath*), with a squadron of Cavy. and two guns, marched to *Dehi-now*, where they were reported to be, or 14 miles N. of *Deh Hajee*, thus taking a different route from Lt.-Col. *Wheeler's* Dett., which went towards *Quilla Futtoolah*. To-day died Dr. *Hamilton*, H. M.'s 17th foot.

This morning Major *Todd*, the Envoy to *Herat* on a friendly mission, marched with his small party from Candahar, under a salute of 11 guns. *Shah Kamran* had written to offer to send his son to Candahar, but *Nujjoo Khan*, Topchee Bashee, or Comdt. of *Kamran's* Artillery, who came in a few days ago with a party, returned with the Major as his *Mehmandar*. This proceeding proved *Shah Kamran* and his vizier, *Yar Mahomed Khan*, to be favorable to the British Government. Two lakhs of rupees (£20,000) were sent with the mission, to be employed in improving the fortifications of the place. (87) *Thermtr.* 3 P. M. 108°.

(86) Owing to the want of camel-drivers, the Europeans were obliged to go out with the cattle, and this was usually done with the Regts. of the Bombay force; but, then, they took their arms with them. Sepoys were sent out from the Bengal Native Regts., the men being armed. I do not think a soldier should ever be employed while on service or in a foreign country, without taking his arms with him to defend himself, as well as his charge. Indeed, I think the Surwans should have been armed, as well as all the servants, as they would often have been a protection to the cattle and baggage, against robbers.

(87) About this time, *Hajee Dost Mahomed* of Gurmseer, with

22nd June.—Thermtr. 4 A. M. 68°. News of the *Lohanee* convoy being safe, reached us to-day. Another skirmish for camels; one prisoner brought in. Thermtr. 3 P. M. 108°.

23rd June.—Thermtr. 4 A. M. 70°. The *Lohanee* convoy of grain came in, all safe, this morning, (88) having been threatened by large bodies of *Ghiljie* horse, night and day, for the last week ; division of counsels existed ; one party proposed to march for *Cabool* and to join *Dost Mahomed;* and the other to proceed to *Candahar* and join the king. Some days before the party under Lt.-Col. *Wheeler* was sent out, 100 of the 4th Bengal Local Horse, under Ressaldar *Uzeem Khan*, had been sent out to gain intelligence of the convoy ; and his presence and firmness of character, turned the scale in favor of the king ; and the detachment coming within feeling distance, decided those who were wavering, to proceed to *Candahar.* It would appear (89) that the convoy had been secretly joined, on this side of *Quetta*, by some emissaries of *Dost Mohamed Khan*, who had endeavoured to seduce its director, *Surwar Khan*, the *Lohanee* Chief, and his followers, to desert our cause, and carry over the convoy to the ex-ruler. The agents had seduced a number of the followers ; and they would probably have gained over the whole convoy to the enemy, but for the determined conduct of the party of the 4th Local Horse under *Uzeem Khan;* who declared *their* determination to oppose such *treachery with their lives;* and maintained night and day so vigilant a guard (90) that the scale was turned, and one of the emissaries was seized and brought prisoner to camp. (91) Owing to the casualties among the private servants by

---

1,000 followers, came in to Shah Shoojah. He is a man of influence, and his having come in, added strength to the Shah's cause.

Major *Todd* reached *Herat* on the 25th of July, 1839.

(88) With Lt.-Col. *Monteath's* detachment.
(89) Outram, p. 83.
(90) They took possession of a village near the convoy.
(91) The convoy experienced much opposition in the *Bolan* and *Kojuk* Passes from predatory hordes, who plundered and wounded many people belonging to it. The people attached to the convoy

deaths, or desertions, and their numbers being reduced, fresh returns were ordered to be sent to the D. C. G. (92) The king to-day shifted his camp preparatory for the march. *Thermtr.* 3 P. M. 108°.

13. *The Lohanee convoy*, (24th June, 1839.)—Thermtr. 4 A. M. 70°. The *Lohanee convoy* having arrived with 20,000 maunds, (93) we expected to march with full rations for the

were all armed, and *Surwar Khan*, the leader, is a most determined man. He said that if he was refused grain at any place, or was plundered near any village, he invariably attacked the place. His plan was to unload and pack the loads; then, leaving a guard, he headed his armed people, and made his attack, and putting all he caught to the sword, he then destroyed the village, &c. Capt. O. says, "had the chief himself remained faithful, of which there is some reason to doubt." The conduct of *Surwar Khan* was of a very doubtful character, for he had entered into a contract to transport grain to the army, and if he, when *alone*, could not control his followers, still, the presence of *Uzeem Khan*, ought to have given him confidence, for there were two parties; and had he exercised his usual firmness and, at once, sided with the *Candahar* party, and with it joined *Uzeem Khan*, he would have compelled the other party to give in; and the evidence of *Uzeem Khan* would in such case, have been conclusive in his favor, for he must have known that, serving the *British* Govt. faithfully, at such a juncture, would have met with its due reward, in such a way as to have rendered him free from any apprehension from the *Cabool Party*.

Sir *J. Keane* was so pleased with the determined, and meritorious, conduct of *Uzeem Khan*, that, having duly inquired into the facts of the case, he sent for *Uzeem Khan*, highly praised his conduct, and presented him with a very handsome pair of English pistols. His conduct was also favorably reported to Govt.; and, here I may observe, that the conduct of the *4th Local Horse* throughout the whole campaign, obtained the approbation of every officer. On every occasion they exhibited the greatest gallantry. They were employed on all occasions, on every duty of fatigue as escorts, and in guarding convoy. They lost 540 horses out of 797 between the 16th Dec. 1838, and 31st Dec. 1839, or, within 35 of the number lost by the rest of the Cavy. of the Bengal column! I trust *Uzeem Khan* will receive the "*Order of British India*," which he so well merits.

(92) And Comg. officers held responsible for these returns being correct.

(93) 1,600,000 lbs., about equal to one month's supplies for the army at half-rations.

whole army all the way to Cabool; but there was an objection raised on the part of the convoy camel *men* to proceed. They objected, that their wives and families were confined by *Dost Mahomed*, and would be sacrificed if they accompanied the army. (94) This was an objection started by *Surwar Khan*, their leader. (95) They wanted us to *buy* their camels, and not to *hire* them, but if we bought them, still *they* would not accompany us: and men could not be procured as drivers. The purchase would have cost more money than could be spared. (96) We still had hopes of bringing them to terms. *Thermtr.* 3 p. m. 110°.

25th June.—Thermtr. 4 a. m. 72°. The first column in orders to march on the 27th instant, in the order detailed in G. O. of the 10th instant. The other columns to move forward in succession. Officers Comg. Brigades not to move their corps on the road, till the troops to precede them in column, have passed on. (97)

Commissariat. "To aid the Commissariat, officers Comg. Regts. to indent immediately on the godown in the city, for as much attah *(flour)* as their bazars can carry, but, till F. O., the troops to be only on the present *(half)* rations." "Officers reminded that the camels brought to Hd. Qrs. by *Surwar Khan*, and other Lohanee merchants, are still in Government employ; and they are not to purchase any of them." (98)

(94) These people lived near *Ghuznee* where their families were.

(95) Capt. *Outram* says, p. 84: "By transporting his charge to the army he fulfilled his contract; but without his assistance the army cannot now be equipped with full rations."

(96) Allowing 20,000 Mds. of grain at 4 Mds. load per camel, 5,000 camels would be required, which, even at 60 Rs. each would have cost 3 Lakhs Rs. (£30,000), and money was scarce. However, part might have been purchased.

(97) There were so many gardens and enclosures near camp, that but for this arrangement, there must have been great confusion and delay, in the movements of the troops.

(98) The Comsst. were in hopes of the camel-men coming into their terms, but they would not *hire* them, and officers, or others, offering to purchase the camels, would induce the owners, who wished to *sell* not to *hire* them: however, as soon as they *positively* refused to hire

Supplies on the march.—" Every encouragement must be given to the people of the country through which the troops are about to march, to bring in *grain* and other supplies, and officers Comg. Regts. will assign some spot in the vicinity of their *standard,* or *quarter-guards,* for the people to sell their goods in. A steady N. C. O., must be present with them, throughout the day, to see that they are not maltreated; but, all must be turned out of camp by sunset." (100)   *Thermtr.* 3 P. M. 110°.

26th June.—Thermtr. 4 A. M. 72°.   "The troops destined to occupy the garrison of *Candahar,* will take up their position this evening at sun-set."

The troops, &c. left at *Candahar* were Capt. *Timing's* Bengal 4th T. 3rd Brigade (native) H. A. and 4th Co. 2nd Bn. Bengal Arty.; the 37th Regt. Bengal N. I.; the 4 18-prs. and such ordnance stores as the Brigr. might see fit to be left at Candahar, under Lt. *Hawkins,* (101) Bengal Arty. A troop of the *Shah's* artillery. (102)   A Battn. of the *Shah's* Infy., (103) and Capt. *Anderson's* Ressallah of Horse. The whole under the command of (late) Lt.-Col. *J. Herring,* C. B. Capt. *J. P. Ripley,* 1st Bengal Eurn. Regt. being the Fort Adjt. and Post Master.

"The Fort Adjt. to receive from the Medical store-keeper such stores as are necessary to be left at *Candahar,* to be sent, the first favorable opportunity, to *Quetta.*"

---

them to the Comsst., officers were at liberty to buy them. In all such cases, the interests of the Govt. must supersede those of private individuals.

5,000 of our camels would require about 1,000 drivers, but, the convoys have often a less number; the *Affghans* usually drive them in flocks, without ropes attached to the tails of the camels; but they must be trained to it.

(100) Without this precaution you might have an enemy in your camp; but even on marches in our own provinces in India, many thefts are committed by not having recourse to the above measure.

(101) Attached to the Shah's force.

(102) Lt. *Cooper's.* Capt. *Anderson,* Comg. both troops of H. A. was stationed at Candahar, on his arrival.

(103) Withdrawn from Quilla Abdoolah Khan, a corps having been raised there.

"The whole of the *Treasure* with the army to move with the 1st (Bengal) Infy. Brigade; and the Pay Master to make over to it all specie in excess to current disbursements."

Major *Leech* (104) was left at *Candahar* as the *Political Agent;* to act, on the part of H. M. *Shah Shoojah-ool-Moolk*, under the orders of the Envoy and Minister at his Court.

About this time an insurrection had been arranged and had commenced in *Kohistan*, a district which partly supplied the city of *Cabool* with grain; and endeavours were being made by us, to cut off the communication between Cabool and Jellalabad. The insurrection in *Kohistan* (recently acquired by the Cabool chief) affected him much, as he did not like to quit his capital under these circumstances, and indeed the city of Cabool was in an unsettled state; while the force at Peshawer, also, rendered it necessary for Dost Mahomed Khan, to keep near the seat of danger; and he had failed to quell the insurrection in *Kohistan*, in his neighbourhood. *Thermtr.* 3 p. m. 110°.

(104) Bombay engineers.

CHAPTER VII.

CANDAHAR.

1. *Candahar* in *Affghanistan* is in *Lat.* 31° 40′ N.; *Long.*
65° 30′ E. (1) It is 370 miles from *Herat*, which lies to the
N. W. in *Lat.* 34° 20′ N.; *Long.* 62° 10′ E., and is 318
miles from *Cabool*, which lies to the N. E. in *Lat.* 34° 30′
30″ N., *Long.* 68° 34′ E. Candahar thus lies to the S. of
and nearly mid-way between *Herat* and *Cabool*. Cabool
and Candahar, have from early antiquity been reckoned the
gates of Hindostan; one affording entrance from *Tooran*,
(2) and the other from *Iran*. (3) Between Candahar and
Herat lies Girishk, (4) nearly W., and distant 75 miles; and
beyond Herat is Ghorian, a place of some strength, 40 miles
on the road from Herat to Meshid. (5) Between Candahar
and Cabool lies Kelat-i-Ghiljie (6) N. E., distant 89 miles;
and Ghuznee N. E. of it, and distant 229 miles from Candahar and 89 miles from Cabool, which lies nearly N. from it.
Thus its position as the capital, at one time, of *Affghanis-*

(1) According to Hamilton's Gazetteer (erroneously) *Lat.* 33° N.
and *Long.* 65° 34′ E.
(2) Toorkistan, or Tartary.
(3) Persia.
(4) It belongs to Candahar; half-way between it and Herat, and
N. W. off the road, is Furrah, to which Kohun-dil Khan of Candahar
laid siege in July, 1838, but was driven from it by Kamran's troops.
In Feb. 1839, the Candaharees sent a force there: they were nearly
starved; and nearly one-half lost by the snow.
(5) It belongs to Herat, and capitulated to the Shah of Persia,
after a siege of 10 days, on the 15th Nov. 1837, on his march to Herat.
(6) A place of some strength in the time of Baber, and surrendered
to him in A. D. 1505. It is now in ruins.

tan was good, being central; particularly when Sindh and the Punjab belonged to it. *Nadir Shah* destroyed the old fortress of Candahar, which stood on the top of a high rocky hill, and founded on a contiguous plain a city named *Nadirabad*, which was completed by Ahmed Shah, Abdalli, but is now only known by the name of Candahar. Two or three miles to the N. W. of Candahar, are the remains of the old fortress on the summit of a rocky mountain. (7)

" In 1737, Nadir Shah, entered Affghanistan with a large army, and took Candahar after a siege, from first to last, of 18 months."

In 1747, Ahmed Shah, Abdalli, an Affghan chief of the tribe of Abdal, on the massacre of Nadir Shah, (8) had acquired so great an ascendance among the troops, that upon this event, several commanders and their followers joined his standard; and he drew off towards his country. He repaired to Candahar, where he arrived with a force not

---

(7) Hamilton, &c. *Baber* got possession of the castle in 1507, by the gates being opened to him. He had only 2,000 men, but defeated the enemy in the field; they had 4 or 5,000 men. (Baber's memoirs, pp. 227—229). In 1650, Shah Jehan sent his eldest son to drive Shah Abbas 2nd out of it, but though his army consisted of 300,000 men, yet the place was so well defended, that he lost the best part of his army before it. The next year he sent another army under the command of *Sultan Sujah*, but he had no better success than his brother." *Tavernier*, p. 258.

Mill, vol. II. p. 334, says, that Abbas 2nd of Persia, " marched to Candahar with a great force, and obtained possession of the city by capitulation, before the Mogul army was able to arrive. The strongest efforts were made for its recovery. Aurungzebe besieged it two several times; and *Dara*, the eldest son of the Emperor, once. It baffled the operations of both."

" *Affghanistan* was held by the posterity of *Aurungzebe* (who in 1678 subdued an insurrection of the Affghans), after which event its subjection was scarcely nominal. About A. D. 1720, the Affghans, under their native chiefs, conquered Persia; but, in 1737, were expelled by *Nadir Shah* from that country, and their own subjugated. In 1739, after the capture of *Delhi* by *Nadir Shah*, Affghanistan was, by treaty, annexed to the Persian Empire." Hamilton, &c.

(8) In his tent not far from Meshed, on the 8th June, 1747.

exceeding 2 or 3,000 horse. He fell in with and seized a convoy of treasure coming from India to Nadir Shah, which had just been seized by the Dooranees, and he immediately claimed it for himself. This enabled him to engage in his pay a still larger body of his countrymen. Candahar submitted to his arms; and he was crowned there in October, 1747. (9)

2. *Town of Candahar.*—The modern city, comprised within an ordinary fortification of 3 miles and 1,006 yards, in circumference, is an irregular oblong-square, surrounded by a ditch 24 feet wide and 10 feet deep; but it was not in good repair. The wall is 20½ feet thick at the bottom, and 14½ feet thick at the top, and 27 feet in height; its western face is 1,967, eastern 1,810, southern 1,345, and northern face 1,164 yards long. It has six gates, but they were not in good order; that to the N. being called the *Eed-gah* gate; that to the S. called the *Shikarpoor* gate. The two gates to the E. called the *Berdouranee* and the *Cabool* gates. The two gates to the W., called the *Tope-Khana*, (10) and *Herat* gates. The Shikarpoor, Cabool, and Herat gates, are towards the roads leading to those places. The length of the city is from N. to S. The gateways are defended by six double bastions, and the angles are protected by four large circular towers. The curtains, between the bastions, have 54 small bastions, distributed along the faces. The citadel and palace, where the kings reside, is in the centre of the N. end, near the gateway. The tomb of *Ahmed Shah*, who was buried here, is to the left of the palace. There are four principal streets running from N. to S. and from E. to W. which meet in the centre, in which there is a large dome, or circular covered space, about 50 yards in diameter, a public market place surrounded by shops where the great merchants live; this is called the " *Char-soo.*" (11)

(9) Mill's History of India, Vol. II. p. 408. Elphinstone, Appx. A p. 337.
(10) Artillery.
(11) *Four roads*, crossing each other.

To the N. and close to the city runs, from W. to E., a canal, which issues from the Urghand-ab river. There is another canal which runs W. to E., through the centre of the city. There is, also, a canal running W. to S. E.; and at about ¾ of a mile to the S. of the city. There is a road which runs, near the W. side of the city to the N., to the "*Baba Wullee*" Pass. The road to old Candahar runs to the W., in continuation of the direction of the S. face of Candahar.

The four principal streets are about 40 yards wide, lined with shops and houses, which are all built of sun-burnt bricks, and are flat-roofed. There are some upper-storied houses. There are smaller and narrower streets which run from the principal ones towards the city walls, (all crossing each other at right-angles,) between which and the houses there is a road about 25 yards wide, all round the city. There is a rampart all round the place, but that round the gateways is separate: to walk round the walls of the city, it is necessary to descend from the gateways, and ascend to the ramparts between each gateway. There was a gun on the bastion near the Shikarpoor gate; but the ramparts are not broad, and it would not have been safe to fire heavy guns from them. The guns were kept, in the city, near the *Tope Khana* gate.

3. *Buildings Houses, &c.*—The tomb of Sultan Ahmed Shah, Abdalli, (12) the founder of the *Dooranee* monarchy,

---

(12) The hero of the battle of Panniput (1761). "The *Dooranees* of Cabool, who were the strength of the Army, being about 29,000, were all men of great bodily vigour, and their horses of the Turkish breed, and very hardy."

The *combined* Mahomedan army consisted of 42,000 horse, and 38,000 foot, besides camels, and 70 or 80 guns. "The regulars of the Mahrattah army consisted of 55,000 horse and 15,000 foot, 200 cannon, and camel pieces and rockets without number. Also, 15,000 pindaries (plunderers), and camp-followers estimated at four times the number of the regulars." See *Hamilton*, &c.

The *Candahar horse* of the present day, is far inferior to that so well known in the History of former Indian warfare: the horses we saw were small and indifferent.

is covered with a gilt cupola, and is held a sacred asylum ; the king himself not daring, it is said, to take a criminal from it. There are said to be 40,000 houses (13) and a population of 100,000 persons. (14) The houses of the rich are enclosed by high-walls, and contain three or four courts with gardens and fountains. Each court contains a building with several small apartments, and three or four large halls, reaching to the roof, supported by wooden-pillars, carved and painted. The apartments open on the halls, and are filled up with paintings on the walls, and looking-glasses let into the recesses.

In the houses of the rich, the walls are plastered with a kind of stucco made of Chunam, (15) and divided into compartments, which are ornamented with flowery patterns, impressed on the stucco by means of a wooden stamp, and then covered over with *Talkh* (16) which gives a silvery, but neat, appearance to the room. The recesses are of plain stucco, and contain glasses or other ornaments. The ceilings are either painted, or formed of many small pieces of wood, carved, and fitting into each other ; and varnished. (17) The houses of the common people are of one story,

---

Ahmed Shah went from Candahar to *Toba* in the Ackukzye country, where the summer is cooler, and died at *Murgha*, in June, 1773, in the 50th year of his age.

(13) The houses are generally small, and many of them in ruins, and uninhabitable.

(14) Some considered that there were only 80,000, giving two to each house. There were said to be 100,000 in 1809 (Elphinstone's Cabool), but as part of the population consists of Hindus and other tribes not *Affghans*, it is probable that, in unsettled times, many would leave the place for a more secure abode. In taking a *census*, it is difficult, in the *East*, to determine the number of *persons* living in each house, though there can be none, in estimating the number of *houses*.

(15) Lime prepared with water, mixed with goor, (molasses.)

(16) *Isinglass*, which is formed into a shining powder.

(17) "One room at least has glazed windows, and several have fire-places. The doors are carved, and covered in winter, with velvet or brocade. The floors are covered with handsome carpets, and thick *felt* seats go all round the room close to the wall, and are covered with silk or velvet."

and usually of a single room about 20 by 12 feet; they have little ornament and scarcely any furniture. (18)

There are several *vapour baths* in the city, as well as *cold-baths,* so that you may enjoy both, proceeding from one to the other. (19) Some are private property, others for public use.

The streets are paved with small stones, but we found them in bad order. (20)

There are some buildings with roofs formed with flat arched domes, with a hole at the top in the centre, and made of sun-burnt bricks; these apertures admit the light. These houses are to be seen, chiefly, in the suburbs outside the city, in ranges containing several together; they have on one side, doors, but no windows, or regular fire-places.

The four principal streets are usually crowded from 8 or 9 in the morning till sun-set. The street from the Shikarpoor (S.) gate-way to the *Char-soo,* is filled with one mass of people, some riding, some walking, proceeding to and from the great market-place; and also, with camels, Yaboos, &c. carrying loads. People of different nations are seen, dressed in various colors, though all assume the *Affghan* dress. The dress of the women is very singular. They wear a white *veil* which is fastened to the top of the head, and reaches nearly down to the feet in front. The *face* is covered, but a fine net-work comes over the *eyes,* which enables them to see without being seen; the eyes alone are seen. The women of *Candahar* are said to be more virtuous than those of *Cabool.* Outside the gates, or in the city, may be bought the *kubab,* (21) the *poolao,* (22) the *nan, &c.* (23) The ac-

(18) " Neither tables nor chairs are used; their place is supplied by coarse woollen carpets, and thick cushions of *felt.*"

(19) Wood being a scarce article, care must be taken to ascertain that those who heat the bath, do not use offensive substances to make the fire with !

(20) The *Shah* ordered a new road to be made down the principal street running from S. to N. towards the palace.

(21) Roasted meats, usually fixed on wooden skewers.

(22) Meat (fowls, &c.) mixed with flesh and rice; sometimes hard boiled eggs are added.

(23) Bread unleavened; it is mixed with milk, and is rolled out to

counts of *Forster* and other travellers regarding the frugal habits of the *Affghans* do not agree with their present mode of living; for man, woman, and child, eat as much animal food as they can procure; no Europeans eat so much. Fruit of all kinds are devoured in great quantities.

4. *Surrounding Country, &c.*—Candahar is on a tableland, surrounded by a well cultivated plain. Detached hills rise from the plain on the S. and E.; on the N. and W. they appear more like a broken range of hills; their height varies from 300 to 2,000 feet. Those to the W. have a singular appearance, they rise up near the top like a wall, are indented, very rugged, and look very bleak, being of a clayey color. To the S. the hills are more distant than in the other directions. There is neither tree, nor shrub, nor herb to be found on them, or, in the language of the Emperor *Baber*, (24) " The mountains are worthy of the men; as the proverb says, ' *a narrow place is large to the narrow-minded.*' There are, perhaps, scarcely in the whole world, such dismal-looking hill countries as *these*." The heat radiates from them during the summer so much, as to warm the breeze as it passes over them; and in the evenings, it is not uncommon to experience a current of *hot* air from the mountains, and one *cool* from the plain—the latter usually succeeding the former; (25) from this and from other causes, there is a great difference between the temperature of the morning and the middle of the day. (26)

a considerable size, and in it they often insert a portion of their curry and rice, &c.

(24) Emperor Baber's Memoirs, p. 152, in his description of the hills of *Affghanistan*.

(25) This we felt in the Bengal Staff camp, which was on a *Chummun* (or green sward) to the S. of the city, and the water was within three feet of the ground; we were at no great distance from the perpendicular hills to the W., which just at one point were low with a curved lime, admitting the W. wind to blow freely towards us: indeed we could nearly see the last of the setting sun. The other camps to our left, being closer to these hills, the warm current would pass over them, and not be felt.

(26) See Table, No. 3. Sometimes 40 and 50 degrees. From the 26th April to 26th June, 1839, both inclusive, at 4 and 5 A. M. it ranged from

From the *Arghund-ab* river being near the city to the W., and there being many canals running from it, and the *Turnuk* river being at some distance to the E., the country about Candahar is susceptible of a high state of cultivation. On the road towards Herat the crops are very abundant, and also in the direction towards *Koosh-ab* (7 miles S.) and between it and the city. But they do not appear to grow more grain than is required for their own consumption.

There are plenty of orchards, and gardens in the vicinity, which contain vines of various kinds; (27) apples, pears, quinces, nectarines, peaches, figs, plums, apricots, cherries. Poplars and willows, surround the orchards; the whole being secured by mud-walls, against the inroads of cattle.

The people have no knowledge of Horticulture, or gardening. Having sown the seed, or planted the tree, their chief attention is paid to irrigation, leaving the rest to nature.

In their various trades, they are far inferior to the natives of Hindostan. They are less educated than the people of India, under British rule, and appear to have changed the habits of pastoral and agricultural tribes, for those of the robber and plunderer; induced no doubt, by the insecurity of property, and constant change of rulers.

5. *Commerce and Politics, &c.*—Candahar, from its position, was, in *Baber's* time, one of the great marts to which caravans resorted, and Cabool was another. To the former came those from Khorasan. In the time of *Dost Mahomed*, owing to his system at Cabool being more liberal than the fiscal arrangements at Candahar, more merchants resorted to Cabool than to Candahar; though from its situation, the trade with Persia, and with the south of India, might be naturally expected to pass through Candahar. The route by the Indus from Bombay, will be that by which the trade from

50° to 72°, and at 3 P. M. from 85° to 110°. From about the middle of May, they reckon two hot periods of 40 days each, the second period hotter than the first. For two or three nights there blew a hot wind all night; but at other times, the nights were cool.

(27) The vines are planted in trenches, ranged in parallel rows, and have nothing to support them.

Views of Candahar. 139

England and India will be carried on ; as the distance from Bombay is less than that from Calcutta, and it is obvious that Indian goods will be sent viâ Cabool, from the upper portion of Bengal alone ; since to go to Persia, the extra distance between Cabool and Candahar (318 miles) must be travelled. (28)

In a Military and Political point of view, Candahar is more exposed than Cabool, for the frontier towards the latter is more easily defended, having several defensible passes ; while the former would be exposed by the fall of *Herat*.

The three brothers, Sirdars, Kohun-dil Khan, Rehm-dil Khan, and Mehr-dil Khan, held 9-10ths of the land, and would not rent it without an immediate return; nor grant a water-lease but on exhorbitant terms ; hence the people were ripe for a change. *Khelat* was free from the influence of the Sirdars, who appear to have looked only to personal advantages ; without regard to the welfare of the state. They had lost their connection with *Sindh*. (29)

The *Moollahs* (priests) were not regarded with respect by the Sirdars, so that they could not succeed in raising a war on the score of religion ; and the *Sheeah* part of the *Kuzzulbashes* not being influential, the Sirdars alone would appear to have desired an alliance with Persia. Though *Dost Mahomed* came to the rescue of Candahar in 1834, when *Shah Shoojah* invaded the country; he on the occasion of our march on Candahar, left his brothers to their fate. It is said that

(28) Candahar forms an outlet to the commerce of the whole of Sindh, and to that by the Indus, from the Punjab. Being at the western extremity of the present kingdom of *Affghanistan*, the trade not only of Cabool, but of the internal parts of the country, would flow to Candahar. There are a number of the passes on the Indus, between *Shikarpoor* and the *Attok*, with roads for caravans; while Cabool labours under the disadvantage of the commerce passing through the *Punjab*, where the duties are not only high ; but, we have no means of regulating the duties to be levied in a *foreign* state.

(29) In the time of Timoor Shah, *Sindh* paid a tribute of 22 Lakhs rupees (£220,000), in subsequent reigns only three Lakhs Rs. (£30,000 ;) but in later years nothing was paid. See Lt. *Leech's* Report.

the *Sikhs* were not so much disliked at Cañdahar, as at Cabool; and that the *Candaharees* would rather have been subject to the court of Lahore, than to that of Persia.

It was by some supposed, that placing *Shah Shoojah* in possession of *Candahar*, would have been a more prudent measure, than that of extending the operations to *Cabool;* but it seems clear that, by such a plan, if ever *Herat* should fall, Candahar would have been placed between two hostile powers, Herat and Cabool; and the passes between Candahar and Cabool would have been in the hands of Dost Mahomed. There never could have been any doubt as to the result of our military operations, had the chiefs of Candahar been joined by Dost Mahomed. (30)

6. *Revenue of Candahar—New Prospects.*—The *Revenue* of Candahar was stated to be not more than eight Lakhs of Rs. (£80,000.) (31) *Forster* (32) says, "The city with a track of dependent territory (under a son of

---

(30) The Surdars of Candahar were said to have had 3,000 good Cavalry, 1,000 Infy. and 15 guns. *Dost Mahomed's* regular force consisted of about 13,180 (of these 3,000 were in Ghuznee), of which about 6,000 were Cavy. He had 40 guns. So that the two, united, could not have brought more than 10,000 men into the field. The *king* in 1834, had 6,000 Hindostanees and many Affghans, and six or eight field pieces, when he fought his battle at Candahar. The *Barukzyes* (Candahar and Cabool forces) had, it is said, 10 or 12,000, and six or eight field pieces. Dost Mahomed acknowledged that he was nearly losing the battle; and must have done so, had *Shah Shoojah* remained on the field. The fact is Mr. *Campbell*, his only officer, (the rest being Natives,) was wounded; the troops got into confusion; and the *king* thought the battle was lost.

From their force being principally Cavy., they could not effectually have opposed us at the *Bolan* or *Kojuk* Passes. Our *Cavalry* were, certainly, out of condition, but then we had good Infantry, and plenty of guns. Had *Dost Mahomed* come to *Candahar*, and had it been necessary to wait for the *Bombay* column, the delay would not have been long. They reached *Candahar*, eight days after us; but, might have moved up sooner; as under this view, they would never have attempted to move by the *Gundava Pass*.

(31) Lt. *Leech's* report.

(32) Travels in 1783, p. 103.

Timoor Shah) produced 18 Lakhs of Rs. (£180,000); so that it is clear that under the *kings*, the country was more productive, than under independent chiefs; and that however well *European* countries may prosper under a republican form of *Government*; still it is inapplicable to *Eastern* Nations. (33) There being no one possessing a general authority in *Affghanistan*, each chief made himself independent. *Shah Shoojah* came to the throne in 1801; *twice* he lost his crown; but he came to the throne at the early age of 20 years, and was obliged to trust to his minister (34) in whom he confided, and who became his worst enemy. The *Shah* twice (35) formed expeditions, and tried to recover his throne. The *British Government* have restored to him his crown, with a diminished kingdom. The king is now about 60 years of age; misfortune ought to have taught him moderation and prudence. He has never committed any act of wanton cruelty; indeed, more firmness and decision would have saved his crown. His chief fault is said to be a certain *hauteur* in his deportment to those under him, which is displeasing to those Affghans, who were accustomed to the indiscriminate frankness, and freedom of converse with their chiefs, who (36) attached their followers to them, by associating with the petty chiefs on terms of equality; regarding less personal character, than the importance they derived from the number of the retainers they could bring into the field. With our Envoy and Minister at the court of the Shah, the influence of British advice cannot fail to

(33) The people being ignorant, cannot appreciate the advantages of a form of Government which gives only one supreme head; and owing to a misrule under two of the last kings, seem to have desired to have had no master. *Niamut Ullah* (a contemporary of *Ferishta*) thus describes the *Affghans* : " We are content with discord; we are content with alarms; we are content with blood; but we *never* will be *content* with a *master*. (Preface Transln. vi. part i.—1829.)

(34) *Akram Khan*, who amassed wealth which he would not (1809) lend to his king to raise and pay troops to defend his throne.

(35) In 1818, and 1834.

(36) Dost Mahomed in particular.

secure to the people, their property, rights, and privileges in undisturbed possession; and the prosperity of *Affghanistan* will be the result: but, it will require time, to restore the habits of peace, after 30 years of constant anarchy and rebellion.

CHAPTER VIII.

MARCH FROM CANDAHAR TOWARDS GHUZNEE.

1. *March to Abdool Uzeez*, (27th June, 1839.)—Thermtr. 4 A. M. 72°. The Hd. Qrs. and the 1st column marched at day-break from Candahar, the Cavalry leading. (1) After a march of nearly six miles encamped near the small village of Abdool Uzeez. The table-land very level and stony. The crops having been cut, the appearance of the valley was dreary. No camel thorn ; water brackish. *Thermtr.* 3 P. M. 108°

As the *Lohanee* merchants would not accompany the army, we were obliged to leave the 20,000 *maunds* (2) of grain brought by the Convoy, in the city of Candahar ; and thus, the troops and followers were obliged to march on half-rations, (3) while could this grain have been brought on, we should have been on *full* rations ; but we wanted carriage for its conveyance.

To-day *Maharajah Runjeet Singh* died, (4) and as his death was early known at Cabool, Dost Mahomed, doubtless, calculated on a change of circumstances in his favor.

(1) In the order detailed in G. O. 25th June, 1839, p. 128. See also, G. O. 10th June, 1839, p. 116.
(2) 1,600,000 lbs.
(3) While at Candahar the issues from the Govt. stores were discontinued ; as the market was open to all, those who had the means, were able to purchase a greater quantity than the half rations.
(4) We did not know of it till the 1st of August ; but it must have been known at Ghuznee and Cabool, before we reached the former. The Gov. Genl. notified the event in a G. O. dated 4th July, 1839, from

In consequence of the great heat of the weather, by which both men and cattle suffered much, and there being *moonlight* in our favor; it was resolved to march early in the mornings.

28th June.—To Quillah Azeem. Thermtr. 2 A. M. 82°. When we marched, in the same order. During the march the wind changed and the temperature became about 12 degrees cooler. With day-light we found a broad and extensive plain to our right, and in our front broken chains of hills, stretching to our left.

At about 10 miles came to Quillah Azeem, a small square mud-fort with round towers at the angles. A small stream of brackish water ran through the village outside the fort. The whole ground covered with camel thorn. Several little streams of brackish water intersected our camp. Plenty of good water in the fort ¾ mile to the left and W. of camp. There were heights in our front, and to the right of camp, where our main picquet was. The road good to-day. This place is 3,945 feet above the sea, and 461 feet above Candahar. *Thermometer* at 3 P. M. 103°.

Simla, and directed minute guns to be fired corresponding with the age (60 years) of the ruler of the Punjab. The event caused some change in the affairs at Peshawer. There was an attempt to conceal his death for some little time, but *Khurruk Singh*, the new ruler, reported it to Lt.-Col. *Wade.* The Sikh troops which were on the frontier under *Konwar Nao Nehal Singh* (the son of Khurruk Singh) left it and crossed the Indus; the son being desirous of being present at Lahore, on his father's accession. They were recommended to stay on the frontier till the present service was over, but could not be induced to stay. There was no commotion among the *Mahomedan* tribes on either side of the Indus; the presence of the mission and the troops under Lt.-Col. *Wade,* was no doubt useful at this juncture. On the 8th July, the Sikh (reserve) troops marched. Genl. *Ventura* (one of the Sikh Generals) also marched to Lahore; he commanded the *Sikh* contingent attached to Lt.-Col. W.'s force: the cause of his going would appear to have been a wish not to be *second* in command; or perhaps, a desire to look after his own interests at Lahore ! On the 10th July accounts were received at *Peshawer* of rumours at Cabool, of Runjeet's death, and a contested succession; so that as a considerable *Sikh* force was withdrawn on this frontier, from the death of the Sikh chieftain, might have been of serious detriment to our operations against Cabool viâ the *Khyber* Pass.

Ghiljie chiefs come in. 145

A *Ghiljie* chief and forty or fifty followers came in and made submission to the king, who to-day marched from Candahar. Another chief, with a number of Ghiljies, reported to have gone over to Dost Mahomed.

Orders to prevent the led-horses of Regts. crowding in front of the column.

29th June.—To Khel-i-Akhoond. Thermometer at 1 A. M. 72°, when we marched in the same order. Full-moon. First part of the road over a dead flat, skirted by broken ranges of mountains. The ascent most considerable after we had passed over the flat; and the road continued rugged, stony, and narrow, with a constant ascent, and descent across the dry beds of mountain streams and ravines, until we came to the valley of the *Turnuk.* The valley is narrow, and on the right bank of the Turnuk river, is the village of Khel-i-Akhoond, about a mile N. W. from camp. The camp on the right bank of the river which was close to, and S. of camp. *Thermometer* 3 P. M. 100°.

This place is 4,418 feet, or 473 feet above the last ground.

The second column, under Brigr. *Roberts*, marched to-day from Candahar. There being the defile of *Pootee* to be passed to-morrow, the sappers and miners, with two Cos. of Infy. and a troop of Cavy., were directed to march an hour before the column; the Comg. Officer of the party to occupy the defile with his Infy., sending his *Cavalry* to the E. extremity of the gorge; the defile to be so held while the sappers and miners are at work, and until the column, and baggage shall have passed over it.

2. *30th June, (the Pootee Defile.)*—To Shuhr-i-Suffa. Thermometer 2 A. M. 68°, when we marched. The road crossed a very wild country, and ran along the bank of the *Turnuk* for 2 miles. Country low, we crossed some watercourses to get to the Pass; the hills in one part so narrowing it, that the pioneers were obliged to widen it, before the guns could pass. A water-course ran close to the right of the road. At about 3 miles was the defile, extending about 200 yards, and 10 to 15 feet broad, on the slope or brow of a hillock. Beyond the Pass, the left of

U

the road was flanked by low hills, close to it, for some distance. From this point the road lay over a low country, with water-courses. The road was then rather stony; the rest of the road more open. One mile W. of camp, a hill and an old fort. Heights in front of camp; to the rear and S. of it, ran the Turnuk. *Thermometer* 3 P. M. 104°.

Distance to Shuhr-i-Suffa 11¾ miles; the elevation above the sea 4,618 or 200 feet above last ground.

G. O.—All guards and picquets to prevent armed parties from passing, or approaching the camp, till they shall have given a satisfactory account of themselves. (5)

The *Ghiljies* had cut the *bunds*, (6) and flooded the road, thus rendering it difficult for the troops to move. Parties of pioneers sent out, to stop them up again.

Maj. Genl. *Willshire's* (or third) column marched from Candahar to-day.

1*st July.* To *Teerundaz.* (7)—Thermometer 2 A. M. 70°, when we marched. We did not experience any difficulty from yesterday's flooding of the road. At 3 miles crossed some water-courses; then an ascent which required 10 *horses* to some of the H. A. guns; moving them with difficulty, owing to the *low condition* of the animals. The road was winding, round the base of low-hills; there was, however, plenty of room in the valley for troops to encamp in.

At 10 miles 3 furlongs, came to *Teerundaz.* There was a range of low hills in front (N.) of camp. The *Turnuk* river, close to the S. There is a small village. *Thermometer* 3 P. M. 100°.

Accounts from *Kelat-i-Ghiljie,* that the *Ghiljies* are as-

(5) "Any such approaching a Post, they are to be stopt by the Officer Comg. it; and a report immediately made to the Brigadier on duty, who will communicate such particulars as he may have been able to elicit to the D. A. G.; who will notify to him the Comr.-in-Chief's pleasure on the case."

(6) Banks to dam up water in channels, &c.

(7) The "*Flight of the Arrow.*" The spot were *Ahmed Shah,* first Dooranee king of the Affghans, shot his arrow to, from the neighbouring hills. There is a round, solid column, to commemorate the event.

sembling there, in great force; 1,000 there and 6,000 more expected. *Chuppaos* (night attacks) to be expected, or attacks on our baggage, or carrying off cattle from the grazing ground. This place is 4,829 feet, or 211 feet above our last ground.

2nd July.—To Tool (or Toot) Gallowgheer. Thermometer 2 A. M. 68°, when we marched. Ravines not far from camp; a little further on, the river ran so close under the hills, that the pioneers were obliged to cut a road in the slope for the guns to pass. At 8 miles a *defile* on the left of the road, which extended about a mile, with a slight ascent, which required the aid of the pioneers to render it passable, and detained the troops for 2 hours. The *Turnuk* and country below, to the right. Re-cross a water-course. At 6 miles the bed of a river : a small stream. Road stony in some places, and in parts, slightly winding. The road generally bad to-day. Confusion among the baggage cattle ; one man killed, and two nearly lost their lives. *Camp.* Range of low- hills in front (N.) distant ¾ mile. The river, Turnuk, to the rear (S.) and close to camp. Hills to the S.; 7 or 8 miles off. Encamped as soon as the valley was sufficiently wide.

The baggage up late; and the troops much exposed. *Thermometer* 3 P. M. 100°. Distance marched 11¾ miles.

3rd July.—To Assia Hazarah. *Thermometer* 2 A. M. 76°, when we marched. A gale of hot wind blew all night ; much heat and dust on the march. The road passable, with the exception of a large ravine, the almost perpendicular sides of which the troops had to ascend and descend. *Camp,* front, the river Turnuk ; rear, low hills ; the corn-fields still not reaped; an increased elevation this march. Reports of enemies. Dost Mahomed's son said to have advanced from Ghuznee towards Kelat-i-Ghiljie. Orders for an increase to the advance party to-morrow. (8) *Thermometer* 3 P. M. 120°.

(8) Picquets and two guns were posted on the road towards Kelat-i-Ghiljie. It was here, on the bank of the river, and from the Comr.-in-Chief's camp, that Capt. *Outram,* A. D. C. to H. E. lost a most

3. *To Kelat-i-Ghiljie,* (4th July, 1839.)—Thermometer at 2 A. M. 62°, when we marched. The sappers and miners with 3 Cos. of Infy., and a squadron of Cavy., and two guns, moved in advance of the column, to prepare the road. The wing H. M. 4th L. D.; the first Bombay, and third Bengal Lt. Cavy., and two guns, went with the D. Q. M. G. (Maj. *Garden*) to feel for the enemy, and prepare the camp for the troops.

Soon after we cleared camp, found the guns and pioneers brought up by a deep ravine, at which the pioneers were employed. At about half-way crossed a ravine which required the aid of the pioneers. The road in other parts good, though stony in some places. At about 2 or 3 miles from Kelat-i-Ghiljie, we found the three Regts. of Cavy. *en bivouac.* A man had passed and given information that a chief had arrived in the town last night. (9) *Sir J. Keane,* immediately ordered the Cavalry to move on. (10)

Having marched nearly 12¾ miles we reached Kelat-i-Ghiljie.

Camp. The Hd. Qrs. were on a height E. of the hill on which stood the old fort. The *Infy.* camp below us to the W. The Cavy., N. E. in the low ground towards the river. The Turnuk river to the E.

Half-way on this march is a small stone bridge; the boundary between the *Ghiljies* and *Dooranees.* Thermometer 3 P. M. 100°.

Kelat-i-Ghiljie, (11) is on a hill, on which a fort once

valuable Arab, the best horse in camp. Capt. O. offered a reward of 2,000 Rs. for the recovery of his charger, without success. The rear was too much exposed.

(9) This was, I believe, a fact; the head-man of the place said so.

(10) Some say 100 or 150 horsemen were seen disappearing over the hills. Capt. *Outram,* says, p. 87, "Except a few mounted *scouts,* who fled at our approach, no signs of Ghiljies." A proposal from one of the chiefs.

(11) The *"forts of the Ghiljies."* It was the Hd. Qrs. of the Ghiljies, there being numerous forts in the country. Being on the high road between Candahar and Cabool, its position was good for the head of the chiefs.

stood. There is no town here, there are two small walled villages not far from it, to the N. W., and some felt tents. The old fort is completely in ruins; it contains two springs of most excellent water. There is a *tradition* that whatever conqueror passed this place without meeting an enemy, might go to Cabool from Candahar (or *vice versa)* sure of success, and meet with no opposition in his advance. (12)

All was quiet during the day, and only a few horsemen were seen near camp in the afternoon, near some hills not far from camp. *Thermometer* 3 p. m. 100°. Kelat-i-Ghiljie is 5,773 feet above the sea.

5th July.—Thermometer 4 a. m. 62°. The Hd. Qrs. and 1st column halted to-day. The Shah's force and the 4th Brigade (13) joined us this morning. Abdool Rehman and Gool Mahomed, *(Gooroo,)* Ghiljee chiefs, marched in columns on our left and right all the way from Candahar, overing on our flanks. The former reported to have had 1,500 and the other 3,000 horse. (14) They were decidedly hostile; but, they waited to be joined by Dost Mahomed, before they would make an attack. These men having refused to submit to the king's authority, two other leading

---

(12) *Baber* took this place and thus describes it: " Kelat-i-Ghiljie, (in the vale of the Turnuk) A. H. 911, A. D. 4th June, 1505."
" When we reached Kelat, without having arrayed ourselves in armour, or erected any engines for an attack, we instantly made an assault. The conflict was severe. Huchek Beg had clambered up a tower on the S. W. of Kelat, and had nearly gained the top, when he was wounded in the eye with a spear; and he died of this wound two or three days after Kelat was taken. The fight continued in this way till about the time of afternoon prayers; when just as the assailants, who had fought bravely and exerted all their vigour, were almost exhausted, the garrison demanded quarter, and surrendered. They came out with their bows, quivers, and scymitars hanging round their necks; and I forgave them." *Memoirs,* p. 171.

(13) They had closed up to join the Shah for his better protection. He was much annoyed by plunderers on the march.

(14) Their numbers were variously reported at from 5 to 1,500. These chiefs are descended from the Ghiljie kings who (from the W.) invaded Persia.

members of the tribe were set up in their stead as rulers.
(15)

The *Shah* left some of his Affghan troops at this place.
(16) *Thermometer* 3 p. m. 98°. A few stray camels carried off.

4. *To Sir-i-Usp*, (6th July, 1839.)—Thermometer 2 a. m. 72°, when we marched. H. M. Shah Shoojah, his force, and the 4th Brigade, halting to-day at Kelat-i-Ghiljie. The road a very passable one, intersected at intervals, by water-courses, which a little delayed the guns. At 3 and 6 miles crossed two nullahs about knee-deep. Road good, but stony in places. Country more open, with low hills. *Camp* close to the Turnuk river. Distance marched 10¼ miles. *Thermometer* 3 p. m. 96°. The elevation above the sea 5,973, or 200 feet above Kelat-i-Ghiljie.

7th July.—To Nouruk. (17) *Thermometer* 2 a. m. 72°. Marched at 3 a. m. On leaving camp, road difficult for guns and camels. Cross, not far off, a water-course 60 feet wide; mud and water, but not deep; an ascent and descent on leaving it which detained the guns an hour; two more afterwards. The country barren, and road stony. At 9⅜ miles reached Nouruk on the bank of the Turnuk; it covered the camp on two sides. On reaching camp, we found the Cavalry *en bivouac;* and had seen no enemy. *Thermometer* 3 p. m. 93°. This place is 6,136 feet, or 163 feet above the last ground.

(15) *Outram,* p. 87. The father of Abdool Rehman, is said to have disputed the empire with *Shah Zeman* (brother of *Shah Shoojah,* who succeeded him as king), at the head of 50,000 horse and foot. On the 6th October, 1839, the fort of this chief (Killa-i-Murgha; a well constructed fort, with a high citadel, and wet ditch) was surrounded by Major *MacLaren's* Dett.; but he escaped during the night. The place was demolished. Shah Shoojah in his former reign, twice, unsuccessfully, besieged this place. See, Capt. O., p. 131.

(16) Major *Leech* recommended the *Shah* to repair the fort, and have a garrison in the place. The object generally is to raze all the forts and strongholds of these Ghiljies; short of which, all operations will be useless, as when defeated in the field they can retire to them.

(17) Or, Tazee Noorook.

G. O.—" A Regt. of Cavy. under the Brigadier of the day, coming on duty, with the sappers and miners and 2 Cos. of Infy. to leave camp an hour before the column." (18)

Prohibition against camels crossing to the other side of the Turnuk river, to graze. (19).

8th July.—To Abee Tazee, $8\frac{3}{4}$ miles. *Thermometer* 2 A. M. 70°. Marched at $\frac{1}{2}$ past 3 A. M. On leaving camp cross a small nullah. At about 2 miles, road narrow and for $1\frac{1}{2}$ mile along the brow of a hillock on the left; road about 20 feet wide. On right, a water-course, and the country low; the Turnuk flowing through it. Cross two or three watercourses, and slight ascents and descents. The rest of the country open, and road good for a hilly-country. The Turnuk in rear, and close to camp.

Some few stray camels carried off, a Ghiljie killed, one wounded, and some prisoners taken. (20) *Thermometer* 3 P. M. 93°. The elevation to-day 6,321 feet, or 185 feet above last ground.

9th July.—Thermometer 4 A. M. 62°. Halted; to give time to the pioneers to level, &c. the banks of some nullahs and ravines, which cross the road. (21) *Thermometer* 3 P. M. 90°.

---

(18) " The two guns, usually sent with this Dett., to move with the *main* column; to provide a place for them at *its* head; to be sent to the front if required."

(19) There were a number of villages across the river, and Gool Mahomed, the Ghiljie chief, was moving on our right flank; the river lying between us.

(20) G. O.—" At the next ground the Brigr. to post picquets to protect the camp, and the *cultivation*."

(21) G. O.—" The *sappers* with their Escort, to continue on their present ground; working parties from the *Infy.* must be in readiness to assist the artillery across the ravines in front."

This morning the son of a Ghiljie chief came into camp, to make submission to the Shah; who overtook us at this place. Some petty chiefs, with about 100 horse and foot, came into camp to the king. Two men were blown from guns, and one spared. The Ghiljies had been guilty of cold-blooded murder, for the sake of plunder.

10th July.—To Shuftul, 6½ miles. *Thermometer* 2 A. M. 60°. Marched at ½ past 3 A. M. Route over a very precipitous line of road, which still required strong working parties, to pass the guns over the steep banks of the nullah and ravines. One gun broke loose, capsized, fractured one man's jaw-bone, and seriously injured several others. Crossed three ascents and descents, with ghauts made over them. *Camp.* The Turnuk close to the rear. *Thermometer* 3 P. M. 96°. *Elevation* 6,514 feet, or 193 feet above last ground.

G. O.—" The Regt. of Cavalry, to go in advance, will proceed, at once, to the new ground, under the Brigadier coming on duty; accompanied by the D. Q. M. G."
"*Safety guards* to be posted, for protection of the fields, and in villages in the immediate vicinity of camp." (22) Another party of *Ghiljies* came in this evening; but none of note among them.

(22) G. O.—" After posting of the picquets and the *Cordon*, all further arrangements, to secure the safety of camp and cattle, to rest with the Brigadier of the day."

" On bodies of plunderers being observed collecting in any direction, it is to be communicated by any one discovering them, to the Brigadier of the day, who will either send out a *support* to the cattle guard, or take such steps as may seem fit, for dispersing, or capturing the robbers."

" *Officers not on duty*, prohibited riding in pursuit of plunderers, carrying with them Detts. not under their orders; thereby unsteadying the men; knocking up the horses; and defeating any systematic arrangements which may be concerted for capturing the thieves, by the responsible authority in camp." (*See G. O.* 1*st April,* 1839.)

" *Quiet* to be observed in camp throughout the night, and officers Comg. corps, to cause *Patrols* to be sent from their rear guards, to put a stop to the shouting of camel-drivers, and other followers." ('The camel-men coming in from grazing make a great noise calling out to each other; by which means they hear from those near the camp, the direction in which they should proceed to their quarter of it.)"

Two troopers were robbed by our own camp-followers, within the picquets. Most of the robberies *in* camp, were committed by our own followers; such is the case in all *Indian Camps.*

5. To Chusma-i-Shadee, 10½ miles ; (11th July, 1839.)—
Thermometer 2 A. M. 58°. Marched at ½ past 3 A. M. Road tolerable, crossed by a nullah with 2 feet water, and several dry ones. Half way crossed a nullah which became a slough by the horses feet stirring up the mud. Country open; considerable extent of table-land. (23) *Camp.* The Turnuk to the rear. Water-courses in rear of the Infy. and Cavy. camps. Some villages, at distance, in front of camp; and across the river. *Thermometer* 3 P. M. 97°. Elevation 6,668, or 154 feet above the last ground.

The people offered no molestation, and we got on very quietly. *Abdool Rehman,* who has been all along moving on our left flank, tendered his submission; but on such impudent terms, that no answer was given him. (24)

12th July.—To Punguk, 6½ miles. *Thermometer* 3 A. M. 70°. Marched at ½ past 4 A. M. At 2½ and 4 miles crossed water-courses. The country open, through a valley about 20 miles in width, crossed by several fine streams of water. Numerous villages, orchards, and much cultivation.

Camp. The Turnuk river a mile, to the rear (E.) of camp. On the other side of the river, about 1 mile, is Quilla-i-Jaffier. Large villages E. and W.; (rear and front) on each side of the river. *Thermometer* 3 P. M. 93°. Elevation 6,810 feet, or 142 feet above last ground.

Report that Abdool Rehman is near us with 500 horse; a reconnoissance ordered, but no enemy seen. (25)

13th July.—To Ghojan 12 miles. *Thermometer* 3 A. M. 66°. Marched at 4 A. M. At 5 miles crossed a deep ravine; rather a hard pull for H. A. horses. Crossed several other ravines. At 11 miles crossed the *Jaffier* nullah, but little water. The river Turnuk 3 or 4 miles off. Road good. The valley widened as we advanced, 10 to 15 miles wide; many

---

(23) About four miles from Chusma-i-Shadee, there is a plain on which 50,000 men might encamp, fronted by a crystal stream and plenty of grass, and wild clover. By halting there, you might make two instead of three marches from Shuftul to Ghojan.

(24) Outram, p. 88.

(25) The Bombay Brigade two marches in our rear.

villages with orchards around them and much cultivation. The villagers reaping and threshing in their fields; springs of water in our camp. An attempt made by some horsemen to carry off camels at graze, and while the picquet was coming up, two troopers of the 4th Local Horse recaptured the camels, and, taking different roads, tried to cut off the robbers from reaching the hills; unfortunately, close to the foot of the hill, their horses ran against each other, both men and horses fell to the ground. The Ghiljies took advantage of this accident, and cut both the helpless men to pieces, before they could recover themselves; and escaped into the mountains. Thermometer 3 P. M. 92°. Elevation 7,068 feet, or 258 above last ground.

14th July.—To Mukoor, or Mookloor, (26) 12¼ miles. *Thermometer* 3 A. M. 64°. Marched at 4 A. M. Road good, over a large table-land (crossed only by two or three small ravines) to the right covered with numerous mud-walled villages, (27) clumps of trees, and orchards near them. At 10 miles, there were 20 or 30 Karezees on each side of our route. (28)

The mountains near this place are about 2,000 feet above the plain; extremely rugged, and from their base the river Turnuk issues in numerous springs, near a clump of trees. Crossed the river, and also a water-course, to enter camp. (29)

(26) The name of the district. It was in Dost Mahomed's country. At this place is the source of the river Turnuk.

(27) These are rendered necessary for their defence against their neighbours.

(28) Said to have but little water.

(29) There is a plain (or *Chumun*) here, covered with a fine green turf, with white and red clover. The plane, poplar, and willow are seen among the fruit trees, and orchards. The Hd. Qrs. camp on the green sward.

Plenty of forage for all the animals. Grain, and some *gram* (a small *white* kind) procured here.

From the mountain near camp, a well cultivated valley was seen on the other side.

Camp. N. of the river, the rear towards it. The left close to the mountain. To the right, distant hills 15 or 16 miles off, on the other side of the valley. The village of Mukoor, S. W., and in rear of our left. *Thermometer* 3 P. M. 87°.

The elevation of this place is 7,091 feet, only 23 feet above the last ground.

The Ghiljies showed themselves to-day, but picquets were thrown out. No attack on *our* line of baggage, was made in that direction. (30)

6. *Halt at Mukoor,* (15th July, 1839.)—*Thermometer* 4 A. M. 56°. The Hd. Qrs. and 1st column halted to-day, in consequence of the indisposition of H. E. Sir J. Keane. The Shah, his troops, and the Envoy and Minister came in to-day. During his last march, the Shah's *Goorkhas* had a skirmish with Abdool Rahman, the Ghiljie chief. (31) *Thermometer* 3 P. M. 87°.

16*th July.*—To Oba, 14¼ miles. Thermometer 3 A. M. 60°. Marched at 4 A. M. At 6 and 10 miles crossed the dry bed of a nullah; rather steep banks the first time. Road generally good, over a flat, and well cultivated country ; few impediments. Numerous small forts, and walled villages,

---

(30) After the rear guard had arrived, many people who kept behind, were murdered and plundered by the thieves. Some of the medical stores of the Bombay troops were carried off. The Bengal medical store-keeper was ordered to supply more medicines. Accounts that the Shah's *Affghans* had surprised a body of *Ghiljies*, killed and wounded many, capturing a standard.

(31) They attacked the Shah's flanks, and were said to have had 1,000 horse and 500 foot. The foot occupied a range of hills commanding the road ; the *Ghoorkha* Battn. went up and attacked them, killed and wounded many, and dispersed the rest. The Shah's party had 1 killed and 2 wounded. The *Ghoorkhas,* are the best troops for hill warfare in *India ;* the mountaineers in *Affghanistan* are very good, but are larger men, and not so active as the little Ghoorkhas. The Shah is, consequently, obtaining more of this class of soldier. They are excellent shots. The *Shah's* camp was attacked in a part protected by a party of the *Ghoorkha* Battn. The Ghoorkhas, at home, on such ground, drove them off, overtook them, killed 13, and wounded many.

and extensive cultivation to the right and left. Numerous groups of villagers, viewing the troops as they passed. Parties of Cavalry thrown out to protect the cultivation; grain, &c. brought into camp.

Camp. Springs of water in camp, a water-course to the rear, beyond which to the N. was the dry bed of a river. Plenty of food for all the animals. The village of *Oba* to the W. was deserted. (32)

G. O.—" The advance guard, of a Regt. of Cavalry; a Wing of Infy., and two H. A. guns, with the sappers and miners to assemble at the main picquet at the 1st Trumpet, and move off under the Brigadier coming on duty, as soon as *day-light* sufficient to discern obstacles on the road." (33)

Rations.—" The D. C. G. to issue from to-morrow, rations of ¾ seer of Attah (flour) to fighting-men; and half a seer (1 lb.) to public establishments, and to camp-followers, instead of that now supplied." (34) *Thermometer* 3 P. M. 92°. The elevation here is 7,325 feet, or 234 above Mookhloor.

17th July.—To Jumrood, (35) 12½ miles. *Thermometer* 3 A. M. 62°. Marched at ½ past 4 A. M. The road crossed by several dry nullahs, and a few ravines, rather heavy for the guns in some places. Numerous forts, and walled villages, with orchards, and much cultivation. About half-way some *Karezees* were passed, some dry, some between them

---

(32) An unfortunate washerman who strayed from the road, was robbed and his left arm cut off. The head-man of the village, near the spot, seized the criminal, and brought him, the wounded man and his property, into camp. After an inquiry and full proof of guilt, the man was shot.

(33) " To leave parties for the preservation of the grain, in the vicinity of the road: to join the rear-guard."

(34) The troops had been on *half*-rations of *half* a seer, and the camp-followers on a *quarter* of a seer, since the 29th March, 1839. (G. O. 28th March, 1839,) or for more than 3½ months; except what little could casually be bought by those followers who had the means, between this place and Candahar; at the latter place there was an open, but dear market, for the poor!

(35) In the district of Kharabaugh.

and the camp; where there were three streams of water. *Thermometer* 3 P. M. 93°. The elevation 7,426 feet, or 101 feet above the last ground.

Many men were now sick, some in consequence of sleeping on the green sward at *Mukoor*. (36) Flour to-day, sold in camp at 22, and barley at 28 seers per rupee.

Accounts from Cabool and Ghuznee most conflicting. That Dost Mahomed's eldest son, (37) with four guns had re-inforced his younger brother (Hyder Khan) at *Ghuznee*.

18*th July*.—To near Musheekee, 8¾ miles. *Thermometer* 3 A. M. 66°. Marched at ½ past 4 A. M. The first 5 miles road rather heavy for guns; intersected by many watercourses, &c. rendering the march difficult for camels; rest of the road good, but rather stony. The whole plain covered with forts, walled villages, and much cultivation. The mountaineers, here, are called *Huzarahs*. (38)

Camp. Heights in front, and Karezees to the front, to the left, and to the rear. The heights N. W. of and close to camp, and a large collection of grave stones in front, and close under the hills. *Thermometer* 3 P. M. 91°. The elevation at this place 7,309 feet or 117 *less* than the last ground.

A party of *Kuzzulbashes* came in to render obedience to the king. (39) Alarms of the enemy, and more picquets

---

(36) 37 men of the 16th Bengal N. I. and many of the 48th N. I. went into hospital. Many of the soldiers European and natives lost their beddings in the *Bolan* and *Kojuk* Passes. H. M.'s 13th Lt. Infy. buried three men last night.

(37) Meer Ufzul Khan. He was in the neighbourhood. But the report that Dost Mahomed had marched from Cabool on the 16th July, for Ghuznee, was not true. He was afraid to leave Cabool without his troops at this time; expecting we should be detained at *Ghuznee* for a long time. The disaffected Ghiljie chiefs were said to be moving with a considerable body of Cavalry on our flanks, intending to aid the *Khan* in resisting our advance; or if *he* did not come to oppose us; then, to tender their submission.

(38) Huzzar means 1,000, the number said to have been sent by one of the conquerors, to people the land.

(39) Said to be the first deserters from Dost Mahomed's army.

thrown out. Authentic accounts received here, that the enemy have assembled in force to oppose us at *Ghuznee*. Rear columns ordered to close up by forced marches. (40) Heavy rain at night.

7. *Troops closing up from the Rear*, (19th July, 1839.)—To Ahmed Khel, (41) 9½ miles. *Thermometer* 3 A. M. 66°. Marched at ½ past 4 A. M. The road first 5 miles heavy sand, (42) and large loose stones; crossing several watercourses: the rest of the road good. Crossed two more watercourses. Many small mud-forts, and villages at the slopes of the hills.

The Infantry, Cavalry, and guns were halted near *Urguttoo*, which was occupied by forty of the enemy's horse, who decamped on the arrival of our advance guard. (43) The Shah, and the force with him, joined us to-day.

Camp. Heights in front; numerous small streams of water near camp. *Thermometer* 3 P. M. 93°. Elevation 7,502 feet, or 193 feet above the last ground.

The 2nd column joined us to-day by forced marches; and Genl. *Willshire* (3rd column) is pushing on to join us. (44)

G. O.—" The 4th Brigade will resume its position in the 1st *(Bengal)* division of Infantry, (45) on the march to-

---

(40) Outram, p. 90.

(41) In the district of Arghistan.

(42) Tents all wet, which increased the weight of the loads of the camels, &c.

(43) The advanced guard were fired upon by a patrol of about 50 of the enemy's horsemen; after a few shots, driven into the hills. A troop of 1st Bombay Lt. Cavy. went after them, but did not come up with them. *Outram*, p. 91.

(44) G. O.—" To be considered a *standing order* that, when the ' alarm' is sounded at night" *(or day)* " the *in-lying picquets* shall immediately turn out, and proceed, under their commander, to the front of the standard, or Qr. guard, of the centre Regt. of the Brigade to which they belong; where they will remain under the Fd. officer of the day of the Brigade; awaiting the orders of the Brigadier on duty. Should the " *Assembly*" be sounded, the Line will get under arms; each Regt. forming in front of its encampment; and remaining in position, till ordered in some particular direction, by competent authority."

(45) It had been marching with the king.

morrow; and the park, with the Dett. usually assigned to it from the 4th Brigade, will follow in column."

" The *Rear Guard* to be increased by a Compy. from the 4th Brigade. The camels carrying the spare ammunition attached to the corps of Infantry, to move on the reverse flanks of their respective Regts." *Thermometer* 3 p. m. 93°. The elevation, here, 7,502 feet or 193 feet above the last ground.

20th July.—Thermometer 3 a. m. 68°. To Nannee 7½ miles. Marched at ½ past 4 a. m. The road sandy, heavy, and stony. At about 6 miles, passed between commanding hills, distant ¼ to ⅛ mile from each other. The road from this, was over table-land, crossed by the dry beds of mountain torrents. (46.)

About fifty or sixty of the enemy were seen on the hills, but they moved off on the approach of our advance guard.

A body of *Huzzarahs* came into camp, and submitted to the Shah. *Thermometer* 3 p. m. 94°. The elevation here was 7,420 feet, or 82 feet less than the last ground.

8. *Preparations for the march to Ghuznee.*

G. O. *Officers quitting camp.* " H. E. calls attention to the impropriety, in the present position of the army, of Officers, quitting camp on *shooting-parties;* and to the unmilitary practice of discharging *fire-arms* within, or in the vicinity, of the lines; the latter practice must be put a stop to." (47)

" The army to move to-morrow, in three columns, in the following order."

" The *Artillery* will march by the main-road, having with it the sappers and miners."

---

(46) To the W. of Nannee there is a small stream, to cross which and encamp on the *Ghuznee* side, is said to give to an army the possession of the country. This must mean, if the river be crossed without opposition; and is something like the *tradition* regarding Kelat-i-Ghiljie.

(47) " To be proclaimed in the different bazars that, any campfollower found discharging fire-arms, within camp, will be severely punished."

" The *Cavalry*, on the *right*, in column of troops, ¼ distance, right in front."

" The *Infantry*, on the *left*, in column of Companies, ¼ distance, left in front."

" Parties of pioneers will move near the head of the columns of Cavy. and Infantry." (48)

" The *Rear-guard* will consist of a company of Infantry from each Brigade, a troop of Light Cavalry, and the whole of the Local Horse ; and will be under the command of the Fd. Officer coming off the duty of the main picquet, who will regulate the march of the baggage, from front to rear." (49)

" The Brigadier Comg. the Artillery, will arrange for the *Mortars*, and a portion of ammunition, moving with the army; the remainder of the *Park*, must immediately precede the *baggage*."

" The *treasure* will move with the *Park*, and will be under the charge of a Company of Native Infy."

---

(48) " As the march of the columns must be simultaneous, they will be formed when the ' *Assembly*' is sounded ; but will await a signal from H. E., to move forward."

" It is the desire of H. E. that corps should muster to-morrow, as strong as possible ; and that all personal guards, and orderlies, and every soldier capable of bearing arms, should join their colors, on the present occasion. H. E. is, also, pleased to permit officers on the *civil* staff of the army, whose Regts. are in the field, to join them to-morrow."

" The *Camp-colormen* must march on the *reverse* flank of the rear troop, or Company, of their respective Regts. The spare ammunition, and two Doolies for each Regt., will be allowed to move in the same position."

" Medical officers must arrange to carry on these Doolies the means of affording ready assistance; and the Supg. Surgeon will make such arrangements as may appear to him expedient, for affording relief to individuals sent to the rear."

" Not an article of baggage, nor a follower, must be permitted to pass the picquets, nor to move from the present ground, until ½ an hour after the rear of the column shall have quitted camp."

(49) " All Detts. of Local Horse now on duty with the different Depts., excepting the detail with the *Baggage Master*, will rejoin their standards, at the first trumpet, to-morrow."

A Bivouac all night. 161

"The *Infantry* must move with *forty rounds* of ammunition in *pouch,* and Qr. Mrs. of corps will be held responsible, that the *spare* ammunition, is kept well up with the column."

"The *sick* of corps are to be collected under a steady N. C. O., and to move in front of the baggage; the *led-horses* will follow the doolies."

"Orders will hereafter be given for an '*advance guard.*' "

Major *Garden* D. Q. M. G. *(Bengal)* returned from a *reconnoissance* to *Ghuznee.* He went within a quarter of a mile of the town, and saw no armed men near the place, and only a few men walking about; nothing to indicate the place being occupied in force. (50) Authentic (though not official) intelligence having reached Lt.-Col. *Wade* at *Peshawer,* of H. M. Shah Shoojah having marched from *Candahar,* the Lt.-Colonel, with the Shah's son, *(Shahzada Tymoor)* moved, to-day, with the force under his orders, from Peshawer to *Jumrood,* near the entrance to the *Khyber* Pass; in order to move through the Pass towards Cabool.

As it was reported that *Meer Ufzul Khan,* (Dost Mahomed's eldest son) who had 3,000 horsemen, was in our neighbourhood, and meant to attack the camp at night, *(Chuppao)* the whole of the troops were *en bivouac* all night. But no enemy appeared, and the only occurrence was the accidental discharge of a musket. The troops rose up with their arms perfectly steady, and without firing a shot. At *midnight*

---

(50) He took about 30 troopers with him; and leaving (as he usually did) his party about a mile or two behind, went on with four troopers up to within ¼ mile of the place. It was afterwards ascertained, that, *Hyder Khan,* the Govr., who had a telescope and saw him advance, had ordered a party to go out in pursuit of Major G.; but they were too late. Major *Parsons,* D. C. G. (Bengal) when riding out on the evening of the 5th July, at Kelat-i-Ghiljie, was nearly falling in with a party of horsemen. The hills concealed them, but Brigr. *Scott* (4th L. D.) who saw them, sent some troopers to intercept them. The Minarets at *Ghuznee* were visible from our camp at *Nanuce.*

Y

Major Genl. *Willshire's* (3rd) column, which had been ordered up from the rear by express, marched into camp; and we were now looking forward to the operations and the events of the coming day.

CHAPTER IX.

MARCH ON; OPERATIONS BEFORE; AND ASSAULT AND CAPTURE OF GHUZNEE.

1. *March from Nannee to Ghuznee* (21st July, 1839.)—
The army marched from Nannee (1) at 4½ A. M., in three columns; Maj. Genl. *Willshire*, and the Bombay column, having joined us last night. The artillery marched, by the main road, as the centre column. The *Cavalry* were the right column, in column of troops, right in front. The *Infantry* formed the left column, in column of companies, left in front. The *Shah's* Cavalry were to the right of all. It was supposed that the enemy would, if they made any attack on us, move from Ghuznee towards our left front; so that the Infantry by being *left* in front, could easily form to the front. *Meer Ufzul Khan* (2) was supposed to be in our neighbourhood, and had he joined the troops under his brother *Hyder Khan* (Govr. of Ghuznee), still the arrangements of the Horse Artillery and Cavalry were suitable to meet the enemy. If he confined his attack to our *right* flank, it was very easy to meet him in that direction; while an attack on our *rear*, was the most probable mode of attack on the plain. There were low hills on our left, which rendered an attack from that side in force, unlikely. The *British* troops amounted to about 8,000. (3) The *Shah's*

(1) Orders were given last night to the *Qr. Guards* not to allow any armed natives of the country to enter the lines; but to direct them to the right flank parties. It was expected that parties would come in; and it is usual to apppoint a place in orders, where they are to be taken to.

(2) Dost Mahomed's eldest son.

(3) I speak of the numbers fit for duty and under arms, and include the Advance and Rear Guards.

contingent to about 2,000, and H. M.'s *Affghans* to about 2,000 men, in all about 12,000 men, and about forty guns, of which eighteen were Horse Artillery. The Comr.-in-Chief formed his advance guard, and we moved off, in parallel columns, preserving such distances between each, as would enable the troops to form to the front, or to either flank. The rear guard (4) consisted of about 800 men. Brigr. *Sale* (5) was Brigadier of the day; and Major *Fitzgerald* (6) Field Officer of the day.

The country over which we marched was undulating, but open; though we crossed some water-courses, still there was nothing to impede our movements, or prevent our acting in concert. Shortly after we had marched, we met a chief (7) with a few followers, who had been in the fort of Ghuznee, and had left it during the night, with the intention of joining us. The route was nearly in a direct line all the way, except the last 3 or 4 miles, when it turned to the *left*, and then the fort of *Ghuznee* burst on our view. It looked formidable with its fortifications rising up, as it were, on the side of a hill, which seemed to form the back ground to it, towards the citadel. We observed as yet no hostile movements. The columns were advancing slowly, but steadily, on the wide plain, and no noise was heard, save that of the movement of the guns, the distant sound of the horses' feet, and the steady tramp of the Infantry; while, there being a slight breeze, the distant clouds of dust indicated, to those afar off, the approach of an army in battle-array. The

---

(4) Consisting of three Cos. of Infy., one troop of Cavy., and the whole of the Local Horse.
(5) Comg. 1st Bengal Brigade.
(6) 2nd Bengal Cavy.
(7) A nephew of Dost Mahomed's. He was sent to *Sir A. Burnes* who was in advance with the Comr.-in-Chief. From him they learnt that Gool Mahomed, the Ghiljie chief, who had been marching on our right flank all the way from Candahar, had gone into the fort and left it again, but that his horses were there. Also, that the Governor meant to resist, and various other particulars. This chief said he had not been well treated by his uncle.

advance of the army was observed by *Hyder Khan* by means of his telescope. As soon as the advance had arrived within a mile of the fortress, it was perceived that preparations were being made by the enemy to stop our advance. (8) The object was, now, to dislodge the enemy from the villages and gardens which they occupied close to, and around the fort.

2. *Enemy driven in—Fire against the Fort.*—The 1st (Bengal) Brigade of Infantry was leading. H. M.'s 13th Lt. lnfy. were ordered to the right in the direction of some gardens near the fort ; the 16th N. I. went to the left, and the 48th N. I. were pushed through the centre of a village, between the above corps. The Light Company of the (Bengal) European Regt. was sent still more to the right, to drive the enemy out of a garden in that direction; while the remainder of the Regt. was kept in ¼ distance column, and as the fire from the fort was heavy, the men were made to sit down. (9) In the direction to the *left* there was a garden within the range of the fort, and completely commanded by an outwork of the fort, about 60 yards distant. The Light Companies of the 16th N. I. (Capt. *Graves*) and of the 48th N. I. (Lt. *Van Homrigh*) were sent to this garden to dislodge the enemy. They soon succeeded in driving them from the garden into the out-work. The above corps were placed in position to prevent the enemy coming out to occupy any ground near the fort; as well as a support to the Light Companies in advance. Some Cavalry were placed in position, to prevent any attack on the Horse Artillery from the country near the gardens : while

(8) "Some scouts were perceived to be hastily evacuating some walled-gardens. The Comr.-in-Chief and staff having passed the gardens, awaited the arrival of the troops in a position overlooking the fort ; observing which, the enemy opened a few guns from the walls and discharging several match-locks from a garden in our vicinity." Capt. *Outram*, (p. 91.)—He was with H. E. in advance. A man near some fields, told us that there were 1,000 armed men in the place. The villagers we met, seemed quite at their ease.

(9) The rest of the troops kept in column ready to move in any direction.

the Infantry protected the guns from any assault by parties issuing from the fort.

The enemy, as soon as their match-lockmen had retired within the outwork, opened a fire from the works with their guns. It was desired by the Comr.-in-Chief to ascertain, what extent of fire the enemy could direct against us from the fort, and accordingly the H. A. guns (10) were brought up, and placed in position as they came up, extending in a line from a village on the right, to the out-work on the left, and opened a fire on the fort with shrapnels and shot at about the distance of 700 yards. The enemy returned the fire, which lasted for about ¾, of an hour. There were some casualties arising from this fire; they had got the range pretty accurately, and could they have sufficiently depressed their guns, would have killed and wounded many. The shots struck close to the Regt. of Infy. (11) posted between a village and the angle of the fort, and many struck the ground close to the Horse Artillery; some shot passing under the horses' bellies, and some reaching to the Cavalry. The position in the garden near the outwork was one of considerable danger, being close to and within musket shot of it; Capt. *Graves*, 16th Bengal N. I. was severely wounded, being shot through the shoulder and hip; (12) and Lt. *Van Homrigh*, 48th Bengal N. I. was wounded in the right arm, slightly. (13) Having ascertained the ex-

(10) There were 18 H. A. guns, and including the camel battery of 9-prs., &c. there were 30 guns employed.
(11) 48th N. I.
(12) At one time his wound was considered to be a dangerous one.
(13) There were one R. and F. and two horses killed; and one Capt., one Lt., six R. and F. and five horses wounded. One R. and F. and 1 horse missing—besides some accidents.

There was one of the enemy who kept mounted on the parapet of the out-work, waving his flag, and calling out to our men to come on; one of our shot knocked off his head, and down went the flag; and the rest became more cautious. Some one contemplated assaulting this out-work at once; but the Comr.-in-Chief would not allow of so hazardous an attack. We afterwards ascertained that our fire had committed havock in the fort, killing and wounding some men, and a great many horses.

tent and power of the enemy's fire from the fort, the troops were ordered to be withdrawn from further exposure; and orders were given not to pitch the camp till a position for the troops was determined on. (14) While the troops were engaged, a report was received that *Meer Ufzul Khan* (15) had gone back, with the whole of his horse, to attack our baggage; in consequence of which, the Wing H. M.'s 4th L. D. and 1st Bombay Cavalry, were sent back to reinforce the rear-guard; this gave the rear-guard, altogether, about 1,600 men. (16) The next operation was, to *reconnoitre* the place; which Capts. (now Majors) G. *Thomson* (Bengal) and *A. G. Peat* (Bombay) the chief *Engineers* immediately commenced. (17) The result of this *reconnoissance* determined the Comr.-in-Chief to change ground to the *Cabool* (S. E.) *side* of the fort.

3. *Move to the Cabool (S. E.) side of the fort.*—The D. Q. M. G. (Major *Garden*) who had accompanied the reconnoitring party, having returned to Hd. Qrs. (18) the following order was issued. *G. O.* " The troops will change ground this afternoon, the 1st trumpet to sound at three; and the '*assembly*' at 4 o'clock, to sound from Hd. Qrs."

" The *Cavalry* will proceed under such directions as Maj. Genl. *Thackwell* may think fit, and take up ground for the

(14) This was not generally understood, for many tents were pitched, and many of the camels were sent out to graze; which turned out to be a very inconvenient measure; but they should not have been sent out to any distance.

(15) With 3,000 horse. Capt. *Outram*, p. 92, says, " The Bombay Cavy. and Infy. Brigade had been halted when within about three miles of the fort, in order to afford protection to our rear."

(16) See para. 1 and note 4.

(17) See the Chief Engineer's report, dated 25th July, 1839, paras. 2 to 6 in this chapter. The party consisted of a Company H. M.'s 13th Lt. Infy. (Capt. *Sutherland*), a Coy. 48th Bengal N. I. (Lt. *Spankie*), and a troop of 2nd Bengal Lt. Cavy. (Major *Fitzgerald*); and not of H. M.'s 16th Lancers, as inserted by mistake in Sir *J. Keane's* Despatch, of the 25th July, 1839, para. 5, in this chapter: one European killed and one man wounded.

(18) They had been established in a garden beyond the village near the fort.

whole of the troops. The D. Q. M. G. (19) will accompany the Cavalry." (20)

"The Maj. Genls. Comg. the Divisions of *Infantry*, will make a corresponding movement, and will cross the river at such points as may be indicated by the Officers of the Qr. Mr. Genl.'s Dept. attached to their respective Divisions." (21)

"In making the change of position, care must be taken to keep the troops *out of fire from the* fort."

"The Artillery, and the whole of the Park establishment will follow the Cavalry."

"A strong *Rear-guard*, consisting of a Regt. of Infy. (22) and the whole of the Local Horse, will form in rear of the centre of the present encampment, and will move under the orders of the Brigadier of the day, (23) who will make suitable arrangements for the protection of the baggage." (24)

"Parties of Pioneers must be attached to each of the columns, and the sappers will move with the Park."

"Two Cos. of Infantry from the 1st Division will also march with the Park, and be prepared to aid in conveying the ordnance across the river."

"Orders for the formation of the *picquets*, and for the protection of the camp throughout the night, will be hereafter issued." (25)

(19) Maj. *Garden*.
(20) The Cavy. and Arty. formed the column moving to the right by the nearest route. The 19th Bombay N. I.. moved with them.
(21) The Infantry and the (Bengal) Comsst. cattle, moved by the route which lay to the left.
(22) The 48th N. I. and 4th Local Horse.
(23) Brigr. *Sale*.
(24) The baggage of each column marched with it.
(25) "Returns of the actual number of R. and F. which marched with each division of Cavy. and Infy., and of the Arty. and sappers this morning, to be sent, without delay, to the D. A. G.; and nominal rolls of this day's casualties among the Comssd. officers, and numerical returns of those of the men and horses, to be sent, as soon as they can be prepared, to the same authority."

As it was reported that Dost Mahomed Khan, had marched from Cabool towards Ghuznee, (26) it was important to make a move towards the Cabool road, to prevent either Dost Mahomed, or his son, Meer Ufzul Khan, pushing into it; or reinforcements, or any parties getting into the place. The *Shah* took a different view of the case; he thought that, in our peculiar situation, we could not take the place with our present ordnance; (27) and his advice was, to leave the fort behind and march on for Cabool: but better judges had determined otherwise; and we were now to move to the Cabool side.

4. *March in two Columns to the Cabool side.*—The troops marched in two columns to take up a new camp on the side of the fort which commanded the Cabool *gate*, and the *road* to Cabool. Thus we were gaining *two* points of great

(26) Capt. *Outram*, p. 90, says, "It was confidently stated that Dost Mahomed Khan, himself, marched on the 16th (July)." The distance is 88 miles (we made seven marches) and by regular marches he would have reached Ghuznee on the 22nd (next day), and as this day (21st) he would have been within *one* march, and would have heard the firing, he would, it was to be supposed, push on; so that there was a great object in not delaying in changing ground. As in 1834, Dost Mahomed had moved from Cabool to defend Candahar against the Shah, the presumptions were in favor of his march to Ghuznee. We knew, from Dost Mahomed's own nephew, that two of the three gates were blocked up, and it was argued by some, that the sudden movement to the *Cabool* gate, which was said not to be built up, would put the enemy on their guard; and cause *that* gate also to be secured. Whereas, by a march in the morning, it would not appear so suspicious. The movement was a delicate one, being a march in two columns by two different routes; for it involved a night march for the rear and much of the baggage, if not for the troops, as we were not to march till four in the afternoon; and the route for both columns could not be well known. The march in two columns would, it was concluded, expedite the movements, but then there were two columns of baggage to protect, and we could not protect that of the column on the right. The march of the baggage at all, that night, was inconvenient; and we gained no time by it.

(27) The king said "I know well that, if you can once breach the place, the fort will be certainly yours; but I cannot understand *how* you are to get into the fort."

moment; but, we, also, had a *third* point,—to protect the rear, while we were uncertain as to the movements of *Meer Ufzul Khan*. The troops of the left column did not march till near 6 P. M. The *right* column marched earlier. The troops arrived at their new position late at night, but the baggage and rear-guard were not so fortunate. (28) The rear-guard (29) did not leave till the moon had risen; it was twelve days old. When we had marched about four miles on the road, nearly the same as that by which we had advanced in the morning, we were obliged to move slowly on account of the rear camels. (30) A Wing of the 48th N. I. was, therefore, ordered to move on to overtake the baggage on a-head, which it did in the course of ½ an hour. We found that the people in advance had lost the road; this was about 10 o'clock at night. We found camels, bullocks, hackeries, (carts,) guards, all jammed up together. People were sent to discover the road, but it could not be found; the moon went down at about ½ past 12, and we could do nothing more than wait for the rear party, and then make the best military disposition of our forces we could; (31) but, it was dark, and we could not well have protected such a number of cattle and baggage had we been attacked. We, therefore, were necessitated to *bivouac* till day-light should show us the road to camp. (32) We

(28) The orders were out late, as it was not decided till late in the afternoon (3 P. M.) how we were to move. Some camels had gone to graze and did not come in till near sunset, and the rear guard could not move till all the baggage was off the ground.

(29) I was with it, and my Regt. 48th N. I.

(30) A Wing of the 48th N. I. and the Local Horse remained under the Brigr. of the day, to bring up the rear, and he sent the other Wing under Major *Thomas* on in advance, to overtake the baggage in advance; as the moon had risen, and a stronger party than they had with them was deemed necessary.

(31) Throwing out flanking parties in different directions.

(32) An officer of the Qr. Mr. Genl.'s Dept. at about 2 A. M. finding we had not arrived, came to us; he had to cross over to our right from the hills near the fort; under these hills runs the river which was to be crossed, as well as about 10 or 12 canals which ran between us and the river, (by the route he came,) an operation which caused many camels to fall in daylight.

heard all night a firing of matchlocks and wall pieces from the fort, about every five minutes, as if the enemy were firing at persons approaching the walls, or ditch. (33)

This firing lasted till day-light: nothing else occurred during the night, except some blue lights were exhibited in the fort, and signal lights were observed in the hills. At *daybreak*, we commenced pushing on the baggage to camp. At *sun-rise* Lt. *Keane,* A. D. C. to the Comr.-in-Chief came across to Brigr. *Sale,* Comg. the Rear-guard, and said that H. E. had perceived parties of the enemy's horse (34) moving towards the baggage, and that he had ordered a Regt. of Cavalry to come and join the rear-guard. Lt. *K.* desired the Brigr. to accompany him to the Comr.-in-Chief who wished to speak to him. (35) Brigr. *Sale* therefore, made over the command to Lt.-Col. *Wheeler,* who took prompt and judicious measures for sending on the baggage to camp. (36) The whole of the baggage did not reach camp till near 12 A. M. on the morning of the 22nd July.

The route of the *left* column was circuitous, and when about half way was parallel to the river, about 1½ miles distant; then moving a mile on from our *bivouac* we came to a village whence the road turned to the right, crossing two streams

(33) The rear guard supposed they were firing at working parties. It was by some thought that the enemy were keeping up a fire to convince us that they were on the alert; and that they might, during the confusion of our troops moving, take the opportunity of escaping from the fort by the hills, after the moon had gone down. In camp they thought they were firing on the rear guard.

(34) Must have been Meer Ufzul Khan. At day-break we perceived parties of eight or ten horsemen to our left about three or four miles off, on some rising ground, watching us; and at sun-rise we heard the firing of matchlocks near our rear, but *we* saw no men.

(35) This was regarding the proposed attack on Ghuznee.

(36) A portion of the baggage was sent in succession, with a suitable guard, by which means all confusion was avoided. The Lt.-Colonel seeing all well across the river, moved with his rear Dett. directly across to the river; thus moving on the centre of the line of baggage. A Regt. of our Cavy. (2nd Bengal) moving towards us.

of the river; then turning to the right the road ran parallel to the river; and a turn to the left up the hills, and another to the right brought us to camp. The route of the *right* column, with which the Comr.-in-Chief went, was a movement to its right, and then turned up the left.

The *right* column did not reach its ground till 10 o'clock, and the *left* column, not till 12 o'clock at night of the 21st July; and the troops had to *bivouac* till next morning; not a single tent up till after sunrise in the *left* column. The distance marched by the *left* column must have been nine miles; that by the *right* column less. (37) The position of the rear guard at the *bivouac* was about one and a half mile in rear of the hills, which divided us at nearly equal distances from our new camp; part of which range of hills commanded the citadel: and between the range and our *bivouac* ran the river, and, besides, ten or twelve canals. The route of the *right* column was across the river, and then turned to the *left*; but they had no hills to cross. (38)

5. *22nd July. Enemy near camp.*—At day-break H. E. the Comr.-in-Chief, accompanied by the Engineers, proceed-

---

(37) Though they moved before the left column, the guns detained them; so that this route may not have been above two miles less than that of the left.

(38) The march of the Cavalry and Artillery by the right, saved the interruption and inconvenience caused by crossing hills, particularly in the night.

While it was desirable to occupy the Cabool road without loss of time, still much confusion would have been saved had about 6 or 7,000 men with the principal part of the guns, been sent to the Cabool road, the troops being ordered to *bivouac* there in position, and the whole of the baggage and Comsst. stores been collected and parked in compact order, guarded by the rest of the troops and some guns; thus, by marching at day-break, the whole of the baggage would have been as early in camp. For, besides *Meer Ufzul Khan's* 5,000 horse (the number stated by Hyder Khan) had the enemy made a *sortie* from the fort, our baggage must have suffered dreadfully. If *Meer Ufzul Khan* had actually gone towards the Cabool road, a less force might have been required on the ground the troops were leaving; but we had to guard against the chance of a *sortie*, and to protect the baggage.

ed to the heights of *Bullal,* on the right of camp to the N. from which a good view was obtained of the E. face of the fort, where the attack was to be made; (39) and confirmed in the opinion formed before, he then resolved to blow open the gate and storm the place. The Engineers had now made further observations as to the nature of the works, and the position of the gate-way. (40) Preparations were, therefore, promptly made for the assault next morning; to be by a false attack to divert the attention of the enemy, while the gate was being blown open.

Attack near Shah's Camp.—The enemy's cavalry under *Meer Ufzul Khan* were said to have been joined by about 3,000 horsemen under the disaffected Ghiljie chiefs (41) and were waiting for an opportunity to fall upon our camp. At about 11 A. M. the hills to the S. of camp were observed to be crowned with numerous bodies of horse and foot, displaying their standards. And as the Shah's troops were in this direction, it was supposed the attack was intended to be made on his camp. (42) Some of H. M.'s guns, the whole of his cavalry, supported by the Lancers, and a Regt. of Bengal Cavy., immediately moved out, and the enemy who had descended into the plains being met by a gallant charge of the Shah's horse under Lt. *P. Nicolson* (43) were compelled to reascend the heights. Capt. *Outram* (44) moved

(39) From these heights he could observe the horsemen going towards the baggage.

(40) The Engineers had the day before observed the position of the gate-way; but on a closer examination, afterwards, Major *Thomson* came to the conclusion that the gate was not blocked up; for at considerable risk, he got as near it as he could undiscovered, and observed people coming out at dusk, which satisfied him that there must be a gate, or wicket, by which an entrance was to be obtained. The Lt. Coy. (1st) Eurn. Regt. were out reconnoitring on the 22nd July.

(41) This would make the above force about 6,000.
(42) It is said they wanted to seize his person.
(43) 28th Bengal N. I.
(44) 23rd Bombay N. I. A. D. C.

with a party to the rear round by the hills, where he posted them to cut off their retreat; but the enemy ascended heights beyond the reach of our horse. Capt. O. then returned and accompanied the Shah's infantry and matck-lock-men, who followed the enemy and, killing the standard-bearer, the *Holy-banner* (45) was captured. They then fled with precipitation. There were 20 killed and wounded of the Shah's troops: and the enemy had 30 or 40 killed and wounded, and 50 prisoners. Capt. *Outram* exerted himself very much on this occasion; and was very actively employed on the previous day.

6. *Orders for the attack of Ghuznee.*—G. O. C. C. Hd. Qrs. camp before Ghuznee, 22nd July, 1839. "The following movements are directed for to-morrow. At 12 o'clock P. M. the *artillery* will commence moving towards the fort, and the Batteries will follow each other, in succession at the discretion of the Brigr. Comg. The *guns* must be placed in the most favorable positions, with the *right* above the village on the hill N. E. of the fortress, and their *left* amongst the *gardens* on the Cabool road. They must all be in position before day-light, and as in the progress down, they cannot avoid being heard, and fired upon, they should make a *return*, sufficient to attract the enemy's attention from the gate-way, about 3 A. M."

2. "The 1st Battery will be accompanied by the *sappers* and *miners*, and by six Cos. of N. I. from the 1st Division; (46) four of these Cos. are intended to close the *gardens* on the *left* of the road, and to support the sappers; and the other two Cos. will be formed on the *right* of the *atillery* for the protection of that flank."

---

(45) This was a green and white flag. The Mahomedan high priest had preached a religious war against the British, and had collected a number of fanatics. The Ghiljie chief, the leader of this army, surrendered himself to Capt. *Outram* on the 28th Sept. 1839, on the occasion of the operations against the Ghiljie chiefs between Cabool and Candahar. The father-in-law of Dost Mahomed was killed in the skirmish of the 22nd July.

(46) 35th Bengal N. I.

3. "The *storming party* will be under the command of Brigr. *Sale*, C. B., and will be composed as follows ; *viz.* The *advance* to consist of the Light Cos. of H. M.'s 2nd and 17th Regts. ; of the (47) European Regt., and of a flank Coy. of H. M. 13th Lt. Infy.—under the command of Lt.-Col. *Dennie*, C. B."

4. "The *main column* will consist of H. M.'s 2nd Regt. of foot, of the (47) European Regt., with the remainder of H. M.'s 13th Lt. Infy. formed as *skirmishers* on the flanks ; the latter will push into the fort with the rear of the main-column. H. M.'s 17th Regt. will be formed in *support*, and will follow the *storming party* into the works."

5. "The whole must quit their respective encampments in column of Companies, at ¼ distance, right in front, so as to ensure their arrival at the place appointed for the *Rendezvous*, by 2 o'clock (A. M.)"

6. "Officers from H. M.'s 2nd, and 17th Regts. and (47) European Regt. to be sent to Brigr. *Sale's* camp this afternoon at 6 o'clock, for the purpose of having the place of *assembly* pointed out to them."

7. "At ½ past 12 o'clock, the Cos. of the 13th Lt. Infy. intended to act as *skirmishers*, will move up to cover, in front of the *gateway*, and be ready to keep down any fire on the party of *Engineers* who proceed to blow it open ; this last party will move up to the *gateway*, before day-break, followed, slowly and at some distance, by the *Assaulting column*."

8. "On the chief Engineer finding the opening practicable, he will have the *advance* sounded, for the column to push on ; when the Head of the column has passed the *gateway*, a *signal* must be made for the *Artillery* to turn their fire, from the walls of the town, on the *Citadel*. The nature of the signal to be arranged by Brig. *Stevenson*."

9. "At 12 o'clock P. M. 3 Cos. of Native Infy. (48) will quit camp and move round the *gardens* on the S. of the

---

(47) 1st Bengal.
(48) 35th Bengal N. I. under late Capt. *J. Hay.*

town, where they will establish themselves; and about 3
A. M. open a fire upon the place, for the purpose of distract-
ing the attention of the garrison."

10. "The Infantry of the Division not warned for duty
in the foregoing part of this Order, will be formed as a
'*Reserve*,' and will be under the personal command of Maj.
Genl. *Sir W. Cotton.*"

11. "A Regt. of Cavy. (49) will quit camp at 12 o'clock
P. M., and will move towards the southern face of the Fort,
to cut off any parties making their escape from the Fort."

12. "These movements must be made without the sound
of *Bugle*, or ***Trumpet***. The remainder of the Cavalry will
be employed in observation on the *Cabool road*, and in such
manner as the Maj. Genl. Comg. may think the best calculated to prevent the operations before the Fort, from being
interrupted; and for the protection of the camp." (50)

13. "The *camp guards* of the Infantry must continue
at their Posts, but it is expected that corps will muster, on
the present occasion, as strong as possible; (51) each Cavy.

---

(49) 3rd Bengal Cavy.

(50) Cavy. D. O. 22nd July, 1839. "A Regt. of Native Cavy. (3rd
Bengal) will quit camp at 12 o'clock to-night, and move towards the
southern face of the fort, to cut off any parties making their escape
from it. The Regt. to assemble and move off without the sound of
trumpet. A guide will we furnished by the A. Q. M. G. of Cavy."

"The remainder of the Cavalry will be formed in column of troops,
right in front, on the *Cabool road*, in rear of the Comr.-in-Chief's camp,
at 3 P. M., to turn out and form without the sound of trumpet."

"The Regts. to turn out as strong as possible. Sufficient guards
for its protection to be left in camp, upon which duty the *dismounted men*
can be employed. Comg. officers of Regts. to be provided with ' *states*'
showing the number of officers, N. C. O. and rank and file, mounted in
the field."

"The 2nd Light Cavy. (Bengal) will remain on the present ground
and be formed on this side of the fort; detaching one squadron to the
rear, for the protection of the camp."

(51) All the sick in hospital, capable of doing any duty, were put on
the inferior camp guards; it was found difficult to keep the men in hospital, they all desired to go.

Assault on Ghuznee.   177

officer to be provided with a return, showing the exact number of Commissioned, N. C. O., and Rank and File under arms with his Regt."

14. "*Suptg. Surgeons* will arrange for having a portion of their Field Hospital Establishments, in the vicinity of the Batteries; but in a hollow of the mountain, and out of range of fire."

15. "The A. Q. M. G. of cavalry and infantry will furnish *guides* to the detachments from their respective divisions, proceeding to the S. of the town."

N. B. "This order to be considered strictly *confidential* for this night, and only such portions of it to be communicated to the troops, as may be absolutely necessary to ensure compliance with its various provisions."

7. *The Assault on Ghuznee*, (23rd July, 1839.)—1. The orders were duly explained by Brigr. *Sale* (52) to the several officers Comg. corps (53) as well as to Lt.-Col. *Dennie* Comg. the "*advance*," the evening before the assault. These orders were for the "*advance*," on the sounding the "*advance*," the signal agreed on, to push into the gate-way. The "*storming party*" to follow, and on entering the fort H. M.'s 2nd Foot, and (1st) Bengal European Regt. to take the road to the *left* leading into the town. H. M.'s 13th and 17th Regts. to take the road to the *right* leading up to the *citadel*. The troops composing the above parties, were ordered to leave camp (54) a little after 2 A. M. The artil-

(52) See No. 6, of Para. 6.

(53) They were explained by Comg. officers to their 2nd in Command, that they might know how to act in case of the death, &c. of the Comg. officer.

(54) The camp was facing the hills which run in a continuation of the heights from the village of *Bullal* close to the fort. Part of the infantry were on the right, on rising ground resting near these hills. The rest of the infantry were on the left (the artillery being in the centre)—on the left of the infantry were the Cavalry; and then came the Shah's camp. The Comr.-in-Chief's camp was in rear of a garden in which there is the tomb of the late Vizier, *Futteh Khan*. The camp represented a curved-line. The *right* was about one and half mile from the fort. The left was nearer, and some shots from the enemy's 68-pr. came into the Cavalry-camp, and killed a horse, and wounded others.

2 A

lery, Engineers, and sappers and miners, and the party for the "*false attack*" moved previously, with their supports, to their assigned positions.

2.—From the *right* of the camp to the fort the distance was about one and half mile ; between this and in a direct line, there are two lofty minarets, which lie perpendicular to the gate-way, so that the troops from the *right*, marched straight down upon them; while those on the *left*, easily moved into the road by crossing into it from camp, by a direct route to their front. The wind was cold, and the temperature about 56°. (55)

As the troops were coming into position there was no sign of any one being in the fort, from the dead silence observed ; nor was a shot fired by the enemy. Some thought the place was evacuated.

The guns of the Horse Arty. and of the Light Field Batteries being already placed in position, by Lts. *Sturt* and *Anderson,* (Bengal) Engineers, to the right and left, commanding a fire on the gate-way, and on the eastern face of the fort ; and H. M.'s 13th Lt. Infy. being employed as *skirmishers,* on each side of the gate, and H. M. 17th foot, on the right of the gate-way as a " *support,*" the troops all being in position ; the attack commenced by a fire from the "*false attack,*" which had been placed to the S. of the fort.

3.—The Engineers then proceeded, with the " *explosion party*" to the gate-way, for the purpose of blowing it open, under a heavy fire ; at length the gate was blown open. The explosion was heard by nearly all. The Artillery now opened their fire, when *blue-lights* appeared all round the walls, which gave *our* party a view of the place. The object was for the guns to play on the works ; and as soon as the *signal* was given for the *advance,* to fire on the *citadel.* The signal being given, the " *advance*" moved forward under Lt.-Col. *Dennie,* accompanied by Lt. *Sturt,* Bengal Engineers, (56) when the *whole* of the troops gave *three cheers.*

(55) Within three days of the full of the moon.
(56) The same officer who distinguished himself at *Pooshoot* on the 18th Jan. 1840.

When the "*advance*" moved forward, it was about 100 yards in front of the "*storming party.*" Before the *advance* got through the gate-way, the enemy advanced sword in hand and opposed the advance, and while repulsing the *Affghans*, and by this detention the "*storming party*" under Brigr. *Sale* had closed up. The enemy being driven back, the "*advance*" charged again into the gate-way. (57) They soon got in, and then commenced a rapid *file firing*. On the "*advance*" getting into the fort (58) the enemy made a rush on the rear of the party on both flanks, wounding Lts. *Broadfoot, Magnay,* and *W. K. Haslewood* of the Light Coy. (1st) Bengal European Regt. and thirty men. (59) Lt. *Haslewood* shot the first man who attacked him, and the second, who had cut him down, was run through the body with a bayonet by a man of his company named "*Kelly ;*" and thus his life was saved. (60) The "*advance*" having entered the body of the place, pushed through into the town ; and then took the road to the *right*.

4.—The "*storming party*" under Brigr. *Sale*, while the above was going on, were exposed to a severe fire, and even when the "*advance*" had entered, the enemy made a rush and attacked the head of the *main column*, which when repulsed, the Brigadier pushed in and was wounded in the gate-way. (61) *H. M.'s 2nd foot* now were moving into

---

(57) The *Affghans* had swords and shields, and received the bayonets on them in the rushes they made at various times ; and cut at their enemy *over* and *under* their shields !

(58) The gate-way was about 150 feet *long* and about 20 feet *wide*. About half way it turned to the *right ;* so that no one could see *through* the whole distance.

(59) I don't know the names of the officers, or number of men belonging to the other Lt. Cos. ; but the chief loss was on the rear of the "*advance*," and front of the "*storming party*."

(60) Lt. *Haslewood* is very anxious to serve this man, and I hope his recommendation will be attended to.

(61) The gate-way was so completely strewed with fallen timbers, that it was difficult to walk through it without any opposition ! The Brigadier on being wounded fell among the timbers and rubbish, and

the fort, but the troops were obliged to move slowly, and as the centre square of the fort was not only not extensive, but crowded with the enemy, the Bengal European Regt. was delayed outside for sometime. On each side of the gateway are bastions, loop-holed, and here this Regt. lost most of their men, and all its officers were here wounded, except Major (now Lt.-Col.) *Warren*, and Lt. *Haslewood*, owing to the cross-fire from the bastions and parapets. As soon as the *storming party* had well entered the centre square, the enemy rushed up the ramps to the citadel, (62) and for the houses in the streets. The ramparts were crowded with *Affghans*.

5.—The *2nd Queen's* and the *Bengal European Regt.*, agreeably to the orders given, pushed into the town, to the *left*. The orders were to keep the men well hugged to the houses, so as to face the ramparts and obtain a fire on them, without suffering from their rear. This order was strictly obeyed. The streets were found empty; but the *Affghans* crowded the tops of the houses, firing at the troops as they advanced; but never came into the streets.

The *advance* of the *storming party*, having all entered, H. M.'s 13*th Lt. Infy.*, which had been *skirmishing* outside, and H. M.'s 17*th foot* (the "*support*") followed into the fort; and they, according to orders, on getting into the square,

---

called out to Capt. *Kershaw* to run the man through, while he (Brigr.) seized the sword of the man who cut him down, with his left hand; and getting up, cut his enemy right through his head, (see Para. 8 of the despatch 24th July, 1839.)

(62) As you entered the fort from the gate-way, you came into a square about 150 yards square. There were houses commanding it on three sides, while on the fourth side was the *Citadel* immediately opposite to the gate-way. There was a 68-pr. which was on commanding ground under the Citadel, while the Citadel itself commanded the square. There were two steep ramps up to the Citadel, one by the right, passing under some houses, high up, which could fire on the spuare, and on troops advancing by that road; the other ramp was to the left towards the entrance to the town. From the gate-way above, and the ramparts on that side, a fire was obtained.

The Storming of Ghuznee.

pushed up the ramp to the right, and moved up towards the *Citadel*, H. M.'s 17th foot leading. They were seen from the outside moving steadily up the second ramp leading to the small gate, the entrance into the upper fort; and every one expected to see a heavy fire from this usually strong-hold of a fortress; but the death and destruction which they saw all around appalled them; and they, here, made no opposition. (63) The *Affghans* seeing so many of their countrymen killed all around, for it commanded a view of the whole town; made their escape from its walls, and the citadel was taken possession of.

6.—The *2nd Queen's* and the *European Regt.* were in the meantime, moving down the streets of the town, towards the *Kenak* (64) *gate-way;* near this gate is the outwork, before mentioned, and in the street leading to it was the heaviest fire, a constant whizzing of matchlock balls. The *2nd Queen's* then went up the ramparts which commanded the above outwork, and from the loop-holes fired into the work; the powder in it shortly afterwards exploded, and killed and scorched many of the enemy. The *European Regt.* from this point, turned off to the *left,* and proceeded down a street which led back to the *Cabool gate,* originally entered; for the purpose of clearing the street. It was, here, that observing the party moving up to the citadel, the troops in the town expected a severe opposition would be made at the upper fort; when all of a sudden, and unexpectedly, the colors of *H. M.'s* 13*th Lt. Infy.* and *H. M.'s* 17*th* were seen flying on the top of the upper fort; and the enemy rushing down from it in all directions, to effect their

---

(63) There was an upper-roomed house to the right, in going up, where a Coy. H. M.'s 17th foot killed 58 *Affghans.* There was a heap of straw here, some stray shot struck it, a moving was observed, a shower of balls was poured in, the straw fired, only one man escaped, and he was shot close to the burning mass. This (citadel) was the residence of the Govr. (Hyder Khan), and the females of the principal people of the place were collected here. Here, too, were the magazine and granary.

(64) By some called the *Candahar* gate, being opposite to the *Cabool* gate.

escape. When about half-way down this street, a firing was heard from a house, Major (now Lt.-Col.) *Warren* turned round to his right, to see from whence the fire came, when he was struck on the left-side by three shots, one carrying away the upper part of the left wrist, the 2nd striking over the left breast, and passing over the chest; the 3rd entering the upper part of the upper right arm, shattering the bone completely. Had he not turned round, he must have been killed, as the three shots would have struck him in front. (65) The caps of almost all the men of this Regt. were riddled, owing to the enemy firing high from the houses, and many were shattered by sabre-cuts. (66)

7.—The "*Reserve*" under Maj. Genl. *Sir W. Cotton*, consisting of the 16th, 35th and 48th Bengal N. I., followed the *storming party* close in; a desultory fire was still kept up by the enemy, from the houses, and from behind walls; some ran along the ramparts to make a rush down to the gateway, and several rushes were made for this purpose, (67) which drew a fire from our troops in the citadel. When the leading Cos. of the 48th N. I., the last corps, had entered, about seventy *Affghans* made a rush between No. 1 and 2, Cos., killed two Havildars, and wounded three sepoys before sufficient space could be cleared to fire on them; when many were killed, and not a man escaped.

8.—The centre square exhibited a scene of blood and confusion; horses, many wounded, were running about in all directions, fighting with each other, kicking, and biting, and running quite furious at any one they saw; so dangerous had these animals become, that, the men were obliged to be ordered to shoot the horses in self-defence, as they

---

(65) The Grenadiers and the rear *Company* of this Regt. suffered most; excepting the Lt. Compy.

(66) A great many men were obliged, afterwards, to wear their forage caps.

(67) The ramparts were not wide, and there was no ramp except by a circuitous road, leading to this gate-way.

endangered the lives of all, and particularly of the wounded men while being carried out in Dhoolies.

9.—Opposition was kept up for some considerable time, from the houses and from behind walls, and a number of men, principally of the 35th N. I. were shot by some desperate *Affghans* who refused quarter; and lay still and concealed, till an opportunity offered of being certain of killing their opponents; and then they met their own deaths, with the satisfaction of having killed so many *Infidels*. Parties of the 16th, 35th and 48th N. I. were sent into the different streets of the town to clear them of any remaining foes.

10.—While the operations were going on *inside* the fort, the *Cavalry* were busily engaged *outside* in pursuit of those who, having descended from the walls, were trying to effect their escape into the country, and into different villages. The arrangements for the Cavalry were good, for the purpose of cutting off the flying enemy; but till day-light appeared *Sir J. Keane*, who expected *Dost Mahomed* would march to Ghuznee to try to relieve it, was desirous of having troops on the *Cabool road* for its protection; besides which, this was a measure of precaution, as a protection to the camp; and even to move against any party which might move in rear of the "*storming party;*" or attack those moving to the rear to camp. In point of fact, *Meer Ufzul Khan*, with 5,000 horse was, afterwards, found to have been *close to our camp very early in the morning*. He heard the firing, and was only waiting for day-light to see the state of affairs in *Ghuznee;* he saw the *British Flag* flying; and he, then, knew that its fate had been sealed. He immediately made the best of his way to Cabool. (68) As soon, therefore, as day-light gave a full view of the state of affairs in and in the neighbourhood of camp, the Cavalry were sent in pursuit of the fugitives. Numbers of them were cut

---

(68) *Hyder Khan*, the Govr. of Ghuznee said, his brother had nearly 5,000 horsemen outside. He abandoned his elephants, and the whole of his baggage at a village about 6 miles off. The *Shah* sent a party to secure them.

up by the Cavalry, by whom they were pursued to some distance. The 1st Bombay Cavalry alone are said to have killed upwards of fifty, with the loss of only one killed, and six wounded. (69) There must have been 150 of the enemy killed by the Cavalry, and a great number of wounded, as many were found next day in all the neighbouring villages.

11.—The "*False attack*" by the three Cos. 35th N. I. to the S. drew many of the enemy to that quarter; and being in an opposite direction from the *citadel* (*N.*) while it operated in our favor by actually drawing the governor and many of the enemy from the upper fort, and from the ramparts near the *Cabool gate*, had, also, the effect of checking the egress of those who were attempting to escape, by the ditches, and close under the walls, where Cavalry could not reach them; the party, therefore, composing the *false attack*, effected two objects; a diversion in favor of the "*storming party*," and the cutting off the garrison's retreat from that quarter, by which they might have securely reached the hills in rear of the camp.

The parties of the Native Infantry, which were sent down the different streets to clear them of any of the enemy who might be seen, had many men killed and wounded by the *Affghans* who had asked for quarter *(Aman, Aman,)* and afterwards kept up a fire from their houses.

12. H. M. *Shah Shoojah*, with the Envoy and Minister, were in rear of the "*storming party*," looking on at the

---

(69) Capt. *Outram* says, p. 99: " I was directed by H. E. to place guns to command the W. face of the fortress, over the walls of which, a number of the garrison were making their escape; after which I rode round to the E. walls to draw on a squadron of the *Lancers*, to intercept their escape by the gardens. While passing under the walls, a large body of the enemy, who were descending by a fallen tower through a breach not before observed, deterred by the sudden appearance of the Lancers, turned back; when a picquet was planted, by which egress was precluded." Some of the enemy likewise tried to push through the 2nd Cavalry, who were stationed near the S. side of the Fort, near the Bazar gate.

operations. As soon as all was quiet H. M., and the Envoy and Minister, went into the fort, and up to the citadel, where they found H. E. the Comr.-in-Chief, and a number of the staff. *Hyder Khan,* the Govr., who was there, having surrendered himself, was introduced to the *Shah* (his uncle); and *Sir J. Keane,* through the Envoy and Minister, asked the king to pardon his nephew, which he did. It was here that we found collected, a great number of prisoners, many badly wounded, and about 300 women belonging to the families of Hyder Khan and the principal men among the Affghans. Here, also, we found the magazine, and granary.

13. It was singular that the enemy should have allowed the guns, and troops to take up their positions without firing on them, and it is only to be accounted for, by relating the following fact derived from *Hyder Khan,* the Govr. himself. *Dost Mahomed* never anticipated that we should resort to the hazardous measure of blowing open the gateway. He conceived that we should proceed in the regular and usual manner by breaching, and then storm the place by *escalade.*

This he fully calculated on, and that it would occupy us a long time, by which delay, also, he hoped to complete the works he had commenced at *Cabool.* In the event of an escalade, the orders were, to man the walls, and not to fire a shot, or use any weapon, till they saw the heads of the British fairly above the walls; thus expecting to destroy a great number at once. *Hyder Khan,* the Governor, when he heard our first firing, from the *"false attack,"* went to that quarter: but, when he learnt that the British troops, were entering the fort, he galloped back to the gateway, where he met some of the Europeans. He had a bayonet run through his *Kummur-bund* (waistband), and one of his attendants, had a shot through his turban. At this moment his horse reared, and he was almost falling; if he had his life was gone. He recovered himself, and dashed away up to the citadel. He saw the place was lost, and he resolved to give himself up to the first British *officer* he saw, fearing the *men* would kill him. Capts. *A. W. Taylor,*

(70) and *G. A. Macgregor*, (71) passing by, he sent to tell them that he was in the *citadel*, and ready to give himself up on his life being spared. (72)

14. *Hyder Khan*, the Govr., who is only now about 21 years old, did not understand the probable effect which the *explosion* would produce; his chief gunner, a native of Hindostan, knew that there would be no use for *his* services any longer, and he escaped from the fort. He afterwards came in to us and said, having served in forts attacked by the British in India, that " as soon as I heard the *explosion*, I knew the gate was blown open, and that you would storm the fort and take it without escalade; and I thought it time to be off." There were a number of *Hindostanees* in the " *out-work*," and many of them were scorched by the explosion of gunpowder in the work, caused partly by the powder being loose, and by the fire of H. M.'s 2nd Queen's. These men said they had been pressed into the service, against their will. At about 8 o'clock the *European* troops were withdrawn, and Brigr. *Sale* was appointed Governor of *Ghuznee*; the 16th and 35th N. I. were left in the fortress and town, under Brigr. *Roberts*, to secure the place, guard the prisoners, and preserve the captured property. A desultory fire was kept up from some isolated houses during the day.

15. *The Loss.*—The loss on our side was seventeen killed, and eighteen Officers, and 147 N. C. O. and rank and file wounded. On the part of the enemy, the loss was very great. *Eight hundred* bodies were buried next day. There were many found dead in the houses three or four days afterwards. Many (about 150) were killed by the Cavalry, and about 300 bodies are said, altogether, to have been found outside (73), probably many of these wounded men who had escaped from the place, died of their wounds: so that

---

(70) 1st Bengal Eurn. Regt. and M. B. 4th Brigade.
(71) Bengal Arty. and Asst. to the Envoy and Minister.
(72) The account given by himself while a prisoner.
(73) 180 were counted round about the gate-way, within 20 yards.

there must have been 1,200 of the enemy killed, and about 300 wounded, and 1,500 prisoners were taken; (some among the wounded,) which, allowing for some to have escaped, will make the garrison to have amounted to 3,000 men; exactly the number stated by *Hyder Khan*, and found in the *Duftur*, or Register of the troops.

16. *Wounded Officers.*—Brigr. (now Maj. Genl. *Sir R. H.*) *Sale* was wounded in the chin, but was able to continue with the troops till the fort was fairly ours, and only left it at the urgent request of the surgeon, as he was bleeding much; after having given the necessary orders to the troops, the Comr.-in-Chief being in the fort himself, at the time. (74)

Major (now Lt.-Col.) *Warren*, 1st Bengal European Regt. was wounded in three different places, one shot carrying away the upper part of the left wrist, which was so far dangerous that for two or three days a lock-jaw was apprehended; a second shot by a ball striking the left breast and passing over the surface of the chest; the third shot entered the upper part of the upper right arm, shattering the bone completely. This was the *same* arm which was very severely wounded by a sabre cut on the shoulder at the escalade of the *Jungeenah-gate,* at *Bhurtpoor,* on the 18th Jan. 1826. (75) The surgeons wished to amputate the arm, thinking it was necessary to save his life; but, he, at once, decided on taking his chance as to the result.

(74) This gallant officer entered the army on the 19th Jan. 1795. Served as Lieut. in the 12th Regt. at the siege and storm of *Seringhapatam,* in May, 1799. Served with great distinction in the *Burmese War,* and was severely wounded on the 15th Dec. 1824 (as senior Major in command of H. M.'s 13th Lt. Infy.) in one of the numerous assaults of the *Burmese stockades.*

(75) He has likewise a severe sabre cut on the left side of his face, lost the upper joint of his left thumb, the cut rendering two of his fingers useless; so that had he lost his *right* arm, he would have had a useless *left* one. On the occasion of the above escalading party by two Cos. 1st Bengal European Regt., Lt. *Candy* was killed, all the officers were severely wounded; of whom Lt.-Col. W. is the only surviving officer.

Lt. *W. K. Haslewood*, 1st Bengal European Regt. was very severely wounded. He received five wounds by sword-cuts. One on the head which knocked him down ; one on the right shoulder joint, very severe ; one lower down, and another crossing it : and a very severe wound in the right hip, several inches in extent. (76)

Capt. *H. M. Graves*, 16th Bengal N. I. was severely and badly wounded in the shoulder and hip. Capt. *O. Robinson*, and Lt. *G. N. K. A. Yonge*, of the 2nd Queen's, were severely wounded ; the former, by a sabre cut on the *head*; and the latter by a match-lock ball in the groin. The other officers were slightly wounded. (77) Major (now Lt.-Col.) *Parsons* was wounded in the cheek near the Comr.-in-Chief, on the heights of Bullal. The Rt. Hon. Earl of Auckland, Govr. Genl. has kindly noticed Lt.-Col. *Warren* and Lt. *Haslewood*, by appointing the former to be officiating Town Major, and the latter to be an A. D. C. on his Lordship's personal; these appointments, while they are gratefully received by them, are duly appreciated by their brother officers ; and afford convincing proofs of Lord Auckland's desire to reward those who suffer in their country's cause. (78)

8. *Orders after the storm.*—(G. O. C. C. 23rd July, 1839.)—1. "Brigr. *Sale*, C. B. is appointed Comdt. of *Ghuznee*, and will immediately order such arrangements as may appear to him necessary, for restoring order in the fort; and for securing the *property* for the benefit of the *captors.*"

(76) From the nature of the wounds it was to be expected that Lt. Haslewood would never thoroughly recover the use of either the arm or leg ; and although returned "*severely wounded*," in order not to cause too much alarm to his friends in England, he might, with propriety, (as declared by the Surgeons) have been returned "*dangerously* wounded ;" the wounds are likely to cause more pain and constitutional disturbance than the loss of a *limb*.

(77) Capt. *Barston*, Bengal 37th N. I. and Lt. *H. Palmer* 48th Bengal N. I. were severely wounded, the former in the "*Bolan Pass*," and the latter before entering the Pass.

(78) Capt. *Graves* has been appointed Offg. Agent for 1st Division of army clothing.

To secure the Place and Property.

2. "The Maj. Genl. Comg. the 1st Division of Infantry, will comply with such requisitions as he may receive from the Brigadier, for troops, for securing the place, until a proper garrison may be provided."

"Every *gate-way* in the fort, with the exception of the *Cabool* gate, is to be effectually blocked up, (79) and the chief Engineer will be pleased to send down parties of Sappers, to carry this order into operation. The Brigr. will direct *patrols* to be sent throughout the *town*, to prevent plundering; and to turn out every camp-follower and soldier, not on duty in the place."

4. "The Maj. Genl. Comg. the *Cavalry* will direct Detts. from the 4th L. D. and 16th Lancers to be sent into the *town*, with fifty syces, (80) for the purpose of bringing out all the *horses, camels*, and *bullocks*, which may be found in the place. These are to be picqetted in some convenient situation in the Bengal Cavy. lines; and a suitable *guard* placed over them, until they can be disposed of."

5. "All the horses, camels, and bullocks, already brought out, either by officers, or their followers, are to be immediately sent to the same place; and any person failing to comply with this order, will be dealt with, as having disobeyed a positive command; and all who may *purchase* horses, &c. which can be *identified* (81) as having been captured, will be required to restore them."

6. "It is believed, that individuals are now offering horses for sale, that were taken out of the *fort;* and all are enjoined to abstain from making purchases of them. Officers in command are required to send all such as may be

---

(79) The other gate-ways were not, as far as I could see, built up with masonry, as I saw no rubbish near the S. gate.

(80) Grooms.

(81) The fact is, that before the order came out, camp-followers and others had taken off a great many horses, &c, and the process of cutting the *tail*, &c. soon prevented *identification*. The *Shah's* camp got its share.

presented in their lines, to the place appointed for their being collected." (82)

7. "Depy. Provost Marshal *Parry*, at present doing duty with the 4th Brigade, is directed to place himself under the orders of the Comdt. of Ghuznee."

8. "A *main picquet* will mount, immediately, on the *Cabool road* consisting of two guns, a squadron of Cavy. (4th L. D.,) and of two Cos. of Infy. the latter to be furnished by the Bengal Division."

9. *Order of thanks.*—G. O. by H. E. Lt.-Genl. Sir *J. Keane*, Comr.-in-Chief of the "*Army of the Indus.*" Hd. Qrs., camp Ghuznee 23rd July, 1839.

1. "Lt.-Gen. *Sir J. Keane*, most heartily congratulates the army he has the honor to command, on the signal triumph they have this day obtained in the capture, by storm, of the strong and important fortress of *Ghuznee*. H. E. feels that he can hardly do justice to the gallantry of the troops."

2. "The scientific and successful manner in which the Cabool gate (of great strength) was blown open by Capt. Thomson of the Bengal Engineers, the chief of that Dept. with this army, in which he reports having been most ably assisted by Capt. *Peat*, of the Bombay Engineers, and Lts. *Durand* and *McLeod*, of the Bengal Engineers, in the daring and dangerous enterprise of laying down powder in the face of the enemy, and the strong fire kept upon them, reflects the highest credit on their skill and cool courage, and H. E. begs Capt. *Thomson*, and the officers named, will accept his cordial thanks. His acknowledgments are also due to the other Officers of the Engineers of both presidencies, and to the valuable corps of sappers and miners under them. This opening having been made, although it was a

---

(82) "Maj. Genl. *Thackwell* will place an officer of Cavy. in charge of these horses, and they will be subsisted by the Comsst. Dept., and the same Dept. will, likewise, supply *rope* to fasten them to their picquets; the expense incurred in their *feed* and in the supply of *rope*, must be charged against the *Prize Fund*, hereafter."

difficult one to enter by, from the rubbish in the gate-way; the leading column, in a spirit of true gallantry, directed and led by Brigr. *Sale*, gained a footing inside the fortress; although opposed by the *Affghan* soldiers in very great strength, and in the most desperate manner with every kind of weapon."

3. "The advance under Lt.-Col. *Dennie*, of H. M.'s 13th, consisting of the Lt. Cos. of H. M.'s 2nd and 17th, and of the (1st) Bengal European Regt., with one Compy. of H. M.'s 13th; and leading column, consisting of H. M.'s 2nd Queen's under Maj. *Carruthers*, and the (1st) Bengal European Regt. under Lt.-Col. *Orchard;* followed by H. M.'s 13th Light Infy., under Major *Tronson*, as they collected from the duty of *skirmishing* which they were to begin with; and by H. M.'s 17th under Lt.-Col. *Croker.*"

4. "To all those officers, and to the other officers and gallant soldiers under their orders, H. E.'s best thanks are tendered, but in particular, he feels deeply indebted to Brigr. *Sale*, for the manner in which he conducted the arduous duty entrusted to him in command of the "*storming party.*" H. E. will not fail to bring it to the notice of His Lordship the Govr. Genl.; and he trusts the wound which Brigr. *Sale* has received, is not of the severe nature, long to deprive this army of his services. Brigr. *Sale* reports, that Capt. *Kershaw* of H. M.'s 13th Lt. Infy., rendered important assistance to him, and to the service in the storming."

5. "Sir J. *Keane* was happy on this proud occasion, to have the assistance of his old comrade Maj. Genl. *Sir Willoughby Cotton*, who in command of the "*Reserve*," ably executed the instructions he had received, and was at the gate ready to enter after the "*storming party*" had established themselves inside; when he moved through it to sweep the ramparts, to complete the subjugation of the place with the 16th Bengal N. I., under Maj. *MacLaren*, Brigr. *Roberts* with the 35th N. I. under Lt.-Col. *Monteath*, and the 48th N. I., under Lt.-Col. *Wheeler*. His arrangements afterwards, in continuation of those Brigr. *Sale*, had made, for the security of the magazine and other public stores, were such as met H. E.'s high approval."

6. "The Comr.-in-Chief acknowledges the services rendered by Capt. *Hay*, of the 35th N. I. in command of three Cos. of the Regt. sent to the *South* side of the fortress to begin with a "*false attack*," and which was executed at the proper time, and in a manner highly satisfactory to His Excellency."

7. "Nothing could be more judicious than the manner in which Brigr. *Stevenson* placed the artillery in position. Capt. *Grant's* troop of Bengal Arty. and camel-battery under Capt. *Abbott*, both superintended by Major *Pew;* the two troops of Bombay H. A. commanded by Capts. *Martin* and *Cotgrave*, and Capt. *Lloyd's* battery of Bombay foot Arty. all opened upon the citadel and fortress, in a manner which shook the enemy, and did execution so as completely to paralize and to strike terror into them; and H. E. begs Brigr. *Stevenson* and the officers and men of that Arm, will accept his thanks for their good service."

8. "The 19th Regt. Bombay N. I. under the command of Lt.-Col. *Stalker*, having been placed in position to watch any enemy that might appear on the *Cabool* road, or approach to attack the camp, had an important post assigned to them; although as it happened, no enemy made an attack upon them."

9 "In sieges and stormings, it does not fall to the lot of Cavalry to bear the same conspicuous part as the two other arms of the profession. On this occasion, Sir J. *Keane* is happy to have an opportunity of thanking Maj. Genl. *Thackwell*, and the officers and men of the Cavalry Division under his orders, for having successfully executed the directions given, to sweep the plain and to intercept fugitives of the enemy attempting to escape from the fort, in any direction around it; and, had an enemy appeared, for the relief of the place during the storming, H. E. is fully satisfied that the different Regts. of this fime arm would have distinguished themselves, and that the opportunity alone was wanting."

10. "Maj. Genl. *Willshire's* Division having been broken up for the day to be distributed as it was, the Maj. Genl.

was desired to be in attendance upon the Comr.-in-Chief. To him and to the officers of the Adjt. and Qr. Mr. Genl.'s Dept. of the Bengal and Bombay army, H. E. returns his warmest thanks for the assistance they have afforded him."

11. "The Comr.-in-Chief feels, and in which feeling he is sure he will be joined by the troops composing the " *Army of the Indus*," that after the long and harassing marches they have had, and the privations they have endured, this glorious achievement, and the brilliant manner in which the troops have met and conquered their enemy, rewards them for it all. H. E. will only add, that no army that has ever been engaged in a campaign, deserves more credit than that which he has the honor to command, for patient, orderly, and correct conduct, under all circumstances; and Sir J. *Keane* is proud to have the opportunity of thus publicly acknowledging it."

By order of H. E. Lt.-Genl. Sir J. Keane, Comr.-in-Chief of the Army of the Indus.

(Signed.) *R. Macdonald*, Lt.-Col., Mily. Secy. and D. A. G. H. M.'s forces, Bombay.

10. *Report of the Chief Engineer.* (83)

1. "*Arrival before Ghuznee.*—The accounts of the fortress of *Ghuznee*, received from those who had seen it, were such as to induce his Excy. the Comr.-in-Chief to leave in *Candahar* the very small *battering train* then with the army, there being a scarcity of transport cattle. The place was described as very weak, and completely commanded from a range of hills to the north."

---

(83) This Report, it is admitted by competent judges, contains so clear an account of the nature of the works; their strength; and of the operations before *Ghuznee*, as well as of the storm, that I have long hesitated in my humble attempt, to describe what I only partially saw myself: but, as I obtained a knowledge of some facts not generally known, or which would not form the subject matter of such a report, or even of a despatch, and thinking the details might be interesting, I made up my mind, to endeavour to relate them as concisely, and in the order in which they occurred.

2. "When we came before it on the morning of the 21st July, we were very much surprised to find a high rampart in good repair, built on a scarped mound about 35 feet high, flanked by numerous towers and surrounded by a *Fausse braye*, and a wet-ditch. The irregular figure of the *enceinte* gave a good flanking fire, whilst the height of the *citadel* covered the interior from the commanding fire of the hills to the N., rendering it nugatory. In addition to this, the towers at the angles had been enlarged; screen walls had been built before the gates; the ditch cleared out, and filled with water (stated to be unfordable), and an outwork built on the right bank of the river, so as to command the bed of it. The garrison was variously stated to be from 3 to 4,000 strong, including 500 Cavalry. From subsequent information we found that it had been over-rated." (84)

3. "On the approach of the army a fire of artillery was opened from the body of the place, and of musketry from the neighbouring gardens. A detachment of Infantry cleared the latter, and the former was silenced for a short time by shrapnells from the Horse Artillery. But the fire from the new out-work on the bank of the river was in no way checked. A nearer view of the works was however obtained from the gardens which had been cleared. This was not at all satisfactory; the works were evidently much stronger than we had been led to anticipate, and such as our army could not venture to attack in a regular manner with the means at our disposal. We had no *Battering train*, and, to attack *Ghuznee* in form, a much larger train would be required than the army ever possessed. The great height of the *Parapet* above the *Plain* (60 *or* 70 *feet*), with the wet ditch were insurmountable obstacles to an attack merely by *mining* or *escalading*."

4. "*Reconnoissance*.—It therefore became requisite to examine closely the whole "*contour*" of the place, to discover if any other mode of attack could be adopted. The Engineers, with an escort, went round the works, ap-

---

(84) Ascertained to have been 3,000.

proaching as near as they could find cover; the garrison were on the alert, and kept up a hot and well-directed fire on the officers whenever they were obliged to show themselves. However, by keeping the *Infantry* beyond musket-range, and the *Cavalry* at a still greater distance, only one man was killed, and one wounded, and the former was hit by the men sent out of the place, to drive off the reconnoitring party."

5. "The fortifications were found equally strong all round, the only tangible point observed was the " *Cabool gate-way,*" which offered the following advantages for a *coup-de-main*; the road up to the gate was clear; the bridge over the ditch was unbroken; there were good positions for the *Artillery* within 350 yards of the walls on both sides of the road; and we had information that the gateway was not built up, a reinforcement from *Cabool* being expected."

6. " The result of this *reconnoissance* was a report to H. E. the Comr.-in-Chief, that, if he decided on the immediate attack of *Ghuznee,* the *only* feasible mode of attack, and the only one which held out a prospect of success, was a dash at the *Cabool gate-way,*—blowing the gate open by bags of powder."

7. " H. E. decided on the attempt; the camp was moved that evening to the Cabool-road, and next morning *(the 22nd)* Sir *J. Keane,* in person, reconnoitred the proposed point of attack;—he approved of the plan, and gave orders for its execution. Preparations were made accordingly; positions for the Artillery were carefully examined, which excited the jealousy of the garrison, who opened a smart fire on the party."

7. *Preparations for and Blowing open the gate.*—" It was arranged that an *explosion party*, consisting of three Officers of Engineers, Capt. *Peat* (Bombay,) Lts. *Durand* and *Macleod,* (Bengal,) three Serjeants, and eighteen men of the sappers, (85) in working dresses, carrying 300*lbs*. *of powder* in twelve sand-bags, with a hose 72 feet long, should be ready to move down to the gateway at day-break.

(85) Native soldiers.

At midnight the first battery left camp, followed by the other four, at intervals of half an hour. Those to the *right* of the road were conducted to their positions by Lt. *Sturt* of the (Bengal) Engineers, those to the *left* by Lt. *Anderson* (Bengal); the ground for the guns was prepared by the Sappers and Pioneers, taking advantage of the inequalities of the ground on the *right*, and of some old garden-walls on the *left*. The *Artillery* were all in position and ready by 3 A. M. of the 23rd; and shortly after, at the *first dawn*, the party under Capt. *Peat* moved down to the gateway, accompanied by six men of H. M.'s 13th Light Infy. without their belts, and supported by a detachment of the same Regt. which extended to the right and left of the road when they arrived at the ditch, taking advantage of what cover they could find; and endeavouring to keep down the fire from the ramparts, which became heavy on the approach of the party; though it had been remarkably slack during the previous operations. *Blue-lights* were shewn which rendered the surrounding objects distinctly visible; but, luckily, they were burned from the top of the parapet, (86) instead of being thrown into the passage below."

8. "The *explosion party* marched steadily on, headed by Lt. *Durand;* the *powder* was placed; the *hose* laid, (87) the *train* fired: and the carrying party, retired to a tolerable cover in less than two minutes. The *Artillery* opened when the *blue-lights* appeared, and the *musketry* from the covering party at the same time, so quickly was the operation performed, and so little were the enemy aware of the nature of it, that not a man of the party was hit."

9. "As soon as the *explosion* took place, Capt. *Peat*, though hurt, his anxiety preventing his keeping sufficiently under cover, ran up to the gate (accompanied by a small party of H. M.'s 13th Lt. Infy.) and ascertained, that it

(86) A shot from the camel-battery cut a man into two, who was holding a *Blue-light* near the top of the gate-way.

(87) On the first application of the port-fire to the hose the powder would not ignite.

was completely destroyed. There was some delay in getting a bugler to sound the ' *advance*,' the *signal* agreed on for the *assaulting* column to push on; and this was the only mistake in the operation."

10. *The Storm*.—" The assaulting column consisted of four European Regts.* commanded by Brigr. *Sale*. The *advance* under Lt.-Col. *Dennie*, accompanied by Lt. *Sturt*, Engineers, moved steadily through the gate-way, through a passage inside the gate, ending in a domed-building with the opening on one side, which made every thing very obscure; and rendered it difficult to find the out-let into the town. They met with little opposition; but a party of the enemy, seeing a break in the column, owing to the difficulty in scrambling over the rubbish in the gate-way; made a *rush, sword in hand*, and cut down a good many men, wounding the *Brigadier* and several other officers. These swordsmen were repulsed, and there was no other regular opposition; the surprise and alarm of the governor and sirdars being so great, when they saw the column occupying the open space inside the gate and firing on them, that they fled, accompanied by their men; even the garrison of the *citadel* following their example. Parties of the *Affghans* took refuge in houses, firing on the column as it made its way through the streets; and a good deal of desultory firing took place in consequence, by which some loss was sustained. The *citadel* was occupied as soon as day-light showed that it had been evacuated by the enemy; and the whole of the works were in our possession before 5 o'clock A. M."

* H. M. 2nd Queen's (1st) Bengal European Regt. H. M.'s 13th Lt. Infy. H. M.'s 17th Foot.

11. *Loss*.—" We lost 17 men (6 Europeans and 11 Natives), *killed*; 18 *officers*, 117 Europeans, and 30 Natives *wounded*; total 182. Of the *Affghans* more than 514 were *killed* in the *town*, that number of bodies having been *buried*; and about 100 outside by the *Cavalry* : 1,600 *prisoners*, were taken; but I have no means of estimating the number of *wounded*."

12. *Guns, Stores, &c*.—" There were nine guns of different calibres, found in the place; a large quantity of good

powder; considerable stores of shot, lead, &c.; and a large supply of attah (flour), and other provisions." (88)

(Signed) *Geo. Thomson,*
Chief Engineer, Army of the Indus.
Camp, *Ghuznee,* 25th July, 1839.
To Colonel *D. MacLeod,*
Chief Engineer, Bengal Army.

11. *Observations of the Chief Engineer, Bombay Column.*
(89)—1. " During the reconnoissance, the *wall-pieces* were particularly troublesome. This weapon is almost unknown in our service, but is a very efficient one, especially in the defence of works; and its use should not be neglected. Every fortified post should be supplied with a proportion of them; and a certain number of men in every Regt. practised in firing them."

2. " The charge recommended by Col. *Pasley,* for blowing open gates, is from 60 to 120lbs., and this is doubtless sufficient in ordinary cases, but in this instance we were apprehensive that the enemy might have taken alarm at our being so much on that side of the place, and in consequence have partially or wholly built up the gate-way. It was afterwards found that some attempts of the kind had been made by propping up the gate with beams." (90)

---

(88) See Table, No. 4, Appendix.

(89) From Capt. *Outram,* pp. 197 to 200. As Capt. (now Major) *Peat's* observations contain some points of interest they are inserted here, as they explain the reasons for the great quantity of powder used, and other matters relative to Asiatic sieges.

(90) The gate-way was strewed with timbers, which lay in it as if they had been placed in nearly parallel lines, with rubbish between them. That the gate was propped up with timbers there can be no doubt; and it is probable (by being fastened across the gate one above the other), that when the explosion took place, those which were uppermost were blown to the greatest distance, thus scattering them along the whole range. The effect of the explosion on the roof, appeared to be about the centre, where there was a *recess* to the *left;* just beyond which, the gate-way took a turn to the *right.*

3. "The charge was so heavy, that it not only destroyed the gate but brought down a considerable portion of the roof of the square building in which it was placed; which proved a very considerable obstacle to the assaulting column, and the concussion acted as far as a tower under which an officer's party of H. M.'s 13th Lt. Infy., were standing at the time, but without occasioning any casualties. In cases of this nature it is of course the first object to guard against any chance of failure, and it is impossible even, now, to say how much the charge might have been reduced with safety."

4. "The enemy appeared so much on the alert, and the *Fausse-braye* was so much in advance of the gate, that we never contemplated being able to effect our object by surprise. The only question was whether it ought to be done by *day*, or *night*. It was argued in favor of the former, that the *Artillery* would be able to make so much more correct *practice*, that the defences would be in a considerable degree destroyed, and the fire so completely kept under, as to enable the "*explosion party*" to advance with but little loss, and with the advantage of being able to see exactly what they were about. *Capt. Thomson*, however, adhered to the latter, and we were afterwards convinced it was the most judicious plan; for although the fire of the *Artillery* was necessarily more general than it would have been in *day-light*, still it was so well directed, as to take up a good deal of the attention of the besieged, and draw upon *their batteries* a portion of the fire which in day-light would have been thrown upon the "*explosion party*," and "*assaulting columns.*"

5. "It would also, even in day-light, have been difficult with our light Artillery to have kept down the fire so completely but that a few match-lock-men might have kept their position near the gate-way, and in that narrow space a smart fire, from a few pieces, might have obliged the party to retire. The obscurity of the *night*, to say nothing of the *confusion* which it must occasion among undisciplined troops, is certainly the best protection to a body of men engaged in

an enterprise of this nature. *Blue-lights* certainly render objects distinctly visible, but their light is glaring and uncertain, especially to men firing through loop-holes." (91)

6. "The party of H. M.'s 13th Lt. Infy. consisted of 18 Officers; 28 Serjeants; 7 Buglers; 276 Rank and File." It was made of this strength, not only to keep up a heavy fire upon the parapets, and thereby divert attention from the party at the *gate-way*, but also, because we were not aware whether the *Fausse-braye* was occupied or not; and as it extends so much in advance as to take the gate completely in *reverse*, it would have been necessary, had a fire opened from it, to have carried it by assault, before the party with the bags could have advanced.

7. "The party with *Lt. Durand* (Bengal) was accompanied by six men of the 13th Lt. Infy. without their belts, the better to secure them from observation, to protect them from any "*sortie*" that might be made from the "*postern* of the *Fausse-braye* on the *right*, or even from the gate itself; while another party under Lt. *P. R. Jennings*, (92) accompanied them as far as the tower, so as to check any attempts that might have been made from the *Fausse-braye*, on the *left*, and at the same time keeping up a fire on such of the enemy as shewed their heads above the parapet; of this party, one man was killed and a few wounded." "Nothing could have been more gallant than the conduct of *Lts. Durand* and *McLeod*, (Bengal Engrs.) and the men under their command, or more efficient than the manner in which they executed their duty."

8. "The *powder* being in bags, of a very coarse, open texture, a long hose and port fire, was thought to be the safest method of firing it. The end of the hose fortunately

---

(91) The ancient use of "*Blue-lights*" was, to place them in such a situation as to be level with the lower part of a wall, so as to throw a light directly forward on the ground, by which the besieged could distinguish any one approaching the wall, or counterscarp of a ditch, &c.

(92) H. M.'s 13th Lt. Infy.

just reached the small "*postern.*" (93) "The casualties during this operation were much fewer than was expected, being in all one private *killed;* 2 Serjts. and 23 rank and file *wounded.*"

9. "The heaviest fire was certainly outside the bridge, for the enemy near the gate-way being marked whenever they attempted to shew their heads above the parapet, were obliged to confine themselves to the loop-holes, the range from which is very uncertain and limited, against men moving about. A high loop-holed wall, although imposing in appearance, is a profile but ill adapted to resist attacks of this nature." (94)

10. "The enemy were perfectly aware that we were in the gateway, but appeared to have no idea of the nature of our operations. Had they been so, they might easily have rendered it impossible to place the powder bags; by throwing over *blue-lights,* of which they had a large quantity in store."

11. "The *powder-pots* and other *fire-works,* so much used by the Natives of *Hindostan,* would certainly have rendered the confined space leading to the gate, much too hot for such an operation; but the ignorance of the besieged was known and calculated upon; the result shows how justly."

12. "Their attempts at resistance were confined to the fire from the *loop-holes,* and throwing over large pieces of earth, some of which appeared to be intended to knock off the portfire."

13. "The *gate-way* appeared from what I had seen from the hills to the N. to lead *straight* into the town. I was led to believe that the gate-way had been blocked up, from seeing in front of the gate that had been destroyed, the

---

(93) Lt. *Durand* was obliged to scrape the *hose* with his finger-nails, finding the powder failed to ignite on the first application of the *port fire.* This sometimes happens owing to the powder getting damp.

(94) In the *citadel* the loop-holes did not command a fire on the works below. The shots fired from the *citadel* would not strike those within 200 yards of the *ditch* round the fort.

outline of an arch filled up with brick-masonry. (95)
The true entrance turned to the right, and would have
been discovered by advancing a few paces, and that in perfect safety; for the interior was secure from all fire."

14. "Lt. *Durand,* on first going up, saw from through
the chinks of the gate—that there was a *light,* and a guard
immediately behind it; and, from that circumstance, was
convinced that no interior obstacles of importance existed."

15. "A party of *Sappers* with felling axes, and commanded by *Lt. Wemyss* (Bombay Engrs.) and two scaling
ladders in charge of *Lt. Pigou,* (Bengal Engrs.) accompanied
the assaulting column, intended for the citadel if required."

16. "Of ten Engineer Officers engaged in this attack,
only one, *Lt. Marriot* (Bombay,) was slightly wounded.
Capt. Thomson (Bengal) however had a very narrow escape,
having been thrown down by the rush of some swordsmen
into the gateway," (96) "and nearly sabred while upon
the ground."

(Signed) A. G. Peat, Capt.
Bombay Engineers.

12. *Despatch from H. E. Lt.-Genl. Sir J. Keane, on the
capture of Ghuznee.*—G. O. by the Comdr. of the Forces,
Head Quarters, Meerut, 27th (97) August, 1839. By
the Right Hon'ble the Govr. General. Simlah ; 27th
August, 1839.

"The Right Hon'ble the Govr. Genl. is pleased to direct,
that the following notification, issued from the *Secret Dept.*
under date the 18th Inst. and the report from His Excy. the
Comr.-in-Chief of the "*Army of the Indus,*" announcing
the capture, by storm, of the important fortress of *Ghuznee,*
therein referred to, be published in Genl. Orders, for the
information of the armies of the three Presidencies."

---

(95) The gate-way took a turn to the *right* when half way through.
(96) When they cut in between the "*Advance*" and the "*Storming
party.*"
(97) Mistake as to date.

Operations before Ghuznee.

Notification.

Secret Department; Simlah, the 18th August, 1839.

The Right Hon'ble the Govr. Genl. of India has great gratification in publishing for general information, a copy of a report this day received from His Excy. Lieut.-Genl. *Sir J. Keane*, K. C. B. &c. Comr.-in-Chief of the "*Army of the Indus*," announcing the capture, by storm, on the 23rd ultimo of the important fortress of "*Ghuznee*."

A salute of twenty-one guns will be fired on the receipt of this intelligence at all the principal stations of the Army in the three Presidencies."

By order, &c.

(Signed) T. H. Maddock,
Offg. Secy. to Govt. of India,
with the Govr. General.

Head Quarters, Camp, *Ghuznee*, 24th July, 1839.

To the Right Hon'ble Lord *Auckland*, G. C. B. &c. &c. &c.

My Lord,

1. "I have the satisfaction to acquaint your Lordship, that the army under my command has succeeded in performing one of the most brilliant acts it has ever been my lot to witness, during my service of 45 years, in the four quarters of the globe, in the capture, by storm, of the strong and important fortress and citadel of *Ghuznee*, yesterday."

2. "It is not only that the *Affghan* nation, and I understand *Asia* generally, have looked upon it as impregnable, but it is in reality a place of great strength, both by nature and art, far more so than I had reason to suppose from any description that I have received of it; although some are from officers from our own service, who had seen it in their travels."

3. "I was surprised to find a high rampart in good repair, built on a scarped mound, about 35 feet high, flanked by numerous towers, and surrounded by a '*Fausse-braye*' and a wet ditch, whilst the height of the '*Citadel*' covered the interior from the commanding fire of the Hills from the north, rendering it nugatory. In addition

to this, screen walls had been built before the gates; the ditch was filled with water and unfordable, and an out-work built on the right bank of the river, so as to command the bed of it."

4. "It is therefore the more honorable to the troops, and must appear to the enemy out of all calculation extraordinary, that a fortress and citadel, to the strength of which, for the last 30 years, they had been adding something each year, and which had a garrison of 3,500 Affghan soldiers, commanded by *Prince Mahomed Hyder*, the son of *Dost Mahomed Khan*, the ruler of the country, with a commanding number of guns, and abundance of ammunition and other stores, provisions, &c. for a regular siege, should be taken by British science and British valour, in less than two hours from the time the attack was made, and the whole, including the Govr. and garrison, should fall into our hands."

5. "My dispatch of the 20th Inst. from *Nannee*, will have made known to your Lordship, that the camp of *His Majesty Shah Shoojah-ool-Moolk*, and of Major-Genl. *Willshire*, with the Bombay troops, had there joined me in accordance with my desire; and the following morning we made our march of 12 miles to *Ghuznee*. The line of march being over a fine plain, the troops were disposed in a manner that would have enabled me at any moment, had we been attacked, as was probable from the large bodies of troops moving on each side of us, to have placed them in position to receive the enemy. They did not however appear, but on our coming within range of the guns of the citadel and fortress of *Ghuznee*, a smart cannonade was opened on our leading columns, together with a heavy fire of musketry from behind garden walls, and temporary field-works thrown up, as well as the strong out-work I have already alluded to, which commanded the bed of the river. From all but the out-work the enemy were driven in, under the walls of the fort, in a spirited manner by parties thrown forward by Maj.-Genl. *Sir W. Cotton*, of the 16th and 48th Bengal N. I., and H. M.'s 13th Lt. Infy. under Brigr.

Sale. I ordered forward three troops of Horse Arty., the camel-battery and one foot-battery, to open upon the citadel and fortress by throwing shrapnell shells, which was done in a masterly style, under the direction of Brigr. *Stevenson.* My object in this was to make the enemy show their strength in guns, and in other respects, which completely succeeded, and our shells must have done great execution and occasioned great consternation. Being perfectly satisfied on the point of their strength, in the course of half an hour, I ordered the fire to cease, and placed the troops *en bivouac.* A close *reconnoissance* of the place all round was then undertaken by Capt. *Thomson,* the chief Engineer, and Capt. *Peat* of the Bombay Engineers, accompanied by Major *Garden,* the Depy. Qr. Mr. Genl. of the Bengal army, supported by a strong party of H. M.'s 16th Lancers, (98) and one of H. M.'s 13th Lt. Infy. On this party, a steady fire was kept up and some casualties occurred. Capt. *Thomson's* report was very clear, (he found the fortifications equally strong all round) and as my own opinion coincided with his, I did not hesitate a moment as to the manner in which our approach and attack upon the place should be made ; notwithstanding the march the troops had performed in the morning, and their having been a considerable time engaged with the enemy, I ordered the whole to move across the river, (which runs close under the fort walls) in columns to the right and left of the town, and they were placed in position on the *north* side, on more commanding ground, and securing the *Cabool* road. I had information that a night attack upon the camp was intended from without. *Mahomed Ufzul Khan,* the eldest son of *Dost Mahomed Khan,* had been sent by his father with a strong body of troops from Cabool to his brother's assistance at Ghuznee, and was encamped outside the walls, but abandoned his position on our approach, keeping however at the distance of a few miles from us. The two rebel

---

(98) A mistake for the 2nd Bengal Lt. Cavy.

chiefs of the *Gilzie* tribe, men of great influence ; viz. *Abdool Rhuman*, and *Gool Mahomed Khan*, had joined him with 1,500 Horse, and also a body of 3,000 *Ghazees* from *Zeinat* under a mixture of chiefs and Moolahs, carrying banners, and who had been assembled on the cry of a religious war. In short, we were, in all directions, surrounded by enemies. These last actually came down the Hills on the 22nd, and attacked the part of the camp occupied by His Majesty Shah Shoojah, and his troops; but were driven back with considerable loss, and banners taken."

6. "At daylight on the 22nd I reconnoitred *Ghuznee*, in company with the chief Engineer, and the Brigr. Comg. the Arty., with the Adjt. and Qr. Mr. Genl. of the Bengal Army, for the purpose of making all arrangements for carrying the place by storm, and these were completed in the course of the day. Instead of the tedious process of breaching, (for which we were ill prepared) Capt. *Thomson* undertook, with the assistance of Capt. *Peat*, of the Bombay Engineers, Lieuts. *Durand* and *MacLeod*, of the Bengal Engineers, and other officers under him, (Capt. *Thomson*) to blow in the *Cabool gate* (the weakest point) with gunpowder ; and so much faith did I place on the success of the operation, that my plans for the assault were immediately laid down, and the orders given."

7. "The different troops of Horse Arty., the camel and foot batteries, moved off their ground at 12 o'clock that night, without the slightest noise, as had been directed, and in the most correct manner, took up the position assigned them, about 250 yards from the walls; in like manner, and with the same silence, the Infantry soon after moved from their ground, and all were at their post at the proper time. A few minutes before 3 o'clock in the morning, the "*explosion*" took place, and proved completely successful. Capt. *Peat*, of the Bombay Engineers, was thrown down and stunned by it, but shortly after recovered his senses and feeling. On hearing the advance sounded by the bugles, (being the signal for the gate having been blown in) the Artillery, under the able directions of Brigr. *Stevenson*, consist-

ing of Capt. *Grant's* Troop of Bengal Horse Arty., the camel-battery under Capt. *Abbott*, both superintended by Major *Pew*, Captains *Martin's* and *Cotgrave's* troops of Bombay Horse Arty., and Capt. *Lloyd's* battery of Bombay Foot Arty., all opened a terrific fire upon the citadel and ramparts of the Fort, and in a certain degree paralyzed the enemy."

8. " Under the guidance of Capt. *Thomson* of the Bengal Engrs. the chief of the Department, Col. *Dennie*, of H. M.'s 13th Light Infy. Comg. the advance, consisting of the light Cos. of H. M.'s 2nd and 17th foot, and of the Bengal European Regt., with one Coy. of H. M.'s 13th Lt. Infy., proceeded to the gate, and with great difficulty, from the rubbish thrown down, and the determined opposition offered by the enemy, effected an entrance and established themselves within the gateway, closely followed by the main column, led in a spirit of great gallantry by Brigr. *Sale*, to whom I had entrusted the important post of Comg. the "*Storming party*," consisting (with the advance above mentioned) of H. M.'s 2nd foot under Maj. *Carruthers*, the Bengal European Regt. under Lieut.-Col. *Orchard*, followed by H. M.'s 13th Light Infy. under Major *Tronson*, and H. M.'s 17th Regt. under Lieut.-Col. *Croker*. The struggle within the fort was desperate for a considerable time; in addition to the heavy fire kept up, our troops were assailed by the enemy sword in hand, and with daggers, pistols, &c., but British courage, perseverance and fortitude overcame all opposition, and the fire of the enemy in the lower area of the fort being nearly silenced, Brigr. *Sale* turned towards the citadel, from which could now be seen men abandoning their guns, running in all directions, throwing themselves down from immense heights, endeavouring to make their escape, and on reaching the gate, with H. M.'s 17th under Lieut.-Col. *Croker*, followed by the 13th, forced it open; at 5 o'clock in the morning, the colors of H. M.'s 13th and 17th were planted on the citadel of *Ghuznee*, amidst the cheers of all ranks. Instant protection was granted to the women found in the citadel, (amongst whom were those of *Mahomed Hyder*, the Governor) and sentries placed over the magazine

for its security. Brig. *Sale* reports having received much
assistance from Capt. *Kershaw*, of H. M.'s 13th Light Infy.,
throughout the whole of the service of the storming."

9. " Major-Genl. *Sir W. Cotton* executed in a manner
much to my satisfaction, the orders he had received. The
Major Genl. followed closely the assaulting party into the
fort, with the " *Reserve,*" namely, Brigr. *Roberts* with the
only available Regt. in his Brigade, the 35th N. I. under
Lieut.-Col. *Monteath;* part of Brigr. *Sale's* Brigade, the 16th
N. I. under Major *McLaren,* and 48th N. I. under Lieut.-Col.
Wheeler; and they immediately occupied the ramparts,
putting down opposition wherever they met any, and making prisoners until the place was completely in our possession. A desultory fire was kept up in the town long after
the citadel was in our hands, from those who had taken
refuge in houses, and in desperation kept firing on all that
approached them. In this way several of our men were
wounded and some killed, but the aggressors paid dearly
for their bad conduct in not surrendering when the place
was completely ours. I must not omit to mention that the
three companies of the 35th N. I. under Capt. *Hay,* ordered to the South side of the fort, to begin with a false attack,
to attract attention to that side, performed that service, at
the proper time, and greatly to my satisfaction."

10. " As we were threatened with an attack for the
relief of the garrison, I ordered the 19th Bombay N. I.,
under the command of Lieut.-Col. *Stalker,* to guard the
Cabool road, and to be in support of the Cavalry Division.
This might have proved an important position to occupy;
but as it was, no enemy appeared."

11. " The Cavy. Divn. under Major-Genl. *Thackwell,*
in addition to watching the approach of an enemy, had
directions to surround *Ghuznee* and to sweep the plain, preventing the escape of run-aways from the garrison. Brig.
Arnold's Brigade (the Brigadier himself I deeply regret to
say, was laboring under very severe illness, having shortly
before burst a blood-vessel internally, which rendered it
wholly impossible for him to mount a horse that day) con-

sisting of H. M.'s 16th Lancers, under Lieut.-Col. *Persse,* momentarily Comg. the Brigade, and Major *McDowel,* the junior Major, the Regt., the senior Major of the 16th Lancers, Major *Cureton,* an officer of great merit, being actively engaged in the execution of his duties as Asst. Adjt. Genl. of the Cavy Divn., the 2nd Cavy. under Major *Salter,* and the 3rd under Lieut.-Col. *Smyth,* were ordered to watch the South and West sides. Brigr. *Scott's* brigade were placed on the *Cabool road,* consisting of H. M.'s 4th Light Drags. under Major *Daly,* and the 1st Bombay Cavy. under Lieut.-Col. *Sandwith,* to watch the North and East sides. This duty was performed in a manner greatly to my satisfaction."

12 " After the storming, and that quiet was in some degree restored within, I conducted His Majesty *Shah Shoojah-ool-Moolk,* and the British Envoy and Minister, Mr. *Macnaghten,* round the citadel, and a great part of the fortress. The king was perfectly astonished at our having made ourselves masters of a place conceived to be impregnable, when defended, in the short space of two hours, and in less than 48 hours after we came before it. His Majesty was of course greatly delighted at the result. When I afterwards, in the course of the day, took Mahomed Hyder Khan, the Governor, first to the British Minister, and then to the king, to make his submission, I informed His Majesty, that I had made a promise that his life should not be touched, and the king in very handsome terms assented, and informed *Mahomed Hyder* in my presence, that although he and his family had been rebels, yet he was willing to forget and forgive all.

13. " *Prince Mahomed Hyder,* the Govr. of *Ghuznee,* is a prisoner of War in my camp, and under the surveillance of *Sir A. Burnes;* an arrangement very agreeable to the former."

14. " From Major Genl. *Sir W. Cotton,* Comg. the 1st Infy. Divn. (of the Bengal Army) I have invariably received the strongest support, and on this occasion his exertions were manifest in support of the honor of the profession and of our country."

2 E

15. " I have likewise at all times received able assistance from Major-Genl. *Willshire*, Comg. the 2nd Infy. Divn. (of the Bombay Army) which it was found expedient on that day to break up, some for the storming party, and some for other duties; the Major-Genl., as directed, was in attendance upon myself."

16. " To Brigr. *Sale*, I feel deeply indebted for the gallant and soldier-like manner in which he conducted the responsible and arduous duty entrusted to him, in command of the storming party, and for the arrangements he made in the *citadel*, immediately after taking possession of it. The sabre wound, which he received in the face, did not prevent his continuing to direct his column until every thing was secure; and I am happy in the opportunity of bringing to your Lordship's notice, the excellent conduct of Brigr. *Sale* on this occasion."

17. " Brigr. *Stevenson*, in command of the Arty. was all I could wish; and he reports, that Brigade Majors *Backhouse* and *Coghlan* ably assisted him; his arrangements were good, and the execution done by the arm he commands was such as cannot be forgotten by those of the enemy who have witnessed and survived it."

18. " To Brigr. *Roberts*, to Col. *Dennie* (who commanded the advance) and to the different officers Comg. Regts. already mentioned, as well as to the officers and gallant soldiers under them, who so nobly maintained the honor and reputation of our country, my best acknowledgments are due."

19. " To Capt. *Thomson*, of the Bengal Engineer, the chief of the Departt. with me, much of the credit of the success of this brilliant " *Coup-de-main*" is due;—a place of the same strength, and by such simple means as this highly talented and scientific officer recommended to be tried, has perhaps never before been taken; and I feel I cannot do sufficient justice to Capt. *Thomson's* merits, for his conduct throughout: in the execution he was ably supported by the officers already mentioned, and so eager were the other officers of the Engineers, of both Presidencies, for the honor of

carrying the powder bags, that the point could only be decided by seniority, which shows the fine feeling by which they are animated."

20. " I must now inform your Lordship, that since I joined the Bengal column in the valley of *Shawl,* I have continued my march with it in the advance, and it has been my good fortune to have had the assistance of two most efficient Staff officers, in Major *Craigie,* Depy. Adjt. Genl. and Major *Garden,* Depy. Qr. Mr. Genl. It is but justice to those officers, that I should state to your Lordship, the high satisfaction I have derived from the manner in which all their duties have been performed up to this day; and that I look upon them as promising officers to fill the higher ranks. To the other officers of both Depts. I am also much indebted for the correct performance of all duties appertaining to their situations."

21. " To Major *Keith,* the Depy. Adjt. Genl., and Major *Campbell,* the Depy. Qr. Mr. Genl. of the Bombay army, and to all the other officers of both Depts. under them, my acknowledgments are also due, for the manner in which their duties have been performed during this campaign."

22. " Capt. *Alexander,* Comg. the 4th Local Horse, and Major *Cunningham,* Comg. the Poonah Auxiliary Horse, with the men under their orders, have been of essential service to the army in this campaign."

"The arrangements made by Superintending Surgeons, *Kennedy* and *Atkinson,* previous to the storming, for affording assistance and comfort to the wounded, met with my approval."

23. " Major *Parsons,* the Depy. Commissary Genl. in charge of the Dept. in the field, has been unremitting in his attention to keep the troops supplied, although much difficulty is experienced, and he is occasionally thwarted by the nature of the country and its inhabitants."

24. " I have, throughout this service, received the utmost assistance I could desire from Lieut.-Col. *Macdonald* my Offg. Mily. Sec., and Depy. Adjt. Genl. H. M.'s forces, Bombay; from Capt. *Powell,* my Persian Interpreter, and

the other officers of my personal staff. The nature of the country in which we are serving prevents the possibility of my sending a single staff officer to deliver this to your Lordship, otherwise I should have asked my Aide-de-Camp, Lieut. *Keane*, to proceed to Simla, to deliver this despatch into your hands, and to have afforded any further information that your Lordship could have desired."

25. "The brilliant triumph we have obtained, the cool courage displayed, and the gallant bearing of the troops I have the honor to command, will have taught such a lesson to our enemies in the *Affghan* nation, as will make them hereafter respect the name of a British soldier."

26. "Our loss is wonderfully small, considering the occasion; the casualties in killed and wounded amount to about 200."

27. "The loss of the enemy is immense; we have already buried of their dead nearly 500; together with an immense number of horses."

28. "I enclose a list of the *killed, wounded, and missing*. I am happy to say, that although the wounds of some of the officers are severe, they are all doing well."

29. "It is my intention, after selecting a garrison for this place, and establishing a Genl. Hospital, to continue my march to Cabool forthwith."

I have, &c.
(Signed)   J. *Keane*,
Lieut.-General.

List of *killed, wounded,* and *missing,* in the army under the command of Lieut.-Genl. *Sir J. Keane,* before *Ghuznee,* on the 21st July, 1839.

2nd Troop Bengal Horse Arty.—3 Horses wounded.

3rd. do. Bombay do. do.—2 Rank and file, 2 horses wounded.

4th. do. do. do. do.—1 Horse killed.

2nd. Regt. Bengal Cavy. 1 Horse killed, 1 rank and file, wounded.

4th. Bengal Local Horse—1 rank and file and 1 Horse missing.

H. M.'s 13th. Light Infy. 1 rank and file killed. (99)
16th. Bengal N. I.—1 Capt. wounded.
48th. do. do. —1 Lieut. and 2 rank and file wounded.
Total killed—1 rank and file, and 2 Horses.
Total wounded—1 Captain, 1 Lieut., 6 rank and file, and 5 horses.
Total missing—1 rank and file, and 1 Horse.

Names of Officers wounded.
Captain *Graves,* 16th Bengal N. I. severely.
Lieut. *Van Homrigh,* 48th Bengal N. I., slightly.
(Signed) *R. Macdonald,* Lieut.-Col.
Mily. Secy, and Depy. Adjt. Genl.
H. M.'s Forces, Bombay.

List of the *killed, wounded,* and *missing* in the Army under the Com. of Lieut.-Genl. Sir J. Keane, K. C. B. and G. C. H. in the assault and capture of the fortress and citadel of *Ghuznee,* on the 23rd July, 1839.

Genl. Staff, 1 Colonel, 1 Major wounded.
3rd Troop, Bombay H. Arty., 1 rank and file wounded.
4th do. do. do. 1 rank and file, and 1 horse wounded.
Bengal Engineers, 3 rank and file killed, 2 rank and file wounded, 1 rank and file missing.
Bombay do. 1 Lieut., 1 rank and file wounded.
2nd Bengal Lt. Cavy., 1 rank and file wounded.
1st Bombay Lt. Cavy., 1 Havr. killed, 5 rank and file, and 7 horses wounded.
H. M.'s 2nd foot, (or Queen's Royal,) 4 rank and file killed, 2 Captains, 4 Lieuts., 1 Serjeant, and 26 rank and file wounded.
H. M.'s 13th Light Infy., 1 rank and file killed, 3 Serjeants and 27 rank and file wounded.
H. M.'s 17th foot, 6 rank and file wounded.
Bengal European Regt., 1 rank and file killed, 1 Lieut.-Col., 1 Major, 2 Captains, 4 Lieuts., 1 Ensign, 1 Serjeant, 51 rank and file wounded.

(99) Reconnoitring on the 21st July.

16th Bengal N. I., 1 Havr., 6 rank and file wounded.
35th do. do., 5 rank and file killed, 1 Havr., 8 rank and file wounded.
48th do. do., 2 Havrs. killed, 5 rank and file wounded.
Total killed—3 Serjts. or Havrs., 14 rank and file.
Total wounded—1 Colonel, 1 Lieut.-Col., 2 Majors, 4 Captains, 8 Lieuts., 2 Ensigns, 7 Serjts. or Havrs., 140 rank and file, 8 horses.
Total missing—1 rank and file.
Grand total, on the 21st and 23rd July, killed, wounded, and missing, 191 Officers and men, and 16 horses.

(Signed) *R. Macdonald*, Lieut.-Colonel,
Mily. Secy. and Depy. Adjt. General,
Her Majesty's Forces, Bombay.

Names of Officers, killed, wounded, and missing.

Wounded.

General Staff.

Brigadier *Sale*, H. M.'s 13th Light Infy. slightly.
Major Parsons, Depy. Commissary Genl., slightly.

Bombay Engineers.
2nd Lieut. Marriott, slightly.

H. M.'s 2nd foot, (or Queen's Royal.)

Captain Raitt, slightly.
„ Robinson, severely.
Lieutenant Yonge, ditto,
„ Stisted, slightly.
Adjutant Simmons, ditto.
Quarter Master Hadley, ditto.

Bengal European Regt.

Lieut.-Colonel Orchard, slightly.
Major Warren, severely.
Captain Hay, slightly.
„ Taylor, ditto.
Lieutenant Broadfoot, slightly.
„ Haslewood, severely.

Lieutenant Fagan, slightly.
„   Magnay, ditto.
Ensign Jacob, ditto.
(Signed)   R. Macdonald, Lieut.-Col.
Mily. Secy. and Depy. Adjt. Genl.
H. M.'s forces, Bombay.
(True copies,)
(Signed)   T. H. Maddock,
Offg. Secy. to the Govt. of India,
with the Govr. General.
(True copies,)
(Signed)   J. Stuart, Lieut.-Col.
Secy. to the Govt. of India, Mily. Dept.
with the Right Hon. the Govr. Genl.

By the Commander of the Forces.

In obedience to the instructions contained in the above notification, a salute of 21 guns to be fired at all the principal Stations of this Presidency, on the receipt of this order.

By order of the Commander of the Forces,
(Signed)   J. R. Lumley, Major-Genl.
Adjt. Genl. of the Army.

13. *Repairs to the Works, &c.*—(G. O. 24th July, 1839.) —1. "The chief Engineer will send in the name of an officer, immediately, with a view to his being employed, professionally, in the garrison of *Ghuznee;* and he will take such measures as may be necessary, for repairing the damage done to the works." (100)

2. *Sick and wounded to be left.* "The Suptg. Surgeons of the Bengal and Bombay columns, will send to the officers of the Adjt. Genl.'s Dept. of their respective Presidencies, returns of the number of *sick* and *wounded,* whom it may be

---

(100) A portion of the wall of the *Citadel* towards the centre square, had been knocked down by the firing of the Artillery. The *Cabool gate* (see para. 3 of G. O. 23rd July) was built up, and a wicket only left, as well as the S. or Bazar gate. The *Kenak* (or Candahar) gate was alone kept open for ingress and egress.

deemed necessary to leave at *Ghuznee;* and they will report the number for which there may be accommodation in the buildings in the fort; and the extent of the Hospital Establishment required to be left with them." (101)

There were 120 Europeans, and some Native soldiers left at Ghuznee. Major (now Lt.-Col.) *G. Warren,* and Lt. *W. K. Haslewood,* of the European Regt., who were so badly wounded that they could not march with their corps, as, also Lt. *Yonge,* H. M.'s 2nd Queen's, were left behind, on the advance of the army to Cabool.

3. *Prize Property, Horse, &c.* "H. E. the Comr.-in-Chief is pleased to direct the following measures to be adopted for the disposal of the horses, mules, and,bullocks, captured in the fort of *Ghuznee.*" (102)

"The whole will be exposed for *sale,* by *Auction,* at 4 o'clock to-morrow afternoon, in the Bengal Cavy. lines; all horses for which a *sum exceeding* 500 *Rs.* may be offered, are to be disposed of, at once; all, *under* that value, (103) are to be transferred to the Comsst. Dept.; for the purpose of being tendered for the *public service.*"

"A Committee of Officers will assemble on the spot at the same hour, for the purpose of *passing* the horses; and will be composed of the following officers, viz." (104)

(101) The houses on three sides of the *Citadel* were given to the sick and wounded men, and the 4th side to the officers.

(102) "In continuation of G. O. of yesterday, officers Comg. corps, and at the head of Depts., are required to cause their lines and bazars, to be searched for captured horses, bullocks or mules; all which may be found, are to be sent at once, to the lines of the Bengal Cavy.; and they will report direct to the D. A. G. of the presidency to which they belong, for the Comr.-in-Chief's information, that they have caused this order to be carried into effect; that not a single captured animal has been allowed to remain in the lines of their corps; and that all found in them, have been disposed of as above directed."

(103) See p. 100.

(104) Brigr. Scott, president, and 4 members (from H. A., H. M. 16th Lancers, the Bengal, and Bombay, Cavy.)

"The horses rejected by the Committee, as unfit for cavalry purposes, together with the mules, and bullocks, are to be sold to the highest

4. " The horses which may be passed into the service by the Committee, are to be *classed* in the usual manner, as for ' *Horse Arty.*,' ' *Dragoons*,' and ' *Lt. Cavy.*' and handed over to the Comsst. Dept. A report of the number of each class to be made to Hd. Qrs. when orders will be given for allotting them to Regts." (105)

5. *Garrison Engineer.*—" Lt. *Broadfoot*, (Bengal) Engineers, to act as Engineer in the garrison; and will place the fort in a proper state of defence; under such instructions as he may receive from the chief Engineer."

6. *Arms, &c. missing.*—" Officers Comg. Regts. having brought with them from the fort, arms and accoutrements, which do not belong to them; will return the same to the Regts. whose *number* they bear; and receive back such as may be the property of their own corps."

bidders. All horses purchased by *Commissioned officers* may be paid for by drafts on their pay for the months of Aug., Sept. and October. Those purchased by *natives*, and others not in the service, must be paid for on the spot."

" Provost Marshal *Wilson* will act as *Auctioneer*, and will furnish the *Fd. Pay Mr.*, of the Bengal Column, with a list of officers who have made purchases on the above terms; and pay into his hands the sums of money collected from other persons." " The D. C. G. will, likewise, furnish the *Pay Master* with a statement of the number of *horses* passed into the service, valuing those attached to the H. A. and Dragoons, and Lt. Cavy., at the sums specified in the Regns. of the service, as a price of a *remount* for those branches." (*See p.* 100.)

" Returns shewing the number of horses required to complete each corps, with reference to the number of men actually present with the army, are to be sent, immediately, to the D. A. G., through whom the president will receive instructions for the allotment of the *remount*."

The Duke of *Wellington* was of opinion that " the nearest approximation to the demand of a Regt. of Cavalry for horses, is to calculate upon one for each N. C. O. and soldier present, and *fit for duty*, and on command." (*Gurwood's* Despatches, vol. 10, p. 103.)

(105) G. O. 25th July, 1839. There were about 800 horses captured (some wounded), but only 39 were *selected* by the Committee altogether, (Ext. from valuation return,) at 550 Rs. each. (See table No. 4, Appx.) There were 1200 originally, including those killed and those too badly wounded to be sold.

7. *Prisoners.* (106)—There were about 1,500 *prisoners*. Except a few, they were all released. Some were *Hindostanees* found in the out-work, who declared they were pressed into the service. With regard to the prisoners, taken on the 22nd July, on the day of the attack on *Shah Shoojah's* camp, twenty-five of the followers of the father-in-law of *Dost Mahomed* who was killed, were brought to the *King*, (I believe, next day,) who offered to pardon them. One of them was very abusive to the *king*, and stabbed one of his own servants who was standing behind him; upon which His Majesty's *attendants rushed on these people and killed them; but this was, by no order from Shah Shoojah.* This, l believe, to be the real fact; and I made particular inquiries. (107)

8. *Pardon and peace proclaimed.*—There was firing from a few houses to-day, but it ceased at 3 p. m., when all resistance was at an end. Pardon was proclaimed and the people came from their hiding-places, and returned to their homes.

Dost Mahomed was reported to be close to us with his army. *Hyder Khan* said that his father had written to him to hold out, and he would come to his assistance. The fall of *Ghuznee* was known at *Cabool* at 5 o'clock on the afternoon of the same day. (108)

(106) At about 9 a. m. on the 23rd July after the European troops had been withdrawn, it was reported that there was another (small) fort not far off, which was occupied by the enemy; it was intended to send the Bengal European Regt. and 2 guns to take it; but it was surrendered on hearing of the fall of *Ghuznee*, from some of those who had escaped from it.

(107) This was the statement given by an officer, a relation of the *Envoy and Minister.* I mention this here, as on the occasion of the vote of thanks to *Sir J. Keane* and the Army of the Indus, (East India House, 11th Dec. 1839,) *Sir C. Forbes* opposed the vote till an explanation was given, of certain prisoners having been " *beheaded on the spot, in cold blood, by order of Shah Shoojah.*"

(108) There had been horsemen stationed at every eight miles between *Ghuznee* and *Cabool*, and the news was speedily conveyed a distance of 88 miles. The messenger gave out the news *publicly*, which quite disconcerted the *Khan*, who wished to have concealed such intelligence as long as he could!

9. *Prize Agents.*—(G. O. 26th July, 1839.) " H. E. The Comr.-in-Chief, is pleased to nominate Lt. *Keane,* H. M.'s 2nd Regt. of foot and A. D. C. to H. E., a Prize Agent to the army of the Indus; and he invites the officers under his command belonging to the Bengal and Bombay Presidencies, to nominate, from amongst their numbers, one officer, in each column, as their Prize Agent; the nomination to be forwarded with the least possible delay, to D. A. Genls. of the Bengal and Bombay armies, by Generals Comg. Divisions." (109)

It was notified in G. O. (110) that the officers of the Bengal troops had voted for Capt. *G. St. P. Lawrence,* 2nd Bengal Lt. Cavy. as their Prize Agent; and those of Bombay, for Capt. *Swanston,* 19th Bombay N. I. (and Pay Mr.) Lt. *Keane,* Capts. *Lawrence,* and *Swanston* were ordered to form the Prize Committee for the capture of *Ghuznee.* The *Prize Agents* were appointed too late, hence we lost some prize property.

Prize Rolls from corps and Depts. employed in the investment and capture of the fortress, were ordered to be prepared in *Triplicate,* and forwarded, without delay, to the D. A. Genls. of the Presidency to which the party sending in the Roll belonged. (111)

14. *Capture of Ali Musjid,* (26th July, 1839.)—1. Lt.-Colonel *Wade,* after a series of operations, (112) obtained possession of the fort of *Ali Musjid* in the *Khyber Pass,* which was in the possession of *Dost Mahomed's* troops.

---

(109) G. O. 29th July, 1839. " H. E. the Comr.-in-Chief invites the officers of the troops of H. M. Shah Shoojah, to join their brother officers of the Bengal and Bombay Armies in the selection of Prize Agents, forwarding their votes in the course of the day, to the Envoy and Minister."

(110) 15th Aug. 1839.

(111) The Prize Act for *India* allows of only *two* Prize Agents. I believe *all* must be chosen by the *army.* I merely mention this as I am not aware of any change since the capture of Bhurtpoor, 18th Jan. 1826. This, however, is a question for the Prize Agents.

(112) Detailed after the description of Ghuznee in this chapter.

Mahomed Akbar Khan, the second son, had a force of 2,500 horse and foot, and fourteen guns, and was stationed at *Jellalabad*, 103 miles from Cabool, and 64 from *Ali Musjid*, and 41 miles from the head of the Pass. Akbar Khan, had repeatedly written to his father to be allowed to join him at Cabool; the fall of *Ghuznee* at length, caused his recall to the capital. This event placed the Lt.-Colonel at a distance of only 167 miles from Cabool, and as the road was now open to his march on the city, while the *British* troops at Ghuznee were within 88 miles of it, the available addition of troops to the amount of 6 or 7,000 men, was important; as the threatening the capital from *two* quarters, at the same time, presented a formidable force against the chief of Cabool. If he resolved to make a stand at his capital, he knew that he would have to contend against two armies; and if beaten he could calculate on a retreat by neither of the roads occupied by them. The most favorable plan would have been to meet the attack before Col. *Wade's* force could join. Had we failed in our assault on *Ghuznee*, we *must* have moved, instantly, and pushed on for Cabool; with a knowledge of the march of another army by the *Khyber Pass*, Dost Mahomed would have been afraid to have moved far from Cabool, as he must, thereby, have endangered its attack on the other side. It would, undoubtedly, have been a *difficult* operation for the army; and would have involved much loss: then, our object would have been, an early action with *Dost Mahomed* in the field, to restore the balance in our favor.

15. *Sick Depôt at Ghuznee*, (27th July, 1839.)—G. O. 1. " Suptg. Surgeon *Atkinson* having represented that sufficient Hospital Establishment for the *whole* of the *sick* and *wounded* of the army, cannot be left at *Ghuznee*, without compromising the efficiency of the field Hospital, H. E. the Comr.-in-Chief is pleased to direct, that such sick and wounded men as could not be removed without risk, be left in the Hospital Depôt at this place; and that all for whom transport is available, shall move with the army. Suptg. Surgeons *Kennedy* and *Atkinson* to send to the

D. A. G. of the Bombay and Bengal columns, *numerical* returns of the sick to be left, and the *names* of the Medical officers, and nature of the establishments recommended to remain."

2. " Fd. Surgeon *Pinkey*, Bombay army, is appointed to the medical charge of the *Ghuznee* Depôt, and is to place himself in communication with the D. C. G. to arrange for provisioning the sick, and for medical comforts."

3. " Camp equipage and carriage must be left for the sick, and their arms and ammunition continued with them. Suptg. Surgeons to see that a suitable proportion of medicines are left." (113)

4. *Force left at Ghuznee.*—" A Dett. of Arty. of the strength noted in the margin, (114) under Lt. *G. P. Sealy*, Bombay Arty. ; a Regt. of Native Infy. (115) Bengal Division, and 200 horsemen in the service of H. M. Shah Shoojah-ool-Moolk to remain at *Ghuznee*."

" The whole to be under the command of the officer at the head of the Regt. of Infy., destined to remain ; special instructions for whose guidance will hereafter be furnished him."

" A Ressalah of 4th (Bengal) Local Horse is to be added to the details to garrison Ghuznee. Four of H. M. Shah Shoojah's guns will, also, be added to the garrison."

" The troops to remain in the fort, will move into camp to-morrow morning at 7 o'clock ; from which hour the command of the garrison will devolve on the officer Comg. the Regt. of Native Infantry (Major (now Lt.-Col.) *MacLaren*), to remain in *Ghuznee*." (116)

5. *Order for march to Cabool.*—" The troops will move

(113) G. O. 28th July, 1839. " The Chief Engineer will give directions for having the buildings selected by the Suptg. Surgeons for the sick and wounded, being prepared in the course of the day, for their reception."

(114) One Subr., one Jemr., three Havs., four Nks, and 27 Privates.

(115) 16th Bengal N. I.

(116) G. O. 28th July, 1839.

forward in the following order. On the morning of the
30th inst., the Hd. Qrs. will quit *Ghuznee,* accompanied by
two troops H. A., the Cavy., No. 6, Lt. Fd. battery, the
Bengal Park, the Engineer Dept., 1st and 4th Brigades of
Infy., the Bengal Local Horse, the Fd. Comsst., and field
Hospital."

" On the morning of the 31st inst., a troop H. A., Capt.
Lloyd's battery, the Bombay Park, the Bombay Brigade
of Infy., and the Poonah Auxy. Horse."

" The officers of the Bengal Staff will move with the 1st
column; those of the Bombay Staff with the 2nd column,
under Maj. Genl. *Willshire.*"

Some chiefs came into camp to offer their services to *Shah
Shoojoh.* Salutes were fired by the Shah.

G. O. 28th July, 1839.—" All colors, and standards captured from the enemy, to be duly reported to the D. A. G.
of the army, and retained till F. O. in the standard and Qr.
guards of the corps to which the captors may belong."

16. *Nuwab Jubbar Khan arrives,* (28th July, 1839.)—
1. To-day about noon Nuwab Jubbar Khan, Dost Mahomed's eldest brother, arrived in camp, with a few *Affghans*
escorted by a party of *Lancers* from the advance picquet, with
overtures from his brother. *Sir A. Burnes* went to meet
him, and accompanied him to the Envoy and Minister. His
nephew, Hyder Khan, was then in a tent close to *Sir A.
Burnes,* but he was not allowed to see him. The proposal
was that his brother, Dost Mahomed, should be the *Vizier,*
or Prime Minister, of the kingdom. The *Shah* received
him with courtesy, and readily offered to confirm the *Nuwab*
in any possessions he might have, and to confer honors on
him. The Nuwab said he wanted nothing for himself, and
that he came on behalf of his brother. He was informed,
that *Dost Mahomed,* if he agreed to terms, would be allowed
a pension, (117) but must reside in *India.* The *Nuwab* said
that his brother would not on any terms consent to reside in
India.

(117) Of, I believe, one lakh Rs. (£10,000) a year.

Claims of Dost Mahomed Khan. 223

2. *Dost Mahomed Khan*, claimed to be *Vizier*, in right of his late brother, Vizier *Futteh Khan*, but this claim had no foundation; because though *Futteh Khan* had been Vizier, to *Shah Mahmood* who usurped the throne; still we have evidence that it was *hereditary* in the person of a *Barukzye*. (118)

3. The conduct of *Jubbar Khan*, on this occasion, was noble; he had at one time been deprived of his estates by his

---

(118) In the time of *Ahmed Shah* (the founder of the *Dooranee* empire) the Vizaret was held by Shah *Wulli Khan, Bamzye*, in whose family it was declared, by the *Dooranees*, on the elevation of Ahmed Shah, to be hereditary.

On the succession of *Timoor Shah*, he did not confer the title of *Vizier* on any one; but appointed Gool Mahomed, Buban, *Amir-ool-Moolk*, (a Peer of the realm.)

Shah Zuman restored the Vizaret, and gave it to Wuffadar Khan, Suddozye, brother to a wife of Shah Shoojah.

When *Shah Mahmood* (the younger brother of Shah Zuman, but the elder brother of Shah Shoojah) was proclaimed king, after Shah Zuman was dethroned, he made Futteh Khan, Vizier.

Shah Shoojah, when he succeeded *Shah Mahmood* as king, ostensibly acknowledged Sheer Mahomed Khan, (the surviving son of *Shah Wulli*) as Vizier, but in reality placed confidence in *Akram Khan, Populzai;* on which Sheer Mahomed retired to Cashmeer. When Shah Shoojah projected an expedition to *Sindh*, he invited Sheer Mahomed Khan to join him, but he refused. Before setting out, Shah Shoojah was joined by *Futteh Khan;* who accompanied the Shah to *Sindh;* and the Shah designed the Govt. of Sikarpoor, and that of *Derajat* (the upper Indus) for him; but the jealousy of *Akram Khan* prevented these appointments: *Futteh Khan* seeing this influence retired.

Now, from this statement it will be seen, that *Futteh Khan*, was never appointed *Vizier* by any of the *Suddozye* kings. That he was appointed by *Shah Mahmood* who deposed his brother, and usurped the throne. All the Viziers were *Suddozyes;* Futteh Khan, was a *Barukzye.* Shah Shoojah, while living in the mountains, had a deputation sent to him from Cabool; and he was crowned king, by the voice of the people; and with the consent and wish of *Shah Zuman;* who being blind, could not, according to the *Mahomedan* Law, reign. Besides, though *Futteh Khan* was Vizier to a *Suddozye* king, still none of his brothers succeeded him; nor was the Vizaret declared to be *hereditary!*

brother; (119) but he said he wanted nothing for himself, and had only come to make a proposal on account of Dost Mahomed. Finding such a result, he took his departure for Cabool, next morning; declaring his determination to follow his *brother's fortunes*.

4. *Dost Mahomed*, it was reported, had assembled his chiefs, and had declared his conviction that *Ghuznee* had fallen through *treachery*. He then asked them as to their intentions, and begged that those who did not *intend to support him, to withdraw at once*. They all replied that *they* were true to his cause, and would support him against the *British*; but could not help suspecting an intention on *his* part to desert *them*. (120) They said, "Let us ask *you*, if you will stick by *us*."

17. *Description of Ghuznee.*—1. "Mahomed, (brother to the Gaurian Usurper,) A. D. 1184, made himself master of the kingdom *of Ghuznee and Candahar*; when the sceptre was transferred from the house of Ghizni, to the house of Gaur."

"The *Moguls* during the reign of Byram 2nd (A. D. 1242) invaded India. They plundered the country as far as Lahore, and then retreated to Ghuzni. In A. D. 1257 *Shere* (Mahmood the Second's nephew) viceroy of Lahore and Multan, expelled the *Mogul* from Ghuznee, and once more annexed that kingdom, to the Indian part of the Gaurian empire." Ghuzni (in the province of Cabool) was once a powerful empire, for four

---

(119) Burnes, 2nd Ed. (1835, vol. 2, p. 115, Travels (1832) to *Bokhara*), says, "He entertains no ambitious views, though he once held the Govt. of *Cashmeer*, and other provinces of the *Dooranee* empire. His brother, the present chief of Cabool, *has requited many services by confiscating his estate; but he speaks not of his ingratitude!* He is a man of amiable character. He has a greater moral influence than any of the *Barukzye* families in *Affghanistan*." He is now about 58 years of age; and styled "*Nuwab*," from having been Govr. of *Derajat* (Upper Indus).

(120) His sending Jubbar Khan they must have looked on as making terms for himself, and he *was* trying to make his own terms.

centuries. It gradually declined to a secondary rank as a city; and at last to total insignificance.

Baber says, (121) 2. "The country of Ghuzni (famous in history as the seat of the Govt. of Sultan Mahomed of Ghaznivi, and of the Ghaznevi dynasty) is often denominated a Tuman (District). By the blessing of Almighty God I gained (A. D. 1504) possession of Cabool and Ghuzni, with the country and provinces dependent on them, without battle, or contest." (122)

3. "Ghuzni was the capital of Subaktegin of Sultan Mahmood, and of the dynasty sprung from them, many call it Ghaznein. Its river may be large enough to drive 4 or 5 mills. (123) The city of Ghuzni and four or five other districts, are supplied from this river, while as many more are fertilized by subterraneous water-courses, *(Karexees.)* The grapes of *Ghuzni* are superior to those of Cabool, and its melons more abundant. Its apples too are excellent, and are carried into Hindustan. Cultivation is (was) carried on with great difficulty and labor, and whatever ground is cultivated, is obliged to have a new dressing of mould every year; but the produce of the crops exceeds that of Cabool. The Madder is chiefly cultivated here, and it is carried over all Hindustan. It is the most profitable crop in this district. The inhabitants of the open country are *Hazaras* and *Affghans*. Ghuzni is a cheap place compared with Cabool."

4. "The tomb of Sultan Mahmood is in one of the Suburbs of Ghuzni, which, from that circumstance, is termed Rozeh (124) the garden. The best grapes in Ghuzni are from Rozeh. The tombs of Sultan Masaud and Sultan Ibrahim, are in Ghuzni. There are many holy tombs at the city." (125)

(121) Memoirs, p. 148.
(122) Do. p. 135.
(123) "The river of Ghuzni runs N. to Lohgar, and joins the Kabul river." They use water-mills in Affghanistan in numbers, according to the *breadth* of a river; hence they describe its size.
(124) Rouzu, a garden—a mausoleum.
(125) "There is a lake S. from Ghuzni."

5. "Ghuzni is but a poor, mean place. I have always wondered how its princes, who possessed also Hindustan and Khorasan, could have chosen such a wretched country for the seat of Govt. In the time of the Sultan, there were three or four mounds for collecting water. (126) One of these, which is of great dimensions, was formed by the Sultan of Ghuzni, on the river of Ghuzni, about three farsangs (12 miles) up the river, on the N. W. of the town." (127)

"Another mound is that of *Sakhen*, which lies to the E. of Ghuzni at the distance of 3 or 4 farsangs (12 or 16 miles) from the city. This also has long been in a state of ruin and is not repairable. (128) Another mound is that of *Sirdeh* (lies S. E. from Ghuzni) which is in good repair."

6. "Ghuzni is celebrated for its cold. The *Kerkend* is a low prickly thorn, that burns alike whether green or dry; it constitutes the only fuel of the inhabitants of Ghuzni." A. D. 1739, Nadir Shah obtained possession of all the provinces on the W. of the Indus, Cabool, Tatta, and part of Multan, from the dominions of the Mogul (Mahomed Shah) after the sacking of Delhi; and in 1747, Ahmed Shah, founder of the *Dooranee* dynasty, became possessed of the whole of Affghanistan, by conquest. (129)

"The land to the W. of the city of Ghuzni at *Heerghaut* is interspersed with low hills, and, except a few cultivated

---

(126) "In the *East*, where success of cultivation depends chiefly on the supply of water, it is usual to dam up the bottom of narrow valleys, or of low meadows, so as to collect all the water into one body, whence it is afterwards distributed for the supply of the country below."

(127) "This mound was destroyed by *Ala-ed-din*, who destroyed many of the tombs of the royal family of the Sultan, ruined and burned the city of *Ghuzni*, and plundered and massacred the inhabitants." In 1525 Baber sent money to rebuild the mound.

(128) Was not in those days considered repairable.

(129) The empire of which Ghuznee was once the capital, reached from the Tigris to the Ganges.

spots, produces little else than a prickly aromatic weed, on which camels feed with avidity." (130.)

7. The *Fort of Ghuznee* is situated on the W. extremity of a range of hills running E. to W.; the W., S. and E. sides are ditched, the water being supplied from the river Ghuznee. There is a bridge over it at the *Kenak* gate, near which there is an outwork. The ditch is deep and formidable. The *Citadel* to the N. is an irregular square; there are two ramps going up to it, and on entering the gate, there is a large square in it. The magazine was in the W. quarter; the granary to the E.; there are other store, &c. rooms below. Above is the Governor's house. The loop-holes from the walls of the citadel, do not command a fire on any ground close to the ditch; hence, only those at a distance would suffer from a fire of matchlocks.

The *town* was said (1839) to contain 3,000 houses, (131) and 150 buneahs, and has an abundant supply of river water. I should think the population was (1839) about 3,000 independent of the then garrison of 3,000 men. (132)

Ghuznee, it is said, once held out nearly a year's siege; and this at a time when not so well defended as we found it.

8. Old Ghuznee is about three miles to the E. of the town and fort of Ghuznee, and is remarkable as containing the tomb of *Sultan Mahmood* of Ghuznee, the conqueror of India. The town is in ruins. The tomb is only deserving of notice from its antiquity; as a building it is not of the first order, either as to the style of the architecture, or the size of the building. The doors, which are large and of *sandal-wood*, are said to have been brought, as a trophy from

(130) See Forster, &c.
(131) The author of a Sketch published in 1838, says, " but it is now reduced to about 1,500 mean dwellings."
(132) The winter has been mild this year (1840). An officer writes, that, "This is a most beautiful climate for Europeans. Hard frost and little snow. Ice on the pools of water and ditch of the fort several feet thick. *Skating* and *sliding* all day long amongst the officers, and some few of the *sepoys* are getting up to sliding."

the renowned temple of *Somnaut* in *Guzerat.* (133) There
are many gardens here, and the most translucent stream of
water I ever saw. The old town is close under the range
of hills which run W. to E. from Ghuznee, but more to the
north. (134) Old Ghuznee has several times been destroyed by snow storms. The elevation of *Ghuznee* above the
level of the sea is 7,726 feet; being 4,242 feet above *Candahar*, and 1,330 feet above Cabool. The range of the *Thermtr.*
from the 21st to the 29th July, 1839, was from 56° to 60° at
4 A. M., and 90° to 94° 3 P. M.

9. We found in the citadel of Ghuznee about 500,000
lbs. (135) Supposing the operations to have failed; and
taking the garrison at 3,000 men, who eat meat also; allowing *one lb.* to each man per diem; and there would have
been rations for 166 days, or say for five months; or, if they
were to rely on the flour alone, full rations for two and a
half months: so that at all events the *garrison* had supplies for three months if besieged. I must omit the non-
combatants (the inhabitants) who could not have been
more than 3,000: they would have left the place; and we
could not well have prevented their doing so, as the river
ran three-fourths round the place.

18. *Operations against Ali Musjid*—(24th, 25th, and 26th
July, 1839).—1. The Mission had arrived safe at Herat on

(133) Maharajah Runjeet Singh, the *Sikh* ruler, wished to stipulate
in the treaty, to which he was a party, that on the conquest of *Affghanistan* by the British for Shah Shoojah, these gates should be given to
him to be restored to the temple; as being a *Hindoo*, he considered
these gates should not remain in the hands of a Mahomedan. On a
tomb-stone of white marble, lies the mace of *Mahmood* of such weight,
it is said (for I saw it not) that few men can wield it. Mahomedan
priests are still maintained, who constantly read the *Koran* over his
grave.

(134) The gardens are walled with stones and mud, but in a
state of ruin. The best grapes are to be had from these gardens.
Many of the wounded of the enemy, were found in this, now, *village*,
instead of *old city* of *Ghuznee.*

(135) Vide Table No. 4; 510,300lbs.; but as only 79,080lbs. were
flour, 500,000lbs. would be about the quantity of wheat and barley, if
reduced to flour.

Capture of Ali Musjid.

25th July, 1839. Lt.-Col. *Wade* having received intelligence, (though not authentic,) of the march of the British army from Candahar towards *Ghuznee* and *Cabool*, calculated that it was time for the force of *Shahzada Tymoor*, to move forward from Peshawer. As Genl. *Ventura* did not accompany the force, Col. *Shaik Bussawun*, was appointed to the command of the *Sikh* contingent ; while Lt.-Col. *Wade* was in the general command of the whole force, amounting to 10 or 11,000 men. On the 9th July, he received information that an insurrection, which had been preconcerted, had already commenced in *Kohistan*, (136) and arrangements had been made to induce the chiefs, in the districts between Peshawer and Cabool, to join the royal cause. Shah Shoojah had, himself, addressed the *Khyber* chiefs, among some of whom he had received an asylum when he lost his throne, and on the occasions of his subsequent flights, when defeated in his endeavours to recover his lost crown. An earlier advance would have been premature ; and the newly raised contingent would not, much earlier, have been ready for the advance. Besides the troops in *Ali Musjid*, *Mahomed Akbar Khan*, Dost Mahomed's second son, was stationed near the head of the Khyber Pass, near Jullalabad with 2,500 men and 14 guns ; while there was no certainty as to what extent the *Khyberees* would join the fortunes of Dost Mahomed. These hill chiefs received him as master, and allowed him to establish a garrison at *Ali Musjid*, in preference to the *Sikhs* having possession of the Pass ; so that it was a choice of two evils, and they chose the least. A certain sum of money was, annually, paid by both parties ; Dost Mahomed paying for the use of the *Pass* ; and the *Sikhs* for the use of the *water* which, from its stream, supplied the fort of Futtehgurh, on the Peshawer frontier, and about five miles from the entrance to the Pass. Lt.-Col. *Wade* was at *Jumrood* (137) on the 20th July. It was

---

(136) Cabool receives much grain from this country.

(137) The fort was destroyed and Futtehgurh built on its site, after the battle of Jumrood in 1837, between the *Affghans* and *Sikhs*. The

necessary to make arrangements to leave the heavy baggage and sick in the fort of Futtehgurh, which the Sikhs allowed him to use as a *Depôt*. *Runjeet Singh* was dead, and though there was the Sikh force at Futtehgurh, the death of the Sikh ruler was to be regretted, (138) while Mahomed Akbar, was urging the *Khyberees* to oppose the advance through the Pass.

2. Before the period for operations had arrived, Lt.-Col. *Wade* employed himself in accepting the offers of the zemindars and other Khyberees whose lands were contiguous to the entrance of the Pass, and whose services he had secured on his arrival at Peshawer (139) to watch the *two* roads leading into the Pass and the entrance to which had been previ-

---

Affghans, were commanded by a father-in-law of Dost Mahomed, (who was killed,) aided by Meer Ufzul Khan, and Mahomed Akbar Khan, (Dost Mahomed's 1st and 2nd sons.) The Sikhs were commanded by *Hurree Singh*, their favorite Sikh General, who was killed; on hearing which Runjeet Singh, shed tears for the loss of his best commander. Dost Mahomed's sons breached and made an attempt to storm the fort of *Jumrood*, and lost there 500 men killed and wounded. The *Affghan* loss was about 1,100 killed and wounded altogether. The *Sikhs* are said to have had 12,000 men, and the *Affghans* less. *Meer Ufzul Khan*, when he found the day gone, and the Affghans had retreated, made a gallant charge as a last effort; but was checked by the *Sikh Infy*. Runjeet was not satisfied with his victory, or the conduct of his troops; and it was observed by one well acquainted with the *Sikhs*, that "*when once a panic has seized the Sikhs*, I have heard, from those whose authority on the subject cannot be doubted, *that it is most difficult to preserve the least order, in their ranks; and the Maharajah himself is well aware of their want of steadiness, and fortitude, before a resolute enemy*." They have no such men as *Hurree Singh*, now, in the *Sikh* army.

(138) At note 4, p. 144, it is stated that the Sikh troops on the Peshawer frontier had retired on Runjeet's death; this did not include the troops of the garrison of Futtehgurh, nor the troops attached to that command encamped near it under *Rajah Goolab Singh*. It would appear that some of the troops which were on the frontier, distinct from the above force, again advanced; for on the 9th August, 1839, they are reported to have retired *to Peshawer*, from the frontier nearer the Pass.

(139) 20th March, 1839.

and against Ali Musjid.

ously reconnoitred. The enemy were beginning to close the narrow defile of *Kafar Tungee*, (140) on one side, and to strengthen themselves in the tower of *Jaghir* (141) on the other. He assigned the duty of confining them within the Pass, to those *Khyberees* who had been gained over, and who lived near the Pass; and posted the rest in the immediate front of his camp.

He lost no time in erecting two stockades, (142) one commanding the principal entrance to the Pass, and the other supporting it. Two other stockades were erected, on the flanks, by which means the position was rendered secure, and the *Khyberees* were shut up in the Pass; and could not get out by this route; while the Khyberees *beyond* Ali Musjid were less hostile.

The *Khyber Pass* is about 28 miles in extent. From the entrance on the Peshawer side it is seven miles to *Ali Musjid*, from which it is two miles to Lalabeg Ghuree, a valley which is about six miles long and one and a quarter broad; hence is the Pass of *Lundeekhana*; in fact, excepting the valley, the rest of the Pass, or for 22 miles, can be commanded by *Jingals* (wall-pieces), or even by the mountain rifle *(Juzzail)* fired with a rest, and in many places by the common musket. The road being stony, the movements of troops with guns is necessarily slow. The first four miles, after the entrance to the Pass, the road is contracted, and the hills on each side, are nearly perpendicular; to the left, two miles up the Pass, there is a road which leads up to the top of the hills. It widens after the third mile, but still the road is exposed to a fire from either side. At about five and a half miles is the town of *Jaghir* on the right, which could fire on any enemy moving by either road. From this

(140) A footpath leading from Jumrood to the right of the main Pass. The part closed was that where the footpath over the hills leads down into the Pass, about 1½ miles from *Ali Musjid*.

(141) A large, high, circular tower which commands the *main* road of the Pass, just before the direct road to Ali Musjid is entered: it is 1½ miles from *Ali Musjid*, which is seen from this spot.

(142) Or Sungahs, from *Sung*, a stone, as they are built of stones.

tower, *Ali Musjid* is one and half mile ; on the left is the range of hills by which you move up to the fort ; on the right is the hill which runs parallel to, and which is commanded by the fort. The range of hills to the left leads to the cantonment of the *Khyberees;* that of *Choorah is about* 8 *miles from* the fort ; that of *Teerah* seven or eight marches off. The tower of *Jaghir* was filled with the enemy. The fort contained a considerable garrison. There were breastworks thrown up on the hills: so that it was necessary to move on slowly, and at each halt (143) to stockade the troops, as well as to protect the position ; and the *left* was the point which required the most exact vigilance. (144)

3. *March from Jumrood,* (22nd July, 1839).—The first move the Lt.-Colonel made, was to a place called *Gagree,* which is between the entrance to the Pass and *Lalacheena,* the latter not far from the tower abovementioned, here it was necessary to stockade ; and the next day was occupied in making arrangements. On the 24th July, he marched to *Lalacheena.* The Lt.-Col. in his operations employed only half the troops, and formed these into two columns. As the left of the position was open to a flank attack, and to secure the rear, it was necessary to have a strong force for this purpose ; as well as to act as supports to the two columns.

The *left* column was that which led the attack on the range of hills on which the fort is situated. The *right* column was to proceed by the hills opposite to the fort, and was previously to dislodge the enemy from the tower, in

---

(143) In the *Nipal* war, the troops were obliged to stockade every day on reaching their position. The Goorkhas would stockade theirs in less than an hour, these, being made of wood close at hand, was an easy operation, as they all worked at it. The *Sungahs* being made of stone are not so quickly made ; but, the *Khyberees* will run up one in a few hours. The *Burmese,* in their entrenched positions, dig rather deep, and not very wide, trenches, and excavate the side, under ground, *next* to the *enemy ;* by which means they are well protected.

(144) See, Chapter XIV, for an account of the *Khyber Pass ;* and the **Khyberees**.

which they were in force; having, also, thrown up *Sungahs* to protect *their* position. Lt. *Mackeson*, (145) who had two guns with him which were carried on elephants, and about 5 or 600 men, was engaged on this service, and had many killed and wounded in an attack made on his Dett.; and the enemy did not quit their position till they had suffered a great loss.

The *left* column (146) moved up the hills which lead to the fort, distant about one and half miles. Thus, the object was to attack the enemy on both sides at once. About 250 of the Maharajah's and Dooranee Horse and some infantry, with a howitzer, occupied the gorge of the Pass which commanded the roads (*Jehaghi* and *Shadee Baggee*) leading *out of* it.

The column on the *right* having driven the enemy from their first position, they retreated to other *Sungahs* half way between it and the fort; where they were attacked and driven from this new position on the 25th July.

The *left* column moved up to a position on the 25th July, near enough to the fort to throw shells into it. Below, in the Pass, there was a *Sungah*, about half a mile from the fort; this was attacked, and the enemy driven from it. The last hold was the fort. It had two or three outposts on commanding hills, from which the enemy were driven; and on the 26th July, they confined themselves to the fort. Early on the morning of the 27th July, 1839, the fort was found to be evacuated by the enemy. They were said to have had 500 Juzzailchees; and several hundred Khyberees supported them.

4. Repeated attempts were made by the chiefs to induce Mahomed Akbar Khan, to join them in opposing the advance of the Shahzada's force; but he evaded to the

(145) 14th Bengal N. I. and Pol. Asst. to Lt.-Col. Wade.
(146) Consisting of 5 Cos. Shahzada's regular Infy., 5 Cos. of the Maharajah's Mahomedan Infy., under Col. *Shaik Bussawun*, and one Coy. of the 21st Bengal N. I. under Capt. *Farmer*, and two guns carried on elephants (1-6 pr. and 1 howit.) under Lt. *Barr*, Bengal Arty.

last the solicitations of two chiefs (147) to come in person to oppose its progress. To encourage the *Khyberees* he had advanced to *Loarghi*, a village in the valley a few miles from the fort, on the 24th July; the day on which the force reached *Lalacheena*. (148) It is probable that he heard of the fall of *Ghuznee* from his father on the 25th July, (149) which caused his recal to Cabool, and probably, caused the early evacuation of the fort of *Ali Musjid*. (150.)

The total loss of killed and wounded of the Shahzada's force was 180. (151) The loss of the enemy was considerable, but I do not know the exact number. In such a warfare the enemy, from a perfect knowledge of every nook and corner, and every rock, near their position, would lose less than the attacking party; and I believe they suffered most from the right column, on which they made attacks; and here confessedly was the most fighting.

The fort is about 150 feet long by 60 feet broad, and has six bastions; but the whole extent of the enclosed place, containing the stores and where the men lived, was about 300 by 200 feet. Water was procured from a well between the fort and the river; the river water is not good in the hot season. It is capable of containing a garrison of 500

---

(147) Khan Bahadoor Khan, and Abdool Rahman Khan. Fyztullub Khan, and Alla Dad Khan, chiefs whose territories lie on the other side of *Ali Musjid* (towards Cabool) came in on the fall of the place.

(148) It was agreed between him and Bahadoor Khan, that the latter should ask for three days cessation of hostilities; for the purpose of collecting their scattered forces. Failing in this, Mahomed Akbar thought it time to retreat.

(149) The distance about 160 miles.

(150) During his retreat he was compelled to abandon the whole of his Artillery (fourteen guns) and baggage; and it is said that after leaving *Gundumuk*, about 70 miles from Cabool, he had effected his escape with difficulty, and with only a few of his followers.

(151) Including British one killed and five wounded. And one camp-follower K. and one W. and 28 of the Maharajah's troops. Total *killed* 22; wounded 158; horses 4 K. and 14 W.

Ammn. and Stores found in it. 235

men. (152) Some ammunition and some grain, and three swivels were found in it. A force was left in the place, and a strong detachment was posted near *Lalacheena*, to maintain the communication between *Ali Musjid* and the *Peshawer* frontier. A proclamation was issued on the fall of *Ali Musjid*, requiring the well-disposed to detach themselves from the disaffected.

The *British* officers employed were Capts. *Farmer*, (21st N. I.) and *Ferris*, (20th N. I.) Lts. *Mackeson*, (14th N. I.) *Rattray*, (20th N. I.) *Maule* and *Barr* of the Artillery, Lt. *J. D. Cunningham*, Engineers (153) of the Bengal Army, and Dr. *Lord*, (Bombay army.) (154) Dr. *Reid* had medical charge. The Sikh Mahomedan troops being commanded by Col. *Shaik Bussawun;* (155) for their services on this occasion, Lt.-Col. (now *Sir C. M.*) *Wade*, and the other officers received the thanks of the Govr. Genl. (156) Arrangements, military and political, being made, the force moved

---

(152) During the engagement with the Sikhs in 1837, it had a garrison of 200 rudely disciplined men, and 200 Juzzailchees. Major *Leech* observes, that "it is situated at too great a height to be of much service in stopping a force passing below; while at the same time the steepness of the hill on which it is built, would be a great obstacle to the same force storming it; which would be absolutely necessary to secure the passage of the main body, or baggage, in safety. There is no cover for the men inside."

There are positions within 300 yards of the fort from which it could be breached. They had no guns, and only three swivels. The garrison could not hold out against an enemy using shells. From the narrowness of the Pass, and the height of the fort there could not be a *plunging*-fire from it. Little of the loss was occasioned by its fire. There is a *Sungah* about half a mile from the fort in the centre of the Pass below: it was from it, and from the *Sungahs*, and from behind rocks, &c. that their fire was most destructive; our force being in a confined position.

(153) Pol. Asst. to Lt.-Col. *Wade*, and Mily. Secy.

(154) Who commanded a party of horse and foot.

(155) He had served with the British Artillery in Egypt under *Sir D. Baird*.

(156) See para. 10th of the G. O. by the Govr. Genl., dated 18th Nov. 1839. Appx. No. 4. *Sir C. M. Wade*, has been in political

forward on the 1st Aug. On the 7th August he heard of the arrival of the *British* army at *Quilla Kazee*, 5 kos (10 miles) from Cabool: while he did not receive the official report of the fall of *Ghuznee* till the 13th of August, 1839.

19. *Order of March from Ghuznee*, (29th July, 1839.)—
" The troops to move to-morrow. The *gun* to be fired at 3½ A. M. when the *General* will sound. The Assembly will sound at 4½ A. M."

2. " At the *General*, a Regt. of Cavy., Engineer's Dept. and a Regt. of Infy., previously assembled in front of the lines of the Bombay Cavy., will move under the Brigr. of the day coming on duty; under the direction of the D. Q. M. G."

3. " The Brigr. to make arrangements to occupy, with two Cos. of his Infy., a *Defile* in advance, and push on with the remainder of his Dett. to the new ground. The two Cos. left in the *Pass*, to be divided into Detts., and remain in possession till the arrival of the Rear Guard, which they will join."

4. " The Cavy. column to be formed left in front, to move round the right of the garden. The *Artillery* with their Detts. formed in their front as an advance guard, will march by the main-road, and through the village (157); followed by the *Infantry* formed right in front."

5. " The sick in Doolies in rear of the Infy.; followed by the treasure, duly protected."

6. " When the ground will admit of it, the Infy. column will be brought up in a line with the Cavy. and Arty., the right flank resting on the left of the latter."

7. " The camel-battery, and Park, will move next in succession; and all the Local Horse, not on duty, assigned for the protection of the train of carriages, and cattle. One Compy. of European Infy., will, as usual, accompany the Park, to render assistance."

---

employ for 17 years, the principal portion of which period, he was in charge of the *Sikh* affairs, and was much esteemed and confided in, by the late Maharajah *Runjeet Singh*. He is, now, resident at *Indore*.

(157) Old Ghuznee.

8. "The Rear Guard to consist of one troop of Cavy., a Ressalah of Local Horse, and a Compy. of Native Infy. from each brigade; under the Fd. officer coming off the duty of the main picquet."

9. "No baggage to move on the main road, till the artillery has passed over it, and nothing to precede the troops on the march."

10. "The Maj. Genl. Comg. the Cavy. to post parties on the road, at stated intervals, for the protection of baggage; they are to join the rear guard."

11. "The troops to move up on the *Assembly*, but not to advance till the Comr.-in-Chief gives orders."

12. "The main picquet, to move to the new ground, to enable the Brigr. to post it soon; the guns, squadron, and Cos. warned for duty, to be brought near the head of their respective columns."

13. "Officers to be left in charge of the sick, one each for H. M.'s 16th Lancers and 13th Lt. Infy.; one for the European Regt. when well enough to take duty."

CHAPTER X.

MARCH FROM GHUZNEE TOWARDS CABOOL.

1. *Ghuznee to Shushgao*, 13¾ miles, (30th July, 1839.)— Thermometer at 3 A. M. 62°. Marched at 4½ A. M. The main road lay through the village of old *Ghuznee*, and over a succession of hills and ravines, very trying for the cattle. At 8 miles passed through a *Defile*, about 2 or 300 yards broad, with low hills on each side, which a few guns and a small body of Infantry could defend against very superior numbers. The elevation here, above the level of the sea, is *estimated at* 9,000 *feet*, or 1,274 feet above *Ghuznee*. The road thence, stony for 2 miles. The rest of the road excellent and hard. Walled villages on the left of the road. The country all waste in the immediate vicinity of the road, till we reached Shushgao; where a cluster of villages, with a mud-fort, and a good deal of cultivation stretched to the N. *Camp;* rear to the hills. A stream of water to the rear (S.) and to the left of camp. Some Karezees in camp; plenty of water. Thermometer 3 P. M. 86°. The elevation of this place is 8,697; a fall of 303 feet from the defile.

G. O. 1. "Officers in command of corps and at the Head of Depts., are reminded of the necessity to repress irregularities among the camp-followers; any found injuring the cultivation, or committing depredations on the corn fields, to be immediately seized, and sent for punishment to the Provost Marshal, his deputy, or any of his assistants; and camp-followers to be warned that any plundering will be most severely visited. Proclamation to this effect to be made in the lines and Bazars."

2. "The Brigr. of the day, will consider it a most important duty to post "*safe-guards*" in the different villages,

and to give every protection to growing corn, and to the inhabitants."

3. "Patrols of Cavy. to be sent round in the vicinity of camp, seizing any found destroying the grain, or injuring the cultivation; after this notice, any man found in the act of plundering will be immediately *hanged*."

4. "The Provost Marshal and his Assts. are required to have the means at hand of giving effect to this order."

We left the Bombay Brigade to follow with *Shah Shoojah* and his contingent.

2. To *Huftosaya*, $8\frac{3}{8}$ miles, (31st July, 1839.)—Thermometer at 4 A. M. 52°. Marched at $4\frac{1}{2}$ A. M. Cavalry leading, followed by the Artillery, and Infantry, the camel-battery, Park, and sick.

"The Brigr. of the day with a Regt. of Cavy., the Engineer Dept., and two Cos. of Infy. to move off from the main picquet at the first trumpet;" ($3\frac{1}{2}$ A. M.) At 3 and 5 miles passed two short defiles, (2 or 300 yards long.) The road much undulating. Crossed some water-courses, and numerous springs of water. The march lay along a narrow valley, which the enemy could easily have defended. Great numbers of the villagers lined the roads to look at the troops. A little before you reach the village and fort of Huftosaya, there is a fine tank of water, fed by a crystal spring which issues from the mountain.

Camp. Several streams of water running through camp; the rear towards the hills. The front, the valley; cultivation, and walled villages. Thermometer 3 P. M. 88°. The elevation here, is 8,420 feet, or 277 feet below the last ground.

The people do not appear apprehensive of ill-treatment. Troops carrying their own supplies might have halted where they pleased.

G. O. "It being necessary that the front and flanks of the advance guard should be perfectly clear of baggage, the officer Comg. the main picquet, will cause videttes and sentries to be posted across the main-road, and to the flanks, an hour before it moves off, to prevent baggage passing him. The Baggage-Master to be on the alert with his sowars, half an hour before the *General.*" (1)

3. To *Hyder Khel,* 11 miles, (1st August, 1839.)—Thermometer at 3 A. M. 60°. Marched at 4½ A. M. The first half of the road good, crossed the dry bed of a river. The rest, stony and rather bad for guns and camels, crossing several water-courses. The road was narrow and much intersected by streams; it ran through a narrow valley, fertile as it was possible to be; extensive fields of beans in flower. The rising sun gilded the tops of the opposite mountains. There were trees on the bank of the river, particularly close to *Hyder Khel.* (2) A Cossid from *Peshawer* brought the official intelligence of *Maharajah Runjeet Singh's* death on the 27th June, 1839, the day we left Candahar, and of Lt.-Col. *Wade* being on the other side of the *Khyber Pass.* Reports of Dost Mahomed's son (Meer Ufzul Khan) being in our neighbourhood; picquets, &c. increased; he was with his father at *Arghundee,* a few miles from Cabool. Thermometer 3 P. M. 94°.

G. O. " Officers Comg. Regts. on the flanks of the Arty. (whence the bugle sounds) to post their trumpeters, or buglers, so that they may readily hear, and repeat the signals from the Arty. Qr. guard." (3)

The elevation here 7,637 or 783 below the last ground.

Camp. To the front of camp was the river; beyond it were some hills distant about 2 miles; a good deal of broken ground between the front and the hills. (4) The next ground in advance was seen from our camp.

(1) " A party of 1 N. O., 2 H., 2 N. and 30 sepoys to protect the Park."

(2) The scene of the treacherous and cruel murder of *Futteh Ali Khan,* the brother of *Dost Mahomed,* (see note in the preceding chapter, regarding the *Vizaret*) by *Mahomed* and his son *Kamran,* the present ruler of Herat; or rather at the instigation of Kamran, on account of a disappointment of his views. This rendered the feud between the *Suddozyes* and the *Barukzyes,* irreconcilable.

(3) " H. E. remarks a remissness on the part of sentries, who move listlessly, conversing with passengers: this is prohibited."

(4) Picquets were posted on the hills.

To *Shahkabad*, 9⅝ miles, (2nd Aug.)—Thermometer 3 A. M. 56°. Marched 4½ A. M. The road only admitting of one column. At Sydabad, half way, to the right, the Cabool river runs, where there is a clump of beautiful willows; the road hence to camp is through a close country, well cultivated. It was one of great difficulty; narrow defiles, loose stones, and broad canals, were numerous. Three rivers were crossed, the last of which, the *Loghar*, near Shahkabad, has a narrow bridge for horse and foot-travellers across it, but a passage across the river was impracticable for guns, till the pioneers sloped the banks on each side; and beyond this was a rice swamp. At this point an enemy might have annoyed the troops, as the movement was obliged to be slow; and the baggage did not reach camp till very late. At about 2 miles from camp there is a village to the left of the road before entering a narrow embanked road leading to the river, and some of the troops took this circuitous route, having to cross the river where it is rapid and rather deep; the road then leads to the village of Shahkabad.

The Thermometer 3 P. M. 98°. The elevation 7,473 feet, or 164 feet less than yesterday.

Camp. Low hills close to the rear. A road in rear of the centre passes into another valley. To the front the hills higher and more distant. The river running to the left, and front of camp. The road hence to *Bameean* is N. E. 123 miles distant by computation. We could see Maj. Genl. *Willshire's* camp at *Hyder Khel*, our last ground.

4. 3rd August.—Halt to-day. Maj. Genl. *Willshire's* column joined our camp this morning. Authentic accounts received of the *flight of Dost Mahomed* towards *Bameean*, and the abandonment of his Artillery at *Mydan*, which is 18¼ miles hence on the road to Cabool; from which it is 25 miles distant. The *Shah* and the Envoy and Minister had now arrived, and it was determined to send a body of *Affghan* Cavalry under *Hajee Khan Kakur*. (5); together with a party of *British* Cavy.

(5) Or Hajee Taj Mahomed. After being in various services he

G. O. "The following officers having volunteered for *special service,* are to place themselves under the orders of the Envoy and Minister." (6)

Capt. Outram, 23rd Bombay, N. I. A. D. C. to Sir J. Keane, Comg.	Capt. Erskine, 1st Bombay Cavy. (Poonah Horse.)
Capt. Wheler, 2nd Bengal Cavy. and M. B.	Capt. Trevor, (6) 3rd Bengal Cavy.
Capt. Troup, 48th Bengal N. I. M. B.	Lt. Broadfoot, 1st Bengal European Regt.
Capt. Lawrence, 2nd Bengal Cavy.	Lt. Hogg, 2nd Bombay Grenadiers.
Capt. Backhouse, M. B. Bengal Arty.	Lt. Ryves, 61st Bengal N. Infy. (Adjt. 4th Local Horse.)
Capt. Tayler, 1st Bengal European Regt. M. B. (6)	Dr. Worral, 4th Bengal Local Horse.
Capt. Christie, 3rd Bengal Cavy., Comg. Shah's 1st Regt. Cavy.	

" Two Detts., twenty-five men each, from the 4th Local Horse, and Poonah Auxy. Horse, to be sent on this duty; these are to be *volunteers,* and officers Comg. those corps are required to permit Capt. *Erskine* and Lt. *Ryves* to make a *selection* from among those who turn out for the service."

" A Dett. of 50 troopers from the 2nd Bengal Cavy. to be added to the above party. To be volunteers and well mounted and will be under Capt. *Wheler."*

"The whole to parade in front of Mr. *MacNaghten's* encampment at *one* P. M. to-day." (7)

---

entered that of *Dost Mahomed,* and was the *Govr. of Bameean.* Shah Shoojah, while at Candahar, created him *Nusser-ool-Doulah,* (Defender of the State.)

(6) I give the whole of the names of the officers, including two who joined the party on the 8th August.

(7) Owing to the delay of the Affghans, or rather of Hajee Khan, they did not move off till 6 P. M. !

The amount of force was as follows:

1st Bombay Cavy.	15*	* Joined Capt. Outram at the Kaloo Pass (from Cabool), about 12 miles from Bameean, with 250 Affghan Horse, under their chiefs; so that Capt. O. started with only 525; besides 200 Affghan followers mounted on Yaboos, (ponies.)
2nd Bengal Cavy.	50	
3rd ditto ditto,	15*	
1st Local Horse,	25	
Poonah Auxy. ditto,	25	
Christie's Horse,	125	
Affghan Horse, (about,)	550	
	805	

G. O. "A Dett. of Cavy. under Major *Cureton* (8) will quit camp at noon to-day on special duty, and go on to Cabool. Lt. *Simpson*, S. A. C. G. will accompany it. The Brigr. Comg. the Artillery will send an officer, and a party with this Dett." (9)

"The whole of the troops to move towards Cabool."

"The Cavy. to lead, followed by the Artillery. The 1st Division of Bengal Infy., and the Bombay, next in succession." (10)

(8) H. M. 16th Lancers, and A. A. G. of Cavy.

(9) To secure the guns left by Dost Mahomed at *Arghundee*, about 18 miles from Cabool, Major C. went with a "*proclamation*" from the King, and Lieut. S. was sent to make Comsst. arrangements; and to cause the liquor shops to be closed.

(10) "The Arty on the main road with the Cavy. on its right in column of troops ¼ distance left in front, and Infy. on left in column of Cos. ¼ distance, right in front. The sappers and miners will move in two columns on the flanks of the artillery."

"The Park, with all the Comsst. carts and hackeries, will move in rear of the Infy., and be under the charge of Major *Pew*, who will have under his orders, three Cos. of Native Infy. and the whole of the Local Horse; and arrange with the D. Q. M. G. the necessary halts for the Park. The whole of the pioneers to be attached to the Park."

"The *rear-guard* of the army to consist of one troop of Cavy. and a Compy. of Infy.; flanking parties will, however, be left at the stated intervals, to reinforce the *rear-guard* as it passes them."

"The Fd. Hospital to march with the Park."

"The officer Comg. the main picquet will post videttes to prevent

Great numbers of Kuzzulbashes came in to the Shah to-day. (11)

4. To *Mydan*, 18½ miles (4th August, 1839.)—Thermometer 1 A. M. 62°. The *gun* fired at 2 A. M., marched 3 A. M. and the troops reached their ground at 9½ A. M. The first part of the road was tolerably good, and open; with the exception of a short defile about 2½ miles from the last ground. The last half rather heavy and confined.

At about a mile from our camp at Mydan, crossed the Cabool river, after crossing which the road turns up to the right, close under low hills. At the point where the hills commence on the right of the road, is an old fort. The valley from its entrance, marked by the fort, is narrow, and well calculated for defence. (12)

Camp. The valley of Mydan is beautiful and well cultivated. Snow seen on the mountains all around. Low hills to the front; the river Cabool to the rear, in which direction the valley has a gradual and shelving slope, and the country is covered with orchards, and cultivation.

Great numbers of *Affghans* were drawn up on the roadside to salute the *Shah*. *Triumphal Arches* were erected, (the *Qoran* surrounding all) for him to pass under. Presents of fruit came in from Cabool; nor would the people, here, *sell* their fruit; it was a day of joy, and they would accept

baggage passing to the front, and the Baggage-Master, with his suwars, will be on the ground before the first ' Trumpet.' "

" Hackeries conveying the *sick* to move with the Park."

" The Camp-Colormen of corps to be formed on the reverse flanks of the leading divisions, prepared to move to take up the ground when ordered."

(11) A party of thieves in the night fired on the rear-guard of one of the corps; shots were exchanged, and a patrol drove them over the hills; when the moon rose they disappeared.

(12) The impediment of broken ground just near the river would delay the movement of guns and Cavy. An enemy would probably occupy the fort, and the heights, as a commanding position; but troops could advance by the right, and get in rear of the hills and ascend them.

of no payment. The *Vizier* of *Dost Mahomed* came in to the Shah at this place. Thermometer 3 p. m. 88°. The elevation here is 7,747 feet or 274 feet above the last ground; but *Quilla Sir Mahomed* between the two is 8,051 feet, so that we made both an ascent and descent from Shahkabad.

To *Moogheera* 13 miles, (5th August.)—Thermometer 2 a. m. 62°. Marched at 3 a. m. A Regt. of Cavy. and 2 Cos. of Infy. moved at gun-fire. The road (13) was constantly intersected by deep ravines, and defiles, and then passed through a very deep cut; which employed the sappers and miners for some time to make it passable for the guns. At 8 miles we entered the narrow valley of *Arghundee,* across which were found drawn up Dost Mahomed's deserted guns, 23 in number. (14) They were loaded and pointed to the front, rear, and flanks. The latter part of the road bad with many deep ravines.

The country near where the guns were drawn up, was much broken and full of ravines. This ground, while it would have opposed obstacles to the movement of guns, and of Cavalry, would have afforded cover for the advance of Infantry close up to the guns; and their fire having been previously silenced by our Artillery, which was nearly double in amount to that of Dost Mahomed; their fate would have been soon decided. (15)

(13) The road lay close under the low hills for about three miles.
(14) Two found afterwards in some places close to the left of the road.
(15) I think the ground at *Mydan* the strongest we met with between Ghuznee and Cabool. Had Dost Mahomed designed to make a stand at all, the range of hills which ran parallel to the right of the road, and close by which was our route to camp, afforded the most commanding position; and as between this range of hills and where we found his guns, the road was very bad, he would have suffered less in his retreat, as Cavalry could not have rapidly pursued him. It offered the best chance of escape: while at *Arghundee,* the ground beyond it was good enough to have admitted of a more successful pursuit. Had he placed his guns on the above range of hills, troops going up to charge them would have suffered more, than in the case

The road from *Arghundee* to *Moogheera* is bad till you reach a village on the right of the road about 3 miles from camp ; from this village the valley is open.

Camp. Cultivation and the river to the front. To the rear, the hills ; from the top of which Cabool is visible. (16)

G. O. " The troops to move to-morrow, Cavalry (left in front). The Artillery with the sappers and miners, on the left flank. The Infy. (right in front)."

" When the ground admits, it will be required to form up the Cavy. on the right of the Arty., and the Infy. on its left; in columns of troops and Cos. ¼ distance. The Artillery will move by the main road."

" Neither followers, nor baggage, to precede the troops. A *gun* at two, *(General.)* At 3 A. M. the Assembly to be sounded. The troops to move up, and to march when H. E. orders." Thermometer 3 P. M. 88°. The elevation here (or at *Quilla Kazee*) is 6,508 feet, or 1,120 feet below the last ground.

5. To 3 *miles W. of Cabool*, 10½ miles. (6th Aug. 1839.)—Thermometer 2 A. M. 68°. Marched at 3 A. M. The troops moved in *one* column ; there being no road for more. The road very stony, with many bad ravines. The first part over rocky ground. Half-way, crossed the stony bed of the Cabool river ; the bed of the river very extensive, and a bad road leading down to it. After passing the river, the road thence passes through confined ground, with culti-

---

of an attack on them at *Arghundee ;* there was *there* the cover of broken ground near them, and they might have been attacked on both flanks, where there were fewer guns, and only two in the rear of the square in which they were formed; and particularly as there was a deep ravine which led from our right to the left of the position in which the guns stood ; and also broken ground in front of it. An attack on the guns *in front,* as at the battle of *Mahidpoor* in 1817, by which Holkar's artillery nearly dismounted the Madras H. A. guns ; would not have been attempted ! But, the *Affghans* do not work their guns so well or so quickly as the *Mahrattas* did and do : and the carriages of Dost Mahomed's guns, were old and bad.

(16) There is a foot-path over the hills to Cabool, by which much distance is saved ; but it is not fit for the march of troops.

vation and gardens on the right. Hence the road is bounded by low-hills on each side. (17) Crossed canals, much stony ground, till we reached the gardens and the high-road. The road passed over canals, swamps, and stony ground, in constant succession. Our camp was 3 miles W. of Cabool, near *Nannochee*, where, on the left, is a salt-water lake. (18)

Camp. On rocky ground, W. of Cabool. To the N. the village of Nannochee, and the salt-water lake. (19) Thermometer 3 P. M. 92°. There is a slight fall from "*Quilla Kazee ;*" the elevation at "*Baber's*" tomb being 6,396 feet or 112 feet less: this place being 1,330 feet lower than *Ghuznee.* Our Artillery fired a Royal salute on H. M. Shah Shoojah's arrival in camp.

G. O. "Officers Comg. Brigades will make suitable arrangements to protect the fields and gardens in the vicinity of their encampments, and will hold Comg. officers of Regts. responsible that no injury be done to fruit trees, or cornfields, by their soldiers or camp-followers, in the neighbourhood of their lines. To send out patrols and plant *safeguards*, at their discretion; and will hand over to the Provost Marshal, his deputy, or any of his Assts., individuals found trespassing, or committing any outrage on the inhabitants. They will afford every protection to the villagers who may enter their camps for the purpose of selling provisions, &c."

2. "No soldier, or camp-follower, to enter the town of *Cabool* without a written *pass* from the Comg. officer of the one, or the master of the other; which are to be returned

---

(17) Our route was to the left of the Cabool road. The artillery went by another road.

(18) The valley of *Nannochee* is of some size. There is a salt-water lake in its centre, and some villages beyond it, surrounded by gardens, orchards, and vineries. The hills between the Camp and Cabool prevented our seeing the city.

(19) The king encamped on a hill to our left. There was a mountain close to our right. The troops were encamped on two sides of the village, and some on the S. and S. E. sides of the mountain.

to the officer signing, to be destroyed, that no improper use may be made of it, by being handed over to another person; as was done occasionally at *Candahar.*" (20)

"Any soldiers entering the town must be properly dressed, and have their side arms on."

3. "A picquet of a squadron of Cavy. will mount this evening at 6, in such position in front of the H. A. and Cavy., as the Brigadier of the day may think fit. Officers Comg. Brigades of Infantry will make their own arrangements."

4. "The Detts. under Major *Cureton* will rejoin their Regts."

6. *The result of the Campaign.*—The "*Army of the Indus*" had, now, arrived at its final destination. After a march of 1,527 miles (21) from *Kurnal,* where the *Bengal* troops first assembled to join the army, they had accomplished, all the objects of the expedition, by fully restoring H. M. *Shah Shoojah-ool-Moolk* to his throne; by obtaining the possession of *Candahar;* by taking the fortress of *Ghuznee* by *storm;* and by reseating the king after a lapse of 30 years, at the *Capital* of the kingdom of *Affghanistan.*

He entered the city on the afternoon of the 7th August, accompanied by the Envoy and Minister; H. E. the Comr.-in-Chief and the Staff, &c., and attended by an escort of Lancers and Dragoons.

Though the troops had much to contend with, owing to various changes of temperature prejudicial to their health; and were for a long time on half-rations; were deprived of

---

(20) See pages 102, 104.

(21) In this distance 145 miles were marched by the *Bengal* column to Lower Sindh, and on its return. Some of the Regts. had marched 16 and 1700 miles. The *Bengal* column made 132 marches from *Kurnal* to *Cabool;* being an average of more than 11½ miles a day! This had been effected from the 8th November 1838 to the 6th August 1839, in less than nine months.

The above does not include the distances marched by corps to join at Kurnal. The *Bombay* troops had marched 293 miles less than we had up to Cabool.

many necessary comforts, owing to the harassing hostility of plunderers; no troops in any warfare, perhaps, ever suffered so much with such soldier-like feeling; and never did any army marching in a foreign country commit so few acts which could prejudice the inhabitants against it; while the people begin to acknowledge the beneficial effects of the change from anarchy to monarchy.

CHAPTER XI.

OCCURRENCES IN THE ARMY OF THE INDUS WHILE AT CABOOL.

1. *Shah Shoojah's entry into Cabool.* (1) (7th August, 1839.)—At 4 P. M. H. M. *Shah Shoojah-ool-Moolk,* accompanied by the *Envoy* and *Minister,* H. E. Lt.-Genl. Sir J. *Keane,* the Major-Genls., Brigadiers, Sir A. *Burnes,* the Staff, and all the officers of the mission and of H. M.'s force, as well as by many other officers, left camp to proceed in state, into the city of Cabool, about 3 miles distant, and to the E. of camp. He was escorted by a troop of Horse Artillery, 1 squadron H. M.'s 4th L. D., and 1 squadron H. M.'s 16th Lancers, who were paraded in review order in front of the lines, and on the road leading to Cabool. A royal salute was fired as H. M. approached the escort, and the squadrons saluted him as he passed; after which, they wheeled up, and followed in procession to the entrance of the town, where they were agained formed; and where another royal salute was fired. The people were very orderly; there were immense crowds, every place in the town was filled with them. As the king advanced, they stood up, and when he passed on they reseated themselves. This was the only demonstration of joy exhibited on the occasion. (2) His majesty led the way into the palace and

---

(1) The king did intend to have gone into Cabool, in the morning, but put it off. Many of the principal people in Cabool yesterday, and this morning, came to pay their respects to His Majesty. For the *report* of arrival at *Cabool,* see Appx. No. 5.

(2) Zumbooruks (swivels) firing from the top of the gate-way, &c. alarmed the cavalcade, and occasioned some scenes of inconvenience to those on horseback, and all were so mounted.

gardens. The former were so much dilapidated after the lapse of nearly 30 years, that the old man (3) wept, while he explained to his grandsons and family, the state of its former splendour. It was difficult to get out of the city again, the whole of the king's baggage passing into it at the time; as the streets do not admit, in many places, of two animals going abreast.

9th August. The Hd. Qrs. Arty., and Cavy. changed ground to-day, and the whole of the Infantry on the following day. (4) The Head Qrs. and all the troops, except the Bengal Infantry Division, were now 6 miles to the W. of Cabool; and moved by the *Quilla Kazee* road, which was good. The Bengal Division of Infy. were half way between us and the city; the Bombay Division were to our right; and all the Cavalry were in our front.

12th August. Owing to instances of irregularities committed by *Europeans* visiting Cabool, officers Comg. Regts., to grant *passes* to enter the city to men only on whose *sobriety* and *steadiness* dependance can be placed; these men to be duly warned, that any abuse of the indulgence will cause the privilege to be withheld from all. This order to be read to each Regt. at three successive parades.

2. *Changed ground.* (13th Aug., 1839.)—The Hd. Qrs. changed ground to within two miles of the city; H. E. the Comr.-in-Chief's camp being close to *Baber's* tomb.

14th August. Lieut.-Col. *Wade's* approach to Cabool, opened the route for the *mails* from India viâ *Peshawer,*

---

(3) Then about 58 years old.

(4) " Maj.-Genls. Comg. divisions to make their own arrangements for the police, and protection of their encampments. The Brigr. of the day, discontinued. A reduction in all guards ordered. Officers Comg. to hold Qr. Mrs. responsible for the cleanliness of their lines, and officers of the Qr. Mr. Genl.'s Dept. not to fail to bring to the notice of the Genl. officers under whom they are serving, any neglect of the proper precautions, to preserve the purity of their encampment."

Two Infy. picquets of one H. and eight Sepoys, each, were posted on the main-road from Cabool, communicating with the right of 1st division of Infy. These were to protect the road against thieves, &c.

and the *Punjab;* instead of by the circuitous route viâ Shikarpore, the Bolan Pass, and Candahar, and Ghuznee.

15th August. To-day, grain ceased to be issued from the Commissariát stores, as rations, to soldiers, and camp-followers. There was an excellent open, and not dear, market in the city.

18th August. The party under Capt. *Outram,* returned this morning after an unsuccessful pursuit of *Dost Mahomed Khan;* no doubt they failed in coming up with the *Ameer* owing to the treachery of *Hajee Khan, Kakur.* There were many reasons to suspect his sincerity. When the army left Candahar, instead of marching with his Affghans, this *" Defender of the state"* (5) made excuses; that he had no money to pay his troops; and when he did march to join the king he kept at a respectable distance; and it was not till the fall of *Ghuznee* convinced him of the *"rising fortunes"* of his master (the *Shah),* that he *hastened* to congratulate him on the *success!* The *intercepted letter* at Candahar, (6) was the *premier-pas* of his line of policy. His object was to serve any chief, whose fortunes would propitiate his own advancement; and this is *Taj Hajee Khan,* chief of the *Kakurs.* Having been, under *Dost Mahomed,* the Govr. of *Bameean, he well knew* the road *he* was going. He knew, too, that if the party failed, his life might be the forfeit; for the *" Dost"* would, most certainly, thus have recompensed his numerous treacheries. Had Capt. *Outram* succeeded; he thought, no doubt, that he would *lose caste* among the Affghans, by any *overt act* against *his old master :* the deserting his (Dost Mahomed's) brothers was, perhaps, he thought a pardonable offence: for the *Dost* had deserted them himself; such is the close tie of brotherhood in Asiatic nations. Whereas, if the *Dost* escaped, and ever regained power, his (the *Hajee's)* star might yet have been in the *ascendant :* at all events he tried

(5) *" Nusseer-ool-Doulah."* The title given him by the king at Candahar. See, also, pages 87, 107 and the 3rd August, 1839, the day of his departure, on the pursuit.

(6) P. 107.

the experiment. However right (politically speaking) in his theory, he was wrong in practice: he had to deal with one (Capt. *Outram*) well known for his zeal, promptitude of action, and indomitable perseverance and courage in the field; and here the *Asiatic* over-reached himself: had he calculated on such a contingency, in his cooler moments at Candahar; he would, certainly, have been staunch to the royal cause from motives of self-interest. (7)

(7) The force sent in pursuit of *Dost Mahomed* was not above 800 horsemen; of these 250 were British, including 125 of the Shah's Cavy. under Capt. *Christie*, but there were 13 most excellent British officers.

	Miles.		Miles.
On the night of the 3d *Aug.* they marched from Shakhabad to Goda, crossing several ranges of hills,		Aug. Return Route.	
		12th, Bameean to a village at foot of Kaloo Pass,	12
		13th, Foot of Hajee-guk Pass,	12
	32	14th, To a short distance of Gurdun Dewal,	18
4th *August*, From Goda to Kadur-i-Suffied,	25	15th, Sir-i-Chusma,	17
5th ditto, Kadur-i-Suffied to Yoort,	16	16th, Kot-i-Ashroo,	17
6th ditto, Yoort to Kalloo,...	26	17th, Over Ooruj Pass, to Cabool,	20
7th ditto, Kalloo to Topchee,	12		
8th ditto, Topchee to Bameean,	12	Computed miles,	96
Computed miles	123		

The 1st *day* (3rd Aug.) few of the *Affghans* were up with the party. The 2nd *day* (4th August) barely 50 *Affghans*. Information was obtained that Dost Mahomed was at *Yoort*, 16 miles off.

On the 3rd *day* (5th Aug.) there were about 300 Affghans. Guides *reported* to have deserted. (*Hajee Khan* wanted no guides, *he* knew the road.)

On the 4th day (6th Aug.) reached *Yoort* at daybreak. Dost Mahomed, 16 miles off, at *Hurzar*; few Affghans forthcoming: nothing could induce them to advance. Capt. O. says, he had no authority to act without them; but to second them: adds " Dost Mahomed's escort being unquestionably too strong for *our* small party, (100; i. e. 50 of 2nd Lt. Cavy. and 50 Local horse; being old soldiers.) By all accounts Dost Mahomed Khan had 2,000 followers, of which 500 were of superior Cavy.; the rest matchlock-men and Juzzailchees; whose progress was retarded by the sickness of his son Akbar."

On the 5th day (7th Aug.) on reaching *Hurzar*, found traces of the Ameer's encampment yesterday. A mile further on met by deser-

The *Hajee* threw every obstacle in the way to prevent Capt. *Outram's* party overtaking Dost Mahomed. Capt. O. told him he would attack the Dost without him. The *Hajee* hinted that whilst many of our *own* Affghans were traitors, on whom no dependence could be placed; the *Ameer's* followers were men whose fortunes were desperate; and bound in honor to sacrifice their lives in defence of their families by whom they were accompanied. If such were

ters from the camp of Dost Mahomed Khan, who had left him early this morning at *Kalloo*, and no signs of his being about to depart. Hajee Khan, Kakur, said he had closed the roads beyond *Bameean*, where, if we were but prudent, he must assuredly fall into our hands. At 3 P. M. reached *Kalloo*. Hajee Khan, Kakur, with the Affghans had remained at *Hurzar*. And as the " *Dost*" must have surmounted the Kalloo Pass, the highest of the Hindoo Koosh, it was useless to proceed. We had crossed the Hajee-guk Pass, 12,000 feet above the ocean.

On the 6th day (8th Aug.) Capt. O. was joined by Capts. *Tayler* and *Trevor*, with 30 troopers, and about 300 Affghans, whose appearance appeared to have inspirited Hajee Khan, Kakur, to come up also; (on the last ground he had predicted a night attack, of which he had entertained great alarm; while we knew the sole object of Dost Mahomed to be, to escape.)

"Again the '*Hajee*' urged us to wait for reinforcements; that Dost Mahomed would make a determined stand at *Bameean;* beyond which there was no prospect of escape; all the roads having been closed, by his (Hajee's) arrangements with the *Huzarahs* and other tribes."

The *Hajee* then (finding Capt. O. determined to go on) had recourse to entreaties and menaces of force, and withholds the guides. The party then went on, and surmounted the *Shutur-i-Gurdun* (the *camel's neck*) Pass.

"Two officers were sent on to reconnoitre *Bameean*. A *council of war* was held in which it was resolved, that on the Ameer's turning to oppose us, the 13 *British* officers, who are present with this force, shall charge in the centre of the little band, every one directing his individual efforts against the person of *Dost Mahomed Khan;* whose fall must, thus, be rendered next to certain. It being evident that the Affghans, on both sides, will turn against us, unless we are immediately successful. This plan of attack appears to afford the only chance of escape to those who may survive; and it is of paramount importance to effect the destruction of the *Ameer* rather than to permit his escape."

his sentiments, why did he not decline to go in the first instance. Had he truly represented the real amount of the *Ameer's* force, more *British* troops would have been sent, and success must have been certain. He now says, " I am a prisoner, and can have no object in speaking a falsehood. Had Capt. *Outram* pushed on with his then force, the whole would have been sacrificed, and the *Ameer* would have escaped. I saved the party." There can be but one opinion; which is, that the *Hajee* ran no risk himself; for, if the *Affghans* would have turned against Capt. O.'s party he (the *Hajee*) would easily have escaped; knowing as he did all the *bye roads and passes.* But he preferred dishonor and a prison.

3. *Return of Hajee Khan, Kakur,* (19th Aug. 1839.)—The celebrated Hajee Khan, Kakur, came into Cabool this morning after the unsuccessful pursuit of *Dost Mahomed.* In consequence of Capt. *Outram's* report of his misconduct, and treachery, the *king* would not see him. The Envoy and Minister saw him, and on a report to the king of the whole of his conduct, Hajee Khan was placed in close confinement in the *Bala Hissar*, with a guard of a Company of Native Infy. over him, and the officer Comg. it received orders, that, in case of a rescue being attempted, the guard were to fire into the room were he was confined, and to destroy him. (8)

20th August. Brigr. *Arnold* died to-day. An officer much respected; he had seen a great deal of service. (9) He was buried next day in the *Armenian* burying ground, S. W. of Cabool, and about 1½ miles from it. (10)

(8) Some supposed his confinement would prevent many influential *Affghans* coming in; but, his character is too well known: and the real facts of the case would be soon known.

(9) He commanded the Bengal Cavy. Brigade. He was formerly in the Infy. and was wounded in the Peninsula, and severely wounded at *Waterloo.*

(10) H. M.'s 16th Lancers, and two guns H. A., attended as the funeral party. The funeral was attended by most of the officers in camp.

22nd August. The Hd. Qrs., H. A. and Cavy. changed ground to the E. of Cabool, distant about 2 miles. The two Divisions of Infy. changed ground, the next day, and encamped half way between the Hd. Qrs. campand Cabool, on the low ground to the right of the road.

25th August. Dr. *Lord* came in to-day, in advance of Lt.-Col. *Wade's* party.

27th August. An order was issued for the disposition of the troops to remain in Affghanistan; which was subsequently changed.

30th August. " H. M. Shah Shoojah-ool-Moolk, having intimated his intention, should Her Britannic Majesty be graciously pleased to permit them to be worn, to confer " *Medals*" on the troops employed in the operations before *Ghuznee,* as a mark of the high estimation in which he holds their gallanty and discipline, H. E. the Comr.-in-Chief is pleased to direct a nominal roll of all *officers* European and Native, and a numerical return of all N. C. O. and privates who were actually present with their corps, or Detts., on the 21*st and* 23*rd of July last,* to be prepared and forwarded, in triplicate, to the D. A. G. of the army of the Presidency to which they belong."

2nd Sept. The Bengal and Bombay Horse Artillery were reviewed before the king this morning, when he was delighted at the rapidity of their movements, and firing.

4. *Arrival of the Shahzada Tymoor and Lt.-Col. Wade's force,* (3rd Sept. 1839.)—Shahzada Tymoor, (the king's eldest son,) with the troops under Lt.-Col. *Wade* marched into Cabool this morning. Maj.-Genl. *Sir W. Cotton,* the principal Staff officers and *Sir A. Burnes,* went to meet the Shahzada, and marched in with him. A guard of honor consisting of a troop of H. A., a squadron H. M.'s 4th L. D., and one of H. M.'s 16th Lancers, and H. M.'s 17th foot, was formed near the camp of the Infantry, facing the highroad, the 17th foot on the left. On the approach of H. H. Prince Tymoor, a royal salute was fired by the Artillery, and the rest of the guard paid him the usual honors. All standard and Qr. guards of Regts. saluted the Prince as he passed.

After he had passed in front of the guard of honor, the squadrons wheeled up, and followed H. H. to the city-gate, and thence returned to their lines: a troop being sent to escort H. H. to the palace of H. M. Shah Shoojah-ool-Moolk in the *Bala Hissar.* (11)

H. M.'s 16th Lancers were reviewed this morning.

5th Sept. This day was buried poor Lt.-Col. *J. Herring*, C. B. Comg. the 37th Bengal N. I. He was marching in charge of a treasure convoy from *Candahar*. On his arrival at *Hyder Khel*, (12) he went up to the hills, near camp, with two other officers of the corps. (Lts. *Rind* and *Carlyon*), a Havildar and one or two Sepoys. He passed a party of Affghans as he was going out of camp. When he got to the top of the hills, a party, concealed, fired at them, and killed the Lt.-Colonel. His body was brought on to Cabool by bearers sent out from our camp, and was buried this afternoon, in the *Armenian* burying ground. (13)

Capt. *Fothergill*, H. M.'s 13th Lt. Infy. was also buried this evening.

(11) The king did not go, at first, to reside in it as it was said he did not like to live in it while Dost Mahomed was at large: but, he overcame his dislike.

(12) Four marches from Cabool, and between it and Ghuznee.

(13) The other two officers escaped with difficulty, and the Havildar was severely wounded. The death of no officer was more regretted. He was highly respected and esteemed in private society. He was an excellent officer. He distinguished himself at the storm of *Bhurtpoor*, (18 Jan. 1826,) in command of the Lt. Coy. of his Regt., for which service he obtained the *Brevet* majority; and subsequently was made a C. B. The day of his death a letter to his address was received in his camp, offering him the command of H. M. Shah Shoojah's Contingent, consisting of 6,000 men and guns. The officers of his Regt. have erected a monument over the remains of their brother-officer, who had been attached to the Regt. for 34 years. They permitted the old friends of the deceased to testify their respect, by becoming subscribers; and on the tablet are inscribed the Brigade and Regtl. orders notifying the melancholy event, and testifying the moral worth, and high professional character of Lt.-Col. Herring.

The native officers and men of the Regt. solicited to be allowed to contribute their mite; for he was beloved by the officers and men of the Regt. His murderers were traced, see note (32.)

Review of the Horse Arty. (6th Sept.)—To-day the Comr.-in-Chief, reviewed the Bengal and Bombay Horse Arty. The object was to test the working of both, and though not an Artillerist, I must say that the detachment system appears to me to be the best. (14)

5. *Camel-battery,* (7th Sept.)—G. O. " No. 6, Lt. Fd. Battery to be prepared for *Horse Draft,* the whole of the camels attached to the battery, and the harness and gear, to be handed over to Major *Pew,* to be taken back to Hindoostan." (15) This was in consequence of the number of

---

(14) The " *Detachment system*" is in use (as in the Royal Arty.) in the Bombay Arty. Shafts are, also, used instead of poles. It was acknowledged by the Bengal Arty. officers, that this system is the best, and no doubt it will be introduced into the *Bengal* Arty. They adopt it at Madras. The Detachment system by giving more horses, renders the H. A. more efficient; gives a protecting party in case there should be no Cavy. at hand; gives more horses for reliefs. The men do not, as in Bengal, ride *all* the horses, but only the *near* horses; they change them, riding, alternately, the *near* and off horses; so that there is less labor, and in case of sore backs the *near* (ridden) can be used as *off* horses. The *shaft* likewise keeps up the horses in descending steep roads; there is less pressure on the wheel horses; and in going down a declivity, the wheels cannot throw down the *wheelers* by the run of the gun on them, which is likely to happen (as I have seen) where the hollow between the descent and ascent is not equal to the length of the four wheels; since, unless the horses, on the *fore* wheels coming to the bottom of the slope, are instantly, pushed up the ascent, must be the result; when riders and horses will be injured. Besides this, there is a pole attached to the shaft, which, being let down, gives ease to the horses. Horse Artillery horses (as well as the Cavy.) should have a light chain with an iron-pin, by which to secure them when their riders are dismounted; this is the *Affghan* arrangement.

(15) "Until grass-cutters can be procured. the Comsst. to furnish forage, each *Yaboo* (pony) to have a ration of *half* that allowed for a horse." (I should doubt if less than 3-4ths would suffice, if in work.)

" The reserve ammunition at present carried in the park, to be conveyed on camels. *Yaboos* (38 required) for the transport of ammunition not being procurable, at the present time, the D. C. G. will comply with the indents of the officer commanding the battery for camels."

" 52 camels with drivers; 20 camels for troop stores; 15 strong grain ags; 20 suleetahs, and 52 strong ropes."

Baugree (16) camels required to complete the complement, not being procurable. The camel-battery worked well during the campaign. The camels were in better condition, than the horses, in going through the Bolan Pass. They had marched 1,600 miles in 10 months. It is only in wet and slippery ground that they ever fail.

Grand Review.—This afternoon there was a grand review of the following troops, *viz.*; 2 troops H. A., H. M.'s 4th L. D., 16th Lancers, 1st Bombay Cavalry, and H. M. 2nd and 17th foot, under the command of Maj.-Genl. *Willshire*, before H. M. Shah Shoojah, and H. E. Lt.-Genl. Sir J. *Keane.* The king was received by a Royal salute on coming to and leaving the ground; the colors being dropped on presenting arms. Several good movements were performed. There was one which had a pretty effect. Guns having been thrown out, were supposed to be attacked by the enemy; the artillery-men retired into the squares of Infy.; and the enemy being driven off, the gunners returned to serve the guns, and play on the retiring enemy.

Capt. *Outram,* (Bombay) and Lt. *P. Nicolson* (Bengal), with a party of Capt. *Christie's* horse and 300 Affghan

---

(16) A particular kind of camel used for *draught.* Major (now Lt.-Col.) *Pew* has since been directed to form another camel-battery at *Nusseerabad.* (No. 1, B. Lt. Fd. battery. G. O. C. C. 3rd March, 1840.) This officer is the original projector of the use of camels for drawing guns. Capt. *A. Abbott,* Bengal Arty. who commanded the camel-battery, is a most zealous, excellent officer; there is no officer more likely to improve the manner of working with them. He suggests that it would be an advantage to carry the ammunition *on camels,* instead of *in* the *tumbrils;* by which arrangement the draught of the four camels would be less; and that the complement of camels should be six to each gun with its limber, to be used when four might not be enough; and that there should be more *spare* camels.

Lt.-Col. *Pew* made the experiment before the campaign took place, and of course experience has suggested improvements. The camels get three seers (6 lbs.) of grain a day. The late Comr.-in-Chief (Genl. Sir *H. Fane*) with his usual foresight, directed this battery to be supplied also with *harness,* &c. for horse draught; we saw the value of his providence; and there was enough to supply some (spare) harness for the Bombay H. Arty.

horse, marched this morning towards *Hyder Khel* the place where the late Lt.-Col. *Herring* was murdered, with orders " to surround the village and mud-fort, and to let no one out, until the murderers, who seemed to be known, were secured ; and if they be not given up, by the chiefs, the place to be stormed, and every *male* put to death." To-day, also, arrived the 37th Bengal N. I. under the command of Capt. *Barstow* with treasure from Candahar. A Committee was appointed for the examination of the treasure.

Cabool Races, (9th Aug.)—The races at Cabool commenced this morning.

Dost Mahomed was reported to have made his appearance near *Bameean.* A Dett. consisting of the 4th T. 3rd. B. H. A. (native) under Lieut. *Murray Mackenzie* (Bengal) Arty., the Shah's Goorkhah Bn., and 200 of the Shah's irregular horse were ordered to be sent to *Bameean* (17).

Recovered Prize property sold to-day.

12th Sept. A Committee (18) ordered to inspect the camels furnished by the Bengal Comsst. for the Bombay column, under orders to march back viâ *Khelat.* The 48th Bengal N. I., Lt.-Col. *Wheeler,* and three guns, No. 6, Lt. Fd. battery (recently horsed) marched this morning for Ghuznee, to escort to Cabool Hyder Khan, and the other prisoners from the above place; and to escort back the wounded officers and convalescent men. (19)

This evening died Capt. *Timings,* Comg. 4 T. 3 B. (Bengal) H. A. He was a most excellent officer; and was completely worn out by the wear and tear of a long campaign.

6. *Occurrences,* (13th Sept. 1839.)—To-day a drunken European soldier struck an *Affghan* in the city and knocked him down, and is said to have defiled the dinner he was

---

(17) They have been there ever since.
(18) President, Lt.-Col. *Croker,* H. M. 17th foot. Members, Lt. Threshy (Bombay), and Lt. Simpson (Bengal) Comsst. Dept. 3,000 camels were furnished.
(19) 54 of the sick and wounded left at Ghuznee, died there.

cooking. The Affghan rose and went to seek for Sir *A. Burnes;* not finding him at home he returned, and clasping the European round the body so as to confine his arms, threw him down, and sitting on his body, beat out his brains with a stone. (20)

14*th Sept.* This *evening* (21) ended the Cabool races, being for a sword given by the king. The king went to see this race. His Majesty was saluted on coming and going away, by his own Artillery.

16*th Sept.* The Bombay column marched this morning to the W. side of the city of Cabool. (22) The 4th Local Horse occupied the ground left by the Infantry of the Bombay column.

7. *Durbar at the Palace,* (17th Sept.)—A *Memo.* in the G. O. yesterday informed us that H. M. Shah Shoojah-ool-Moolk, would hold a *Durbar* to-day, at the palace at the "*Bala Hissar.*" Accordingly at 5 o'clock this evening all officers off duty were invited to attend. The object of this Durbar was to confer the order of the *Dooranee* (23) *Empire* on certain officers. His Majesty invested H. E. Lt.-Genl. Sir *John Keane,* Mr. (now Sir W. H.) *Macnaghten,* and Maj.-Genl. Sir W. *Cotton* with the 1st class of the order; and informed the other officers present, on whom the order was to be conferred, that a sufficient number of stars of the order had not yet been prepared, to enable him to invest, on the spot, all the Civil and Mily. officers, on whom he was anxious

---

(20) On the 26th August an European sentry in front of the Infy. camp was shot dead by an Affghan, whose brother had been killed at *Ghuznee,* and as he concluded by the Europeans. The man was seized, and said he was content to die, having killed an European. A 2nd sentry was wounded in the hand.

(21) The last heat between Maj. *Daly's* Arab and another horse was run at 7 or near 8 o'clock.

(22) A soldier of one of H. M. Regt. found dead on the ground they left; supposed to have been killed by his comrades in a drunken quarrel.

(23) " Ahmed Shah took the title of *Door dowran,*" or pearl of the age; which being corrupted into " *Dooranee,*" gave one of their names to himself and his Abdallees."

to confer the honor of knighthood; but that the order should be speedily sent to them. The names of the officers selected for this honor, were then read over, and each, on being named, went up and made his bow to the king. Sir J. Keane made a speech to the king, declaring that if his sovereign would permit him, he should be proud to wear the order. This was translated to His Majesty in Persian by Capt. *Powell*, the Persian interpreter.

1st Class of the Order.

The Earl of Auckland, G. C. B. Gov. Genl. of India.

Lt.-Genl. Sir John (now Lord) Keane, G. C. B. and K. C. H. Comr.-in-Chief.

Maj.-Genl. Sir W. Cotton, G. C. B. and K. C. H. *(Queen's)* Comg. Bengal Infy. Division.

Mr. (now Sir W. H.) Macnaghten, Envoy and Minister.

Lt.-Col. Sir A. Burnes, Knt. (Bombay.)

Lt.-Col. (now Sir C. M.) Wade, Knt. and C. B. (Bengal.)

2nd Class.

Maj.-Genl. (now Sir T.) Willshire, *(Queen's,)* Comg. Bombay Infy. Division.

Maj.-Genl. (now Sir Jos.) Thackwell, *(Queen's,)* Comg. the Cavy.

Maj.-Genl. C. H. Simpson, (Bengal,) Comg. Shah's Contingent.

Brigr. (now Major-Genl. Sir R. H.) Sale, *(Queen's.)*

Brigr. A. Roberts, (Bengal.)

Brigr. (late) R. Arnold, (Queen's.)

Brigr. Beaumgardt, (Ditto.)

Brigr. Scott, (Ditto.)

Brigr. Stevenson, (Bombay.)

Lt.-Col. Macdonald, C. B. (Queen's), Mily. Secy. D. A. G. H. M. F. (Bombay.)

Major Keith, D. A. G. Bombay.

Major Parsons, D. C. G. Bengal.

Major A. Campbell, Offg. Q. Mr. Genl. Bombay.

Major Garden, D. Q. Mr. Genl. Bengal. [Bengal.

Major Craigie, D. A. G.

Major Todd, Arty. (Mily. Secy. to the E. and M.)

Capt. (now Maj.) G. Thomson, Bengal Engineers, C. B. Capt. (now Major) Peat, Bombay Engineers.

Capt. *Outram*, (24) Bombay, A. D. C. to Sir J. Keane, &c.

3rd Class.

Lt.-Col. *Dennie*, C. B. (Queen's,) H. M. 13th Lt. Infy. (25)

Lt.-Col. Orchard, C. B. 1st Bengal European Regt.

Lt.-Col. (late) Herring, C. B. Bengal 37th N. I.

Lt.-Col. Monteath, Bengal 35th N. I.

(24) To Captain Outram, &c. &c. &c.

" Sir,—I am desired by H. M. Shah Shoojah-ool-Moolk, to convey to you his acknowledgment of the zeal, gallantry, and judgment displayed by you in several instances during the past year, whilst employed in H. M.'s service."

" H. M. desires me to specify three instances, on which your merits and exertions were particularly conspicuous."

" *First*, On the occasion of your gallantry in placing yourself at the head of H. M.'s troops engaged in dispersing a large body of rebels who had taken up a threatening position above H. M.'s encampment on the day previous to the storm of *Ghuznee*."

" *Secondly*," On the occasion of your commanding the party sent in pursuit of *Dost Mahomed Khan*, when your zealous exertions would in all probability have been crowned with success, but for the treachery of your Affghan associates."

" And *Thirdly*, For the series of able and successful operations, conducted under your superintendence, which ended in the subjection or dispersion of certain rebel Ghiljee and other tribes, and which have had the effect of tranquillizing the whole line of country between *Cabul* and *Candahar*, where plunder and anarchy had before prevailed."

" For these signal and important services H. M. has commanded me to signify to you that he has been pleased to confer on you the *second class* of the order of the " *Douranee Empire*," as a mark of his royal approbation.

I have, &c.

(Signed) W. H. Macnaghten,
Envoy and Minister.

Jellalabad, 7th Jan. 1840.

(25) Lt.-Col. *Dennie*, C. B. had commanded a Brigade at one period of the campaign. He entered the army on 28th October, 1801. As Ma-

Lt.-Col. Wheeler, Bengal 48th N. I.
Lt.-Col. Persse, (Queen's) 16th Lancers.
Lt.-Col. Croker, (Queen's) 17th foot.
Lt.-Col. Smyth, Bengal 3rd Cavy.
Lt.-Col. Sandwith, Bombay 1st Cavy
Lt.-Col. Stalker, Bombay 19th N. I [Cavy.
Major Salter, Bengal 2nd
Major (now Lt.-Col.) Warren, 1st Bengal Eurn. Regt.
Major Thomson, Ditto.
Major (now Lt.-Col.) Carruthers, (Queen's) 2nd foot.
Maj. (now Lt.-Col.) Tronson, (Queen's) 13th foot.
Major (now Lt.-Col.) Pew, Bengal Arty.
Major (now Lt.-Col.) Cureton, (Queen's) 16th Lancers.
Major (now Lt.-Col.) McDowell, (Queen's) 16th Lancers.
Major (now Lt.-Col.) Daly, (Queen's) 4th L. D.
Major (now Lt.-Col.) McLaren, Bengal 16th N. I.
Major (now Lt.-Col.) Pennycuick, (Queen's) 17th foot.

Major Deshon, (Queen's) 17th foot.
Major Thomas, 48th Bengal N. I.
Major Handcock, Bombay 19th N. I.
Major (now Lt.-Col.) C. J. Cunningham, Bombay 1st Cavy.
Major Leech, Bombay Engineers, Pol. Asst.
Capt. (late) J. Hay, Bengal 35th N. I.
Capt. Davidson, 17th Bombay N. I. A. Comy. Genl.
Capt. Alexander, 5th Bengal Cavy., Comg. 4th Local Horse.
Capt. Sanders, Bengal Engineers.
Capt. McSherry, 30th Bengal N. I., M. B. Shah's Contingent.
Capt. Johnson, 26th Bengal N. I. Pay Mr. &c. Shah's Contingent.
Lt. G. H. Macgregor, Bengal Arty., Asst. to the E. and M.
Lt. F. Mackeson, 14th Bengal N. I., A. P. A.
P. B. Lord, Esq. M. D. Bombay, Pol. Asst. (26)

jor, he was wounded on the 15th Dec. 1824, in one of the many attacks on the stockades, during the Burmese war. This officer led the "*Advance*" at the storm of Ghuznee, 23rd July, 1839. He *declined* the 3rd class of the order (being already a C. B.) Except four, Lt.-Col. D. had been much longer in the army than those honored with the 2nd class of the order.

(26) The officers (except Lt.-Col. *Dennie*) in this class, are not ar-

I omitted to mention that Sir R. H. *Sale* was, as Captain, in the 12th foot, engaged with the party which attacked the *French* guns, on the landing of the *British* troops, at the *Mauritius*, 1810.

8. *March of Bombay column*, (18th Sept. 1839.)—The Bombay column marched this morning en route for Quetta and *Khelat*. They took the route by Ghuznee and *Toba*, the direct line on Quetta, leaving Candahar to their right; by which the distance was 85 miles less. (27)

G. O. " The *Transport Train*—bullocks and hackeries now with the Park are to be made over to the D. C. G. to be employed in Comsst. purposes. (28) The whole of the *Park*, except such as is to be left at Cabool, to return to the provinces, under the orders of Capt. *Day*, Commissary of Ordnance.

2. *Warm clothing*.—"The D. C. G. to make arrangements to supply every soldier remaining in *Affghanistan*, with two pairs of worsted stockings, and one pair of gloves; those at *Jellahabad*, and *Ghuznee*, and *Cabool*, each with a *Pooshteen*." (29)

" *Order of Merit*.—A Court was assembled (30) to

ranged according to seniority. This order was intended to represent the three classes of the Bath. (G. C. B., K. C. B., and C. B.) Selections were made as follows. Those for the political officers and officers of the *Shah's* force by Sir W. H. Macnaghten; those for the *British* officers by Lord Keane.

(27) See Chapter XVIII.

(28) A Committee was held to determine whether they should be left at Cabool, or not. It was resolved to bring them on. The argument was that they had been brought from the provinces, and should be taken back, as they never contemplated being kept in *Affghanistan*. They certainly carried the soldiers' beddings, &c.; but it would have been better to have bought the hackeries, and have left them at Cabool, and to have used the *draught*, as *carriage*-bullocks to carry loads, for we found the hackeries a great nuisance on our march back, in bad roads; and it is a wonder that they ever got safe back.

(29) Jackets made of sheep-skins dressed, and the wool worn inside, with arms to them.

(30) Under G. O. G. G. in C. No. 99 of 1st May, 1837; consisting of a F. O. and four members (two Capts. and two Subadars.) The D. J. A. G. conducted the proceedings, and recorded the evidence of the chief and other Engineer officers.

record the claims, of certain Native officers and soldiers of the Bengal *sappers* and *miners*, to obtain the Order of Merit for distinguished conduct at Ghuznee." The chief Engineer and Lts. Durand and Macleod, and the claimants, attended the court.

23rd Sept.—Officers Comg. corps remaining in Affghanistan, to send reports to the D. Q. M. G. shewing what tents are required to complete their corps to the prescribed complement. This afternoon H. M. Shah Shoojah reviewed the *Sikh* troops arrived with Lt.-Col. *Wade's* mission, under the command of Col. *Shaik Bussawun;* when they performed a series of movements in good style, keeping up a good fire from two field-pieces and musketry.

27th Sept.—The 3rd Cavy. marched towards Jellalabad to reinforce a convoy of treasure in progress to Hd. Qrs.; taking ten days' supplies.

29th Sept.—G. O. " The result of an attack on a horde of Banditti by a Dett. under Major *MacLaren*, Comg. 16th N. I., is published in orders."

" That officer with a promptitude highly creditable to him, at the requisition of the Political Agent, Capt. *Outram*, moved with a wing of his Regt. from the fortress of *Ghuznee*, and after a march of 50 miles in little more than 24 hours, joined Capt. O. at *Killoogoo*, on the morning of the 18th inst., and assumed command of the troops; having heard that the *Kujuck* tribe of plunderers had descended from the mountains, he marched at midnight on the 21st to attack them, with the details in the margin." (31)

" The Dett. came in sight of the robbers at day-light on the 22nd, when Major *MacLaren*, made such admirable disposition of his force, as completely to hem them in."

" The robbers are described to have defended themselves with bravery, but were speedily overpowered by the gallan-

---

(31) A wing 16th N. I., 50 Skinner's horse, under Lt. J. S. *Broadfoot*, Bengal Engineers; 150 Christie's horse, under Lt. P. *Nicolson;* and 150 Affghans, under *Mahomed Osmar Khan*.

try of the troops; and the whole band has been either killed or taken prisoners." (32)

9. *Troops to remain in Affghanistan.* G. O. 2nd Oct. 1839.—1. " The whole of the 1st (Bengal) Division of Infantry, the 2nd (Bengal) Lt. Cavy., and No. 6 Lt. Fd. battery, will continue in Affghanistan, and a Dett. of 30 sappers under an Engineer officer." (33)

2. " Maj.-Genl. *Sir W. Cotton* will command the troops in Affghanistan, and all reports to be made to him after the 10th inst."

3. " Capt. J. D. *Douglas* A. A. G. will perform the duties of the Adjt.-Genl.'s Dept. Capt. *J. Paton,* A. Q. M. G. will have charge of the duties of the Qr. Mr. Genl.'s Dept. Capt. *Watt,* A. C. G. will be the senior officer of that Dept. Supg. Surgeon *Atkinson* will remain. Orders hereafter will be issued for cantoning the troops."

4. " The 2nd T. 2nd B. H. A., H. M.'s 16th Lancers, and 3rd Lt. Cavy., 4th Local Horse, (34) the remainder of the sappers and miners, a Coy. of 20th N. I., with Capt. *Farmer's* Cos. 21st N. I., and the Dett. now in progress to Hd. Qrs. under Capt. Hopkins, 27th N. I., will move towards *Hindostan,* on such day and order, as will be hereafter issued."

5. " Indents for *Pooshteens,* gloves, and socks for the corps and Detts. to remain in Affghanistan, to be supplied without delay."

6. " The Fd. Hospital will be broken up, such portion

---

(32) " Major M. reports that amongst the captors, are some of the murderers of the late Lt.-Col. *Herring,* and that articles have been discovered in their possession which prove that from this horde of Banditti, issued the parties which, by plundering our cattle, and murdering our defenceless followers, occasioned annoyance to the troops on their advance upon Cabool."

" H. E. returns his thanks for the patient endurance of fatigue and for the gallant bearing of the troops in the skirmish, which he will not fail to report to the Govr. Genl." (See note 24.)

(33) Lt. J. L. D. Sturt.
(34) The 4th Local horse by G. O. 4th Oct. 1839.

of the Estbts. not necessary, will be sent to *Ferozpoor*, and there be discharged."

7. "The medical stores remaining in Affghanistan, to be under charge of such officer to be selected by the Suptg. Surgeon, and hold with it that of the corps."

8. "Assts. Baggage-Master abolished from this date."

9. "Capt. *F. Wheeler*, 2nd Cavy., to be D. J. A. G. to the troops in Affghanistan, from 10th inst." (35)

10. "The Dy. Provost Marshal, and Provost Serjt. *Harman*, will remain under the orders of Capt. *Douglas* A. A. G."

11. "Maj.-Genl. *Sir W. Cotton*, will be pleased to nominate an officer to act as Post-master to the troops under his command."

12. "Capt. *Bygrave* will continue as Pay-master; subject to the pleasure of the Govr. Genl."

13. "A special Committee, (36) to assemble on the 5th inst., for the purpose of reporting on men of H. M.'s 13th Lt. Infy. and of the European Regt., who are deemed unfit for further service. No man to be presented, who is likely to recover his health by a residence in *Affghanistan*." (37)

(35) Majors *Hough*, D. J. A. G. and *Sage*, Post-master, permitted to rejoin their staff situations in Hindostan, and to act in those situations with the troops proceeding with Hd. Qrs. The Rev. *A. Hammond* was permitted to return to India. The Fd. Surgeon and Medl. store-keeper to rejoin their corps.

Asst. Baggage Mr. *Hicks* to proceed under the orders of the D. Q. M. G. Provost Serjts. *J. Farnham* and *J. Harris* to rejoin.

The Provost Marshal, and Provost Serjt., to accompany Hd. Qrs. The tents of the Fd. Hospital to be made over to the D. Q. M. G. to complete corps remaining.

(36) President, Supg. Surgeon, and one Surgeon, and three Asst. Surgeons, members.

(37) Proceedings in the case of H. M.'s service to be guided by the rules prescribed for invaliding in H. M. S. For company's troops by those laid down in G. O. 6th March, 1835.

On the 6th inst., as to natives, under the rules laid down in G. O. 1st June, 1835.

14. "Officers Comg. corps in the 1st and 4th Brigades to furnish the drafts for the 9th Cos. with arms and accoutrements, to march to the provinces."

15. "The annual Committee on arms, (38) will now be assembled; and indents to be made on the Delhi Mag^{ne}." (39)

10. *4th October*, 1839.—G. O. "The D. C. G. is directed to comply with the Indents of the officer Comg. the 2nd Cavy., for an extra blanket, for every horse."

"The Maj. Genl. Comg. the Cavy. will order a casting Committee on the horses of the 2nd Cavy."

5th Oct.—Lt.-Col. *Wade* marched from Cabool on his return to Loodianah.

8th Oct.—Treasure amounting to 13 Lakhs Rs. (£130,000) arrived to-day at Hd. Qrs., under convoy of 2 Cos. 27th N. I. commanded by Capt. *Hopkins,* together with some troops from Jellalabad. This convoy came through the Khyber Pass with 2 Cos. The 3rd Lt. Cavy. came in with the convoy having met it at *Jugduluk,* six marches from Cabool.

A special Committee (40) was held at the Comsst. Fd. Depôt, to inquire into and report on the cause of the loss of carriage and supplies, sustained by a late convoy.

Passes.—"To guard against irregularities, officers Comg. corps will withhold, for the present, (41) *passes* to enter the town. Men desirous of making purchases, to signify their wish to the orderly Serjts. of troops or companies, at evening parade, and those deserving of the indulgence are to be marched down to the city, under N. C. O., to be held responsible for conducting the whole of the men back to Camp."

---

(38) Usual in December.

(39) The indents to be forwarded through Genls. of divisions to D. A. G.; with copies of survey reports.

(40) One F. O. and two Capts. On the convoy just arrived.

(41) Pay about to be issued.

"The Provost Marshal, with his Deputy, and Assts., supported each by a small guard, will patrol in the town, at intervals throughout the day; with instructions to arrest disorderly persons."

11. *Disposition of troops in Affghanistan, Cabool,* (9th Oct. 1839.)—G. O. "H. M.'s 13th Lt. Infy., three guns of No. 6 Lt. Fd. battery, and the 35th Native Infy. to remain at Cabool, and to be accommodated in the *Bala Hissar.*" (42)

The Hd. Qrs. of the Shah's 1st Cavy. were also left, and some of his Artillery. (43)

Lt.-Col. (now Brigr.) *Dennie,* C. B. was left in command at Cabool.

"The public cattle, as well as the Rewarree camels, to be sent for grazing to Jellalabad; and the Envoy and Minister will be solicited to place a body of *Affghan* horse to keep up the communication between Cabool and that place."

Jellalabad. "The 48th N. I., the 4th Brigade, and Dett. of sappers and miners, and 2nd Cavy., with a Ressalah of Skinner's horse, to be cantoned at Jellalabad."

Three guns of No. 6 Lt. Fd. battery to be stationed at Jellalabad. (44)

Ghuznee. "Ghuznee to be garrisoned by the 16th N. I., a Ressalah of Skinner's Horse; and such details of H. M. Shah Shoojah's available, the whole to be under the command of Major *MacLaren.*" (45)

"The Kajawahs now in use to be retained with corps."

Candahar. "Candahar will have for its garrison the 42nd, 43rd N. I., 4th Co. 2nd Bn. Arty., a Ressalah of 4th Local Horse, and such details of H. M. Shah Shoojah's troops

---

(42) Lt. *Sturt,* Engineers, built the barracks.

(43) The doolies (except 1 per Coy. H. M.'s 13th Lt. Infy., Golundaz, and 35th N. I.) to be sent to Jellalabad for the winter; but the full proportion of *Kajawahs,* to be retained at Cabool.

(44) The party furnished for duty in the *Khyber* Pass, to be relieved periodically, at the pleasure of the Maj. Genl. Comg.

(45) "Two doolies to remain there, and such public, and Rewaree camels, as cannot be provided at Ghuznee."

as may be available. Major-Genl. *Nott*, will command. Orders will be sent through the D. Q. M. G. to Lt.-Col. *Stacy*, senior officer, to put the troops under cover. (46)

12. *Troops returning to India*, (11th Oct. 1839.)—
" The troops to return to the provinces will move in the following order." (47)

" *1st Column*. Hd. Qrs., H. M.'s 16th Lancers, Capt. *Farmer's* Coy. 21st N. I., and a Ressalah of 4th Local Horse," (completed to 100 suwars.)

"*2nd Column*. 2nd T. 2nd B. H. A., 3rd Lt. Cavy.; 4th Local Horse; Capt. Hopkins's Dett., 27th N. I. and Detts. under Majors *Squires*, (48) *Warren*, (49) and Capt. *Prole*, (50); under the command of Maj.-Genl. *Thackwell*."

13*th Oct*. " Officers Comg. corps in Affghanistan, to transmit to the Commissary of Ordnance, Delhi Mag$^{ne.}$, statements, countersigned by Brigadiers, (51) for articles urgently required." (In anticipation of the annual indents.)

---

(46) A Bn. of the Shah's Infy. some horse, and his two troops of Horse Arty. were at Candahar.

" On the operations in *Shawl* and its vicinity being over, the 31st N. I. and two Ressalahs of 4th Local horse, now at *Quetta*, to move to *Dadur*, where they will receive F. O."

" The Coy. of Bombay Arty. with the battery of 9-prs. will join Maj.-Genl. *Willshire's* column, and move towards the Bombay presidency."

" The Mily. stores at Quetta to be made over to Capt. *Bean*, Pol. Agent, (receipts in duplicate.)"

(47) It was necessary to march in two columns, as the road viâ Peshawer was known to be incapable of affording forage for all the cattle. We had on leaving Cabool, 3,100 public and Rewaree camels, and Govt. lost 1,300 of these between Cabool and Peshawer, a distance of 193 miles; besides a great many belonging to officers and private individuals ! ! !

(48) Invalids H. M.'s 13th Lt. Infy.
(49) 82 Drafts for the 2nd European Regt.
(50) Drafts for the 9th Cos. of native Infy. Regts. then at Cabool.
(51) " Those of the 1st and 4th Brigades (G. O. 11th Oct.) were directed, according to the Regulations, to inspect the men of their Brigades recommended for the invalid Estbts; and to strike out of the rolls such as they considered fit for further field service; communicating the names to the D. A. G."

Capt. *John Hay*, 35th N. I. and M. B. 4th Brigade, died, and was buried this afternoon in the *Armenian* burying ground. This officer was *Persian Interpreter* to the late Sir H. *Fane*. He joined his Regt. on this expedition and commanded the *false attack* at *Ghuznee*. He was a good officer; and much esteemed.

14*th Oct*.—G. O. "The Ressalah 4th Local Horse to be attached to the 1st Column, half as a rear guard, and the remainder to be in rear of H. M.'s 16th Lancers, followed by Capt. *Farmer's* 2 Cos. 21st N. I."

"The 1*st Column* to march to-morrow."

"The 2*nd Column* to march on the 16th inst." (52)

Lieut. *Palmer* Intr. and Qr. Mr. 48th N. I. was appointed Post-Master to the force remaining in Affghanistan. Major *Sage* continued as Post-Master with the troops returning to India.

Mahomed Hyder Khan, Dost Mahomed's son, the late Govr. of Ghuznee, and Hajee Khan, Kakur, returned with the 2nd Column, under charge of Capt. (now Major) *Mc-Sherry* to India.

(52) The native details over H. M.'s 16th Lancer's Comsst. store, to be furnished from the 3rd Lt. Cavy.

CHAPTER XII.

DESCRIPTION OF THE COUNTRY OF CABOOL.

1. *Nature of the country.*—The province of Cabool lies between the $32\frac{1}{4}$ and $35\frac{1}{2}$ degrees of N. Latitude; and between the $62\frac{1}{4}$ and $71\frac{1}{2}$ degrees of E. Longitude.
The city of Cabool is in 34° 30' 30" Lat. N. and 68°, 31' Long. E. It has to the N. the Hindoo Koosh; to the S. the Sufed Koh; to the E. Peshawer, and to the N. W. and W. Bameean, and the Hazara mountains. *Cabool* is one of the gates to Hindostan; and *Candahar* is the other. *Baber* (1) describes the country of Cabool as situated in the 4th Climate, (2) in the midst of the inhabited part of the world. (3) It is a narrow country, but stretching to a considerable extent. Its length is in the direction of E. and W. It is surrounded by hills on all sides.

(1) Memoirs, p. 136. The names of places, &c. are spelt according to Sir W. *Jones's* plan, except I have used C for K in *Kabul* and *Kandahar*.

(2) Ghuznee is in the third climate, or division. *Asiatics* say there are seven. The Uqulem are reckoned from China W., extending, more or less, to the N. and S. (Moofurruh-ool-Qooloob.)

(3) " He confines the term *Affghanistan* to the countries inhabited by *Affghan* tribes. These were chiefly the hill tracks to the S. of the road from Cabûl and Ghazni; the low country of Lamghan, and in general all the places and low grounds, with the towns, were inhabited by Tajuks, men of a different race." An Armenian told me that Cabool and Ghuznee were considered in Hindostan, and Mukoor, six marches from Ghuznee on the road to Candahar, was in *Khorasan*. Baber says, that the people of Hindostan call every country beyond their own Khorasan. Forster, p. 121, says, (according to Sir W. Jones,) "*Khor*," in ancient Persian, signifies the *last*." On entering the *Bolan* Pass, you are in Khorasan.

"The country of Cabûl (4) is very strong, and difficult of access, whether to foreigners or enemies. Between Balkh, Kundooz, and Badakhshan, on the one side, and Cabûl on the other, is interposed the mountain of Hindû Kûsh, the Passes over which are seven in number."

"During the summer, when the waters are out, you can go by the Pass of *Shibertu,* only by taking the route of *Bamian* and *Seighan;* but in the winter season they travel by the way of *Abdereh.* In winter all the roads are shut up for four or five months, except this alone; such as then proceed to Shibertu through this Pass, travel by way of Abdereh. In the season of spring when the waters are in flood, it is as difficult to pass these roads as in winter; for it is impossible to cross the water-courses, on account of the flooding of the torrents, so that the road by the water-courses is not passable; and as for passing along the mountains, the mountain track is so difficult, that it is only for three or four months in autumn, when the snow and the waters decrease, that it is practicable." (5)

"The road from Khorasan leads by the way of Candahar. It is a straight level road, and does not go through any hill Passes."

"From Hindustan there are four roads which lead up to Cabûl. One of these is by the way of Lamghanât (the great road from Cabûl to Peshawer) and comes by the hill of *Kheiber,* in which there is one short hill Pass. In all the rest of the roads there are Passes of more or less difficulty." (6)

---

(4) P. 139.

(5) Zuman Shah (brother of Shah Shoojah) crossed over the Hazâra mountains on his march from Herat with a body of horse, and reached Cabool in twelve days; but heavy guns cannot come by this route. Caravans travel this route in summer; but the ascents of innumerable hills are such, that it is said to be very fatiguing to the cattle. Major *Pottinger* crossed over these mountains from Herat to Cabool in October, 1839.

(6) See, Chapters XIII. and XIV. for the route between Cabool and Peshawer.

Its Divisions. 277

"In the country of Cabûl there are many various tribes. Its valleys, and plains are inhabited by Tûrks, Aimâks, and Arabs. In the city and the greater part of the villages, the population consists of Tâjiks. Many others of the villages and districts are occupied by Pashâis, Parâchis, Tâjiks, Barekes, and Afghans. In the hill country, to the W. reside the Hazâras (7) and Nukderis. Among the Hazâra and Nukderi tribes, there are some who speak the Moghol languages. There are eleven or twelve different languages spoken in Cabûl; Arabic, Persian, Tûrki, Mogholi, Hindi, Áfghani, Pushtoo, Pashâi, Parâchi, Geberi, Bereki, and Lamghani. It is dubious whether so many distinct races, and different languages, could be found in any other country."

2. *Divisions of the country.*—" The country of Cabûl is divided into fourteen Tumâns (districts.) On the E. lies the Lamghanât, which comprehends five Tumâns and two Balûks *(Talooks.)* The largest of the Tumâns of Lamghan is Nangenhâr. (8) It lies to the E. of Cabûl, 13 farsangs (more than 50 miles) of very difficult road. In three or four places there are some very short Kotuls, or steep hill Passes, and in two or three places there are narrows or straits. The Gurmsîl (or region of warm temperature) is divided from the Surdsîl (or region of cold temperature) only by the steep Pass of Badam-cheshmeh, (i. e. Almond-spring.) The Pass of Badam-cheshmeh lies S. of the Cabûl river, between little Cabûl and Barik-âb. Snow falls on the Cabûl side of this Pass, but not on the Kuruk-saî and Lamghanât side. The moment you descend this hill Pass, you see quite another world. Its timber is different, its grains are of another sort, its animals of a different species, and the manners and customs of the inhabitants are of a different kind. Nan-

---

(7) They inhabit the hill-country between Cabool and Herat. Those on the Cabool side are Sheeahs; those on the Herat side, Soonees.

(8) "Lies along the Cabûl river on the S. It is the Nunnehaura of Mr. Elphinstone's map."

genhâr has nine streams. (9) Its rice and wheat are excellent. Oranges, citrons, and pomegranates, are very abundant and of good quality." (10)

"There are a number of other districts belonging to Cabûl. (11) On the N. W. of Cabûl is Kohi-Baba. (The Helmund and the river of Cabûl both rise there. The river of Balkh rises in the N. W. of the same mountain. The river of Eibak, and the Surkhrûd, which descends by Kundoz, rise at no great distance.) It is a high snowy mountain, on which the snow of one year generally falls on the snow of another." (12)

"The different districts of Cabûl lie amid mountains which extend like so many mounds; with vales and level plains expanding between them. The greater part of the villages and population is found on these intermediate spaces."

3. *Eastern and Northern Mountains.*—" The mountainous country (13) on the E. frontier of Cabûl is broken and of two kinds, and the mountainous country on the W. of Cabûl is also of two sorts, in which it differs from the hilly country

(9) " Whence said to derive its name ; which in Affghani means nine streams."

(10) Baber says, " after conquering Lahore, and Debâlpûr (a town in the province of Mooltan, 80 miles S. by W., from Lahore Lat. 30° 43′ N. Long. 73° 41′ E.) A. D. 1524, I brought plantains and planted them here; they grew and thrived. The year before I planted the sugar-cane in it, which throve remarkably well. I sent some of them to Badakhshân and Bokhara. It is on an elevated site, enjoys running water and the climate in the winter season is temperate." (Consult the *map* beyond Hindoo Koosh.)

(11) P. 146.

(12) " It happens very rarely that the old snow has disappeared before the new falls. When the *Ice-houses* of Cabûl are exhausted, they fetch ice from this mountain to cool their water. It is three farsangs (12 miles) from Cabûl. This hill and that of Bamian are both exceedingly lofty. The Helmund, the Sind, the Daghabeh of Kundoz, and the river of Balkh, all take their rise in this mountain, and it is said, that in the same day a person may drink from the streams of all these five rivers."

(13) P. 151.

in the direction of Anderab, Khost, and the Badakhshanat, which are all covered with the Archeh, or mountain pine, well watered with springs, and abounding with soft and smooth heights; the vegetation on these last, whether on the hills, the gentle heights or eminences, or the valleys, is all of one sort, and is of good quality. It abounds with grass named Kah-but-keh, which is excellent for horses." (14)

"Nijrow, (15) and the hilly country of Lamghanât, Bajour, and Sewad, are of another kind, having many forests of pine, fir, oak, olive, and mastick, but the grass is by no means equal to that of the hill-country just mentioned. (16) Though these mountains are not nearly so elevated as those that compose the other hill country, and appear diminutive in comparison, yet they are singularly hard hills; and there are indeed slopes and hillocks which have a smooth, level, surface; yet the hillocks and hills are equally hard, are covered with rocks, and inaccessible to horses."

Western Mountains.—" The mountainous country which lies to the W. is composed of the hills which form the valley of Zindan, the vale of Suf, with Gurzewan, and Gharjestan, which hills are all of the same description. Their grazing grounds are all in the valleys; the hills, or hillocks, have not a single handful of grass such as is to be found on the mountains to the N., nor do they even abound with the Archeh pine. The grass in the grazing ground is very fit for both horses and sheep. Above these hills, the whole country is good riding ground, and level, and there all the cultivated ground lies. The courses of the streams are generally profound glens, often quite perpendicular, and incapable of being descended. (17) The hill countries of

(14) " Said to be so called because it grows in *buteh,* knots, or patches."

(15) " Ferghana and Moghulistan."

(16) " It is abundant enough and likewise tall enough, but good for nothing, and not kindly either for horses or sheep."

(17) " It is a singular circumstance, that, while in all other mountainous tracks, the strengths, and steep and rugged places, are at the *top* of the hills, in these mountains the strong places are all towards the *bottom.*"

Ghûr, Karbû, (18) and Hazâra, are all of the kind that has been described. Their pasture grass is in the valleys and plains. They have few trees, and even the *Archeh* pine does not grow in them. The grass is nutritive to horses and sheep. The deer are numerous; and the rugged, and precipitous places, and strengths of these hills, are also near the bottom."

Southern Hills.—"This hill country, however, bears no resemblance to the hills of Khwajeh Ismael, Desht, Daman, Duki, (19) and Affghanistan, which have all an uniformity of aspect, being very low, having little grass, bad water, and not a tree; and which are an ugly and worthless country. There are, perhaps, scarcely in the whole world such dismal looking hill countries as these."

4. *Trade, Fruits and Climate.*—"On the road between Hindustan and Khorasan, there are two great marts; the one Cabûl, and the other Candahar. (20) Caravans, from Ferghana, Tûrkestan, Samarkand, Balkh, Bokhara, Hissar, and Badakhshan, all resorted to Cabûl; while those from Khorasan repaired to Candahar. The productions of Khorasan, Rûm, (Turkey), Irâk (Persia), and Chin (all China), may be found in Cabûl, which is the very emporium of Hindustan."

Fruits.—" In the districts dependent on Cabûl there is a great abundance of the fruits both of the hot and cold climates, and they are found in its immediate vicinity. The fruits of the cold districts in Cabûl are grapes, (21) pome-

---

(18) " Some times called Gaznee, some times Karnûd."

(19) " Duki is the Hindi for a hill. *Baber* always uses it for the S. E. hills of Affghanistan."

(20) Baber's Memoirs, p. 137.

(21) Said to be 36 kinds and even more, they each come in at different times during the season. They are in season from about the middle of July till the end of October. "There is a species of grape they call the *water*-grape, that is very delicious; its wines are strong and intoxicating; that produced on the skirt of the mountain of Khwajeh Khan Saaid is celebrated for its potency." *Baber* adds, " *The drinker knows the flavor of the wine; how should the sober know*

granates, (22) apricots, peaches, (23) pears, apples, quinces, jujubes, damsins, almonds, and walnuts; all of which are found in great abundance. The cherry (24) is also here. The fruits it possesses peculiar to a warm climate, are the orange, citron, (25) the amlûk, the sugar-cane, which are brought from the Lamghanât. (26) They bring the Jelghûzek (27) from Nijrow. They have numbers of bee-hives; but honey is brought only from the hill country on the W. The Rawash (Rhubarb) of Cabûl is of excellent quality; (28) its quinces and damask plums are excellent, as well as its badrengs." (29)

The *potato* was introduced by *Sir A. Burnes*, at Cabûl, in 1837. He found some in 1839, in the garden of the Nuwab Jubbar Khan; and it is his intention to send some to Ghuznee, Candahar, and Jellallabad.

Grain.—" Cabûl is not fertile in grain; (30) a return of four or five to one is reckoned favorable. (31) The *melons* too are not good, but those raised from seed brought from *Khorasan* are tolerable." (32)

---

it?" He was in his younger days fond of wine. The grapes of *Ghuznee* are superior to those of *Cabool;* though the former is 1330 feet more elevated than Cabool.

(22) Some we saw weighed 36 Co.'s Rs. (40 Co.'s Rs. are about a lb.) nearly *one* lb.

(23) Some weighed 22 Rs., more than half a lb.

(24) *Baber* says, " I caused the sour-cherry tree (*Aloo-baloo*) to be brought here and planted; it produced excellent fruit, and continues thriving." It is acid, not sour.

(25) And a berry like the Karinda *(Kurounda)* used in tarts in India.

(26) The country E. of Cabool. *Baber* caused the sugar-cane to be brought, and planted it there.

(27) "The seed of a kind of pine, the cones of which are as big as a man's two fists."

(28) When sweetened with sugar, it is equal to the best apple-tart.

(29) " A large green fruit."

(30) The city of Cabool is partly supplied with grain from Kohistan.

(31) *Baber* says, that the produce of the crops of Ghuznee exceeds that of Cabool.

(32) The melons of *Bokhara* are said to be so good, that after tast-

Climate.—" The climate is extremely delightful, and in this respect there is no such place in the known world. In the nights of summer you cannot sleep without a *posteen*. (33) Though the snow falls very deep in the winter, yet the cold is never excessively intense." (34)

" In the spring the N. winds blows incessantly ; they call it bade-perwan, the pleasant breeze, (but probably it means the breeze of Pérwan, from the town of that name N. of Cabûl.) From the 6th August to the 14th October, 1839, we had the wind from the N. W., E., N. E., and N. W. The N. W. wind in September and October caused falls of snow in the mountains."

Valleys—Plains—Meadows.—" In the neighbourhood of Cabûl (35) there are four fine Aulengs, or meadows. (36)

ing them, no person would eat one of Cabool; but the Cabool melons, both the musk and water melons, are good.

(33) " A sheep, or lamb-skin cloak." We arrived at Cabool on the 6th August, the hottest time of the year; and a blanket at night was acceptable.

(34) The Thermometer at Cabool this last winter 1839-40, was often 4° and 6° below *zero!* Though *Ghuznee* is 1330 feet above Cabool, the last winter *there* has been mild. The first fall of snow *we* saw on the mountains was on the 3rd Sept. 1839. *Baber* says that " Though the cold is intense, and much snow falls in winter, yet there is plenty of firewood, and near at hand. They can go, and fetch it in one day. The fuel consists chiefly of mastick, oak, bitter-almond, and the kerkend. The best of these is the mastick, which burns with a bright light, and has also a sweet perfume; it retains its heat long, and burns even when green. The oak (belût is a kind of oak, and bears acorns, but has prickly leaves, from which circumstance it is probably here confounded with the holly) too, is an excellent firewood, and though it burns with a duller light it affords much heat and light; its embers last a long time, and it yields a pleasant smell in burning. It has one singular property; if its green branches and leaves are set fire to, they blaze up and burn from the bottom to the top briskly and with a cracking noise, and catch fire all at once. It is a fine sight to see this tree burn. The bitter almond is the most abundant and common of all; but it does not last. The kerkend is a low, prickly, thorn, that burns alike whether green or dry.

(35) Baber, p. 138.

(36) Aulung, or ulung, a plain, or meadow.

On the N. E. is the Auleng of Sung-Korghan, at the distance of about 2 kos, (4 miles.) It is a fine plain, and the grass agrees well with horses; there are few musquitoes (37) in it. To the N. W. lies the Auleng of Châlak, about one kos (2 miles) from Cabûl. It is extensive; but in summer the musquitoes greatly annoy the horses. (37) On the W. is the Auleng of Deveren, which consists properly of two plains; the one the Auleng of Tibâh, the other that of Kush-Nâdir, which would make the Aulengs of Cabûl 5 in number. (38) The Auleng of Siah-Seng lies on the E. of Cabûl. Between this last Auleng and the currier's gate, stands the tomb of Kutluk Kedem. (39) Adjoining to this last valley is that of Kemri. By this computation it appears that there are six Aulengs about Cabûl, but we hear only of the four Aulengs."

The Cabûl river runs through the plain, and there are numerous springs of water by means of which the valleys can be highly cultivated, to support a larger population, as soon as the country shall become settled, and the distinction between "*meum* and *tuum*" be rightly understood.

About 15 or 20 miles to the S. E. of Cabool there is a very extensive forest which supplies the city with timber, and fire-wood.

6. *The City of Cabool.*—1*st*. The city of Cabool is not as described by *Forster* a walled-town; (40) and is about 3

---

(37) It is said that they as well as gnats, attack the bellies of the camels and cattle, during the hot weather, and by creating a sore cause their death. Hence it is usual to send camels to graze to a distance of 25 or 30 miles from the city.

(38) "Each of these 2 aulengs is about a farsang (4 miles) from Cabûl. Though but of small extent, they afford excellent pasture for horses, and are not pestered with gnats. There is not in all Cabûl any auleng equal to these."

(39) "This auleng being much infested with musquitoes in the hot weather, is not in such high estimation as the others."

(40) Forster, vol. ii., p. 79. He says, it is 1½ mile in circumference; he wrote in 1783. He could not have included the *Bala Hissar*. *Candahar* is more than 3 miles in circumference.

miles in circumference. It is situated on the E. and between two ranges of hills, which protect it from the N. and S. winds, owing to which circumstance its site appears to have been been selected. From the Candahar side, you enter by the W., passing through a winding range of hills till you meet the entrance, between the hills on each side of it; they rise up nearly perpendicular and are fortified, in the Asiatic style, by double-walls with small bastions, the walls being loop-holed. (41) On the S. W. of the city there is a small hill, which is called Baber Badshah. (42) Baber's tomb is just below this hill. It is not large, nor in a good style of architecture. From the above hill a clear crystal stream issues. The ground on which the tomb stands is higher than any in the city, and is enclosed by a wall all round. South from the city and to the E. of Baber Badshah, there is a lake nearly 4 miles in circumference. (43) The view from the E. side of the city is the best. (44) From the E. the city of Cabool is seen to advantage; the Bala Hissar being to the S. E., and from the hills to the N. E. you obtain the entire view of both; the whole of the city being seen, with the Bala Hissar to the left of the landscape.

2nd. The length of the city is from E. to W.; the N. and S. being contracted by the hills. On the E. and S. E. side is the Bala Hissar, (45) which, now, as formerly under

---

(41) Said to have been built by Ahmed Shah. These are of no defence to the place; but a fire from them might annoy the inhabitants.

(42) " Called (formerly) Shah Cabûl (where Baber himself is buried) from the circumstance of a king of Cabûl having built a palace on its summit. This hill may be about a farsang (nearly 4 miles) in circumference."

(43) This lake irrigates the lands on the E. side of the city, and by it the country may be flooded.

(44) The west side is not seen on account of the hills closing in, by which there is the appearance, as stated by *Forster*, of the city " describing generally the figure of a semicircle;" the base of which is to the E.: the country to the W. is the most picturesque.

(45) The palace is in the centre of the walled part. There is an entrance from the E. side, and there is a gate-way which leads

the kings, is the residence of the Governor; and even in the time of Dost Mahomed. The Bala Hissar division is about ½ mile long and ¼ mile broad, the length being from E. to W. (46); and has a stone-wall all round. Just on entering you come to the spot where the barracks are built, beyond which on the left is a large square for stables. There has been a small gate built to the E. entrance into the square, on passing into which, a road leads down to the left to the palace in which the Envoy and Minister lives. The king's palace is on the right side of the great square; the S. and N. sides of which to the rear, are occupied by the palaces and gardens. The large square is about 200 yards square. Beyond this square there is another in which the *Shah's* troops were encamped. Then you come into the street containing the bazar. The Bala Hissar (or upper fort) is to the S. of the side where the Envoy and Minister lives; it is on a high commanding hill, overlooking the city. (47)

from it to the W., from which the road turns to the right, runs along the river, and passes over a bridge into the city. The " *Bala Hissar*" itself is to the S. on a hill which overlooks the city, and would contain a corps of 800 or 1,000 men. The Bala Hissar division contains a bazar and two or three palaces. The barracks for our troops were built not far from the king's palace.

(46) On entering from the E. side after proceeding about 200 yards, the road turns off to the right leading to the Bala Hissar. The road straight on, leads into the city.

(47) In the time of Timoor Shah, his brothers and other state prisoners were confined here. Timoor Shah lived at Candahar usually. From the following Persian lines of the poet Moolla Mahomed Taleb Meeamaee, it would seem, that the kings lived actually in the citadel, or upper fort. " Drink wine in the *citadel* of Cabùl, and send round the cup without stopping. For *it* is at once a *mountain* and a sea, a town, and a desert."

Baber says, " In the N. part of the citadel there are houses with windows, which enjoy a delightful atmosphere." The palace in the *Bala Hissar*, where Shah Shoojah lives, cannot be the *citadel* referred to in the above lines; for a " *mountain*" must apply to the *hill* on which the upper part, or citadel, stands. The present palace therefore, is in the Bala Hissar *Division*.

The *Kuzzulbashes* have a division of the city to themselves on the W. side. After entering the city from the W., and proceeding about ½ a mile to the E., there is a road which turns to the left, (N.) and leads into the *Seistan* road, running to the N., and the first turn to the right takes you to the E. passing a village, bringing you out of Cabool; the city then being to your right, and gives a front view of the king's palace. There is an entrance into the city, from the S. W. side leading from *Baber's* tomb, which, on your reaching the outskirts, turns to the left to get to the W. entrance. The road to the right leads to the S. side of the city.

3rd. There are no gates to the entrances to the city. That to the Bala Hissar division could easily be protected. The other entrance on the E. side, is called the Lahore entrance. The entrance by the N. is by the *Seistan* road. There is none directly from the S. There are four spacious bazars in the centre of the city, (48) where articles and goods of all kinds, English, Russian, Indian, and from almost every part of the world, are to be sold. The entrance on the Lahore side (E.) leads into the most crowded bazar I ever saw. The streets are narrow, and in some parts do not admit of two horsemen passing abreast. The streets are paved with large stones, but are much out of order; particularly in that part leading from the Bala Hissar entrance into the city, and the road outside the gate-way towards the river, and after passing through the first bazar in the direct line from the bridge; in many places there are deep hollows in the centre of the road. The houses have two, some three stories; and at the top of the houses a wattled framework is erected to render them more private; here the people sleep in the warm weather. Many of the houses of the princi-

---

(48) Said to have been built by Ali Murdan Khan, a celebrated nobleman in the reign of Jehangeer, who reigned from A. D. 1605 to 1628. These bazars have covered passages, so that the sun does not shine on them. There were fountains in these bazars, in the days of the ancient kings.

pal people have gardens attached to them. The shops are on the ground-floor, and the traveller procures an excellent dinner for about *one penny*. Fruit of all kinds are to be had. The grapes and other fruits are to be seen piled up in tiers in the front of the shops. Fruit and cook-shops are to be met with in, or near all the bazars; but iron, &c. wares, clothes, &c. are in particular quarters. Ice and sherbet and all the luxuries of an *Affghan* dinner may be had for about three halfpence.

4th. The Citadel, Suburbs, &c.—Dost Mahomed had commenced to build a *Fausse braye* to the *Bala Hissar*. He commenced it from the S. side, (49) and this is the *only* part of Cabool which *could* be defended. There is a wet-ditch round it, deepest on the S. side; to the E. it may be 3 or 4 feet deep. To the S. W. distant about 1½ mile, is the *Armenian* (50) burying ground which is surrounded by a wall, and where all our officers were buried. A Cemetery should be, and no doubt will be built at Cabool.

In the *Mahomedan* burying ground near and to the S. E. of the city, there is a tomb-stone with this inscription, "*Here lyeth the body of John Hicks, son of Thomas and Edith Hicks, who departed this life, the Eleventh of October 1666.*" (51) Near the hills to the N. E. of the city are some mosques close under the hills. To the S. E., on the

(49) It was said he would have completed it in 5 months more; had we delayed the expedition, he would have been so far the better prepared.

(50) Dost Mahomed was the cause of a great number of the Armenians leaving Cabool. They were the manufacturers of spirits. The Cabool-spirit, which is very strong, is made from grapes. When from fresh grapes, it is not unlike whiskey, and its color is white; when prepared from the dried grapes, owing to the bruising of the seeds, it has an unpleasant flavor; it is dear, being about 4 or 5 shillings a quart bottle. It is not a bad drink with warm water and sugar, in the absence of brandy, &c., but it is said to possess deleterious qualities, why I cannot understand, as a pure spirit ought to be the produce; I should apprehend this not to apply to fresh grapes.

(51) The time of Aurunzebe. There is no tradition of who John Hicks was.

hills distant about 8 or 9 miles from the city, are two lofty pillars, said to have been built by *Alexander the Great*: the inscriptions on them have not yet, I believe, been decyphered. To the N. E. of Cabool about 5 miles there is a beautiful plain where the *races* were held and the troops reviewed. To the W. and N. W. of the city distant about 2 and 4 miles, there are several summer houses, enclosed with walls and gardens; and there are villages in various directions. The view, therefore, from the Bala Hissar, and from the hills which enclose the city, is very extensive and grand.

5th. Revenue, Population, Army.—The Revenue of Cabool, (52) Bootkhak and Koh Damun is said to be about 5 Lakhs Rs. (£50,000.) The last year of Dost Mahomed's rule, the whole revenue of the *Province* of Cabool was 26 Lakhs Rs. (£260,000) including Ghuznee, Jellalabad, &c. The *district* of Cabool on his accession yielded 50 or £60,000. Out of this revenue he had to pay his army 21 Lakhs Rs. (£210,000) so that he had little left for other purposes. The *population* has been variously stated at 60,000 and 100,000, and *Sir A. Burnes* thinks it exceeds 100,000; and that it was never so high as in Dost Mahomed's time. It appeared to me to be greater than that of Candahar; and the houses at Cabool contain more stories. The army was paid partly in money, by grants of lands, and by giving so much grain. (53) Dost Mahomed's regular Army was

---

(52) Of the city of Cabool was in Baber's time £33,333, but it is said to be more now. The extreme amount of the Revenue of Affghanistan which must have included Cabool, Candahar, and Herat under the *Suddozye* prince was, it is said, 80 or 90 Lakhs Rs. (800, or £900,000.) *Elphinstone*, vol. ii., p. 258 (new edition) states it to have been three crores of rupees, but only two crores available to the crown, of which one crore (one million sterling) went in Jaghires, or grants to the military chiefs. This must have included Balkh, Sindh, Cashmere, Lahore, &c.

Mr. *Elphinstone* must refer to the reign of Ahmed Shah; and Sir *A. Burnes*, to the latter part of that of Timoor Shah.

(53) Sir *A. Burnes* says—" The quantity of grain received in former times by a soldier as his pay, or by a proportion from his lands,

about 14,000 men, of which 6,000 were Cavalry, with about forty guns, besides those in *Ghuznee*, &c. The fear of invasion by the *Sikhs*, and his proximity to the country of, and disputes with *Moorad Beg*, caused him to maintain an army much beyond his means. (54) The sytem of paying the troops was, that a Sirdar, or Chief, received so many villages, or so much land, and a portion of money, and grain, for the maintenance of his quota of troops. (55)

is (1837) unaltered, but such is the complaint of a want of money, that the value of grain is deteriorated by a *third* and often by one *half.* lt was, at one time, unusual and even considered a disgrace, to part with land in Cabool, but it may be now (1837) had at from six to seven years' purchase, and is for sale everywhere. During the *monarchy,* the *Affghans* went, in the course of their service, to *Peshawer, Sindh, Cashmeer,* and to the other provinces, and brought back with them their savings. No such opportunities now present themselves : the *Koh-Damun, Jellalabad* and *Lughman*, are their *Sindh* and *Cashmeer.*"

(54) It was reported (Sept. 1838) that the envoy sent by Dost Mahomed to the king of Bokhara to seek his aid and alliance had been intercepted, on his return, by Meer Morad Beg of Kundoz, who after plundering him of his horses, sent back to Bokhara the presents he was bringing to Cabool, and had since seized several villages N. of *Bameean,* which were added by Dost Mahomed to his own possessions about the year 1833 ; and in consequence Dost Mahomed had sent the greatest part of his disposable troops to that quarter ; and ordered the reinforcement which had been despatched towards *Ali Musjid,* to halt at Gundamuk (about 34 miles from Jellalabad, and 07 miles from *Ali Musjid*). Overtures of peace were subsequently made by *Morad Beg :* but, their proximity to each other, rendered it necessary for Dost Mahomed to keep up a large force.

(55) When these troops were serving at other places than near their homes, or stations, there was a difficulty in providing for the men and horses, for in the winter the Cavalry and most of the Juzzailchees were stationed at Jellalabad, which being distant from the Jagheers granted to the chiefs, there were not the means to obtain forage for a large body of Cavy.

On the occasion of the last march to Peshawer (1837) one Regt. was one and a half year in arrears, and only received two Rs. it is said, per man : such a system must have naturally occasioned plundering to be common, to provide for their wants. From this cause it is *well known* that he could not *long* keep an army together. The chiefs would meet for any concerted operations ; but if any considerable delay ensued, they dispersed !

To meet the contingencies of increased demand on his treasury, he, of late years, had recourse to increasing the taxes paid by the merchant and trader ; as well as to borrowing money by way of loan : these acts naturally tended to lower his dignity, and would, in time, have placed him in the hands of his chiefs and subjects: there could be no stability in such a Govt. (56)

6th. Provisions, Police, &c.—Provisions are said to have been more plentiful and cheaper under the rule of Dost Mahomed, than under the kings. This may have been caused by the kings granting the most valuable lands to their favorites, and thus a monopoly would result ; but, the necessities of the state had brought Dost Mahomed to a low financial ebb ; and it does not seem to me how it would have been *practicable* to have supported him in a high and useful position in Affghanistan, without a great pecuniary sacrifice, and without the aid of a subsidiary force, on nearly as expensive a scale as that which will be the cost under a king; who must feel gratitude to the *British* for an asylum and pension for nearly 24 years from our Govt., by whose means he has recovered his throne. (57) The country was

(56) It is, also, said that in many instances two or three years' rent had been taken from the *Ry'yut* (cultivator of the soil) in advance ; on the plea of supporting the war against *Runjeet Singh* (Sikh ruler.) *We* heard at Cabool, that before he left it, he had fore-stalled the Revenue for three years! This could scarcely have been done in so poor a country ; but that he *did* fore-stall as much as he *dared* to exact is most probable. The chiefs of Candahar (his brothers) did so. It is said that 40,000 people had during his rule left Cabool and its vicinity and emigrated to Bokhara. I should attribute this fact, if true, to the state of the country in a great measure.

(57) The British Government could not have relied on any *half-*measure to have effected the regeneration of *Affghanistan*. Candahar must have been added to Cabool, these being the two *keys* to Hindostan ; this would have involved two subsidiary forces and two British Political agents at the two cities, to have rendered the measure complete ; while Dost Mahomed would never have had the same motives for remaining staunch to the British Government.

Dost Mahomed wished to have Peshawer ; but, I believe, he would have foregone that demand. He pretended that as the English would

infested with robbers immediately the troops were withdrawn from Jellalabad ; and though they were employed about two months in the year to collect the Revenue, still no steps seem to have been taken, to secure the safety of the roads by stationing troops, or by any police arrangements.

Indeed even in the city of Cabool during the summer months, it is said not a night passed without several houses being broken into. This (58) was usually practised by the *Affghans* who brought their flocks into the neighbourhood of Cabool ; and by others who repaired there to avoid the heat of the surrounding country. (59)

not aid him, he was compelled to throw himself on Persia. Now the aid he required was clearly to augment his dominions. Had he been sincere in his wish for an alliance with the *British Government*, by which his circumstances would have been improved, he would at once, have given up the demand : the Nuwab Jubbar Khan (his brother) advised him " *to strengthen friendly relations with the British Government;* but, when he decided to adhere to his policy and entertained a Persian alliance, the Nuwab, said, in council, " *the time is now gone by, it is no use to consult me, or any of the Sirdars now,*" that the Ameer might follow the course he considered safest, that there was no other alternative than to fight !

Affghanistan was merely held in military possession by Dost Mahomed, and his brothers at Candahar. Dost Mahomed, no doubt, hoped that the Persian alliance would secure him Peshawer, or some advantage. Under such a ruler there was no security against intrigue. Jubbar Khan, from being attached to the British Government, said *he* was suspected, and at one time received from our Govt., the means to enable him to leave the country. His son Abdool Ghias Khan had been sent to Loodianah for education, so that the Nuwab himself was desirous to retain our friendship.

(58) Declared to have been the case in 1837.

(59) " The usual mode of operation was for 10 or 12 to attack a house, when, if any opposition was shewn, they invariably committed murder ; and then effected their escape, which they easily did, owing to their number. Such was the dread they inspired, that the inhabitants of a house, on finding thieves had entered, feigned to be asleep, and allowed them to carry off what they pleased. It is said, that 20 houses have been known to be broken into in a night ; and for several nights in the hot weather, the inmates in every house kept watch during the night !"

Cabool is a healthy place, though it is said that the people do not attain a great age. Here as well as at Candahar the people are subject to fever during the autumn. (60) The elevation of *Cabool* above the level of the sea is (at *Baber's* tomb) 6,396 feet, which is 1,330 feet below *Ghuznee,* and 2,912 feet above *Candahar.* This gives Cabool a temperature of nearly 21½ degrees lower than at the level of the sea, (61) and from 16 to 17 degrees lower temperature than at most of the military stations in India. (62)

The range of the thermometer at Cabool from the 6th to the end of August, at 4 A. M. was from 46° to 74°, and at 3 P. M. was from 72° to 96°.

In the month of September, at 4 A. M. 50° to 64°, and from 3 P. M. 70° to 90°.

From the 1st to 14th October, 1839. At 4 A. M. 30° to 56°, and from 3 P. M. 64° to 92°.

I have myself heard it declared, that Dost Mahomed had no control beyond the city ; and while our army was encamped close to it, we had ample evidence of the state of the road between our camp and the city. If any officer dined in the city, he had 3 or 4 horsemen as a guard to protect him on his way back ; and our sentries were even shot at on their posts ! I impute all this to the absence of all control under the rule of the Ameer, whose schemes of aggrandizement caused him to neglect the "*Home Dept.*"

(60) An Armenian told me it was owing to the too free use of grapes ; the Affghans drink a decoction of wild thyme as a cure. The cold of Cabool in the winter causes those complaints which are prevalent in cold countries. This winter (1839-40), the temperature has been 4 and 6 degrees below *zero!* The sepoys have stood the cold well ; those who have died have been the weak and sickly ; warm clothing, and fires were used in the barracks and hospitals.

(61) Allowing 300 ft. of altitude to decrease the temperature *one* degree.

(62) See Appx. Table, No. 3.

CHAPTER XIII.

MARCH OF THE HEAD QUARTERS FROM CABOOL TO THE KHYBER PASS.

1. *Cabool to Boot-khak,* 8½ miles, (15th Oct. 1839.)—H. E. Lt.-Genl. Sir J. Keane, Comr.-in-Chief of the army of the Indus, and Hd. Qrs., with the first Column, consisting of H. M. 16th Lancers, 2 Cos. 21st N. I. and a Ressalah of 4th Local Horse, quitted Cabool this morning under a salute. Thermometer 4 A. M. 44°. Marched at 6 A. M. The road, after descending from the high ground near the E. of Cabool, proceeds by the famous plain to the N. E., and passes through some low ground. At about 3 miles (1) it crosses to the left by bridges over the Loghar and Khoord (small) Cabool rivers; it thence runs through a swamp. The road is raised and covered with stones, rendering it difficult for horses and camels. This compelled us to take the road close to the left of the raised road. The latter part of the road is much better, though so narrow, being confined between ravines and a high bank, that it is bad for guns. The appearance of cultivation was lost after the sixth mile; and the road ran to the right close to the hills, to the S. and was free of stones, but the whole was barren, no vestige of grass, or any sort of vegetation was to be seen. Our camp was a mile beyond the village of Boot-khak, which is a small place. The Khoord Cabool river E. and close to camp. Thermometer at 3 P. M. 64°. Lieut. *F. Mackeson,* Pol. Asst. accompanied our column. The elevation here is 6,247 feet or 153 below Baber's tomb at Cabool.

To *Khoord Cabool,* 9 miles 1 furlong, (16th Oct. 1839.)—Thermometer 4 A. M. 36°. Marched at day-break. The

(1) Or 5 miles from Cabool; our camp was two miles from the city.

2nd column, under Maj.-Genl. *Thackwell* left Cabool to-day (2) with the state prisoners, *Mahomed Hyder Khan*, and *Hajee Khan, Kakur*, in charge of Capt. *McSherry*. Shortly after leaving camp the road lay close under the hills to the S. From Boot-khak there is a Kafila (caravan) road (the *Luttabund* Pass) which runs about S. E. from camp and passes over the mountains to the left of the entrance to the Pass. (3) At 1½ mile from camp you enter the Pass of " *Kotil Khoord Cabool*." (4) The Pass is formed by two chains of high mountains between which runs the Khoord Cabool river, confined within a very narrow channel. The cold was intense; the height of the mountains kept the rays of the sun from us. The length of the Pass is about 6 miles, and the width not more than from 100 to 200 yards, the road crossing the river 23 times. The mountains are of the most barren description, of *basalt*, and *iron-stone*, broken into precipices, and crags, and without a particle of vegetation. On leaving the Pass, there is a perceptible ascent. The entrance to the Pass is about S. E. and its termination about E. (5) Having debouched from the Pass the village of Khoord Cabool is about 1½ mile distant, the road taking a turn

---

(2) It consisted of 2nd T., 2nd B. H. A., 3rd Lt. Cavy., 4th Local Horse, two Cos. 27th N. I. Detts. under Majors Squires and Warren, consisting of the invalids of H. M.'s 13th Lt. Infy. and 82 men for 2nd European Regt. and the Drafts for 9th Cos. (of Native Infy. Regts. left at Cabool) under Capt. *Prole* 37th N. I.

(3) It comes out at the 3rd march from Boot-khak, at the giant's tomb, about 30 miles distant. It is not fit for the passage of an army; nor for heavily loaded camels.

(4) The little Cabool (river) Pass.

(5) I could perceive no place, in the Pass, by which a person could ascend these mountains. The streams were frozen in many places, and as the water splashed up on our cloaks it froze on them. On getting out of the Pass to a spot where the sun's rays shone on it, I saw a trooper of the 1st Bombay Cavy. who was nearly frozen.

In a military point of view this pass is a very formidable obstacle to the march of an army to or from Jellalabad and Peshawer; and the Kafila path is out of the question in military operations: but the passage of either could be easily disputed.

to the left, and there being a perceptible ascent. The elevation at the village is 7,466 feet, or 1,219 feet above our last ground. Thermometer 3 p. m. 64°. *Camp.* The river to the rear. Hills to the front. The village about a mile to the rear of the left. Many camels lost to-day.

The *Tezeen* 12⅛ miles, (17th Oct.)—Thermometer 4 a. m. 30°. Marched at 6 a. m. The road was a moderate ascent to the E. for about 3 miles and good. About half way crossed several slight ascents and descents and some few streamlets. Thence commences the *Huft Kotil,* (6) or so many ranges of hills over which the road runs. It then enters the bed of the Rood (7) Tezeen, running nearly due N., after a winding descent through mountains variously stratified, it opens into the valley of Tezeen. The last descent is about ¾ of a mile and very steep. The first half forms nearly a semicircle to the left, and the last half is nearly direct to the valley, the direction of the march was E. and then N. (8) There is another road to the left which leads into the valley lower down, and beyond our camp, which was opposite to the debouche of the Pass. The Rood-i-Tezeen which runs down the Pass, discharges itself into the Cabool river at Tarobi. (9) The village of Tezeen was about a mile S. from camp.

Further S. the valley is crossed by a range of mountains, wooded from their base to their summit. To the W. of N. and to the E. are other mountains. The valley is not above 1,000 yards broad, and is barren, with the exception

---

(6) Or seven passes; the descents are long, and the declivities steep, two of the descents are considerable, and six others in succession, so that it should properly be called the "*Husht-kotil,*" or eight Passes. The last is a very stony Pass (like the *Bolan*) with water-courses.

(7) *Rod* or *Rood* river (of the *Tezeen* or *narrow* valley).

(8) An enemy might dreadfully annoy a column moving down this last descent, as they would have a flanking fire on it.

(9) The Gorbund, the Uzbeen, and Rood-i-Tezeen, all join and fall into the Cabool river, near the same place; and the bed of these three rivers form so many Passes to the high ridge, between Cabool and Jellalabad.

of a few patches of cultivation. (10) Thermometer 3 P. M. 66°. The elevation of the Tezeen *Pass* is 8,173 feet, 707 feet above the last ground ; that of the Tezeen *valley* 6,488, or 1,685 feet *below* the Pass ; and as the chief descent is in the last 5 miles, it would give a fall of one foot in sixteen; the greatest we had yet met with. (11)

2. The *Giant's* (or Fuqueer's) *Tomb at Ararent on the Tezeen*, 8½ miles, (18th Oct. 1839.)—Thermometer 4 A. M. 50°. Marched at day-break. The road descended the bed of the Rood-i-Tezeen due N. generally, or ascended some spurs of the mountains which ran into it. The valley was about 1,000 to 1,200 yards wide, crossing the same streams frequently as on the last march. The whole of the way was covered with round, loose, stones, and more difficult than the *Bolan* Pass, over a continual ascent and descent of loose stones, splitting the bullocks' feet, and rendering them incapable of moving. The valley widened a good deal during the march ; but, still, it was a *valley of stones*, and worse than the " *Bolan Pass,*" equally sterile, with *bad*, instead of *good* water : (12) the latter part of the road worse than the first. The only forage were a few stunted bushes, and coarse grass for the camels. (13) About half-way there is a small tower, on the hills to the left. The Tezeen empties itself into the Cabool river, about 15 miles to the N. of Tarobi. The Kafila road (Luttabund Pass) passes down from the hills to the left, by a steep descent about a mile beyond the Giant's tomb. A descent in to-day's march. Thermometer at 3 P. M. 75°.

(10) The Holly, and some few stunted shrubs were observed among the rocks.

(11) Many hackeries came up late at night ; some did not come to camp for two days, and were plundered.

(12) There is a spring of water on the other side of the hill on the right, distant about 3 miles. The water of the Rood-i-Tezeen, at our camp, ran over, it is said, a vein of iron.

(13) We lost a great many camels, and many were said to have died from eating some poisonous bushes. Grain was procurable, in small quantities, from the villages in the valley beyond camp (Seroobee, &c. 4 or 5 miles off).

To *Rood-i-Kutta-Sung*, 4¾ miles, (19th Oct.)—Thermometer at 4 A. M. 48°. Marched at day-break. The road straight in a continuation of the valley of Tezeen. We took the road to the right, nearly due E. For half a mile passed over a stony level road. Then commenced the first ascent. There are four ascents and descents. At the end of the second descent, and between it and the third ascent, is a stony valley, and a small stream, called the "*Bareek-ab.*" (14) There is an old fortification on a hill by the side of the stream. The third ascent is the steepest. The last is the longest and greatest descent. The whole road stony, and must be very difficult going to Cabool. The valley in which the camp was, is called "*Rood-i-Kutta-Sung.*" No village, nor cultivation seen. "Bareek-Ab," (15) is 5,313 feet, or 1,175 feet below the valley of *Tezeen*. Thermometer 3 P. M. 72°.

To *Jugdulluk*, 7½ miles, (20th Oct.)—Thermtr. 5 A. M. 54°. Marched at day-break. The road lay first 3 miles E. over some steep spurs, or hillocks, running down to the Kutta-Sung. Then the valley widens, and you pass a Chokee on the left. At 4 miles enter the gorge of the "*Puree-Duree*" (16) Pass, taking a direction to the S. The Pass is the bed of the Jugdulluk river. It is about 3½ miles in extent. It is very narrow and stony, with an ascent. The Pass winds several times almost at right-angles. The average width is about 40 or 50 yards; but there are three places where it is less than 10 feet, indeed one only 6 feet, so that if any animal fell, the road would be stopped till it should be removed. The almost perpendicular cliffs, on both sides, appear as if

---

(14) "Fine" or "small-stream."

(15) The country around belongs to Aughur Khan, the chief. It is a succession of barren hills, deep ravines, and small rivulets running to the Cabool river, through valleys of stones rarely exhibiting a few patches of cultivation. From the hills which bound the Kutta-Sung, the snowy range is visible in the S. E. and the "*Sufed-koh*" is also seen rising in majestic grandeur above the rest. The scenery is very grand.

(16) Literally, the "*Fairy Valley*" Pass.

threatening the destruction of the traveller. A small party
of armed men would stop the passage of any force which
had entered it. The road passes so much over water that,
in certain seasons, it would much impede the march of
troops. This difficult Pass is, in some respects, not unlike
the defile of the *" valley of hell"* between *Neustadt* and
Fribourg. (17) To the W. of the Pass, a road crosses the
mountains, which completely turns the Pass. (18) Lt.-Col.
Wade moved by the road over the hills, but his *guns* went
through the Pass. From the entrance to the Khoord
Cabool Pass to Jugdulluk, a distance 42 miles, there is a
succession of Passes and defiles, more difficult than any
road we had yet seen. They beggar description. (19)

The Jugdulluk country belongs to the Jeebhar Khel tribe,
of which Uzzeez Khan, the chief, was, at this time, adverse
to the *Shah's* Govt. There is a garden here, to the W. in
a grove of mulberry trees. There are the remains of four
bastions on the raised mound it occupies. We found some
of the 3rd Cavy. here whose horses had been left on the
return of the Regt. with the convoy to Cabool ; having been
knocked up. It was at Jugdulluk that *Sir A. Burnes*,
received his last letter from *Dost Mahomed*. Thermometer
3 p. m. 72°. Jugdulluk is 5,375 feet, or 62 feet above

---

(17) "To traverse the black-mountains, from *Neustadt* to *Fribourg*,
you have for two hours to travel along a narrow valley between perpendicular rocks. This valley, or rather this crevice, (at the end of
which there is a torrent) is only a few paces wide, and is named the
valley of hell. By this terrible defile, the greater part of the *French*
army traversed the black-mountains with an enemy in its front, its
rear, and on its flanks." (Campaign 1796, between the Archduke
Charles and Genl. Moreau.) Moreau's life by Philippart, p. 89 *note*.

(18) The road is parallel to the Pass and leads over the hills to the
left as you come from Jellalabad, and ends in the valley by which you
enter the pass from Cabool (near the above named Chokee) ; and is
said to be a better road ; but not for guns. It is about 4 miles long.
The command of the Pass would secure this road from the hills by
which the Pass is formed.

(19) The country is more barren than any we had yet seen, and
our camels got less to eat. The feet of bullocks were knocked to pieces.

Bareek-ab. We buried this afternoon Capt. *W. Hackett*, H. M.'s 17th foot, who died last night.

3. To *Soorkh-ab* (20) 13 miles, (21st Oct. 1839.)—Thermometer 4 A. M. 40°, when we marched. The road E. for the first 1½ mile was an ascent up the river. Then came a very steep ascent for about 300 yards, very trying for loaded animals. This can be avoided by passing over a small kotil (Pass) to the right, on descending which there is a ruined fort, but it is a circuitous route; some baggage went that way.

On attaining the top of the steep ascent you are on the crest of the ridge of the Kotil-i-Jugdulluk, where the river has its rise: thence there is a rather precipitous descent for about 3 miles. (21) For 7 miles the road crossed a succession of steep ravines, covered, with loose pebbles, and of a most dreary aspect. To the S., the mountains of the " *Sufedkoh*" covered with deep snow, bounded the view. At about 1 mile from the valley of *Hissarah*, there is a very steep descent over ledges of rocks, (22) into the bed of the Soorkhab river, which is crossed by a bridge of one arch, through which the river rushes a perfect torrent. Though only 1½ foot deep it was difficult to cross the stream below to the left of the bridge. To the right near the ledge of rocks, are the ruins of an old fort. To the N. E. of camp is a small tower on the hills. To the S. W. is the bridge. The river here runs from W. to E. The direction of our route to-day was E., and last half a little N. The valley still stony, and the width from ½ to ¾ of a mile. The valley particularly to the S. W. and village of Hissarah, has many orchards, vineyards and cornfields on the banks of the river, affording a pleasing

(20) Water of a reddish color.

(21) A stream comes from this side of the Pass, and running parallel to the road for about 2 miles, crosses it, and passes to the N. to the Cabool river.

(22) At this place the hackeries were obliged to stay till late at night, and the people were fired on all night; the Ghiljies being on the watch, came down and plundered them. The baggage did not get into camp till the middle of the night.

contrast to the country we had hitherto passed through. The camp was supplied with corn, bhoosa, and abundance of the finest grapes, pomegranates, and vegetables. At about half-way from the last ground Lieut. *F. Mackeson*, recovered two of the guns left by Mahomed Akbar Khan, on his retreat from Jullalabad to Cabool. Thermometer 3 P. M. 80°. The elevation at Soorkh-ab is 4,373 or 1,002 feet less than at our last ground.

It was here that *Shah Shooja*, "having marched from Peshawer (23) to attack Cabool, met the army of *Mahmood* (who deposed Shah Zeman) consisting of 3,000 men, at *Eshpaun*, in a narrow plain surrounded with hills and having the brook of *Soorkh-ab* in their front. Shah Shoojah had at least 10,000 men, was at first victorious; but his troops took to plundering, and got into confusion. The Bareekzyes under Futteh Khan (24) defeated him, and Shah Shoojah escaped with difficulty to the Khyber hills, where he remained till a fresh opportunity offered of asserting his claim to the throne." (25)

4. To *Sufed-Sung*, 9¾ miles, (22nd Oct. 1839.)—Thermometer 4 A. M. 56°. Marched at day-break. The road ran to the E. through the valley, 800, or 1,000 yards wide, and for about two miles was as stony and difficult with ascents and descents as any we had passed over; and crossed by several rivulets winding their way to the Cabool river. The valley now widened. At about 4 miles a tolerable road, crossing ravines and rivulets running from S. to N.; then a steep ascent, a mile beyond which is *Gundumuk*, on the left of the road. The elevation is 4,616 ft. or 243 ft. above our last ground. Thence the road is good till within 3 miles of Sufed-Sung, when it has most rugged descents crossing the Gundumuk river with a stony bed. There is a bridge with a broken arch at Sufed-Sung. The road to our camp crossed the stream to the left of the bridge, with a steep ascent up to it. *Camp* S. W. ½ mile from the bridge, which except

(23) On 10th Sept. 1801. He was then 20 years old.
(24) The Vizier and Dost Mahomed's father.
(25) Which he did in 1803.

the arch, is repairable. The walled village of *Gundumuk* is prettily situated. It is surrounded with wheat-fields, cypresses and a considerable forest group, through which the river issues, and with the distant snow-capped *Sufed-koh*, formed a beautiful scene, and a contrast to the bleak hill on which our camp was pitched. Thermometer 3 p. m. 78°.

23rd October.—Thermometer 5 a. m. 54°. Halt. No account of the baggage-wagons. The rear column lost one jemadar, one havildar and three sepoys, by the fire of the thieves at the last ground. They halted, to-day, at Gundumuk, the usual stage. Thermometer 3 p. m. 75°.

To Futehabad, 12 miles, (24th Oct. 1839.)—Thermometer 5 a. m. 52°, when we marched. The road to-day lay to the N. of E., and leaving the valley of *Neemla* on the right, ascending the heights along which it wound. In the valley of *Neemla,* 2½ miles from the last ground is a celebrated garden. It is a square and contains some magnificent plane and cypress trees. There are four raised planes of masonry for pitching tents upon, surrounded by the largest cypresses, planted at equal distances. *Shah Shoojah* occupied this garden, in 1809, and his army was encamped in the valley where he was defeated about the end of June 1809, shortly after Mr. *Elphinstone's* mission had left Peshawer. (26) The king fled to the mountains, losing his kingdom the *second,* and last time, his jewels, and treasure. The river Neemla runs through the valley of that name, and leaves it crossing the road, and runs into the Cabool river, at its N. extremity.

The road hence has a precipitous descent (the valley along it to the right) over loose round stones, and crossing the Neemla, turns to the S. E. (left) and ascends an opposite hill, the steep of which is difficult for loaded camels, and wheeled carriages. The next 6 miles the roads are ascents and descents; there are three passes or defiles,

---

(26) The Shah is said to have had 14,000 men and a train of artillery. It is said that *Futteh Khan,* the Vizier of Mahmood had only 2,500 men, only half of which were engaged. The Shah's army was surprised, and it was straggling and mixed with the baggage.

crossing so many streams, over loose stones of all sizes, until it enters the valley of *Rood-Croad*, (27) covered with grass. Camp at Futehabad the elevation of which is 3,098 feet, or 1,518 feet *below* our last ground. A fine view of the " *Sufed-koh*" to the S. W. Thermometer 3 p. m. 80°.

5. To *Sooltanpoor*, 7½ miles, (25th Oct. 1839.)—Thermometer 4 a. m. 54°. Marched at day-break. The road just after leaving camp passed over a water-course, then over a low flat, sometimes of loose stones and again crossing a slight sandy soil. To the S. is seen the " *Sufed-koh.*" To the N. flows a rivulet (Soorkh) running to the Cabool river. Along the banks of this stream were villages, and patches of sugar-cane. The last ¾ of a mile is a deep, heavy sand. The *camp* near the village of Sooltanpoor. The elevation, here, is 2,286 feet, or 812 feet lower than our last ground. Sooltanpoor, from the ruins near it, appears to have been a large place. The cultivation extends to the banks of the river, about 3 miles N. Lieut. *F. Mackeson* went into Jellalabad to-day. Thermtr. 3 p. m. 90°. As we were now approaching the *Sikh* frontier the following G. O. was issued. (Adverting to the steady discipline which, during the present campaign, had secured the approbation of Govt.) "While passing through the " *Punjab*" and protected Sikh states, all are required to abstain from killing *pea-fowl*, the *Neelghy,* or the domestic pigeons, or from offending, in any way, the prejudices of the *Sikhs ;* and the D. C. G. will prohibit, in the strictest manner, the slaughtering of cattle." (28)

" Major-Genl. *Thackwell*, (29) and Brigr. *Persse* (30) will use every means in their power, in restraining camp-followers from injuring, or trespassing on the cultivation ; and parties under the Provost Marshal and his assistants

---

(27) Beyond the valley the stream is called " *Karsee*," and comes from the *Viseree* District, in the *Khajeearee* territory.
(28) *Runjeet* wished us not to kill bullocks in Affghanistan.
(29) Comg. the 2nd, or Rear Column.
(30) Comg. 1st column.

must be early on the new ground, daily, to place safeguards in the villages, and over the corn-fields."

"The Provosts are enjoined to deal strictly with those they may find tresspassing, or committing any act of oppression."

"Officers Comg. must remind their men that the army is passing through the territory of an ally, and that as the soldiers of that prince, from not possessing the same degree of discipline of which the *British* army can boast, may be more ready to enter into quarrels, and to make use of offensive expressions; it will be the duty of all, to keep a guard on their temper, and to be careful not to allow themselves to be forced into collision, with those whom the Government requires that they shall look upon as friends." (31)

To *Jellalabad*, nine miles, (26th Oct.)—Thermtr. 4 A. M. 54°. The road the first part sandy, the next part stony, and the last part sandy. There is a sandy plain E., W. and S. of Jellalabad. This was once a flourishing town. The elevation, here, is 1,964, or 322 feet below our last ground. Thermtr. 3 P. M. 92°.

We here, found some troops which had been left by Lt.-Col. *Wade* and Lieut. *W. R. Hillersdon* (32) the Assist. Pol. Agent.

It was at this place where Dost Mahomed kept his Cavy. and the greatest portion of his Juzzailchees. The town we

(31) "From the date of the arrival of the troops within the Sikh territory, a main picquet, consisting of Cavy. and Infy. according to the strength of each arm, with the different columns, must mount daily on reaching the new ground, and be in readiness to move in any direction, to quell disturbances, or to preserve order."

"No soldier to be allowed to quit camp after passing the Sikh frontier, except on duty; and all camp-followers are to be prohibited entering the towns and villages in the neighbourhood of the camp; guards must, invariably, be planted at the gate-ways of towns and villages, to ensure this order being complied with."

"When it may prove indispensably necessary, in pitching the camp, to encroach on the cultivation, the D. Q. M. G. will take care that the proprietors of the fields are reimbursed to the fullest extent for the property which may be injured."

(32) 53rd Bengal N. I.

found to be a small dirty place, with mud-walls, round towers, and narrow streets. It stands on the right bank of the Cabool river. The inhabitants are said to be about 2,000. It is bounded by sterile mountains.

27th and 28th October, halted.—(Thermtr. the same as on the 26th.) While we were here the *Khyber Pass* was attacked. (33)

6.—To *Ali Boghan*, 6¾ miles, (29th Oct. 1839.)—Thermtr. 4. A. M. 56°. Marched at day-break. The road ran due E., first part sandy, over a level plain, the greater part of which was under cultivation, for nearly 3 miles. Thence crossed over a bed of stones; the rest of the road good, excepting two not difficult ravines, and two or three water-courses, then a thick jungle of reeds through which there was a path, which terminated in ravines and sandy hills, about the sixth mile. At 42 minutes past 3 P. M. a shock of an earthquake. Thermt. 3 P. M. 92°. The elevation, here, is 1,911 ft. or 53 ft. below the last ground.

(33) On the 25th October, 1839, Capt. *Ferris's* post was attacked and the Khyberees carried off 40 horses. The post was just under the fort, in which there was a party. On the 26th, they made a slight attack, and left four men dead on the ground. On the 28th, they made a grand attack on the Sikh post (the party composed of Mahomedans), at some *Sungahs* near the tower of *Jaghir*, about one and a half mile from Ali Musjid and Capt. F.'s post. The Khyberees stationed a party on the hill between the post and Ali Musjid to prevent any troops being sent to their aid; they thus commanded the road.

The Khyberees appear to have been, principally, swordsmen; but few armed with matchlocks. They made seven attacks on the Sikhs, and were repulsed six times by musketry. At last, they attacked sword in hand. It is said that, on the Sikhs leaving the Sungah to attack them, the Khyberees attacked the weak point where the sick were; and then cut up those that remained. There were said to be 60 of the Sikh Bn. killed in the Sungah and 150 below it; and many were cut up on the road; and that out of about 800, only 250 reached Peshawer. The Dett. is said to have been in a sickly state. Had they kept to the *Sungah*, they might have beaten off the Khyberees, whose attack was said to have originated in a desire to get plunder; the Sikhs having their money (their pay recently received) in the stockade: but, it is highly probably that the *real* cause was, the settled *antipathy* of the Khyberees to the Sikhs.

To *Char Deh,* 14 miles, (30th Oct.)—Thermtr. 4 A. M. 56°, when we marched. The road lay almost due E. and for the first 3 miles was good and level, but on ascending a small hill, we entered a wide, barren valley or stony desert, called the "*Soorkh-Denkor,*" (surrounded with low hills,) where in the months of April and May, the deadly *simoom* prevails. This track was marched over for 9 miles, and there seemed to be desolation all around. About 1½ mile from camp was the small dilapidated village of *Bareek-ab;* water-courses near it. The road then was sandy and brought us to the banks of the *Rood-Buttur-kot* and cultivation; and crossing this stream, we reach the village of that name, and in the valley was our *camp.* The Cabool river running to the N., the desert to the W., the "*Sufed-koh*" to the S., and to the E. the *Khyber* range. The elevation at *Bareek-ab* is 1822 ft. or 89 below our last ground. Thermtr. 3 P. M. 88°.

To *Huzarnow,* 11¾ miles, (31st Oct.)—Thermtr. 4 A. M. 54°. There were two roads leading out of camp. (34)

The first part sandy. At about 3 miles crossed the dry bed of a nullah, and crossed between this and Huzarnow, two dry stony beds of hill streams. The middle part of the march, the road stony for 2 or 3 miles. The road generally pretty good, but sandy and stony, and crossing several small water-courses. Direction the last half E. The road passing over the *Dusht* (plain) led to Huzarnow, a cluster of villages, some of which have mud-walls and towers; and a good deal of cultivation around the villages. (35)

The village of *Basool* is at an elevation of 1,509 feet or 313 feet below Bareek-ab.

---

(34) The nearest had a direction nearly E., but was found to be intersected by numerous ditches full of water. The other took a S. E. direction, round some low hills until it entered the "*Dusht*" (plain) about 3 miles off, over a good, even, country, when it turned to due E.: the two roads meet at Basool, a village to the left about half-way.

(35) On the mountain to the N. there is a black stratum (of slate) regarding which the natives have a tradition of the annual exit of a snake for food, and his return to the mountain.

To the N. of Huzarnow, distant 2 or 3 miles is the village of Chuhkouree. Thermometer 3 P. M. 88°. Good grass, and grazing for the cattle. Bhoosa procured.

To *Dakka*, 9 miles, (1st Nov.)—Thermometer 4 A. M. 56°. Marched at day-break. The road skirted the hills for some distance avoiding a swamp, when it turned to the E. along a level, gentle rise, over a good country for about 4 miles; then crossed several very small rivulets, and some arable lands, and at 6 miles ascended the Pass, or narrow defile, of *Kum* or *Khoord Khyber*, or *little Khyber*. (36) On quitting the defile, the road lies through the valley, and at two miles you come to *Dakka*, where are two walled villages, to the left of the road and distant about a mile; the Cabool (37) river runs by them from W. to E. (38) The ground at *Dakka* is covered with an efflorescence of Soda for some distance from the river, and the ground is in consequence very damp; the surrounding land is covered with stones and hard sand. We found supplies here and a party of troops recently raised by Mr. *Mackeson*. The elevation, at Lalpoora is 1,404 feet, or 105 feet lower than Basool. It was N. W. and Dakka, E.

---

(36) The defile is very narrow, in some places not admitting of two horsemen going abreast. It is about three quarters of a mile long. It is more like a deep narrow ravine, with high banks in some parts. We found the road through it good, and the descent in it not difficult. But if the heights were occupied by troops, it would stop the advance of any force, till the enemy were dislodged.

(37) Here called the *Lunda*, or *Lundee*.

(38) At the back of the mountains through which the road runs, are numerous small forts, and the whole of the country is a succession of hills.

At *Lalpoorah* N. W. on the other side of the river, distant one and half mile, is the fort of Saadut Khan, the most powerful of all the petty chiefs in the country; but he has no authority over the country between Peshawer and Dakka, called the Ab-khana. He receives Budrika (money for passports or Purwanahs) from all travellers, which is divided among the Ooloos, or clan. *Dakka* has about 200 families, and the place can furnish supplies for a considerable body.

of our camp. Thermtr. 3 p. m. 87°. The Khyberees on the side of the Pass towards Peshawer, were hostile to the Shah, and it was only on the 28th October, that they had ceased from their attacks on the Sikh Dett.; hence the " Post" had been delayed for some days: and we were to move through the Pass with caution.

CHAPTER XIV.

THE MARCH OF THE HEAD QUARTERS AND TROOPS THROUGH THE KHYBER PASS TO PESHAWER.

1. To *Lundee-Khana*, 9 miles, (2nd Nov. 1839.)—Thermometer 4 A. M. 48°. Marched at day-break. The entrance to the Pass was a mile distant from camp. The road was to the S. of E., over beds of loose stones, and up a gradual ascent. The mountains on the N. and S. gradually contracting the Pass, which turned at several points, being the bed of a mountain torrent. At about half-way in the Pass, the road was good, and less stony. The width of the Pass varies from 100 to 200 yards in the centre. In the last half there is a sensible rise. The Pass narrows the latter part. The hills are generally precipitous, covered with stunted bushes. Our direction the last part of the march was E. The hills are not very high; on the highest to the S. near camp, there is an old fort. (1) The village of Lundee-Khana is S. E. of camp, close under the hills on rising ground, distant about a mile, near which there is some cultivation; our camp was on high broken ground to the N. The Pass near camp about ¼ mile wide. Water close to camp. (2) The elevation, here, is 2,488 feet, or 1,084 feet above Lalpoora. Thermometer 3 P. M. 78°. As the Pass is no where above 200 yards wide, it is clear that it can be commanded by the native rifle from either side. (3)

(1) Called by some Alexander's fort.
(2) On our arrival we found the sappers, who had been ordered on in advance, and had been halted here.
(3) The native mountain rifle fired with a rest will kill at 800 yards. From the entrance to Lundee-Khana, is about 7½ miles, and in the centre, in the widest part, there is on the left rising ground at

To *Ali Musjid*, 13¾ miles, (3rd Nov.)—Thermometer 69°. Marched before day-break. There are two roads from Lundee-Khana, which, after the ascent of the Pass, unite at the bottom of the descent. The lower is in the bed of the river, and is the most precipitous. The commencement of the steepest ascent was close to camp, and very abrupt for about 150 yards, (4) after which the rise is moderate, excepting two rather steep parts of no great extent. The road is about 12 feet wide, and to the right there is a precipice towards the valley. After an ascent of about 2 miles you reach the top of the Pass, at an elevation of 3,373 feet, or 885 feet above Lundee-Khana, or, a rise of about *one in fifteen feet* the greatest we had yet met with. The direction from the ascent was about E., and the road described a portion of a circle to the S. E., where there is a Police Chokee stationed. (5) The descent from the hill is for about three miles, and the road and country more open. At the bottom of the descent you enter the valley of Lalbeg, or, Lalbeg-gurhee. (6)

After entering the valley there is an old fort on the hills to the right, which if in repair would annoy any troops moving towards Lundee-Khana. (7) The valley of Lalbeg-gurhee

Huft-chah on which *Sungahs*, or stockades, could be erected; so that parties, by crowning the hills, on both sides, would inflict great havock among troops advancing, for there is no *cover*.

(4) Difficult to walk up.

(5) When we reached the tôp we could see the camp we had left. The road is formed very much like those at Simla. The top of the hill, (as observed by Major *Leech*) is an admirable position for a fort, which could enfilade with the most destructive effect, both the road from *Dakka*, and that from *Lalbeg* (coming from Ali Musjid). From the top of the hill, a fire could be thrown on the winding road coming up to it; while it commands, more directly, the road going down from it.

(6) The road up the ascent was good, and that of the descent had been repaired lately by Mr. *Mackeson*, and was good; there are some ascents, also, in this road. The rock of "*Aornus*" is supposed to be the summit of the Pass at Lundee-Khana.

(7) There is a plain of the Shanwarees running to the N. of this plain, in which is the village of Luadgai, distant about 2 miles, whence

is about 6 miles long and 1¼ broad and is cultivated. (8) There are small villages on each side of the road, and you cross two dry stony beds in the valley. At the end of the valley towards Ali Musjid there are towers (9) on either side of the road. On the left on the top of an isolated hill is a Tope (or Barrow) somewhat resembling that at *Munikiala*, but is disfigured by a tower, said to have been built by Aurungzebe, on the top of it. Just before you leave the valley and to the W., is Lohwargee, which it is said would answer for a cantonment; hence 1½ mile to Ali Musjid.

The valley was soon lost, and the bed of the stream was confined by rugged hills, until the road narrowed to about 70 feet, and did not widen much near Ali Musjid. We passed several springs, one of large volume issuing from the rocks, which formed a considerable stream, down which lay the road to Ali Musjid. The Pass, here, very much contracts, and in one place is not above 40 or 50 feet wide, (10) crossing almost entirely the rocky stream, till you arrive at Ali Musjid, which is situated on a hill to the right. We encamped about a mile to the E. of it. Thermometer 3 P. M. 82°. (11)

a cross road leads to the *Tatara* Pass, but it is not a gun road. This is the left road; the right goes to Dakka. Luadgai is N. W. from Tatara, and 9 miles in a direct line.

The *Kadapa* is another Pass and is a gun road—and goes by Moosa Jod to Goshta; the left, which is not a gun road, goes to Lalpoor, a distance of 7 kos; this road is not so difficult as the Tatara one.

The 3rd or Ab-khana Pass (water route) is a Kafila road, but difficult for the last two stages, obliging horsemen to dismount sometimes.

But, these Passes are connected with the main Pass, and could be secured very easily by Sungahs, &c.

(8) There are few springs in this valley, and two tanks to collect water in, one was dry, and the other did not contain much water; they have wells in the villages.

(9) These belong to the Malaks of the Khyber tribes.

(10) Within pistol shot.

(11) The baggage was coming up all night and next day!

Halt 4th Nov. 1839. We halted to-day in consequence of the non-arrival of our baggage, and it being thought advisable to take steps to protect the line of march between this and the *debouché* of the Pass, (12) in consequence of which the second column under Major-Genl. *Thackwell*, moved close to us, and encamped to-day, between us and Ali Musjid.

2. *Ali Musjid.*—The fort of Ali Musjid is situated on a hill to the right coming from Jellalabad. The elevation above the level of the sea is 2,433, or 940 feet below the summit of the Pass at Lundee Khana. The fort is about 150 feet long and 60 feet wide, but the whole of the enclosed place is about 300 by 200 feet. There are three hills within from 200 to 300 yards of the fort, on which there were posts. The width of the Pass here is about 150 yards. On the opposite side, the hills are not high. In the centre of the Pass below is a *Sungah*. There were likewise Sungahs on the hills opposite to the fort. From the fort to where our camp was (the road taking a turn to the left) is the most important section of the Pass. Our camp had to its front, S. W., some heights on which there was table-land. This table-land leads to the fort to the W., and to the Khyberee cantonments. (13) To the rear of camp N. E. was a detached hill on which there was a Sungah; beyond this is a valley and a high range of hills, a road leading over it to the left rear. The width of the Pass here is about 150 yards. To the E. of camp is the foot-path leading over the hills to Jumrood. To the S. E. is a tower *(Jaghir)* and a Sungah which commands the main Pass, which led from the left of our camp in that direction. (14) In the fort of *Ali*

(12) Genl. *Avitabile*, Govr. of Peshawer was written to, and he sent some Sikh troops to move up the Pass.

(13) Teerah distant about 7 marches to the S., and at an elevation of about 7,000 feet Choorah about 4 miles in a direct line S. Bazar 8 or 9 miles in a direct line S.

(14) In this section of the Pass, about 1½ mile in extent, was the principal opposition given to Lieut.-Col. *Wade's* force in July, and where the Khyberees attacked the Sikhs in October, and opposed our parties in November, 1839.

Musjid there is no water, but there is a covered passage leading down to a well. Thermometer 3 p. m. 82°.

To *Kuddum* beyond the Pass, 10 miles, (5th Nov.)—Thermometer 4 a. m. 60°. Marched at 5 a. m. The road lay through the bed of the river. After leaving camp our route was to the right, leaving the tower *(Jaghir)* on our left, on which side there is high ground, and two other towers within 3 miles of camp, and close together. The Pass from camp was for 3 miles from 200 to 150 yards wide, sometimes only as many feet. It then narrows to about 60 or 80 yards in some places; widening again at the *debouché*. The hills are higher for the first 3 miles, after which they are lower and rocky, and more perpendicular. The road the first 3 miles over stony ground, crossing the river often; the latter part over shingles with a slight descent to the valley of Peshawer. The Choorah stream, which issues from the Pass, irrigates the country near Kuddum. From our last ground to the *debouché* of the Pass is 7 miles. There is a foot-path which leads over the hills from *Jumrood*, and is three miles shorter than the route by the main-road of the Pass; but, it is not a gun-road. Thermometer 3 p. m. 86°. Capt. *H. P. Burn,* (15) the officer left in Political charge at Peshawer, came to our camp. Our camp was close under some low hills on which there is table-land to the W., *Jumrood* (where the Sikh camp is) is a mile off, and close to the fort of Futehgurh. We met some Sikh Battalions entering the Pass, as we were leaving it.

3. *The Khyber Pass and its Defence.*—The Khyber Pass from the entrance, on the Jellalabad side, to the *debouché* (2 miles short of and from Kuddum), is 28 miles in length, and excepting the valley of *Lalbeg-gurhee,* (16) 6 miles long and 1¼ broad, there are 22 miles of Pass which can be commanded, and in which there are few places where an army advancing could find cover.

---

(15) First Bengal N. I.
(16) Most probably so called, owing to the *Towers* of the Malaks.

Suppose a convoy to enter the Pass from Peshawer, by the main road of the Pass to Ali Musjid. At about 2 miles on the left, there is a small road which turns into the left and re-enters the main-road about ¼ mile higher up. From this to where the two first towers are seen on the right of the road, is about 2 miles. When the Khyberees had possession of the road, attacks were made from the *left*, by parties coming from Ali Musjid, or from the neighbouring cantonment. Those from the *right* were made by the troops in possession of the towers and Sungahs. Our possession, therefore, of the towers and Sungahs on the right, while holding Ali Musjid and the hill on the left opposite to the great tower *(Jaghir)*, would prevent them occupying the hills in any numbers between the entrance to the Pass and these points. There might be Sungahs erected on the right and left of the hills to render these more secure.

In that portion of the Pass from the tower *(Jaghir)* to Ali Musjid, Sungahs, on the hill running from the left to the fort, might be erected to secure that line. On the opposite (right) side of the Pass, the detached hill might have a Sungah to command the valley on the other side; the entrance into which by the gorge, should be closed up by another Sungah. The path-way which leads to Jumrood should be protected by a Sungah.

As on entering the Pass from the Jumrood (or Peshawer) side, attacks from the *left* are most likely to be made, *there should be towers, at certain intervals, along the whole line up to the fort; as on that line are the cantonments of the Khyberees.*

In the valley of Lalbeg-gurhee there is open space. The possession of the summit of the Lundee-Khana Pass, with a good work, would secure it. There is a hill beyond it on which there are the ruined walls of an old fort; (17) on which might be erected a small work if necessary.

---

(17) Said to have been built by Alexander. I would fortify this, as it could, I think, fire on a work on the summit of the Pass.

The remaining portion of the Pass from Lundee-Khana to the *debouché* near Dakka, might have a tower erected about half-way, on some rising ground at *Huft-chah*. The Tatara, Kadapa, and Ab-khana Passes, being narrow, might be easily secured by Sungahs.

Now that a corps of *Khyberees* has been raised, it would seem that these men would be the best to employ, to garrison the towers and Sungahs proposed to be erected.

As the point to be chiefly guarded is the line on which Ali Musjid stands, the object appears to be, to have a proper garrison for the fort, with some work on the plain leading to *Choorah*, sufficient to hold a body of men equal to repulse an attack.

Owing to the sickness of our troops in the hot months and rainy season after its capture in July, 1839, Lt.-Col. Sir *C. M. Wade* directed Dr. *A. Reid* to report upon the best site for a cantonment, (18) as *our* troops could not live in *Ali Musjid* during the hot, or the rainy season, in fact only in the cold months; *Lohwargee* seems to offer the best

(18) Dr. *Reid*, on the 27th October, 1839, made the following report.

" 1st. The village of *Chardeh* (elevation of about 1,800 ft.) 20 miles E. of Jellalabad.

" 2nd. The village of *Bussool* (elevation of 1,509 feet) about 26 miles E. of Jellalabad.

" 3rd. *Lohwargee* (3,500 feet) about 15 W. of Ali Musjid, and three miles from Lalbeg-gurhee is a valley of considerable extent within the Khyber mountains; it is well supplied with water, both from springs and wells, and is beautifully cultivated, the air pure and salubrious; and the climate is so good that it is resorted to by the sick in search of health, and is nearly 3,500 feet above the level of the sea, and would be a most eligible spot for a cantonment."

" The sickness at *Ali Musjid* is attributable to the water, which is said to be impregnated with antimony; the spring from which the fort is supplied rising from under a rock of the sulphuret of that metal; other water was for some time used by the troops, but it is said that all in the neighbourhood is impregnated with it."

" That the troops ought not to be kept there will, I think, be evident from the number of sick and casualties that have occurred since the place has been occupied by our's and the Maharajah's troops, as shown in the accompanying table.

place for a cantonment, and is sufficiently near to afford constant relief to the parties in *Ali Musjid,* and at the posts; and the troops would be able to move, at a short notice, to take up any position that might be required to protect any convoy, &c. passing through the Khyber Pass.

4. The Khyberees are divided into two classes, the *Afreedees* and the *Shanwarees,* and are all Mahomedans. In the time of the kings of Affghanistan they are said to have received the following sums, viz.

		Annually.
Abdal Rahman's Ancestors, Kukee Khels, *Afreedee,*	Rs.	25,000
Khan Bahadar's, ditto, (Malakdeen Khel,) *Afreedee,*	,,	25,000
Mahomed Ameer Khan, (Lepa's ancestors,) *Afreedee,*	,,	25,000
The brothers of Mintaza Khan and Sardalla Khan, Zakee Khel, *Afreedee,*	,,	25,000
The Malak of the Meerdad Khel, *Shanwarees,*	,,	10,000
The Malak of the Peroo Khel, *Shanwarees,*	,,	10,000
The Malak of the Khuga Khel, *Shanwarees,*	,,	10,000

(£13,000) Rs. 130,000

The body of Khyberees supported themselves by theft, and when called into service, they only received rations.

The Grenr. Co. 20th N. I. of	60	died since 1st Sept.	23
Capt. Ferris's levies, ...	760	ditto ditto, ...	43
Ramgoles, ...	640	ditto ditto, ...	45
Nujeebs, ...	682	ditto ditto, ...	104
Suwars, ...	200	ditto ditto, ...	19
Goolab Sing's Suwars, ...	50	ditto ditto, ...	5
Heera Sing's ditto, ...	50	ditto ditto, ...	4
	2,442		243

which is a loss in 57 days of nearly *one-tenth!*

" The unhealthiness of *Dakka,* which is much less than that of *Ali Musjid,* is to be attributed to its low and damp situation, which can be avoided by crossing the troops to the opposite side of the river to *Lalpoorah;* where the ground is dry, and where there is a good position for the camp.

Tax, or toll, levied. 317

Before the engagement with the Sikhs in 1837, the Khyber Pass did not cost *Dost Mahomed,* more than 10,000 Rs. a year; but, after the above affair he paid nearly 20,000 Rs. yearly, viz.

Alladad Khan, and Fyzullah *(Fyztullub)*	Rs.	No. of Sword and Matchlockmen.
Zakee Khel,	4,000	3,000
Khan Bahadar, Malakdeen Khel,	5,000	4,000
Abdul Rahman Khan, (19) and Jangeer Khan, Kukee Khels,	3,000	3,000
Salem Khan, Lepa, Sadulla Khan, Gango, and Anar Khan, *Shanwarees,*	1,500	6,000
Noor Mahomed, Kambar Khel,	750	1,500
Samandar Khan, and Bakar Khan, Aka Khel,	750	1,500
Alif Khan, Kambar Khel,	1,500	3,000
	Rs. 19,500	26,000

However, subsequently, he paid, it is said, 28 or 32,000 Rs.

It would seem that under the kings the Khyberees did not collect the tax, or toll, levied on the passage of animals laden or unladen, and on passengers; but under Dost Mahomed this was permitted. (20)

Lt. Dowson's corps, of 359 died since 6th Aug.   7   143 present sick.
Maharajah's troops, 1,500 ditto ditto, ... 28   200 ditto.

         1,859   35 343
A loss in 83 days of 1 in 53.   (27th October, 1839.")

(19) He was not sincere in the first negociations. Occupies the Pass between Ali Musjid and Jumrood. Alladad Khan and Fyztullub Khan came in after the fall of Ali Musjid.

(20) A camel laden with Rs. cloth, or khajahwah, ... 5
Grocery, ... 3
A Horseman, ... 3
A load of leather, ... 2
A Hindoo foot passenger, 1½
A Moosulman ditto, ... 1½
A load of salt, ... 1

This was for the whole extent of the Pass; but, as it has been known that the toll paid at one end of the Pass, did not secure the merchant or traveller from a demand at the other end, there was dissatisfaction to the party paying, and of course delay; besides which it must have diminished the number of animals and passengers passing through, as well as the annual amount collected.

I believe the Shah has agreed to pay Rs. 120,000 (£12,000) annually, but insists on collecting the tax, or toll. Without this arrangement there could be no certainty of the use of the Pass for the transit of commerce; and in a military point of view, the Shah's Govt. would have been liable, on any change of policy at the court of *Lahore*, to an unsettled state of the Pass. The Sikhs paid a certain sum of money, annually, for a supply of water from the Pass; this, under the treaty with Shah Shoojah, was to be adjusted with his Govt. In viewing the conduct of the Khyberees, regard must be had to the sum offered them in the first instance, which was less than has since been allowed them; and which is about that which they received under the kings; then, to the depriving the chiefs of the collection of the tax, or toll, to which they had been accustomed for 30 years; and in fact to an alteration of their mode of existence. (21) *Nadir Shah*, in 1739, paid £100,000 for the passage of his army through this Pass !

(21) The Duke of *Wellington* in a letter to the Secy. to Govt., Bombay, 5th Nov. 1803, writes, " Col. *Murray* with great truth, says, 'It is not to be expected the *Bheels*,' (a hill-tribe) 'and Chieftains will remain attached to us without some prospect of advantage.' "

His Grace adds, " The question is whether it is an object to obtain such *Military advantage as the possession of the defiles* in the countries of the *Bheels*, and the assistance of these people, even at the expense of the remission of the tribute which they paid to Dowlut Rao Scindiah, before we obtained possession of the country?" and " Experience teaches that tribute of this description, cannot be collected from the inhabitants of the hilly and jungly tracts of India, without frequent appeals to arms."

" I have but little doubt the company would have been richer, and I am convinced that the military reputation of the British nation would have stood higher, and that the power of Government would have been greater, if all tribute payable by hill polygars and rajahs, had been originally remitted." (Despatches—Gurwood, Vol. I. p. 486.)

The question with respect to the *Khyberees* seems to be this, whether in the best times the sum of money they received, together with the collection of the tax, or toll, was or was not more than they now receive? If the military possession of the Pass, thereby increasing its use in a commercial point of view, and the collection of the tax, or toll, realise, to the Shah's government, a greater annual sum than is

5. To *Koulsir*, 7 miles, (6th Nov. 1839.)—Thermometer 4 A. M. 58°. Marched at 6 A. M. The road lay E. over a level plain; shortly after leaving *Kuddum*, the country is more open, the hills are more distant, and run into a low and distant range to the right. On the left about one mile is *Jumrood*, where the Sikh force is encamped, and beyond it is the fort of Futehgurh, about 2 miles from Kuddum, and reaching which a salute (22) of 17 guns was fired in honor of H. E. *Sir J. Keane's* passing it. The fort has a double wall, and a white pukka citadel in the centre, and has two or three guns in it. The road was over a sandy level, and then stony plain, on which were seen many *Tumuli*. The road towards Koulsir was sandy with small stones; there is cultivation near where our camp was, and a round circular breast-work erected by Lt. *F. Mackeson* on the Shahzada's troops marching from Peshawer. There was a descent in this day's march. *Jumrood* is 1,670, or 763 feet below *Ali Musjid*. Thermometer 3 P. M. 86°.

The second column under Maj.-Genl. Thackwell moved, to-day, out of the Pass to our last ground (Kuddum); some of the Sikh troops were sent to the Pass to protect its bag-

paid to the *Chiefs* (besides paying the ordinary military expenses for its defence), the question is whether it will not be better to satisfy them rather than to seek, by force, to carry the point as to a *minimum* payment, when the doing so must occasion an additional expense, and when such a measure may raise a spirit of opposition to the Shah's government.

It cannot be expected that a few months will obtain all the objects contemplated; it must require time to induce these people to give up their lawless pursuits. Offers were made by the late Lt.-Col. *Tod*, in 1818, to induce some *Bheel* tribes to cultivate the soil by paying each so much a month for a certain period, (gratuitously,) for this purpose; their reply was, "Our ancestors did as we do: we have never been accustomed to toil, but to live on plunder." They have been reclaimed, and the new generation has adapted habits of industry.

(22) Jumrood was taken by the Sikhs, under *Hurree Singh*, early in January, 1837, before the battle in 1837, in which *he* was killed in the action with the Affghans. As it was commanded, Futehgurh (the fort of Victory) was built.

gage. Some 50 or 60 Khyberees showed themselves on the hills, but made no attack.

To *Peshawer*, 8¾ miles, (7th Nov.)—Thermometer 5 A. M. 62°. Marched at day-break. The road was due E., crossing two small canals, which were bridged, and which appeared to take a direction to the N. to join the Cabool river. We also crossed some ravines. As we neared Peshawer we saw the Sikh cantonments on our left, where, leaving the main-road, we passed round them, and saw the king's garden to the N. E. of the fort; we passed to the left of the town, keeping the fort on our left. Our camp was to the E. of the city of Peshawer. We breakfasted with Genl. *Avitabile*, the Govr. Thermometer 3 P. M. 92°. The elevation above the sea at Peshawer is 1,068 feet, or 602 feet below Jumrood, which gives a fall of about 1 in 76 feet. Maj.-Genl. *Sir W. Cotton*, the Hd. Qr. Staff, and the officers with the 1st Column, dined in the evening with Genl. *Avitabile*, who illuminated his house, and exhibited fire-works before dinner; after which he gave the party a *nautch* and produced all the best vocalists of Peshawer.

CHAPTER XV.

PESHAWER—MARCH FROM IT TO ATTOCK.

Peshawer, (8th Nov. 1839.)—Thermometer 5 A. M. 52°. The 2nd Column, under Maj.-Genl. *Thackwell* marched in this morning. Our camp was to the E., and that of the 2nd column beyond our's to the S. E.

The following Genl. Order, (1) was issued regarding the conduct of the troops marching through the Sikh territories. " The leading column having entered the *Sikh* territory, H. E. the Comr.-in-Chief calls the attention of Comg. officers to the injunction laid down in G. O. 25th ult." (2)

" All officers are specially enjoined to lend their utmost aid to preserve order among the followers, and to bring to punishment any one found plundering the fields, or committing acts of oppression."

" H. E. is requested by the Govr. Genl. to give publicity to the following despatch (3) and to require strict obedience to the instructions it conveys on the part of the troops."

1. " The Govr. Genl. has noticed in the *Lahore Akbars* the circumstance of British officers who happen to pass through that capital, and visit the *Durbar*, receiving *Khilluts*

(1) Dated 5th Nov. 1839, before reaching Peshawer.
(2) Prohibiting the going into the towns, and villages. To be published daily by beat of tom-tom, till F. O. G. O. 8th Nov. 1839. " One N. C. O. per troop, or company, permitted to visit the town, to make purchases, but Comg. officers to take care, that they are accompanied by some of the Sikh horsemen ; on application to Capt. Mackeson."

(3) " Addressed in the *Secret Dept.* on the 21st ultimo, by his Lordship's desire to the Offg. Pol. Agent at Loodianah (G. R. Clerk, Esq.) by T. H. Maddock, Esq. Offg. Secy. to Govt. of India, with the Govr. General."

(4) from the Maharajah, and that sums of money, as *Zeafut*, (5) are, also, sent to their tents, or the places where they reside during their stay at Lahore."

2. " The practice being contrary to the established Regulations of the British Govt., applicable to all its servants, and highly objectionable, on many accounts, and being likely, if permitted to continue, to entail a heavy expense on the Lahore Govt., his Lordship requests that you will take prompt and effective measures to ensure its total discontinuance, and explaining to the Durbar that the custom is prohibited in the case of the servants of this Govt., at all Native Courts; and that it is the particular wish of the Govr. Genl. that the Lahore Durbar should conform to the general practice, when British officers visit that place."

" His Lordship would acknowledge with all courtesy, and gratitude, the spirit of kindness in which the practice has originated; but, would hope that the Maharajah will readily consent to prohibit its repetition; particularly on your explaining that this prohibition is not meant to extend to those occasions of interviews between the Heads of the two Govts., or the reception of special notifications of officers of high rank; or of missions from one Govt. to the other, on which such observances have been already established, and will remain in force as heretofore; and in which there is a due observance of reciprocity." (6)

2. *The city of Peshawer.*—The city of Peshawer is in Lat. 34° 6′ N. Long. 71° 45′ E.; it was founded by the Emperor *Akbar*, (7) who encouraged the inhabitants of the Punjab to resort to this new settlement, as the Affghans

---

(4) Honorary Dresses.

(5) *Ziyafut*, means a feast; also hospitality.

(6) "A copy of this letter will be forwarded to Mr. Macnaghten, and to the Comr.-in-Chief of the Army of the Indus, in order that the attention of officers may be specially drawn to his Lordship's direction on this occasion, as well as to the orders of Govt. prohibitory of the practice of Govt. servants accepting presents from Natives of any description." Simla, 21st Nov. 1839.

(7) About A. D. 1590; he died in 1605.

were averse to commerce. From the convenience of its position, it unites Persia and Affghanistan, by a commercial intercourse, with India. The markets are abundantly supplied with provisions. The city is said to be about 5 miles in circumference, and consequently more extensive than Candahar and Cabool. The principal streets are much like those of Cabool, but are not so clean, and have narrow gullies leading into the enclosures, with gates and walls; and the town is much larger and more compact than Cabool, not being increased by orchards, gardens, canals, and water-mills. There is a mosque outside to the N. wall, which is the chief place of worship; and two others, with only a single dome, to distinguish them from the other buildings of the city.

The Govr. (Genl. *Avitabile*) states that there are 10,000 houses inhabited by Mahomedans and 1,400 by Hindoos, and that there are 100,000 inhabitants. (8)

Since the time of Mr. *Eliphinstone* a great change has taken place. When Shah Shoojah-ool-Moolk fitted out his last expedition to recover his throne (1833-34) he promised Peshawer to Maharajah Runjeet Singh. In 1834 when the Shah was defeated at Candahar, he fled towards *Khelat*. The Sikhs having taken possession of Peshawer, Sultan Mahomed Khan, (the Govr.) (9) retreated to Cabool, where Dost Mahomed collected a force of Ghazees, crusaders,) and accompanied Sultan Mahomed Khan to Peshawer, and the Sikh and Affghan armies remained opposite to each other for fifteen days; when Runjeet Singh intrigued with Sultan Mahomed Khan, to get Dost Mahomed to retire, which he did; himself remaining more dependant than before on Runjeet Singh: and Peshawer is now a province of the Punjab.

---

(8) The Hon. Mr. *Elphinstone*, whose mission was there from 25th Feb. to the 14th June, 1809, states the amount at about 100,000. New Edition, Vol. II. p. 46.
This would give more than eight souls to each house.
(9) And brother of Dost Mahomed.

The present Govr. (Genl. *Avitabile*) has built a fort on the site of the *Bala Hissar*, or former palace of the king, which is to the N. of the city. The whole of the W. E., and N. faces are covered with low swampy ground. The only gate it has is to the N. The lower part of the fort is commanded by the citadel. The ditch was not finished. (10) The south face seems to afford the only assailable point; this would first render necessary the occupation of the city, on the N. side, as owing to its nearness to the fort, it would take the breaching batteries in reverse. A salute was fired from the fort on our arrival on the morning of the 7th inst.

3. The city is to the S. of the fort and is walled all round, and Genl. *Avitabile* is constructing a *second* wall, about 100 yards outside the inner one. The Govr. lives, in a large square, or Caravanseraee, in which he has built a large three-storied house, the walls of which, as well as of the large square, are loop-holed; and the bastions of the square have guns in them. The Govr.'s house overlooks the whole city. The houses of the city are built of brick, and about three stories high. The streets are narrow, and have a gutter in the centre, but are not paved. Part of the town is said to be flooded during the spring rains, which makes it then an unwholesome residence. The shops display for sale, dried fruits, nuts, bread, meat, boots, shoes, saddlery, bales of cloth, hardware, ready-made clothes, books, sheep-skin cloaks, &c. The general keeps the inhabitants in good order. (11) The revenue of Peshawer has been

---

(10) It will require a good deal of time and expense to complete it, as from the nature of the soil, and the mound on which the fort is built being artificial, both the scarp and counterscarp, would require to be faced with masonry.

(11) We found a great many men hanging on gibbets. He shews no partiality to any class, whether Mahomedan or Hindoo, and on some occasions hangs eight or ten at a time; by which *discipline,* life and property are safe at Peshawer!

variously estimated. *Forster* (12) says, " seven lakhs were remitted to the capital.' At present the province may yield about 15 lakhs Rs. (£150,000;) though it is said to be capable of yielding £250,000 yearly. The Affghans had a force of 3 or 4,000 men, and several guns ; but the Sikh force kept up is said to be more than 12,000 : (13) sufficient to absorb the whole Revenue.

The soil of the plain is a black mould, and abundantly supplied with water. The orchards scattered over the country produce a profusion of plum, peach, pear, quince, and pomegranate trees, and the greatest part of the plain is in a high state of cultivation, being irrigated by many watercourses. Thirty-two villages have been counted within a circuit of 4 miles. These are generally remarkably neat, adorned with mulberry and other fruit-trees ; and over the streams are bridges of masonry, having two small towers at each end.

The wheat and barley crops are off the ground by the month of April.

During the summer the heat is very great, and in the height of the solstice the atmosphere is almost insupportable, although in the immediate vicinity of everlasting snow: but the simoom, does not, I believe, prevail at Peshawer. (14) From the plain of Peshawer four ranges of mountains are distinctly seen to the N. Towards the end of February the snow disappears from the lowest, the tops of

(12) A. D. 1783, Vol. II. p. 51. Sir A. *Burnes* in 1832, states it at less than nine lakhs Rs. Vol. II. p. 319. Genl. *Avitabile* has very much raised the amount.

(13) They keep 3 or 4000 men at the Camp at " Jumrood ; the rest at Peshawer ;" but the numbers vary according to circumstances.

(14) Shahzada Tymoor's force with Lt.-Col. Sir *C. M. Wade* was encamped at Peshawer from the 20th March to the 20th July, 1839, when the heat was so great that most of the officers were laid up with fever ; the Lt.-Col. used a *kus-kus* tent presented to him by Maharajah Runjeet Singh, which diminished the temperature. The heat, unlike that of India, is suffocating, being unaccompanied by any strength of wind. In June, 1809, when Mr. *Elphinstone* was there, the Thermtr. stood at 113°!

the second continue covered, and the third half-way down. The height of one of these peaks was estimated by Lieut. *Macartney* at 20,493 feet, and in June, 1809, was covered with snow.

4. *9th Nov.* 1839. Thermometer 5 A. M. 52°.—The Column to halt till F. O. Thermometer 3 P. M. 82°.

10th Nov. Thermometer 5 A. M. 60°.—This morning a Dett. consisting of two guns 2nd T. 2nd B. H. A., a squadron of the 3rd Cavy., two Cos. of sappers and miners, and every available soldier of the Cos. of the 20th and 21st N. I. marched as an escort to provisions intended for the garrison of *Ali Musjid*. It was not intended that the Artillery and Cavalry should enter the Pass, unless circumstances should render the measure absolutely necessary. (15) Six days' supplies were taken with the Dett. (16) While we remained at Peshawer the issue of grain from the Comsst. stores, was suspended. Officers wishing to visit the city were instructed to apply to Capt. *Burn's* servant at the gate-way leading to Genl. *Avitabile's* house, for persons acquainted with the town, to attend them. Thermometer 3 P. M. 68°.

11th Nov. Thermometer 5 A. M. 50°.—Accounts came in that the convoy had arrived at Ali Musjid, and the grain had been thrown into the fort yesterday afternoon; but that on the return, the *Khyberees* had attacked the party and carried off 4 or 500 camels. Lt. *F. Mackeson*, the Pol. Asst. who accompanied that party lost all his property. There was a Regt. of Sikhs with this party, who, immediately the Khyberees made the attack, ran off and never stopt till they got out of the Pass; this misconduct of the Sikhs threw the whole into confusion. The loss of the camels was serious, as we could not supply others, and much crippled our means of transport; having lost, before,

---

(15) They did not enter, but were kept near the mouth of the Pass, ready to advance if required.

(16) The infantry were directed to take 30 rounds of Ammn. in pouch, and 70 rounds in reserve.

Loss of Camels, &c. 327

1,300 out of 3,100 camels since we left Cabool. Thermometer 3 P. M. 76°.

14*th Nov.* Thermometer 5 A. M. 52°.—This morning marched a Dett. consisting of the drafts proceeding to join the 2nd European Regt., one Coy of sappers and miners, (17) Capt. *Farmer's* two Cos. 21st N. I., the two Cos. of the 20th N. I. and Capt, *Prole's* Dett. of drafts for the 9th Cos. of Regts., to reinforce the garrison of *Ali Musjid*, and to hold it till the arrival of the 37th and 48th Regt. N. I. under Lieut.-Col. Wheeler, from Jellalabad. The Infantry to take 200 *rounds* per man (40 in pouch), and eight days' provisions.

Memo. " The Govr. of Peshawer has requested it might be intimated to the troops, that he cannot be responsible for the safety of officers going out of camp to shoot, unless they apply to him for a guard." (18) Thermometer 3 P. M. 85°. Dr. *A. C. Gordon*, Pol. Asst., joined the Hd. Qrs. for the purpose of accompanying the troops through the *Punjab*. The party sent the second time, took a quantity of ammunition for the troops at Ali Musjid. They succeeded in this object, but on their return were attacked, two officers were wounded and several men killed and wounded. Lieut. *N. Macleod*, Engineers, made a gallant charge up a hill and drove off the Khyberees. (19) The Dett. of Europeans (63 men) alone fired 3,000 rounds.

5. 29*th Nov.* 1839. Thermometer 5 A. M. 54°.—The Hd. Qrs. changed ground to the E. of Peshawer, camp, dis-

---

(17) Sent on both occasions, as we had so little infantry with the two columns; two guns were sent on in the afternoon to join the above Dett.

(18) " Officers Comg. Regts. directed to communicate with Capt. *Burn*, and obtain from him parties of Sikh horsemen, when they, or their officers are desirous of going from camp."
We never suffered any inconvenience from the people on any occasion.

(19) Capt. *W. S. Prole*, 37th N. I. was shot in the arm, and Lt. *F. S. MacMullen*, 1st European Regt. was shot in the thigh. Two Europeans and several sepoys were killed, and several were wounded. The sappers and miners suffered the most.

tant from the city 2¾ miles. Crossed a stream about a mile
from Peshawer, also some water-courses, and two bridges;
the bridge to the left of the road destroyed, the arches entire.
The river to the S.   To-day Lt.-Col. *Wheeler's* Dett., two
guns, and 37th and 48th N. I. arrived at Ali Musjid. The
Lieut.-Col. had been directed to march on the *Khyberee*
cantonment of *Choorah,* instead of coming direct; but his
march was countermanded. (20)   Thermometer 3 P. M. 79°.
21st Nov. Thermometer 5 A. M. 44°.—Lieut. *Mackeson*
reported that he expected the *Khyber* chiefs to come in as
negociations were being entered into.   Terms were agreed
on late in the evening. (21)   Thermometer 3 P. M. 75°.
22nd Nov. Thermometer 5 A. M. 42°.—The Khyberees
broke the treaty they had entered into. Lt.-Col. *Wheeler's*
Dett. was to have marched to *Choorah;* but owing to
pending negociations, was directed to move on *Ali Musjid.*
On the 19th November, it entered the Pass and marched
to Lundee Khana. An advance party of 43 men (37th
and 48th N. I.) with the Qr. Mr. Serjts. of both corps,
was attacked, on clearing a Pass, at day-break, by at least
500 men. The enemy was most gallantly repulsed, and
thrice charged with the bayonet, and ultimately driven off,
without the loss of any thing. The cool and daring
courage of Qr. Mr. Serjt. *Wallace,* 48th N. I., was most
conspicuous. The 37th N. I. had three sepoys killed, two
naicks and two sepoys wounded. The 48th N. I. one
sepoy wounded. Two Cos. 37th N. I. were sent round the
hills to try to cut off their retreat, and 50 men were
pushed up a hill under Lieut. *H. Palmer,* 48th N. I.; and
the enemy were driven off.

Ou the 23rd Nov. the Lieut.-Col. marched for *Ali
Musjid,* with the Fd. Comsst. treasure, and about 3,000
camels. On his arrival there, he assumed command of all
the troops.

(20) As Lt. *Mackeson* was negociating with the chiefs. But, it was
found, also, that the cross-road from Jellalabad was not a gun-road.
One of the carriages of the guns (the Shah's) broke down.

(21) They promised, 1 believe, to restore the property stolen.

Negociations were being carried on, but the tops of the hills close outside camp were covered with large bodies of the enemy. The troops halted on the 21st; negociations still going on; late at night it was intimated by Capt. *Mackeson*, that the chiefs (of Choora and other chiefs, between Ali Musjid and the Jumrood side) had acceded to the terms; but that they were not to be trusted. The cattle had been without forage for two days, and it was resolved to march for Jumrood next morning.

22nd Nov.—The Dett. marched at 7 A. M. The hills were, on every height, covered with people. The chiefs had promised to assemble with the more influential of their followers, to prevent any infraction of the treaty. They were waving flags demonstrative of amity. The Dett. had marched about 4 miles, when it was halted to close up the baggage. Two parties of 20 men each from the two corps, were placed at a point which covered a broad ravine in which and its neighbourhood, a great many had assembled; but still preserving every appearance of being friendly, telling the people to move on without fear; that no one would hurt them. The Dett. had scarcely moved, when a most treacherous attack was made on the baggage. (22) The Lt.

(22) The camels were taken up the ravine already mentioned, and another leading towards Choora. The camels were mostly hamstrung; most of those that were not, were recovered. The baggage on the disabled camels fell into the enemy's hands ultimately, as, though secured at the time, there was no means of removing it. Several officers and men lost every thing. Of the 91 camels lost, there were 14 Govt., Rewaree (hired) 38, and 39 private. Some young sepoys of the 37th N. I. used their bayonets, and killed several of the Khyberees. The 2 Europeans were killed while pursuing the Khyberees to recover some baggage; but they were not engaged on the above occasion. Lieut. *Collinson* was afterwards killed at *Pooshoot* on the 18th Jan. 1840, and was a most gallant officer. When Capt. *Mackeson's* baggage was carried off some days before during one of the attacks, he had, as Asst. Pol. Agent, a *Toshuk-khanu* (or *Toshu-khanu*) or wardrobe (in which honorary dresses, &c. are kept for presents); the women who were on the heights are supposed to have urged the men to plunder the loaded camels; hoping to get some more. The Khyberees, however, were

Coy. 48th N. I. was thrown up the height, took the enemy in flank, and drove them off. The sepoys at the ravine, though hotly opposed, pursued, recovered and brought off most of the camels.

Having full confidence in the Native troops, the Lieut.-Colonel determined not to employ the European Dett., unless as a last resource.

The Lieut.-Colonel reported that the rear guard under (late) Lt. *Collinson*, 37th N. I., and the Lt. Coy of that Regt. under Lt. *Steer*, Lt. *H. Palmer*, (48th N. I.) Dett. Staff, Lt. *Hasell*, (Adjt.) and Lt. Thomas, 48th N. I., who commanded parties, behaved with great gallantry. Lieut. *N. Macleod*, with a Dett. of sappers and miners, without orders, followed the Lt. Coy. 48th N. I. and gave great assistance. The whole of the troops behaved exceedingly well. The Lieut.-Colonel also highly praised the conduct of Capt. *J. Paton*, (58th N. I.) A. Qr. Mr. Genl.

The European Dett. had one Serjt. and one private killed. The 37th N. I. had three killed, one naick and four sepoys wounded. The 48th N. I. one Havr. one naick, and sixteen sepoys wounded. Total five killed, and 23 wounded. Of the enemy eighteen killed were counted in one spot. 91 camels were lost. Thermometer 3 p. m. 76°.

6. *To Pubbee*, 12 miles, (23rd November, 1839.)—Thermometer 5 A. M. 46°. Marched at 6 A. M. We had moved 3 miles from Peshawer on the 20th inst. The road from Peshawer had been laid under water to prepare the fields for the plough. (23) The crops of Indian corn on the ground were most luxuriant, and the villages had a few scattered trees near them. The road from last camp was due E. over a country covered with cultivation in most parts. The soil was of the finest garden mould. The

---

severely handled; and have been more cautious ever since : and I doubt much, if they could be, as some say, rooted out: 26,000 armed men in their own hills, are not to be so easily put down ; and *where are the troops to come from ?*

(23) Very little rain falls in this country, and several crops are raised during the year by irrigation.

Noushera. 331

country is well watered, as we crossed a river about halfway, being the third, since leaving Peshawer. (24) Some camels carried off at this ground, but recovered. The Cabool river 4 or 5 miles N. W. of camp. Thermometer 3 P. M. 66°.

A *Memo.* in G. O. "The sword of the Govr. of Ghuznee, is now in the hands of the Prize Agents, and will be sold for the benefit of the Captors, by auction, on the arrival of the Hd. Qrs. at Ferozpoor, which will probably be about the 7th Jan. next." (25)

To Noushera, 9¾ miles, (24th Nov.)—Marched at daybreak, the road first part rather sandy for 2 or 3 miles. The middle part good, the last part a little stony. At about 4½ miles on the left is a circular loop-holed building. At about 7 miles there is another. (26) About half a mile before reaching Noushera, on the left, are the ruins of an old cantonment. Marched through the bazar to camp S. E. distant ¼ mile, on the right bank of the river which runs N. W. to S. E., and has a bend lower down to N. E. A low range of hills N. W. to S. E., on which there is table-land. (27) The fort, here, to the right of the village of Noushera, was built by Genl. *Avitabile*. It has four bastions, and double rows of loop-holes. (28)

---

(24) To the left of the road, 3 miles from the last camp, there are distinct remains of a canal, near a walled village, parallel to the road for some miles. At about 4 miles crossed the dry bed of a nullah. There were several villages and clumps of trees, on both sides of the road. The Persian wheel is used at the wells.

(25) The sword was *claimed* by Sir *J. Keane* as a *right*, which was disputed, it was made over to the Envoy and Minister pending a reference, the answer to which caused the *Memo.* The delay in the sale was to give the *Bombay* column, and the officers at Cabool, &c. time to write to get some one to bid for them.

(26) These have been built by the Governor of Peshawer as police stations.

(27) These hills ran from Peshawer to our right all the way, and are infested by *(khuttuk)* robbers.

(28) Single in the walls.

2 u 2

Battle of Noushera, (1823).

On the other side of the river is the town of Noushera, the field of battle between Runjeet Singh and the Eusufzyes in 1823, in which the Sikhs gained the victory. There is a low range of hills beyond the town of Noushera, where there are graves which mark the scene of action. Sir A. *Burnes* states, (29) "He *(Runjeet Singh)* here encountered the Affghans for the last time; but their chief, *Azeem Khan*, was separated from the greater part of his army by the river of Cabool. The Sikhs defeated the divisions on the opposite side" (left bank) "mainly through the personal courage of Runjeet Singh, who carried a hillock with his guards," *(Akalees)* "from which his other troops had three times retreated. Azeem Khan, of Cabool, fled without encoun-

---

(29) Burnes, Vol. II. p. 73, 2nd edition. In January 1823, Runjeet Singh having desired Mahomed Azeem Khan to resign all claims to Cashmeer, he (Dost Mahomed's eldest brother and Governor of Cabool) had advanced from Peshawer to Noushera, while Mahomed Zeman Khan with 4,000 Ghazees (crusaders) was posted on the opposite or left bank of the river. Maharajah Runjeet Singh, who had about 24,000 Sikhs, attacked the Ghazees with a large portion of them; Mahomed Azeem Khan and Mahomed Zeman Khan being separated by the river, the former could not cross the river to assist the latter. Numbers of Mahomedans were slain; and Mahomed Zeman Khan fled and joined Mahomed Azeem Khan with a few survivors. The principal *Akalee* (Sikh) general was killed. Runjeet Singh urged the Akalees to make a last attack, and finish the battle, as night was coming on.

Encouraged by their defeat, Konwar Sher Singh attacked the Sirdar (Mahomed Azeem Khan), and a general battle ensued, but night soon coming on, both parties retired from the field.

Mahomed Azeem Khan proposed to Dost Mahomed Khan and Yar Mahomed Khan, to attack the right flank of the enemy, while at the same time Habeeboollah Khan, Vale Meer Akbar, and Futeh Mahomed Khan, should charge the left; but *Dost Mahomed Khan* and Yar Mahomed Khan, did not approve of the proposal: Mahomed Azeem Khan, finding himself helpless, committed his artillery to the care of *Dost Mahomed Khan* and Yar Mahomed Khan. *They* retired in the darkness of the night, and sent all their troops to Peshawer. The Sirdar (Mahomed Azeem Khan) then assembled his artillery and fled to Peshawer. The enemy hung on and annoyed his rear till he entered the city. He proceeded to Cabool, where he shortly afterwards died.

tering the successful army, which had partly crossed the river to oppose him."

The 2nd Column marched from Peshawer this morning; joined by the two Cos. 20th N. I. Thermometer 3 p. m. 76°.

To Akorah, 12 miles, (25th Nov.)—Thermometer 4 a. m. 50°. The road rough and stony, intersected by numerous dry nullahs and deep ravines, cut by the rains, and draining the water from the country into the Cabool river. Though the road ran close by the river for some distance, there was little cultivation to be seen, till we came near the village of Akorah, where there is a table-land of the finest mould, which was under irrigation. (30) The village, built of white stone with mud cement, is of a good size. It has a stone square, the walls of which are closely pierced with loop-holes. The camp was 2½ miles E. of Akorah. Thermometer 3 p. m. 76°.

To Attok, 10¾ miles, (26th Nov.)—Thermometer 4 a. m. 46°. The first part of the road tolerably good. At 5 miles crossed the bed of a hill stream. Then entered a narrow road running through low hills. At 6 miles entered the *Geedur Gullee* (31) defile, of about two miles in length. From

---

(30) Several Persian wheels were at work, and there were numerous vegetables of the freshest green. The crops were just rising out of the ground, which prevented the camp being near the village.

(31) Literally the "*Jackal's Pass,*" i. e. figuratively, so narrow as only to admit of a jackal: *gulee* meaning, a pass, or way; we were obliged to pass singly. It was about 7 miles from the last ground.

The G. O. directed the Asst. Baggage Mr. to proceed and post his party at an early hour, at the entrance to the defile, to prevent any wheeled-carriages entering it, till the troops had moved through it. Camels were to be allowed to file through it singly.

It is very narrow, ten or twelve feet in some places, with rather high and broken hills. There are two ascents and descents in it. At the end of it, on a hill to the right, is a small fort overlooked by the higher hills; here the road turns to the left; but there is another straight on passing under the fort.

The officer Comg. the advance guard, was directed to leave a detail of Lancers at the entrance to the bridge across the river, to prevent

the hills on the left, is a commanding view of the *Cabool* river, running into the *Indus*. A mile from the bridge on the left side of the road is a large Baolee. (32) The bridge over the *Indus* at the Attok. (33) The bridge was an excellent one and was constructed with 24 boats. (34)

The fort of Attok is on the left bank; there is another on the right bank at Khyrabad, opposite to the former; both are commanded by the neighbouring heights. H. M.'s 16th Lancers crossed the bridge mounted. The town is contained in the fort of Attok, which is not a strong place. From the bridge the road to our camp passed under the fort over the deep sandy bed of the river; at the end of the range on which the fort stands, the road to camp turned to the right. Thermometer 3 P. M. 74 . Some officers, on the application of Dr. *Gordon*, the Asst. Pol. Agent,

any crowding among the cattle, and to see that they followed each other with regularity across the bridge. (See the note on the passage of the bridge of boats over the Indus to *Sukkur* on the 15th Feb. 1839. Chapter II.) The plan is always to keep an open space between the bridge, and the cattle.

(32) A well with a flight of steps going down to it; some have 100 steps to them.

(33) Or " *Utuk*." Prevention, or obstacle. The name of a river. In former times, *Hindoos* were said to be prohibited by their religion from crossing the Indus at the *Utuk*, the direct road from Hindostan; this, I believe, was a *Mahomedan* plan of policy invented by some political bramins, to keep the Hindoos from leaving their country.

(34) In 1837, there were only 17 boats used ; the number depends upon the season. The Sikh Govt. build it annually, after the rainy season, about the 20th of October. The river is very rapid where the bridge is formed. The road-way of the bridge was covered with mud and straw over the planks. The anchors to the boats are made of wooden frame-work, and filled with stones, weighing 25 cwt. each. The junction of the Cabool river with the Indus was a grand sight. The Indus runs in several streams until it is joined by the Cabool river, when it rushes past the fort like a torrent. The river contracts in the cold season. There are nine fords, all except two *said* to be available every year, but only to bodies of men ; only three are properly fordable as *five feet* is too deep a ford. The Indus has been forded by *Shah Zeman*, and by Runjeet Singh; but the latter is said to have lost 7,000 men in effecting the passage ; but it was 5 miles higher up the river.

to the Govr., went in the afternoon to see the fort; and found the people very civil. There are plunderers near Attok called Khuttuks.

27th Nov. Halt. Thermometer 5 A. M. 46°.—The 2nd Column, under Major-Genl. *Thackwell* marched in this morning. Thermometer 3 P. M. 76°.

Shah Shoojah lost his throne after the battle of Neemla, (1809); during his subsequent flight, Maharajah Runjeet Singh offered him Attok as a place of refuge. This was an act of gratitude rendered, no doubt, to Zeman Shah (the brother) who had left Peshawer with the females of the royal family, on Shah Shoojah's marching from it, and had entered the *Punjab:* Zeman Shah had, when king of Affghanistan and in possession of the *Punjab,* made Runjeet Singh his viceroy at Lahore. Runjeet obtained possession of Attok, after the battle of *Chuch* in 1811.

CHAPTER XVI.

THE MARCH OF HEAD-QUARTERS FROM ATTOK TO FEROZPOOR.

1. *Attok to Shumsabad*, 9¾ miles, (28th Nov. 1839.)—Thermometer 4 A. M. 40°. The first part rather sandy for 2 or 3 miles, crossing two dry water-courses. Passed two small villages within 4 miles. Passed over much fine arable land. Camp E. of the village; there is another village N. E. of Shumsabad, and of the same size (300 houses); both built on mounds. The Himalayas are seen to the N. E., and the Cashmeer range below them. Thermometer 3 P. M. 76°.

To *Boorhan*, 13 miles, (29th Nov.)—Thermometer 4 A. M. 34°. The road lay a little to the S. of E. The road first part good; at 2nd to 3rd mile rather sandy. At 3rd mile a small village. At 5 miles cross the sandy bed of a stream, beyond which, on the right, is a Fuqueer's house. Cultivation here and there near the road, and villages in the distance. At 7 miles the road runs through some ravines, for a mile. At 8 miles cross the *Harroo* river, a small, clear stream, (1) 3 feet deep, which has considerable velocity; 1½ mile further cross a water-course: 2 miles further on is a nullah of some depth with steep banks. Camp E. of Boorhan. Thermometer 3 P. M. 78°. There was no grass here.

To *Vah*, 8 miles, (30th Nov.)—Thermometer 4 A. M. 33°. The road lay principally through a jungle of Byr, (2) and thorny shrubs, full of gullies, and ravines, and many turns to the S. and N. of E. for about 3 miles, when the *Chumlah* river is crossed, about 60 yards wide and 3 feet

---

(1) Sixty yards wide, but at some seasons must be deep and wide.
(2) Ber, or Byr, a wild plum.

deep. (3) The road thence lay E. for a mile through ravines. At 6 miles Hussun Abdool a small village; ½ mile beyond cross the *Dhoomrah*, a small stream near camp to the E. of Vah. (4) We were now in a well cultivated valley, surrounded by considerable hills, (5) over which the snowy peaks of the Himalaya are seen. Thermometer 3 P. M. 74°.

To *Janee-ka-Sung*, 14 miles, (1st Dec.)—Thermometer 5 A. M. 36 . The road (6) marched over to-day was the roughest we had yet travelled. The ascent considerable over bare rocks, dangerous for man or beast, if they missed their footing. Thence the country more open; direction E. At half-way is the *Kalee-ka-Seraee*, before reaching which on the left is a large *Baolee* with 100 steps. Here the road turns to the right or S. of E., with broken ground. Hence through a low, thin, *Byr* jungle. At 8 miles is a stone bridge (7) over the *Kalee* river, a deep stream, thence broken ground on each side, and low jungle. At 10 miles there is a stone causeway (8) of some extent, beyond this many ravines, so deep and narrow, that only one camel could pass. (8) The road thence through a rather

(3) Some places deep on each side of the two fords—the second ford ¼ mile to the left of that by the road.

(4) Much cultivation between Husun Abdool, and Vah. On the right of the road near Vah is Fuqueer's house in the raised village, where there is a stone with the mark of the hand of *Nanuk*, (name of a Fuqueer, founder of the sect of *Sikhs*.) It is said that a large rock fell from heaven, and that he put up the *back* of his hand, and thus by the weight of the stone was the mark on the stone caused! An Indian would exclaim, *wah! wah!* (wonderful). The ignorant believe in these stories.

(5) All round, except to the N. W. In the N. and S. they are about a mile between. In the hills to the N. there is a white pukka building.

(6) There are two roads, the left, or lower, for hackeries. The right road above, 12 to 18 feet wide; both roads are narrow, and bad for 200 yards. A hill to the right, and to the left low ground.

(7) An old bridge, the road-way in very bad order, only in part passable.

(8) Called " *Margullee*." It is paved with large stones and has parapets, to the sides. It is about 250 yards long, and in the centre has a turn to the left.

thick jungle, and very stony. Camp S. E. of Janee-ka-Sung, after crossing the *Baboodra* river. Thermometer 3 p. m. 72°.

G. O. " The practice of breaking down hedges and removing thorns from them for burning is prohibited, and the Provost Serjt. and Asst. Baggage Mr., will inflict summary punishment on the spot, on any camp-follower infringing this order, to be proclaimed by beat of tom-tom in the different bazars."

To *Rawul Pindee*, 13¾ miles, (2nd Dec.)—Thermometer 5 a. m. 34°. The jungle and ravines rendered it difficult to get out of camp into the road, the first 6 miles of which are full of ravines, narrow and difficult, obliging the camels and cattle to pass through singly. The country to the left is low with distant villages. At 7 miles cross the stony ghat of the *Seel* (or, *Chehul Jungee*) river. It is partially dry. The ghat bad for hackeries; not far hence on the right is a dry tank, on the left ½ mile beyond it is another tank filled with water. (9) To the right the country low, and distant villages. Crossed the *Leh* river, and encamped N. of the town of *Rawul Pindee*. It is a large town surrounded with walls with bastions, and has an old castle from which a *salute of four guns* (10) was fired. It is a celebrated place for old coins. (11) There is a house here, built, Sir A. *Burnes*

We met Mrs. (now Lady) *Macnaghten* en route to join Sir W. H. M. at Jellalabad, with Lieut. *Conolly* and Dr. *Berwick*. They had a great convoy of camels, and as they were marching one way and we another, there was great confusion, and delay in the arrival of our baggage.

(9) These tanks are 80 to 100 yards square, and the sides are faced with round stones.

(10) The Sikhs have curious rules for firing salutes; they fire three guns for a Colonel. Elsewhere Sir J. Keane had the compliment of 17 guns; but there is no regular force here; and the poor Govr. knew no better.

(11) Though no antiquarian and unlearned in coins, I would advise caution in buying these coins, as they are often *made for the market*. A friend of mine got a Greek coin, the head on which was tolerably perfect. The gold and silver coins are of the most doubtful character; and I believe the copper coins had most claim to antiquity.

states, (12) by the ex-king of Cabool. Thermometer 3 p. m. 75°.

G. O. " A Duffadar's party of the Local Horse will proceed to-morrow morning, under the orders of Naeb Russaldar Hussein Beg, towards the *Jheelum* river. The Naeb Russaldar will receive his orders from the D. Qr. M. G."

3rd Dec. Halt, and the 2nd Column closed up, and encamped on the other side of the river. Thermometer 5. a. m. 40°; 3 p. m. 64°.

2. To *Hoormuk*, 9 miles, (4th Dec. 1839.)—Thermtr. 5 a. m. 48°. The road passed over much broken and raviny ground. About half-way, to the left, the country is very low; we were on high table-land. At about 5 miles the ravines were so deep and narrow that only one camel could ascend and descend at a time. To the river the descent was so difficult, that a single horseman was alone able to pass through the *defile*. To the plains below, is a descent ½ mile long, close to the end of which we crossed the river *Sawun*, a stony-bed, not broad, and one foot of water. Our camp was near the village of Hoormuk. (13) Thermometer 3 p. m. 76°.

To *Muneekyala*, 10 miles, (5th Dec.)—Thermometer 5 a. m. 36°. Shortly after leaving camp, the road passed through ravines for 2 or 3 miles. (14) The country was under cultivation, the divisions of the lands are marked

---

(12) 2nd Edn. vol. ii. p. 59. " We alighted at the house which the ex-king of Cabool built in his exile. It was a miserable hovel." Mr. Elphinstone states, (vol. i., Introduction, p. 126, 2nd Edn.) " While at Rawul Pindee, the haram overtook us, and with it came *Shah Zeman*." The ex-king was Shah Shoojah, but I believe he never lived in it, but *Shah Zeman* only. This was the place of asylum offered by Runjeet Singh to *Shah Shoojah*, when he lost his throne in 1809.

(13) Hoormuk was about a mile off; we obtained water from a spring between it and our camp.

(14) The road was very narrow and stony, and the crowd of camels and men rendered it difficult to pass through.

by hedges of thorns. (15) The ravines and deep chasms caused by the periodical rains made the march a tedious one. At 6 miles, on the left of the road, is a very large *Seraee*, now quite in ruins, called " *Rabat-ke-Seraee.*" There is also a temple to the N. of considerable size. From the Seraee we saw the *Tope* of *Muneekyala*. The country became more open as we approached the *Tope*. Our camp was S. of and close to it, and N. of the village. There is another and larger village of the same name N. of the *Tope*. The *Tope* is a circular building; it is about 60 or 70 feet high from the top of the mound to the top of the building, whose circumference is 375 feet. It is arched over, the outer coating is of plain hewn large stones; the inside is of rough stone and mud: there is a well in the centre. The stones are all polished. (16) It is erected on a mound about 20 or 25 feet high; a flight of steps lead you to the top of the building. Thermometer 3 P. M. 74°.

(15) They make no embankments, consequently the thorny bushes are of value in a country producing little wood. The Sikhs allow all trees to be cut except the *Seeso (Dalbergia Sissoo, Roxb.)* usually pronounced *Sissoo;* which Runjeet always preserved for gun-carriages and other Military purposes; the destruction of which he severely punished.

(16) The difficulty in the execution of this work consists in the great size of the stones, which it would be difficult to remove from a quarry; but the raising them in the operation of building must have required a superior description of machinery than the *natives* themselves possessed more than 2,000 years ago. Mr. *Elphinstone* (vol. i., Introduction, p. 131, 2nd Edn.) says, " There is nothing at all of a *Hindoo* character in the appearance of the building ; most of the party thought it decidedly *Grecian*. It was, indeed, as like Grecian Architecture as any building which Europeans, in a remote part of the country, could now construct by the hands of unpractised native builders. The *natives* called it the Tope of Maunicyala, and said it was built by the *gods*." They have no tradition of the building assigning it to a *native* Architect. There is a temple built of stone at Oodeepoor (Lat. 24° 28' N., Long. 74° 5' E.) in the time of *Vicramaditya*, who reigned before the time of the Christian Era, and as observed by Mill, " the name by which chiefly

To *Seraee Pukkee*, 12¾ miles, (6th Dec.)—Thermometer 5 A. M. 48°. The road over a fine broad plain for about 4½ miles, whence there is a considerable descent through a ravine into the bed of a dry nullah, beyond which there is a small village to the right. Near this the ravines were of great size and depth and very tortuous. Near camp came through a deep, narrow, ravine, about a mile in length. Thence the road went up the bed of the Kasee river, only a few inches deep, (17) crossing which the road turned up to the left, and the camp was at a place called Mull, E. of Seraee Pukkee. Thermometer 3 P. M. 82°.

To *Tameehak*, 14¾ miles, (7th Dec.)—Thermtr. 5 A. M. 38°. Crossed the river Kasee near camp by descending into the bed of the river. The direction to the E. At 1¼ mile ascended a difficult, and in places, dangerous ravine. (18) This obstacle surmounted, the road was tolerable, the

the idea of the universal sovereignty of India, and of the glory of art and science is combined." (Mill's British India, vol. i. p. 429.) Of this building they have a tradition as to the period, and I presume such would have been the case had Muneekyala been built by a native; and that it was not may be inferred from there being no similar buildings of native structure.

Sir A. *Burnes* (2nd Edn. vol. ii. p. 58) says, " It stands on a spacious plain, and the 'Tope' is to be distinguished at a distance of 16 miles. Various surmises have been thrown out regarding this site, but I do not hesitate to fix upon it as '*Taxilla*,' since '*Arrian*' expressly tells us that 'that was the most populous city *between* the Indus and Hydaspes;' which is the exact position of Manikyala." Dr. *Vincent*, (Voyage of Nearchus,) p. 10, says, the *Attok* is *Taxilla*. See, note 41.

It is supposed to have been built by *Alexander* to commemorate his exploits in this part of India. The Tope was entered from the top by *M. Ventura*, a general in the service of the Sikh Govt., some time ago, and in the well, a gold box, containing a bottle of some dark fluid was found, and also a great number of *Greek* coins, and other curiosities. A piece of plate like a salver, on which "in relief" was the triumph of Bacchus, drawn in his chariot by tigers, and the wheels urged on by Cupids, &c. *M. Ventura* first tried to enter from below; but failed owing to the great solidity of the structure.

(17) The river must be extensive in the rains.

(18) The proper road was to the left, but some hackeries having got to the gorge of the road, could proceed no further, and the whole

country falling to the E., in a succession of regular levels, here and there with deep ravines, and rocks protruding above the surface. At 11 miles descending into the bed of the *Kasee* (19) river a few inches deep, then ascended another ravine, and crossing two or three smaller, reached camp. The village of Dhumuk was on the rising ground N. W. of our camp; water procured from a spring near the village of Boorj a mile S. of camp. There were towers to both villages. (20) Thermometer 3 p. m. 74°.

To *Bakerala*, 9⅔ miles, (8th Dec.)—Thermometer 5 a. m. 42°. With much difficulty a road, or path-way, was found down a steep, stony, ghat which led to the river, the road into the bed of which was very narrow and precipitous; (21) the Lancers were obliged to dismount and moved by twos leading their horses. On the left was a fearful precipice into the bed of the *Kasee* river. The banks of the river, were cliffs of perpendicular red and grey sand, and its bed was narrow and winding. (22) The rest of the road was through the bed of the river to camp, on high ground. The village

ravine soon became crowded by camels, bullocks, yaboos, asses, mules, &c. none of which could move on, till the hackeries were passed through. The staff went up by a natural causeway with fearful precipices on each side, the Lancers followed. The width of the roadway only admitted of one horseman passing at a time, being in some places about 2 feet wide; if any horse had made a false step both horse and rider would have been seriously injured, if not killed. One horse of the Lancers in getting up a ravine fell, and died in consequence of the fall.

(19) By some called *Bowlee;* it is the river we crossed before.

(20) This was the largest and worst march from Cabool. When you got on table-land you looked back on the most frightful ravines ever seen, those about the *Chumbul* river are as nothing in the comparison. In such a country, small parties could cut up the baggage cattle of an army in detail.

(21) It only allowed of one camel passing at a time, and was soon choaked, while the entrance to the descent, for nearly half a mile, was crowded with camels, asses, bullocks, mules, &c. It was difficult to pass them; and there was a precipice to the left.

(22) A small body of troops might defend this spot, against a large force.

W. of camp, a mile distant. (23) Low hills on each side of the river half a mile distant. Thermometer 3 P. M. 75°. Rather confined ground for a camp.

To Udhurana, 8¾ miles, (9th Dec.)—Thermometer 5 A. M. 48°. The road lay almost due S. along the bed of the river, which was sandy and heavy in many places, but open for the baggage cattle. (24) At 6 miles the Dhamoyl river falls into the Kasee, and in the rains must form a considerable stream. The camp close to the bed of the river. The village close and N. W. Confined ground for a camp. (25) The bed of the river ran about N. W. to E. round camp. Crossed the river near camp. Thermometer 3 P. M. 80°. No village, or cultivation here. The hills were covered with stunted trees and bushes; and some fine Oleanders were to be seen.

3. To *Rhotas*, 8⅜ miles, (10th Dec. 1839.)—Thermometer 5 A. M. 38°. The road lay through the bed of the river, occasionally crossing some spurs of hills and ravines. Rhotas was built by *Shere Shah*, the Affghan, the same who took the fortress of Rhotas in the province of Behar, in A. D. 1542 by stratagem. It is a walled town nearly half a mile long, running N. E. to S. W. The walls are of great thickness. It was in former times, a frontier post. It is a place of no strength against European science. Its site is on a hill of gentle declivity and overlooks the

---

(23) No water in the bed of the river except small shallow pools. We dug many wells in the bed of the river; water close to the surface. Near the village is a well containing the best water in the *Punjab*. Runjeet Singh always used the water from this well. The Kasee river, here changed its name to Bukeralee *Khoord*, or *Kahun*, (or *small* Bukeralee.)

(24) There is a road a mile shorter by moving straight from camp, on the high bank, through the jungle of Dhak and grass; but 3 or 4 places of heavy sand, between the patches of jungle.

There is a ravine half-way; the road crosses into the bed of the river 2 or 3 times.

(25) The two columns could not have encamped in many of our halting-places. The ground, here, was jungly. There are some *Sissoo* trees in the neighbourhood, (see note 15.)

river Kasee, (26) the bed of which is a Pass into the strong country between the Jheelum and the Attok.

The camp was on the left bank, N. W. of Rhotas, and N. W. of camp was a garden ¼ mile distant, and a *durgah* (27) is just beyond it. Lower down the river, on the right bank on which Rhotas stands, is a large white mosque. Thermometer 3 P. M. 76°.

G. O. "The Asst. Baggage-Master, with a suitable party, will take post at the *ferry* (28) early to-morrow morning; and will prevent the people crowding into the boats."

"The Provost Serjt. will be posted at the *Ford*, with his Dett. and will see that the camels are sent across the river in the order they come up to its bank; and that no crowding is allowed."

To *Jheelum*, 12 miles, (11th Dec.)—Thermometer 5 A. M. 40°. The road lay through the bed of the river Kasee, for about 6 miles, when the route turned to the N. E. and crossed a well-cultivated country, extending to the bank of the Jheelum. The river Jheelum runs close past the town, from E. to W. The ford lies about ¾ mile higher up the river, (E.) There is a village ½ mile from the town, between it and the ford. From the point a little above the village, the ford takes a diagonal direction to the left down the river to the centre, and then takes another diagonal direction up to the left; so that the ford describes two sides of a triangle, which, where the two sides meet, points down the stream: the fords at each side of the river being opposite to each other on the N. and S. side of the river. The ferry is close to the town, where there were 20 large and six small boats. H. M.'s 16th Lancers arrived near the town of Jheelum at about ½ past 8 A. M. From the report of the Duffadar who had been sent on some days before, the depth of water was reported to be up to the middle of a man, and was not considered too deep for cavalry to ford. Stakes had been driven in to mark the direction of the ford. From the

(26) And Dhamoyl.
(27) Mosque, or place of Mahomedan worship.
(28) Of the *Jheelum*.

information obtained also from Lt. *Conolly*, (29) whose party had crossed about 23rd Nov. it was concluded that the ford was practicable. The Adjt. of the Lancers had ridden across, and came back announcing it to be practicable. The Regt. entered the ford by *threes*, and passed to the centre of the river without any accident; but on arriving at the centre, there being a number of camels crossing at the time by which a sight of the stakes was lost, the leading portion of the Regt. tried to pass them by going beyond them to the right, going *lower down the stream*; they immediately got into deep water, and the strength of the stream. So deep was the river, here, that the horses began to swim. From the opposite (Jheelum) side, the scene was most awful and distressing, to witness the struggle of the animals on getting suddenly into deep water; we could observe horse after horse and rider disappear, and suddenly rise again; the impression was that a troop at least would be lost. The remainder of the Regt. averted the danger by taking the ford to the *left*. Boats were despatched to the ford, but could not arrive in time to save many. On mustering the Regt. it was found, that Capt. *Hilton*, a corporal and nine privates and their horses were drowned. The bodies of Capt. H. and of two or three men were brought on shore, and every medical aid tried in vain to restore them to life; but failed, except in the case of one or two privates. Lt.-Col. *Cureton* was nearly drowned by his horse being frightened at some camels, and falling back in the water, thus compelling him to swim hampered with his sword and cap fastened under his chin; and he with difficulty reached the bank. Lt. *Pattle* had a very narrow escape, and was saved by private *Dobbin*. (30)   *Sir J. Keane* came to the spot and remained for some time; evidently affected by the distressing scene. The river was about 300 yards wide opposite the town, but more at the ford; and by the

---

(29) Who with Dr. *Berwick* accompanied Mrs. Macnaghten.

(30) He was Chaplain's clerk, and had crossed before the Regt. The Rev. Mr. *Hammond* solicited the Colonel to promote him to Serjt. which I hope has been done.

The river Jheelum. 347

circuitous direction the ford extended over a line of about 500 yards, and had more than 3 feet of water, and a strong current near the S. bank; and what made it worse was, the water was very cold, and the crossing being made after a long march. This sad event cast a gloom over the whole camp; nor were its results confined to the past. (31) Thermometer 3 P. M. 72°.

(31) Several men died from catching cold. It is to be observed that since the Duffadar had crossed the river (some days before) the river had risen, for it fell 18 inches during the night, as next morning a sandbank covered with water the day before, was distinctly visible: and at this season such a fall could only be occasioned by a previous sudden (unaccountable) rise; since in the cold season rivers do not usually fall suddenly. It fell six inches more the day after. The Lancers had their caps fastened under their chins (by which Col. *Cureton* was nearly drowned) which impeded the men swimming, and having their swords and accoutrements on, if they fell they could not recover themselves, they were weighed down. The horses with all their trappings, and martingals, and bridled up, were fettered; and the least check threw the horse over. Fording a broad river after a long march, when the horses were tired and heated, moving through (as on that morning) very cold water, both horse and man were chilled and benumbed!

Where a ford is in a direct line, it is most easy, by staking the ford and planting two flags on each side, to give a perfect direction. In a case like that at the *Jheelum*, it would require to give the two cross directions. Thus, the banks of the river being N. and S. the directions would be from N. E. to S. W. and from N. W. to S. E. Capt. *Macauly*, Royal Engrs. p. 247 (Mily. Reconnoissance, &c.) observes, " Fords should not be deeper than three feet for infantry, four feet for Cavy. and two and half feet for Arty. and Ammn. wagons. If a ford be situated where the current is rapid, its depth should be diminished in proportion, from *half* to *one* foot for cavalry, and from nine inches to one and half feet for infantry. Having reconnoitred a ford, it will be prudent to plant upright pickets in the stream, notched to show the variation of the depth at different times. In mountainous countries these variations will be considerable in winter; large stones are also frequently found in fords among hills, rendering the passage difficult for cavalry; insurmountable for carriages. In sandy countries, and where alluvial deposits are frequent, fords may be found for infantry in small numbers, but impracticable for cavalry, more so for carriages, sometimes appearing to have a firm and solid bed, but proving, on critical

4. Left bank of the *Jheelum*, (12th Dec. 1839.)—Thermometer 5 A. M. 38°. Halt. The 2nd Column, under Maj.-Genl. *Thackwell*, arrived on the opposite bank this morning; encamped on the right bank, close to the town of Jheelum. Thermometer 3 P. M. 64°.

G. O. "It is with much sorrow that H. E. the Comr. in-Chief notifies to the troops, that, in fording the Jheelum river, yesterday morning, Capt. *Hilton*, H. M.'s 16th Lancers, one corporal and nine privates of the same Regt. unfortunately lost their lives. H. E. deeply deplores the circumstance, and sympathizes with the afflicted friends, and comrades of the deceased."

examination, soft and shifting. The best have a gravelly bottom. Great care must be taken in the examination of fords, across streams or rivers threading a morass, or boggy district. A brown rushy bottom may generally be trusted; but bright green spots are more delusive."

"A row of pickets planted on either side of the ford, and retained by cordage, will be found useful, as well in the crossing as for the indication of its direction. When a river offers a ford of sufficient width, and the stream is rapid, it is sometimes expedient to use the cavalry to cut the current of the water obliquely, and make the infantry cross lower down." p. 248.

Burnes says, (vol. ii. p. 42,) "Arrian speaks of the Hydaspes as a muddy and rapid river with a current of 3 or 4 miles an hour, which is correct." Burnes crossed it about the end of February, we on the 11th December. He crossed it lower down and says, "It had rained the day preceding our arrival; the stream was discolored, and the water bubbled in eddies at various places." But where a ford has picquets laid down, the rule is not to pass *below* but *above* the picquets, as below is the deepest water; by passing *below* the stakes, the Lancers got into deep water. The ford was over a sand-bank, and by getting off it, in any direction, the horses got into deep water and floundered. When the English entered France in March, 1814, the river *Adour* was fordable, owing to a strong wind blowing against the stream and raising up the sand; but on a change of wind, the stream caused the full flow of the river and the sand to fall with it, and deepened it so much as to render the river not fordable: nor was it forded. The *Jheelum*, I believe, has quicksands, and from its direction, the most difficult ford I ever saw. *Lances* driven into the river would always, with the white and red flags, be better than stakes.

"Brig. *Persse* will be pleased to give such orders for the interment of the bodies, this afternoon at ½ past 4 o'clock, as may be proper."

"All officers off duty belonging to the troops are requested to attend."

The funeral took place accordingly, and the bodies of the late Capt. *Hilton* and four men (the rest have never been found) were interred close to our camp, opposite to the town of Jheelum: his body being placed in the centre grave. Steps have since been taken by the Regt. to build a tomb on the spot. This was indeed a melancholy event at the close of our campaign; it cannot fail to be remembered, as a lesson of dear-bought experience: and as *Napoleon* said, "Les passages des rivière de cette importance sont les opérations les plus critiques." (32)

Left bank of the *Jheelum*, (13th Dec.)—Thermometer 5 A. M. 30°. (33) The 3rd Cavalry crossed over this afternoon at 3 P. M. to prevent the horses suffering from the cold water in the morning, particularly after a long march. The officers were ordered by *Sir J. Keane*, to come over in boats, as well as all of the troopers who could not swim. The horses were ordered to come over in *watering order*, (the saddles, &c. being sent over in the boats.) The horses of each troop came over singly, with a horse's length between each; each troop being led by a guide (Mullah) procured from the town. There was no accident. The Asst. Qr. Mr. Genl. (Lt. *Becher*) was sent with boats to station them in a position on each side of the centre-point of the river near the ford, to prevent any horses or camels, &c. passing below the line of demarcation: and the river had been fresh staked. We went to the ford to witness the passage; the horses did, at times, get into deep water. At the time of crossing, two or three elephants belonging

---

(32) Napoleon's Mem. par Montholon, Tome 3, p. 165.

(33) In the open air 22°, and at 8½ A. M. 36°. The water of the river was scarcely warmed at the surface by the sun; it was a very cold day.

to *Lenah Singh*, (34) were driven straight across the river, at the imminent risk of frightening the horses : luckily such an event did not occur. We saw the advantage of the horses crossing *singly*.

There were many camels lost, owing to their becoming benumbed with cold; they were seen to stand with their loads, or without them, incapable of moving : they sat down in the river, rolled on their sides, and were carried down the stream, floating for a time, and then sinking. Thermometer 3 P. M. 68°.

The town of *Jheelum* (35) is on the N. bank of the river, and extends about ½ a mile on the right bank, running from E. to W. In the centre, between the town and river, is a

---

(34) Sikh Mehmandar.

(35) By some written Jhylum *(Vahuda)*. " It is the most W. of the Punjab streams, and is by Abal Fazel, named the Behut, or Bedusta: in ancient Hindoo mythological poems the Indrani, and is the famous Hydaspes of Alexander."

Sir A. Burnes, vol. ii. p. 58, 2nd Edn. says, (alluding to *Maneekyala*,) "M. Ventura decides on *it* as *Bucephalia*, from a derivation that interprets Manikyala to mean the city of the *horse;* but this is not founded on history, as *Bucephalia* stood on the banks of the *Hydaspes*."

But at page 50 he says, again, " about 15 miles *below* Jelum," (i. e. the town and right bank,) " and about 1000 yards from the Hydaspes (the river Jelum) near the modern village of *Darapoor*, we hit upon some extensive ruins called *Oodeenuggur*, which seem to have been a city that extended for 3 or 4 miles. The traditions of the people are vague and unsatisfactory, for they referred us to the *deluge,* and the time of the prophet *Noah*." And " on the opposite side of the Hydaspes," to *Darapoor*, (i. e. on the *left* bank) " stands a mound said to be coeval with Oodeenuggur, where the village of Moong is built." And " I do not conceive it impossible that *Oodeenuggur may* represent the site of *Nicœa*, and that the mounds and ruins on the W. bank" (clearly not *at* the town of *Jheelum*) " mark the position of *Bucephalia*." So that we cannot assign the town of Jheelum, as the ancient site of either Nicœa or Bucephalia, according to the above reasoning; so that learned antiquarians must decide.

The river takes its name from the town. In India, usually, a river changes its name as often as it passes through a new district; the Ganges and Jumna form exceptions. (Vide Note 41.)

large mosque. To the W. is a garden and temple for Hindoo worship. There is a village to the E., distant ½ a mile. Some of the houses are of pukka brick, and of considerable height. The *Punjab* here commences; the country between the Attok and Jheelum, contains no Sikhs, the population being all Mahomedan; though under Sikh rule.

Lieut. (now Major) *Pottinger*, from Herat, came into camp to-day, en route to Calcutta.

5. To *Khoar*, 12¼ miles, (14th Dec. 1839.)—Thermometer 5 A. M. 32°. The direction of the road varied often. The country a low flat, intersected by seven or eight heavy dry, sandy, beds, which are so many streams in the rains. At 3 miles a village on the left. Half-way, ascend and descend a ridge of hills. At 7 miles a village on the left with a small mud fort. Half a mile beyond another village, near which is a pukka well. No cultivation seen except near the villages, which are small. Crossed several ravines, and a low grass jungle on the road. We saw *byr*, *sissoo*, and *neem* (36) trees, around the villages. It was a heavy march. *Camp* ¼ mile N. of Khoar. The troops had to file through and round the village, by a narrow road. There is a small mud fort here. Fine young crops of wheat and barley near the town. Thermometer 3 P. M 73°.

To *Dheengee*, 14¼ miles, (15th Dec. 1839.)—Thermometer 5 A. M. 42°. The road more to the E. but at no great distance from the Jheelum, for 5 or 6 miles, crossing the dry sandy beds of several water-courses, in some parts deep sand. The road then passed through Dhak and grass jungle, and then over a low ridge of hills, when it ran due E., and after crossing it, we entered on a very extensive plain. (37) Four miles from this we came to Noor Jheelum; the country tolerably well-cultivated. From the ridge of hills is seen the *Ascesines* (Chenab) winding along in the distance. Passed four villages on the road; they are raised on mounds, with walls and mud towers. The town of

---

(36) The *Neem*, (Melia azadirachta.)
(37) Where the largest armies might manœuvre.

Dheengee said to contain 2,000 houses, some built of brick and high. A small pukka-walled garden, near it. *Camp* S. of it ¼ mile : plenty of hogs and hares at this place. Thermometer 3 p. m. 68°.

To *Pareewallah*, 11½ miles, (16th Dec.)—Thermometer 5 a. m. 40°. The road good, ran nearly E. and for the first 5 miles through a Dhak and grass jungle, some places thick. Passed four villages, on mounds. Other villages seen in the distance. Passed the village of Lalah with a square mud fort; beyond it, one mile, is Pareewallah, a large village of a similar description. The late Maharajah Runjeet Singh kept his stud here, the water and grass being esteemed excellent. The famous horse *Lylee* (38) was here. Camp N. of Pareewallah. *Thermometer* 3 p. m. 72°.

An order was issued to-day against igniting patches of grass on the road. (39) Any camp-follower found lighting a fire by the road-side, and in a situation where flames were likely to spread, was severely punished. (40)

G. O. "The Head Qrs. and sappers to move across the Chenab and encamp at Ramnuggur; no baggage of the 16th Lancers to go across till the whole of that of Hd. Qrs. and the sappers has passed over."

To *Ramnuggur* on the left bank of the Chenab 10 miles, (17th Dec.)—Thermometer 5 a. m. 40°. The road lay over the same extensive plain, bare of trees. Passed three or four villages; 7¾ miles to the ghat (right bank.) The ford is lower down to the right, a round of 2½ miles, with three streams; and 3 feet of water in the middle one. The ghat

---

(38) Runjeet fought a pitched battle with Sultan Mahomed of Peshawer for this famous horse " whose speed was like the wind." The Sultan lost it and secured peace by surrendering the horse. This is, I believe, the first battle fought for a *horse* ever known. The fact is worthy of record: but Runjeet was so fond of horses, that he would have given £10,000 for a horse of high character.

(39) This grass (or rather reed) is valuable, being used in making hedges to the fields. They lighted these fires to warm themselves; but were warmed in another way if they disobeyed the order.

(40) The same order in both columns.

is good, and has not high banks. Cross over heavy sand for 1¼ mile, at the end of which cross four beds which would be 3 or 4 feet deep with water on the rise of the river.

Our camp was about 2 miles from the left bank, and about 2 miles N. W. of the town of Ramnuggur, and ½ mile S. of a large clump of trees. There were 12 or 14 large and some smaller boats at the ghat. The *Chenab* must be more than a mile broad in the rains, and have a depth of from 14 to 16 feet of water ; and is said to be free of rocks, so it is well suited for the passage of boats of a large size in the rainy season, and for good-sized boats at other periods. Ramnuggur is a large walled town. (41) Some

(41) Ramnuggur has been thought to be the site of the ancient town of *Bucephalia*. Sir A. Burnes, vol. ii. p. 50, says, that there is a *mound* where the village of Moong is built, and some *extensive ruins* beyond Moong, near Huria Badshapoor, and adds, " I do not conceive it improbable that Oodeenuggur may represent Nicæa, and that the *mound* and ruins on the W. bank of the Hydaspes *(Jheelum)* mark the position of Bucephalia." But Ramnuggur is on the *Chenab* !

Dr. *Wm. Vincent*, 1797, (Voyage of Nearchus down the Hydaspes or Chelum to the north of the Indus,) p. 94, says, " the discovery (of *Nicæa*) is not difficult ; for though the present road from Attok to Lahore crosses the Chelum at Rotas," " we are directed by *Arrian* with so much precision to another point, that we can hardly be mistaken. On a *bend* of the Hydaspes, he says, there is an island *(Jamad)* surrounded by the river, with a second branch, or artificial canal, on the E. side." " Below the S. point of the island, and the re-union of the river, *Porus* had drawn up his forces on the E. side. *Alexander* leaving Craterus with a considerable body of forces opposed to Porus, marched in the night to effect a passage under cover of this island, to the opposite shore. He embarked himself in a galley, and conveyed his troops in boats brought overland from the Indus. He had scarcely disembarked them, when he found himself encircled by another channel which, being swelled by the solstitial rains, he forded with great difficulty : then turning to his right, he followed the course of the stream, and, after defeating the *son* of Porus, advanced to the spot where the *king himself* had drawn up his forces opposite to *Craterus*. Here the battle was fought, and *here must be the site of Nicæa*." (Major *Rennell*, in his Memoir, p. 93,) " concludes that Alexander passed the *Chelum* at *Rotas ;*" (i. e. by the direct road, 12 miles distant ;) " but in the accompanying map places *Nicæa* lower down 28 miles." Again, p. 95, " The natives here remarked to us that we had *surrounded* (42) *the country* (Punjab), *taken Candahar, Ghuznee, and Cabool, and said " how can Lahore and Umritsir escape ?"* Thermometer 3 p. m. 76°.

To-day was published the G. O. of the Govr. Genl. of India, (in the Secret Dept.) dated 18th Nov. 1839, expressive of the sense entertained by His Lordship of the soldier-like spirit and conduct, of the Army of the Indus, throughout the late campaign: and granting a donation of six months' full, or Field Batta, to every officer, European and native, and to the N. C. O. and privates of the native troops.

G. O. " H. M.'s 16th Lancers to send forward their baggage, in the course of the afternoon, and to cross the river, to-morrow morning; the men, with their saddles, &c.

distance from his camp on the W. side of the river to the head of the island is given by *Arrian*, and may be estimated at 9 miles. If, therefore, we can find an island in modern geography which will correspond with this of Arrian, we have a precise point given and have only to fix *Nicæa* at the requisite distance below. Such an island *(Jamad)* is found, and situated on the bend of the Chelum or Hydaspes, *about* 28 *miles below Rotas,"* (while Rotas from the present town of Jheelum *is only* 12 *miles !)* " and in a more direct line between *Attok* and Lahore than *Rotas itself*. The road probably passed at this place in earlier times, and has diverted to Rotas only because the island afforded a strong post which in India is always a source of exaction. This *island* is called *Jamad* by *de la Rochette*, and by Major *Rennell* in his second map." Dr. V. says, p. 99, that the Longitude of *Jamad*, by Maj. *Rennell* is 71° 50' E.; and that *Bucephalia* is supposed to have been on the *opposite* side of the river; and p. 110, " The distance from the lower point of *Jamad* to the confluence (with the *Acesines*) is from 60 to 70 miles." He (p. 100) fixes the time of departure of the fleet under *Nearchus* on the 23rd October, A. C. 327.

At p. 10 he assigns *Taxilla* as the ancient site of the modern *Attok*, "being in the kingdom of the *Taxiles*."

(42) The British dominions, Affghanistan, and the Himalaya mountains surround the Punjab, see p. 3, note 7.

At Rawul Pindee a Mahomedan asked some of our principal staff officers, to give him a certificate that his village was his property, for he said *" I know this country will be yours, and I wish to have a paper to show, in such an event, that I may not be deprived of it !"*

are to be sent by the ferry; the horses by the ford in charge of the syces." (43)

" The Artillery and Cavalry horses (of the 2nd Column) to be sent by the ford in charge of the syces; and the men, guns, harness and saddles by the ferry."

Burning of grass.—" The corporal's party of Lancers with the Provost Serjt., for the purpose of preventing this practice, to be increased, and the men composing it to be furnished with whips, to use them on all followers they may find standing over burning grass, by the road-side, even although they may not be the individuals who set it on fire."

(44) 18th Dec. Halt. Lenah Singh waited on Sir J. Keane to sound him as to his intention of visiting Lahore. Sir John replied that he had received no invitation. Dr. *Gordon* was sick; he was, strictly speaking, the channel of communication.

6. To *Naeewalla*, 12⅝ miles, (19th Dec. 1839.)—Thermometer 5 A. M. 38°. Shortly after leaving camp crossed a small dry nullah, which must be rather deep in the rains; thence the road sandy for a mile. Then over a flat plain with villages, on mounds, at intervals, in the distance. The soil rich and highly cultivated around the villages. About half-way on the right, is the large town of *Akaligurh;* (45) having passed it we saw four or five white Hindoo temples close under the walls. There were several villages passed on the same side of the road. Camp ½ mile S. of Naeewala, which was surrounded by fine crops of wheat,

(43) Grooms.

(44) " Proclamation of the penalty to be made, daily, in the different bazars." It was next to impossible to find out of a crowd, who did set fire to the grass.

(45) It is a walled town with gates, and the inhabitants are *Akalces* who are a very independent and brave people. The Akalees rendered Runjeet Singh important services in several of his battles, in which they often led the troops into action. (See the battle of *Noushera* in Chapter 15.) They are considered sacred by the Sikhs, and have been known to threaten even the life of Runjeet. At this place it is said, they pay no revenue. The Sikhs are in great fear of these fanatics, whom it is dangerous to affront; they are regardless of their own lives.

&c. There is a very extensive plain, here, and on our route to-day. Thermometer 3 p. m. 78°.

To *Thabool*, 10¾ miles, (20th Dec.)—Thermometer 5 a. m. 38°. The direction of the route S. and S. E. and then E. Passed two villages on the road, which was good, and the country very open; but little cultivation. Camp ½ mile S. W. from the village. About ½ mile N. W. of it is a Hindoo temple, and some trees. We lost our road to-day. (46)

Memo. " It is to be proclaimed by tom-tom, in the different bazars, that the cutting down of Peepul (47) trees, for feeding elephants, or camels, is prohibited; and any follower detected in destroying such trees will be severely punished."

The people, here, said that the Sikh troops rob them of all they have, when they are marched across the country. I believe the Sikh people are not averse to the British; the Sikh soldiers are: they have every thing to lose; the former every thing to gain! Thermometer 3 p. m. 72°. About this time we heard of the capture of *Khelat* by the troops under Maj.-Genl. *Willshire;* and all were glad that the gallant general, had an opportunity of distinguishing himself in the Affghanistan campaign.

To near *Mutta*, 8½ miles, (21st Dec.)—Thermometer 5 a. m. 38°. The route over the same extensive plain, road excellent. About 7 miles from *Thabool* are two large villages, called Nyshara, (48) between which the road passes;

---

(46) The road properly lay in a nearly direct line to the left, instead of which we marched straight on to a village to the N. W. of Thabool, and had to turn to our left to reach camp S. W. of it.

(47) (Ficus Religiosa), a species of fig-tree (wild). It is a tree held sacred by Hindoos.

(48) We passed two other villages on the road. Low jungle on parts of the road. Cultivation near the villages. There were two villages in front and S. E. of camp. There are some Bramins and a temple near this place, and a rather thick grass jungle, in which the Rev. Mr. *Hammond* nearly lost his way.

two miles further was camp N. W., about a mile short of Mutta. Thermometer 3 P. M. 72°.

To *Mullyan*, 15 miles, (22nd Dec.)—Thermometer 5 A. M. 38°. The road lay over the same extensive plain. Passed two villages. A village about 2 miles short of Mullyan, passing which we had some ravines to cross; from which we passed through some low jungle, after which there was an extensive plain. Camp S. W. of Mullyan. At this place an invitation came to *Sir John Keane* to pay a visit to Lahore, which was accepted. Thermometer 3 P. M. 70°.

23rd Dec. *Halt*. Thermometer 5 A. M. 36°. G. O. "The 2nd Brigade H. A., H. M.'s 16th Lancers, a Ressalah of the 4th Local Horse, will accompany H. E. as an Escort to Lahore; the remainder of the troops will move towards Ferozpoor, under Maj.-Genl. *Thackwell*. In addition to H. E.'s personal staff, the following officers of the General staff, are directed to move with Hd. Qrs. to Lahore, *viz*. The D. A. G., D. Q. M. G., D. C. G., D. A. Q. M. G., the Offg. A. A. G. and S. A. C. G."

" Such officers of the staff, and those not belonging to the troops forming H. E.'s Escort, as may be desirous of visiting Lahore, are requested to communicate the same to the D. A. G., through the Maj.-Genl. Comg. the Column, and if their services can be dispensed with, they will have permission to accompany Hd. Qrs." (49) Thermometer 3 P. M. 76°.

7. To *Dhingee*, 13¼ miles, (24th Dec.)—Thermometer 5 A. M. 36°. H. E. Sir J. Keane, and his Escort marched this morning, taking the direct road to *Lahore;* (50) we took the

---

(49) "No bullocks, tattoos, or cattle of any description to precede the troops on the march. Syces, &c. to remain in the rear."

(50) Rajah Lenah Singh, who came with the invitation from Lahore, wished Sir J. Keane to proceed by a different route, declaring that boats had been prepared at another ghat; however, it was determined to take the shorter route. When permission for the return of the troops through the Punjab had been granted, it was stipulated that they should not pass within 25 miles of Lahore; but this was by their own

route to Ferozpoor. Our route, the direction varying, was over arable land for about 5 miles, passing several villages. At about 6 miles passed round a village, then over some broken ground, and thence, by a path-way, through much cultivation: the last 3 or 4 miles, the road lay through jungle grass. Crossed near camp a nullah, with a few inches of water. Camp N. E. of the village. (51) Thermometer 3 P. M. 68°.

To *Surrukpoor*, 10 miles, (25th Dec.)—Thermometer 5 A. M. 44°. The road lay over a grass jungle for 2 miles, then over arable land. About the middle of the march, cultivation and two villages were passed. Then we arrived at the village of Surrukpoor. There being symptoms of rain, the order to cross the Ravee (Hydraotes) was issued after breakfast, to move at 12 o'clock. The ghat on the right bank was 2½ miles distant. At 1½ mile crossed a nullah, with rather steep banks. (52) The Ferryghat is a mile from it. The river about 250 yards wide. The ford was a good one, the river there, wider. After crossing the river to the left bank, passed over a bed of sand for ½ mile to camp, pitched in some Jow jungle. On

invitation. The Govr. Genl., I believe, wished Sir John to accept the invitation if asked: I do not think the latter had any personal wish to go there (he was sick); but his staff wished to go there.

(51) The villages on this march more numerous, and the cultivation more forward and extensive. Some of the Mahomedan inhabitants of the villages of Cawnpoor, Aktah, &c. asked when we were going to *take the country*. The Sikhs will not allow the Mahomedans to call those of their faith to prayers, publicly, (usually by a crier from the top of a mosque, who may be heard a mile off;) but they will receive them as proselytes.

(52) It was a bad ghat and deep mud with the water. Some found a better crossing 100 yards to the left, the banks being lower, and little water. Thence the road to the Ferry ghat is to the right (those going to which should have kept the direct road from Surrukpoor); the ford to the left, higher up the river. The ford was marked off with reeds and grass in two rows, and was about two and half or three feet deep, but broad and firm bottom. Camels and Yaboos went over loaded. The 3rd Cavy. forded over. The hackeries went in the boats.

this march there was, half-way, a cross-road to Lahore. The wind (N. E.) threatened to blow down our tents.

There was a rumour to-day that the Sikhs intended to attempt the rescue of our prisoners, Mahomed Hyder Khan, and Hajee Khan, Kakur; but no such attempt was made. (53) Thermometer 3 p. m. 64°. We spent our Christmas dinner, in the mess-tent of the sappers and miners; and with the aid of a little good wine (which had been a scarce article) passed a pleasant evening; and went to bed without any fears of our slumbers being disturbed, unless the wind should blow down our tents.

26th Dec. *Halt.* Thermometer 5 a. m. 36°. No fresh alarms. Thermometer 3 p. m. 70°.

To *Gunjatee*, 11½ miles, (27th Dec.)—Thermometer 5 a. m. 40 . The first part of the road was through low jungle. (54) Crossed the first mile, two dry beds of nullahs. The road then ran E. At 4 miles there is a village; thence the road turns to the left, or N. of E. About half-way we found a great expanse of plain, or desert, and some low jungle. To the right, distant 5 miles is a village, with high

---

(53) There were some Sikh sepoys in most of the villages, probably their homes, and no doubt they spread the report as a good joke. However Hajee Khan, Kakur, thought it none. He begged to have a sword to defend himself, as he knew the Sikhs detested him cordially. However, the guards over the *Hajee* were loaded as a measure of precaution. An officer wrote from Ferozpoor, that it was said 25,000 men and 100 guns, were to attack us, to release the prisoners ; and to seize the Comr.-in-Chief, so that some thought, we had only come "to the end of our beginning," and a war in the Punjab was foretold ; the force required was laid down at from 15 to 20,000 men. New regiments to be raised as a matter of course. The Punjab was to be annexed to the British dominions in the cold season 1839-40. The expedition to China was at a discount; and a war with Nepal, or the Burmese, was deferred till a future period.

(54) We lost our road, or rather could see none. The trumpets and bugles were sounded from the advance, " *we have lost our road,*" (for five or six minutes) to give intimation to the troops, and camp-followers. We at length succeeded in finding our way, about day-break.

houses. *Camp* E. ¼ mile from the village. (55) Thermometer 3 P. M. 70°.

To *Sulleeanee*, 13¾ miles, (28th Dec.)—Thermometer 5 A. M. 44°. The direction varied little from E. The road the first half over an open country, with low jungle. No regular road. About half-way the village of Ahphur. (56) At 10 miles the village of Nuddeepoor (both small villages.) From the last village the jungle is thicker. *Camp* ¼ mile W. of the village. Thermometer 3 P. M. 75°.

8. To *Kussoor*, 10 miles, (29th Dec. 1839.)—Thermtr. 5 A. M. 40°. The road first half over a jungly country, a village on the right half-way; hence the road is free from jungle, and a well cultivated country is entered. *Camp* to the E. close under the walls of Kussoor. It is as ancient as Lahore; there are, or rather were, 12 divisions, and the inhabitants are all Mahomedans. (57) It is of great extent. An army might make a good stand here; as not only are there heights here, but each division of the town might be turned into a fortified position. Thermtr. 3 P. M. 75°.

30th Dec. To the right bank of the Sutluj, (9⅔ miles.)—Thermometer 5 A. M. 44°. The road to the E., and first part over the ruins of Kussoor, about one mile in extent; the road then descends into a low, flat, tract, taking a direction to the S. E. Passed by much cultivation, and a village on the road. Breakfasted on the right bank, which is not very high; encamping ground sandy. After breakfast crossed over, and encamped on the left bank. There were 60 or 70 boats of sizes. The stream was of no strength, and the bed is shelving, to the left bank. It was about

---

(55) Half-way on this march, there is a cross-road to Lahore.

(56) Hence a cross-road to Lahore.

(57) The city was founded by a Nuwab who gave each of his 12 sons, a fort, or walled place, to reside in. It is said to have been conquered from the Moghul Emperors 70 years ago. The divisions (such as remain) are surrounded by pukka brick walls, with bastions. There are several mosques, and palaces. The surrounding country is covered with ruins; and garden-houses are scattered over a great extent.

The Visit at Lahore.

400 yards wide. After crossing to the left bank, at about ¼ mile, crossed some water, in some places 2½ to 3 feet deep. Camp on the left bank, on sandy ground with low jungle, distant from the Ferozpoor-ghat, about 1½ mile (deep sand between); and about 5 miles from the cantonment. Thermometer 3 P. M. 75°.

Left bank near Ferozpoor, (31st Dec.)—The 3rd Cavalry crossed over this morning, by boats. Halted for the arrival of *Sir J. Keane*, from Lahore. We did not cross the *Beah*, (or Hyphasis) which you do in the regular route from Lahore to Loodianah.

1st Jan., 1840. H. E. Sir J. Keane reached the *right* bank of the *Sutluj* (Hysudrus) and crossed over next morning to the *left* bank, and encamped between us and the ghat. We now learnt the result of the visit to Lahore.

Sir John Keane, being unwell, he sent a deputation, consisting of Brigr. *Persse* and ten or twelve other officers, to wait on the *Maharajah, Kurruk Singh*, (58) and the visit was returned; the deputation also waited on *Konwar Nao Nihal Singh*, the son. The party before leaving Lahore, were shewn a large portion of the Sikh army; consisting of 32 Battns. of *Infantry* each of eight Cos. of 100 men each, 6,000 *Cavalry*; 96 Horse Artillery, and 64 Foot Artillery guns; and a large body of Irregular troops. This gives a regular force of 31,600 men and 160 guns. The real amount of the Sikh regular army is about 50,000, of whom one-fifth are Mahomedans, the rest Sikhs. (59) The regular

---

(58) The invitation was in the name of the Maharajah (son of the late Runjeet Singh), but his son (Konwar Nao Nihal Singh) has the supreme control of all affairs. In October last, the Maharajah left Lahore, on his road to Loodianah; he made one march, and was brought back. *Rajah Dhian Singh*, who was the minister, about January last left the court, and went to his estate in the hills. I believe *Rajah Goolab Singh*, has adopted the same mode of retirement.

(59) " The Sikh troops can undergo great fatigue and make long marches. *Forster* says, p. 289, "A body of their cavalry has been known to make marches of 40 and 50 miles, and to continue them for many successive days." I was told by Col. *Courtlandt* that two or three

Sikh force was drawn up in line, the Artillery on one flank, and the Cavalry on the other: the Irregular troops were drawn up at right angles with them. The Maharajah sent a present of 26,000 Rs. (£2,600) to be distributed among the British troops. The British Govt. gave 11,000 Rs. (£1000.) A G. O. was issued on the 2nd Jan. 1840, by H. E. Lt.-Genl. Sir J. *Keane*, breaking up the "*Army of the Indus;*" the Bengal portion of which had marched 2,070 miles, (60) between the 8th Nov. 1838, to the 31st

years ago, a considerable body of *infantry* marched from *Lahore* to *Peshawar* in seven days, a distance of about 250 miles. They are free from prejudice, they will carry seven or eight days' provisions on their back; and, as *Runjeet* said, " dig a well, or build a fort, if required."

They used to have *messes* of ten men each, but Runjeet, of late years, discontinued the system as being too expensive; as he granted an extra allowance, on this account: he had now no more conquests to make; and might, like *Alexander*, have cried because he had no more kingdoms to conquer.

The *Sikhs* are disciplined after the French manner, but they have no knowledge of European tactics on the grand scale. A Sikh officer of high rank, thought that the strength of a position consisted in drawing up a force in order of battle with many guns, in *one line*, superior to their opponents; assuming that the enemy would attack them in line (as at the battle of Mahidpoor!) and asked Genl. *Ventura* if such would not be the case. This was begging the question, but the General adroitly answered: "In *European* armies, it is a battle of position," leaving the *Sikh* to guess at the mode of executing the movement!

They use the French words of command, move at quick time, marching to the beat of drum, fife and cymbals. I saw the Sikh troops at *Roopur*, on the Sutluj, at the interview between (late) Lord *W. Bentinck* and (late) *Runjeet Singh*, in October, 1831; and it was observed on the occasion of their review before Lord *Auckland* and (late) Sir *H. Fane* at Ferozpoor, in Dec. 1838, that their movements were quicker and manœuvring better: but, competent judges were of opinion that they were (1838) inferior to the troops of Scindiah's regular battalions.

When we consider that Peshawer, and the country between it and the Jheelum, Mooltan, Dera Ghazee Khan, and Dera Ismael Khan, &c. (a very considerable portion of the country) are inhabited by *Mahomedans* who detest the Sikhs, we reduce the strength of the Sikh power by more than one-half: for the Mahomedans must desire to free themselves from the Sikh yoke.

(60) Including 145 miles marched in Lower Sindh.

Dec. 1839; the longest distance ever marched by an Indian army.

On the 7th Jan. Sir J. *Keane* embarked on boats at Ferozpoor for Bombay; (61) on which and on the following day, the troops, &c. marched to their respective destinations: and thus terminated the "*March and Operations of the Army of the Indus.*"

I shall, in the following Chapter, endeavour to exhibit the state of affairs, Political and Military, in *Affghanistan*, since Mr. *Elphinstone* left *Shah Shoojah* at his court at *Peshawer* in June, 1809, to the time of his full restoration at *Cabool* in August, 1839; which will prove, that owing to the distracted state of that country for 30 years, it was impossible without the aid of the expedition, to have regenerated that kingdom.

(61) Taking with him Mahomed Hyder Khan, late Govr. of Ghuznee. I must not omit to mention that the famous "Ghuznee Sword" was sold by auction at Ferozpoor for 4,250 Rs. (£425); and purchased by Sir John (now Lord) Keane. Subsequently I hear it was purchased by the Bombay Column for 6,000 Rs. and presented to H. Excy.

CHAPTER XVII.

THE HISTORY OF THE DOORANEE DYNASTY.

1747.—1. Ahmed Shah, Abdalee, (1) was the founder of the Dooranee empire. He fought his way through the greater part of Khorasan, and passing the fortified places without attacking them, repaired to Candahar, where he arrived with 2 or 3,000 horse. He there found and seized a treasure coming from India to *Nadir Shah.* In October 1747, he was crowned at Candahar, (2) and was said to have been only 23 years old. He spent the winter at Candahar, settling the country, and preparing his army for future expeditions: he had to found a monarchy over a warlike, and independent people, not attached to the kingly form of government; such as prevailed in Persia. (3)

---

(1) The history of the Dooranee Empire, during the reigns of Ahmed Shah (the founder), Timoor Shah, Zeman Shah, Mahmood Shah, and of Shah Shoojah, till he lost his throne in 1809, is an abstract taken from Elphinstone's Cabool, vol. ii. App. A. p. 337, &c. The continuation from 1809, to 1839, is by Moollah Jaffer (who was Shah Shoojah's Moonshee Bashee, or head Moonshee) and from other sources.

(2) Dooranee, Kuzzlebash, Belochee, and Hazara chiefs assisting at the coronation.

(3) Which he is said to have taken as a model. They had never been united under a Native king, and from the love of equality conspicuous in their character, were likely to view the exaltation of one of their nation, with even more jealousy, than the tyranny of a foreign master. His object was to secure the affections of his own tribe; he confirmed all the Dooranees in the possession of their lands; only requiring the attendance of their contingent of troops as fixed by Nadir. He distributed all the great offices among the leading Dooranees, and established them in particular families, and fixed the crown on his own. He left the hereditary chiefs in possession of their privileges, and

1748.—He marched from Candahar in the spring of 1748 with 12,000 men, composed of Dooranees, Belochees, and others. He reduced the Ghiljies, and appointed Dooranee Governors over them, and proceeded to Cabool. His army increased by the Affghans of Peshawar, he proceeded to the invasion of Hindostan, advanced rapidly through the Punjab; defeated the Indian troops, and entered Lahore in triumph, and prepared to advance upon Delhi. He crossed the Sutluj, and defeated, at Sirhind, the army of Mahomed Shah. Affairs in the Punjab being arranged, he marched back to Candahar; settling on his way the Governments of Dera Ghazee Khan, Dera Ismael Khan, Shikarpoor, and Mooltan. (4)

1749.—In the spring of this year he assembled an army of 25,000 men, from the western part of his dominions. He first marched against *Herat*, which surrendered. He then advanced to Meshed; reducing all the places on his route.

seldom interfered with the government of their clans, except it was necessary to keep up his army, which he effectually maintained. He took pains to improve the advantages he derived from the respect of the Dooranees for the Suddozyes, of which he was the head. With the other tribes (except the Ghiljies) he endeavoured to form a spirit of attachment to their native king, which he hoped to accomplish by delivering them from foreign dominion, and by a moderate and gradual introduction of his power.

He felt, or pretended to feel, a strong attachment to his nation. His popular manners, courage, activity, vigilance, and other military virtues, impressed all ranks with respect; and strongly attached his soldiers to his person.

The Dooranees had acquired experience and discipline by their long and active warfare with the *Persians*, and afterwards under *Nadir*, and the preference shewn towards them, had raised their spirit and confidence; so that, with reason, they considered themselves the best troops in *Asia*. Their enemies, the Ghiljies, had been broken and dispirited by a long course of defeat and disaster. The remaining *Affghans* had learned, by past events, to despise the *Indians*, and to hate the *Persians*, and were, therefore, more likely than formerly, to favor a king of their own nation.

(4) It is probable that, at this time, the south of Affghanistan acknowledged him as king. He reached Candahar about the end of winter.

From Meshed he marched against Neeshapoor; and detached a force against Muzeenaun and Subzewaur; he failed in his attacks against those places, and was compelled to retreat to Meshed, and retire to Herat.

1750.—In the spring of this year he marched against and took Neeshapoor (5) and returned to Herat.

1751.—In the winter, (1750) or early in the spring of this year, he was recalled to, and crushed a rebellion at Meshed. At this time, also, he made an attempt on Asterabad, which was repelled by the Kudjirs.

1752.—In the summer of this year, Ahmed Shah marched into the Punjab, and reduced a revolt; conquered *Cashmeer* and obtained, by cession, the country as far E. as Sirhind, from the great Mogul: he returned to Candahar; and appears to have spent the years 1753-4-5 in tranquillity, except quelling an attempted insurrection of the Ghiljies.

1756.—The Emperor of Delhi sent a large force into the Punjab, and annexed it to the Mogul empire. Ahmed Shah left Candahar, crossed the Indus, recovered the Punjab; marched to and entered Delhi. He sent a sirdar who took Bullumgur, and Muttra; but was repulsed at Agra by the Jauts. Ahmed Shah returned to his own dominions at the end of the year. On the marriage of his son Timoor (at Delhi) with a princess of the royal family, the Emperor was compelled to bestow the Punjab and Sindh on Timoor Shah; who was left to command the provinces on the E. of the Indus. The king wintered at Candahar.

1757.—2. The Mahrattahs took Sirhind; and drove Timoor Shah from the Punjab, in the middle of 1758, and obtained possession of the whole of it to the E. of the Jheelum.

1758.—Ahmed Shah marched in person into Belochistan, and took Kelat, after a siege of 40 days; during which the Dooranee Cavy. suffered severely from the scarcity of forage.

1759.—Ahmed Shah, during the winter, entered the Punjab; and crossed the Jumna, near Seharunpoor. He next

(5) It is believed that the Dooranee Empire never extended much beyond Neeshapoor on the W.

took Delhi. He pursued the conquest of the Dooab, and marched as far as Anoopshuhr. The Mahrattahs besieged Delhi which was surrendered after a spirited defence, by a small party of Dooranees.

1761.—On the 7th January, Ahmed Shah fought the celebrated battle of *Paniput*, which was fatal to the Mahrattah power; and many years elapsed before they resumed their enterprise under *Madhojee Scindia*; (6) whose troops were disciplined in the European manner. After this battle the whole of Hindostan appeared to be at Ahmed Shah's mercy. He contented himself with the portion formerly ceded to him, and bestowed the rest of the country on such of its Native chiefs who had assisted him; and in the spring of 1761, returned to Cabool. From its remoteness, he could with difficulty retain the Punjab, where the Sikhs had become very powerful; and their successes compelled him to return to India in the beginning of 1762.

1762.—He now completely expelled the Sikhs from the plain country, but in 1763 he was obliged to quit the Punjab, and in the course of a few years the country was in greater confusion than ever.

1763.—This year he was obliged to return to Candahar where there was an insurrection. (7)

1767.—The Sikhs had become masters of all the open country as far W. as the Jheelum.

1771.—He went in person against them, and drove them again into the mountains; but this expedition, the last he made in India, was attended by no permanent benefit: as

---

(6) Sevajee, the first Mahrattah commander, died in 1680.

(7) He was at Sirhind when he heard of the insurrection, and though at the height of summer, he marched by the route between the left bank of the Sutluj and the desert, to Mooltan, and thence to Ghuznee. His army, composed of Affghans, Uzbeks, Belochees, and natives of cold climates, suffered great hardships during the first part of this march; and he lost an incredible number of men from *heat*, before arriving at Mooltan: the winter set in before he reached the mountains of Affghanistan, and many of his troops perished from the cold and snow.

soon as the Shah quitted the country, the Sikhs appeared in greater force than ever, and before the end of the year they crossed the Jheelum, and took the famous fortress of Rhotas from the Dooranees. (8)

1773.—In the spring of this year, he left Candahar for the hills of Toba, in the Atchukzye country. (9) Here his malady (a cancer in his face) increased, and in the beginning of June, 1773, he died at Murgá, in the 50th year of his age.

His military courage and activity are spoken of with admiration, by his subjects and by those of other nations with whom he was engaged in wars or alliances. The memory of no eastern prince, is stained with fewer acts of cruelty and injustice.

With the Dooranees, he kept up the same equal and popular demeanour, which was usual with their Khans, before they assumed the title of king.

His policy was to conciliate the Affghans and Belochees. *He applied himself to the whole people of Affghans, and only to the chiefs in the other.*

At his death (after a reign of 26 years) his dominions extended, from the W. of Khorassan to Sirhind, and from the Oxus to the sea.

1773.—3. *Timoor Shah.*—Timoor Shah, the son and successor of Ahmed Shah, was born at Meshed in Dec. 1746. He was educated at his father's court, and accompanied him on many of his expeditions. He came to the throne at the age of 27 years. It was owing to his system of policy, that the power of the Dooranees first became stationary, and has since declined. Timoor Shah removed the seat of

---

(8) A rebellion in Khorassan prevented his proceeding to recover Rhotas. The Shah defeated the Persian army near Meshed, (the valour of Nusseer Khan, the chief of the Belochees restored the battle when its issue was doubtful;) it being impious to fire on Meshed, he therefore reduced it after a blockade of several months. Tubbas also was taken. He returned to Candahar.

(9) Where the summer is cooler than at Candahar.

government from Candahar, in the midst of the Dooranee country, to Cabool, which is inhabited by Taujeks, the most quiet and submissive of all the subjects of the Affghan monarchy.

1774-5.—He defeated a rebellion of his relation Abdool Khaulik Khan, which probably happened in 1774-5, who was defeated and blinded ; and the tranquillity of the Dooranee country was soon restored.

1779.—In 1779, there was an insurrection for the purpose of murdering Timoor Shah, and placing his brother, Prince Secunder, on the throne; from this till 1781, there were insurrections of various extent and consequence in Balkh, Khorassan, Seistan, and Cashmeer. ,

1781.—In 1781 Timoor Shah went in person to recover Mooltan, which had been betrayed by the governor into the hands of the Sikhs. The city was taken after a siege of a few days.

About this time broke out the rebellion of the Talpoorees, which ended in the expulsion of the Governor of Sindh. (10) The Talpoorees again recovered the whole of Sindh.

1786.—It was probably as late as 1786, before Timoor Shah sent another army into Sindh. On the Talpoorees again agreeing to pay the former revenue to the king, (11) Meer Futeh Ali was appointed Governor. The reduction of Azaud Khan's rebellion in Cashmeer, took place during the interval between the expeditions to Sindh, and that against Bahawul Khan, in the beginning of 1788.

(10) The Talpoorees expelled the Calorees in 1783.

(11) 12 lakhs Rs. (£120,000) regularly paid till his death in 1793, when it was reduced to seven lakhs Rs., and subsequently during the internal dissensions of his successors withheld altogether. The revenues of Sindh, during the Caloree government, were estimated at 80 lakhs (£800,000) ; but since reduced to 42 lakhs Rs. Regarding Sindh consult Sir A. Burnes, 2nd Edition, vol. i. p. 223. The Narrative of Dr. Jas. Burnes, K. H. &c. visit to Sindh, and Col. (now Sir H.) Pottinger.

1788.—Nothing of general importance to the kingdom occurred till the summer of this year, when a war broke out with the Uzbek Tartars. (12)

1789.—In the spring of this year, Timoor Shah marched from Cabool with an army which his subjects reckoned at 100,000 men, against Shah Morad; who sued for peace which was granted; Shah Morad retaining all his possessions. Timoor Shah failed in every object of this expedition, except securing his remaining possessions. (13) He allowed to be put to death Arsilla Khan, chief of the Upper Memunds, who had rebelled against him.

1793.—In the spring of 1793, Timoor Shah was taken ill on a journey from Peshawer, and died at Cabool, on the 20th May, 1793, aged 47; and after a reign of 20 years.

4. *Character of Timoor Shah.*—His finances were well regulated, and he observed the strictest economy; by which means he rendered himself independent of military expeditions for the ordinary expenses of his government; and was able to lay up a treasure against any unexpected emergency. He retained the Dooranee chiefs about his court; but as he had no troops of their tribe at the capital, they were entirely in his power, and had no means of disturbing his government. The only troops he kept at all times embodied, were his own guards, the *Gholam-i-Shauhs;* which were strong enough to keep the country in order, and being mostly *Persians* and *Taujeks,* were unconnected with the *Affghan* chiefs or people, and entirely devoted to the king. These troops were well paid, and received much countenance from

---

(12) Shah Morad Beg, king of Bokhara, had long been encroaching on the Dooranee dominions, and, during the king's expeditions to Bahawulpoor, he carried his aggressions so far, as to oblige Timoor Shah to take decisive measures for the defence of his Northern provinces.

(13) The winter was so far advanced before he marched on his return, that he was forced to leave his artillery in Balkh; and many of his troops perished from the cold and snow in crossing the *Indian Caucasus.*

the king; and were invested with some privileges, of a nature which tended to separate them from the rest of the people.

This policy succeeded moderately well in maintaining *internal* tranquillity; the provinces immediately under the king remained quiet, and though there were some conspiracies during this reign, and two rebellions of pretenders to the throne, they were either discovered by the king's vigilance, or defeated by his full treasury and his well-appointed guards; but the *remote* provinces gradually withdrew from the control of the court: the government lost its reputation and influence abroad; and the states which had been obliged to preserve their own territories by submission to *Ahmed Shah*, now began to meditate schemes for aggrandizing themselves at the expense of the *Dooranees*.

The decay was not severely felt in Timour Shah's time, but its commencement was even then observable; and it has advanced by rapid strides, under the reigns of his successors.

He had named no heir to the throne, and at the time of his death the succession was not settled. The eldest and most conspicuous of his sons (14) was absent, and Governor of Candahar. Mahmood (15) held the same office at Herat. Prince Abbas (16) was Governor of Peshawer, but had joined his father, on hearing of his illness. The other princes (17) were all at Cabool, except Feeroz, the full brother of Mahomed (18) who was with that prince at Herat.

1793.—5. *Shah Zeman.*—Timour Shah was no sooner dead, than an intrigue was set on foot to secure the crown to *Shah Zeman*. It was carried on by Timour Shah's favorite queen, who prevailed on Sirafrauz Khan, the head of the Barukzyes, to join in her scheme; and by his means

---

(14) Humayoon.
(15) Third son, but only half-brother.
(16) Fifth son.
(17) i. e. Zeman and Shoojah.
(18) Mahmood and Feeroz were both only half-brothers. Feeroz governed sometime at Herat, and became a Hajee or pilgrim.

secured the interest of most of the Dooranee Khans. (19) He was immediately proclaimed king, a largess was issued to the guards, the princes were sent into confinement in the upper fort of Cabool; and from that moment *Shah Zeman* entered quietly on the administration of the government. Means were taken for assembling an army to establish the authority of the new king, and to subdue the rebellions that might be expected from his brothers. Shah Zeman could not have been above 28 or 29 years of age at this time. (20)

Shah Zeman took possession of Candahar, and soon after received the submission of prince Mahmood, (21) and then set off for Cabool.

As soon as Shah Zeman had secured himself from his competitors for the throne, he appears to have determined on an invasion of India. (22)

(19) The princes of the royal family made an attempt to raise Abbas to the throne, but, though they behaved with much spirit, they shewed little skill: their persons were secured by a stratagem: the gates of the Balla Hissar, or Citadel of Cabool, were seized by *Zeman's* partizans; and that prince was declared king in a hasty meeting of the Dooranee chiefs.

(20) His greatest apprehension was from *Humayoon*, who was certainly entitled to the throne, if primogeniture gave a claim; and he commanded at Candahar, in the heart of the Dooranee country. He was, however, unpopular; he was deserted by some of his adherents, was defeated by a small force commanded by prince *Shoojah* (who succeeded Shah Zeman as king); and was compelled to take refuge in Belochistan.

(21) Governor of Herat; and his younger and half-brother.

(22) To which he was stimulated by *Meerza Ahsun Buksh*, a prince of the royal family of Delhi, who had fled to Cabool in Timoor's reign; as well as by ambassadors who had arrived, about this time, from *Tippoo Sultan*, and who made great pecuniary offers to the king, on condition that he should attack the British. Mr. *Elphinstone* in his Introduction, p. 68, says, " The king of Cabool had always been the resource of all the disaffected in India. To him Tippoo Sultan, Vizier Ally, and all other Mahomedans, who had a quarrel either with us or the Mahrattahs, had long been in the habit of addressing their complaints."

In December, 1793, Zeman Shah marched to Peshawer with the intention of immediately invading India; but he was convinced his own dominions were not sufficiently settled to admit of foreign expeditions. (23)

Shah Morad (24) invaded Balkh immediately on Timoor Shah's death. The extensive and ruinous city of Balkh was abandoned; but the fort held out for three or four months, notwithstanding the utmost exertions of the enemy. (25) Shah Zeman, after his success in Khorassan, arrived at Cabool.

1794.—The rest of 1793, and part of 1794, was occupied in reducing *Cashmeer*, which had rebelled on Timoor's death; and in settling the S. provinces, whither the king went in person: on that occasion he compelled the Ameers of Sindh, to pay 2,400,000 Rs. (£240,000), on account of the tribute due from them; after which he returned to Cabool.

6. Mahmood (his brother) again rebelled. The king marched against him with 15,000 men. They met at the Helmund (26) and Shah Zeman (narrowly escaping a defeat) obtained a complete victory: Mahmood fled, and reached Herat in safety. The king sent a force to take possession of Furrah, returned to Candahar, (27) proceeded to Peshawer, and again began to collect an army for the invasion of India; but his designs were again frustrated by fresh disturbances

---

(23) The most serious danger on the side of Toorkistan, had passed over by this time.

(24) King of Bokhara.

(25) There is no fort now. It is an open town. The inhabitants are, even now, *Affghans*. Shah Morad offered to give up his claim to Balkh, on condition of Zeman's observance of the treaty concluded with Timoor Shah, to which he consented, and peace ensued.

(26) A river between Candahar and Herat.

(27) Before leaving it he sent Sheer Mahomed Khan to settle the government of Belochistan, who put Mahomed in possession of all the strong places, and left the Belochee government apparently restored: but it had received a shock it never recovered. The tribes in the S. W. had been lately conquered, and were never perfectly subdued.

excited by his brother *Humayoon*; who captured Candahar: but Zeman, returning to the West, Humayoon's troops deserted him, and he escaped to the hills. (28) Zeman returned to Peshawer. His claim to the throne was now undisputed, and his authority was established over all the country left by Timoor Shah.

1795.—Shah Zeman's first invasion of the *Punjab*, was commenced at the close of the year 1795. He crossed the Indus by a bridge of boats at Attok, got possession of Rhotas: but the invasion of the W. of Khorassan, by Agha Mahomed Khan, Kujjur, king of Persia, recalled him to the defence of his own dominions. (29)

1796.—He returned to Peshawer on the 3rd January, 1796. He proceeded to Cabool and prepared for war against the Persians, but Agha Mahomed's return induced him to change his mind. No sooner had the king of Persia withdrawn, than Zeman set out for Peshawer, and prepared to return to the Punjab. He assembled 30,000 men, (one half Dooranees,) and in the end of November, began his march for India. This alarmed all India. (30)

(28) He made another attempt, fled, was seized at Leia, on the E. of the Indus, blinded, and passed the rest of his life in confinement.

(29) The Persian invasion was to capture Meshed. Agha Mahomed entered it, dug up Nadir Shah's bones, and sent them to Teheran.

(30) It alarmed the Mahrattahs, the whole of whose forces were drawn to the S. of India by their own dissensions. The government of Oude was feeble, and most of its subjects were disposed to insurrection and revolt. The Mahomedans' looked to the restoration of the house of Timoor; the emperor Shah Alum being in the hands of the Mahrattahs. Zeman's march on Delhi would have thrown the whole country into a state of disorder and anarchy. The Mahrattahs, struck with dismay, solicited the assistance of their neighbours. The *British* Government adopted vigorous measures. An army was assembled at Anoopshuhr, (70 miles S. E. from Delhi,) to defend the frontier of Oude, no less than its own dominions. The present Bengal 4th Light Cavalry and the 26th, 27th, 28th and 29th Regts. N. I. were raised on this occasion.

The partisans of Shah Zeman set on foot intrigues in many parts of Hindostan. The Rohillahs assembled in arms. Every Mussulman from Delhi to the Deccan, anxiously looked for the Champion of Islam. Zeman's expedition failed, but the impression of his advance was paramount.

1797.—He advanced unopposed to Lahore, which he entered on the 3rd Jan. 1797; but news of a rebellion in his own dominions caused his retreat. Prince Mahmood, still Govr. of Herat, had 20,000 men, and but for Zeman's speedy return would probably have attacked Candahar. On the 8th September, 1797, Zeman marched from Candahar, and by the treachery of Mahmood's adherents, he became master of Herat; and Mahmood fled to Toorshish with his son Kamran.

1798.—7. Shah Zeman, a 3rd time, turned his attention to the Punjab. He left Peshawer on the 25th October, 1798, and advanced without molestation to Lahore; (31) and Runjeet Singh (late king of the Sikhs) did him homage in person. About the end of 1798, the Shah received news of the invasion of Khorassan by Futeh Ali Shah, (the new) king of Persia, and set out on his return to Peshawer; before which, however, he wrote to the Emperor of Delhi to state that, at present, circumstances prevented his marching to Delhi; but, that he would embrace the earliest occasion of returning, to replace him on his throne, (32) and cause the Mahomedan to be the paramount power in India.

1799.—Zeman reached Peshawer on the 30th January, 1799. His guns were lost in the Jheelum, on his return, by a sudden rising of the river; but they were dug out and restored by Runjeet Singh and Sahib Singh. About this period, it would seem, Zeman appointed Runjeet Singh, his viceroy at Lahore.

After a short stay at Peshawer, Zeman repaired to Herat. Futeh Ali Shah, failed in his attempts in Khorassan, and retreated. Zeman withdrew to Candahar during the winter

(31) This caused increased alarm in India, and the present Bengal 30th, 31st, 32nd, 33rd, 34th and 35th Regts. N. I. were raised.

(32) Shah Alum was under British protection till 1771, when he ascended the throne of Delhi. He was blinded by Gholam Kadir in 1788. Delhi was subject to Madhojee Scindia from about 1770 till 1803, when on the 11th Sept. Lord Lake's battle, placed the emperor again on his throne.

of 1799. An unsuccessful attempt was made on Herat by Shah Mahmood, with 10,000 men : Prince Kyser (33) was then Govr. of Herat; Shah Mahmood fled.

During this time six of the principal Dooranee and Kuzzlebash lords, disgusted with the power and insolence of *Wuffadar Khan*, (34) conspired to assassinate that minister, to depose Zeman, and to place his brother Shoojah on the throne. Sirafrauz Khan, (35) and other conspirators were beheaded. These sanguinary measures increased the danger of the king and his minister; from this time the spirit of rebellion, which occasioned Zeman's downfall, took its rise. (36)

1800.—In the spring of 1800, Futeh Ali Shah a second time invaded Khorassan, (37) accompanied by Mahmood, whom he promised to place on the throne of Cabool. Zeman marched to Herat, remained there during the summer, and in early autumn set off with all expedition for Cabool. (38) Mahmood with Futteh Khan repaired to Candahar and with a large army besieged it 42 days. He obtained posses-

(33) Son of Shah Zeman.

(34) Minister, and brother to Shah Shoojah's favorite queen (Wuffadar Begum.)

(35) The Barukzye chief who caused Zeman to be placed on the throne.

(36) Sirafrauz Khan, was the Head of the Barukzyes.

(37) Mehdee Ali Khan, at Bombay, well known at the king of Persia's court, was deputed by the British Govt. to induce the king to make this invasion. It had before in the end of 1798, caused Zeman's return to Peshawer.

(38) Sending his army by the usual route ; he went himself, with 2 or 3,000 choice troops, through the *Eimauk* country, and the almost inaccessible mountains of the Hazaurehs, (lying between Herat and Cabool.) He reached Cabool in fourteen days. When Zeman left Herat, Futeh Ali Shah retired from Subzwar. Shah Mahmood retired to Tubbus in despair of Persian assistance. The arrival of Futeh Khan, Barukzye, from his castle of Girishk, gave a new direction to his councils. Shah Mahmood left Tubbus, and with 50 horsemen, crossed the desert into Seistan, and advanced to Jellalabad, the capital of that province.

3 c

sion of it by a stratagem of Futeh Khan, and the treachery of the Govr. Zeman heard of this event at Peshawer, which caused him to lay aside a fourth and last attempt to invade Hindostan, and he returned to Cabool.

8. At this time Zeman seized and tortured Abdoollah Khan, Alekhozye, Govr. of Cashmeer, on which his brother Sydaul Khan, who was at Candahar, went over to Mahmood with his whole clan. Instead of employing his army to quell the rebellion of Mahmood, Zeman detached 15,000 men to Cashmeer. He left a considerable force at Peshawer, under his brother Shoojah-ool-Moolk (present king of Cabool), and went to Cabool; where security was succeeded by the utmost disquiet and alarm.

The king marched against the rebels with 30,000 men. He kept a march or two in rear of his army. Ahmed Khan who commanded the vanguard, deserted; the king gave up all for lost and fled towards Cabool. Mahmood sent 2,000 men under Futeh Khan to Cabool, and soon after marched there himself. Shah Zeman pursued his flight till he reached the Shainwarree *(Khyber)* country, worn out with hunger and fatigue. He attained an asylum at *Moollah Ashik's* castle; who took measures to prevent his escape, and sent intelligence to Mahmood at Cabool, who sent a surgeon to put out his brother's (Zeman's) eyes. (39) Zeman was taken to Cabool and confined in the Bala Hissar, during all Mahmood's reign, after a reign of about 7½ years.

Character of Shah Zeman.—Notwithstanding some defects in his character, and some erroneous maxims in his policy, Shah Zeman would probably have succeeded, if he had resolved to govern for himself; but committing the whole powers and duties of Govt. to an unworthy favorite (Wuffadar Khan), he involved the ruin of his own fortunes, and of the prosperity of his nation. Instead of obtaining the support of his own tribe, the original plan

---

(39) Assud Khan, a brother of Futeh Khan, was sent. It will be recollected that Shah Zeman owed his rise to Sirafrauz Khan, whom he beheaded for rebellion. (See paras. 5 and 7.)

adopted by Ahmed Shah, and thereby securing the internal quiet of his country; he widened the breach between the Dooranees and the court. In his foreign policy he should have defended Khorassan against Persian encroachment, in place of weakening his resources in vain attempts to invade *India*. (40) The more desirable object of reducing the *Punjab* was not to be accomplished by a hasty incursion. (41)

The source of all his errors was his choice of *Wuffadar Khan* for the office of Vizier, and the implicit confidence he reposed in him. He was a Suddozye (42) who had gained the king's confidence, and had used his ascendancy to overturn the power of Sirafrauz Khan (43) and all the great officers of the army and state. Shah Zeman, though proud and imperious, was easily led by flatteries; and with all his fondness for activity and enterprise, he had not patience or application to manage the details of state affairs. (44) Nor had he any share of the order and economy which distinguished his predecessor. (45) He caused his elder

(40) Which was much altered since the time of his grandfather (Ahmed Shah), and nothing to be gained there, but by long and uninterrupted operations. Even Ahmed Shah contented himself with what had been ceded to him.

(41) The plan opposed by the Sikhs to Ahmed Shah, was by evacuating their country on his approach, and returning when his army was withdrawn, which could only be baffled by keeping a force in the country sufficient to retain possession; and that measure could only be accomplished, when the *Western* frontier of Affghanistan was secure.

(42) The tribe to which Shah Zeman and Shah Shoojah belong.

(43) Head of the Barukzyes, and to whom Shah Zeman greatly owed his crown.

(44) Wuffadar Khan was timid when exposed to personal danger; and this was the distinctive difference between him and Akram Khan, who was the minister of Shah Shoojah. The governments of Provinces and other offices were sold openly, for his own profit; and his embezzlements caused a decline of the revenue.

(45) Had he invaded India, he would probably have had to contend with the Mahrattahs, as well as the English; for in any reverse of fortune, the former would have been glad to have taken revenge for their defeat by Ahmed Shah, in 1761, at Panceput.

brother, Humayoon, to be blinded for his rebellion. The execution of Sirafrauz Khan, was the punishment due for his attempt to dethrone him. [*This I apprehend caused the original feud between the Suddozyes, and the Barukzyes.*] Shah Zeman took the life not only of Gool Mahomed Khan but of eight others the principal officers of his court. (46)

1800.—9. On the flight of Shah Zeman, Mahmood Shah sent Futeh Khan, with 2,000 men to Cabool, whither he himself followed. Mahmood's accession was at first joyfully welcomed by all ranks of men. The Govt. was left entirely to Akram Khan, Alizye, (47) and Futeh Khan, Barukzye. Mahmood's Govt. was now fully established in the capital; but the provinces were as yet by no means under his authority. The utmost licentiousness prevailed among the soldiery, on whom the court relied; and his reign more resembled the temporary success of a military adventurer, than the establishment of a regular government.

Herat was given to his brother *Feeroz*, who acknowledged his authority, but governed as if he were an independent prince. The N. E. tribes still held out for Zeman: the other provinces declared for neither party.

The principal opponent to Mahmood who now remained, was prince Shoojah-ool-Moolk, (48) who was about 20 years of age, and had been left at Peshawer with a small party of guards. (49)

After the first panic that followed his brother's defeat, Shoojah-ool-Moolk proclaimed himself king, and prepared for a regular contest with the usurper. He distributed large sums among the tribes round Peshawer; and soon

---

(46) See article *Vizarat*. Shah Zeman had been blinded by order of his brother Shah Mahmood; but when Shah Shoojah succeeded Zeman as king, and entered Cabool in triumph in 1803, Mahmood being then in his power, Shoojah spared his brother's eyes: and Zeman even requested him to do so.

(47) Not Akram Khan, Populzye, and Shah Shoojah's minister.

(48) The full brother of Zeman.

(49) In charge of Zeman's family, the jewels and property of the crown.

Mahmood Shah.

saw the greater part of the *Berdooranees* (50) flock to his standard.

This caused alarm to Mahmood who had already become unpopular, from the general relaxation of all Govt., which left the bulk of the inhabitants of the country at the mercy of the courtiers, and the soldiery. The arrest of Mookhtar Oodowlah, who had formed a plot in favor of Shoojah, put an end to present danger.

1801.—On the 10th September, 1801, Shooja-ool-Moolk, marched from Peshawer to attack Cabool. About half-way he found Mahmood's force consisting of 3,000 men, commanded by Futeh Khan, at Eshpaun. Shoojah who had at least 10,000 men, was at first victorious, but he lost the battle, and the royal treasures; and escaped with difficulty to the Khyber hills. (51)

An insurrection at this time broke about among the *Ghiljies*. They offered Abdooreheem (52) the crown, who accepted the proposal with reluctance. Their operations extended to Candahar, Ghuznee, and Cabool. Mahmood's army left Cabool on the 12th November, it met the Ghiljie army (20,000 men) (53) at Sejawurd. The Dooranees drew up in line in three Divisions, with their camel-swivels in front. The Ghiljies rushed on in a confused mass, regardless of the fire kept up, (54) seized the guns and

---

(50) The tribes who inhabit the N. E. quarter, between the Hindoo Koosh and the Indus, the salt range and the Soliman range: they are mostly agriculturists.

(51) See the battle described, (Soorkh-ab, 21st Oct. 1839, Chapter XIII.)

(52) The representative of their royal family, who had a pension from Zeman, besides his paternal estates; but had lately been injured by the government.

(53) Almost entirely of Infantry, ill-armed and some with only clubs.

(54) In the action on the 15th May, 1840, Capt. *Wm. Anderson*, Bengal H. A. in command of a Dett. of about 1,200 men and guns (of which the Horse under Capt. Tayler and Lieut. Walker were ahead

made a furious charge on the line : the victory seemed in
favor of the Ghiljies, till the unbroken Dooranees wheeled
in on the flanks of the enemy. Though broken, the Ghiljies retreated in a body to Killaee Zirreen, a fort of their
own in the hills, 6 miles from the field of battle, (55) the
winter setting in, prevented further hostilities.

1802.—10. In the spring of 1802, the Ghiljies rose as
suddenly as before, and with more arrangement. (56) Their
force is said to have amounted to 50,000 men. They were
defeated by the Dooranees in three actions, in the month
of March. (57) On the 11th May, part of Mahmood's
force defeated 10,000 Ghiljies at Moollah Shaudee; the
last stand that tribe made.

The severities of the Govt. ceased with the campaign;
when tranquillity was restored, the Ghiljies were treated as
before their rebellion.

Shah Shoojah who had advanced against Peshawer, sustained a great defeat in March of this year, at the head of

and not then engaged) defeated about 2,500 Ghiljies, near Tazee, 25
miles N. E. of Kalat-i-Ghiljie. Though exposed to a well-directed,
and destructive fire of shrapnel and grape, the Ghiljies came down
twice, in a body of 200, riding up to the centre of Lieut. Spence's
company, and died on the men's, bayonets. They had 200 killed, and
40 or 50 were cut up by the Cavalry afterwards. Capt. A.'s loss was a
Jemadar and 8 men killed, and 50 wounded; some mortally, and many
severely. Except a few of the 4th Local horse, the Dett. was entirely
composed of the *Shah's* contingent raised in August, 1838!

(55) They subsequently, re-inforced, marched to Killaee Shahee,
within a few miles of Cabool, the next evening; but, broke out into
rapine and violence, which Abdooreheem could not restrain. They
attacked the Dooranees without orders and lost 3,000 men; the
Dooranees returned to Cabool, where they erected a pyramid of the
heads of the Ghiljies killed in the battle.

(56) Almost the whole of the clans were now engaged. Abdooreheem was to attack Cabool from the S.; Futeh Khan, Babukurzye, with
an equal body, from the E.; while 10,000 should keep the Dooranees
employed within their own boundaries. To each of these, a Dooranee
army was opposed.

(57) It is said that these three separate battles, the defeat of the
Khyberees under Shah Shoojah, and a victory over the Uzbeks in
Balkh, took place on the same day.

Mahmood Shah.

2,000 Khyberees, by the regular troops of the city; they suffered great slaughter, and vast numbers perished from heat and thirst, before they reached their mountains. Shoojah with difficulty, escaped to his former retreat (Khyber hills).

Shah Shoojah remained at Choora, (58) in the Afreedee country, till the arrival of Futeh Khan at Peshawer rendered it unsafe; when he retired further S. and took refuge in the mountains of the Kakurs. (59)

1802.—He was in this condition in the depth of the winter of 1802, near the town of Shawl, or Quetta, (60) in Belochistan. In this extremity he was advised to plunder a Caravan just arrived; his troops surrounded it, the merchants gave up their property, and received notes, in his name, promising to pay the value at a future time. (61) He raised troops and made an attack on Candahar, which failed, and he retired, (a third time,) into the Khyber hills, where his army soon after dispersed. Quiet was restored to the kingdom; but the government was deplorably weak; few of the provinces had been reduced; the Khan (62) of the Belochees, and many of the Affghan tribes, refused to acknowledge so unsettled a government, and an empty treasury left Mahmood destitute of the means to restore his authority.

The Persians in one campaign, almost completed the con-

---

(58) About 8 miles S. of Ali Musjid. See Chapter XIV. for the Khyber Pass, &c.

(59) Wandering about, subsisting himself and followers on the sale of his jewels and casual hospitality.

(60) Properly Koth; which is the name for a fort.

(61) He paid many of them after his accession; most probably he could not find out the other claimants.

The Caravan was worth 3 lakhs Rs. (£30,000); it relieved his present wants, and enabled him to assemble troops for an attack on Candahar.

(62) Mahmood Khan, son of Nusseer Khan, whom Nadir Shah rewarded for some important services by the donation of several adjacent provinces. See Chapter IV. Note on *Shawl*.

quest of Persian Khorassan. (63) The last place they took was Meshed.

Though the court was freed from all immediate danger from without, dissensions arose among the ruling party, particularly between the two great leaders, *Akram Khan, Alizye,* and *Futeh Khan.* (64)

1803.—11. In the meantime *Mahmood's* government was hastening to decay. Frequent complaints were made of the conduct of the Gholam-i-Shahs (king's Kuzzlebash guards), but were disregarded by Mahmood.

On the 4th and 5th June a serious tumult and battle took place between the *Soonees* and Kuzzlebashes (65) at Cabool.

On the 8th July, Mookhtar-Oodowlah, (66) who was in favor of Shoojah, (67) fled from Cabool. When Mookhtar-Oodowlah (Akram Khan) returned with Shoojah-ool-Moolk, on the 12th July, he found *Shah Mahmood* besieged in the Bala Hissar, which was closely invested by the populace. *Shoojah* encamped outside the city, engaged in collecting troops to oppose *Futeh Khan* who drew near with 8 or 10,000 men. An action took place soon after; Futeh Khan was at first successful; he routed the part of the enemy immediately opposed to him, and was advancing to the city when the desertion of a great lord to *Shoojah,* threw the whole into confusion; his own party then fell off by degrees till he found himself almost alone; and was obliged to fly.

(63) The whole lost at this period; except Toorshish, reduced in 1810.

(64) The latter was sent to settle the S. E. of the kingdom. He went to Peshawer, and then to the S. through Cohaut, Bunnoo, and Damaun, levying revenue; he spent a long time in endeavouring to reduce the *Vizierees;* and, after plundering their lands, he marched, settling the country, to Candahar, where he arrived in the summer of 1803.

(65) Who are Sheeahs, the opponents of the Soonees.

(66) Vizier Akram Khan, Alizye.

(67) Having instructed Meer Waez to renew the tumults in the city. I have before said that he was called to the throne "by the voice of the people." See Chapter XI.

Next morning (13th July) Shah Shoojah entered Cabool in triumph. (68)

The gates of the Bala Hissar were thrown open on the king's approach; and Mahmood, deserted by all his adherents, suffered himself to be quietly conducted to the upper fort, where the princes of the blood were confined. His eyes were spared by Shah Shoojah, (69) and even poor blind Zeman made a personal request to preserve the eyes of a brother by whom he had himself been deprived of sight.

The character of Shah Mahmood.—The character of Shah Mahmood was calculated to disappoint the expectations of all ranks; unprincipled, indolent, and timid, he shared as little in the cares of government, as in the toils and dangers of war; and while his own care and safety were secure, he was indifferent to the conduct of his ministers and to the welfare of his people. Shah Zeman had deprived of sight his elder brother, *Humayoon*, who had rebelled against him when his king; but *Mahmood* dethroned his king, and elder brother, and also deprived him of sight. These are the only two instances in the Dooranee dynasty. Shah Mahmood reigned about two years.

12.—*Shah Shoojah* had been for two years a fugitive in his own dominions, during which period he had made several attempts to expel his rival. He had consequently incurred great obligations to the *Dooranees* and other chiefs. These were rendered of the more importance by his own disposition, which was susceptible of gratitude and permanent attachment.

All the honors and appointments in the gift of the crown, were insufficient to reward the king's adherents, and he gave away a large portion of his permanent revenue, in grants to such as remained unprovided for: thus almost the

---

(68) The second time on 7th August, 1839.

(69) Mr. *Elphinstone* says, p. 393, " but Shooja has unfortunately, had sufficient reason to regret this clemency; of which he probably, afforded the first example in his country." According to *Mahomedan* Law, a blind sovereign is not a legal king.

whole of the revenue of *Peshawer* was settled on the *Khyberees* as the reward of their attachment; (70) and much of the royal dues were alienated in other places in favor of Dooranee chiefs. What remained of the revenue passed through the hands of the Vizier (Mookhtar Oodowlah, *Akram Khan*) who, as soon as his interests were separated from those of the king, applied a large portion of the public money to his own use. (71) The first act of his reign was to release his brother Shah Zeman; and soon after *Moollah Ashik* who had betrayed Zeman, was apprehended, and suffered the punishment of his perfidy and ingratitude. This was the only execution that followed the change of government. All the other measures of the Vizier's internal administration, were calculated to conciliate, and to efface the memory of the civil dissensions which had so long prevailed. He applied himself with great vigor and success to reduce the rebellious provinces; and to bring the empire into its ancient state.

(70) The Chiefs in 1839 did not evince much attachment to the Shah.

(71) Had the king given his confidence entirely to the vizier, many of the inconveniences which were afterwards felt, might have been avoided. It would have been the interest of that minister to raise the king's power; and his success in the beginning of Shoojah's reign, showed that he had talents and influence requisite for such an undertaking. This plan was not tried. The king (then about 22 years of age,) was not disposed to resign his own power to his minister; and his old adherents, who were anxious to succeed to their share of power, early inspired him with jealousy of the vizier; and induced him to adopt a system of counteraction to his measures; the absence of harmony between the king and his minister, prevented the adoption of measures of vigor against their common enemy; and each lavished the resources of the state to secure partizans to himself.

The slightest provocation from the court drove a nobleman into rebellion: the least offence from one of the rebels, sent him back to the court; or led him to form a new party.

The jealousies between the king and the vizier did not, however, shew themselves till some time after Shoojah's accession (the second time); and the commencement of his reign was quiet and prosperous. [It must, too, be recollected that he owed his throne to this minister.]

The first expedition was sent to *Candahar*, still held by prince *Kamran* (72) and Futeh Khan; it was taken without difficulty, and Futeh Khan submitted to the king, but retired from the court in disgust. (73)

1804.—13. His defection was early and severely felt. In January, 1804, the king assembled 30,000 men, at Peshawer, and was about to complete the settlement of his dominions, by intimidating the chiefs of Cashmeer and Sindh, when he heard of a rebellion at Candahar, which obliged him to relinquish his design. (74)

The whole of the *West* being now settled, the king marched from Candahar in the end of September to Sindh, compelled the chiefs to acknowledge him, and to pay 17 lakhs Rs. (£170,000); after which he moved up his *Eastern* frontier, and settled all the provinces in his route.

(72) Son of Mahmood, and Shah Shoojah's nephew.

(73) An opportunity now offered to secure the attachment of this powerful and active chief; but it was allowed to escape, and hence arose the misfortunes which disturbed the rest of Shah Shoojah's reign; and which drove him, at length, from his throne. Futeh Khan's demands were the offices held by his father *(Poyndar Khan)*; but those were withheld; and Futeh Khan, after a short residence at court, quitted it in disgust, and retired to his castle of Girishk. Wuffadar Khan, was Zeman's Minister: Sirafrauz Khan (Barukzye) was beheaded for heading a conspiracy to depose Zeman. It is most probable that Akram Khan, jealous of the talents of Futeh Khan, prevented the king giving him office.

(74) The government of Candahar was now held by Prince *Kyser*, (son of Shah Zeman) under the guidance of Ahmed Khan, Noorzye. Futeh Khan persuaded the young prince to imprison Ahmed Khan. Ahmed Khan's son gave up Candahar to Kamran, (son of Mahmood Shah,) whom he invited from Furrah; but *Kyser* and Futeh Khan recovered Candahar, and again assembled troops. Shoojah returned towards Candahar, which was evacuated on his approach, and Kyser soon after threw himself on the king's mercy, was affectionately received, and reinstated in his government. Futeh Khan, finding his schemes at Candahar defeated, went to Herat, and persuaded Prince Feeroz (Shoojah's youngest brother) to assert his claim to the throne of Cabool. Feeroz appeared in arms, Shoojah sent Kyser to oppose him, offering terms which Feeroz accepted: while Futeh Khan left him in indignation, and again retired to Girishk.

1805.—He reached Peshawer in April, 1805, and soon after received an ambassador from the king of *Bokhara* who came to propose a renewal of the alliance concluded by Zeman, (75) and to negociate the marriage of *Shoojah* to the daughter of the king of Bokhara, which was agreed to.

Kyser continued to serve the king with zeal and fidelity in the government of Candahar. He seized Futeh Khan, and had nearly been persuaded to gratify the revenge of his father (Shah Zeman), by putting him to death; (76) but Kyser set him free.

Futeh Khan repaired to Girishk, where he made preparations for placing Kyser on the throne; but on his return to Candahar, he found Kyser had been dissuaded from the design of rebelling.

Futeh Khan now engaged to deliver up Candahar to Kamran (Mahmood's son), whom he invited to occupy it. Kamran advanced with troops to the Eedgah, a few miles from Candahar. Kyser was about to quit the city, when Futeh Khan *changed to his side,* and recapitulated his designs *in favor of Kyser.* (77) Futeh Khan's plan of placing Kyser on the throne, was now resumed; apparently with the prince's full concurrence; but its execution was artfully delayed by Khojeh Mahomed.

Shoojah had prepared an expedition at Peshawer for the reduction of Cashmeer, the only province in rebellion.

Akram Khan, the Vizier, marched with 10,000 men. He encountered the first opposition at Mozufferabad, where he

(75) This embraced the marriage of the king of Bokhara to a princess of Cabool, but (it is said) it is contrary to custom to give a princess to foreigners.

(76) For sending his brother Assud Khan to seize him, after which he was deprived of sight. Zeman had beheaded Sirafrauz Khan, head of the Barukzyes, for a rebellion.

(77) Next morning Kyser and Futeh Khan moved out to oppose Kamran. Futeh Khan, charged him sword in hand; Kamran's troops were broke, and he with difficulty effected his escape to Furrah.

This caused I think, chiefly, Kamran's enmity to Futeh Khan, and his pursuading his father (Mahmood) to put him to death in 1818.

found the high and rocky bank of a rapid branch of the Jheelum occupied by the Cashmerian army: he effected his passage in four divisions; and drove the enemy from their position. One of his sons was wounded in this battle. The rest of the road to Cashmeer was through steep and barren mountains, and often along the face of precipices. The vizier's advance was consequently slow, and his provisions began to fail long before he reached the valley. (78)

He, therefore, began to treat with *Abdoolah Khan*. (79) The armies were still separated by the Jheelum. At length Abdoolah Khan threw a bridge over the river in the night, and crossed it without delay. The Cashmeer army was routed, and driven back on the river. (80) Great part of the army, and Abdoolah Khan, were forced to swim, and many were cut to pieces by the victors, or drowned in the river.

Abdoolah Khan took refuge in his fort, and prepared for a long siege; the king's troops were prevented by the season and by the fatigues they had suffered, from attempting any operations during the rest of the winter.

1806.—14. Early in the spring (1806) the fort was attacked, and had held out for two months, when Abdoolah Khan died. It held out now, for two months, but surrendered on condition (81). Cashmeer was then reduced under the king's authority.

The reconciliation between Futeh Khan and Kyser was of no long duration; Futeh Khan retired to Girishk; and once more renewed his intrigues with Kamran; who joined Futeh Khan, and they advanced towards Candahar: Kyser fled into Belochistan. The king, then at Peshawer, sent to

(78) So great was the distress of his troops, that when he came to a defile beyond which the enemy's army was encamped, he was not able to hold out till he tried the chance of a battle.

(79) The Governor of Cashmeer.

(80) The bridge was choaked by the crowds of fugitives.

(81) That Abdoolah Khan's family and the chiefs in the fort, should be allowed to reside, unmolested, at Cabool, or Peshawer. These terms were strictly observed.

recall his vizier from Cashmeer; but, was obliged to command in person against the rebels. Before he reached Candahar, his troops had been again defeated by Kamran, who was reinforced by 6,000 men from Herat, under the son of Prince Feeroz. (82)

The Persians threatened an attack on Herat. The success of the Persians at first excited a strong sensation among the Dooranees; and the king at one time, intended to have moved to Herat in person, but the internal state of the kingdom did not admit of foreign enterprises. (83)

The king now heard that the vizier had proclaimed Prince *Kyser*, king at Cabool; and not long after learnt that Peshawer had fallen into the hands of the rebels.

1807.—The king succeeded in recovering Peshawer by the end of February, 1807. About this time the vizier and Kyser arrived in its neighbourhood with 12,000 men.

1808.—After a fruitless negociation, the parties engaged on the 3rd March, 1808. The royal troops were broken on the first onset, and the king himself was about to quit the field, when the vizier imprudently charged him at the head of a few men. The Khans about the king made a desperate resistance, and the vizier was shot in the struggle. The king's troops rallied on this event, and the battle was soon turned in their favor; and the king entered Peshawer in triumph. (84) This victory entirely restored the king's affairs in Peshawer; but Cashmeer still held out, for the

---

(82) Cassim was his son, but must have been a boy; his father was about 23 years old.

(83) There was an open rapture between the king and the vizier, who became disaffected; and it has been suspected that he was the author of an attempt to raise *Abbas* (the next brother to Shoojah), one of the confined princes, to the throne. The plan failed; but Mahmood (deposed in 1803) effected his escape during the confusion it occasioned. He proceeded to Sindh, and entered into an arrangement with the governors, which so much offended Futeh Khan, that he quitted the army, with 3,000 troops under his command.

(84) The vizier's head borne behind him on a spear.

Shah Shoojah. 391

vizier's party, under his son Atta Mahomed Khan; but more urgent difficulties at Cabool and Candahar, prevented any operations against that province.

15. Meer Waez, who had remained at Cabool, no sooner heard of the defeat and death of his friend (vizier), than he set all the imprisoned princes at liberty; and prepared the capital for a vigorous defence. He was obliged to desert the city on the king's approach; but he retired with Kyser into the strong country of Kohistan, where he continued, for some time, to resist the troops sent against him. At length Kyser came in, and was freely pardoned, and the king marched against Mahmood, who had been joined by Futeh Khan, and had taken Candahar. The rival kings met on the E. side of the city, Mahmood was defeated, and Candahar fell into the hands of the victor.

The king was, now, about to move towards Sindh, but was anticipated by a payment from that province.

1809.—He left Candahar, and reached Peshawer on the 10th January, 1809.

From Peshawer he immediately despatched Akram Khan with all the force he could collect, against Cashmeer. On the 23rd April, he received intelligence of the entire defeat and destruction of Akram Khan's army. (85) Akram

---

(85) Mr. *Elphinstone's* mission was there; it arrived on the 25th Feb. 1809. Akram Khan reposed confidence in Motawullee, the hill chief of Mozufferabad, and had depended on him for supplies and guides. His ungovernable pride and avarice led him to offend this very man, and he was betrayed. Motawullee undertook to show him a Pass by which he might turn the flank of the enemy's work. Akram moved up the valley, securing the mountains on each side, by parties of Khyberee and Ghiljie Infantry. His march was soon discovered, and his Infantry out-numbered and driven in; besides which, it was ascertained, or rumoured, that the upper part of the valley was choaked with impassable snow. Akram, now, lost all confidence; he remained for a day in the valley without supplies and exposed to the fire of the enemy's infantry, which, though too distant to be effective, disheartened his troops, and caused many desertions: this completed the vizier's alarm. Akram Khan, knowing his unpopularity in the army feared being seized and delivered to the chief of Cashmeer, whose

Khan after his flight from Cashmeer, crossed the Indus, and reached Akorah, (86) where he received those who went to meet him, without the smallest abatement of his former pride. Of the whole army, not above 2,000 men arrived at Peshawer, dismounted, disarmed, and almost naked.

At the same time authentic intelligence arrived of the advance of *Shah Mahmood,* (the deposed king,) of the capture of *Cabool;* and of the immediate advance of the enemy towards Peshawer. (87) The enemy were found to have remained at Cabool, and it was now certain that they were disputing among themselves. Akram Khan had returned to Peshawer, and began to assemble the wreck of the Cashmeer army, together with such troops as had been left at Peshawer, or could now be raised. The king's situation, however, was still far from promising. Every thing depended on money with which he was very ill provided. Many of the chiefs could have, at once, remedied this evil, but few were zealous at this crisis; and even *Akram Khan,* the vizier, who had occasioned most of the king's misfortunes, and who knew he must stand or fall with his master, was so blinded by his avarice, that he refused to give or lend any part of the father's death he had occasioned. He resolved to fly, and in the course of the night, all the chiefs abandoned the army, and each endeavoured to effect his escape through the Passes of the mountains. Most were plundered by Motawullee's mountaineers before they passed Mozufferabad; and Akram is said to have been surrounded, and to have escaped by scattering pieces of gold among the plunderers, and flying during the scramble.

(86) Three marches from Peshawer.

(87) Some of the neighbouring tribes who were in favor of *Mahmood,* were said to be armed, and ready to start up at a moment's warning. The troops were represented to be on the eve of a *mutiny,* and it was rumoured that the king had sent off his most valuable jewels, and was about to fly from the city. The Mehmandar to the mission, frankly avowed to them, that in the event of any general confusion, they would be attacked by the Khyberees and other plunderers. The people talked openly of the state of affairs; but nobody acted as if a revolution were at hand. This panic at length subsided.

large treasures which he had inherited from his father, and had amassed himself. (88) During this time the king was exerting himself to get together an army. The army, indeed, was generally disaffected.

16. It was at length (June, 1809) determined by *Shah Shoojah*, to march to Cabool, and taking leave of the king, the mission marched from Peshawer towards India on the 14th June, 1809. (89) The king's affairs were now in a highly prosperous condition. He had equipped a tolerable army, and was ready to move against the enemy, whose dissensions had come to such a pitch, that *Futeh Khan* had seized his rival (90) in the midst of the court, and had thus occasioned the defection of two of the great Dooranee clans. Accordingly all parties seemed to look forward, with certainty, to the success of *Shah Shoojah's* cause ; an event which was called for by the prayers of the people, to whom the Shah's moderation and justice had greatly endeared him.

The king marched from Peshawer, with an army of about 14,000 men, and a train of Artillery. The army was attacked by a small force under *Futeh Khan*, as it was straggling on, mixed with the baggage, after a very long march through the mountains. The king and Akram Khan (vizier) were

---

(88) The character of this minister was the great cause of the king's weakness. Though so deficient in political courage, even his enemies allowed that he was endowed with the greatest personal bravery, and that he was sincere in his attachments, true to his word, a strict observer of justice, and perfectly direct and open in his dealings; but on the other hand, he was extremely avaricious, and of a haughty, sullen and suspicious temper; arrogant and irritable to those around him; difficult of access; and tenacious of respect.

Mr. *Elphinstone* says, " In my own intercourse with him, however, I found him to possess all the good qualities ascribed to him; without any one of the bad." He was killed, at the battle of Neemla, in about two months afterwards.

(89) It not being the policy of the British Government to take any share in the civil war, the Govr. Genl. (Lord *Minto*) recalled the mission.

(90) Mahmood Shah.

in the rear; but the latter who had on his armour, rode straight to the scene of action. He had not above one or two hundred men when he set off, and most of these were left behind as he advanced. The day was decided before he arrived; but he, nevertheless, pushed on, and had penetrated to the place where *Futeh Khan* was, when he was overpowered and slain, after a very brave resistance. (91) The king fled and returned to Peshawer, hence he hastened to Candahar, which he at once recovered, without a battle. Shah Mahmood, having settled his authority at Peshawer and Cabool, proceeded to Candahar, where, in the battle between him and Shoojah, the latter was again defeated, and took refuge at Rawul Pindee. (92) The battle at Candahar was fought four months after that at Neemla.

1810.—This year Toorshish (N. of Tubbus) the last place belonging to the Affghans in Khorassan, was taken by the Persians.

17. Ata Mahomed Khan (1) who was still at Cashmeer, (2) fearing his independance, and to strengthen his position, deputed his brother Jandad Khan, to Shah Shoo-

---

(91) Futeh Khan had only 2,500 men, not more than 1,300 of whom were engaged. See an account of the battle of *Neemla* at Chapter XIII.—Futehabad. The loss of this battle is most unaccountable, for he had six times a larger force than the enemy. Shah Shoojah wrote a letter himself in which he says that " His troops had behaved with fidelity; but that he was defeated ;" so that he lost the action owing to the absence of the ordinary military precautions. Akram Khan, by being in the rear, could not arrange his troops in time. This occurred in the end of June. Mr. *Elphinstone* says, " all the king's partizans were depressed, while some adversaries of his started up where they were little expected ;" no doubt in consequence of the loss of this action. The loss of this battle was even less to have been expected than that of Eshpaun in 1801.

(92) This closes the abstract from Mr. *Elphinstone's* history, and here commences a continuation extracted from the works of Sir A. *Burnes*, Dr. *Burnes;* and Moollah Jaffer, head Moonshee of Shah Shoojah, who accompanied the Shah to Loodianah.

(1) Son of late Akram Khan, (vizier.)

(2) Finding Shah Mahmood had recovered Peshawer, Cabool, and Candahar; Herat being in his possession.

jah at Attok, and offered, if the Shah would resign that place (3) to his brother, they would replace him on the throne. Jandad Khan obtained the fort of Attok, took the ex-king to Peshawer, of which he possessed himself; but proposed such degrading terms of allegiance to Shah Shoojah, that he would not consent to them. Ata Mahomed Khan, being informed of Shah Shoojah's resistance to their will, laid a plot, seized and carried Shoojah, captive, to Cashmeer.

1811.—*Futeh Khan* was appointed by Shah Mahmood to the *Vizarat* of his kingdom; while Azeem Khan, the vizier's next brother, was sent to recover Peshawer from Jandad Khan, who retired to Attok. Shah Mahmood and Futeh Khan now came to Peshawer, and designed the invasion of Cashmeer. They opened a negociation with Runjeet Singh, who gave them an auxiliary force. (4)

The Sikhs and Affghans both advanced in force to Cashmeer. Ata Mahomed was seized; and Shah Shoojah set at liberty, by both parties. On the release of Shah Shoojah, Futeh Khan entreated him not to trust himself to the Sikhs but to accompany him to Affghanistan, where he would provide for him; but the Shah was afraid of treachery; (5) and preferring the offer of the Sikhs, accompanied their commander, Dewan Mokun Chund, to Lahore. (6)

About this time (7) the Governor of Cashmeer, after being blockaded in the citadel for a few days, surrendered himself and was treated with distinction. The eldest brother of the

(3) Which was yet in his possesion.

(4) *Burnes*, vol. iii. p. 237, states, that 10,000 Sikhs marched, and that nine lakhs of Rs. of revenue were to be set aside; the Affghans subdued the valley before the Sikhs arrived; and did not fulfil their promise to the Sikhs, who left the country in disgust.

(5) He had refused Futeh Khan office in 1803; still so earnest was the Khan, that he attended the Shah, on foot, and holding his stirrup for a considerable distance after his departure from the city, he urged him to return with him.

(6) Shah Zeman had also taken refuge in the Punjab.

(7) *Burnes*, vol. iii. p. 238.

vizier, Mahomed Azeem Khan, was now appointed Governor of Cashmeer. At this time, the Ruler of the Punjab received secret overtures from the commandant of *Attok*, for the cession of that fortress. It was held by (8) a brother of the ex-governor of Cashmeer, and the offer was at once accepted. Runjeet Singh acquired this valuable possession at the small sacrifice of a lakh Rs. (£10,000), and prepared to defend his new acquisition. Futeh Khan quitted Cashmeer and marched on Attok. He found the Sikh army encamped on the plains of *Chuch*, about two miles from the fort. (9) The vizier had a contempt for his opponents. Dost Mahomed Khan, who headed a body of 2,000 Affghans, commenced the conflict by an advance on, and the capture of the whole of the Sikh artillery. He had dismounted two of their guns, and was proceeding to improve his victory, when he found himself without support, and that the whole of his brother's army had fled. (10) It only remained for him to retreat, which he effected with honor, and crossed the Indus. Since this disaster, the power of the Affghans has ceased on the eastern side of the Indus, and that country has been ever since annexed to the dominions of the Sikhs.

1814.—18. About this time the king of Persia demanded a tribute from Herat. The government was held by a brother of Mahmood (Hajee Feeroz) who was requested to treat the demand with scorn ; and the vizier (Futeh Khan) marched there to oppose the Persians. On reaching Herat, Futeh Khan made himself master of the person of the Governor, though a brother of his sovereign, and not only extracted the whole of his wealth from him, but violated his harem in searching for it. He then seized Herat, and

---

(8) Jandad Khan.

(9) The heat of the season was oppressive, and the Sikhs had both the advantage of position and water.

(10) On the attack of Dost Mahomed Khan, some evil-disposed persons brought a report to the vizier, that he had been made prisoner, with the whole of his division ; and an equally treacherous intimation was conveyed to Dost Mahomed Khan, that his brother had fallen.

prepared to meet the Persians. A battle ensued, which was not decisive. The Persians fled, but the Affghans also left the field, and their victory, with the greatest precipitation. (11) The vizier reaped the full harvest of the campaign, since he refused the tribute and beat off the army sent to enforce it. He strengthened the western frontier of the kingdom, by seizing the Governor of Herat, who, though he professed allegiance to his brother Mahmood, was at best a dubious friend. By this war, however, the garrison of Cashmeer was much weakened; since he drew levies from it, which in the end proved most injurious to the interests of Mahmood in that part of the kingdom.

1815.—Shah Shoojah had, since his defeat at Neemla (1809), being wandering as a fugitive in various corners of his dominions. (12) He was as before stated, released at Cashmeer, (13) and permitted to join his family at Lahore. His queen, *Wuffadar Begum*, (14) the most influential lady of his harem, had used every persuasion to prevent his placing himself in the power of Runjeet Singh; but he disregarded her advice, which he had ample reason to regret having neglected. She was of the most bold and determined character; and her counsel had often proved valuable to her husband, in the days of his power and adversity.

While at Lahore, and absent from the Shah, she preserved her own and his honor in an heroic manner. Runjeet pressed her to surrender " *the Diamond,*" and evinced intentions of

---

(11) The vizier was struck by a spent ball in the face, and fell on his horse's neck, on which the troops became disheartened.

(12) After his defeat at Candahar, he was seized by Ata Mahomed Khan (son of his former vizier), and subjected to much indignity. He was for sometime confined in the fortress of Attok. The lancet was frequently held over his eyes; and his keeper once took him into the middle of the Indus, with his arms bound, threatening him with instant death. The object was to extract from him the celebrated diamond, called " Koh-i-Noor," or *mountain of light.*

(13) By Futeh Khan.

(14) Whose brother (Wuffadar Khan) had been vizier to Shah Zeman.

forcing it from her. He also desired to transfer the daughters of the unfortunate king to his own harem. (15) She succeeded in the end in escaping from Lahore, disguised as a *Hindoo*, and planned the deliverance of her husband, which shortly followed. This was only effected at the expense of the great diamond. (16) Imprisonment of the closest nature, insult, and even hunger, fell to the lot of this unfortunate monarch.

(15) The disgrace in this case would have been double; for they were *Mahomedan* ladies, and *Runjeet* was a *Hindoo*. She seized the person who brought the message, and had him soundly chastised; and intimated to the Maharajah, that, if he continued his dishonorable demand, she would pound the diamond in a mortar, administer it to her daughters, and those under her protection, and then swallow it herself; adding, " May the blood of all of us be on your head!" Sir A. *Burnes*, vol. ii. p. 138. (1st. Edn.) says, that " the late King of Persia (Futeh Ali Shah) used the essence of pearls and precious stones as a tonic, to support declining strength ; in which the oriental faculty have great faith." Runjeet used pounded pearls in the spirits he drank ; it was very costly and potent.

(16) It has been valued at 3½ millions sterling. I saw it in 1831. Runjeet at the evening durbar shewed it to the Governor General and lady *W. Bentinck;* but he kept his (one) keen eye watching to see into whose hands it went. It was as big as a pigeon's egg. It weighed 3½ rupees (40 rupees being one lb.); and one weighing 2 carats is said to be worth £128.

It is not irrelevant here to state that, on Runjeet's death (27th June, 1839,) he desired to give this diamond to the brahmins (priests). Natives are impressed with a belief that the deity may be propitiated by such means! Rajah Dhian Singh, his minister, dissuaded him from this measure. Runjeet had joined the treaty and furnished his quota of troops in aid of Shah Shoojah's restoration ; getting, however, £150,000, (part of the tribute due from Sindh) for his aid. Runjeet, when only one of many chiefs, in the Punjab, had been made viceroy at Lahore by Shah Zeman the brother of Shah Shoojah. As Runjeet was disposed to part with the diamond, Dhian Singh would have done honor to himself and to his master, had he advised its restoration, and thus put to him on his death-bed, he would probably have complied with the advice. I blame *Dhian Singh,* for not recommending such an act of generosity, when he found the Maharajah willing to part with it, and when he might have impressed on his mind, that an act of *justice,* though ren-

The queen had established herself at Loodianah. She caused horses to be placed on the road; and Shoojah and his people, made every exertion in Lahore. They hired all the houses adjoining those in which they lodged; and opened a passage into the street by cutting through seven walls. A few hours after the household had retired to rest, the king descended by the aperture, and issued into the street in the dress of a native of the *Punjab*. The city wall had yet to be passed, and the gates were shut. Shoojah crept through the common sewer of the city, and fled, with two or three servants, towards the hill country of Kistwar. Here he once more raised the standard of a monarch, and planned an attack on *Cashmeer*, in which he was assisted by the Rajah of Kistwar. The expedition would have been successful, for the Governor of Cashmeer had evacuated his frontier position, but an untimely season blocked the roads with snow, interrupted the arrival of supplies; and once more frustrated the hopes of Shah Shoojah. Wandering by a cheerless and ungenial country, the Shah at length reached the British station of *Sabathoo* (17) in the outer Himalaya, from which he repaired to Loodianah, in Nov. 1815, where his family had found an asylum.

1816.—19. The reign of Mahmood was thus far successful beyond the most sanguine expectations of his partisans; he held *Cashmeer*, the revenues of which afforded the means of

---

dered after a lapse of 24 years, was more likely to propitiate the deity, than giving to others what he had obtained by *fraud and almost violence!*

The Sikh ruler gave away a million sterling to the brahmins, and six or seven ladies burnt themselves on his death! The English reader must recollect, that, *the Punjab not being in the East India Company's possessions, the British Government cannot there abolish Suttees;* I mention this as an E. I. proprietor once exclaimed against the Honorable Court for not interfering. The *Suttee* (or person burning) is *not* directed in *any* Hindoo Law Book; all that *Munnoo* says is, that "it is better for the widow not to marry again." The suttee was instituted by brahmins to prevent wives destroying their husbands: it was a political and domestic rule; but never was a religious rite.

(17) Twenty-four miles from Simla.

protection to his other provinces. He exacted the usual tribute from *Sindh*, and warded off an attack from *Persia*, the only quarter from which he apprehended danger. The king himself, rioting in debauchery, owed his successes to his vizier, who managed the whole affairs of the kingdom. Futeh Khan distributed the different governments of Cabool among his numerous brothers. He evinced no want of respect or allegiance to his sovereign; and *Mahmood* seemed satisfied, but his son, *Prince Kamran*, was discontented at the vizier's proceedings, and resolved to rid himself of a person so formidable, opposed as he was to some ambitious designs which he himself entertained. The prince at last worked upon his father, and persuaded him that he might govern his country, now that it was consolidated, without the aid of his vizier. He, therefore, determined on ridding himself of that powerful chief, his friend and benefactor. Kamran availed himself of an early opportunity, seized Futeh Khan at Herat, and gave an immediate order for his eyes being put out. (18)

1818.—When Shazada Kamran confined Futeh Khan at Herat, and deprived him of sight, his brother Peer-dil Khan of Candahar, seized and imprisoned Mahomed Rahm Khan, the Amir-ool-Moolk, while Sher-dil Khan, another brother (19) of Futeh Khan, fled to Girishk, where he took shelter in the fort of Now Ali, one of the possessions of his family.

Kamran, meanwhile, negociated peace with Futeh Ali Shah (late) king of Persia, on which he placed his own (second) son, Syf-ool-Moolk and Yar Mahomed Khan, in charge of Herat; and went to Candahar. (20)

This year (1818) Mahmood Shah, claimed for himself the sovereignty of *Cutch*, and required the renunciation of all interference with that country, as a component part of the Affghan dominions. The vizier, *Futeh Khan*, wrote

(18) Moollah Jaffer's History.
(19) Of Candahar and since dead.
(20) Futeh Khan, Peer-dil Khan (another brother) and Mahomed Khan (the Amir-ool-Moolk) were also conveyed there.

a letter more explicit to Capt. McMurdo, the Political Agent. This demand did not alarm the mind of the Govr. Genl. (Marquis of *Hastings*), who wrote a reply, treating it as a forgery; at the same time, in express terms, informing the king that the British Government, while it did not "misuse its strength by wantonly trespassing on its neighbours, it has never been attacked without destroying those who unjustly assailed it." (21)

20. Shah Mahmood, nominal king, sent for the vizier (Futeh Khan) and observed that having lost his sight, it was advisable for him to send for his brothers. Futeh Khan advised him to send for Peer-dil Khan, who was made vizier, but fled to his brother Sher-dil Khan at Girishk. It was then conferred on Ata Mahomed Khan (son of Mokhtar Oodowlah.)

Shah Mahmood despatched Shazada Jehangeer (22) and Dost Mahomed Khan, son of Bedil Khan, Populzye, and Bagar Khan, Karota, with the Kuzzlebash chiefs in attendance, to Cabool. Nuwab Samad Khan, Governor of Cabool, no sooner heard this news, than he left the city and repaired to Peshawer, while Jehangeer advanced and entered Cabool.

When Mahomed Azeem Khan, the next brother to the vizier (Futeh Khan) heard of his brother's imprisonment, and Nuwab Samad Khan's flight, he appointed his brother,

---

(21) "The messenger overtook the vizier at Peshawer ready to take the field against the Sikhs, who were threatening the frontier at Attok. Futeh Khan fired a salute on its reception, and proclaimed aloud through his Camp, that despatches had been received from the Governor General of India, the friend of the Cabool Government! Futeh Khan replied to Capt. *McMurdo*, that he did not expect an enemy in the English; but looked for their support; that in due time he meant to bring *Sindh* to its former state of dependence on Cabool; and if the *British* had any views towards that country, he would afford assistance. Professed ignorance of the letter written, as if some one had procured, by bribery, and affixed his seal." Dr. *James Burnes*, K. H. History of Cutch, 1839, p. 45.

(22) His grandson and eldest son of Kamran.

the *present Dost Mahomed Khan* (23) to the government of Peshawer, and proclaiming *Shahzada Sooltan Ali* as his sovereign; Azeem Khan proceeded with him to Cabool.

Ata Mahomed Khan, the new vizier, meanwhile, wrote to *Dost Mahomed Khan*, that if he, also, would advance with his troops towards Cabool, he would betray the Shahzada into his hands. Dost Mohomed Khan, with his brothers, left Peshawer, and by hasty marches arrived at Bootkhak; (24) where he had a secret interview with Ata Mahomed Khan.

Shahzada Jehangeer, hearing of his arrival, retired within the palace of the Bala Hissar, while *Dost Mahomed Khan* and Ata Mahomed Khan occupied the city. Hearing this, Shah Mahmood hastened with (25) a considerable army towards Cabool. (26) He did not advance beyond *Ghuznee*, where the Shahzada and his immediate adherents rejoined him.

Shah Mahmood, accompanied by Shahzada Kamran, left Ghuznee, at the head of his collected troops, and on arriving at Sydabad (27) put *vizier Futeh Khan*, with every studied cruelty to death. (28)

(23) Who now appears for the first time to take an active part in the troubles and revolutions of his country.

(24) Nine miles E. of Cabool.

(25) Two days after this Dost Mahomed Khan heard that Ata Mahomed Khan intended to invite him to a feast, and make him a prisoner. Dost Mahomed Khan seized Ata Mahomed Khan, and ordered him to be blinded; and then laid siege to the Bala Hissar.

(26) The inclemency of the season, and probably want of confidence of success, delayed his arrival.

(27) Forty-eight miles from Cabool.

(28) Sir A. *Burnes*, vol iii. p. 241, says, " After a lapse of five or six months," (*i. e.* after he was deprived of sight) " Kamran put the vizier to death, between Cabool and Candahar, with the full consent of the king. This rash act was perpetrated in the year 1818, and drove the whole of Futeh Khan's brothers into rebellion." At p. 271, he says, alluding to there being 60,000 (more properly 6,000) families of Barukzyes, " *Hajee Jumal*, the most powerful of its chiefs, willingly bowed to the authority of Ahmed Shah; and contributed to fix him

21. From hence the Shah proceeded viâ Obaguk to the fort of Door Bannu.

Dost Mahomed taking his newly-acknowledged sovereign with him, moved from Cabool to oppose Shah Mahmood. While both parties were engaged watching each other's motions, Dilwas Khan, Nawaz Khan, and Akbar Khan, joined Dost Mahomed. Shah Mahmood lost all confidence and returned towards Ghuznee, while Dost Mahomed Khan returned to Cabool in triumph. Mahomed Azeem Khan quitted Cashmeer, returned to Peshawer, and left Cashmeer in charge of his brother Nuwab Jubbar Khan. (29) On his

---

on his throne. The successors of that monarch rewarded his services, by the murder of his son *Poynda Khan;* and we have related the atrocious assassination of his grandson the vizier," (Futeh Khan.)

" The tragedy which terminated the life of *Futeh Khan,* Barukzye, is, perhaps, without parallel in modern times. Blind and bound he was led into the Court of Mahmood, where he had so lately ruled with absolute power. The king taunted him for his *crimes,* and desired him to use his influeuce with his brothers, then in rebellion. He replied without fear, and with great fortitude, that he was now but a poor, blind-man, and had no concern with affairs of state. Mahmood irritated at his obstinacy, gave the last orders for his death, and this unfortunate man was deliberately cut to pieces by the nobles of the court; joint was separated from joint, limb from limb, his nose and his ears were lopped off; nor had the vital spark fled, till the head was separated from the mangled trunk. Futeh Khan bore these cruel tortures without a sigh; he stretched out his different limbs to those who thirsted for his blood, and exhibited the same cool indifference, the same reckless contempt for his own life, which he had so often shown for that of others. The bloody remains of this unfortunate person, were gathered in a cloth and sent to Ghuznee, where they were interred."

I have heard from one well qualified to know the fact from having resided at *Herat,* that *Futeh Khan* was engaged in a plot to depose Shah Mahmood, which if true (though every one must deprecate the cruelty of the vizier's death) taking his life would have been according to the custom of the country.

It will be recollected that he seized Mahmood's brother (Feeroz) at Herat, and if he *did* depose *one* brother, there is fair reason to believe that he would try to displace *another ;* and we have examples among his brothers of such acts.

(29) Dost Mahomed's elder brother.

way, Mahomed Azeem Khan had an interview with *Shah Ayoob*, (30) and sent his brother Peer-dil Khan and Madad Khan to conduct *Shah Shoojah-ool-Moolk*, (31) from Dera Ghazee Khan (where he had arrived on his first expedition) to Peshawer. Shortly after the Shah's arrival, Azeem Khan demanded the dispersion of the Shah's troops, and delivery of his artillery. The Shah refused, and leaving Peshawer he stationed himself at *Takal* where he was attacked; one of his magazines of gunpowder exploded; and many persons lost their lives, and a defeat was the result. The Shah then, once more, escaped to the *Khyber hills*. Mahomed Azeem Khan and Shahi engaged to declare *Shah Ayoob*, viceroy of Peshawer, to which they retired.

When Mahomed Azeem Khan, eldest survivor of the family, returned from Cashmeer, he resolved to dethrone the *murderer* of his brother; *Mahmood*, afraid to encounter the rebels, fled to Herat, which involved a virtual resignation of his power; he retained *Herat* and the title of king; but sunk into a vassal of Persia.

Azeem Khan, says Sir *A. Burnes*, "now took the extraordinary step of recalling Shoojah-ool-Moolk from his exile. He offered him the crown of Cabool, and sent a *Koran* to the ex-monarch, under his *seal*, according to the custom of the country, as proof of his sincerity. Shoojah repaired with every despatch to Peshawer." (32)

Dost Mahomed Khan hearing of these events, wrote requesting his brother Mahomed Azeem Khan, if he had any regard for him, to depose *Shah Ayoob;* as he (the Dost) had declared *Sooltan Ali*, the king at Cabool.

---

(30) Brother of Shah Mahmood.

(31) He had left Loodianah on the 13th October, 1818, on his first expedition to try and recover his throne. He returned to Loodianah in 1821, when his pension of £4,800 a year was again paid to him. The Government gave no support or public sanction to the enterprise, which failed. In 1819, also, *Shah Zeman* came to reside at Loodianah.

(32) Vol. iii. p. 243; but he adds p. 246—" Shoojah after all his misfortunes, might have now re-ascended the throne of his ancestors; but

Mahomed Azeem Khan wrote that, if he, Dost Mahomed Khan, had any intention to aspire to the chief authority, he would retire to Peshawer: Dost Mahomed, finding he could not gain the ascendancy, abandoned the cause of Sooltan Ali; and owned the supremacy of Mahomed Azeem Khan. Mahomed Azeem Khan, then, accompanied by Shah Ayoob, entered Cabool; and soon after his arrival, he advised Shah Ayoob to *sanction* the murder of Sultan Ali. (33)

1819.—22. On leaving Cashmeer, Mahomed Azeem Khan, entrusted the government of it to *Nuwab Jubbar Khan*, (34) and about this period Runjeet Singh contemplated the reduction of Cashmeer. When news of the approach of the Sikh troops reached Cashmeer, Nuwab Jubbar Khan marched out of the city at the head of his forces, and after various operations, being reinforced, the Nuwab boldly attacked, and struck terror into the ranks of the enemy. Next day he made a night attack (35) in which he failed, was wounded, and fled with 1,000 suwars: he reached Peshawer, and afterwards moved to Cabool.

The murder of *Sooltan Ali*, gave great offence to Dost Mahomed Khan; (36) but he concealed his anger, (though

before Azeem Khan had reached Peshawer, he (Shoojah) prematurely displayed his notions of royal authority, by insulting some friend of his benefactor, whom he considered to be encroaching on his dignity, *by using a palankeen.* The whole Barukzye family took offence at such ill-timed pride; and Azeem Khan determined to place a more compliant master on the throne." " A favorable opportunity presented itself in the person of *Ayoob* (or Job), a brother of Shoojah. He entered the camp of Azeem Khan, and sued for the throne as the most abject of slaves. ' Make me but king,' he said, ' permit money to be coined in my name, and the whole power and resources of the kingdom may rest with yourself; my ambition will be satisfied with bread, and the title of king.' This was just the the person the Barukzyes wanted, and his conditions were accepted."

(33) His brother.
(34) The brother next in succession to himself.
(35) Chupao, and for which the Affghans were famed.
(36) He wished to raise him to the throne; and govern as vizier.

he tried to raise troops to oppose him;) and at length acknowledged the supremacy of his brother (Mahomed Azeem Khan), and became reconciled. (37)

Dost Mahomed Khan proceeded from Cabool towards Candahar. On his arrival at Ghuznee, he *disguised* himself in the habit of a *khidmutgar*, and entered the fort (under the pretence of buying provisions) with a few followers. Abdoorrehman Khan, the Governor of Mahomed Azeem Khan, went up to Dost Mahomed Khan, in order to ascertain who he was. No sooner were they confronted, than Dost Mahomed Khan *shot his visitor dead on the spot, and made himself master of the place.* (38) Mahomed Azeem Khan proceeded with his troops to Ghuznee. Dost Mahomed Khan fortified himself within the fort, and prepared for a vigorous siege.

For some days an irregular cannonade was kept up on both sides. At length Dost Mahomed wrote to Nuwab Samad Khan his determination never to resign the place; adding that he came there with the view to take away the Governor's life, and would omit no opportunity to take his *(the Nuwab's)* unless he were allowed to keep possession. The Nuwab conciliated Mahomed Azeem Khan, and Dost Mahomed Khan, who, leaving Ghuznee under Ameer Mahomed Khan, went to Cabool.

23. When Mahomed Azeem Khan received (39) intelligence of the arrival of *Shah Shoojah-ool-Moolk* at Shikarpoor, he proceeded to Candahar accompanied by Dost Mahomed Khan, Nuwab Jubbar Khan, and his other brothers. He despatched half his army under his brother Sher-dil

---

(37) Mahomed Azeem Khan retraced his steps to Cabool; and Dost Mahomed Khan, leaving his partizans at his brother's mercy, fled to Peshawer. Dost Mahomed afterwards came to Cabool; but Mahomed Azeem Khan ordered him to leave it; as he was of *no service to him*; and to go where he pleased.

(38) This is one of the most prominent acts of this man's life to rise to power.

(39) Said to have been six months after the above events. This would bring the transaction to the end of 1819.

Khan. At Dadur, Sher-dil Khan was overtaken by Mahomed Azeem Khan, with the rear of his army ; and here the Sirdar was visited by Mehrab Khan, the Beloochee chief, who came to do him homage. (40)

1822.—About the end of this year a deputation was sent by Maharajah Runjeet Singh to Sirdar Mahomed Azeem Khan, desiring him to resign all claim to *Cashmeer*. (41)

(40) Which he refused to Shah Shoojah in March, 1839, and on 13th Nov. 1839, he was killed at the storming of his fort (Khelat). A letter was addressed to the Sindhians enjoining them to expel Shah Shoojah from their country. They compelled him to leave Sindh, and the king returned to Loodianah, viâ Jesselmere and Jypore, in the year 1821.

(41) It is a curious historical fact, that about this period, the Governor of Cashmeer sent a message to the resident at Delhi, offering to deliver up that fertile valley to the British Government. But, it was found that, by an article of the treaty (1809) the acceptance of the offer would have involved its infraction ("not to occupy any territory to the N. of the Punjab," and Cashmeer is N. E.) Whether the treaty was so worded advisedly, or without looking at remote contingencies, I do not know. Mr. (now Sir C.) *Metcalfe* stood too high as a politician not to have foreseen the probability of its falling into the hands of the Sikhs. I will venture at a solution of the problem.

In the beginning of the years 1810 and 1811, the Govt. sent expeditions to the *Isle of France* and to *Java ;* and, we had too much on our hands to force a treaty. Major-Genl. *St. Leger's* force (accompanied by Sir D. *Ochterlony* and Mr. *Metcalfe)* had reached the Sutluj, and returned in April, 1809. Runjeet declined the article, usual in our treaties with all native powers, requiring the giving up all European deserters.

It is to be regretted that so valuable a valley, said to be, in reality, as beautiful as ascribed by *Moore,* should have fallen into such hands. Sher Singh (Runjeet's adopted son) the Govr. it was supposed, would, on the Maharajah's death, declare his independence; it is not an improbable event ; and the difficult nature of that country, as already mentioned in *Akram Khan's* retreat, renders the measure of easy accomplishment. When the offer was made to our Govt., the Govr. was prepared to lead our troops by a road through the hills, avoiding the route by the Punjab. In our possession, in a commercial point of view, no less than on the score of humanity, we might soon have regenerated a country, called by the natives, with truth, the " *Paradise of the East.*"

1823.—Sirdar Mahomed Azeem Khan proceeded to *Noushera*, in January, 1823, where was fought the action already described (42) in which the Affghans were defeated, and on which occasion Dost Mahomed Khan did not support the character which might have been expected from his conduct at the battle of Chuch, in 1811.

Runjeet Singh wrote to Mahomed Azeem Khan that, if he would send a deputation to him, he would restore Peshawer; he did so, and Runjeet fulfilled his promise. Mahomed Azeem Khan then proceeded towards Cabool, and was taken ill on the road; Dost Mahomed Khan repaired to Cabool, and Sirdar Mahomed Khan died shortly afterwards, to the great sorrow of the people. (43).

On the fourth day after this event, Dost Mahomed Khan and Yar Mahomed Khan, conferred on the son (Habeeb Oollah Khan) the robe of Sardaree; and declared him the Ruler of Cabool, in the place of his father. Owing to the intrigues carried on by the above Khans, Habeeb Oollah Khan sent a message to them to inform them that they were of no service to him, in consequence of which Dost Mahomed Khan and Yar Mahomed Khan, quitted Cabool, and joined *Shah Ayoob*; between whom and Habeeb Oollah Khan, they began to sow the seeds of ill-will; and seduced the simple Ayoob into their view, and plans. He (Ayoob) conferred the office of vizier on Yar Mahomed Khan, and that of Sirdar on Dost Mahomed Khan, which were duly proclaimed.

Habeeb Oollah Khan ordered his troops to lay siege to the Bala Hissar. When Shah Ayoob heard of this, Dost Mahomed Khan began to raise commotions, but failing in his object, he fled to Ghuznee, still in his possession; and Yar Mahomed returned to Peshawer.

24. Four months after this insurrection Dost Mahomed Khan set out on his return to Cabool, with the view of creating fresh disturbances, but on his approach to the fort

---

(42) See Noushera (24th Nov. 1839) at Chapter XV.

(43) He and Jubbar Khan appear to have been the most moderate of the whole of the brothers.

of Hashif, his progress was checked by Habeeb Oollah Khan's troops; peace was restored between the combatants; and Dost Mahomed Khan and Habeeb Oollah Khan returned together to Cabool; where the former went to reside in the Muhalla of Jawan Sher.

A few days afterwards, Habeeb Oollah wrote to (his uncle) Peer-dil Khan of Candahar, and entreated him to come to his aid with troops; he marched immediately, and on reaching Ghuznee left his party there, and hastened on with only a few followers (suwars). He confirmed the reconciliation between the contending parties. The mountain tracts were conferred, in Jaghier, on Dost Mahomed Khan, on which he retired to Chareekar. Peer-dil Khan next went with 400 suwars to the Bala Hissar, and on the pretence of a *visit* to Shah Ayoob, he seized him (Ayoob); put one of his sons to death, and secured the whole of his property. (44)

Shah Ayoob was then released. He went to Peshawer, and afterwards to the court of Runjeet Singh, who gave him a stipend, which he enjoyed till the day of his death some time last year. (45)

Peace and order being established at Cabool, Peer-dil Khan returned to Candahar. (46)

Habeeb Oollah Khan, as soon as his suspicions were raised by Dost Mahomed's proceedings, desired the latter to appear before him; but, he, fearing he would be seized and imprisoned, made his escape, and went towards Mydan; (47) and induced a majority of the Ghiljie tribe to adopt his cause.

---

(44) His father (Azeem Khan) left three crores of rupees (three millions sterling).

(45) In 1837, at Lahore.

(46) Forty days after his departure, news arrived of the march of Mehr-dil Khan towards Cabool, which once more excited the restless spirit of Dost Mahomed Khan. Peer-dil Khan, and Mehr-dil Khan were his brothers; the latter left Candahar as we (1839) approached the city.

(47) Two marches from Cabool.

Habeeb Oollah, hearing of this, proceeded, at once, with his army to Mydan, and besieged Dost Mahomed Khan (in his fort) who made a good defence. Ameer Mahomed Khan shortly after arrived from Ghuznee to the relief of his brother. An action took place which ended in the total defeat of Ameer Mahomed Khan; and Dost Mahomed Khan surrendered the fort to the enemy; and went to Ghuznee. Mehr-dil Khan at the same time, left Candahar, and joined Habeeb Oollah. Six months after this defeat, Dost Mahomed Khan was joined by Hafiz Jee at Ghuznee. Dost Mahomed Khan and Ameer Oollah Khan proceeded to the fort of Khairandesh, where Habeeb Oollah Khan soon made his appearance; and an action took place. Meanwhile Habeeb Oollah received intelligence that Cabool had been attacked and occupied by Hafiz Jee. He resolved however, to risk a battle; was defeated, and fled to Cabool.

25. Mehr-dil Khan, who had joined Habeeb Oollah Khan wrote to Sher-dil Khan (48) and Peer-dil Khan to come to Cabool. Sher-dil Khan came with a few attendants. He reproved Dost Mahomed for his past conduct, and soon reconciled him with Habeeb Oollah Khan. Dost Mahomed Khan was to keep Chareekar and the mountain tracts; and the rest of the country (49) was to be held by Habeeb Oollah Khan; Sher-dil Khan to be appointed Naeb (50) to Habeeb Oollah Khan, who was to reside in the Bala Hissar; and Sher-dil Khan to reside in the house of Habeeb Oollah Khan inside the city. (51)

(48) Another of the numerous brothers of Dost Mahomed. He died on an expedition to Khelat.
(49) Of Cabool.
(50) Deputy.
(51) Scarcely had three months elapsed before *Sher-dil Khan* proposed to Dost Mahomed Khan to seize Habeeb Oollah Khan, and divide his territory and property between them. *Dost Mahomed readily agreed to the proposal.* This is the conduct of two uncles to an unfortunate nephew; son of their respected brother!

Sher-dil Khan.

Some time after this iniquitous transaction, Sher-dil Khan invited both Dost Mahomed Khan (52) and Habeeb Oollah Khan, to his house, and *treacherously* put them in confinement. Having thus secured the person of Habeeb Oollah Khan, he liberated Dost Mahomed Khan; and then laid siege to the Bala Hissar, which was captured the fourth day. (53)

No sooner had he settled himself in the Bala Hissar, than Dost Mahomed Khan (54) asked him to fulfil their agreement. In consequence of which Sher-dil Khan sent him some valuables and a sum of ready money, altogether equal to about one lakh Rs. (£10,000), as well as *one of the wives of Mahomed Azeem Khan.*

At the same time Dost Mahomed Khan was desired by his brother (Sher-dil Khan) to meet him in the Bala Hissar, when, in concert with each other, they would consider and settle the matter. (55)

---

(52) Then at Chareekar.

(53) Sher-dil Khan entered the palace and seized and imprisoned Imam Virdi, and also Akram Khan, the brother of Habeeb Oollah Khan, who had just arrived from Candahar.

The next object of Sher-dil Khan, to secure his newly acquired possession, was to remove the prisoners from Cabool, where their presence might occasion disorder, (Shah Mahmood, p. 390 Note (83) had once escaped from the Bala Hissar)—and to confine them very strictly in the fort of Mawa, in the valley of Khiwat. The family of the late Mahomed Azeem Khan was driven out of the Bala Hissar in *a very ignominious manner*, and lodged in the house of Habeeb Oollah, inside the city. Having thus secured himself from every danger from his enemies, Sher-dil Khan took up his residence in the Bala Hissar; and *made himself master of all the wealth* which had been accumulated by (his brother) Mahomed Azeem Khan, during his long and prosperous rule. This is the conduct of an uncle. The usurper, notwithstanding his strict precautions, could not long remain without a rival.

(54) With whom he had entered into engagements to divide the property of Mahomed Azeem Khan.

(55) The division of the property. Dost Mahomed Khan replied that it was not fair to send him only *one* lakh rupees out of *three crores* (three millions sterling); the reported wealth which Mahomed Azeem Khan left at his death. However, he added, " should you be inclined

This affair not being adjusted to his satisfaction, Dost Mahomed Khan commenced hostilities, by raising commotions in the house of Ameer Oollah, where an action ensued between him, on the one side, and Mehr-dil Khan (another brother), Ameer Oollah Khan, and Abdoolah Khan, on the other; but the contest was of very short duration, because the latter soon feeling their inability to overcome Dost Mahomed Khan, fled to the Bala Hissar, setting the house of Ameer Oollah Khan on fire. This success induced the citizens, the mountaineers (Kohistanees) and the people of the Ghiljie and Kuzzlebash tribes (except Ameer Oollah Khan and Hafiz Jee, who still continued attached to Sher-dil Khan) to embrace and support the cause of Dost Mahomed Khan, who, encouraged by the general rise in his favor, (56) proceeded to lay siege to the Bala Hissar.

26. Sher-dil Khan, finding himself unable to resist Dost Mahomed Khan, sent a message to his brothers at Candahar, desiring them to send him a re-inforcement. (57)

to preserve the union and good understanding which subsist between us, either come to me yourself; or send the remainder of the money that is due as my share, without delay."

Sher-dil Khan returned answer that the money which he had already remitted to him, was sent entirely out of *personal regard*, and not upon any other consideration—for what pretension could he (the Dost) have to property acquired by another person's sword? This message enraged Dost Mahomed Khan, and soon after collecting the mountaineers (Kohistanees) and the Kuzzlebashes, he prepared to make war on *Sher-dil Khan*.

This was indeed, taking the *lion's* share. (*Sher-dil Khan*, means the Khan with a *Lion's heart*).

(56) Probably owing to his brother's avarious conduct.

(57) Dost Mahomed Khan proposed to Yar Mahomed Khan, (Barukzye) and Sooltan Mahomed Khan, who were at Peshawer, to come immediately to his aid; and if successful, he would share his acquisitions with them: (contrast this with Sher-dil Khan's avaricious conduct.) They proceeded to Cabool, where they arrived within the course of a month; while Peer-dil Khan and Mehr-dil Khan (brothers of Sher-dil Khan and of the Dost), were forty days in reaching it.

Dost Mahomed Khan holds the reins. 413

For more than three months, civil war raged in Cabool, which now became a scene of general anarchy and confusion. Numerous lives were lost on either side, and still there was no end to their disputes. At last the people, reflecting that neither of the rival parties was subdued, while thousands of their followers fell victims in their quarrel, came to the resolution of putting, first Dost Mahomed Khan, and then Sher-dil Khan, to death; but if the former would go, alone, to the camp of the latter, and kill him with his own hand, his life would be spared.

When intelligence of this design reached Dost Mahomed Khan, he sent word to Sher-dil Khan, urging him to an interview on the following day, and threatened, with an oath, that he would take his life, if he refused to come.

Early next morning, when both parties were drawn up in sight of each other, Sher-dil Khan, with two attendants, went to the tent of Nuwab Samad Khan, where a meeting was held. (58)

A treaty was concluded between the parties, by which Dost Mahomed Khan was to hold the reins of government, and Habeeb Oollah, to do him homage.

The whole property belonging to Mahomed Azeem Khan was to be retained by Sher-dil Khan and Peer-dil Khan; for the purpose of meeting the expenses of foreign wars. (59)

Sher-dil Khan and Peer-dil Khan, returned to Candahar with the property which they had plundered, and sent Habeeb Oollah Khan, Akram Khan, and Imam Verdi,

---

(58) Afterwards Dost Mahomed Khan and Sher-dil Khan, in company with Nuwab Samad Khan, Yar Mahomed Khan, and Sooltan Mahomed Khan, went to visit the mother of Habeeb Oollah Khan. They affected to condole with her, and promised to restore her son to liberty, and to place him in the hands of Dost Mahomed Khan. They had frightened the poor mother into compliance, by threatening to blow her son from a gun.

(59) By means of this wealth (gained through this fraternal robbery), they were enabled to become possessed of nine-tenths of the lands and revenues of Candahar.

under charge of Moollah Peer Mahomed, the Qazee of Jawan Sher, and Dost Mahomed of Jawan Sher, to Sirdar Dost Mahomed Khan. (60)

1824.—27. The whole of the country of Cabool was, now, divided into five unequal portions, and possessed by each brother, according to his means and pretensions, *viz.*

1st. The territory of the Ghiljies was held by Jubbar Khan.

2nd. The Kohistan and Koh-i-Damun, together with one half of Cabool, by Dost Mahomed Khan.

3rd. Sukar, Loghur, and the other half of Cabool by Sooltan Mahomed Khan, and Yar Mahomed Khan.

4th. Jellalabad, by Mahomed Zeman Khan.

5th. Ghuznee, by Ameer Mahomed Khan. For two years this arrangement lasted.

1826.—At this time Dost Mahomed Khan, combining with Habeeb Oollah Khan, compelled Sooltan Mahomed Khan to retire from Cabool; and made himself sole master of that place.

He also deprived his brother, *Jubbar Khan,* of the Ghiljie country, and Mahomed Zeman Khan of Jellalabad.

At the request of Habeeb Oollah Khan, Dost Mahomed conferred *Sukar* on him; he held it only for six months, was deprived of it, and turned out of Cabool.

Habeeb Oollah Khan proceeded to Peshawer, where Yar Mahomed Khan settled on him an annual allowance of 50,000 Rs. (£5,000), which he held till the death of Yar Mahomed Khan. (61) Habeeb Oollah Khan quitted Peshawer, and went to Mahomed Zeman Khan, the Ruler of Jellalabad; where he incited the *Bujor* tribe to espouse his cause; and prepared to take vengeance upon Sooltan Maho-

---

(60) Yar Mahomed Khan despatched all his troops commanded by his younger brother, Peer Mahomed Khan, to Peshawer; while he himself and Sooltan Mahomed Khan, remained at Cabool.

(61) Slain in the action with Syud Ahmed (the fanatic) with the Sikhs in 1831; when Sooltan Mahomed Khan ceased to pay the allowance.

med Khan. (62) Being deserted on all sides, on account of his crimes, Habeeb Oollah went towards Candahar to join, it is said, Shah Shoojah; on his arrival at Dera Ismael Khan, Habeeb Oollah became insane and murdered some of his slave girls.

1829.—28. This year Shah Mahmood died at Herat (63) and was succeeded by his son, Shah Kamran, who now reigns there.

1830.—This year Syud Ahmed, the fanatic made his appearance in Cabool, and was treated by Dost Mahomed with the respect he thought his avocations (64) ought to secure for him. He retired to Peshawer where he was joined by Sultan Mahomed Khan, (65) Yar Mahomed Khan also joined him, and several engagements took place with the Sikhs.

1831.—This year Syud Ahmed was killed in an action with the Sikhs; and thus terminated the religious warfare.

1832.—This year Sir A. Burnes went to Cabool (in the progress of his travels into Bokhara) and for the first time became acquainted with Dost Mahomed Khan, and his brother Jubbar Khan.

1833.—On the 17th Feb. 1833, Shah Shoojah left Loodianah on his second expedition to endeavour to recover his throne. In the month of May he obtained possession of Shikarpoor, with the consent of the Ameers of Sindh.

1834.—Shah Shoojah (66) fought a very severe action

(62) In the mean time, Habeeb Oollah fell in love with his brother's wife. In order to become possessed of the object of his heart, he took the life of his brother, by poison; which atrocious crime roused the indignation of the people who had joined his party; and they refused supporting his cause any longer.

(63) I thought he had been blinded; but it is said that he never lost his sight.

(64) A religious war against the Sikhs as infidels. He had proclaimed a religious war before in India.

(65) Who had been ejected from Cabool by Dost Mahomed.

(66) Having been refused money (he had already sold many of his jewels) by the Ameers, he threatened to plunder Shikarpoor and Larkhana.

with the Sindhians, on the 9th January, 1834, seven kos from Rohree. The Sindhians lost 1,370 horse and foot soldiers. On the Shah's side a considerable number were killed and wounded. The army of the Talpoorians fairly fled from the field of battle, and the Shah got possession of Shikarpoor. (67)

The Shah, then, marched to Candahar, where he was defeated on the 2nd July, by Dost Mahomed Khan, (68) and was obliged to fly, and take refuge at Khelat.

About the end of this year (69) Dost Mahomed Khan assumed the title of "*Ameer Shah Ghazee*," and offered the viziership to Nuwab Jubbar Khan. (70)

1835.—The Shah was expected to go to Bombay, and that Government was authorized, in such case, to give a *Zeafut* of 100 Rs. a day. (71)

(67) They consented to a pecuniary aid of five or seven lakhs rupees in preference to hazarding another battle; and to farm Shikarpoor from the Shah. See *Shikarpoor*, Chapter II. Before going to Sindh it is said that Shah Shoojah threatened the Ameers (privately, through Meer Ismael Khan) that if they did not immediately accede to his request (demand of Shikarpoor) it was his intention to *transfer his undoubted sovereignty over Sindh to his faithful allies the British!* Dr. *Burnes's* visit to Sindh, p. 151. Sindh paid to Cabool a tribute of fifteen lakhs Rupees (£150,000).

(68) Who came from Cabool to the assistance of his brothers. Had not Mr. *Campbell*, the Commander of the Shah's Hindostanee troops been wounded, the king would have won the battle: but this event threw all into confusion. The Shah lost all hope, and fled, and the army dispersed. The Dost said that the Shah lost 4,000, and that the Affghans lost 7 or 800 men only; but, that had the Shah remained on field he (the Dost) must have lost the battle. See the account in Chapter V.

(69) Reported on the 17th January, 1835.

(70) Which I believe he declined. See the account of his arrival at Ghuznee in July, 1839. Chapter IX.

(71) Equal to three-fourths of the allowance he received at Loodianah. The Govt. of India reported to the Court of Directors the failure of the expedition as quite unexpected; "As the army of the *Shah* was known to be superior, both in numbers and in discipline, to the *Barukzye* troops, the most confident expectations were entertained of his success."

This year Dost Mahomed Khan sent a mission to Persia, the object of which has since been made manifest. Had it been to seek protection, he had, in 1837, an opportunity of seeking it from the British, instead of from the Persian Government. This year, also, Abdool Ghias Khan, son of Nuwab Jubbar Khan came to Loodianah, under the sanction of the Government of India; and the Home authorities approved of his hospitable reception. (72) Such a measure was a proof of the desire of the British Government to cultivate terms of friendship with the ruler of Affghanistan; free from all distrust arising from the residence of his nephew at our frontier post. (73)

1837.—29. This year Sir *A. Burnes* was sent on a mission of a purely commercial nature to Cabool, (74) but affairs took a political turn, the result of which proved that Dost Mahomed Khan was determined to adhere to his Persian alliance; and which caused the mission to leave his court.

1838.—Lt. *Leech* had in 1837 been sent to Canhadar on a commercial mission which, like that to Cabool and from the same cause, was converted into one of a Political cast. In 1838, he was sent to Khelat.

This year the Persian army was before Herat, but owing to the remonstrances of the British Govt., the king withdrew from the siege of that fortress on the 9th Sept., though the event was not known to the Govt. of India till the 22nd of October. On the 1st of October the Govr. Genl. of India published his Proclamation, declaratory of the object of the expedition into Affghanistan.

When Dost Mahomed Khan heard of the retreat of the Persians, he was absorbed in thought and speculation; always engaged in holding consultations. He was engaged with the chief Koondooz. At one time he stopped the march of his troops to Jellalabad; and then he recalled his son and party from Balkh.

(72) A village was, I believe, assigned for his support.
(73) Whence he, or his instructor, might have conveyed intelligence, which the jealousy of many Govts. desires to conceal.
(74) Major *Leech* and Dr. *Lord* accompanied him.

On the 10th Dec. 1838, the "*Army of the Indus*" marched from Ferozpoor.

1839.—On the 26th of April, 1839, Shah Shoojah arrived at Candahar. On the 8th of May he was installed in that city. On the 23rd July the fortress of Ghuznee was carried by assault; on the 6th he arrived at Cabool, which he entered in triumph, on the 7th of August, 1839. (75)

Thus, after having been the ruler of Cabool for 13 years, Dost Mahomed Khan's ambition lost him the power, to attain which had occupied as many years; and which he might have retained, had he possessed the prudence of his brother Nuwab Jubbar Khan, who advised him "*to cultivate friendly relations with the British Govt.*" (76)

Affghanistan was governed by the kings for about 62 out of the 92 years since the foundation of the empire by Ahmed Shah in 1747; (77) so that there have been 30 years of anarchy; a longer period than falls to the fate of other empires. It is now but the shadow of its former greatness. But time and good Govt. will, I hope, restore it to tranquillity and prosperity.

30. *Character of Dost Mahomed Khan.*—Dost Mahomed Khan came to power in troubled times, when each man's hand was raised up against his neighbour. He tried to propitiate the soldier more than the citizen,—a course which can never last beyond a time of warfare. Though liberal in his commercial policy, his exigencies made him

(75) The first time on the 13th July, 1803.

(76) Azeez Khan (brother-in-law of the Dost) a Ghiljie chief, wrote in October, 1838, that Dost Mahomed repented of having dismissed Capt. Burnes. He preferred the policy of Capt. *Vikovitch*. I am very incredulous as to this gentleman having committed suicide, because his acts were renounced by his Govt. My belief is that his was only a *civil and diplomatic* death; and that he enjoys a pension under some other cognomen. I am no politician; but the *corps diplomatique* is anti-suicidal; and one of its members can enjoy a pension under a *change of name*.

(77) Ahmed Shah 1747 to 1773. Timoor Shah 1773 to 1793. Shah Zeman from 1793 to 1801. 1801 to 1803, disputed succession. Shah Shoojah 1803 to 1809. 1809 to 1839 anarchy, rebellion and confusion.

exact more from the merchants than was consistent with good policy, or was beneficial to trade. His revenue did not admit of his keeping up an army equal to the accomplishment of his views of external policy, and conquest. History should have instructed him to view a Persian alliance, as that kingdom was then situated, as the forerunner of his ultimate subjugation. He presided in the court of justice, and added its emoluments to his own treasury. When in want, he borrowed money from the wealthy, which he often neglected to repay, though from time to time called upon to redeem his pledge, and bond. His failing to keep his promise, had at times, caused a rebuke from the lowest Affghan : when he would renew his promise, which was not confided in. He is about 45 years of age, 5 ft. 9 inches in height, with a fair complexion and intelligent countenance. When intent upon any scheme, he would observe his company by furtive glances, as if desirous of penetrating into their characters, unknown to themselves. When relating his past deeds of arms (which he delighted to make known) his large black eyes would first dilate to an unusual size, the sockets reddened ; the eye-balls revolved, exhibiting but a small portion of the eyes, with a glare most piercing, but as unpleasant as extraordinary. The frankness of Dost Mahomed was, probably, natural ; but he was too familiar for the dignity of his situation ; or to command the respect of his inferiors.

He owed much to the chiefs of his own tribe (Barukzyes) ; but he had no control over them. His mother was, by birth, a Persian ; so that he might have secured the attachment of the Kuzzlebashes. He is connected, by marriage, with Shah Shoojah ; both having married sisters.

The *Barukzyes* were not more numerous than the *Suddozyes*; therefore, there was no pretence to pre-eminence, in virtue of the importance of his tribe. He placed but little confidence in his eldest son, who is said to possess most talent. He placed two of his sons in the Govts. of Ghuznee and Jellalabad, of whose fidelity he was secure ; but he effected his object by the unseasonable removal of others, and thereby lost the confidence of those, whose merits gave them claim to retain appointments, which had been the rewards of their services.

His Military character partook more of the partizan than of a skilful general. The battle of *Chuch* (1811) proved his bravery; but he should not have left the field on the report of Futeh Khan's defeat. At the battle of Noushera (1823) he evinced no desire to renew the action next day : but he never liked to act under the command of another.

He might have retired with honor, had he accepted a liberal provision, instead of being, now, a prisoner at Bokhara; and he should have learnt from the Emperor *Baber*, the dignity of submission when resistance was hopeless.

" If you are fettered by your situation, submit to circumstances. If you are independent, follow your own fancy." (78)

31. *Shah Shoojah's claim to the throne, and character.*—As to the claim of Shah Shoojah to the throne, it is sufficient to state that he was its last legal possessor. He succeeded Shah Zeman who was declared king, his father (Timoor) not having nominated a successor. The usurpation of Shah Mahmood (the half-brother who stood between Zeman and Shoojah) must be set aside. Shoojah, therefore, was the next brother, (79) and I have the best authority for saying that, Shah *Zeman* declared him to have *the best right to the throne*.

The character of Shah Shoojah has been already given by the *Hon. Mr. M. Elphinstone*, so that it were almost presumption to add to what he has pronounced in such favorable terms. When he came to the throne in 1803, he was about 23 years of age, (80) so that much allowance was to

(78) Erskine's translation of Baber's Memoirs, p. 391.
(79) Shah Zeman being blind could not, according to Mahomedan Law, reign. His son Kyser attempted to displace Shah Shoojah ; so did Kamran (Mahmood's son) but he is the son of an usurper.
(80) When Mr. Elphinstone says about 20 years old, I understand him to refer to 1800, when he proclaimed himself king. He entered Cabool in triumph, in 1803.

be made for his inexperience in the art of Govt., and for his placing too much confidence in his minister (Akram Khan). Even at that time, during the absence of Akram Khan, he took the field in person; and his two several attempts to recover his throne, evince much energy of character.

I have endeavoured to continue the state of affairs since 1809, to explain the state of anarchy and misrule in Affghanistan for the 30 years preceding the Shah's restoration. I have only given, in an abstract form, as much of the Dooranee dynasty of the former period, as was necessary to give a connected series of events for 92 years, the whole period of its duration; for *Barukzyes* being Dooranees as well as the *Suddozyes*, the rule of the former, though an usurpation, is embraced in the history of its dynasty. I trust that, with the rising generation, the Shah's kingdom will continue to prosper; it must be the work of time; the old leaven of faction must die away, and " *good measures and men,*" must take the places of misrule, ambition and habits of plunder.

The chief defect in Shah Shoojah's character, is the exhibition of a certain hauteur, which is no element of greatness of mind, or even a symbol of royalty. Let him but reward his true friends, and requite the services of all, whether *Suddozye* or *Barukzye*, who by their allegiance, or by the performance of any service to the state in any civil or military office; have claims to his consideration, without partiality, or favor. (81)

---

(81) *Baber* said, Memoir, p. 155, referring to his capture of Cabool in 1504: " I always regarded and provided for those Begs and soldiers who were strangers and guests, in the first place; and in a superior manner, to the *Baberians*, and those who were of Andejan." By strangers and guests, he means to designate the Caboolees, or people of the country. They were strangers to him.

At present there are about 50 British officers employed in his service. It has been a necessary measure; though it is said to be viewed with jealousy. Those who serve a Govt. well have claims to preferment, which is a return due from the state as an act of gratitude to a

The Shah is about 60 years of age. His personal appearance is commanding. His demeanor is that of a nobleman of high birth, accompanied with much dignity, and his manners are affable. Of all the kings of the Suddozye race he is the most humane. (82)

From having found an asylum under the British Govt. for 24 years, gratitude is, I believe, his predominant feeling. The residence of a British Envoy and Minister at his court, is well calculated to give a superior tone to his Govt., and to guard His Majesty from any act, which might be likely to weaken the moral effect of the change. His restoration may be viewed both in the light of justice and policy. Those who are admirers of a *democracy*, may exclaim with *Baber* (83) in favor of *Dost Mahomed Khan*.

"*Ambition admits not of inaction;
The world is his who exerts himself.*"

Those who are in favor of *kingly* power; will hope, as I do, that *Shah Shoojah* may never experience the Emperor's picture of a king.

"*In wisdom's eye, every condition may find repose;
But royalty alone.*" (84)

---

deserving subject: and is never esteemed as a personal favor conferred: it is a reward to stimulate others to exertion, and not to please the solicitations of private individuals.

(82) Some Ghiljie chiefs are said to have been executed lately, after their surrender; if true, the Shah is not, I am convinced, to blame. As *Baber* said, "You cannot shut the mouth of an enemy."

(83) Memoirs, p. 391.

(84) I must not omit to mention his literary acquirements. During his residence at Loodianah, *Sir C. M. Wade* (the Pol. Agent, through whom he corresponded) induced the Shah to write his own "*Life and Adventures,*" in Persian. A translation was made by Lieut. *Ellis*, 23rd N. I. I hope to see the publication of this work, which is said to be written in elegant Persian. The life and adventures of the King, of which I have given a faint out-line, are interesting. We ought to take such an interest in the cause of legitimacy, as to free us from the imputation of a mere selfish policy. Our object should be to increase the prosperity and happiness of all nations, from motives of good-will to all men, and a desire to enlighten them, without doing violence to their prejudices.

CHAPTER XVIII.

TABLES OF ROUTES.

Reference to the Tables of Routes, marched by the "Army of the Indus," *from 8th Nov. 1838, to 31st Dec.* 1839.

Tables.	M.	F.	Y.
No. 1. From Kurnal to Loodianah,	124	6	0
No. 2. ,, Loodianah to Ferozpoor	81	0	0
No. 3. ,, Ferozpoor to Bhawulpoor,	229	6	40
No. 4. ,, Bhawulpoor to Rohree (Bukkur)	224	6	20
No. 5. ,, Rohree to Lower Sindh and back to Sukkur,	145	6	0
No. 6. ,, Sukkur to Candahar,	404	6	150
No. 7. ,, Candahar to Cabool,	318	0	0
No. 8. ,, Cabool to Peshawer,	193	4	30
No. 9. ,, Peshawer to Ferozpoor,	347	1	40
Total number of miles marched by Bengal column, nearly 11¼ miles per march,	2,069		60
Digression to Lower Sindh,	145		0
In the direct Route,	1,923	6	60
No. 10. ,, Route of Bombay Army from Bominacote to Dadur,	476	0	0
No. 11. ,, Ditto, from Cabool to Khelat,	494	2	0
No. 12. ,, Ditto, from Khelat to Kotree (Sindh)	173	5¼	0
Total,	1,103	7¼	0
Add from Dadur to Cabool,	551	0	0
Add from Kotree to the Sea Coast,	402	¾	0
Total march of Bombay column, miles,	2,057	0	0

So that the two columns marched nearly the same distance during the campaign, in a little more than a year.

N. B. The distance of Calcutta from Cabool is viâ Meerut and Kurnal, by the Punjab route (Nos. 8 and 9) ...... 1713 miles.
Ditto by the Bolan Pass, and Candahar, ... 2350 do.
The route from Calcutta to Candahar through the Bolan Pass is, ... 2033 do.
Ditto viâ Ferozpoor, Punjab, and Cabool, ... 2031 do.

424   *From Kurnal to Loodianah and Ferozpoor.*

TABLES OF ROUTES. (1)

No. 1.—*From Kurnal to Loodianah.*

1838.	Nos.	Stages.	M.	F.	Y.	Remarks.
Nov.						
8	1	Leelokheree,	11	0	0	Road good—plenty of water.
9	2	Thanesur,	12	4	0	Ditto do. do.
10	3	Shahabad,	14	2	0	Ditto do. Stage bungalow.
11	4	Kotkuchwa,	8	0	0	Cross the river Gumbur on leaving Shahabad.
13	5	UMBALLA,	9	4	0	A large town—plenty of supplies and water.
14	6	Rajpoor,	13	0	0	3 miles from Umballa, cross the Kuggur river 2½ feet water, bad ford for guns.
15	7	Patarsee,	8	4	0	Road good—plenty of water.
16	8	Sirhind,	9	0	0	Ditto do.
17	9	Kunhaka Seraee,	11	0	0	Ditto do.
19	10	Douraka Seraee,	14	0	0	Ditto do.
20	11	LOODIANAH,	14	0	0	Ditto do. A large town.
		Total,	124	6	0	

No. 2.—*From Loodianah to Ferozpoor.*

21	12	Ghouspoor,	10	0	0	From this to Bahuk Bodla ke Mohun ke—in the Protected Sikh states, except marches 14, 15 and 16.
22	13	Boondree,	7	0	0	
23	14	Tehara,	11	0	0	Sikh territory—Aloowalla.
24	15	Dhurumkote,	10	0	0	Ditto Kurruk Singh.
26	16	Jheerah,	15	0	0	Ditto Sher Singh.
27	17	Maleewalla,	12	0	0	Ditto.
29	18	FEROZPOOR,	16	0	0	Marched 3 miles short of it on the 28th Nov.
		Total,	81	0	0	

No. 3.—*Route from Ferozpoor to Bhawulpoor.*

Dec.						
10	19	Mumdote,	14	0	0	Road rather heavy—plenty of water.
11	20	Mohun ke,	12	3	90	Road good—do.
12	21	Bagge ke,	12	4	16	Ditto do.
13	22	Bahuk Bodla ke Mohun ke,	10	6	60	Ditto do.

(1) The road being described in the days' marches in chapters I. to XVI., the reader is referred to them for particulars.

No. 3.—Continued.

1838.	Nos.	Stages.	M.	F.	Y.	Remarks.
Dec.		*Bhawulpoor country.*				
14	23	Lukke ke,	17	0	170	Road good—plenty of water.
15	24	Tawukkul,	11	6	70	Ditto do.
17	25	Ruhmoo ke,	10	2	0	Ten kos W. across the river is Pauk Puttun.
18	26	Chukko ke,	13	0	110	Road good—plenty of water.
19	27	Mamoo ke,	13	4	190	Ditto do.
20	28	Kasim ke.	13	5	30	Ditto do.
21	29	Mahtah Jhedoo,	13	7	130	Ditto do.
22	30	Bhadere,	14	0	120	Camp 1 mile S. of
24	31	Hussilpoor,	11	0	200	Do. ¾ mile S.
25	32	Kaem Raees ke got,	10	3	30	Do. 1¾ mile S.
26	33	Khyrpoor,	13	3	110	Do. 1¼ mile S.
27	34	Gote Noor Mahomed,	12	3	150	Do. 1 mile S. W.
28	35	Bakkeda ke Dera,	11	5	0	Do. E. of it.
29	36	BHAWULPOOR,	13	3	180	Do. the W. of the town.
		Total,	229	6	40	

No. 4.—Route from Bhawulpoor to Rohree on the Indus.

1839.						
Jan.						
1	37	Khairpoor,	13	3	16	Camp 1½ mile beyond: 18 wells.
2	38	Husseen ke Bustee,	9	1	0	Do. ½ mile beyond: water abundant.
3	39	AHMEDPOOR,	9	7	80	Do. 1 mile S. of the town, do. 40 wells.
5	40	Chuneekhan ke Gote,	15	0	90	21 wells.
6	41	Choudree,	11	4	130	45 do.
7	42	Mamoodee kundee,	12	0	0	16 do.
8	43	KHANPOOR,	17	6	140	11 do. A canal near it coming from the Indus. Camp 1½ mile from the town.
10	44	Sumabada Gote,	14	2	200	24 wells.
11	45	Noushahra kalan,	13	3	0	13 do.
12	46	Kathee ka Bustee,	14	4	0	11 do.
13	47	Sarwaee,	11	4	200	21 do.
		In Sindh.				
14	48	Subzeel ka Kote,	5	3	40	⅔rds belong to Ameers of Hyderabad, and ⅓rd to Khyrpoor. A great improvement in the country on entering Sindh. The river 20 miles of.

To Rohree on the Indus.

No. 4.—*Continued.*

1839.	Nos.	Stages.	M.	F.	Y.	Remarks.
Jan.						
15	49	Oobowrah,	10	1	100	Camp E. of it*.
17	50	Bagoodrah,	14	3	100	12 wells. The river 3 miles off.
18	51	Surhud,	8	3	0	Last half road through low jungle.
19	52	Gothee,	8	0	80	Road through low jungle.
21	53	Malodee,	11	3	80	Ditto do.
22	54	Choonga,	8	7	90	Ditto do., but country more open. A Lake N. of Camp.
23	55	Uzeezpoor,	4	4	30	Heavy sand on this march. The ghat on the Indus 5 miles distant.
24	56	ROHREE, (Bukkur,)	11	4	0	On the left bank of the Indus.
		Total,	224	6	20	

No. 5.—*Route from Rohree to Lower Sindh and back to Sukkur, in Upper Sindh.*

30	57	Mahomed Ludanee,	9	0	0	Enclosed country—cross water courses.
31	58	Beeraloo,	7	0	0	Country more open, but jungly.
Feb.						
2	59	Peer Gote,	10	2	0	Do. more open than last march—cross water-courses.
3	60	Bhara khundee,	11	4	0	Road through jungly country. Cross water-courses.
4	61	Nova Gote,	13	4	0	Ditto do. do.
5	62	Dera Mohobut,	12	4	0	1st part close country—then through an open country. Cross water courses.
6	63	Khundearee,	11	0	0	At 7 miles cross a dry nullah: move up its bed for 2 miles.
		Hence returned.				
10	64	Dera Mohobut,	12	0	0	Did not encamp on our old ground, marching back.
11	65	Nova Gote,	12	0	0	To the old ground.
12	66	Leleh ke,	10	5	0	
13	67	Peer ke Gote,	11	7	0	
14	68	Beeraloo,	9	4	0	
15	69	SUKKUR,	15	4	0	Crossed the bridge of boats to Sukkur, on the right bank.
		Total,	145	6	0	

* The Dundah Nuddee distributes the water of the Indus for irrigation.

To Dadur and Quetta. 427

No. 6.—*Route from Sukkur to Shikarpoor and Dadur through Bolan Pass to Quetta, and Candahar.*

1839.	Nos.	Stages.	M.	F.	Y.	Remarks.
Feb.						
19	70	Kaee,	14	2	0	First part bad road in rainy weather. Cross a dry nullah 3 miles from it.
20	71	SHIKARPOOR, 250 feet above level of the Sea. In Sindh.	12	0	0	
23	72	Jagan,	17	6	170	Road through a jungly country.
24	73	Janeedera,	11	7	120	Ditto do.—was deserted.
27	74	Rajhan,	11	1	70	But little water. The country from this to Noushera, a desert for 96 miles.
Mar.						
3	75	Barshore,	26	4	40	Over the desert. In Beloochistan.
4	76	Meerpoor,	14	4	30	In Beloochistan.
5	77	Ustad,	13	6	0	Do.
6	78	BHAG,	9	5	100	Do.
8	79	Myhesur,	16	1	130	Do.
9	80	Noushera,	15	6	0	Do.
10	81	DADUR, 743 feet,	7	4	0	Do. near the entrance to the Pass—but little forage between this and Shikarpoor.
		Total,	171	1	100	
11		Bolan Pass.				
16	82	Kohan Delan, 964 feet,	11	0	0	1st march in the Pass, plenty of water.
17	83	Kirta,	10	5	0	Plenty of water.
18	84	Beebee Nanee, 1,695 feet,	9	1	0	Do.
19	85	Abeegoom, 2,540 feet,	8	5	0	Do.
20	86	Sir-i-Bolan, 4,494 feet,	9	5	0	Do.
21	87	Dusht-i-Bedoulut 5,793 feet,	12	6	0	The march out of the Pass, into the valley. Want of water.
22	88	Sir-i-Ab,	15	5	0	Plenty of water (Karezees)
26	89	QUETTA, 5,637 ft.,	8	7	0	Properly *Kot*, (in the province of Shawl.) There are 3 roads hence to Candahar.
		Total,	86	2	0	
Apl.						
7	90	Kutchlak,	11	6	0	The Kutchlak Pass 7 miles from Quetta.
8	91	Hyderzye, 5,259 feet,	10	2	0	Bad nullahs to cross.
9	92	Hykulzye, 5,063 feet,	10	7	0	Cross a river.
10	93	Rt. bank of the Lora,	7	6	130	Cross the Lora river—steep [banks.

To Candahar.

No. 6.—Continued.

1839.	Nos.	Stages.	M.	F.	Y.	Remarks.
Apl. 11	94	Arumbee,	7	5	0	Road good.
12	95	Quilla Abdoolah Khan,	7	4	0	The fort 4 miles N. of Camp.
14	96	Khojuk Pass, the summit of 7,457 feet,	11	0	0	The halt in the Khojuk Pass—foot of the main ascent 6,848 feet: see Chapter V. The valley of Candahar at Chumun Chokee 5,677.
18	97	Dundee Goolaee, 4,036 feet,	14	2	110	1st part road stony—an open plain.
21	98	Quilla Futtoollah, 3,918 feet,	10	4	0	Road over undulating stony ground.
22	99	Mahel Mandah,	12	0	0	Through a pass, and thence over very stony and rocky ground.
23	100	Near the Doree river, 3,630 feet,	15	4	0	First 3 miles over undulating ground—then over good road.
24	101	Deh Hajjee,	8	4	0	The road stony, but good.
25	102	Khoosh-ab, 3,484 feet.	12	1	0	Cross dry bed of Kudany river: road good—country open.
26	103	Candahar, 3,484 feet,	7	4	0	The grand total is 1005 miles from Kurnal, but we went 145¾ down to lower Sindh, (see No. 5) out of our direct route.
		Total,	147	3	50	
		Grand Total,	1005	0	210	

No. 7.—Route from Candahar to Ghuznee and Cabool.

Jun.			M.	F.	Y.	Remarks.
27	104	Abdool Uzeez,	5	7	210	Country open, and barren.
28	105	Quilla Azeem, 3,945 feet,	9	7	40	The road good—Camp ¾ mile E. of the fort.
29	106	Quillah Akhoond, 4,418 feet,	16	3	160	Road good, rather stony. Camp 1 mile S. E. on right bank of the Turnuk river.
30	107	Shuhur-i-Suffa, 4,618 feet,	11	6	0	At 3 miles a defile. Cross water courses. Camp 1 mile E. of the fort—Turnuk river to the rear.

From Candahar towards Ghuznee.

No. 7.—Continued.

1839.	Nos.	Stages.	M.	F.	Y.	Remarks.
July 1	108	Teerundaz, 4,829 feet,	10	3	10	At 3 miles water-courses to cross—some very steep ascents. The Turnuk S. of camp.
2	109	Tool or Toot,	11	5	210	At 3 miles a defile. At 6 bed of a nullah. The Turnuk S. of camp.
3	110	Assia Hazareh,	10	2	30	Road good. Camp near the river.
4	111	Kelat-i-Ghiljie, 5,773 feet,	12	5	180	Half-way cross a nullah. Camp near the ruins of the fort, and country below it. The river 1½ mile off.
		Total,	78	6	0	
6	112	Sir-i-Usp, 5,973 feet,	10	2	0	At 3 miles a wet nullah, At 6, water-courses. At 8, another wet nullah. Camp near the river.
7	113	Nouruk, 6,136 feet,	9	3	0	Cross a broad water-course, ascents and descents—Camp near the river.
8	114	Ab-i-Tazee, 6,321 feet,	8	7	0	Cross a nullah. At 2 miles road along the brow of a hillock—cross water-courses; ascents and descents. Camp near the river.
10	115	Shuftul, 6,514 feet,	6	4	0	Cross 3 ascents and descents. Camp near to the Turnuk.
11	116	Chusma-i-Shadee, 6,668 feet,	10	4	0	Half-way cross a nullah. Camp near the river.
12	117	Punguk, 6,810 ft.,	7	0	0	At 2½ miles a nullah. At 4 miles a water-course. The river near and E. of camp.
13	118	Ghojan, 7,068 feet,	12	0	0	At 5 miles a deep ravine, and several others, bad for guns. At 7 miles a nullah (Jaffirs.) Springs of water. The river 3 or 4 miles off.
		In the Cabool country.				
14	119	Mukoor, 7,091 ft.,	12	3	0	At 10 miles 20 or 30 karezees; cross ravines. Here is the source of the Turnuk. Camp N. of the river.
16	120	Oba, 7,325 feet,	14	2	40	At 6 and 10 miles cross a dry nullah, the first with steep banks. Springs of water.

3 K

No. 7.—*Continued.*

1839.	Nos.	Stages.	M.	F.	Y.	Remarks.
July 17	121	Jumrood, (Karabaugh district,) 7,426 feet.	12	3	160	Cross ravines and dry nullahs 2 or 3 times—road heavy for guns. Half-way karezees, and some near camp.
18	122	Musheekee 7,309 feet,	8	6	120	Road heavy first 5 miles—several water-courses. Camp S. of the heights—springs of water.
19	123	Arghistan, 7,502 feet,	9	4	110	First 5 miles sandy. Water-courses. Heights in front of camp.
20	124	Nannee, 7,420 feet,	7	4	0	Road sandy, heavy and stony. At 6 miles pass between two low ranges of hills.
21	125	GHUZNEE, 7,726 feet,	11	0	0	
		Total,	150	6	0	
30	126	From Candahar, Shushgao, 8,699 feet,	229 13	4 5	28 160	Road undulating. At 8 miles a Pass, (9,000 feet.) Camp rear to the hills. A stream of water.
31	127	Huftasaya, 8,420 feet,	8	3	0	At 3 and 5 miles defiles—road much undulating. Camp rear to the hills. Streams of water.
Aug. 1	128	Hyder Khel, 7,637 feet,	10	7	180	Half-way cross a dry nullah—cross water-courses.
2	129	Shakkabad, 7,473 feet,	9	5	0	Road contracted and difficult—particularly last part. Cross the river.
4	130	Mydan, 7,747 feet,	18	3	140	Last half rather heavy, and confined. Cross a defile. The river Cabool to the rear of camp.
5	131	Moorgheera,	12	7	10	The road bad and confined. Camp, cultivation and water to the front; hills to the rear.

To and from Cabool.

No. 7.—Continued.

1839.	Nos.	Stages.	M.	F.	Y.	Remark.
Aug. 6	132	CABOOL, 6,396 feet,	14	0	0	Camp W. of Cabool—first encamped 2½ miles from it at Nannochee.
		From Ghuznee,	88	0	0	
		Do. Candahar,	318	0	0	
		Grand Total,	1530	0	0	
		Deduct for No. 5,	145	0	0	March to lower Sindh.
		From Kurnal to Cabool,	1385	0	0	

No. 8.—Route from Cabool to Peshawer.

	Nos.	Stages.	M.	F.	Y.	Remark.
Oct. 15	133	Boot Khak, 6,247 feet,	8	7	0	Cross the Laghar and Khoord Cabool rivers.
16	134	Khoord Cabool, 7,466 feet,	9	0	0	Through a pass 6 miles long. Cross the stream 23 times.
17	135	Tezeen, the Pass, 8,173; Valley, 6,488 feet,	12	7	0	The road crosses over 7 Kotils (Passes). Camp in the valley. Water from the river.
18	136	Ararent, or the Giants' tomb,	8	6	0	Road over a valley of stones. Water not good.
19	137	Rood-i-KuttaSung	4	6	0	Ascents and descents, road over stones. Cross the Bareekab 5,313 feet.
20	138	Jugduluk, 5,375 feet,	7	4	120	A contracted Pass for 3½ miles, crossing the stream often.
21	139	Soork-ab, 4,373 feet,	13	0	210	Ascents and descents. Last part very difficult road. Camp near the heights.
22	140	Sufed Sung (Gundumuk, 4,616 ft.)	9	6	0	Ascents and descents. Enter valley of Gundumuk (usual halting place.) Last 3 miles bad road.
24	141	Futehabad, 3,098 feet,	11	7	180	Valley of Neemla to the right. Ascents and descents. Cross the river Neemla. Ascents and descents (defiles.)

No. 8.—Continued.

1839	Nos.	Stages.	M.	F.	Y.	Remarks.
Oct. 25	142	Sultanpoor, 2,286 feet,	7	4	210	Road over a low flat and stony desert.
26	143	Jellalabad, 1,964 feet,	8	7	70	Road over a sandy tract. The Cabool river ¾ mile to S. of the town.
29	144	Alee Boghan, 1,911 feet,	6	6	200	First part sandy. Last 3 miles over stony road. A jungle of rushes 3 miles from camp.
30	145	Chardeh, (Bareek-ab, 1,822 feet,)	14	1	100	First part an ascent, thence enter a wide valley, where the *simoom* prevails in the hot season. At 9 miles village of Bareek-ab. Cross the Rood-i-Butter Kot.
31	146	Huzarnow, (Bassool, 1,509 feet,)	11	6	0	There are 2 roads which join at Bassool. The nearest in an E. direction, the other S. E.
Nov. 1	147	Dakka,(Lalpoora, 1,404 feet,)	9	0	0	At 6 miles the small Khyber Pass, Dakka on right. Lalpoora on the left bank of Cabool river.
2	148	Khyber Pass, Lundee Khana, 2,488 feet, Summit of Pass 3,373 feet.	8	7	160	At 1 mile from Dakka, enter the Pass.
3	149	Ali Musjid, W. 2,433 feet,	13	6	0	In the Pass, 12 miles, we encamped 1½ beyond it.
5	150	Kuddum, out of the Pass, (Jumrood, 1,670 feet,)	10	1	0	Road through and out of the Pass.
6	151	Koulsir,	7	0	0	Pass on left the fort of Futehgurh. The road sandy and stony.
7	152	Peshawer, 1,068 feet,	8	5	100	
		From Cabool.	193	4	30	

From Peshawer to Rawulpindee.

No. 9.—*Route from Peshawer to Attok, and through the Punjab to Ferozpoor.*

1839.	Nos.	Stages.	M.	F.	Y.	Remarks.
Nov. 23	153	Pubbee,	12	1	30	First part road swampy. Cross 2 bridges. At 4 miles cross a stream. A ruined pukka bridge. The Cabool river 4 or 5 miles N. W. of camp.
24	154	Noushera,	9	7	170	Camp close to the village on right bank of the Cabool river.
25	155	Akorah,	11	7	120	The road rough and stony, runs close to the Cabool river. Camp 2½ miles beyond and E. of Akorah.
26	156	Attok,	10	5	0	At 6 miles the narrow Geedur-Gullee Pass—cross the Indus over a bridge of boats (in the rainy season by ferry-boats). Camp beyond the fort.
28	157	Shumsabad,	9	6	0	First part sandy. Cross 2 beds of streams. Camp E.
29	158	Boorhan,	13	1	0	First part good. Then sandy. At 7 miles a defile. At 8 miles the river Haroo, knee-deep.
30	159	Vah,	8	0	140	At 2½ miles cross the Chumlah river, deep in some places—2 fords (the left ford best). Ravines. At 6 miles the village of Hussunabdal. Cross a wet nullah close to Vah — camp to the E.
Dec. 1	160	Janee ka Sung,	14	0	40	2 roads, the left for hackeries. The road narrow at first. Country then opens, direction E. Half-way is Kallee ka Seraee, hence road to right, through a Byr jungle. At 8 miles a pukka stone bridge. At 10 miles a stone causeway. Last 4 miles thick jungle. *Camp S. E.*
2	161	Rawul Pindee,	13	6	0	Road through jungle and difficult ravines. At 8 miles cross the Seel (or Chehul Jungee) partially dry. Cross the Leh river. Camp N. of the town.
4	162	Hoormuk,	9	0	0	Road good for 5 or 6 miles, thence bad ravines. Cross the river Sawn. Camp near Hoormuk.

No. 9.—Continued.

1839.	Nos.	Stages.	M.	F.	Y.	Remarks.
Dec. 5	163	Muneekyala,	10	1	0	Extensive ravines for 2 or 3 miles; thence country open. At 6 miles Robat ke Seraee in ruins. At 8½ miles ravines. Camp S. of the *tope* of Muneekyala.
6	164	Seraee Pukkee,	12	5	0	At 4½ miles a deep ravine. Then a village: 3 or 4 ravines. Camp E. of Seraee Pukkee. The Kasee river close to it.
7	165	Tameehak,	14	9	0	Cross the Kasee river near camp. Road along the bed of it. At 1¼ mile, a dangerous ravine; thence descends into the bed of the river—an ascent. Camp N. W. of Tameehak.
8	166	Bakerala,	9	5	40	Bad road to the river; the road through its bed. Camp E. of the village. The best water in the Punjab from a well here.
9	167	Udhurana,	8	6	0	Road along the bed of the river. Camp close to it and S. E. of the village.
10	168	RHOTAS, left bank,	8	5	20	Road along the bed of the river. First 3 miles 2 ravines. Half-way a ravine. Camp N. W. of Rhotas.
11	169	JHEELUM, on right bank of the *Jheelum*, Here commences the Punjab.	12	0	0	First 3 miles through the bed of the river; thence good road across the county. The river runs from E. to W. The town on the N. and right bank. The *ferry* opposite the town; the *ford* is nearly a mile up the river, and is a dangerous one, and deep. Crossed and Camp on left or S. bank.
14	170	Khoar,	12	2	0	The road crosses 7 or 8 beds of sand, (hill-torrents in the rains.) Half-way ascend and descend a ridge of hills. At 7 miles a large pukka well. Camp ¼ mile N. of Khoar.

No. 9.—Continued.

1839.	Nos.	Stages.	M.	F.	Y.	Remarks.
Dec. 15	171	Dheengee,	14	1	140	For 5 or 6 miles over a sandy road. Pass through a dhak jungle. Camp ¼ mile S.
16	172	Pareewala,	11	4	0	For 5 miles through a dhak jungle. A ravine 1½ mile from camp. Camp N. of some trees.
17	173	Ramnuggur, left bank of the *Chenab* river,	10	0	0	It is 8 miles to the Ghat on the right bank. Crossed and camp 2' miles N. W. of and from the town, and S. ½ mile from a clump of trees. After crossing, 1¼ mile of heavy sand.
19	174	Naeewala,	12	5	0	Road crosses a dry nullah, then sandy. Half-way is the town of Akaleegurh. Camp ½ mile S. of the village. Country open this march.
20	175	Thabool,	10	6	0	The road good and country open. Camp ½ mile S. W.
21	176	Mutta,	8	4	0	Good road over a very extensive plain. Low jungle on parts of the road. Camp N. W. a mile distant.
22	177	Mullyan,	15	1	0	Over a large plain. Camp S. W.
24	178	Dhingee,	13	7	0	Cross a wet nullah near the village. Camp S. W. of it mile.
25	179	Surrukpoor, 3 miles across the *Ravee*,	13	0	0	At 10 miles a village where we encamped. Moved and at 1½ mile crossed a wet nullah. Crossed the river Ravee; 2⅓ miles to the Ghat. There is a ferry and ford; the latter good. Camp on the left bank.
27	180	Gunjatee,	11	4	0	First part cross 2 dry nullahs. Half-way great expanse of plain, or desert; low jungle. A cross road half-way to Lahore. Camp ¼ mile E.
28	181	Sullianee,	13	7	0	Half-way village of Ahphur. A cross road hence to Lahore. At 10 miles Nuddeepoor. Camp ¼ mile W. of the village.

From the Sea coast through Sindh.

No. 9.—Continued.

1839	Nos.	Stages.	M.	F.	Y.	Remarks.
Dec. 29	182	Kussor,	10	0	0	First half of road jungly. Camp E. close to the town.
30	183	Left bank of Sutluj,	10	6	0	Road first part over the ruins of Kussoor. 9½ miles to the right bank; cross the river to left bank. Camp 1½ mile from the Ghat, and 5 miles from Ferozpoor.
		From Peshawer,	347	1	40	
		From Cabool,	540	5	70	

No. 10.—Route of the Bombay Army from Bominakote to Dadur.

1838.					
Dec. 24		Bominakote,			A small village 2 miles from Vikkur and Gorabaree.
	1	Julalkote,	9	1	A small village, crossed the river on Pontoons.
25	2	Somanakote,	7	7	Moderate village, fine Tope of trees.
26	3	Goolamshaw,	18	4	A large village on N. B. of Bugaur river: crossed the Bugaur branch of the Indus.
28	4	Tattah,	11	4	Camp on S. W. of the city.
1839. Jan. 23	5	Shaik Radaw Peer,	9	2	No village, 2 large tanks, and Peer on small hills.
24	6	Soonda,	13	3	A large village, 2 miles from the Indus.
25	7	Jirrikh,	9	5	Ditto do. on bank of the river.
Feb. 3	8	Mozauwur,	9	2	Camp on do. do.
4	9	Kotree, near Hyderabad,	13	6	A large village on do. do.
10	10	Bada,	9	2⅚	A village do. do.
11	11	Oonderpoor,	11	3½	A large do. do.
12	12	Kassye and Gopang,	11	1	2 villages do. do.
13	13	Majinda,	10	0	A large town on a creek 1½ mile from the main river.
14	14	Sun, or, Sen,	12	1	A large place, ½ mile from the river.
15	15	Amree,	10	7½	A small village on bank of the river.
16	16	Lukkee, (a Pass,)	11	1	A large village, and fine sheet of water.

Viâ Larkhana to Dadur.

No. 10.—Continued.

1839.	Nos.	Stages.	M.	F.	Remarks.
Feb. 21	17	Sewun,	13	1	A large town. Arrul and branch of the Indus rivers, cross.
23	18	Terooty and Bullalpoor,	8	1	One mile apart, both small villages. An extensive lake.
24	19	Bombia Jullow,	9	4	A moderate village, 1½ mile from the river.
	20	Moondra,	11	3	A large town, wells, and standing water.
25	21	Rookun,	6	7	A large village on the bank of the river.
26	22	Gulloo,	10	2	A moderate village, a small lake.
27	23	Nowadera,	15	6½	Camp 1½ mile on left of the village—bank on the Indus.
28	24	Chunna,	6	2	A moderate village, on a branch of the river.
Mar. 1	25	Futehpoor,	7	0	A large village, and fine sheet of water.
2	26	Bukranee,	15	6	A moderate village near the Narrah river.
3	27	Larkhana,	9	7	A large town, and Larkhana river now dry. (The Maiee river not fordable on the 26th and 27th Jan.)
12	28	Kumber,	15	1½	A large town with good wells.
13	29	Dost Ali,	9	7½	A moderate village where Kafilahs assemble going N.
14	30	Shudautpoor,	15	4	Do. near the Runn, or desert—lately deserted.
16	31	Keechee,	30	0	Cross the Cutch Gundava desert. A village near the hills.
18	32	Jhull,	19	1	A large town, the principal one of the Moongassee Belooches, and fine streams of water.
20	33	Punjook,	13	5½	Do. village of the Moongassee Belooches.
21	34	Gundava,	11	3½	A large town do. do.
31	35	Gugur,	5	3½	Do. village do. do.
Apl. 1	36	Shoorun,	14	3	A moderate village, but the principal one of the Rind Belooches.
2	37	Sooner,	23	3½	A small village—cross a perfect desert.
3	38	Noushera,	18	1	A large place, with a good Bazar.
5	39	Dadur,	7	4	A large town, the principal of the district.
		Total miles,	476	0	

3 L

No. 11.—*Route of the Bombay Column from Cabool viâ Ghuznee, and Quetta (leaving Candahar to the right) to Kelat.*

1839.	Nos.	Stages.	M.	F.	Remarks.
Sep. 18	1	Urghundee,	14	4	(Reckoned from 2½ miles E. of Cabool.) Several killahs, and a good stream on the right of the road.
19	2	Mydan,	12	4	An extensive cultivated valley, with many killahs, and a fine river.
20	3	Benee Badam,	7	4	4 killahs on right, and a small stream of water.
21	4	Shakabad,	11	3	A large place, fine river, and cultivated valley.
23	5	Hyder-khel,	7	5½	1 killah, on left, and 1 killah and river 1 mile on right.
24	6	Tukea,	6	4	Several populous killahs, much cultivated ground, and good stream of water.
25	7	Shushgao,	13	5	6 killahs on right, aqueduct of water, and considerable cultivated ground.
26	8	GHUZNEE,	14	4	A fortress, important bazar, fine river, and many populous killahs, and villages.
29	9	Siriwana,	6	4	Several killahs, fine cultivated plain, and aqueduct of water.
30	10	Nanee,	7	0	The town 1½ mile on left, a small river with good stream crosses the road from the hills on right; the plain on left highly cultivated.
Oct. 1	11	Mooshakee, *(Road turns off from the Candahar road.)*	12	4	Several populous killahs and villages in a cultivated plain. The road runs to the left of the *Candahar road* from this.
2	12	Bushkee,	10	2	Several populous killahs, cultivated plains, and streams of water.
4	13	Ootuk,	10	0	A large killah, some villages near, and aqueduct of water.
5	14	Mookoor, (Road entirely diverges from the Candahar road.)	13	3	Many killahs and villages in an extensive cultivated plain, the road diverges to the left, here, entirely from the *Candahar road*, and the valley of the *Turnuk river*.
6	15	Tajh	12	2	A killah and village 2½ miles from the road on right, and aqueduct of water.

No. 11.—*Continued.*

1839.	Nos.	Stages.	M.	F.	Remarks.
Oct.					
7	16	Munsoor Karez,	12	5	3 small villages on the banks of the Abistada lake which is salt, and some aqueducts of water.
8	17	Bara-khel,	13	2½	Several large villages in the cultivated plain, and aqueduct of water.
10	18	Jumaet,	11	0	2 or 3 small villages in the same plain, and aqueduct of water.
12	19	Kishainee,	8	0	A small village in the same plain, and small stream of water.
13	20	Ghoondan,	11	0½	An aqueduct stream, and some cultivated ground at Ghoondan mountain, several villages 3 or 4 miles to the right, the road across a low range of hills very difficult for guns.
15	21	Moossu-khel,	10	0	3 small villages, and small stream of water, the road crosses another low range of hills.
16	22	Speenwarree,	11	5½	A mound (ruins of a city) near a river in a cultivated valley : the inhabitants encamp generally in the hills.
18	23	Soorkh-ab,	10	2	A few huts on the banks of the river Soorkh-ab, which winds through a range of hills; road difficult for guns.
19	24	Sir-i-Soorkh-ab.	10	0½	A few huts and places of native encampment near the bed of the Soorkh-ab river, the road winding by the river bed through the same range of hills, laborious and difficult for guns.
20	25	Khoodoo Chumun,	13	3½	Some cultivated ground (the natives encamp) on the banks of a small river ; at the foot of another range of hills, the road reaches the summit of the Soorkh-ab range half-way ; then descending, crosses an undulating valley, in general very difficult for guns.
21	26	Kudinee,	7	6	A few huts on the bank of a small river, the road winding by the river bed, and crosses another range of hills, also difficult for guns.
22	7	Koturrik,	11	0½	A few huts and places of native encampment on the banks of the Koturrik river, the road crosses another range of hills, mid-way

No. 11.—*Continued.*

1839.	Nos.	Stages.	M.	F.	Remarks.
Oct.					ascent and descent, rugged, stony, and very difficult for guns.
24	28	Cutch Toba,	12	3	Some huts and several places of native encampment, and cultivated ground on the banks of a small river. The road winds by the river bed, through a very hilly country, nearly all the way.
25	29	TOBA, See the MAP and direction leaving *Candahar* to right.	7	3	Camp 2½ miles W. of Toba killah, at a few huts, and small stream of water. The killah, the residence of *Hajee Khan, Kakur's* family; the road winds through another range of hills.
26	30	Shahur Gullaee,	12	6	Several small villages on the banks of a small river, in a very hilly country. The road winding over another range of hills, stony, rugged, and very difficult for guns.
27	31	Burshahra,	8	2	5 or 6 killahs, and several small villages along the Burshara river. The road along the river bed, nearly all the way.
28	32	Soorkh-ab Paunde Khan Killah,	16	4	A large killah, open village, and aqueduct of water; at 7 miles the road, which winds through the hills by the river bed, reaches the extensive, and cultivated plains of *Pisheen*.
29	33	Hyderzye,	14	2	2 large villages. River and cultivated plains.
30	34	Kuchlak,	9	4	Several villages and killahs, cultivated plains, and fine streams of water.
31	35	QUETTA (or Kot) in province of SHAWL,	10	4	Several villages and killahs, cultivated plains and fine streams of water.
					N. B. By this Route the Bombay Column saved 85 miles of march to Quetta. The Bengal Column made 43 marches from *Quetta* to *Cabool*.
Nov. 3	36	Ispunglee,	5	4	A large village, and aqueduct of water.

To Kelat. 441

No. 11.—Continued.

1839.	Nos.	Stages.	M.	F.	Remarks.
Nov.					
4	37	Burg Karez,	7	8	An aqueduct of water, 4 or 5 small villages at 2 or 3 miles distant on right, towards the hills.
5	38	Kanuk Karez,	12	6	An aqueduct of water, some huts, much cultivated ground; the village of Kanuk 2½ miles on S. W.
6	39	MOOSTOONG,	15	2	A large walled-town, many villages near, in an extensive cultivated plain.
8	40	Sheereen-ab,	11	6	The bank of Sheereen-ab river, a small but good stream, no village near.
9	41	Dost Mahomed Karez,	9	3½	A small village, and aqueduct of water.
10	42	Zirid,	12	2	About 8 small villages and aqueduct of water, in an extensive cultivated valley.
11	43	Burem Chinao,	9	4½	An aqueduct stream and much cultivated ground, in an extensive plain, 2 or 3 small villages from 2 to 3 miles distant.
12	44	Guranee,	17	7	A small village and aqueduct stream; about 2 miles short of the large villages of Zyarut, there was no water on the road from Burem Chinao.
13	45	KELAT,	8	2	A strong fortress and lofty citadel, a considerable town, outside, on the right; and another on the left, with many villages, in a cultivated valley.
		Miles from Cabool to Kelat,	494	2	By this route the Bombay Column saved 85 miles of march to Quetta.

No. 12.—*Route of Bombay Column from Kelat to Kotree in Sindh (viâ the Moollah Pass) 7 miles from Gundava.*

		In Kelat territory.			
Nov.	46	Rodenjo,	14	7	A village of about 50 houses, and a fine stream of water.
	47	Soorma Singh,	12	0	Name of a river, 1 mile W. of the halting place.
	48	Sohrab,	16	3	A collection of several villages; wate in streams from the hills.

No. 12.—*Continued.*

1839.	Nos.	Stages.	M.	F.	Remarks.
Nov.	49	Anjeera,	14	1	3 or 4 houses, and a stream of water. The *Sonmeanee* road runs off to the right from this.
	50	Bapow,	11	6¾	A moderate village, 1 mile to the N. of the road. The road runs along the bed of the Moollah river, which runs through the Pass, water in pools.
	51	Pesee Bent, (the Moollah Pass,)	12	5	No village, but means an opening in the valley. At 10½ miles the hills on each side, suddenly closed and approached to within 20 or 30 feet, and at least 500 feet high, almost perpendicular.
	52	Putkee,	11	7	No village, but at 7 miles the deserted village of Mordana. Crossed the river several times, which has now a good stream running; with a good deal of Tamarisk jungle.
	53	Paeesht Khana, (Out of the Kelat territory.)	10	4	No village near. The first 5 miles very tedious, having to cross the river several times, and is very stony. The hills from this opened into a large plain, with better road. The river meets another stream from the N. from Pandarang.
	54	Nurd,	11	6	At 3 miles pass Peer Luttoo, a Fakeer's tomb. Cross the river several times in the first part of the march. Another stream joins in from the right, by which a road comes in from Khozdar by Guzgooroo and Zehree. A few huts; some supplies were brought in here.
Dec.	55	Jungi-kooshta,	12	2	From Bapow to Nurd the direction was S. E. when it changed to N. E., with considerable descent. At 6½ miles pass the tomb of Sokka, the adopted son of Shah Bhaz.
	56	Bent-i-Jah,	10	4	At 7 miles pass the village of Katachee. The road good leaving the river to the right. A village here and some supplies.

No. 12.—Continued.

1839.	Nos.	Stages.	M.	F.	Remarks.
Dec.	57	Camp 1½ mile short of Kohow,	11	2½	The valley is very confined here. The river is left to the right the first part of the way, but is crossed several times in the last 2 miles, passing the halting-place, called Paneewan, about mid-way.
	58	Kullaz or Keelan (a Pass,)	10	2¼	The first mile of road very bad, when it ascends some elevated ground, descending into the river bed again at 6 miles, and enters the pass of Nowlung— this is a ruined village and the end of the Pass.
	59	Kotree, (See Route No. 10, march No. 34 for the route back to the sea coast.)	13	2¾	Left the river which runs E. into the plain at Keelan Pass. Peerchuttai at 6 miles, where there are some fine trees and cultivation, with a fine stream of water, or small river, which runs to Kotree. For a short distance from Peerchuttai, the road is indifferent and stony where it crosses the river. Passing half-way from Chuttai the tomb (a handsome building) of Mahomed Ettazai. Kotree is a large place, with a good bazar, principally inhabited by Hindoos from *Shikarpoor*. It is 7 miles from *Gundava*, and the 7th Camp from *Larkhana* of the (Bombay) army in its advance in March, 1839. See Route No. 10, march No. 34, then Nos. 33 to No. 1.

APPENDIX.

APPENDIX.

No. I.

Proclamation.

1. The Right Hon'ble the Govr. Genl. of India having, with the concurrence of the Supreme Council, directed the assemblage of a British force for service across the Indus, His Lordship deems it proper to publish the following exposition of the reasons which have led to this important measure.

2. It is a matter of notoriety that the treaties entered into by the British Govt. in the year 1832, with the Ameers of Sinde, the Nawab of Bahawulpore, and Maha Rajah Runjeet Singh, had for their object, by opening the navigation of the Indus, to facilitate the extension of commerce, and to gain for the British Nation, in Central Asia, that legitimate influence which an interchange of benefits would naturally produce.

3. With a view to invite the aid of the *de facto* rulers of Afghanistan to the measures necessary for giving full effect to those Treaties, Capt. Burnes was deputed, towards the close of the year 1836, on a mission to Dost Mahomed Khan, the Chief of Cabul. The original objects of that officer's mission were purely of a commercial nature.

4. Whilst Capt. Burnes, however, was on his journey to Cabul, information was received by the Govr. Genl. that the troops of Dost Mahomed Khan had made a sudden and unprovoked attack on those of our ancient Ally, Maha Rajah Runjeet Singh. It was naturally to be apprehended that His Highness the Maha Rajah would not be slow to avenge this aggression; and it was to be feared that the flames of war being once kindled in the very regions into which we were endeavouring to extend our commerce, the peaceful and beneficial purposes of the British Govt. would be altogether frustrated. In order to avert a result so calamitous, the Govr. Genl. resolved on authorizing Capt. Burnes to intimate to

Dost Mahomed Khan that, if he should evince a disposition to come to just and reasonable terms with the Maha Rajah, His Lordship would exert his good offices with His Highness for the restoration of an amicable understanding between the two powers. The Maha Rajah, with the characteristic confidence which he has uniformly placed in the faith and friendship of the British nation, at once assented to the proposition of the Govr. Genl. to the effect that, in the meantime, hostilities on his part should be suspended.

5. It subsequently came to the knowledge of the Govr. Genl., that a Persian Army was besieging Herat; that intrigues were actively prosecuted throughout Afghanistan, for the purpose of extending Persian influence and authority to the banks of, and even beyond, the Indus; and that the Court of Persia had not only commenced a course of injury and insult to the officers of Her Majesty's mission in the Persian territory, but had afforded evidence of being engaged in designs wholly at variance with the principles and objects of its alliance with Great Britain.

6. After much time spent by Capt. Burnes in fruitless negotiation at Cabul, it appeared, that Dost Mahomed Khan, chiefly in consequence of his reliance upon Persian encouragement and assistance, persisted, as respected his misunderstanding with the Sikhs, in using the most unreasonable pretensions, such as the Govr. Genl. could not, consistently with justice and his regard for the friendship of Maha Rajah Runjeet Singh, be the channel of submitting to the consideration of His Highness; that he avowed schemes of aggrandizement and ambition, injurious to the security and peace of the frontiers of India; and that he openly threatened, in furtherance of those schemes, to call in every foreign aid which he could command. Ultimately he gave his undisguised support to the Persian designs in Afghanistan, of the unfriendly and injurious character of which, as concerned the British power in India, he was well apprized, and by his utter disregard of the views and interests of the British Govt., compelled Capt. Burnes to leave Cabul without having effected any of the objects of his mission.

7. It was now evident that no further interference could be exercised by the British. Govt. to bring about a good understanding between the Sikh Ruler and Dost Mahomed Khan, and the hostile policy of the latter Chief showed too plainly that, so long as Cabul remained under his Govt., we could never hope that the tranquillity of our neighbourhood would be secured, or that the interests of our Indian Empire would be preserved inviolate.

Appendix.

8. The Govr. Genl. deems it in this place necessary to revert to the siege of Herat, and the conduct of the Persian nation. The siege of that city has now been carried on by the Persian Army for many months. The attack upon it was a most unjustifiable and cruel aggression, perpetrated and continued, notwithstanding the solemn and repeated remonstrances of the British Envoy at the Court of Persia, and after every just and becoming offer of accommodation had been made and rejected. The besieged have behaved with gallantry and fortitude worthy of the justice of their cause, and the Govr. Genl. would yet indulge the hope that their heroism may enable them to maintain a successful defence, until succours shall reach them from British India. In the meantime, the ulterior designs of Persia, affecting the interests of the British Govt., have been, by a succession of events, more and more openly manifested. The Govr. Genl. has recently ascertained by an official despatch from Mr. McNeill, Her Majesty's Envoy, that His Excellency has been compelled, by the refusal of his just demands, and by a systematic course of disrespect adopted towards him by the Persian Govt., to quit the Court of the Shah, and to make a public declaration of the cessation of all intercourse between the two Govts. The necessity under which Great Britain is placed, of regarding the present advance of the Persian Arms into Afghanistan as an act of hostility towards herself, has also been officially communicated to the Shah, under the express order of Her Majesty's Govt.

9. The Chiefs of Candahar (brothers of Dost Mahomed Khan of Cabul) have avowed their adherence to the Persian Policy, with the same full knowledge of its opposition to the rights and interests of the British Nation in India, and have been openly assisting in the operations against Herat.

10. In the crisis of affairs consequent upon the retirement of our Envoy from Cabul, the Govr. Genl. felt the importance of taking immediate measures, for arresting the rapid progress of foreign intrigue and aggression towards our own territories.

11. His attention was naturally drawn at this conjuncture to the position and claims of Shah Soojah-ool-Moolk, a monarch who, when in power, had cordially acceded to the measures of united resistance to external enmity, which were at that time judged necessary by the British Govt., and who, on his empire being usurped by its present Rulers, had found an honorable asylum in the British Dominions.

Appendix.

12. It had been clearly ascertained, from the information furnished by the various officers who have visited Afghanistan, that the Barukzye Chief, from their disunion and unpopularity, were ill fitted, under any circumstances, to be useful Allies to the British Govt., and to aid us in our just and necessary measures of national defence. Yet so long as they refrained from proceedings injurious to our interest and security, the British Govt. acknowledged and respected their authority. But a different policy appeared to be now more than justified by the conduct of those chiefs, and to be indispensible to our own safety. The welfare of our possessions in the East requires that we should have on our Western Frontier, an ally who is interested in resisting aggression, and establishing tranquillity, in the place of chiefs ranging themselves in subservience to a hostile power, and seeking to promote schemes of conquest and aggrandizement.

13. After a serious and mature deliberation, the Govr. Genl. was satisfied that a pressing necessity, as well as every consideration of policy and justice, warranted us in espousing the cause of Shah Soojah-ool-Moolk, whose popularity throughout Afghanistan had been proved to His Lordship by the strong and unanimous testimony of the best authorities. Having arrived at this determination, the Govr. Genl. was further of opinion, that it was just and proper, no less from the position of Maha Rajah Runjeet Singh, than from his undeviating friendship towards the British Government, that His Highness should have the offer of becoming a party to the contemplated operations. Mr. Macnaghten was accordingly deputed in June last to the Court of His Highness, and the result of his mission has been the conclusion of a Tripartite Treaty by the British Government, the Maha Rajah, and Shah Soojah-ool-Moolk, whereby His Highness is guaranteed in his present possessions, and has bound himself to co-operate for the restoration of the Shah to the throne of his ancestors. The friends and enemies of any one of the contracting parties, have been declared to be the friends and enemies of all. Various points have been adjusted, which had been the subjects of discussion between the British Govt. and His Highness the Maha Rajah, the identity of whose interests with those of the Hon'ble Company, has now been made apparent to all the surrounding states. A guaranteed independence will, upon favourable conditions, be tendered to the Ameers of Sinde; and the integrity of

Herat, in the possession of its present ruler, will be fully respected; while by the measures completed, or in progress, it may reasonably be hoped that the general freedom and security of commerce will be promoted; that the name and just influence of the British Govt. will gain their proper footing among the natives of Central Asia, that tranquillity will be established upon the most important frontier of India; and that a lasting barrier will be raised against intrigue and encroachment.

14. His Majesty Shah Soojah-ool-Moolk, will enter Afghanistan surrounded by his own troops, and will be supported against foreign interference, and factious opposition, by a British Army. The Govr. Genl. confidently hopes that the Shah will be speedily replaced on his throne by his own subjects and adherents, and when once he shall be secured in power, and the independence and integrity of Afghanistan established, the British Army will be withdrawn. The Govr. Genl. has been led to these measures, by the duty which is imposed upon him of providing for the security of the possessions of the British crown; but he rejoices that, in the discharge of this duty, he will be enabled to assist in restoring the union and prosperity of the Afghan people. Throughout the approaching operations, British influence will be sedulously employed to further every measure of general benefit; to reconcile differences; to secure oblivion of injuries; and to put an end to the distractions by which, for so many years, the welfare and happiness of the Afghans have been impaired. Even to the Chiefs, whose hostile proceedings have given just cause of offence to the British Govt., it will seek to secure liberal and honorable treatment, on their tendering early submission; and ceasing from opposition to that course of measures, which may be judged the most suitable for the general advantage of their country.

By Order of the Right Hon'ble the Govr. Genl. of India,

(Signed) W. H. MACNAGHTEN,
Secy. to the Govt. of India,
with the Govr. Genl.

NOTIFICATION.

With reference to the preceding declaration, the following appointments are made.

Mr. W. H. Macnaghten, Secretary to Govt., will assume the functions of Envoy and Minister on the part of the Government of

India at the court of Shah Soojah-ool-Moolk. Mr. Macnaghten will be assisted by the following officers.

Capt. Alexander Burnes, of the Bombay establishment, who will be employed under Mr. Macnaghten's directions as Envoy to the chief of Kelat, or other states.

Lieut. E. D'Arcy Todd, of the Bengal Artillery, to be Political Assistant and Military Secretary to the Envoy and Minister.

Lieut. Eldred Pottinger, of the Bombay Artillery; Lieut. R. Leech, of the Bombay Engineers; Mr. P. B. Lord, of the Bombay Medical Establishment, to be Political Assistants to do. do.

Lieut. E. B. Conolly, of the 6th Regt. Bengal Cavalry, to command the Escort of the Envoy and Minister, and to be Military Assistant to do. do.

Mr. G. J. Berwick of the Bengal Medical Establishment, to be Surgeon to do. do.

(Signed) W. H. MACNAGHTEN,
Secy. to the Govt. of India,
Oct. 1st, 1838. *with the Govr. Genl.*

No. II.

To T. H. Maddock, Esq. Offg. Secy. to the Govt. of India, with the Govr. Genl. (1)

SIR,

In my letter to your address of the 12th instant, I ventured to record an opinion to the effect, that the lapse of a few days would suffice to show the high estimation in which H. M. Shah Soojah-ool-Moolk is held by his countrymen, as well as the wisdom of the policy pursued by the British Govt., throughout the whole of the proceedings in which we are now engaged.

2. Yesterday the Shah, with his disciplined troops, made a march of 22 miles to Deh Hadjee, where we had the satisfaction of learning that the Sirdars were about to decamp. We have since ascertained that they actually set out about 3 o'clock yesterday evening, attended by about 200 followers. Their conduct to the last was marked by meanness and rapacity. Whilst with one hand they were selling their stores of grain to the merchants of the city, they

(1) Political Dept. (Simla.)

Appendix.

were practising every species of extortion and violence towards the peaceable inhabitants, and they departed amidst the execrations of all classes.

3. This morning we marched upon Candahar, a distance of about 18 miles, and we are now encamped within 2 miles of the city. The spectacle which presented itself to us on the road, was the most interesting one it ever fell to my lot to witness. H. E. Lt.-Genl. Sir J. Keane, with the army of the Indus, was one march in our rear, our advance having been made on an erroneous calculation of the distance, which, owing to the heat of the weather, was too great to be performed by the European troops. The Shah's disciplined troops were behind us, and H. M. advanced, attended only by the officers of the Mission and his own immediate retainers. At every 100 yards of our progress, we were met by bands of well-mounted and well-armed men all tendering their allegiance to His Majesty, whilst the peaceable inhabitants of the country assembled in crowds, and manifested their joy at the Shah's restoration in the most unqualified terms.

4. Tranquillity is restored—the people flock to our Camp with the greatest confidence. There is no longer any apprehension of scarcity, and even the confidential servants of the Sirdars, several of whom have visited me, declare their satisfaction at the change of Govt., and state that they would sooner have joined the Shah, but for the dread that some evil would have been inflicted on their families, whom they must have left in the city.

5. H. M. proposed to send out a party in the hope of overtaking the fugitive Sirdars, and they certainly appear deserving of little consideration after the wickedness and folly which they have displayed, in spite of repeated and solemn warnings. It doubtless would be dangerous to allow them to remain at large and excite disturbances in the country; but I was apprehensive that in the present excited state of men's minds, they might be seized by the Shah's party, and be subjected to unnecessary cruelty; I therefore prevailed upon H. M. to permit me to make the Sirdars one more offer, which, if accepted, will enable them to retire to our territories in safety. Any provision which His Lordship the Govr. Genl. may please to assign to them will, of course, fall far short of what they would have received had they at once come into our terms; and I am of opinion that 500 Rs. (2) per mensem for each of them, would be an ample provision.

(2) £50.

6. It is my intention, therefore, to write to the Sirdars, through *Moollah Nussoo*, their confidential adviser, and I am not without hope that they will come into my terms—deserted as they are by nearly all the followers who left the city with them, and surrounded as they must be by dangers and difficulties of every description.

7. I now proceed to detail the progress of events from the date of my last communication.

8. Since the despatch of my letter to your address, dated the 12th instant, giving the substance of my communication with the Sirdars, nothing of sufficient importance occurred to require a separate report.

9. In the *Kojuk Pass*, we found a natural obstacle of a much more formidable nature than we anticipated: it was speedily surmounted by the energy of the British troops. Brigr. Arnold, who went to reconnoitre the Pass, suddenly came upon a small party detached by the Sirdars, and was fired upon; the party however made a precipitate retreat; and it was evident that the Sirdars had been surprised by the rapidity of our advance.

10. In the same Pass, letters were intercepted from the Sirdars, addressed to the authorities in *Sevee* and the eastern provinces, stating that they intended to advance and oppose us in *Pesheen*, and calling upon all true *Mahomedans* to join in a religious warfare against the invading *infidels*. We further learnt that the Sirdars were still unremitting in their endeavours to excite the same feelings of animosity, against us at *Candahar*.

11. It subsequently came to our knowledge, that *Rahim Dil Khan* and *Mehr Dil Khan*, with a number of other chiefs, and a body of between 2 and 3,000 Cavalry, had quitted *Candahar* with a view of annoying us in every possible way,—leaving Kohun Dil Khan to guard their interests in the city. The main body advanced as far as *Killa Futtoollah*, whence they detached parties to the vicinity of *Dunda-goolaee*. These parties succeeded in killing several of our followers who had incautiously strayed; and in carrying off two of my elephants which had been, against orders, taken for the purpose of procuring fodder, to a great distance from the Camp. They also put us to considerable inconvenience, for a short time, by *diverting the stream* which supplied our Camp with *water*.

12. On the morning of the 20th instant, *Hajee Khan, Kakur*, who had accompanied the Sirdars from *Candahar*, and who is decidedly the most powerful chief in these parts, reported his arrival, with about 200 horsemen, to pay his respects to the *Shah*.

He was escorted into Camp, and received with all honor both by H. M. and myself. This defection, it was obvious, would at once prove fatal to the hopes of the Sirdars.

13. On the same day, two other persons of considerable influence came in, namely, *Abdool Mujeed Khan*, the son of *Shah Pussund Khan*, Govr. of *Lash* and *Gholam Akhoondzada*, a moollah, who, I have good grounds for believing, was one of those who were most violent in stirring up the population to oppose us.

14. The secession of these individuals, and the near approach of our troops, filled the Sirdars with consternation ; and they fell back rapidly on Candahar.

15. The *ancient nobles* of the land have been nearly exterminated by the *rapacious tyranny* of the *Barukzye* usurpers ; but it was gratifying to find that the advent of the *Shah*, was cordially welcomed in every stage of his progress, by every man of respectability who has been left in the country ; and H. M.'s reception at Candahar, as above detailed, has fully justified the opinions that have been pronounced, as to his popularity with all classes of his subjects.

16. I shall report further proceedings in the course of to-morrow.

I have, &c.

(Signed) W. H. MACNAGHTEN,

Envoy and Minister.

Camp at Candahar, the 24th April, 1839.

By order of the Hon'ble the President in Council,

(Signed) H. T. PRINSEP, *Secy. to Govt.*

Political Dept. 3rd June, 1839, *(Calcutta.)*

No. III.

G. O. by H. E. Lt.-Genl. Sir. J. Keane, K. C. B. and G. C. H. Commanding the Army of the Indus.

Hd. Qrs. Camp, Candahar, 4th May, 1839.

The combined forces of Bengal and Bombay being now assembled at Candahar, the Comr.-in-Chief congratulates all ranks on the triumphant, though arduous, march which they have accomplished, from distant and distinct parts of *India*, with a regularity and discipline which is much appreciated by him, and reflects upon themselves the highest credit. The difficulties which have been surmounted have been of no ordinary nature, and the recollection of what has been overcome, must hereafter be a pleasing reflection to those concerned who have so zealously, and in so soldier-like a manner, contributed to effect them, so as to arrive at the desired end. The engineers had to make roads, and, occasionally, in some extraordinary steep mountain passes, over which no wheeled carriage had ever passed. This was a work requiring science and much severe labor; but so well has it been done, that the progress of the Army was in no manner impeded. The heavy and light ordnance were alike taken over in safety, by the exertions and good spirit of the Artillery, in which they were most cheerfully and ably assisted by the troops, both *European* and *Native*, and in a manner which gave the whole proceeding the appearance, that each man was working for a favorite object of his own.

2. H. E. shares in the satisfaction which those troops must feel (after the difficult task they have accomplished, and the trying circumstances under which they have been placed, the nature of which is well known to themselves, and therefore unnecessary for him to detail), at knowing the enthusiasm with which the population of *Candahar* have received and welcomed the return of their lawful sovereign, *Shah Shoojah-ool-Moolk*, to the throne of his ancestors in *Affghanistan*. Sir J. Keane will not fail to report to the Rt. Hon. Lord Auckland, Govr. Genl. of India, his admiration of the conduct and discipline of the troops, by which means it has been easy to effect, and to fulfil the plans of his Lordship, in the operations of the campaign hitherto.

3. The Comr.-in-Chief has already, in a G. O. dated the 6th ultimo, expressed his acknowledgment to Maj.-Genl. Sir W. Cotton for the creditable and judicious manner in which he conducted the *Bengal* column to the valley of Shawl. H. E. has now a pleasing duty to perform in requesting Maj.-Genl. Willshire, Comg. the *Bombay* column, to accept his best thanks for his successful exertions in bringing the troops of that Presidency to this ground, in the most efficient and soldier-like state.

4. The Comr.-in-Chief entertains a confident expectation, that the same orderly conduct which has gained for the troops the good-will of the inhabitants, of the states and countries through which they have passed, will continue to be observed by them during their advance upon *Cabool,* when the proper time for the

adoption of that step shall have been decided upon, by H. E. in concert with H. M. Shah Shoojah-ool-Moolk, and the Envoy and Minister, W. H. Macnaghten, Esq. representing British interests at the Court of the King of Affghanistan.

G. O. 5th May, 1839.

On the occasion of H. M. Shah Shoojah-ool-Moolk taking possession of his throne and receiving the homage of his people of *Candahar*, the following ceremonial will be observed:—

The whole of the troops now at Head Quarters will be formed in order of Review at day-light on the morning of the 8th inst. on ground which will be pointed out to Asst. Adjts. Genl. of Divisions to-morrow afternoon at 5 o'clock, by the D. Adjt. Genl. of the Bengal Army.

2. The troops will take up their ground in the following order from the right.

3. *Bengal*. Horse Artillery; Cavalry Brigade, Camel Battery; 1st Brigade of Infantry; 4th Brigade of Infantry.

Bombay. Horse Artillery; Cavalry Brigade; Infantry Brigade.

4. The 4th (Bengal) Local Horse will take up a position in front of the right flank, and the Poona Auxiliary Horse in front of the left flank, for the purpose of keeping the space in advance of the troops, clear of the populace.

5. A platform will be erected for H. M. Shah Shoojah-ool-Moolk, in front of the centre of the Line, on either flank of which detachments of H. M.'s Cavalry will take post, to prevent the intrusion of the populace.

7. The troops of H. M. Shah Shoojah will be drawn up in a street in the most convenient situation, between the gate and the British Army, and will salute H. M. as he passes. The king's Artillery will be formed near the palace, and will fire a royal salute on the departure, and return of His Majesty.

8. On His Majesty approaching the platform, a royal salute is to be fired from one of the batteries in the line; and on his appearing in front of the troops, he will be received with a *General Salute* from the whole line,—the colors being lowered in the manner that is usual to crowned heads; and as soon as the infantry have shouldered, 101 guns are to be fired from the batteries in line, under directions from Brigr. Stevenson.

9. The Envoy and Minister, and officers attached to the mission, the Comr.-in-Chief and his personal staff, and the officers at the heads of departments, and Affghan Sirdars, are to be station-

ed on the right of the throne; and Syuds and Moollahs on the left—the populace on both sides and in rear of the Shah, restrained by H. M.'s Cavalry, 4th Local Horse, and Poona Auxiliary Horse.

10. The Envoy, and the Comr.-in-Chief will present Nuzzurs,—as representatives of Govt.

11. The officers of the Shah's force will also present Nuzzurs, leaving their troops for that purpose, after the Shah has passed, and returning to receive His Majesty.

12. The Shah's subjects will then present Nuzzurs. At the close of the ceremony, the troops will march past, the cavalry in columns of squadrons,—the infantry in columns of companies, in slow time; the columns will move up to the wheeling point in quick time. The columns having passed, will continue their route towards the encampment, the 4th Brigade of Bengal Infantry moving on to the Cabool gateway, at which His Majesty will enter the city, where it will form a street, and salute His Majesty as he passes.

13. The troops are to appear in white trousers, the officers of the general staff in blue trousers and gold lace.

14. Corps will parade on the occasion as strong as possible, and the encampments will be protected by the convalescents, and by Quarter and Rear guards; such extra-guards as may be considered essentially necessary, to be placed over treasure, at the discretion of Brigadiers Comg. Brigades.

15. Officers Comg. divisions are to be supplied with field states, showing the actual number of troops there are under arms in their respective commands, to be delivered when called for.

16. His Majesty having expressed a wish that H. E. the Comr.-in-Chief should be near his person during the ceremony, Maj.-Genl. Sir W. Cotton will command the troops in line.

***

G. O. 8th May, 1839.

Lieut.-Genl. Sir J. Keane has received the gracious commands of H. M. Shah Shoojah-ool-Moolk, to convey to Major-Genl. Willshire, Comg. in the field, (3) to the Generals and other officers, and the N. C. O. and soldiers who were present and assisted at the splendid spectacle of the king taking possession of his throne this day, the deep sense His Majesty entertains of the obligations he owes to them, and to the British nation. The king added, that he would request W. H. Macnaghten, Esq., Envoy and Minister at

(3) Sir W. Cotton was sick.

H. M.'s Court, to convey these his sentiments, to the Rt. Hon. Lord Auckland, Govr. Genl. of India.

No. IV.

Fort William, 6th Sept. 1839, Political Dept.—The Hon'ble the President in Council has much satisfaction in publishing, for general information, the following official papers received, by express, from the Head Qrs. of the Rt. Hon. the Govr. Genl., announcing the desertion of Dost Mahomed Khan by his Army on the 3rd August, and the possession obtained, in consequence, of all his guns; also the subsequent advance of the Army under H. E. Sir J. Keane to Cabool, which city was entered in triumph by H. M. Shah Shoojah-ool-Moolk on the 7th ultimo. (4)

A Royal salute will be fired from the Ramparts of Fort William in honor of this important event; and a *feu de joie* will be fired in the afternoon, upon the occasion of the intelligence being communicated to the troops in garrison.

By order of the Hon'ble the President in Council,
(Signed) H. T. PRINSEP,
Secy. to the Govt. of India.

NOTIFICATION.

Secret Dept. Simla, 26th August, 1839.—The Govr. Genl. of India publishes for general information, the subjoined copy and extracts of despatches from H. E. the Comr.-in-Chief of the Army of the Indus, and from the Envoy and Minister at the Court of H. M. Shah Shoojah-ool-Moolk, announcing the triumphant entry of the Shah into Cabool on the 7th instant.

In issuing this notification, the Govr. Genl. cannot omit the opportunity of offering to the officers and men composing the Army of the Indus, and to the distinguished leader by whom they have been commanded, the cordial congratulations of the Govt. upon the happy result of a compaign, which, on the sole occasion

---

(4) The last time he entered in triumph was on the 13th July, 1803.

when resistance was opposed to them, has been gloriously marked by victory, and in all the many difficulties of which, the character of a British Army for gallantry, good conduct and discipline has been nobly maintained.

A salute of 21 guns will be fired on the receipt of this intelligence at all the principal stations of the Army in the 3 Presidencies.

By order of the Rt. Hon'ble the Govr. Genl. of India,
(Signed) T. H. MADDOCK,
Offg. Secy. to the Govt. of India,
with the Govr. Genl.

(True copy,)
(Signed) H. T. PRINSEP, *Secy. to Govt.*

(Copy.)
To the Rt. Hon'ble Lord Auckland, G. C. B.

MY LORD,

We have the honor to acquaint your Lordship, that the Army marched from *Ghuznee* on route to Cabool, in two columns, on the 30th and 31st ultimo, H. M. Shah Shoojah-ool-Moolk, with his own troops, forming part of the second column.

2. On the arrival of the Comr.-in-Chief with the 1st column at Hyder Khail, (5) on the 1st instant, information reached him, and the same reached the Envoy and Minister at Huftasaya, (6) that Dost Mahomed with his Army and Artillery were advancing from Cabool, and would probably take up a position at *Urghundee* or *Midan* (the former 24, the latter 36 miles from Cabool). Upon this, it was arranged that His Majesty, with the second column, under Maj.-Genl. *Willshire,* should join the 1st column here and advance together, to attack Dost Mahomed, whose son, Mahomed, Akbar had been recalled from Jellalabad, with the troops guarding the Khyber Pass, and had formed a junction with his father; their joint forces, according to our information, amounting to about 13,000 men.

3. Every arrangement was made for the king and the army marching in a body from hence to-morrow, but in the course of the night messengers arrived, and since (this morning) a great many chiefs, and their followers, announcing the dissolution of Dost

(5) Four marches from Cabool.
(6) Five marches from Cabool.

Mahomed's army by the refusal of the greater part to advance against us with him, and that he had, in consequence, fled with a party of 300 horsemen, (7) in the direction of *Bameean;* leaving his guns behind him; in position as they were placed at *Urghundee.*

4. H. M. Shah Shoojah has sent forward a confidential officer, with whom has been associated Major *Cureton,* of H. M.'s 16th Lancers, taking with him a party of 200 men and an officer of Artillery, to proceed direct to take possession of those guns, and afterwards such other guns, and public stores, as may be found in Cabool and the Bala Hissar, in the name of, and for H. M. Shah Shoojah-ool-Moolk; and the king's orders will be carried by his own officer with this party, for preserving the tranquillity of the city of Cabool.

5. A strong party has been detached in pursuit of Dost Mahomed under some of our most active officers. We continue our march upon Cabool, to-morrow, and will reach it on the 3rd day.

We have, &c.

(Signed) JOHN KEANE,
Lt.-Genl. Comr.-in-Chief.
W. H. MACHAGHTEN,
Envoy and Minister.

Extract from a Letter from H. E. Lt.-Genl. Sir J. Keane, K. C. B. and G. C. H. dated Hd. Qrs., Camp Cabool, 8th August, 1839.

It gives me infinite pleasure to be able to address my despatch to your Lordship from this capital, the vicinity of which, H. M. Shah Shoojah-ool-Moolk, and the Army under my command, reached the day before yesterday. The king entered his capital yesterday afternoon, accompanied by the British Envoy and Minister, and the gentlemen of the mission, and by myself, the generals and staff officers of this army, and escorted by a squadron of H. M.'s 4th L. D. and one of H. M.'s 16th Lancers, with Capt. Martin's troop of Horse Artillery. H. M. had expressed a wish that British troops should be present on the occasion, and a very small party only of his own Hindoostanee and Afghan troops. After the animating scene of traversing the streets, and reaching the Palace in the Bala Hissar, a Royal salute was fired, and an additional Salvo, in the Afghan style, from small guns resembling wall-pieces, named Jinjals,

(7) Major Outram makes them much more.

c

and carried on camels. We heartily congratulated His Majesty on being in possession of the throne and kingdom of his ancestors; and after taking leave of His Majesty, we returned to our camp.

I trust we have thus accomplished all the objects which your Lordship had in contemplation, when you planned and formed the Army of the Indus, and the expedition into Afghanistan.

The conduct of the army, both European and Native, which your Lordship did me the honor to place under my orders, has been admirable throughout, and, notwithstanding the severe marching and privations they have gone through, their appearance and discipline have suffered nothing; and the opportunity offered them at *Ghuznee* of meeting and conquering their enemy, had added greatly to their good spirits.

The joint despatch addressed by Mr. Macnaghten and myself to your Lordship on the 3rd instant, from Shakkabad, (8) will have informed you, that at the moment we had made every preparation to attack (on the following day) Dost Mahomed in his position at Urghundee, where, after his son Mahomed Akbar had joined him from Jellalabad, he had an army amounting to 13,000 men, well armed and appointed, and 30 pieces of Artillery, (9) we suddenly learnt that he abandoned them all, and fled with a party of horsemen on the road to *Bameean;* leaving his guns in position as he had placed them to receive our attack.

It appears that a great part of his army, which was hourly becoming disorganized, refused to stand by him in the position, to receive our attack, and that it soon became in a state of dissolution. The great bulk immediately came over to Shah Shoojah, tendering their allegiance, and I believe H. M. will take most of them into his pay.

It seems, that the news of the quick and determined manner in which we took their stronghold, *Ghuznee*, had such an effect upon the population of Cabool, and perhaps also upon the enemy's army, that Dost Mahomed, from that moment, began to lose hope of retaining his rule for even a short time longer, and sent off his family and valuable property towards *Bameean*, but marched out of Cabool with his army and artillery, keeping a bold front towards us, until the evening of the second, when all his hopes were at an end, by a division in his own camp, and one part of his army abandoning him.

(8) Three marches from Cabool.
(9) Only 25 were found.

So precipitate was his flight, that he left in position his guns with their ammunition and wagons, and the greater part of the cattle by which they were drawn. Major Cureton, of H. M.'s 16th Lancers, with his party of 200 men, pushed forward on the third, and took possession of these guns, &c. There were 23 brass guns in position and loaded, two more at a little distance, which they attempted to take away, and since then, three more abandoned still further off on the Bameean road. Thus leaving in our possession 28 pieces of cannon, with all the material belonging to them, which are now handed over to Shah Shoojah-ool-Moolk.

(True Extract)
(Signed) T. H. MADDOCK,
Offg. Secy. to Govt. of India,
with the Govr. Genl.

(True Copy)
(Signed) H. T. PRINSEP,
Secy. to the Govt.

(Copy.)

Extract from a Letter from W. H. Macnaghten, Esq. Envoy and Minister to the Court of Shah Shoojah-ool-Moolk, dated Cabool, 9th August, 1839.

By a letter signed jointly by H. E. Lieut.-Genl. Sir J. Keane and myself, dated the 3rd instant, the Right Hon'ble the Govr. Genl. was apprized of the flight of Dost Mahomed Khan.

The ex-chief was not accompanied by any person of consequence, and his followers are said to have been reduced to below the number of 100 on the day of his departure. In the progress of Shah Shoojah-ool-Moolk towards Cabool, H. M. was joined by every person of rank and influence in the country; and he made his triumphant entry into the city on the evening of the 7th instant. H. M. has taken up his residence in the *Bala Hissar*, where he has required the British Mission to remain for the present.

(True Extract)
(Signed) T. H. MADDOCK,
Offg. Secy. to Govt. of India,
with the Govr. Genl.

(True Extract)
(Signed) H. T. PRINSEP,
Secy. to Govt. of India.

Appendix.

By order of the Comr. of the Forces.

In obedience to the above notification, a salute of 21 guns, to be fired at all the principal stations of this Presidency, on receipt of this order.

(Signed) J. R. LUMLEY, *Maj.-Genl.*
Adjt.-Genl. of the Army.

No. V.

General Orders by the Commander of the Forces: Head Quarters, Meerut, 22nd Nov. 1839. *By the Right Hon'ble the Governor General, Camp Somalka, 19th Nov.* 1839.

The following General Orders, issued by the Right Hon'ble the Govr. Genl. in the Secret Department, under date the 18th instant, are published for general information to the army:

General Orders by the Right Hon'ble the Governor General of India.

Secret Department; Camp Paniput, the 18*th November,* 1839.

1. Intelligence was this day received of the arrival, within the Peshawer territory, of His Excellency Lt.-Genl. Sir John Keane, K. C. B. and G. C. H. Commander-in-Chief of the Army of the Indus, with a portion of that force on its return to the British provinces. The military operations under the direction of His Excellency having now been brought to a close, the Right Honorable the Governor General has, on the part of the Government of India, to acquit himself of the gratifying duty of offering publicly his warmest thanks to His Excellency, and to the officers and men who have served under his command, for the soldier-like spirit and conduct of all ranks throughout the late campaign, and he again cordially congratulates them on the attainment of the great objects of national security and honor, for which the expedition was undertaken.

2. The plans of aggression, by which the British empire in India was dangerously threatened, have, under Providence, been arrested. The Chiefs of *Cabool* and *Candahar*, who had joined in hostile designs against us, have been deprived of power, and the territories which they ruled have been restored to the government of a friendly monarch. The Ameers of Scinde have acknowledged the supremacy of the British Government, and ranged themselves

under its protection; their country will now be an outwork of defence, and the navigation of the Indus within their dominions, exempt from all duties, has been opened to commercial enterprise. With the allied government of the *Seikhs*, the closest harmony has been maintained; and on the side of *Herat*, the British alliance has been courted, and a good understanding, with a view to common safety, has been established with that power.

3. For these important results, the Governor General is proud to express the acknowledgments of the Government to the Army of the Indus, which alike by its valor, its discipline, and cheerfulness under hardships and privations, and its conciliatory conduct to the inhabitants of the countries through which it passed, has earned respect for the British name, and has confirmed in central Asia a just impression of British energy and resources.

4. The Native and European soldier have vied with each other in effort and endurance. A march of extraordinary length, (10) through difficult and untried countries, has been within a few months successfully accomplished; and in the capture of the one stronghold where resistance was attempted, a trophy of victory has been won, which will add a fresh lustre to the reputation of the armies of India.

5. To Lieut.-Genl. Sir John Keane, the Comr.-in-Chief of the army, the Govr. Genl. would particularly declare his thanks for his direction of these honorable achievements. He would especially acknowledge the marked forbearance, and just appreciation of the views of the Govt., which guided his Excellency in his intercourse with the Ameers of *Scinde*. He feels the Govt. to be under the deepest obligations to His Excellency, for the unshaken firmness of purpose with which throughout the whole course of the operations, obstacles and discouragements were disregarded, and the prescribed objects of policy were pursued; and above all, he would warmly applaud the decisive judgment with which the attack upon the Fortress of *Ghuznee* was planned, and its capture effected; nor would he omit to remark upon that spirit of perfect co-operation with which His Excellency gave all support to the political authorities with whom he was associated. Mr. Macnaghten, the Envoy and Minister at the Court of Shah Shoojah-ool-Moolk, and Col. Pottinger, the Resident in Scinde, have been chiefly enabled by the cordial good understanding which has throughout subsisted between them and His Excellency, to

(10) More than 1,700 miles; on arriving at Ferozpoor 2,070 miles.

render the important services by which they have entitled themselves to the high approbation of the Government: and his Lordship has much pleasure in noticing the feelings of satisfaction with which His Excellency regarded the valuable services of Lieut.-Col. Sir A. Burnes, who was politically attached to him in the advance upon *Ghuznee*.

6. The Govr. Genl. would follow His Excellency the Commander-in-Chief, in acknowledging the manner in which Maj.-Genl. Sir Willoughby Cotton, K. C. B. and K. C. H., exercised his command of the Bengal division throughout the campaign, and supported the honor of his country on the 23rd July; and His Lordship would also offer the thanks of the Government to Maj.-Genl. Willshire, C. B., commanding the 2nd Infantry division; to Maj.-Genl. Thackwell, C. B. and K. H., commanding the Cavalry division; to Brigr. Roberts, commanding the 4th Infantry brigade; to Brigr. Stevenson, commanding the artillery of the army; to Brigr. Scott, commanding the Bombay Cavalry brigade; and to Brigr. Persse, upon whom, on the lamented death of the late Brigr. Arnold, devolved the command of the Bengal Cavalry brigade; as well as to the Commandants of corps and detachments, with the officers and men under their respective commands; and to the officers at the head of the several departments with all of whom His Excellency the Commander-in-Chief has expressed his high satisfaction.

7. To Brigr. Sale, C. B. already honorably distinguished in the annals of Indian warfare, who commanded the storming party at *Ghuznee*; to Lieut.-Col. Dennie, C. B. who led the advance on the same occasion; and to Capt. George Thomson, of the Bengal Engineers, whose services in the capture of that fortress have been noticed in marked terms of commendation by his Excellency the Commander-in-Chief; and to Capt. Peat, of the Bombay Engineers, and Lieuts. Durand and Macleod, of the Bengal Engineers, and the other officers and men of the Bengal and Bombay Engineers under their command, the Governor General would especially tender the expression of his admiration of the gallantry and science which they respectively displayed, in the execution of the important duties confided to them in that memorable operation.

8. In testimony of the services of the army of the Indus, the Governor General is pleased to resolve, that all the corps, European and Native, in the service of the East India Company, which proceeded beyond the " *Bolan Pass*," shall have on their regimental colors the word " *Afghanistan*," and such of them as were employ-

ed in the reduction of the fortress of that name, the word "*Ghuznee*" in addition.

In behalf of the Queen's regiments, the Governor General will recommend to Her Majesty, through the proper channel, that the same distinction may be granted to them.

9.—The Govr. Genl. would here notice with approbation, the praiseworthy conduct, during this expedition, of the officers and men attached to the disciplined force of His Majesty Shah Shoojah-ool-Moolk. This force was newly raised, and opportunities had not been afforded for its perfect organization and instruction; but it shared honorably in the labors and difficulties of the campaign, and it had the good fortune, in repelling an attack made by the enemy in force, on the day prior to the storming of *Ghuznee*, to be enabled to give promise of the excellent service which may hereafter be expected from it.

10.—His Lordship has also much satisfaction in adding, that the best acknowledgments of the Govt. are due to Lieut.-Col. Wade who was employed upon the *Peshawer frontier*, and who, gallantly supported by the officers and men of all ranks under him, and seconded by the cordial aid of the Seikh Govt., an aid the more honorable because rendered at a painful crisis of its affairs, opened the "*Khyber Pass*," and overthrew the authority of the enemy in that quarter, at the moment when the advance of the forces of the Shah Zadah Tymoor could most conduce to the success of the general operations.

By command, &c.

(Sd.) T. H. MADDOCK,   (Sd.) J. STEWART, *Lieut.-Col.*
Offg. Secy. to Govt. of India,   *Secy. to the Govt of India Mily. Dept.*
with the Govr. Genl.   *with the Rt. Hon. the Govr. Genl.*

By order of the Comr. of the Forces,

(Signed)   J. R. LUMLEY, *Major-Genl.*
Adjt.-Genl. of the Army.

No. VI.

G. O. by the Comr. of the Forces; Head Quarters, Meerut, 12th December, 1839.

The following General Orders, issued by the Rt. Hon'ble the Govr. Genl., in the Secret Department, under date the 4th instant, are published for general information to the army:

G. O. by the Right Hon'ble the Govr. Genl. of India.

Secret Department; Camp Deothanee, the 4*th December,* 1839.

The many outrages and murders committed, in attacks on the followers of the army of the Indus, by the plundering tribes in the neighbourhood of the "*Bolan Pass,*" at the instigation of their chiefs, *Meer Mehrab Khan,* of *Kelat,* at a time when he was professing friendship for the British Government, and negociating a treaty with its representatives, having compelled the Govt. to direct a detachment of the army to proceed to Kelat, for the exaction of retribution from that chieftain, and for the execution of such arrangements as would establish future security in that quarter, a force under the orders of Maj.-Genl. *Willshire,* C. B. was employed on this service; and the Rt. Hon'ble the Govr. Genl. of India having this day received that Officer's report of the successful accomplishment of the objects entrusted to him, has been pleased to direct that the following copy of his dispatch, dated 14th ultimo, be published for general information.

The Rt. Hon'ble the Govr. Genl. is happy to avail himself of this opportunity to record his high admiration of the signal gallantry and spirit of the troops engaged on this occasion, and offers on the part of the Govt. his best thanks to Maj.-Genl. Willshire, and to the officers and men who served under him.

By command, &c.

(Signed) T. H. MADDOCK,
Offg. Secy. to Govt. of India,
with the Govr. Genl.

Despatch.

Camp near Kelat, 14*th Nov.* 1839.

To the Rt. Hon'ble Lord Auckland, G. C. B. Govr. Genl. of India, &c.

MY LORD,

1. In obedience to the joint instructions furnished me by H. E. the Comr.-in-Chief of the Army of the Indus, and Envoy and Minister to H. M. Shah Shoojah, under date Cabool, the 17th Sept. 1839, deputing to me the duty of deposing *Mehrab Khan* of *Kelat,* in consequence of the avowed hostility of that chief to the British nation during the present campaign, I have the honor to report, that on my arrival at Quetta, on the 31st ultimo, I communicated with Captain *Bean,* the Political Agent in Shawl, and arranged with him the best means of giving effect to the orders I had received.

2 Guns Bombay Horse Artillery.
4 ditto Shah's ditto.
2 Ressallahs 4th Ben. local horse.
2nd Queen's Royal
H. M. 17th Regt.
31st Bengal Native Infantry.
Bombay Engineers.

2. In conseqence of the want of public carriage and the limited quantity of Commisst. supplies at Quetta, as well as the reported want of forage on the route to Kelat, I was obliged to dispatch to *Cutch Gundava*, the whole of the cavalry and the greater portion of the Artillery, taking with me only the troops noted in the margin, leaving Quetta on the 3rd instant.

3. During the march the communications received from *Mehrab Khan* were so far from acceding to the terms offered, that he threatened resistance if the troops approached his capital. I therefore proceeded, and arrived at the village of *Giranee* within eight miles of Kelat, on the 12th instant.

4. Marching from hence the following morning a body of horse were perceived on the right of the road, which commenced firing on the advanced guard commanded by Maj. Pennycuick, H. M. 17th Regt. as the column advanced; and skirmishing between them continued until we came in sight of *Kelat*, rather less than a mile distant.

I now discovered that three heights on the N. W. face of the fort, and parallel to the north, were covered with infantry, with five guns in position, protected by small parapet walls. Capt. *Peat*, Chief Engineer, immediately reconnoitred, and having reported that nothing could be done until those heights were in our possession, I decided upon at once storming them simultaneously, and if practicable, entering the fort with the fugitives, as the gate in the northern face was occasionally opened to keep up the communication between the fort and the heights.

5. To effect this object, I detached a company from each of the European regiments, from the advanced guard with Maj. Pennycuick H. M.'s 17th Regt., for the purpose of occupying the gardens and enclosures to the N. E. of the town, and two more companies in the plain midway between them and the column; at the same time I ordered three columns of attack to be formed, composed of four Cos. from each corps under their respective commanding officers, Maj. Carruthers, of the Queen's; Lt.-Col. Croker, H. M.'s 17th Regt., and Major Weston, 31st Bengal N. I., the whole under the command of Brigr. Baumgardt, the remainder of the regiments

d

forming three columns of reserve under my own direction, to move in support.

6. A hill being allotted to each column, Brigr. Stevenson, commanding the artillery, moved quickly forward in front towards the base of the heights, and when within the required range opened fire upon the infantry and guns, under cover of which the columns moved steadily on and commenced the ascent, for the purpose of carrying the heights, exposed to the fire of the enemy's guns, which had commenced while the columns of attack were forming.

7. Before the columns reached their respective summits of the hills, the enemy, overpowered by the superior and well directed fire of our artillery, had abandoned them, attempting to carry off their guns, but which they were unable to do; at this moment it appearing to me the opportunity offered for the troops to get in with the fugitives, and if possible gain possession of the gate of the fortress, I dispatched orders to the Queen's Royal, and H. M.'s 17th Regt. to make a rush from the heights for that purpose, following myself to the summit of the nearest to observe the result; at this moment the four companies on my left, which had been detached to the garden and plain, seeing the chance that offered of entering the fort, moved rapidly forward from their respective points towards the gate-way, under a heavy and well-directed fire from the walls of the fort and citadel, which were thronged by the enemy.

8. The gate having been closed before the troops moving towards it could effect the desired object, and the garrison strengthened by the enemy driven from the heights, they were compelled to cover themselves, as far as practicable, behind some walls and ruined buildings, to the right and left of it, while Brigr. Stevenson having ascended the heights with the artillery, opened 2 guns under the command of Lt. Forster, Bombay H. A. upon the defences above the gate and its vicinity, while the fire of two others commanded by Lt. Cowper, Shah's artillery, was directed against the gate itself, the remaining 2, with Lt. Creed, being sent round to the road on the left leading direct up to the gate, and when within 200 yards commenced fire for the purpose of completing the blowing it open, and after a few rounds they succeeded in knocking in one half of it; on observing this, I rode down the hill towards the gate pointing to it, thereby announcing to the troops it was open, they instantly rose from their cover and rushed in, those under the command of Maj. Pennycuick, being the nearest, were the first to gain

Appendix. 27

the gate, headed by that officer, the whole of the storming columns from the three Regts. rapidly following and gaining an entrance as quickly as it was possible to do so, under a heavy fire from the works and from the interior, the enemy making a most gallant and determined resistance, disputing every inch of ground up to the walls of the inner citadel.

9. At this time I directed the reserve columns to be brought near the gate, and detached one company of the 17th Regt. under Capt. Darby, to the western side of the fort, followed by a portion of the 31st Bengal N. I. commanded by Maj. Weston, conducted by Capt. Outram, acting as my extra Aide-de-camp, for the purpose of securing the heights, under which the southern angle is situated, and intercepting any of the garrison escaping from that side; having driven off the enemy from the heights above, the united detachments then descended to the gate of the fort below, and forced it open before the garrison (who closed it as they saw the troops approach) had time to secure it.

10. When the party was detached by the western face, I also sent 2 companies from the reserve of the 17th under Maj. Deshon, and 2 guns of the Shah's artillery, under the command of Lt. Creed, Bombay artillery, by the eastern to the southern face, for the purpose of blowing open the gate above alluded to, had it been necessary, as well as the gate of the inner citadel; the infantry joining the other detachments, making their way through the town in the direction of the citadel.

11. After some delay, the troops that held possession of the town at length succeeded in forcing an entrance into the citadel, where a desperate resistance was made by *Mehrab Khan* at the head of his people, he himself with many of his principal chiefs being killed sword in hand; several others however kept up a fire upon our troops from detached buildings difficult of access, and it was not until late in the afternoon, those that survived were induced to give themselves up on a promise of their lives being spared.

12. From every account I have every reason to believe the garrison consisted of upwards of 2,000 fighting men, and that the son of Mehrab Khan had been expected to join him from *Nowskey* with a further reinforcement. The enclosed return will show the strength of the force under my command present at the capture.

13. The defences of the Fort, as in the case of *Ghuznee*, far exceeded in strength what I had been led to suppose from previous

d 2

report, and the towering height of the inner citadel was most formidable both in appearance and reality.

14. I lament to say, that the loss of killed and wounded on our side has been severe, as will be seen by the accompanying return; that on the part of the enemy must have been great, but the exact number I have not been able to ascertain; several hundreds of prisoners were taken, from whom the Political Agent has selected those he considers it necessary for the present to retain in confinement: the remainder have been liberated.

15. It is quite impossible for me sufficiently to express my admiration of the gallant and steady conduct of the officers and men upon this occasion; but the fact of less than an hour having elapsed from the formation of the columns for the attack, to the period of the troops being within the fort, and this performed in the open day, and in the face of an enemy so very superior in numbers, and so perfectly prepared for resistance will, I trust, convince your Lordship how deserving the officers and troops are of my warmest thanks, and of the highest praise that can be bestowed.

16. To Brigr. Baumgardt, commanding the storming columns, my best thanks are due, and he reports that Capt. Wyllie, acting A. A. G. and Capt. Gilland, his A. D. C., ably assisted him and zealously performed their duties; also to Brigr. Stevenson, commanding the artillery, and Lts. Forster and Cowper, respectively in charge of the Bombay and Shah's artillery, I feel greatly indebted for the steady and scientific manner in which the service of dislodging the enemy from the heights, and afterward effecting an entrance into the fort, was performed; the Brigr. has brought to my notice the assistance he received from Capt. Coghlan, his Brigade Major, Lt. Woosnam, his A. D. C., and Lt. Creed, when in battery yesterday.

17. To Lt.-Col. Croker, commanding H. M.'s 17th Regt., Major Carruthers, commanding Queen's Royal, Maj. Weston, commanding the Bengal 31st N. I., I feel highly indebted for the manner in which they conducted their respective columns to the attack of the heights, and afterwards to the assault of the town, as well as to Maj. Pennycuick, of the 17th, who led the advanced guard companies to the same point.

18. To Capt. Peat, Chief Engineer, and to the officers and men of the engineer corps, my acknowledgments are due; to Maj. Neil Campbell, acting Qr. Mr. Genl. of the Bombay army; to Captain Hagart, acting D. A. G; and to Lt. Ramsay, acting A. Q.

Mr. Genl., my best thanks are due, for the able assistance afforded me by their services.

19. It is with much pleasure I take this opportunity of acknowledging my obligations to Maj. Campbell, for relieving me from the necessity of returning by the route by which the army advanced to Cabool, which being entirely exhausted, must have subjected the troops to great privations, and the horses to absolute starvation. The Q. M. G. took upon himself the responsibility of leading my column through the heart of the *Ghiljie* and *Koroker* countries, never hitherto traversed by Europeans, by which our route was considerably shortened, a sufficiency obtained, and great additions made to our geographical knowledge of the country, besides great political advantages obtained in peaceably settling those districts.

20. To my Aide-de-camps, Capt. Robinson and Lt. Halket, as well as to Capt. Outram, who volunteered his services on my personal staff, I received the utmost assistance, and to the latter officer I feel greatly indebted for the zeal and ability with which he has performed various duties that I have required of him upon other occasions as well as the present.

21. It is with much satisfaction I am able to state that the utmost cordiality has existed between the political authorities and myself, and the great assistance I have derived from Capt. Bean in obtaining supplies.

22. After allowing time to make the necessary arrangements for continuing my march, I shall descend into "*Cutch Gundava*" by the "*Moona Pass*," having received a favorable report of the practicability of taking guns that way.

23. I have deputed Capt. Outram to take a duplicate of the despatch to the Hon'ble the Govr. of Bombay, by the direct route from hence to "*Soomeanee Bunder;*" the practicability or otherwise of which, for the passage of troops, I consider it an object of importance to ascertain.

I have, &c.

(Signed.)   T. WILLSHIRE, *Maj.-Genl.*
Comg. Bombay column, Army of the Indus.

Return of Casualties in the army under the command of Maj.-Genl. Wilshire, C. B., employed at the Storming of Kelat on the 13th November, 1839.

	Killed.				Wounded.										Total killed and wounded.	Horses.	
	Lieut.	Soobadars.	Rank and file	Total.	Capts.	Lieuts.	Ensigns.	Adjts.	Jemadars.	Sergts.	Drummers.	Rank and file	Regtl. Bheesties.	Total.		Killed.	Wounded.
Dett. 3rd troop of Horse Artillery,	0	0	0	0	0	0	0	0	0	0	0	0	0	0	0	0	0
1st troop of Caboul Artillery,	0	0	0	0	0	0	0	0	0	0	0	2	0	2	2	0	6
Gun Lascars attached to ditto,	0	0	0	0	0	0	0	0	0	0	0	1	0	1	1	0	0
H. M.'s 2nd or Queen's Royal Regt.	1	0	21	22	1	2	0	1	0	2	0	*40	0	47	69	0	1
H. M.'s 17th Regt.,	0	0	6	6	1	0	0	0	0	3	1	29	0	33	39	0	0
31st Bengal Native Infantry,	0	1	2	3	2	0	1	0	2	3	0	14	1	22	25	0	0
Sappers, Miners and Pioneers,	0	0	0	0	0	0	0	0	0	0	0	1	0	1	1	0	0
Two Ressallahs of the 4th Bengal L. H.	0	0	0	0	0	0	0	0	0	0	0	1	0	1	1	0	0
Total,	1	1	29	31	4	2	1	1	2	8	1	87	1	107	138	0	7

* One Corporal since dead.

Missing—none.

Names of Officers killed and wounded.

Killed.		
Corps.	Rank and Name.	
H. M.'s 2nd or Queen's, Royal Regiment,	Lieut. T. Gravatt,	

Wounded.		
Corps.	Rank and Names.	Remarks.
H. M.'s 2nd or Qn.'s Roy. Regt.	Capt. W. M. Lyster,	Severely.
ditto,	,, T. Sealy,	Ditto.
ditto,	Lieut. T. W. E. Holdsworth,	Ditto.
ditto,	,, D. I. Dickenson,	Slightly.
ditto,	Adjt. J. E. Simmons,	Severely.
H. M.'s 17th Regt.,	Captain L. C. Bourchier,	Ditto.
31st Bengal N. Infantry,	,, Saurin,	Slightly.
ditto,	Ensign Hopper,	Severely.

(Signed)   C. Hagart, Capt., Actg. Dy. Adjt. Genl., Bombay Column, Army of the Indus.

Appendix.

State of the corps engaged at the storming of Kelat, on the 13th November, 1839, under the command of Major-General Willshire, C. B.

Camp at Kelat, 14th November, 1839.

Corps.	Major General.	Brigadiers.	Aides-de-Camp.	Actg. Dy Adjt. Genl.	Actg. Qr. Mr. Genl.	Dy. A. Qr. Mr. Genl.	Brigade Majors.	Sub. Asst. Com. Genl.	Lieut. Cols.	Majors.	Capts.	Lieuts.	Ensigns.	Adjts.	Quarter-Masters.	Surgeons.	Asst. Surgeons.	Native Officers.	Sub-Conductors.	Sergeants.	Drummers.	Farriers.	Rank and file.
Staff,	1	2	5	1	1	1	2	1	0	0	0	0	0	0	0	0	0	0	0	0	0	0	0
Dett. 3rd Troop Horse Artillery,	0	0	0	0	0	0	0	0	0	0	0	2	0	0	0	0	0	0	0	2	0	0	36
1st Troop of Cabool Artillery,	0	0	0	0	0	0	0	0	0	0	0	1	0	0	0	0	0	0	0	8	1	1	58
H. M.'s 2nd or Queen's Royal Regiment,	0	0	0	0	0	0	0	0	0	1	3	7	1	1	0	1	0	0	0	31	10	0	290
H. M.'s 17th Regiment,	0	0	0	0	0	0	0	0	1	2	4	13	2	0	1	1	0	0	0	29	9	0	336
31st Regiment Bengal Native Infantry,	0	0	0	0	0	0	0	0	0	1	2	3	2	1	1	1	0	12	0	30	14	0	329
Total,	1	2	5	1	1	1	2	1	1	4	9	26	5	2	2	2	0	12	0	100	34	1	1049

Note.—Two Ressallahs of the Bengal Local Horse remained in charge of the Baggage during the attack.

(Signed) C. HAGART, Captain,

Act. Dy. Adjt. Genl., Bombay Column, Army of the Indus.

List of Belochee Sirdars killed in the assault of Kelat, on the 13*th November,* 1839.

Names.	Remarks.
Meer Mehrab Khan, ...	Chief of Kelat.
Meer Wullee Mahomed, ...	The Muengul Sirdar of Wudd.
Abdool Kureem, ...	Rushanee Sirdar.
Dad Kureem, ...	Shuhwanee Sirdar.
Mahomed Ruzza, ...	Nephew of the Wuzzeer Mahomed Hoosen.
Khysur Khan, ...	Ahsehire Sirdar.
Dewan Buchah Mull, ...	Financial Minister.
Noor Mahomed, and Tajoo Mahomed, ...	Shagpee Sirdars.

Prisoners.

Mahomed Hoosen, ...	Wuzzeer.
Moola Ruheem Dad, ...	Ex-Naib of Shawl.

With several others of inferior rank.

(Signed) J. D. D. BEAN, *Political Agent.*
(Signed) J. STEWART, *Lieut.-Col.*
Secy. to the Govt. of India, Mily. Dept. with the Rt. Hon. the Govr. Genl.

By order of the Comr. of the Forces,
(Signed) J. R. LUMLEY, *Major-Genl.*
Adjt.-Genl. of the Army.

No. VII.

London Gazette.

Downing street, 12*th August,* 1839.

The *Queen* has been graciously pleased to nominate and appoint Lt.-Genl. Sir John. *Keane*, K. C. B. of the most Hon'ble Order of the Bath; to be a G. C. B.

Whitehall, 11*th Dec.* 1839.

The *Queen* has been pleased to direct *Letters Patent* to be passed under the *great seal,* granting the dignitaries of Baron and Earl of the united kingdom of Gt. Britain and Ireland, unto the Rt. Hon. George *Auckland*, G. C. B. and the heirs male of his body lawfully begotten; by the names, styles, and titles of Baron *Eden*, of Norwood, in the county of Surrey, and Earl of *Auckland*."

Appendix. 33

The Queen has also been pleased to direct Letters Patent, &c. granting the dignity of a baron of the U. K. of Great Britain and Ireland, unto Lt.-Genl. Sir J. *Keane*, G. C. B., and the heirs male of his body lawfully begotten, by the name, style, and title of Baron *Keane*, of Ghuznee, in Afghanistan, and of Cappoquin, in the county of Waterford.

The *Queen* has also been pleased to direct Letters Patent, &c. granting the dignity of a Baronet of the U. K. of Great Britain and Ireland, unto the following gentlemen, and the heirs male of their bodies lawfully begotten, *viz.* Wm. Hay Macnaghten, Esq. of the Civil Service of the E. I. C., on the Bengal establisement, Envoy and Minister from the Govt. of India to H. M. Shah Shoojah-ool-Moolk; and Col. Henry Pottinger, in the service of the E. I. C., on the Bombay establishment, Political Resident in Cutch.

The *Queen* has also been pleased to direct Letters Patent, &c. conferring the honor of knighthood upon Lt.-Col. *Claud Martine Wade*, of the Mily. Service of the E. I. C., on the Bengal establishment, Pol. Resident at Loodiana.

War office, 13*th Dec.* 1839.

Brevet. The undermentioned commissions are to be dated 23rd July, 1839, Col. Rob. Hen. Sale, 13th foot, to have the local rank of Maj.-Genl. in *Affghanistan.*

To be Lieut.-Col. in the *Army* :

Majors C. R. Cureton, 16th Lt. Drs.   F. D. Daly, 4th L. D.
Jno. Pennycuick, 17th Foot.   R. Carruthers, 2nd Foot.
E. T. Tronson, 13th Do.   G. J. McDowel, 16th L. D.

To be *Majors* in the Army :
Capt. T. S. Powel, 6th Foot.   Capt. Jas.Kershaw, 13th Foot.

To be *Lieut.-Cols.* in the *East Indies* only :

Majors Jas. Keith, Bombay N. I. (D. A. G.)   Geo. Warren, Bengal Eurn. Regt.
Jas. MacLaren, Bengal N. I.   C. M. Wade, Bengal N. I. H. F. Salter, Bengal Cavy.
P. L. Pew, (Do.) Arty.   David Cunninghame, Bombay Cavy.
J. D. Parsons, (Do.) D. C. G.

To be Majors in the *East Indies* only :
Capts. N. Campbell, Bombay N. I. (D. Q. M. G.)   Jno. Lloyd, Bombay Arty.
Geo. Thomson, Bengal Engrs.   Pat. Craigie, Bengal N. I. (D. A. G.)
   A. C. Peat, Bombay Engr.

e

Capts. W. Garden, Bengal N. I.   W. Alexander, Bengal Cavy.
(D. Q. M. G.)
Jno. Hay, Bengal N. I.
To have the local rank of Major in *Affghanistan :*
Lieut. Eldred Pottinger, Bombay Arty.

Downing street, 20th Dec. 1839.

The *Queen* has been graciously pleased to nominate and appoint—
Col. T. Willshire, Comg. the Bombay troops, and serving with the rank of Maj.-Genl. in *India ;*
Col. J. Thackwell, Comg. the Cavy. and serving with the rank of Maj-Genl. in *India ;* and Col. R. H. Sale (11) Comg. 13th Lt. Infy.

(11) Entered the Army as Ensign in 36th Foot, 24th Feb. 1795. Lieut. Feb. 1797. Exchanged into 12th Foot in Feb. 1798, served with it at the battle of Mallavelly 27th March, 1799. At siege and storm of Seringapatam 4th May, 1799, and served throughout the campaigns in the Wynnaud country in 1801. Received a medal for Seringapatam, and promoted to a company without purchase, 6th March, 1806. At the storming of the Travancore lines in 1809, and at the capture of the Mauritius in 1810. On 31st Dec. 1813, a Majority, without purchase. In Dec. 1818, placed on Half Pay, by the reduction of the 2nd Bn. In June 1821, received a Majority in 13th Lt. Infy., paying the difference. At the capture of Rangoon in 1824 (in the command of his Regt.) drove the enemy from the vicinity of Rangoon, 14th May, 1824. Stormed the stockades near " Kemmendie," 10th June, 1824, for which " distinguished conduct," he received the thanks of Sir A. Campbell, on the field of battle. Stormed the seven stockades, on 8th July, 1824, and thanked for his " gallant conduct," and noticed in G. O. On 1st Dec. 1824, stormed the enemy's lines with the 13th Lt. Infy. and 200 Sepoys; on 5th Dec. commanded 1600 men, and drove the enemy from every position. On 15th Dec. 1824, commanded 800 men in an attack on the rear of the enemy's lines in front of the great Pagoda, near Rangoon, and received a very severe wound on the head; and noticed in G. O. for the actions of the 5th and 15th Dec., as also for the capture of the intrenchment, at Holkeun. Commanded a brigade employed in the reduction of Bassein, and subsequent operations from 10th Feb. to 2nd May, 1825. Lt.-Colonel, 13th Lt. Infy., without purchase, 2nd June, 1825. On 1st Dec. 1825, commanded 1st Brigade, and repulsed the Shauns and Burmese at Prome. With same Brigade, stormed the heights and lines near Prome, next day; and stormed Mallown, where he received a severe wound. For his " gallant conduct," and " distinguished services," made a C. B.

On 28th June, 1838, promoted to Colonel. In October, 1838, appointed to the command of the 1st (Bengal) Brigade " Army of the Indus," which formed the " *Advance*," throughout the campaign, in Affghanistan. Com-

Appendix. 35

and serving with the rank of Maj.-Genl. in *Affghanistan* to be Knts. Comrs. of the most Hon. Mily. Order of the Bath.

H. M. has also been pleased to nominate and appoint the following officers, in H. M.'s Service, to be companions of the said most Hon. Mily. Order of the Bath.

Lt.-Cols. J. Scott, 4th L. D.   W. Croker, 17th Foot.
W. Persse, 16th Lancers,   R. Macdonald, 4th Foot, D. A. G. (Q. T.) Bombay.

H. M. &c. following officers, in the service of the E. I. C. to be companions of the said most Hon. Mily. Order of the Bath:

Lt.-Cols. A. Roberts, Bengal N. I.   B. Sandwith, Bombay Cavy.
T. Stevenson, Bombay Arty.   F. Stalker, Do. N. I.
T. Monteath, Bengal N. I.   C. M. Wade, Bengal Do.
H. M. Wheeler, Do. Do.   Geo. Thomson, Do. Engineers.
C. C. Smyth, do Cavy.   E. Pottinger, Bombay Do.

Downing street, 21st Jan. 1840.

The *Queen* has been pleased, &c. Maj.-Genl. Sir W. Cotton, K. C. B. to be a G. C. B.

The Brevet for Khelat.

2nd June, 1840. To be Lieut.-Col. in the Army: Major Chas. John Deshon, 17th Foot.

To be Majors in the Army: Capts. Geo. D. I. Raitt, and J. G. S. Gilland, of the 2nd Foot. Capt. J. Darley, 17th Foot, and Capt. O. Robinson, 2nd Foot.

To be Lieut.-Col. in the East Indies only: Major J. S. H. Weston, 31st Regt. Bengal N. I.

To be Majors in the East Indies only: Capts. Sir A. Burnes, (12) 21st Bombay N. I., C. Hagart, Jas. Outram, and W. Wyllie, Bombay N. I. and Capt. W. Coghlan, Bombay Artillery.

The only officer who has not been noticed, is Lieut.-Col. *W. H. Dennie,* C. B., H. M.'s 13th Lt. Infy. who led the "Advance," at the storm of Ghuznee, who was wounded in the Burmese War, and for his services there was made a companion of the Bath. He has been in the Army since the 28th Oct. 1801.

---

manded a Dett. of 2,500 men sent to Girishk. On 23rd July, 1839, commanded the " *Storming-Party* at Ghuznee, where he received a Sabre-cut on the chin, and a contusion on the chest and shoulder, from a musket ball.

(12) Since made a C. B, I hear.

No. VIII.

Lord Auckland, Govr. Genl. of India to the Secret Committee of the East India Company.

Camp at Bhurtpoor, 12*th Dec.* 1839.

I do myself the honor to forward copies of the despatches noted in the margin, (13) relative to the assault and capture of the Fort of Kelat.

2. The decision, the great military skill, and excellent dispositions of Maj.-Genl. Willshire, in conducting the operations against Kelat, appear to me deserving of the highest commendation. The gallantry, steadiness, and soldier-like bearing of the troops under his command, rendered his plans of action completely successful, thereby again crowning our arms across the *Indus* with signal victory.

3. I need not expatiate on the importance of this achievement, from which the best effects must be derived, not only in the vindication of our national honor, but also in confirming the security of intercourse between *Scinde* and *Affghanistan*, and in promoting the safety and tranquillity of the restored monarchy; but I would not omit to point out that the conduct on this occasion of Major-Genl. *Willshire;* and of the officers and men under his command (including the 31st Regt. of Bengal N. I., which had not been employed in the previous active operations of the campaign), have entitled them to more prominent notice than I was able to give them in my General Order of Nov. 18th, 1839; and in recommending these valuable services to the applause of the Committee, I trust that I shall not be considered as going beyond my proper province, in stating an earnest hope that the conduct of Maj.-Genl. *Willshire* in the direction of the operations, will not fail to elicit the approbation of Her Majesty's Govt.

I have, &c.

(Signed)   AUCKLAN

(13) India Board, 13th Feb. 1840.—*London Gazette.*

No. IX.

From the Rt. Hon'ble Lord Hill, Genl. Comr.-in-Chief, H. M.'s Forces, Horse Guards, 4th Dec. 1839, *to H. E. Lieut.-Genl. Sir John Keane, G. C. B. &c.*

Hd. Qrs. Bombay, 28th Feb. 1840. (14)

(Ext.) I have perused with the deepest interest the particulars, as detailed by you, of the capture by storm, of the important Fortress of *Ghuznee*, together with its citadel, by the army under your command, and I have the greatest satisfaction in conveying to you the sense I entertain of your conduct upon that occasion, marked and distinguished as it was, by a display of skill, judgment and valour; and most gallantly supported throughout every part of the difficult and dangerous operation, by the admirable courage and discipline of all the troops.

In submitting these important despatches to the *Queen*, I did not fail to solicit Her Majesty's attention, not only to the undaunted spirit and gallantry of the troops under your command; but likewise, to the exemplary behaviour immediately subsequent to this daring as successful achievement, behaviour which could only have resulted, as you have justly observed, from the maintenance of a high state of discipline, combined with British courage, and British character; and you will be so good as to avail yourself of an early opportunity to make known to the army under your command, that the *Queen* has been pleased to express her most gracious approbation of their brilliant and important services.

(Signed)   HILL.
By Order of H. E. the Comr.-in-Chief,
(Signed)   R. MACDONALD, *Lt.-Col.*
Dy. Adjt. Genl. H. M.'s Forces in India.

No. X.

Head Quarters, Calcutta, 22nd April, 1840.

No. 36. G. O.—H. E. the Comr.-in-Chief in India has been honored by receiving the commands of Her Majesty, contained in a

(14) G. O. by H. E. Lieut.-Genl. Sir T. MacMahon, Bart., K. C. B.

letter from Genl. Lord Hill, commanding the army in Chief, dated 4th March, 1840, to express Her Majesty's high satisfaction at the judgment, skill, gallantry and discipline, displayed by Major-Genl. Sir Thomas Willshire, K. C. B. and by the Officers and Men of H. M.'s 2nd and 17th Regts. of Foot, in the glorious and successful assault upon the Fortress of Kelat.

His Excellency is aware that these most gracious expressions of the Queen's approbation, are equally intended to be conveyed to the Detachment of the Bombay Horse Artillery, to the 31st. Regt. Bengal Native Infantry, and to the other Detchments engaged ; and he is quite certain that Her Majesty's Officers and Men will freely and liberally share with them, the applause thus bestowed, upon their united, and gallant exertions, and upon their splendid, noonday achievement.

No. XI.

To Major P. Craigie.

Dy. A. G. of the Army, with the Army of the Indus.

Mily. Dept.

SIR,

It has been brought to the notice of the Rt. Hon. the Govr. Genl., that the wives and families of officers attached to the *Bengal Column* of the Army of the Indus, have been, in some instances, subjected to much inconvenience, by the delay, or interruption, of the remittances on which they are dependent for support, occasioned by the irregularity, or interruption by robbers, of the Dâk Communication between the Army and the Company's Provinces.

2. *(Ext.)* The Govr. Genl. has been pleased to determine, that such portion of their pay and allowances as officers of the Bengal Column of that army may authorize the deduction of, by the field Pay Master, shall be paid to their wives, or families, in the provinces; under such arrangements as shall be made for that purpose, in the Pay Dept. to which the necessary reference will be made.

3. In the mean time, to obviate delay, I am directed to request H. E. the Comr.-in-Chief of the Army of the Indus, will cause *Rolls* to be prepared, of the officers wishing to avail themselves of this indulgence ; specifying the amount to be deducted from each,

Appendix. 39

and the month from the pay of which the first deduction has been made.

4. These Rolls may be sent in the first instance, by the Fd. Pay Master, to the Depy. Pay Mr. of the district in which the *Payees*, the officers' wives or families, are residing; and full instructions will be furnished, hereafter, for Capt. *Bygrave's* guidance, by the Accountant in the Mily. Dept.

(Signed) JAS. STUART, *Lt.-Col.*
Offg. Sec. to Govt. of India Mily. Dept.
with the Rt. Hon. the Govr. Genl.

Simla, 4th June, 1839.

No. XII.
Dooranee Order. (15)

Secret Dept. 3rd August, 1840.

The Rt. Hon. the Govr. Genl. in Council is pleased to publish the following list of officers who have been invested with the Order of the Dooranee Empire, by permission of Her Most Gracious Majesty the Queen.

Members of the 1st Class of the Order of the Dooranee Empire.

Sir W. H. Macnaghten, Bart., Envoy and Minister at the Court of Cabool.

Lt.-Col. Sir C. M. Wade, Kt. C. B. Resident at Indore.

Lt.-Col. Sir Alex. Burnes, Kt. Envoy to Kelat and other states.

Members of the 2nd Class.

Maj.-Genl. Simpson, late Comg. Shah Shoojah's Force.

Brigr. A. Roberts, C. B. Hon. Company's Eurn. Regt. Comg. Shah Shoojah's Force.

Brigr. Stephenson, C. B. Lt.-Col. Bombay Arty.

Lt.-Col. Parsons. Depy. Comy. Genl., Bengal Army.

Major Garden, Dy. Qr. Mr. Genl. Bengal Army.

Major Thomson, C. B. Bengal Engineers.

Major Peat, Bombay Engineers.

Major E. D'A. Todd, Bengal Arty., Envoy to Herat.

(15) The names given at p. 263 are correct, but Capt. *Anderson's* is added to this List. Lord *Auckland* has accepted of the Order, though not detailed in the present List.

Major Craigie, Dy. Adjt. Genl., Bengal Army.

Capt. (now Major) J. Outram, Pol. Agent Lower Sinde.

Members of the 3rd Class.

Lt.-Col. Orchard, C. B. Bengal European Regt.

Lt.-Col. Wheeler, C. B. 48th Bengal N. I.

Lt.-Col. Monteath, C. B. 35th Bengal N. I.

Lt.-Col. Smyth, C. B. 3rd Bengal Lt. Cavy.

Lt.-Col. Sandwith, C. B. 1st Bombay Lt. Cavy.

Lt.-Col. Stalker, C. B. 19th Bombay N. I.

Lt.-Col. Salter, 2nd Bengal Lt. Cavy.

Lt.-Col. Warren, Bengal European Regt.

Lt.-Col. Cunningham, 2nd Bombay Lt. Cavy. Comg. Poonah Auxy. Horse.

Lt.-Col. Pew, Bengal Arty.

Lt.-Col. McLaren, 16th Bengal N. I.

Major (now Lt.-Col.) Weston, 31st Bengal N. I.

Major Thomson, Bengal Eurn. Regt.

Major Thomas, 48th Bengal N. I.

Major Hancock, 19th Bombay N. I.

Major C. J. Cunningham, 1st Bombay Lt. Cavy.

Major Alexander, Comg. 4th Local Horse.

Major McSherry, late Major of Brigade, Shah Shoojah's Force.

Major Hagart, Bombay Eurn. Regt.

Major Leech, Pol. Agent, Candahar.

Major E. Pottinger, C. B. Bombay Arty.

Capt. Davidson, 17th Bombay N. I.

Capt. Sanders, Bengal Engineers.

Capt. Johnson, Pay Mr. and Commsst. officer, S. S. Force.

Capt. Anderson, Bengal H. A. Comg. Horse Arty. S. S. Force.

Capt. Macgregor, Pol. Agent at Jellalabad.

Capt. E. B. Conolly, Mily. Asst. and Comg. Escort, Envoy and Minister.

Lt. F. Mackeson, Pol. Agent, Peshawer.

Mr. P. B. Lord, Pol. Agent, Bameean.

N. B. The following Members of the Order have died since its institution.

Brigr. Arnold, Lt.-Col. H. M.'s 16th Lancers, 2nd class.

Lt.-Col. Keith, Dy. Adjt. Genl. Bombay Army, 2nd Class.

Lt.-Col. Herring, C. B. Bengal Infy. 3rd Class.

Capt. Hay, 35th Bengal N. I. 3rd Class.

(Signed) H. TORRENS,
Offg. Secy. to the Govt. of India.

Appendix. 41

No. XIII.

List of Officers of the "Army of the Indus," dying from 1st November, 1838, to 1840.

Nos.	Rank and Names.	Corps.	Dates.	Where and how died, &c.
1	Lt. Halliday,	S. S. O. M.	Nov. 1, 1838.	Loodianah.
2	Lt. Kewney,	D. A. Q. M. General,	Nov. 5,	Kurnal, Suicide.
3	Lt. F. C. Fyers,	H. M. 4 L. D.	Dec. 14,	In Sindh, Suicide.
4	Lt. E. W. Sparkes,	2d Q.'s Foot,	Jan. 30, 1839,	} Ditto, accidentally burnt to death.
5	Lt. T. A. Nixon,	Ditto,	Ditto,	
6	Asst. Surg. W. E. Hibbert,	Ditto,	Ditto,	
7	Lt. E. C. Campbell,	Bombay 1st Lt. Cavy.	Feb. 19,	} In Sindh.
8	Capt. H. J. Keith,	2d Q.'s Foot,	March 3,	
9	Capt. Hand,	2d Bombay Grenrs.	April,	Kurachee, murdered by the Beloochees.
10	Lt.-Col. J. Thomson,	31st Bombay N. I.	April 19,	1st march from Shikarpoor—Apoplexy.
11	Lt. Inverarity,	H. M.'s 16th Lancers,	May 28,	Candahar—murdered by Affghans.
12	Lt. J. H. Corry,	17th Foot,	June 4,	Proceeding to join. Heat of weather.
13	Asst. Surgeon J. Halloran,	Bombay Foot Artillery,	...	Ditto, ditto.
14	Lt. Chalmers,	43d Bengal N. I.	June,	Bagh, ditto.
15	Ensn. Beaufort,	42d ditto,	Ditto,	Ditto, ditto.
16	Dr. Hamilton,	17th Foot,	June 21,	Candahar.
17	Lt. Baynes,	Bombay Arty.	Aug.	Quetta.
18	Capt. Meik,	31st Bengal N. I.	Ditto,	Ditto.
19	Brigr. Arnold,	H. M.'s 16th Lancers,	Aug. 20,	Cabool.
20	Lt.-Col. J. Herring, C. B.	37th Bengal N. I.	Sept. 3,	At Hyder Khel, near Cabool, murdered by Ghiljies.
21	Capt. Fothergill,	13th Foot,	Sept. 5,	Cabool.
22	Capt. Gould,	42d Bengal N. I.	Sept. 6,	Quetta.
23	Capt. Timings,	Bengal H. A.	Sept. 12,	Cabool, worn out.
24	Bt. Major Hart,	43d Bengal N. I.	Oct. 11,	Candahar.
25	Capt. J. Hay,	35th ditto,	Oct. 13,	Cabool.

Appendix.

Nos.	Rank and Names.	Corps.	Dates.	Where and how died, &c.
26	Major Keith,	D. A. G. Bombay Army,	Oct. 19,	Between Cabool and Quetta, sore throat.
27	Capt. Hackitt,	17th Foot,	Ditto,	Jugduluk, between Cabool and Jellalabad.
28	Lt. T. Gravatt,	2d ditto,	Nov. 13,	Killed at the storm of Khelat.
29	Capt. Hilton,	H. M.'s 16th Lancers,	Dec. 12,	Drowned fording the Jheelum, in the Punjab.
30	Capt. Ogle,	H. M.'s 4th L. D.	Dec.	At Shikarpoor.
31	Dr. Forbes,	V. Bombay Lt. Cavy.	Ditto,	Ditto.
32	Dr. Walker,	42d Bengal N. I.	Dec. 22,	Candahar.
33	Lt. Collinson,	37th ditto,	Jan. 18, 1840,	Died of wound received in action at Pooshoot near Jellalabad.
34	Capt. Sutherland,	13th Foot,	April,	Cabool.

Appendix.

No. I.

Return of all Death Casualties (killed, &c.) in the Bengal Column of the Army of the Indus, from 10th Dec. 1838 to the 31st Dec. 1839. Hd. Qrs. Camp at Ferozpoor, 1st Jan. 1840.

Average Strength in year 1829.	Arm.	Corps and Detachments.	Eurn. Comssd. Officers.								European N.C.O., Rank and File.		Native Comssd. N.C.O., Rank and File.					Cattle.	
			Colonels.	Lt.-Cols.	Capts.	Lieuts.	Ensigns, &c.	Assist. Surgeons.	Sergeants.	Corporals.	Bombrs.	Trumpeters, &c.	Rank and File.	Soobadars.	Jemadars.	Havrs. &c.	Naicks, &c.	Trumpeters, &c.	Rank and File.	Horses.	Gun Camels.
102	Arty., ..	2nd T. 2nd B. H. A.......	0	0	0	0	0	0	0	0	2	0	10	0	0	0	0	0	1	30	0
93		4th Co. 2nd B. A.	0	0	0	0	0	0	0	0	0	0	4	0	0	0	0	1	0	0	0
161		2nd Co. 6th B. A.	0	0	0	0	0	0	0	0	0	0	0	0	0	1	0	1	18	0	44
463		H. M. 16th Lancers.....	1	0	1	1	0	0	2	0	0	1	62	0	0	0	0	0	0	219	0
440		2nd Lt. Cavy.,	0	1	0	0	0	0	0	0	0	0	0	0	0	3	0	0	20	206	0
450	Cavalry,	3rd do., ...	0	0	0	0	0	0	0	0	0	0	0	0	0	3	0	0	12	76	0
160		Dett. 1st local Horse,......	0	0	0	0	0	0	0	0	0	0	0	0	0	0	0	0	4	75	0
879		4th Local Hrs.	0	0	0	0	0	0	0	0	0	0	0	0	0	0	0	0	37	540	0
254		Sappers and Miners, ...	0	0	0	0	0	0	0	0	0	0	0	0	0	0	0	0	15	0	0
502	1st Brigade Infy.	H. M. 13th Lt. Infantry, ..	0	0	1	0	0	0	2	4	0	2	85	0	0	0	0	0	0	0	0
728		16th Regt. N. I............	0	0	0	0	0	0	0	0	0	0	0	0	1	2	7	0	53	0	0
741		48th do. do. ..	0	0	0	0	0	0	0	0	0	0	0	0	0	6	6	0	42	0	0
676	2nd do..	31st do. do. ...	0	1	1	0	0	0	0	0	0	0	0	1	0	6	4	0	43	0	0
617		42nd do. do. ...	0	0	0	1	1	1	0	0	0	0	0	2	1	8	5	2	59	0	0
744		43rd do. do. ...	0	0	1	1	0	0	0	0	0	0	0	0	0	0	0	0	24	0	0
566	4th do..	1st European Regt.	0	0	0	0	0	0	1	0	0	0	27	0	0	0	0	0	0	0	0
730		35th Regt. N.I.	0	0	1	0	0	0	0	0	0	0	0	0	0	2	2	0	25	0	0
703		37th do. do. ...	0	1	0	0	0	0	0	0	0	0	0	0	0	5	1	0	27	0	0
9007		Totals,..	1	3	5	3	1	1	5	5	2	3	188	3	2	36	25	4	380	1146	44
(1)		Total of each,				14							203				450				

N. B. The H. A. marched with 169, 16th Lancers 463, 2nd Cavalry 440, 3rd Ditto 450. Dett. 1st Local Horse with 160, and 4th Local Horse, with 797. Total 2,479 Horses. *The loss of* 1,146 *being* 46 *P. C.* (including cast, &c. &c.) The *Bombay Column,* out of about 1700 horses, lost 418, equal to more than 27¾ P. C. Total Bengal and Bombay horses lost 1564, or nearly 38 P. C. The Bombay loss is calculated up to its return. The transport train lost 195 out of 500 bullocks. Hackery bullocks 326. Total loss of 521 bullocks.

(1) Add park of artillery 684. Also 4th T. 3rd B. H. A. (lent to the Shah's force) 140, making the total 9,831 men.

Observations on Table No. 2, Admissions into Hospital, and Deaths in the " Army of the Indus," for the year 1839.

The sickness in the 31st and 42nd Regts. N. I. is to be ascribed more to the fatigue and privations the men underwent before their arrival in *Shawl* (May 1839), than to any peculiar unhealthiness in the situation of *Quetta*. These Regts. marched from Shikarpoor by Detts. in charge of Convoys, during the months of April, May, June and part of July ; and suffered greatly from incessant fatigue, daily, indeed hourly, exposure to intense heat, (the thermometer one day stood at 135° in a tent,) and severe privations arising from want of water ; which, when procurable, was for the most part very bad.

On these parties reaching *Shawl*, they were in a comparatively cold climate, and incapable of protecting themselves against its chilling effects, in consequence of many of them, (the whole of the 31st N. I. certainly,) having been compelled to throw away all their bedding and warm clothing, such as *meerzaees* (quilted jackets) and *ruzaees* (quilts) from want of carriage, arising from casualties among their camels.

The men not being able to procure vegetables, milk, and other articles of diet considered necessary by them, must have had an injurious effect; more particularly as for some time they had no dhall, (split peas.)

The 43rd N. I. arrived at Quetta in March, 1839, consequently continued healthy.

The 43rd N. I. arrived at Quetta in March, the 31st and 42nd N. I. not till May, 1839. The 37th N. I. reached Candahar in May, 1839. The rest of the Bengal troops reached Candahar in April, 1839.

The climate of Shawl is variable, the changes of temperature sudden, and the range of the thermometer great, *viz.* about 45° within the 24 hours in tents, and about 90° in the open air. Nevertheless, if the sepoys arrived there in good health, had sufficient clothing (extra to what is customary in Hindostan during the cold season); abundance of warm-bedding ; good huts ; and wholesome food, it is the opinion of medical men, that they would remain as healthy as Native troops generally are in *India*.

Appendix. 45

Around the town of *Quetta*, the water lies near the surface, and forces itself upwards by many springs which stagnate, and cause numerous small morasses. These and the constant irrigation of the fields, may account for the *intermittent fevers* which always prevailed at *Quetta* in autumn.

This part of the valley, however, is capable of being drained, which operation would, it is said, decidedly add much to the salubrity of the place, and probably would free it altogether from fevers.

The Bolan Pass is open for travellers during the whole year. The difficulty and danger lies between Dadur and Shikarpoor in the hot weather.

The cold this winter at *Quetta* has stood at $10°$, and $50°$ in a tent with a fire.

No. 2.—*Monthly Numerical Return, shewing the number of Admissions and Deaths, in the European and Native Troops of the "Army of the Indus," from 1st Jan. to 31st Dec. 1839, inclusive. Camp Jellalabad, 1st Jan. 1840.*

(1) 1839. Months.	H. M.'s 16th Lancers, average strength 463½.									2nd Troop 2nd Bgde. H. Arty., average strength 102½.									
	Admissions.				Deaths.					Admissions.				Deaths.					
	Fever.	Dysentery.	Cholera.	Other Diseases.	Total Admissions.	Fever.	Dysentery.	Cholera.	Other Diseases.	Total Deaths.	Fever.	Dysentery.	Cholera.	Other Diseases.	Total Admissions.	Fever.	Dysentery.	Cholera.	Other Diseases.	Total Deaths.
January,	5	1	...	34	40	...	...	...	1	1	2	2	...	10	14	...	...	...	...	...
February,	1	...	...	57	58	...	...	...	...	...	1	3	...	11	14	...	...	...	...	...
March,	21	...	...	41	62	...	...	...	...	...	1	...	...	4	5	...	...	...	1	1
April,	13	1	...	116	130	...	...	...	2	2	2	5	...	27	34	...	...	...	...	...
May,	6	1	2	97	105	2	1	...	4	7	1	4	...	18	23	...	2	...	2	4
June,	16	2	...	85	102	1	1	...	4	6	4	11	...	14	25	...	...	...	...	...
July,	15	1	...	67	84	1	...	...	7	8	6	3	2	12	21	1	...	...	2	3
August,	9	...	...	38	48	...	...	...	1	1	3	...	...	10	16	1	...	...	1	2
September,	14	2	...	18	32	...	...	...	7	7	2	1	...	5	9	...	...	...	...	...
October,	17	...	...	45	64	...	...	...	5	5	4	1	...	4	7	...	...	...	1	1
November,	14	1	...	34	49	1	...	...	2	3	5	3	...	...	7	1	...	...	1	1
December,	8	1	...	37	46	2	...	...	4	6	...	...	...	6	11	...	...	...	...	...
Total,	139	10	2	669	820	7	2	...	37	46	30	33	2	121	186	2	2	...	7	11
Ratio p. c. per annum,	32	2	4⁄9	144 to 1	2 to 1	1½	½	...	8	10	30	33	2	118 to 1	2 to 1	2	2	...	7	11

(1) For range of the Thermometer, see Table, No. 3.

No. 2.—*Continued.*

1839. Months.	(2) 4th Co. 2nd Arty. Bn. average strength 93 7/12.										(3) H. M.'s 13th Lt. Infy., average strength 502.									
	Admissions.					Deaths.					Admissions.					Deaths.				
	Fever.	Dysentery.	Cholera.	Other Diseases.	Total Admissions.	Fever.	Dysentery.	Cholera.	Other Diseases.	Total Deaths.	Fever.	Dysentery.	Cholera.	Other Diseases.	Total Admissions.	Fever.	Dysentery.	Cholera.	Other Diseases.	Total Deaths.
January,	2	3	1	7	13	—	—	—	—	—	15	8	—	51	74	—	—	—	—	—
February,	2	3	—	9	14	—	—	—	1	1	11	10	—	70	91	1	—	—	—	1
March,	2	—	—	9	11	—	—	—	—	—	23	10	—	61	94	—	—	—	—	—
April,	8	1	—	19	28	—	—	—	—	—	55	8	1	97	161	—	—	—	1	1
May,	5	—	—	11	16	—	—	—	1	1	38	10	3	126	177	—	1	—	—	1
June,	4	—	—	9	13	—	—	—	1	1	45	27	2	100	174	—	1	—	4	5
July,	8	—	—	10	18	—	—	—	—	—	33	15	1	106	155	3	2	—	21	26
August,	12	—	—	10	22	1	—	—	—	1	12	8	1	52	73	1	3	—	10	14
September,	30	2	—	8	40	—	—	—	—	—	16	1	1	26	44	—	—	—	4	4
October,	43	—	—	5	48	1	—	—	—	1	11	10	—	49	70	—	—	—	5	5
November,	23	—	—	6	29	—	—	—	—	—	9	2	—	21	32	1	1	—	1	3
December,	11	—	—	7	18	—	—	—	1	1	18	2	—	44	64	1	1	—	8	10
Total,	150	9	1	110	270	2	—	—	4	6	286	111	9	803	1209	7	9	—	54	70
Ratio p. c. per annum,	1 3/5 to 1	10	1	1 1/5 to 1	3 to 1	2 1/5	—	—	4 1/4	6 1/2	58	22	2	1 1/2 to 1	2 1/4 to 1	1 1/4	2	—	11 1/2	14

(2) Left at Candahar when the Army marched on 27th June, 1839. (3) Left at Cabool the whole winter.

No. 2.—*Continued.*

1839. Months.	(4) Hon. Comp. 1st Eurn. Regt., average strength 566.										(4) 2nd Regt. Lt. Cavy., average strength									
	Admissions.					Deaths.					Admissions.					Deaths.				
	Fever.	Dysentery.	Cholera.	Other Diseases.	Total Admissions.	Fever.	Dysentery.	Cholera.	Other Diseases.	Total Deaths.	Fever.	Dysentery.	Cholera.	Other Diseases.	Total Admissions	Fever.	Dysentery.	Cholera.	Other Diseases.	Total Deaths.
January,	18	7	...	57	82	...	...	...	1	1	9	...	...	24	33	...	...	...	1	1
February,	23	10	...	38	71	...	...	...	...	...	13	...	...	18	31	1	...	...	...	1
March,	24	18	...	48	90	...	...	...	1	1	10	...	...	20	30	2	...	...	1	3
April,	65	13	...	86	164	...	...	...	...	...	16	...	...	47	63	1	...	...	1	2
May,	45	30	...	78	153	2	1	...	1	4	10	...	...	52	62	2	...	...	...	2
June,	49	19	...	50	118	1	...	...	2	3	9	...	...	24	33	1	...	...	...	1
July,	49	22	...	119	190	1	...	...	4	5	9	...	...	42	51	1	...	...	...	1
August,	21	3	...	60	84	...	...	...	2	2	11	...	...	36	47	...	...	...	...	...
September,	9	5	...	45	59	...	...	...	1	1	8	...	...	15	23	...	...	...	...	...
October,	7	4	...	44	55	...	...	...	3	3	7	...	...	16	23	...	...	...	...	...
November,	4	1	...	60	65	...	...	...	...	...	2	...	...	14	18	...	...	...	...	...
December,	3	3	...	39	45	...	...	...	...	...	8	...	...	22	30	...	...	...	...	...
Total,	317	135	...	724	1176	4	1	...	15	20	112	...	...	332	444	8	...	...	3	11
Ratio p. c. per annum,	68	28	...	1¼ to 1	2⅛ to 1	¾	⅕	...	2¾	3½	27	...	...	76	100	2¼	...	...	1⅗	3

(4) Marched from Cabool in October 1839 for Jellalabad. The Eurn. Regt. is at Kujyah (now), 25 miles from Jellalabad.

Appendix.

No. 2,—Continued.

1839. Months.	(5) 3rd Regt. Lt. Cavy., average strength 450.									(5) 4th Regt. Loc. Hse., average strength 879 8/12.								
	Admissions.					Deaths.					Admissions.					Deaths.				
	Fever.	Dysentery.	Cholera.	Other Diseases.	Total Admissions.	Fever.	Dysentery.	Cholera.	Other Diseases.	Total Deaths.	Fever.	Dysentery.	Cholera.	Other Diseases.	Total Admissions.	Fever.	Dysentery.	Cholera.	Other Diseases.	Total Deaths.
January,	16	...	...	32	48	1	...	...	...	1	10	5	...	23	38	...	...	...	1	1
February,	14	8	...	26	48	...	...	...	...	...	18	15	...	13	46	...	...	...	...	...
March,	10	8	...	20	38	...	1	...	2	3	14	9	...	18	41	...	...	...	...	...
April,	5	...	...	58	63	2	...	...	2	2	3	...	...	18	21	...	...	...	1	1
May,	15	...	...	39	54	...	...	...	...	...	26	...	...	58	84	...	...	...	...	...
June,	11	...	...	24	35	...	...	...	...	...	19	...	...	32	51	...	...	...	...	...
July,	10	...	...	48	58	1	...	...	1	1	20	...	...	29	49	...	...	...	1	1
August,	7	...	...	27	34	...	...	...	...	...	20	1	...	23	43	1	1	...	1	1
September,	6	...	...	11	17	...	...	...	...	...	12	...	...	18	31	...	...	...	...	...
October,	6	...	...	24	30	1	...	...	1	1	5	...	...	15	21	1	...	...	1	1
November,	10	...	...	15	35	2	...	...	1	2	9	...	...	5	14	...	...	...	1	1
December,	17	...	...	7	24	3	...	...	...	3	10	...	...	6	16	2	...	...	1	3
Total,	127	16	...	331	474	5	1	...	7	13	167	30	...	258	455	2	1	...	5	8
Ratio p. c. per annum,	29	3¼	...	66	100	1⅛	...	...	1	1¾	18	3½	...	27	48	¼	⅛	...	⅔	1

(5) 3rd Regt. Lt. Cavy., average strength 450.
(5) 4th Regt. Loc. Hse., average strength 879 8/12.
(5) Marched from Cabool on 16th October, 1839, and returned to India.

No. 2.—Continued.

1839. Months.	(6) 2nd Co. 6th Bn. Arty., average strength 161½.										(7) 16th Regt. N. I., average strength 728½.									
	Admissions.					Deaths.					Admissions.					Deaths.				
	Fever.	Dysentery.	Cholera.	Other Diseases.	Total Admissions.	Fever.	Dysentery.	Cholera.	Other Diseases.	Total Deaths.	Fever.	Dysentery.	Cholera.	Other Diseases.	Total Admissions.	Fever.	Dysentery.	Cholera.	Other Diseases.	Total Deaths.
January,	5	..	..	12	17	..	..	..	..	..	26	1	..	48	74	..	..	..	..	..
February,	4	..	..	11	15	..	..	..	..	..	25	..	..	27	53	..	..	..	..	..
March,	5	..	..	10	15	..	..	..	..	..	33	..	..	32	65	1	..	..	..	1
April,	10	..	..	24	34	..	..	..	..	..	38	4	..	129	167	..	..	..	2	2
May,	6	..	..	11	17	1	..	..	..	1	30	..	..	111	145	..	..	..	..	..
June,	6	1	..	5	11	1	..	..	1	2	28	..	..	58	86	1	..	..	..	2
July,	10	..	..	26	37	..	..	..	..	..	42	..	..	158	200	2	..	..	13	15
August,	14	1	..	20	34	..	..	..	2	2	39	..	..	48	87	1	..	..	10	11
September,	6	..	..	5	12	..	..	..	..	..	6	..	..	7	13	2	..	..	1	3
October,	2	..	..	6	8	..	..	..	..	..	29	..	..	29	58	2	..	..	2	4
November,	5	..	..	4	9	..	..	..	1	1	43	1	..	15	59	1	..	..	1	12
December,	3	..	..	4	7	..	..	..	1	1	41	..	..	5	46	14	..	..	1	15
Total,—	76	2	..	138	216	2	..	..	5	7	380	6	..	667	1053	34	..	..	30	64
Ratio p. c. per annum,—	50	1⅓	..	90	1½ to 1	1⅓	..	..	3¼	4⅓	65	⅞	..	90	1¼ to 1	4¾	..	..	4¼	9

(6) Left Cabool for Jellalabad in Nov. 1839—returned to Cabool in April, 1840.
(7) Left at Ghuznee on 30th July, 1839, and there ever since.

No. 2.—Continued.

1839. Months.	(8) 31st Regt. N. I., average strength 676½										(9) 35th Regt. N. I., average strength 730 6/12									
	Admissions.					Deaths.					Admissions.					Deaths.				
	Fever.	Dysentery.	Cholera.	Other Diseases.	Total Admissions.	Fever.	Dysentery.	Cholera.	Other Diseases.	Total Deaths.	Fever.	Dysentery.	Cholera.	Other Diseases.	Total Admissions.	Fever.	Dysentery.	Cholera.	Other Diseases.	Total Deaths.
January,	20	10	..	30	60	..	..	..	..	..	5	11	..	35	51	1	..	..	..	1
February,	20	2	..	22	44	..	..	..	..	..	20	3	..	25	48	..	..	..	2	2
March,	19	1	..	20	40	1	..	..	..	..	19	7	..	21	47	..	..	..	..	..
April,	11	4	..	21	36	..	..	..	..	..	18	2	..	43	63	..	..	..	2	2
May,	36	14	..	32	82	..	..	..	..	..	26	7	..	61	94	..	1	..	2	2
June,	36	20	..	28	84	..	..	..	..	..	27	5	..	34	66	..	1	..	..	1
July,	38	22	..	167	227	1	..	..	1	1	24	11	..	84	119	..	..	..	2	3
August,	62	23	48	74	207	1	1	21	1	24	40	14	..	49	103	..	..	..	..	..
September,	33	14	4	37	108	..	..	..	..	..	18	3	..	19	40	..	..	..	1	1
October,	28	7	..	65	100	2	1	..	2	5	17	2	..	19	38	1	..	..	1	1
November,	25	7	..	59	91	..	..	..	1	1	14	1	..	26	41	..	1	..	4	5
December,	165	1	..	40	206	2	..	..	1	3	15	2	..	16	33	..	..	..	1	1
Total,	503	135	52	595	1285	6	2	21	5	34	243	68	..	432	743	2	3	..	14	19
Ratio p. c. per annum,	75	20	8	89	2 to 1	¾	¼	3	¾	5	33	10	..	61	100	¼	¾	..	1¾	2¾

(8) Arrived at Quetta in May and left it for Khelat in Nov. 1839. Now in India.
(9) Left at Cabool the whole winter.

52   *Appendix*

No. 2.—*Continued.*

1839. Months.	(10) 37th Regt. N. I., average strength 703 8/14.								(11) 42nd Regt. N. I., average strength 617 8/13.							
	Admissions.				Deaths.				Admissions.				Deaths.			
	Fever.	Dysentery.	Cholera.	Other Diseases.	Total Admissions.	Fever.	Dysentery.	Cholera.	Other Diseases.	Total Deaths.	Fever.	Dysentery.	Cholera.	Other Diseases.	Total Admissions.	Fever.	Dysentery.	Cholera.	Other Diseases.	Total Deaths.
January,	13	..	..	58	71	..	..	..	..	..	11	11	..	50	72	..	..	..	1	1
February,	28	..	..	38	66	2	..	..	..	2	38	7	..	38	83	1	..	..	1	2
March,	27	1	..	25	53	1	..	..	1	2	29	10	..	28	67	..	..	..	..	..
April,	24	..	..	30	54	1	..	..	..	1	7	1	..	18	26	..	..	..	..	..
May,	21	..	..	40	61	..	..	..	..	..	19	12	..	40	71	..	..	..	..	..
June,	18	3	..	53	74	1	1	..	..	1	19	1	..	40	60	..	..	..	..	..
July,	33	..	..	50	83	1	..	..	4	4	80	4	..	89	173	..	..	..	..	..
August,	26	..	..	51	77	1	..	..	..	1	123	..	22	77	222	1	1	18	1	21
September,	20	..	..	54	74	2	..	..	..	2	88	2	..	76	166	..	..	..	..	..
October,	11	..	..	33	44	..	..	..	1	2	62	1	..	111	174	1	1	..	1	1
November,	3	..	..	10	13	..	..	..	..	..	34	2	..	59	95	..	1	..	..	1
December,	1	1	..	47	49	..	..	..	2	2	18	..	..	20	38	3	..	..	1	4
Total,	231	5	..	489	719	7	1	..	8	16	528	51	22	646	1247	5	3	18	4	30
Ratio p. c. per annum,	32	1/7	..	70	100	1	1-7	..	4	2 1/4	84	8 1/4	3 1/2	1 5/7 to 1	2 1/7 to 1	1 p.c. 1/4	1/2	3	3/4	5

(10) Marched from Cabool to Jellalabad in October, 1839—returned to Cabool in April, 1840.
(11) Reached Quetta in March, 1839, went to Candahar in October, 1839, and is now there.

Appendix.

No. 2.—Continued.

1839. Months.	(12) 43rd Regt. N. I., average strength 744.									(13) 48th Regt. N. I., average strength 741 3/12.								
	Admissions.				Deaths.					Admissions.				Deaths.			
	Fever.	Dysentery.	Cholera.	Other Diseases.	Total Admissions.	Fever.	Dysentery.	Cholera.	Other Diseases.	Total Deaths.	Fever.	Dysentery.	Cholera.	Other Diseases.	Total Admissions.	Fever.	Dysentery.	Cholera.	Other Diseases.	Total Deaths.
January,	21	10	...	62	93	...	...	...	...	...	34	...	...	103	137	...	...	...	...	...
February,	27	5	...	39	71	...	...	...	...	...	28	...	...	55	83	...	...	...	...	...
March,	26	8	...	16	50	...	...	...	...	...	21	...	...	40	61	...	...	...	...	...
April,	33	4	1	28	66	...	...	...	...	...	51	4	...	189	244	...	...	...	1	1
May,	48	8	...	18	74	1	...	...	1	3	21	3	...	170	194	...	1	...	...	4
June,	63	3	...	28	94	...	1	...	...	...	23	...	...	102	125	1	...	...	4	6
July,	47	5	...	35	87	1	...	...	...	...	35	...	...	226	261	...	...	...	5	15
August,	45	15	...	42	102	...	...	...	1	2	32	2	...	117	151	2	...	...	...	2
September,	52	9	1	14	76	...	1	...	...	...	32	4	...	107	143	2	...	...	2	4
October,	55	3	...	17	76	2	...	...	...	3	32	...	...	62	94	...	...	...	1	1
November,	66	4	...	11	81	...	...	...	...	...	20	...	...	66	86	...	...	...	...	...
December,	47	2	...	9	58	1	...	...	...	1	21	2	...	54	77	...	...	...	3	3
Total,	531	76	2	319	928	5	2	...	2	9	350	15	...	1291	1656	5	1	...	31	37
Ratio p. c. per annum,	74	84	1/4	43	124 4/10 to 1	1	1/3	...	1/2	1 1/2	50	2	...	1 1/2 to 1	2 to 1	3 3/4	1/7	...	4 1/7	5

(12) Arrived at Quetta in March, and went to Candahar in September, 1839.
(13) Left Cabool in October, 1839—and since then with the European Regt. at Kujyar near Jellalabad.

No. 2.—Continued.

1839. Months.	(14) Sappers and Miners, average strength 254.										(15) 4th Tp., 3rd Bde. Ilse. Arty. avge. strength 140.									
	Admissions.					Deaths.					Admissions.					Deaths.				
	Fever.	Dysentery.	Cholera.	Other Diseases.	Total Admissions.	Fever.	Dysentery.	Cholera.	Other Diseases.	Total Deaths.	Fever.	Dysentery.	Cholera.	Other Diseases.	Total Admissions.	Fever.	Dysentery.	Cholera.	Other Diseases.	Total Deaths.
January,	4	2	..	14	20	..	..	..	..	..	..	..	..	..	..	..	..	..	..	..
February,	3	..	..	24	27	..	..	..	..	..	..	..	..	..	..	..	..	..	..	..
March,	7	2	..	12	21	..	..	..	1	1	..	..	..	..	..	..	..	..	..	..
April,	4	3	..	9	16	..	..	..	..	..	..	..	..	..	..	..	..	..	..	..
May,	14	28	..	16	58	1	..	..	1	2	..	..	..	..	..	..	..	..	..	..
June,	11	4	..	17	32	..	..	..	..	..	1	1	..	4	5	..	..	..	..	..
July,	21	13	..	31	65	..	..	..	..	..	6	..	..	8	15	..	..	..	..	..
August,	9	4	..	10	23	..	..	..	..	..	16	5	..	18	39	..	1	..	1	1
September,	6	3	..	1	10	..	..	..	..	..	2	3	..	16	21	..	1	..	..	1
October,	2	3	..	7	12	1	..	..	..	3	12	2	..	8	22	..	..	..	..	..
November,	13	..	..	22	35	..	..	..	..	..	9	1	..	11	21	..	..	..	..	..
December,	9	7	..	10	26	..	..	..	..	..	..	..	..	..	..	..	..	..	..	..
Total,	103	69	..	173	345	2	..	..	4	6	46	12	..	65	123	..	1	..	1	2
Ratio p. c. per annum,	43	28	..	46	1½ p.c. to 1 & ¼ 1	1¼ p.c. & ¼	..	..	1 1/9	2¾	33	9	..	50	88	..	¾	..	¾	1½

(14) Left Cabool on 16th Oct. 1839 and returned to India; except a small part left in Affghanistan.
(15) Left at Cabool. Wintered at Bameean; and a native Troop of H. A.

No. 2.—Continued.

(16) Park of Artillery, average strength 684.

1839. Months.	Admissions.				Deaths.			
	Fever.	Dysentery.	Cholera.	Other Diseases.	Total Admissions.	Fever.	Dysentery.	Cholera.	Other Diseases.	Total Deaths.
January,	..	..	..	..	..	..	..	..	..	..
February,	..	..	..	..	..	..	..	..	..	..
March,	..	..	..	..	..	..	..	..	..	..
April,	..	..	..	..	..	..	..	..	..	..
May,	..	..	..	..	..	..	..	..	..	..
June,	8	1	..	15	24	..	..	..	2	2
July,	2	3	..	13	18	..	1	..	4	3
August,	2	1	..	10	13	..	..	..	..	4
September,	3	..	..	7	10	..	1	..	..	1
October,	..	..	..	..	..	..	..	..	..	..
November,	..	..	..	..	..	..	..	..	..	..
December,	..	..	..	..	..	..	..	..	..	..
Total,	15	5	..	45	65	..	2	..	6	8
Ratio p. c. per annum,	2¼	¾	..	6¾	10	..	¼	..	½ p. c. and ¼	1¼

(16) Left Cabool on 16th October, 1839, and returned to India.

Appendix.

Admissions into the Hospital of the 35th Bengal N. I., at Cabool, during the months of January, February, March, and April, 1840.—About 700 men.

1840. January.	Diseases.	Remaining on 1st January, 1840.	Admitted in January.	Total.	Discharged in January.	Died in January.	Remaining.
	Cutaneous diseases,.........	..	2	2	2	..	..
	Dislocations and sprains,........	1	..	1	1	..	..
	Intermittent fevers,............	3	11	14	10	..	4
	Gonorrhœa,.................	1	1	2	2	..	..
	Thoracic Inflammation,........	2	9	11	3	6	2
	Rheumatism,................	..	1	1	..	..	1
	Syphilitic affections,...........	..	2	2	1	..	1
	Ulcers,.....................	4	3	7	6	..	1
	Wounds,....................	2	..	2	1	..	1
	Other diseases,..............	3	5	8	1	2	5
	Total,........	16	34	50	27	8	15

1840. February.	Diseases.	Remaining on 1st February.	Admitted in February.	Total.	Discharged in February.	Died in February.	Remaining.
	Diarrhœa,...................	..	1	1	..	..	1
	Cutaneous diseases,............	..	1	1	1	..	..
	Fevers { Remittent,...........	..	1	1	1	..	..
	{ Intermittent,.........	4	2	6	5	..	1
	Thoracic Inflammations,........	2	7	9	2	1	6
	Rheumatism,................	1	3	4	4	..	..
	Syphilis,....................	1	..	1	1	..	..
	Ulcer,......................	1	..	1	..	..	1
	Wounds,....................	1	..	1	..	..	1
	Other diseases,...............	5	6	11	5	..	6
	Total,........	15	21	36	19	1	16

Appendix.

1840. March.	Diseases.	Remaining on 1st March.	Admitted in March.	Total.	Discharged in March.	Died in March.	Remaining.
	Cutaneous,	...	2	2	2	...	...
	Diarrhœa,	1	1	2	...	1	1
	Fevers, { Remittent,	...	15	15	11	...	4
	{ Intermittent,	1	1	2	1	...	1
	Thoracic inflammation,	6	...	6	5	...	1
	Rheumatism,	...	3	3	1	...	2
	Ulcers,	1	1	2	...	...	2
	Wounds,	1	...	1	...	...	1
	Other diseases,	6	13	19	9	1	9
	Total,	16	36	52	29	2	21

1840. April.	Diseases.	Remaining on 1st April.	Admitted in April.	Total.	Discharged in April.	Died in April.	Remaining.
	Cutaneous diseases,	...	1	1	...	...	1
	Diarrhœa,	1	...	1	1	...	...
	Sprains,	...	1	1	...	...	1
	Fevers, { Remittent,	4	22	26	20	1	5
	{ Intermittent,	1	16	17	12	...	5
	Thoracic Inflammation,	1	3	4	2	...	2
	Rheumatism,	2	2	4	3	...	1
	Syphilis,	...	1	1	1	...	...
	Gonorrhœa,	...	1	1	1	...	...
	Ulcers,	2	...	2	1	...	1
	Wounds,	1	...	1	...	...	1
	Other diseases,	9	25	34	29	...	5
	Total,	21	72	93	70	1	22

N. B. About 150 of this Regt. were on duty on an average, during the winter. H. M. 13th Infy., it is said, had about 60 men, on duty. The sepoys of the 35th N. I. stood the cold admirably well; though the thermometer was often 4 and 6 degrees below zero, and though exposed as sentries day and night. They had barracks, and fires were kept up in them. The men had charpoys (beds), but were crowded, and the floor is said to have been damp. Out of 700 men 12 died in 4 months; about 1¾ p. c. They lost 14 men in all 1839.

No. 3.—*Range of the Thermometer during* 1838-39. *For the Month of Dec.* 1838.

Places.	1838 Dec.	4 & 5 A. M.	3 P. M.	Differ.	Remarks. (1)
In the Bhawulpoor Country.	18	45	84	39	
	19	45	84	39	
	20	48	86	33	
	21	48	86	38	
	22	53	80	27	
	23	53	80	27	
	24	50	70	20	
	25	34	70	36	Ice ¼ inch thick.
	26	54	66	12	A cold westerly wind and heavy clouds, succeeding to the heat of the morning.
	27	54	72	18	
	28	40	70	30	
Bhawulpoor,	29	50	68	18	
	30	50	68	18	
	31	50	68	18	

(1) The range of the Thermometer was kept inside a small 12 feet square Hill-tent, with 2 flies (roofs) but only one set of Qunats (walls).

The difference between this tent and a Subaltern's single-poled-tent (14 feet square) gave a lower temperature of about 5 to 8 degrees.

At Candahar we used *Tatties* in the months of May and June, 1839.

The tents of the sick were about 5 degrees hotter than the hill-tents; but the European sick were quartered in mud houses, in which the temperature was reduced 18 to 20 degrees below that in a hill-tent.

At *Bameean*, on the Feb. 1840, the cold was excessive, being 10° below zero, for several mornings, and the maximum temperature at noon was 15° to 20° of the thermometer in the shade. In the forts, there, with a good fire raised to 50°. The Goorkha Battn. had lost 30 men since their arrival there. But Jellalabad, between Cabool and Peshawer, offered this year the most curious fact as to temperature. On the 6th January, 1840, the thermometer stood *at* 28° *at sunrise, and at* 92° *at* 2½ P. M. *in the open air; being a difference of* 64 *degrees*, a variation greater than reported from any other station in Affghanistan. Jellalabad and Kujyar are the most trying situations for troops, European or native. Their relief would, consequently, be desirable.

No. 3.—Continued.

For the Month of January, 1839.

Places.	1839 Jan.	4 & 5 A. M.	3 P. M.	Differ.	Remarks.
The Bhawulpoor Country.	1	55	68	13	
	2	45	60	15	
	3	46	60	14	
	4	34	60	26	
	5	48	60	12	
	6	44	74	30	
	7	44	74	30	
	8	44	80	36	
	9	44	80	36	
	10	44	82	38	
	11	44	84	40	
	12	54	68	14	
	13	58	84	26	
	14	44	76	32	
In Upper Sindh.	15	40	62	22	
	16	50	70	20	
	17	54	72	18	
	18	40	80	40	
	19	38	76	38	
	20	44	80	36	
	21	38	74	36	
	22	38	72	34	
	23	37	78	40	
Rohree.	24	44	84	40	
	25	56	78	22	
	26	48	78	38	
Lower Sindh.	27	47	80	33	
	28	50	80	30	
	29	48	80	32	
	30	55	82	27	
	31	60	82	22	

Maximum 84°. Minimum 34°. Mean 59°.

No. 3.—Continued.

For the Month of February, 1839.

Places.	1839 Feb.	4 & 5 A. M.	3 P. M.	Differ.	Remarks.
Lower Sindh.	1	48	78	30	
	2	47	76	29	
	3	55	78	23	
	4	58	84	28	
	5	58	78	20	
	6	40	80	40	
	7	44	80	36	
	8	50	86	36	
	9	45	89	44	
	10	55	91	36	
	11	54	92	38	
	12	65	92	27	
	13	54	90	36	
	14	60	90	30	
Sukkur.	15	60	92	32	
	16	50	90	40	
	17	48	85	37	
	18	44	78	34	Threatened rain. Thunder and large drops fell in showers.
	19	50	78	28	Rain fell heavily at 4 A. M.
Shikarpoor.	20	55	86	31	Altitude above the sea 250 feet.
	21	55	86	31	
	22	48	78	30	
	23	58	86	28	
Upper Sindh.	24	48	78	30	
	25	36	76	40	Ice this morning.
	26	50	80	30	
	27	45	90	45	
	28	50	92	42	

Maximum 92°.   Minimum 36°.   Mean 64°.

Appendix.

No. 3.—Continued.

For the Month of March, 1839.

Places.		Altitudes.	1839 Mar.	4 & 5 A. M.	3 P. M.	Differ.	Remarks.
Upper Sindh.		Feet.	1	50	94	44	
			2	50	94	44	
			3	50	94	44	
			4	60	98	38	
			5	56	96	40	
	Beloochistan.		6	60	98	38	
			7	60	98	38	
			8	60	96	36	
			9	60	88	28	
Dadur.		743	10	60	88	28	
			11	55	82	27	
			12	50	82	32	
			13	50	84	34	
			14	55	82	27	
			15	50	86	36	
		904	16	62	86	24	
		1,081	17	60	86	26	Very close and cloudy.
The Bolan Pass.		1,695	18	60	72	12	Rain poured all night, and at 4 A. M. heavily.
		2,540	19	50	66	16	A gale of wind, and some heavy showers during the night. Cold considerable. Many tents blown down.
		4,494	20	52	66	14	Wind N. W. and cold.
		5,793	21	44	60	16	
			22	38	75	37	
			23	50	68	18	Heavy clouds—threatening snow.
			24	55	72	17	
			25	44	66	22	
Quetta.		5,637	26	34	60	26	
			27	40	62	22	Clouds and wind.
			28	30	58	28	Rain at day-break. Snow in the hills, and rain in the valley, whole day and night.
			29	38	60	22	
			30	38	72	34	A beautiful day.
			31	40	70	30	

Maximum 98°. Minimum 34°. Mean 66°.

No. 3.—*Continued.*

For the Month of April, 1839.

Places.	Altitudes.	1839 Apl.	4 & 5 A. M.	3 P. M.	Differ.	Remarks.
		1	44	76	32	
		2	50	76	26	
		3	55	76	21	Heavy rain at night.
		4	56	76	20	The weather cleared up in the morning. In the evening a strong gale, with heavy rain.
		5	40	64	24	Cold clear sky and wind. 3 P. M. bleak wind; bitter cold all night, and strong wind.
		6	38	64	26	
Kuchlak.		7	46	76	30	
Hyderzye.	5,259	8	62	79	17	Close cloudy morning.
Hykulzye.	5,063	9	52	82	30	
		10	52	88	36	
		11	48	83	35	
		12	60	80	20	
		13	55	84	29	
Kojuk Pass.	6,848	14	60	94	34	The summit of the Pass 7,457.
Chumun Chokee.	5,677	15	60	86	26	
		16	60	87	27	
Dundee Goolaee.		17	62	89	27	
	4,036	18	62	97	35	
		19	54	102	48	
Quilla Futoolah.		20	54	102	48	
	3,918	21	54	102	48	
		22	52	102	50	
Tukht-i-pool.	3,630	23	60	102	42	
		24	62	100	38	
		25	68	99	31	
Candahar.	3,484	26	62	94	32	
		27	62	88	26	
		28	50	90	40	
		29	50	97	47	
		30	64	96	32	

Maximum 102°. Minimum 38°. Mean 70°.

Appendix. 63

No. 3.—Continued.

For the Month of May, 1839.

Places.	Altitudes.	1839 May	4 & 5 A. M.	3 P. M.	Differ.	Remarks.
Candahar.	3,484	1	54	98	44	
		2	54	94	40	
		3	55	96	41	
		4	54	99	45	
		5	56	102	46	
		6	60	100	40	
		7	62	100	38	
		8	62	102	40	
		9	60	98	38	
		10	56	98	42	
		11	56	100	44	
		12	56	102	46	
		13	56	102	46	
		14	56	102	46	
		15	58	102	44	
		16	60	104	44	A violent storm of wind at night.
		17	62	104	42	Weather getting more oppressive every day.
		18	66	104	38	
		19	66	100	34	A gale of wind from S. W. with clouds of dust ; but cool in the middle of the day.
		20	50	86	36	Cold wind from S. W. cloudy—threatening rain.
		21	54	85	31	Strong S. W. winds and heavy clouds.
		22	56	85	29	
		23	59	92	33	
		24	58	95	37	
		25	56	96	40	
		26	58	97	39	
		27	56	99	43	
		28	62	98	36	
		29	62	100	38	
		30	64	102	38	
		31	54	102	48	

Maximum 104°. Minimum 50°. Mean 77°.

No. 3.—Continued.

For the Month of June, 1839.

Places.	Altitudes.	1839 June	4 & 5 A. M.	3 P. E.	Differ.	Remarks.
Candahar.	3,484	1	52	104	52	
		2	54	104	50	
		3	54	105	51	
		4	66	106	40	At 10 A. M. 100°. Noon 102°. In the sun 122°.
		5	58	106	48	
		6	60	106	46	
		7	54	106	52	
		8	54	106	52	
		9	62	106	42	A close heavy atmosphere. At night a gale of hot wind.
		10	74	100	26	Strong wind and cloudy.
		11	56	102	46	Very chilly early in the morning.
		12	52	100	48	
		13	62	104	42	A very windy hot day.
		14	62	100	38	A gale of hot wind all day with clouds.
		15	60	100	40	
		16	52	100	48	
		17	54	106	52	
		18	60	106	46	At 9 A. M. 90°. Noon 98°. In the sun 128°. Hot wind at night.
		19	70	108	38	Do. Noon 100°.
		20	66	108	42	10 A. M. 100°.
		21	68	108	40	
		22	68	108	40	
		23	70	108	38	
		24	70	110	40	
		25	72	110	38	
		26	72	110	38	
Abool Uzecz.		27	72	108	36	Left Candahar.
QuillaAzeem.	3,945	28	82	103	21	12°, cooler during the march.
Quilla Akhoond Shuhr-i-shuffa.	4,418	29	72	100	28	Full moon. Cool during the night.
	4,618	30	68	104	36	

Maximum 110°.   Minimum 52°.   Mean 81°.

Appendix.

No. 3.—Continued.

For the Month of July, 1839.

Places.	Altitudes.	1839 July	4 & 5 A. M.	3 P. M.	Differ.	Remarks.
Teerundaz,	4,829	1	70	100	30	Great change in the temperature which increased much towards dawn.
		2	68	100	32	
Jugduluk,	5,396	3	76	102	26	A gale of hot wind blew all night. A hot march.
Khelat-i-Ghiljie,	5,773	4	62	100	38	
		5	62	98	36	
Sir-i-usp,	5,973	6	72	96	24	A cold, cutting, breeze sprung up on the march.
Tazee Nouruk,	6,136	7	72	93	21	
Tazee,	6,321	8	70	93	23	
		9	62	90	28	93° noon. Thunder, cooled atmosphere.
Shuftul,	6,514	10	60	96	36	
Chusma-i-Shadee,	6,668	11	58	97	39	Heavy clouds and wind.
Punguk,	6,810	12	70	93	23	Strong gusts of wind, heavy clouds—evening cool.
Ghojan,	7,068	13	66	92	27	In the sun 12 to 2 P.M. 110°. After 3 P.M. heavy gale of wind and clouds.
Mukoor,	7,091	14	64	87	23	
		15	56	87	31	
Oba,	7,325	16	60	92	32	
Jumrood,	7,426	17	62	93	31	
Musheekee,	7,309	18	66	91	25	Heavy rain in the middle of the night.
Arghistan,	7,502	19	66	93	27	Close day with distant thunder.
Nannee,	7,420	20	68	94	26	
Ghuznee,	7,726	21	68	94	26	
		22	66	92	26	
		23	56	94	38	The wind cold, and chilling.
		24	58	90	32	
		25	58	92	34	
		26	58	93	35	Thunder storm in the night, and light rain.
		27	62	90	28	Ditto ditto, lightning and rain in the evening.
		28	58	92	34	
	(2)	29	60	90	30	
Shushgao,	8,697	30	62	86	24	A furious wind all day, with hazy weather.
Huftasya,	8,420	31	52	88	36	At 4 A. M. in open air 47°. Cold S. wind and cool night.

Maximum 102°. Minimum 52°. Mean 77°,
(2) Gundi Shere Pass, estimated 9,000 feet.

Appendix.

No. 3.—Continued.
For the Month of August, 1839.

Places.	Altitudes.	1839 Aug.	4 & 5 A.M.	3 P.M.	Differ.	Remarks.
Hyderkhel,	7,637	1	60	94	34	
Shakabad,	7,473	2	56	98	42	
		3	60	94	34	
Mydan,	7,747	4	60	88	28	
Urghundee,	7,628	5	62	88	26	
Cabool,	6,396	6	68	92	24	Thunder storm after 3 P. M. which reduced it to 86°.
		7	68	92	24	
		8	72	94	22	
		9	74	96	22	
		10	72	96	24	
		11	72	96	24	
		12	74	96	22	A gale of wind in the evening.
		13	54	92	38	A gale of wind all night, reducing temperature next morning.
		14	48	90	42	
		15	48	86	38	
		16	46	86	40	Cloudy and windy night.
		17	58	88	30	
		18	48	86	38	
		19	50	88	38	
		20	48	91	43	
		21	50	96	46	
		22	60	96	36	
		23	66	94	28	Heavy gale, and some rain during the night.
		24	62	90	28	Thunder, lightning, and wind, and sharp rain after 3 P. M.
		25	62	76	14	Thunder, rain, and N. W. wind, succeeded by dampness all night.
		26	58	72	14	Heavy clouds, some peaks covered with snow.
		27	56	83	27	Great mist, and rawness in the atmosphere. Sudden gusts of wind from opposite directions, and hazy weather.
		28	60	88	28	
		29	60	87	27	A fog A. M. Heavy gusts of wind, almost blowing down the tents, and hazy weather.
		30	60	84	24	Heavy gale of wind till 11 P. M.
		31	59	83	24	High winds, and mist.

The thermometer often 96° in a single-poled tent at Candahar, during this month.

Maximum 98°.   Minimum 46°.   Mean 72°.

Appendix. 67

No. 3.—*Continued.*
For the Month of September, 1839.

Places.	Altitude.	1839 Sep.	4 & 5 A. M.	3 P. M.	Differ.	Remarks.
Cabool,	6,396	1	58	82	24	
		2	60	83	23	Clouds and strong gales.
		3	62	84	22	Heavy clouds, with a gale of wind. Snow fell on the mountains, lowering temperature.
		4	54	84	30	Cold N. W. winds. Snow melted during the day.
		5	54	86	32	
		6	56	88	32	Winds from E. with sultry lulls—close night gale of wind and thunder.
		7	64	84	20	The gale all night, cooled the atmosphere.
		8	60	82	22	
		9	58	82	24	Heavy rain, and strong gales of wind.
		10	58	76	18	Heavy winds, and deep fall of snow on the mountains.
		11	52	80	28	
		12	54	80	26	The snow disappeared. The natives said the late gales caused by the change of the moon.
		13	54	80	26	
		14	60	82	22	A gale of wind with the setting sun, and lasted best part of the night.
		15	56	84	28	
		16	54	90	36	
		17	56	88	32	A heavy gale of wind from N. E. after 3 P. M.
		18	50	88	38	
		19	52	88	36	
		20	54	88	34	A gale of wind and clouds in the evening.
		21	56	82	26	A cool summer breeze. Fresh breeze at dusk.
		22	54	84	30	Strong wind at night.
		23	54	88	34	
		24	54	90	36	Black clouds and high winds
		25	62	80	18	Heavy clouds, wind, and slight rain.
		26	56	72	16	Ditto ditto and strong gale of wind all night.
		27	54	70	16	Ditto ditto and wind. Heavy fall of snow on the mountains obscuring the sun. The highest peaks covered with snow; all darkness below.
		28	54	78	24	Strong wind in the evening, and night.
		29	50	78	28	The Autumn arrived.
		30	50	82	32	A gale of wind from 4 P. M. till 11 P. M. almost blew the tents down.

The thermometer often 96° in a single-poled tent at Candahar, during this month.
Maximum 90°. Minimum 50. Mean 70°.

68   Appendix.

No. 3.—Continued.

For the Month of October, 1839.

Places.	Altitudes.	1839 Oct.	4 & 5 A. M.	3 P. M.	Differ.	Remarks.
Cabool,	6,396	1	50	82	32	Fine temperate weather.
		2	50	80	30	
		3	50	80	30	A gale of wind, half the night.
		4	50	78		
		5	48	76	28	Gales of wind.
		6	47	73	26	A heavy gale of wind in the night.
		7	47	70	23	A N. W. wind, cold at night 54°.
		8	40	68	28	A. M. Ice outside ¼ inch thick, bracing weather, and clear sky.
		9	40	72	32	Fine weather, bracing cold.
		10	40	76	36	A. M. extremely cold.
		11	40	70	30	Ice outside the tent.
		12	40	68	28	Heavy clouds in evening, and cold E. wind, threatening a snow storm.
		13	48	72	24	Change to warm and close weather.
		14	48	72	24	
Boot Khak,	6,247	15	44	64	20	
Khoord Cabool,	7,466	16	36	64	28	Must have been below zero all night. The water bags having nothing but ice in them. Cold intense in the Pass, piercing E. S. E. wind.
Tezeen Valley,	(3) 6,488	17	30	66	36	
		18	50	75	25	A change of wind dispersed the frost.
Pareek-ab,	5,313	19	48	72	24	During the march the wind changed from S. to N., and froze the water.
Jugduluk,	5,375	20	54	72	18	
Soorkh-ab,	4,373	21	40	80	40	
Gundamuk,	4,616	22	56	78	22	
		23	54	75	21	
Futeh-ab,	3,098	24	52	80	28	
Sultanpoor,	2,286	25	54	90	36	
Jellalabad,	1,964	26	54	92	38	
		27	54	92	38	
		28	54	92	38	
Alee Boghan,	1,911	29	56	92	36	At 42 min. past 3 P. M. 2 distinct shocks of an earthquake, preceded by a rumbling noise.
Bareek-ab,	1,822	30	56	88	32	
Bassool,	1,509	31	54	88	34	

Maximum 92°.   Minimum 30°.   Mean 61°.
(3) Tezeen Pass, 8,173.

Appendix.

No. 3.—*Continued.*

For the Month of November, 1839.

Places.	Altitudes.	1839 Nov.	4 & 5 A. M.	3 P. M.	Differ.	Remarks.
Dhaka,	1,404	1	56	87	31	
Lundeekhana	2,488 (4)	2	48	78	30	Change partly owing to elevation, and partly to damp ground surcharged with Soda.
Ali-musjid,	2,433	3	60	82	22	A change of wind.
		4	60	82	22	
Jumrood,	1,670	5	60	86	26	
		6	58	86	28	Heavy clouds; atmosphere close and hazy.
Peshawer,	1,068	7	62	92	30	
		8	52	82	30	
		9	52	82	30	
		10	60	68	8	Heavy clouds and slight rain—no clouds at night.
		11	50	76	26	A fine clear morning.
		12	50	82	32	
		13	50	82	32	
		14	52	85	33	
		15	48	82	34	
		16	46	82	36	
		17	48	78	30	
		18	48	80	32	
		19	50	81	31	
		20	54	79	25	
		21	44	75	31	
		22	42	76	34	
		23	46	66	20	Heavy clouds threatening rain. Heavy clouds all night.
		24	56	76	20	
		25	50	76	26	
Attok,		26	46	74	28	Heavy wind from W.
		27	46	76	30	
		28	40	76	36	
		29	34	78	44	
		30	33	74	41	

Maximum 92°.   Minimum 33°.   Mean 62½°.

(4) The summit of the Pass, 3,373.

No. 3.—Continued.

For the Month of December, 1839.

Places.	1839 Dec.	4 & 5 A. M.	3 P. M.	Differ.	Remarks.
Rawul Pindee,	1	36	72	36	The cold severe, weather rather cloudy.
	2	34	75	41	
	3	40	64	24	Heavy clouds.
	4	48	76	28	
	5	36	74	38	A cold N. W. wind.
	6	48	82	34	
	7	38	74	36	
	8	42	75	33	
	9	48	80	32	
Rhotus,	10	38	76	38	
Jheelum,	11	40	72	32	
	12	38	64	26	Cloudy and threatening rain.
	13	30	68	38	In open air 22° 5 A. M. ; 36° at 8½ A. M.
	14	32	73	41	
	15	42	68	26	Cloudy morning.
	16	40	72	32	
Chenab,	17	40	76	36	
	18	38	76	38	
	19	38	78	40	
	20	38	72	34	
	21	38	72	34	Very cold on the march.
	22	38	75	37	Hoar frost.
	23	36	76	40	
	24	36	68	32	Heavy clouds threatening rain.
Ravee,	25	44	64	20	
	26	40	70	30	
	27	40	70	30	
	28	44	75	31	
	29	40	75	35	
Sutluj,	30	44	75	31	
	31	36	74	38	

Maximum 82°. Minimum 30°. Mean 56°.

Appendix.

No. 3.—Continued.

Register of Thermometer at Quetta.

For the Months of May and June, 1839.

1839 May.	Sun-rise.	3 P.M.	Differ.	Wind.	1839 June	Sun-rise.	3 P.M.	Differ.	Wind.
1	66	91	25	W.	1	47	94	47	N. W.
2	64	87	23	ditto.	2	58	96	38	ditto.
3	63	83	20	ditto.	3	63	95	32	ditto.
4	55	93	38	ditto.	4	65	94	29	ditto.
5	64	96	32	ditto.	5	66	94	28	ditto.
6	60	98	38	N. W.	6	57	94	37	ditto.
7	64	96	32	ditto.	7	55	95	40	ditto.
8	64	93	29	ditto.	8	53	94	41	ditto.
9	63	91	28	W.	9	57	98	41	ditto.
10	61	91	30	ditto.	10	64	91	27	N. W. & S. E.
11	61	95	34	ditto.					
12	61	96	35	ditto.	11	56	90	34	ditto.
13	65	95	30	ditto.	12	52	90	38	ditto.
14	67	97	30	ditto.	13	62	90	28	Variable.
15	66	100	34	ditto.	14	64	94	30	ditto.
16	66	97	31	ditto.	15	62	90	28	N. W.
17	67	96	29	ditto.	16	54	91	37	ditto.
18	68	94	26	ditto.	17	54	93	39	ditto.
19	56	84	26	N. W.	18	60	96	36	N. W. & S. E.
20	54	86	32	ditto.					
21	53	82	29	ditto.	19	64	99	35	ditto.
22	55	80	25	W.	20	62	96	34	ditto.
23	52	86	34	ditto.	21	63	87	24	ditto.
24	53	89	36	N. W.	22	66	99	33	ditto.
25	49	91	42	ditto.	23	66	99	33	ditto.
26	49	92	43	ditto.	24	69	98	29	ditto.
27	52	92	40	ditto.	25	69	95	26	S. E.
28	55	93	38	ditto.	26	68	94	26	S. E. & N. W.
29	56	92	36	ditto.					
30	65	92	27	ditto.	27	65	95	30	N. W. & S. E.
31	56	92	36	W.					
					28	65	94	29	ditto.
					29	63	92	29	N. W.
					30	65	94	29	S. E. & N. W.

Maximum 100. Minimum 49.
Mean 74½.

Maximum 99. Minimum 47.
Mean 73.

No. 3.—Continued.

Register of Thermometer at Quetta.

For the Months of July and August, 1839.

1839 July.	Sun-rise.	3 P.M.	Differ.	Wind.	1839 Aug.	Sun-rise.	3 P.M.	Differ.	Wind.
1	70	92	22	Variable.	1	58	94	36	W.
2	72	93	21	ditto.	2	61	94	33	ditto.
3	69	93	24	ditto.	3	63	95	32	ditto.
4	71	93	22	S.&N.W.	4	63	95	32	ditto.
5	69	93	24	ditto.	5	64	94	30	ditto.
6	70	92	22	ditto.	6	63	90	27	N. W.
7	68	88	20	S.	7	64	95	31	S.
8	67	73	6	ditto.	8	64	95	31	W.
9	59	92	33	ditto.	9	63	94	31	ditto.
10	68	93	25	N. W.	10	63	95	32	ditto.
11	61	94	33	ditto.	11	65	95	30	ditto.
12	62	94	32	W.	12	66	96	30	Variable.
13	66	92	26	ditto.	13	66	97	31	ditto.
14	60	91	31	ditto.	14	67	95	28	N. W.
15	56	92	36	Variable.	15	65	90	25	N. W. &. S
16	62	92	30	ditto.					
17	65	95	30	S.	16	64	88	24	W.
18	68	79	11	ditto.	17	66	88	22	N. W.
19	65	92	27	Variable.	18	64	87	23	Variable.
20	64	92	28	ditto.	19	63	91	28	W.
21	60	92	32	N. W.	20	62	94	32	ditto.
22	62	94	32	ditto.	21	64	95	31	ditto.
23	62	96	34	ditto.	22	64	93	29	ditto.
24	64	96	32	ditto.	23	64	94	30	Variable.
25	66	96	30	ditto.	24	65	95	30	ditto.
26	68	95	27	ditto.	25	65	89	24	ditto.
27	68	88	20	Variable.	26	59	90	31	ditto.
28	64	94	30	N. W.	27	53	90	37	ditto.
29	62	93	31	ditto.	28	57	88	31	ditto.
30	62	94	32	ditto.	29	53	91	38	ditto.
31	62	94	32	ditto.	30	53	90	27	ditto.
					31	57	91	34	ditto.

Maximum 96. Minimum 56.
Mean 76.

Maximum 97. Minimum 53.
Mean 75.

No. 3.—Continued.

Register of Thermometer at Quetta.
For the Month of September, 1839.

1839. Sept.	Sun-rise.	3 p.m.	Differ.	Wind.
1	62	91	29	Variable.
2	63	90	27	ditto.
3	62	87	25	W.
4	52	88	36	ditto.
5	47	89	42	Variable.
6	49	89	40	ditto.
7	58	90	32	S.
8	60	88	28	S. & S. W.
9	61	82	21	ditto.
10	52	67	15	N. W.
11	50	70	20	N. & S. W.
12	51	83	32	W. & S.
13	54	85	31	N. W.
14	55	85	30	W.
15	54	85	31	ditto.
16	56	87	31	ditto.
17	53	88	35	ditto.
18	52	89	37	ditto.
19	50	84	39	N. W.
20	51	88	37	ditto.
21	50	88	38	ditto.
22	50	89	39	ditto.
23	47	87	40	ditto.
24	48	88	40	W.
25	58	87	29	N. W.
26	57	87	30	ditto.
27	47	83	36	ditto.
28	45	80	35	N.
29	42	80	38	ditto.
30	43	79	36	W.

Maximum 91, Minimun 42, Mean 66½,

N. B. The Table for October was lost at Khelat. It would give a lower temperature than that in September,

No. 4.

Barometrical Heights in feet. Observations with an Englefield Barometer, without an attached Thermometer. (1)

Places.	Feet.	Places.	Feet.
Shikarpoor,	250	Quilla Kazee,	6,508
Dadur,	743	Cabool, (Baber's Tomb,)	6,396
Kohun Delan, (Bolan Pass,)	904	Boot Khak,	6,247
Gurm-ab, (ditto,)	1,081	Khoord Cabool,	7,466
Beebee Nanee, (ditto,)	1,695	Tezeen Pass,	8,173
Abi-goom, (ditto,)	2,540	,, Valley,	6,488
Sir-i-Bolan, (ditto,)	4,494	Bareek-ab,	5,313
Munzilgah, (out of Pass,) } Dusht-i-Bedoulut, }	5,793	Jugdulluk,	5,375
		Soorkh-ab,	4,373
Quettah,	5,637	Gundamuk,	4,616
Hyderzye,	5,259	Futtehabad,	3,098
Hykulzye,	5,063	Sultanpoor,	2,286
Halt in Khojuk Pass, Foot of main		Jellalabad,	1,964
ascent,	6,848	Ali Boghar,	1,911
Summit of Khojuk Pass,	7,457	Bareek-ab,	1,822
Chumun, (in the valley,)	5,677	Bussoolah,	1,509
Dundee Goolaee,	4,036	Lalpoorah,	1,404
Quilla Futtoolah,	3,918	Lundee Khana, (Khyber Pass,)	2,488
Tukht-i-Pool,	3,630	Summit of Pass,	3,373
Khoosh-ab,	3,484	W. of Ali Musjid,	2,433
Candahar,	3,484	Jumrood,	1,670
Quilla Azeem,	3,945	Peshawer,	1,068
Turnuk, (29th June,)	4,418	Summit of Khaki Sufed Pass,	8,670
Shuhr-i-Suffa,	4,618	Kot-i-Ashruf, (Mydan Valley,)	7,749
Teerundaz,	4,829	Sir-i-Chushm, (Head of Cabool	
Julduk,	5,396	river,)	8,836
Khelat-i-Ghiljie,	5,773	Foot of main ascent of Oonnye Pass,	10,522
Sir-i-usp,	5,973	Summit of Oonnye Pass,	11,320
Tazee Noorook,	6,136	Youart,	10,618
Tazee,	6,321	Helmund river,	10,076
Shuftul,	6,514	Halt in Siah Sung River,	10,488
Chusm-i-Shadee,	6,668	Kurzar,	10,939
Punguk, (12th July,)	6,810	Foot of main ascent of Hajee Guk,	11,370
Gojhan,	7,068	Summit of Hajee Guk Pass,	12,190
Mookhloor,	7,091	Kulloo,	10,853
Oba,	7,325	Sooktar, or Kulloo River,	9,839
Jumrat, (Jumrood,)	7,426	Summit of Kulloo Pass,	12,481
Mahshookee	7,309	Topchee,	9,085
Urguttoo,	7,502	Bameean,	8,496
Near Nanee,	7,420	Zohawk at junction of Kulloo and	
Ghuznee,	7,726	Bameean River,	8,186
Gund-i-Sher Pass, (estimated,)	9,000	Lesser Erak Pass, (very steep,)	9,155
Shushgao,	8,697	Erak Valley, upper end of culti-	
Huftasya,	8,420	vation,	8,914
Hyder Khel,	7,637	Halt in Erak Ravine, near foot of	
Shakabad,	7,473	main ascent,	11,545
Quilla Sir Mahomed,	8,051	Summit of the greater Erak Pass,	12,909
Mydan,	7,747	(Here we came on our first route	
Urghundeh,	7,628	at Kurzar.)	

(1) As taken by Dr. Geo. Griffiths, Madras establishment.

Appendix.

No. 5.—*Guns, and Ordnance Stores, and Grain, captured at Ghuznee on the 23rd July ;—at Arghundee on the 1st, and at Cabool on 4th August ; and near Jellalabad.* By Lieut.-Col. Wade.

Ghuznee.	Brass Guns.			Iron Guns.					Total.
	68-Pr.	6-Pr.	¾-Pr.	6-Pr.	3½-Pr.	1½-Pr.	Rifled wall pieces.	Ginjals or wall pieces.	
Taken in the Fort on the 23rd July, 1839.	1	1	2	1	1	2	1	21	30 (1)

Shot.

8 Inch.	48-Pr.	42-Pr.	32-Pr.	24-Pr.	12-Pr.	9-Pr.	6-Pr.	4-Pr.	3-Pr.	Chain. 6-Pr.	Grape 6-Pr.	Ditto 4-Pr.	Ditto 3-Pr.	Total.
6	164	47	7	4	250	40	1103	353	437	7	18	13	7	2358

Balls, Cartridges, Port-fires, Blue lights, &c.

Ginjal Balls.	Leaden Balls.	Cartridges with Ball 6-Pr.	Ditto 4-Pr.	Light 6-Pr.	Ditto 4-Pr.	Ditto 3-Pr.	Rockets large.	Ditto small.	Port fires.	Blue Lights.	Flints.
1940	2180(2)	186	54	253	61	231	491	55	400	74	4418

Iron.	Lead.	Powder fine.	Bayonets.	Swords.	Shields.	Powder Horns.	Match and flint locks.
1308 lbs.	2304 lbs.	22,612	12	50	67	60	238 (3)

There were 39 horses selected for the public service, by a committee, for the H. A. and Dragoons.

(1) Carriage and limbers—the large Gun, a carriage.
(2) Balls leaden Musketry of sizes 4,144.
(3) Shovels 42 ; Picks 14 ; Iron Axle 1 ; Cylinders 15 ; Copper Cauldrons 2. Felloes, wheel, rough 10 ; Cow-hides 9 ; Lashing (pieces 12) yards 200 ; Line-Cotton tent white 60 lbs. ; Oil (country) Gallons 15 ; Steelyard 1 ; Wheels 2 ; Wood for charcoal 60 cwt. ; Iron 56 lbs.

No. 5.—*Continued.*

Grain Captured at Ghuznee and taken by the Commissariat for the use of the army.

Flour.	Wheat.	Barley.	Peas.	Bhoosa.	Wood.
79,080 lbs.	353,780 lbs.	74,000 lbs.	3520 lbs.	57,760 lbs.	2560 lbs. (4)

Guns, &c. taken at Arghundee on the 4th August, 1839.

Brass.							Iron.		Total.
24-Pr.	12-Pr.	10-Pr.	9-Pr.	8-Pr.	6-Pr.	Howit. 6-Inch.	4-Pr.	¾-Pr.	
2	8	2	4	5	1	1	1	1	25 (5)

Guns, &c. taken at Cabool on the 4th August, 1839.

Guns Brass 4-Pr., Carriages, &c. 4

Guns taken near Jellalabad.

By Lieut.-Colonel Wade, ... 14

(4) Rice 288 lbs. ; Salt 32 lbs. ; Raisins 160 lbs.
(5) Gun Carriages 20. Limbers 16. Iron Axletrees 10½. Wooden yokes 27. Gun-Carriage bodies 7. Do. wheels 8. Do. Block-wheel 1. Collars and harness 94. Saddles 9. Infantry pouches 50. Horse-traces 75. Sponges 7. Ammn. boxes 18. Pall-tents 5. Draught bullocks 139. Powder destroyed (by accidental explosion, *owing to some men smoking near the spot*) about 300 lbs. N. B. Two of the guns were found in a house not far from where the other 23 guns were parked.

No. 6.—Return of Month's supply for the Army of the Indus.

Candahar, 1st June, 1839.

Columns.	Fighting men.	Mustered followers.	Miscellaneous followers.	Horses.	Bullocks.	Gun camels.	Abstract of men and cattle.	Otta or Rice. Mds.	Dall. M. S.	Ghee. M. S.	Salt. M. S.	Gram for cattle. Mds.	Remarks.
Bengal Column,...	6,460	11,474	12,852	2,100			10,406 Fighting men, 14,621 Mustered followers,	7,804	975 23	487 36	162 22		Otta,....24,031 M. S. C. Otta,....24,031 0 0 Dall,.....3,656 22 0 Ghee,....1,170 26 0 Salt,.......609 0 0 Barley,..14,237 0 0
Bombay Column,...	3,946	3,147	1,180	1,350	481	97	14,032 Miscellaneous followers, 3450 Horses, 481 Bullocks, 97 Gun camels,	10,965	1365 30	682 30	227 10	12,937	Mds., 4)43,704 8 0
								5,262	1315 20	,, ,,	,, 219 8	1,082	
												218 (1)	
	10,406	14,621	14,032	3,450	481	97	974 Mds. per camels,..	24,031	3656 22	1170 26	609 0	14,237	Camels, 10,926 Add spare, 656
								6008	914 0	292 0	153 0	3,559	Camels, 11,582

Fighting Men and mustered Establishments.   *Miscellaneous Followers.*   *Cattle.*

Otta or Rice at 1 seer ea.=2 lbs.   Otta at ½ seer ea.   Horses at 5 seers ea.
Dall   at 2 ch. ea.=¼ ,,   Dall at 2 ch. ea.   Camels   } 3 seers ea.
Ghee   at 1 ch. ea.=⅛ ,,   Salt at ⅓ ch. ea.   Bullocks }
Salt   at ⅓ ch. ea.

N. B. Thus for an Army of 10,406 men it requires 1 1/20 camel per man to carry provisions for one month. A Cavalry soldier requires 7 times as much as an Infantry soldier. The latter only wants his *one* seer, the former requires one for himself, one for the groom, and 5 for his horse. Let those who think an Invasion of *India* an easy operation, study this Table.

(1) A maund is 80 lbs.

No. 7.—Return of Ordnance (1) and ordnance stores belonging to the Bengal Park with the Army of the Indus.

Kurnal, 31st October, 1838.

	Bomb shot.			Spherical Case.					Cannister, or grape.					Carcass shells.				Carcasses.		Light Balls.		Balled Ammunition.			Gunpowder Barrels 100 lbs. each.	
	18-pr.	9-pr.	6-pr.	18-pr.	9-pr.	6-pr.	24-pr. Howr.	12-pr. Howr.	18-pr.	9-pr.	6-pr.	24-pr. Howr.	12-pr. Howr.	8-Inch.	5¼-do.	4⅖-do.	8-Inch.	5¼-do.	8-Inch.	5¼-do.	Musket.	Carbine.	Pistol.	Musketry.	Ordnance.
Moved with the Army,	2000	1428	1920	100	620	720	144	180	200	124	240	24	24	600	708	144	20	32	20	20	1,529,040	26,520	1,04,520	47	425
In Depôt at Ferozpoor for 3d & 5h Brigades,...	,,	816	960	,,	112	360	70	90	,,	68	120	12	12	,,	54	72	,,	,,	,,	,,	560,236	4,800	,,	4⁶⁄₁₀	59

(1) N. B. *Ordnance*. Mortars, 2—8 Inch, 2—5½ Inch. Howitzers, 1—24-pr.; 1—12-pr. Guns, 4—18-pr.; 2—9-pr.; 2—6-pr. Mortar Beds, 2—8.Inch; 2—5½ Inch. Carriages, Gun and Howitzer with Limbers, 5—18-pr.; 4—9-pr.; 4—6-pr.; 2—24-pr. Howit.; 2—12-pr. Howit. Ammn. Carriages, 33. Ammn. Tumbrils 5. Transport Carriage 1. Platform carts 5. Store carts 11.

(1) I have been obliged to insert the Guns, &c. in this form, owing to the number of Columns. The expenditure of Ammn. was not great, being chiefly used at Ghuznee, and the greatest part unconsumed was left in Affghanistan. See loss in the Khojuk Pass, p. 90.

No. 8.—*Loss of Public and hired Cattle in the Bengal Column "Army of the Indus."*

In 14 Months.	Public camels died.	Public camels, abandoned, strayed, stolen, &c.	Total public camels.	Cavalry & H. A. horses.	Bullocks.	
					Transport train.	Hackery.
From Nov. 1838 to Dec. 1839, both included, ...	6,109	2,864	8,973	1,146	195	326
Add for Gun camels, (Bhagree,)	44	,,	44	,,		
Add for Loss of Rewaree or hired camels, ...	,,	,,	10,983	,,		
Total, ...	6,153	2,864	20,000	1,146	521	

N. B. I cannot estimate the loss of hired camels at less than 10,983. The Dy. Comy. General said, the loss of camels by Government, including the hired camels, could not be less than from 25 to 30,000, (all the returns not yet collected;) but I believe he included both the Bombay as well as Bengal Column. The Bombay Column was supplied with 7,266 camels by the Bengal Commissariat up to the time of their leaving Cabool. (1)

The value of the public camels at 70 rupees, (£ 7)........	63,119
Ditto Rewaree ditto, ditto 25, (2).....................	27,457
Ditto Horses at medium value 425 rupees, ...	48,705
Ditto 195 Train Bullocks, at 30 rupees, ...	585
Ditto 326 (3) Hackery Bullocks, at 20 rupees, ...	652

For Bengal Column, £140,518

(1) Grain of sorts, more than 40,000 maunds (3,200,000 lbs.) and 6,759 gallons of Rum.

(2) Government paid a monthly hire, and on proof of the death of a camel 25 rupees were paid to the owner.

(3) Hired by Government.

No. 8.—Continued.

Loss of Cattle, &c. by Officers and Men in the Bengal Column from Nov. 1838 to Oct. 1839, (4) Army of the Indus.

Corps and Departments.	Elephants.	Camels died.	Camels stolen, &c.	Horses.	Ponies, Yaboos, &c.	Bullocks.	Tents.
General Staff,	...	58	29	2	5	..	1
Cavalry Brigade ditto,	...	2	35	1	2	9	...
Infantry ditto ditto,	...	48	4	...	...	...	...
2nd T., 2nd B., H. A.	...	26	1	1	...	1	2
H. M.'s 16th Lancers, (5)	...	250	50	...	100	30	4
2nd Light Cavalry,	...	25	35	2	3	...	1
By the men,	...	7	4	...	...	4	...
3rd Light Cavalry,	...	105	4	...	5	11	8
By the men,	...	46	12	...	2	1	...
4th Local Horse,	...	25	1	2	1	...	1¼
By the men, (6)	...	30	...	...	56	29	11
Artillery,	...	29	30	1	...	...	½
H. M.'s 13th Light Infantry,	...	129	99	...	2	...	3½
By the men,	...	33	71	...	...	...	...
1st Bengal European Regiment,	...	112	52	7	...	5	17½
By the men, (7)	...	69	14	...	...	...	...
37th Native Infantry,	1	100	10	2	...	...	2
By the men,	(8)	58	40	2	...	...	...
42nd Native Infantry, (9)	...	98	5	...	...	...	1½
By the men,	...	150	29	...	2	3	...
43rd Native Infantry, (9)	...	46	...	...	...	...	...
By the men,	...	96	...	...	...	...	...
48th Native Infantry,	...	40	10	...	...	...	...
Total,	3 (8)	1585	465	20	178	83	53¼
Total,	...	2,050		...	...	...	...

(4) Up to October, 1839.
(5) Only obtained from one squadron and estimated for the other 3.
(6) Of only 3 out of 8 Ressallahs.
(7) They lost the greater part of their bedding; and nearly all their property not carried in their knapsacks.
(8) Killed in action, Sir W. H. Macnaghten's two elephants were carried off; Lieut.-Colonel Wheeler had two elephants; we had with the army only five elephants.
(9) Did not march beyond Quetta till September, 1839.

No. 8.—*Continued.*

N. B. I have no return from the Engineers, 31st N. I., nor from the Shah's force, and the losses of the men in 4 corps are not given. If we allow for these omissions, I should estimate the loss of Camels, at 2,500 for the Bengal Column and Shah's force.

Value of 2,500 Camels at 70 rupees,	£17,500
Ditto 20 Horses at 400 rupees,	800
Ditto 178 Ponies or Yaboos at 40 rupees,	712
Ditto 83 Bullocks at 30 rupees,	249
Ditto $53\frac{1}{4}$ Tents (large and small) at 250 rupees,	1,331
Add 3 Elephants at 1,000 rupees,	300
	£ 21,092

But, as before explained, the full return has not been furnished me. There are 3 months more to be included, (Oct. Nov. and Dec. 1839.) Many Officers lost property of value, not included in the columns; the losses of the clothes, &c. of the men are to be added:—hence, including the Shah's force, I estimate our loss at, ...£50,000

No. 8.—Continued.

Loss of Cattle, &c. by Officers and Men in the Bombay Column " Army of the Indus." (10)

	Camels died.	Camels stolen.	Horses.	Ponies, Yaboos.	Bullocks.	Tents.
General Staff,	74	20	1	8	..	½
Staff 1st Infantry Brigade,	5	2	1	2	..	..
Engineers,	2	1	..	2	..	..
Artillery,	68	10	1	26	..	1
Wing, H. M.'s 4th L. D.,	63	27	..	17	7	3
2nd Queen's Royal Regiment of Foot,	76	22	2	5	2	2½
By the Men,	34	..	..	..	..	..
H. M.'s 17th Foot,	57	31	3	7	6	8
19th Native Infantry,	58	13	1	17	4	3
By the Men,	96	6	..	..	..	..
Total,	533	132	9	86	19	18
Total,	665		9	86	19	18

N. B. There is no return for the 1st Light Cavalry or Poonah Horse. The losses of the men in several corps not stated. I should, therefore, estimate the loss of Camels at 800.

Value of 800 Camels, at 90 rupees, (11).	£7,200
Ditto 9 Horses, at 400 rupees,	360
Ditto 86 Ponies, at 40 rupees,	344
Ditto 19 Bullocks, at 30 rupees,	57
Ditto 18 Tents, at 250 rupees,	450
	£8,411

For the same reason as assigned in regard to the Bengal Column, I would estimate the loss at, ... 20,000

(10) Only up to middle of September, 1839.
(11) Some Officers gave 150 rupees for each camel.

No. 8.—Continued.

Recapitulation of the loss of animals, and their value.

Public and private losses.	Elephants.	Camels died, stolen, &c.	Horses.	Ponies, or Yaboos.	Bullocks.	Tents.
The Government loss in both Columns,..	..	26,700 (12)	1564 (13)	..	521	(14)
Officers and men in the Bengal Column, and Shah's Force, ...	3	2,500	20	178	83	53¼
Ditto Bombay Column, ...	..	800	9	86	19 (15)	18
Total,....	3	30,000	1564	264	623	71¼

N. B. Making a total loss of 32,483 animals, which may be called in round numbers 33,000 in an army of about 13,000 men including the corps left at Quetta; and without including any of the corps left in Sindh.

The value lost by Government, ...£140,518
Add 418 Horses, (Table No. 1,) Bombay Column, medium price
    450 rupees, (16) 17,810
Loss of officers and men, Bengal Column, ... 50,000
Ditto ditto Bombay ditto, ... 20,000

                        Aggregate amount,....228,328

Which in round numbers is, ... 229,000

This is one branch of the expense of the expedition. The rest is comprised in the extra, or full batta to the Native Troops, the money rations to them while serving beyond the Indus; (see p. 9,) and the difference between the feeding, &c. troops in a cantonment: and on a march in a distant foreign country.

(12) i. e. 20,000 for the Bengal Column; 6,700 for the Bombay; and our Commissariat actually furnished them with 7,266 camels.
(13) 1,146 Bengal Column; and 274 (Table No. 1.) Bombay Column, up to 15th September, 1839.
(14) No return of. Some were lost.
(15) No return of the Bombay public Bullocks; some died, &c.
(16) At Bombay they give 500 and 450 rupees per horse.

INDEX.

A.

	Page
ABBAS, attempt to make king,	390
ACHUKZYES, mountaineers,	78
ADJUTANT, of the Day,	86
ADVANCE GUARD, ... 86, 94, 117,	240
AFFGHANISTAN, Expedition, formation of	1
Object of it,	6
And Appendix,	3
Prejudices of people respected	59
Result of the expedition,	249
Disposition of troops in 257, 268,	271
Troops returned from,	268
Staff appointed, ... 269,	273
Warm clothing for troops,	266
Extra blanket for horses,	270
Stores indented for,	272
Necessity for the expedition,	290
AHMEDPOOR, arrival at,	12
AHMED SHAH'S reign,	365
AKALEES, Sikh fanatics, ... 332,	355
ALARM, false,	18
When sounded,	158
ALI MUSJID, capture of, ... 219,	228
Arrival at,	310
AORNUS, rock of, position,	310
AMMUNITION, sent with the army, see Table, No. 7.	
Sent with each man, ...107,	120
Spare, on reverse flank,	159
ARGHUNDEE, position of,	246
ARORE, ancient capital of Sindh,	21
ARMS, Committee on,	270
ARMY OF INDUS, Corps arrive at Kurnal,	1
Rendezvous at Ferozpoor,	2
Reduction of force,	ib.
Its component parts,	5
Disposable force,	6
March from Ferozpoor,	7
Arrive at Bhawulpoor,	11
Enter Sindh territory,	13
Arrive at Rohree on the Indus,	14
March to lower Sindh,	22
Return, treaty signed,	25
Cross the bridge at Sukkur,	26
Sir J. Keane appointed Commander-in-Chief—new arrangements,	31
Equal pay, &c. to Bengal and Bombay troops,	31
Arrive at Shikarpoor,	32

	Page
March from Shikarpore,	38
Arrive at Dadur,	42
March through Bolan Pass,	48
Arrive at Quetta,	61
Half rations,	64
Sir J. Keane joins,	69
March from Quetta,	75
The Kojuk Pass,	79
Arrive at Candahar,	99
Dett. sent to Girishk,	106
Orders for march on Cabool,111,	116
Return of Girishk Dett.,	119
Preparations for march,	120
March of Herat Mission,	125
Grain convoy arrives,	126
Troops left at Candahar,	129
March from Candahar,	143
Arrive at Kelat-i-Ghiljie,	148
Enter Dost Mahomed's country,	154
Increased rations,	156
Orders for march on Ghuznee,	159
March on Ghuznee,	163
Operations before it,	165
Change ground to Cabool side,	167
Attack near Shah's camp,	173
Orders for storm of Ghuznee,	174
Storm of Ghuznee,	177
G. O. of thanks,	190
Report of chief Engineer,	193
Observations on the operations,	198
Despatches,	202
Capture of Ali Musjid, ... 219,	228
Force left at Ghuznee,	221
Mission arrives at Herat,	228
Orders for march from Ghuznee,	236
March from Ghuznee,	239
Flight and pursuit of Dost Mahomed, ... 242,	253
Arrival at Cabool,	247
Result of the expedition,	249
Bombay column leaves Cabool on its return,	266
Troops to remain and return,	268
Orders breaking up the Army of the Indus,	362
ARTILLERY under Brigr. Stevenson,	72
Advantage of the detachment system of horse artillery,	259
ATTOK, Bridge of boats at,	333
Hindoo prejudice regarding it,	334
Is ancient TAXILLA,	342
AYOOB, death of,	409

Index.

B.

	Page
BAGGAGE, too much with the army,	9
Heavy left at Bukkur,	30
Mode of marching, 44, 70, 80,	90
Parties on road to protect,	117
Kept in the rear,	160
BAGGAGE MASTER, thanked,	26
Duties of, 28, 44, 70, 80, 117, 241,	333
BALKH, condition of,	374
BAOLEE, (well,) 100 steps,	338
BAYONET, used by Native soldiers,	329
BAZAR, REGTL., difficult to carry 3 days' supplies,	43
BEARERS, Dhoolee, run away,	44
BELOOCHEES, troublesome plunderers, 40,	47
Attacks on baggage, 43, 45, 63, 74, 78,	84
BHAWULPOOR, arrive at,	11
Conduct of the Khan,	11
The town, &c.	12
March from it,	12
BHEELS, and Khyberees compared,	318
In former times,	75
BOATS, difficult to procure in numbers,	8
Those on the Indus,	20
Monthly sent to and from Ferozpoor,	30
Superintendant of	30
In the Punjab rivers,	353
BOLAN PASS, desirable to hold it,	32
Order of march in,	43
Entrance to it,	48
Season to enter it,	53
March out of,	54
Elevations,	56
Attacks in, 78, 79,	84
Corps of Rangers,	78
BOMBAY, troops sent to Sindh,	4
Landing there,	5
Near Hyderabad, 14, 15,	25
Reserve lands at Kurachee,	23
Arrive at Candahar,	103
March to Cabool, 116,	144
Leave Cabool on return,	266
BRIDGE, timber and boats for,	8
Of boats on the Indus, 26,	27
Ditto at Attok,	334
BRIGADIER of Day, 85, 94, 117, 125, 152,	239
Discontinued,	252
BRIGADE MAJOR,	124
BUCEPHALIA, position of, 350,	354
BUKKUR, treaty regarding,	16
Possession of,	19
Description,	21
Force left in, 29,	30
BULLOCKS, carriage, procurable,	43
Taken back to India,	266
BURNES, Sir A. joins the army,	13
Plan to murder,	74
At Cabool in 1832 and 1837, 415,	417

C.

	Page
CABOOL, preparations at,	121
Grain from Kohistan,	130
Dett. sent to in advance,	244
Arrival at,	247
Report, Appx.,	15
Soldiers not enter without passes,	248
Occurrences at, 251,	261
Grand review at,	260
Races at,	261
Durbar at,	262
Troops left at,	271
Description of,	275
March from to India,	293
Division of country into 5 shares,	414
CAMELS, India drained of,	7
Few obtained in Sindh,	36
Number with the Army,	9
Dying and carried off,	13
Required by Bombay troops,	36
Carried off, 41, 63, 68, 83, 109, 112, 114, 115, 122, 123, 124, 150,	151
Over driven, 42, 58,	66
Dying in numbers,	53
Overloaded,	80
Sent to graze,	100
Compensation to owners of,	109
Purchased at Candahar,	113
Trial for stealing,	114
Serjts. &c. in charge of,	117
Cordon to protect at graze,	118
Corps send parties with,	ib.
Where kept in camp,	ib.
Recovered from robbers,	120
Marked to identify,	151
Lost by leaving the cordon,	151
Baugree (draft),	260
CAMEL BATTERY, (Arty.) gets on well,	53
Horse drafted,	259
Improvements proposed,	260
CAMP, Noise in prohibited,	18
Dead animals removed from, 66, 68,	252
Duties in,	85
No arms discharged in on service,	159
Plan of to Brigr. of day,	86
People turned out at sun-set,	129
Armed parties not to enter,	146
Quiet in, at night,	152
CAMP COLORMEN, on reverse flank,	245
CAMP FOLLOWERS, number marched with the army,	8
Summarily punished,	45
Killed and wounded, 67, 68, 84 85, 93, 103,	156
Distresses of, 74,	106
Deaths among,	127
CAMP POLICE, vested in Brigadiers,	252
CANDAHAR, arrival at, 93,	95
See Report of, Appx. p.	8
G. O. Appx p.	11
People not to enter,	94
Passes granted to enter, 102,	104
Bombay troops arrive,	103
Installation of king,	105
G. O. Appx. p.	13

Index. 87

	Page
Grain dear at—riot,	106
King's levee,	108
Crops reaping, 109,	112
Garrison left at, 111, 112, 116.	129
Order of march from,	116
Money spent at,	122
Staff left there,	123
Candahar described,	131
March from,	143
Battle of (1834),	416
CASHMEER, offer of to British Government,	407
CATTLE, loss of, see Table	viii.
Sent for winter to Jellalabad,	271
CAVALRY, all under Genl. Thackwell,	72
Dismounted how used,	118
CHENAB, cross river of,	352
CHUCH, battle of,	396
COINS, caution in buying,	339
COLORS, dropped to the Shah,	260
COMMISSARY GENL. duties of, 25, 41, 43, 45, 64, 65, 100, 109, 115· 217, 221,	302
COMMISSARIAT, D. C. G, of Bengal, General control of, ..31, 71,	72
Bengal supplies, Bombay army, 36,	261
Duties of Dept., 66, 70,	72
Native agents require checks,	104
European N. C. O. advantageous,	110
Purchase on credit, sometimes necessary,	122
COMMITTEE, to purchase horses,	100
To adjust compensation,	109
On treasure, and camels, 261,	270
To invalid soldiers, 269,	272
COMPENSATION, for rations not issued 41, 45,	64
CONVOY, of grain attacked, 39,	104
Ditto arrives,	104
Ditto in danger, 123,	125
Arrives,	126
Of treasure reinforcement sent to,	267
COTTON, Sir W. commands. the Bengal column,	8
Thanks on giving over the command,	69
COURT, to record claims to Order of Merit,	266
CRIMINALS, Affghan mode of execution, 123,	151
CROPS, protection to, 41, 58, 60, 86, 94, 151, 152, 239, 302,	321
When assigned as food for horses, 41, 43, 65, 87,	89
At Candahar,	112

D.

DEFILE, how occupied,	236
DENNIE, Lt.-Col. commands advance at Ghuznee,	264
DEPOTS, for supplies at Ferozpoor,	8
At Sukkur,	30

	Page
At Shikarpoor,	37
At Dadur,	46
At Ouetta,	71
DESERT, how crossed,	39
Country between Shikarpoor and Dadur,	47
Through the Bolan Pass,	57
Death caused by,	113
DOMES, men to carry away dead animals, &c.	66
DONATION, to the troops,	38
To the army of the Indus,	354
DOOLIES, for surgical instruments on reverse flank,	160
DOORANEE ORDER, and Durbar to install,	262
Officers selected,	263
Declined by one officer,	264
History of the Empire,	365
DOST MAHOMED KHAN, Ex-ruler of Cabool, as in 1834,	32
Came to Candahar in 1834,	108
Claims Vizarat,	223
Accounts of his flight,	242
Dett. sent in pursuit, 243,	254
Returns unsuccessful,	253
Reported at Bameean,	261
His Mily. character,	332
First comes into power,	413
His general character,	418
DRAFT, for 9th companies,	270
DHAMS, extra to working parties	54
On Queen's Birth-day,	110
To officers, and staff Sergts.,	110
DURBAR, at Candahar,	108
At Cabool,	262

E.

ENEMY, Reports of being near, 83, 85,	241
ENGINEERS, thanks to, 27, 28,	210
ENTRENCHMENT, Burmese,	232
ESHPUN, battle of, 300,	381

F.

FAMILY REMITTANCES, Appendix, No. XI.	38
FAMINE, sometime before the expedition,	7
FANE, Sir H. to command the army of the Indus,	1
Resigns the command to Sir W. Cotton,	3
Goes by water to Bukkur,	9
Requested to remain in India,	14
Takes leave—order of thanks,	29
FEROZPOOR, army assembled at,	2
2nd Division to remain at,	3
Army marches from,	7
Depôt of Grain, &c.	8
FIELD OFFICER of the day, 85,	124
FORAGING parties, caution required	67
FUTEHGURH, near Peshawer, 229,	319
FUTEH KHAN, hostility to Shah Shoojah explained,	223
Place of his murder,	241
Where and how murdered,	402

Index

G.

	Page
GHILJIES, Shah sends money to,	120
Refuse it, to be considered enemies, 120 123, 141,	149
Come in to the king, 151, 152,	222
Military character of,	381
GHORIAN, near Herat,	131
GHUZNEE, preparations to receive us,	121
Enemy said to be in force,	158
Preparations for the march on,	159
March on,	163
Operations before,	165
Attack on Shah's camp, 173,	206
Orders for the storm,	174
The storm of Ghuznee,	177
Orders after the storm,	188
Orders of thanks,	190
Report of Chief Engineer,	193
Observations of Bombay Chief Engineer,	198
Despatch of Sir J. Keane,	202
Killed and wounded at,	212
Orders consequent,	215
Prisoners captured,	218
Prize Agents,	219
Depôt for sick and wounded,	220
Force left at,	221
Orders for march from, 221	336
Dost Mahomed's brother arrives at to ascertain terms,	222
Description of the place,	224
Supplies found in,	228
Medals poposed for	257
Sick and wounded die at,	261
Troops ultimately left there,	271
GIRISHK, Dett. sent there,	107
Description of,	107
Return from,	119
GORDON, Dr. procures grain for the army,	8
Joins Hd. Qrs. at Peshawer,	327
GRAIN, difficult to collect large quantities, 7,	11
From Mooltan, 8,	35
From the Punjab,	11
At Shikarpoor,	34
Plenty there,	36
Little between Shikarpoor and Candahar,	36
A little at Bhag,	41
Ditto at Quetta,	63
Sent to Mooshtung valley for,	67
Convoys arrive at Candahar, 104	127
Left at Candahar,	143
When dearest,	108
GRASS, order against burning, 43,352,	355
GUARD, advance duty of,	333
Rear, increased,	159
Duty on,	160
Qr. and Rear of Regiments,	118
GUARDS reduced at Cabool,	252
GUN fired at noon,	109
Carried on Elephants,	233
Fired before march of troops,	245

H.

	Page
HABEEB OOLLAH KHAN, temporary rule of,	408
HAJEE KHAN, KAKUR, comes in to the king; his character,	87
Intercepted letter of,	107
Sent in pursuit of Dost Mahomed,	242
His treacherous conduct,	253
Return to Cabool and confined	256
Brought to India,	294
HEDGES, not to be destroyed,	339
HELL, valley of (pass),	298
HERAT, Persians retire from, 2,	417
If threatened, how to act, 6,	104
Gallant defence by Pottinger,	6
Report of advance on,	102
Mission sent to,	104
Party ditto, 119,	125
Persians no designs on,	121
Money sent to,	125
Mission reaches it,	228
HOOMAYOON, rebels against Shah Zeman,	373
HORSES, falling off in condition of,	25
Want of grass, kurbee issued,	39
Want of kurbee, extra barley,	41
Green barley how used,	43
Additional to gun horses,	53
On half rations,	59
Regts. purchase forage for,	65
Knocked up by over-work, 67,	107
Shot unable to march, 75,	90
H. A. Bombay begin to knock up,	90
Lost on a march,	92
Various modes of feeding,	96
Committees to buy, 100,	216
Difficult to procure,	101
Number lost, 101,	102
Grain issued again,	109
Reduced rations again,	115
Led, to march in rear,	145
Iron pins to picket,	259
Extra blanket for, in winter,	270
Casting Committees,	270
HORSE ARTILLERY, reviewed,	257
Detachment system best,	259
See *Artillery*.	
HOSPITALS, buildings for sick, at Candahar, 106,	108
HUZZARAHS, origin of them,	157
Come into the king,	159

I.

	Page
INDIA, invasion threatened by the Affghans, 373,	375
INDUS, Shah Shoojah crossed in boats in seven days, 14,	15
British troops, by the bridge of boats,	26
INSPECTION, of troops before a march,	37

J.

	Page
JELLALABAD, Dost Mahomed's troops wintered there,	121
Troops to be left there,	271
Hd. Qrs. arrive at,	303

Index. 89

JHEELUM, Hd. Qrs. arrive at, ... 345
    Loss in crossing the river, ... 346
    Hence begins the Punjab, ... 351
JUMROOD, and battle of, ... 229
    Belongs to the Sikhs, ... 319
JUZZAEL, Native rifle, ... 49

K,
KAKUR'S, a hill tribe, ... 66
    Plunderers, ... 67, 76
KEANE, Sir J., assumes command, 31
    Arrives in camp, ... 69
    Order of thanks, ... 70
    Quits and returns to Bombay, 363
KAMRAN, first appears, ... 387
    Reigns, ... 415
KAREZEES, Water-courses, &c. .. 58
KHELAT, conduct of chief, 45, 48, 66, 73, 83, ... 106
    Capture of, ... 356
KHOJUK PASS, preparations to pass, ... 78
    Order of march through, .. 79, 95
    Confusion in, ... 81
    Extent of descent, ... 82
    Losses in, ... 90
    Attacks in, ... 95
KHOORD CABOOL Pass, ... 294
KHOORD KHYBER, ditto, ... 306
KHUJAWAHS, ... 108, 119
KHUTTUKS, tribe of hill robbers, 331 335
KHUZZULBASHES, come in to the Shah, ... 157 245
KHYBER PASS, march through, .. 309
    Proposed defence, ... 313
    Corps raised for, ... 315
    Sickness in, ... ib.
    Use of the Pass, ... 318
    Nadir Shah paid for the passage of, ... ib.
    Loss of camels in, ... 326
    Officers wounded, ... 327
    Attacks and losses, ... 329
KHYBEREES, two classes of, ... 316
    Attack by, ... 229, 234, 304
    Payments to, ... 316
    Number of armed men, ... 317
    Tax, or Toll, levied by them under Dost Mahomed, ... ib.
    Compared to the Bheels, ... 318
    Ingratitude of, ... 386
KOH-I-NOOR, diamond, account of, 397
KOHISTAN, insurrection in, ... 130
    Furnishes grain to Cabool, ... 229
KUJJUK, tribe of plunderers, ... 267
KURACHEE, troops landing at—fort destroyed, ... 5
    Description, ... 23
KURNAL, army first assembles at, 1
KYSER, Zeman's son, ... 387

L.
LAHORE, invitation to, ... 357
    Return from, ... 361
LARKHANA taken; Sindh grain mart, ... 24

LEECH, Major, opinion of Kurachee, ... 24
    At Khelat in 1838, ... 417
    Joins Hd. Qrs. 38
    Left as P. A. at Candahar, (see also p. 417,) 130
LEVEE, at Candahar, and presents, 108
LOCAL HORSE, 4th, meritorious conduct, ... 127
LORD, Dr. opinion of Kurachee, .. 24
    Arrives at Cabool, ... 257
LYLEE, a famous swift horse, ... 352

M.
MACKESON, Capt. collects grain, . 8
    Joins Hd. Qrs., ... 11
    Ditto ditto from Cabool, ... 293
    Loses his property, ... 326
MAHIDPOOR, battle of, ... 247
MAHOMED AZEEM KHAN, when ruler of Cabool, ... 406
HYDER KHAN, son of Dost Mahomed, ... 294
MARCHING, before daybreak hazardous, ... 49
    Troops to move on one point, .. 128
    Through the Sikh country, ... 302
MEDALS, proposed to be given by the Shah, ... 257
MEDICAL officers with their surgical instruments, ... 160
MONEY, want of, felt, ... 122
MULES, with the Bombay guns, knock up, ... 83
MUNEEKYALA, tope of, ... 341, 350
MURHEES, plunderers, ...51, 73
MYDAN, nature of the position at, 245

N.
NATIVE TROOPS, money rations to, 9
NEEMLA, battle of, ... 301
NICÆA, true position of, ... ,..... 353
    (See, also 350.)
NIGHT ATTACKS, threatened, 77, 88 161
    MOVEMENTS, bad, ... 169
NOUSHERA, battle of, ... 332
NUWAB JUBBAR KHAN, comes to ask terms, ... 222
    His excellent character, ... 223

O.
OFFICERS, too many cattle, and too much baggage, ... 9
    Native invested with order, ... 10, 11, 17
    Not to accompany parties sent out, ... 66, 152
    Not to leave camp without swords, ... 110
    Not to quit camp on service, .. 159
ORDER of Dooranee empire, ... 263
    Of Merit 266
    Of British India, ... 10
ORDERS, made known by beat of Tom Tom to followers, 87, 94

Index.

P.

	Page
PARK, Arty. returns to India,	266
PASSES, through mountains, &c. Bolan, &c. 48, 76, 79, 91, 239, 294, 295, 207, 306, 309,	333
PASSES, or leave in writing, 102, 104, 248, 252,	270
PATROLS, sent from picquets, &c. 85	152
PAY, to troops how issued, 115,	120
PAY MASTER, disposal of surplus Cash,	130
PESHAWER, arrive at,	320
City described,	322
New fort built,	324
March from,	330
Sickness in hot season,	114
PICQUETS, duties on, 18, 85,	240
Position of,	54
Inlying and outlying, 86,	124
Advance,	85
Main, 117,	124
Advance party from it,	117
Very distant,	123
Additional,	147
How posted, 241,	249
On road to city of Cabool,	252
PLUNDERERS, seized and shot,	75
Killed, 103,	152
PLUNDERING, by troops, damage paid for, 94,	321
POOSHTEEN, sheep skin Jacket, 266,	268
POST OFFICE, new arrangements for,	38
Mails attacked, 39,	66
Ditto robbed, 43, 45, 60, 119,	121
Candahar to Girishk,	107
Road open viâ Peshawer,	252
Delayed in Khyber Pass,	307
PRESENTS, order against taking,	321
At king's levee,	108
PRISONERS, how treated,	218
Brought from Ghuznee,	261
Ditto to India,	273
PRIZE property, 216,	261
Agents,	219
See Appendix, Table, No. V.	
PROVISIONS, attempt to regulate the price of,	67
Protection to people bringing in, 94,	129
PROVOST MARSHAL, Assts. and Sergts. duties of, 18, 44, 70, 87, 94, 117, 240,	271
PUNJAB, commences at the Jheelum river,	351
Remarks of people as to the British Govt., 354,	358
British troops were not (by treaty) to go near Lahore,	357
Rumour of a rescue of state prisoners,	359
Nao Nihal Singh, virtual ruler,	361

Q.

	Page
QUARTER MASTER GENERAL, and duties of the Dept., 25, 26, 41, 42, 43, 86, 89, 91, 94, 117, 118, 148, 241, 244, 252,	349
QUARTER MASTER, duties of, 68, 89, 116,	252
QUETTA, arrival at,	61
Little grain at,	63
Depôt at,	71
Corps of Kakurs raised at,	75
March from,	75
Troops left at,	111
Mily. stores left at,	272
QUILLAH ABDOOLAH KHAN, corps raised at,	78

R.

	Page
RAMNUGGER, town of, in the Punjab,	353
RATIONS, half, to mustered followers,	41
Half to troops,	63
Increased,	156
Not issued at Candahar,	95
Ditto ditto at Cabool,	253
Ditto ditto at Peshawer,	326
RAVEE, crossing the river,	358
RAWUL PINDEE, town of,	339
REAR GUARD, 86,	117
REPORTS, made by Bengal and Bombay Troops,	72
Of movements at Cabool,	121
Ditto Ghuznee and Cabool,	157
Ditto from Ghuznee,	241
Ditto of Dost Mahomed,	261
RETURNS, made to Bengal and Bombay,	72
See Appx. for Returns.	
REVIEW of 16th Lancers,	258
Of Horse Arty.,	259
Grand Review,	260
Of Sikh troops,	267
RIFLES, Affghan, great range of,	309
RIVERS, how forded,	347
ROAD, losing, to give the sound,	359
Roads made for the Army, 8,	32
ROHREE, (Bukkur,) arrive at,	15
Order of March from,	17
Troops left at,	ib.
Description of the town,	20
March from to Lower Sindh,	22
RUM, three months' supply taken from Shikarpoor,	37
Served out to officers, &c.,	110
RUMOURS, of various kinds,	122
RUNJEET SING, joins in the treaty,	3
The death of, 122,	143
Effects of his death,	230
Official reports of,	241

S.

	Page
SAFETY GUARDS, 94, 152,	239
SENTRIES, duties of,	18
To be alert,	241
SHAH MAHMOOD, death of,	415
SHAH SHOOJAH-OOL-MOOLK, restoration resolved on,	1
His force,	3
Arrival at Candahar,	93
Ditto Cabool,	251

Index. 91

	Page
Called to the throne (1803)	223
In 1834,	414
Character of,	220
SHAHZADA TIMOOR, arrives at Cabool,	257
SHAWL, the place a gift, ...71,	383
SHERDIL KHAN, death of,	411
SHIKARPOOR, arrive at,	32
Description of,............33,	34
March from and troops left at,	38
SICK, and Hospital stores sent by water,	8
Khujawahs for,..........108,	119
Increase of,	157
Left at Ghuznee,	215
Officers left with,	237
Sent from Ghuznee,	261
See Table, No. 2, Appx.	
SIGNALS, to be repeated,	241
SIKH CONTINGENT,	4
Troops, Runjeet's opinion of, 230,	332
Arrive at Cabool,	257
Conduct in Khyber Pass, ...	326
Make long marches,	361
Discipline of,	362
Detested by Mahomedans, ..	4
Territory, orders on marching through it, ... 302, 321,	327
SINDH, operations in,..........5,	17
Trade with Mooltan,	12
State of affairs, ... 16,	48
Mily. knowledge of the people,	22
Treaty signed,	48
Cavalry raised in,	111
SNOW storm, kills cattle,	53
SPRINGS dry up,	83
STOCKADES, how made,......231,	232
SUDDOZYES, and *Barukzyes*, cause of feud between,	360
SUKKUR, Description of,	22
SUNGAHS, how made,........231,	232
SUPPLIES, taken from Ferozpoor,..	8
Few at Bhawulpoor,	11
Plenty at Shikarpoor,......13,	36
Taken from it,	37
By land and by water,	25
Ordered on to the army,	39
Difficulty bringing on,	41
How served out,	43
With each column,	44
Few at Dadur,	45
None from Khelat,	73
With each corps,	128
Collected on march,	129
SUTLUJ, names of the river,	9
Crossed at Ferozpoor,	360
SWORD of Ghuznee, prize property,	331
Sold by public auction,	363
SYUD AHMED, death of,	415

T.

TAXILLA, true position of,	342
TENTS, ropes fastened to stones, 50,	52
TIMOOR SHAH, reign of,	369
TIRHUN, Govr. sent to,	113
TOM TOMS, (drums) not to be beaten at night,	18

	Page
To proclaim orders, &c., ..	87
TOPE, (Barrow) in Khyber Pass, .	311
Of Muneekyala, ...	341
TREASURE, how disbursed,	30
Arrives at Candahar,	115
Protected on a march,	117
Want of felt,	122
Surplus made over,	130
Arrives at Cabool,........261,	270
TREES, fruit not to cut,	59
Peepul, Neem, and Sissoo, not to cut,	356

U.

UZEEM KHAN, meritorious conduct of,	126

V.

VENTURA, Genl. commands the Sikh Contingent,	4
Resigns the command,	144
VIDETTES, duties of,	18
VILLAGES, armed men not to go into, ...65,	68
VIZARAT, of Affghanistan in Bamzye family,	223
VOLUNTEERS, selections to be made from,	243

W.

WADE, Lt.-Col. moves towards Peshawer,	4
Arrives at Peshawer,	54
Hears of occupation of Candahar,	105
Operations in the Khyber Pass, ...219,	228
Arrives at Cabool,	257
Leaves it for India, ...	270
Thanked by the Gr. Gl. App.	30
WARM CLOTHING. for troops remaining in Affghanistan, 266,	263
WATER, supplies, &c. ordered down by,	25
Bombay troops in Sindh, stores proceed by,	36
Scarcity of, ...38,	90
March by Detts.	47
Diverted by the enemy,....85,	87
Canteen required to be used on service,	40
Cavalry require more than Infantry,	47
Guards to be placed over, ...	83
Channels opened and closed by the enemy,..........85,	87
Distress and search for, and loss of horses,	91
Road flooded with, by the enemy,	146
WOOD, Lt. I. N. Supt. of boats, ..	30
WORKING parties how armed, ..	82
WAFFADAR BEGUM, noble character of,	397
Khan, minister, character of,	379

Z.

ZEMAN SHAH, reign of,	372

ERRATA AND ADDENDA.

Page 8—the number of camels carrying grain were nearly 16,000.
45—note (37) " Bolan" not " Balan."
49—*for* " Rifes," *read* " Rifles." *For* " Conally," *read* " Conolly."
50—*for* " Kalifa," *read* " Kafila."
54—note (19) line 13—before " Staff," dele " Déjéuné."
63—note (1) line 2—dele " Lt."
79—top line, *for* " order," *read* " ordered."
    note (34) *for* " 1 A. M.," *read* " 1 P. M."
83—line 6, *for* " 14th," *read* " 4th Brigade ;" dele the figure 1.
119—note (67) *for* " selecton," *read* " selection."
144—note (4) line 3 bottom, should be " withdrawn from this frontier, on the death," &c.
149—line 17, *for* " overing," *read* " hovering."
172—line 5, should be " up *to* the left."
174—line 3, add " the :" line 16, after " succession," a comma.
188—line 18, after " personal," add " Staff."
189—before " every gateway," add " 3."
193—note (83) line 8, dele " as."
223—line 6, should be " have *no* evidence."
228—note (52) line 4, should be " princes."
233—line 13, *for* " Jahaghi and Shadee Bagge" *read*, " Bagadee Tungee, and Shadee Tungee."
251—line 15, *for* " agained," *read* " again."
272—line 8, *for* " Coy.," *read* " Cos."
312—note (13) line 2, full stop after " feet."
318—line 18, *for* " 100,000," *read* " £10,000."
334—note (34) line 6, should be 250 Cwt.
343—note (20) top line, should be " longest," not " largest."
369—note (8) line 5, should be " Tubbus also."
400—line 6, after " kingdom," *read* the 4th line from the bottom. " This year (1818)" to " assailed it," page 401—then, line 6, page 400. " Futeh Khan, &c."—as the writing the letter, &c. must have been before he was blinded ; though in the same year.

Appendix, page 35, line 14, Major not Lieut.-Colonel George Thomson, Bengal *Engineers*.

Major E. Pottinger, Bombay *Artillery*.

ADDENDA.

Downing Street, June 6th, 13th, and 16th, 1840.

Major General Sir Thomas Willshire, to the dignity of a Baronet of the United Kingdom, for the Capture of Khelat.

Col. J. G. Baumgardt, of the 2nd (Queen's Royal) Regt. of Foot; and Lieut.-Col. J. Pennycuick, of the 17th Foot; and Lieut.-Col. R, Carruthers, 2nd Regt. of Foot, to be Companions of the most Hon'ble Mily. Order of the Bath.

Major Alexander C. Peat, Bombay Engineers, and Bt. Major Sir Alexander Burnes, Knt. Bombay N. I. to be Companions of the Bath.

On the Invasion of India.

The new edition (1840) of the work *(On the British Empire in India)* of Lieut.-General *Count Bjournstjerna,* Swedish Ambassador at the Court of London, was received by me in Calcutta, some days after the article I had written on the invasion of India was printed. The Count points to the route *viâ* Herat, Candahar, Ghuznee, Cabool, Peshawer, and the Indus for an invading Army. The route, therefore, of the Army from Candahar to Cabool, and of the Head Quarters from Cabool to India, will be a subject of interest to all. I give a few extracts from the work.

Routes. " That which leads from the province of *Fars* and *Kerman* (1) along the Eastern Coast of the Persian Gulf, through *Beloochistan,* to *Sindh,* at the mouth of the Indus." P. 217. " There is only *one* example on record of an Army having followed it, that of Alexander the Great." Page 218.

" Alexander was, however, master of the Persian Gulf, and was accompanied on the left bank by his fleet, under the command of Nearchus, conveying water and other necessaries. This assistance could not be enjoyed by an army marching the same route now to India, the English being, by means of their naval force stationed at Bombay, sole masters of the Persian Gulf, and without such support an enterprise in that quarter would be quite impossible: we see thus that India is perfectly safe on that side." P. 219.

---

(1) It was marching through this desert that Alexander quenched (as it is said) the thirst of his army, by throwing away the water brought to him by a soldier in his helmet!

Addenda.

"What has been here said of the roads to India seems sufficient to show that the only *possible* route, for an army organized in the *European* manner, is that which passes through *Herat, Kandahar, Ghuznee, Cabool,* and *Peshawer* to *Attok,* on the *Indus*: it is the road taken by *all* former conquerers of India, by *Alexander, Tamerlane,* and *Nadir Shah.*"

" Every military expedition, however, undertaken on this road, pre-supposes, as an indispensable condition, the co-operation of *Persia*. I say co-operation, for Persia alone is unable to undertake any thing of importance against the British power in India. Its Infantry and Artillery are inconsiderable, its Cavalry undisciplined, and its treasury empty; consequently, it could only be in conjunction with some greater power, and as its vanguard, that *Persia* could possibly, venture on an expedition against British India; that this power can be no other than *Russia* is scarcely necessary to repeat here." P. 227.

"After having crossed the Indus at the *upper* part, it enters the *Punjab,* (the kingdom of *Lahore,)* a marshy country, intersected by five great rivers of very difficult access; crossing the Indus at the *middle* part, it finds the sandy desert of *Bikaneer,* with want of water and of supplies; and if the passage be made at the *lower* Indus, the country of *Sindh* presents equally great difficulties: it is but after having surmounted all those difficulties, that the conqueror would arrive at the *real British Dominions,* where the burning *sun* of *India* would be equally fatal to the soldiers of a Northern people as the *Ice* and *cold* of *Russia,* was in 1812 to those of France and Italy."

" From these various data it may be concluded how very large that army must be, which, after having secured its communications with the necessary corps of reserve along the whole distance of 2,000 English miles, which separates the *Araxes (Arras)* from the *Indus,* could arrive in sufficient strength at the latter, to engage there with the *Anglo-Indian Army,* amply supplied with all the necessaries of war, &c. &c." P. 232.

N. B. I must not omit my thanks to Capt. *De Budé,* Engineers, Offg. Secy. to the (Bengal) Military Board, for Table No. 5, at page 75 of the Appendix.